Analytical Writing Handbook

新东方GRE名师团多年教学精华倾囊相授

解密GRE
写作论证思维

丛书主编◎万炜　　编著◎万炜　高炜松

机械工业出版社
CHINA MACHINE PRESS

本书目标是使GRE考生在短期内分析性写作达到4分，以及为想要提升学术分析性写作的同学提供帮助。全书共分为六大部分。前两部分详细讲解了GRE写作考试两个部分（Analyze an Issue 与 Analyze an Argument）的备考技巧和方法。后四部分提供了官方题库 Issue 和 Argument 写作所有题目的详细思路分析，其中 Issue 部分包含两个版本的思路：4分简化版思路和追求更高分数的更充分的思路；Argument 部分提供了题目译文、文章结构图和各步推理分析思路。在帮助考生拓展思路的基础上，书中还提供了 Issue 与 Argument 各20道题的范文，每道题配两篇范文，一篇定位在4~5分，一篇定位在5.5~6分，共计80篇范文。其中，Issue 部分的高分范文还配有针对重要语言点的音频讲解，以帮助大家切实有效地提升语言能力。

图书在版编目（CIP）数据

解密GRE写作论证思维 / 万炜，高炜松编著. —北京：
机械工业出版社，2019.8（2023.1重印）
（娓娓道来出国考试系列丛书）
ISBN 978-7-111-63404-1

Ⅰ.①解… Ⅱ.①万… ②高… Ⅲ.①GRE-写作-自学参考资料 Ⅳ.①H315

中国版本图书馆CIP数据核字（2019）第165077号

机械工业出版社（北京市百万庄大街22号　邮政编码100037）
策划编辑：苏筛琴　　责任编辑：苏筛琴
责任印制：刘　媛
涿州市般润文化传播有限公司印刷
2023年1月第1版第2次印刷
210mm×260mm·30.75印张·1插页·839千字
标准书号：ISBN 978-7-111-63404-1
定价：88.00元

电话服务　　　　　　　网络服务
客服电话：010-88361066　机　工　官　网：www.cmpbook.com
　　　　　010-88379833　机　工　官　博：weibo.com/cmp1952
　　　　　010-68326294　金　书　网：www.golden-book.com
封底无防伪标均为盗版　　机工教育服务网：www.cmpedu.com

丛书序 PREFACE

"娓娓道来出国考试系列丛书"诞生于2017年,包含了从一开始的《笔尖上的托福:跟名师练TOEFL写作TPO真题》《舌尖上的托福:跟名师练TOEFL口语TPO真题》《托福高分万能思路:跟名师练TOEFL口语/写作》,到2018年的《解密GRE阅读逻辑线》,再到如今的《解密GRE写作论证思维》《解密GMAT数学出题点》,未来还会陆续出版北美留学考试各科目书籍。

无论是我亲自动笔,还是邀请其他作者主笔,我都一直坚持一个核心的理念,那就是拒绝"马后炮"式的方法论,要呈现第一视角的考场心态。在编写过程中,我们所有作者都试图把自己还原到正在考试的学生的角度,去感受考场上学生实际面对的思路上的困难,而不仅仅是呈现一个漂亮的答案解析。比如说,在GRE写作中,作为学生的我不想只看到老师给我呈现一篇思路完美的文章,因为老师想这个思路可能用了两个小时,最后写出的文章确实无懈可击,但考场上我们根本没有这样的奢侈条件可以设计出这么精美的结构。再比如,在GRE阅读中,也许一道题选C,因为ABDE在文章中没有提过,但是C在原文的第七行出现了。真正的问题不是知道答案选项在第七行但看不出来,而是我当时不记得这个信息在哪里,所以我需要知道为什么第一遍阅读时应有第七行的意识,以及我看到C选项时应该能够回到第七行,毕竟,我读完文章后不可能记住所有的东西,我也不希望老师告诉我必须练到所有句子和词都记得住,我希望老师能够给我一套普适性强的方法论,教我阅读时如何区分什么该理解,什么不需要关注。就像初中平面几何课程,我不希望老师告诉我在∠A上做辅助线可以解决某道题,我希望老师能够告诉我,当我看到这道题的时候,应该靠什么样的普适性强的方法论才能意识到应该在哪里做辅助线。

为了达到这个目的,我们要求作者们不仅仅讲出自己做题时的第一视角的思路,而且要更进一步深挖自己的直觉。因为,作为一个熟练的考生,很多习惯是下意识的——自己没有意识到自己其实已经做了某种思考,已经在潜意识里完成了这个步骤。我们都知道很多时候学霸给学渣讲题的时候会说"这很明显啊",但是学渣感觉步骤并不明显。我们希望老师们的讲解不要高高在上,不要把自己觉得想当然的步骤当作真正理所应当的。我们要求老师能够解构自己做题潜意识里的习惯,用清楚的语言去呈现给读者们。

　　这套丛书的另一个重要目的就是摒弃过去横行在出国考试培训当中的一系列"奇技淫巧",一些根本上来自于国内应试教育的习惯。这些习惯在中国的高考和考研等考试当中也许有用,之前的一些培训从业者把它们用在了出国考试中,并且忽悠了无数学生,但其实这些习惯对于托福、GRE、GMAT等考试毫无用处。比如在 GRE 阅读中,很多人宣称"原文没说的就不能选";在 GRE 和托福写作当中,很多人倡导学生写长句,用"高级词"替换"低级词"……这些做法不仅不会有帮助,实际上还严重坑到了很多学生。

　　总而言之,本系列丛书试图以一种全新的视角把做题方法呈现给广大读者,力求做到新颖、诚实、细致、全面、可操作。祝愿考生们在拥有了这套利器之后能顺利攻克出国深造路上的层层难关。

万　炜

2019 年 4 月

序言 PREFACE

2007 年，我参加了人生中第一次 GRE 考试，那时的 GRE 我们现在称为"老 GRE"，当然写作部分和如今形式差别不大。我当时没做什么准备，算是半"裸考"，考前一天发烧难以入眠，5 点才入睡，一大早迷迷糊糊去考试，心里抱着考多少是多少的准备。结果几周之后成绩出来，发现写作部分得了个 5 分，心情还颇愉悦。那个时候我上大四，读了两年的哲学双学位，比较喜欢看英美分析哲学（Analytic Philosophy）的东西，所以该领域的原版论文看了不少，比较习惯西方人的思维和论证方式。后来我在北大读了哲学硕士，毕业后去了美国 Syracuse 大学读哲学博士，读了一学期后我做了一个比较突然的决定：回国到新东方教书。做出这个决定的重要原因是在 Syracuse 大学我需要做逻辑课的助教，需要给学生上习题课，上课的过程中发现了教书的激情，当然这有点跑题了。

到了北京新东方我申请当 GRE 写作讲师，咨询并请教了前辈们，包括市面上主流的讲法。在这里我隔空感谢一下当年的第一个培训师徐亮老师，他可能已经离开这个行业很久了，他是唯一一个思路和我高度契合的前辈，并且给了我很多启发。除此之外我听到的大部分 GRE 写作理念都令我感到震撼，或者说惊愕吧。追求词数、追求华丽辞藻、追求长难句、追求名人案例……我心想，好难啊，我完全做不到啊。而且，照这么写，学生考多少分啊？一看，大家都是华丽丽的一堆 3 分。

然而，市面上还流传各种说法（一直流传至今）。什么要得 4 分（甚至还有说要得 3 分）必须要写五六百词，要变换句型、长短句结合、要替换高级词……想一想我的 5 分怎么来的呢，我的 Argument 几个正文段落句型都是一样的，比如：开头句都是 Even if it is true that…/ It doesn't necessarily mean that … 然后，能利用原文句子我就利用原文句子。想一想我在美国读哲学博士，分析亚里士多德的论证时，用的都是妥妥的非常无聊的语言风格，翻译成中文就是"亚里士多德的论证首先基于两个前提：一是……，二是……。由这两个前提，他得出了……结论，他假设了……；接着基于这个新的结论，加上第三个前提……，他进一步推出了……，其中他假设了……"我就不再赘述了，你们应该明白我的意思了。这是个思维考试，不是语言考试，尤其不是文学考试，你们都在写什么？这就萌发了我最初的小理想：让 GRE 写作教学走向正路。

我其实早就该写这样一本书了。但期间算是我自己耽搁了这件事情，因为我先转去教 TOEFL 写作，然后又去教 GRE 阅读了。因为对于赴美学习的中国考生来说，一般情况下 GRE 阅读和 TOEFL 写作比 GRE 写作相对更重要一些（除极个别特殊专业外），而且 TOEFL 写作和 GRE 阅读在市面上也有很多错误的理念在流传，以至于我也想要去改变一下（我想法多了点，不然为什么会有"娓娓道来出国考试系列丛书"呢）。一些读者可能已经知道了，我和团队中的老师们在过去两年间分别出版了《笔尖上的托福：跟名师练 TOEFL 写作 TPO 真题》与《解密 GRE 阅读逻辑线》两本书。

完成那两本书后，我终于有时间来酝酿这样一本 GRE 写作教程。但对于它的定位我是很犹豫的，我考了很多次 GRE，写作得了一堆 5 分，从来没有得过 6 分，所以我可不敢夸口说我能写出来一堆满分文章。但我知道我确实能够帮助很多学生，我也带出过很多学生（即便是在我教 GRE 阅读期间），哪怕是看了我短短的 45 分钟写作视频，甚至连一篇写作都没有练过，有些学生的写作分数也迅速从 3 分突破到 4 分。因为，我知道 GRE 写作不像市面上很多谣传所说的那样难。3 分其实就是垃圾文章，4 分只是非常普通的文章，我的 5 分就是还不错的文章，但算不上优秀的文章。我没有谦虚，我的言语中应该是充满骄傲的，GRE 写作 4 分的学生，语言水平在 TOEFL 写作上可能也就是 25 分，显然不算什么特别厉害的水平。所以，我虽然写不出什么帮助大家得满分的教程，但是我想帮助大家快速突破，达到申请需要的分数就好了，而且我确定，这并不是一个难以做到的事情。大部分人考 3 分，而且花了很多复习时间，那不是因为他们差，而是因为他们用在 GRE 写作上的时间其实根本和 GRE 写作所需要的东西无关。我可以帮他们改变这一点，当然，我也不是万能的，前提是，大家在不追求辞藻华丽的情况下能够把基本的意思说清楚。

在我刚开始教写作的年代，市面上流传一个叫"北美范文"的东西，据说是北美考官写的，不知道是不是真的。很多老师上课用那个，也鼓励学生看那个。不是我觉得那个材料不好，人家写得特别好，但是我不用那个教学，也完全不鼓励学生模仿，因为大部分同学的英语水平模仿那个就是东施效颦。我认为我们学生就应该学习不完美的文章——平时看来不完美，但是在考场上仍然算是优秀的文章。GRE 考场上大部分人不可能写出完美的文章，因为只给 30 分钟的时间。这个考试期望的东西叫 draft，也就是初稿。初稿中有单词拼写错误，有语法错误，有不严谨的地方，甚至写不完，都是正常的，并不妨碍文章是一个优秀的初稿。我们"娓娓道来出国考试系列丛书"有一个统一的理念，就是给大家呈现第一视角的考试体验，不是马后炮式的分析，而是让大家去学习优秀考生第一视角做题时所经历的思考过程。所以我亲自写范文，而且给自己严格限时，真实地告诉大家考场上 5 分水平的文章是什么样子的，在这个写作考试当中，最重要的是抓住哪些元素，不要把精力花在根本不相关的妄想上（最终呈现给大家的范文，为了避免引起误解，我还是把明显的拼写和语法错误纠正了一下）。

我是一个怕被骂的人，我也知道我写出这些文章会被骂，因为不是每个人都会理解我的初衷。而且，说实话，很多拿起一本写作教程的同学也有非功利的目的，他们想要真的学习学术写作，而中国的大学教育大部分情况下是没有提供这个机会的，GRE 写作考试给他们创造了第一个机会。抱有这种目的的同学想要看到更好的文章，我深感无能为力，也许我不能帮助他们了。

不过我很庆幸，去年联系到了我的老朋友、老同事、高帅富——前新东方 GRE 教师高炜松老师。当时我去他在 Gainesville 的家里作客，那会儿他还在读英文文学专业（English Literature）的博士，主攻方向是文化研究（Cultural Studies）和批判理论（Critical Theory）。我一直都知道他的英语功底以及英文写作功底都比我厉害得多，而且他在读博士期间教的课程就是文学课（Literature）及批判性写作课（Critical Writing），完美符合 GRE 的写作需要。非常庆幸他居然答应在百忙之中和我一起合作完成这本书，真的是百忙之中，要不然这本书我们也不会写了一年，因为他既要忙博士毕业，还要找工作。在我写这个序言的时候，就是现在，我正坐在他在加州的新家的椅子上，我要恭喜他已经当上了 University of California, Merced 的教师，仍然是在英文系（English Department），教授"亚裔美国文学"（Asian American Literature）、"20 世纪女性作家"（20th Century Women Writers）、"文学与性别"（Literature and Gender）等课程。今天下课的时候，还有学生问他："高老师，你能和咱们系里别的老师聊聊吗？你能教教他们如何教写作吗？"他的班里全是美国大学生，但是他深受所有人欢迎，而他是在教美国人用自己的母语进行学术写作啊，可能在历史上也没有多少中国人能做到这一点。我从高中到本科前几年主要以理科为主，即便学习哲学也是主攻跟逻辑相关的方向，所以我更熟悉的领域还是在自然科学方向；高老师在人文方面的专长也算是帮助我实现了更完整的拼图。了解 GRE Verbal 部分的同学，应该知道，很多 ETS 的阅读文章背景是基于美国人文社会的，所以高老师写的很多文章也是考虑了这种社会环境的。虽然不需要同学们接受什么样的社会价值观，但是了解美国的人文价值对于参加整个 GRE 考试都是非常重要的。简而言之，我觉得我真的是捡到宝贝了。

有了高老师的帮助，我才终于让这本即将问世的 GRE 写作书实现了我希望的双重定位。既能够帮助有功利需求的同学快速找到考试的方向，又能为真正想要快速提高英文学术写作能力的同学提供指导。所以，这本书当中每一个话题的范文我们都呈现两个版本：一个功利性的，定位在 4~5 分的版本；一个更符合学术标准的，定位在 5.5~6 分的版本。而且，对于高分版本的 issue 文章，我还要求高老师能够对其中地道的、重要的语言点进行音频授课，希望他能够把他渊博的知识分享给更多想要学习学术英语的中国大学生。

我不想只做一个功利的培训师，这不是我快乐的来源；我想真的能够让同学们提高能力。我个人能力也许不足了，所以这次要特别感谢高老师，能够帮我实现这个愿望。也希望同学们能够超越功利心，去扎扎实实学一些真正帮助写作能力提升的东西。毕竟，这简直是用最廉价的方式上了美国原版的学术写作课程，和美国大学生一道学习。这次写书过程中，每一篇范文我都和高老师反复切磋（其实是一直被他指点），对我本身就是一次回炉再造，一次重要的提升。由于能力所限，在写作过程中我们不可避免还会出现或大或小的错误，也望广大读者谅解和指正。

希望读者们能够像我一样，在使用这本书的过程中收获满满！

万炜

2019 年 4 月 9 日于 Merced, California, U. S. A.

如何使用本书

这本书有两个目标：帮助想要尽快解决 GRE 考试的同学达到写作 4 分，以及帮助真正想要学习英语学术写作的同学提高分析性写作能力。下表是对两种目标的同学分别给出的学习建议。

GRE 写作快速提分		提升学术写作能力	
Analyze an Issue	Analyze an Argument	Analyze an Issue	Analyze an Argument
阅读全部方法论	阅读全部方法论	阅读全部方法论	阅读全部方法论
读 20 篇以上的 Issue 写作题目分析思路，保证至少能够完成简化版思路，尽量挑选自己不擅长的话题	读 20 篇以上的 Argument 写作题目分析思路，自己先主动尝试列出文章推理结构，并找到至少三个推理步骤，指出假设和反例	读所有的 Issue 写作题目分析思路，并逐渐学会按照相似的步骤去自主分析	读 20 篇以上的 Argument 写作题目分析思路，自己先主动尝试列出文章推理结构，对所有推理步骤，指出尽可能多的假设和反例
读所有 Good 范文	读 5 篇以上的 Good 范文	读所有的范文和点评，对比 Outstanding 范文与 Good 范文的区别，学习两篇范文当中好的语言点以及写作思路，听针对 Outstanding 范文配套的重点语言点音频讲解	读 5 篇以上的 Outstanding 范文和相应的 Good 范文，比对两篇范文之间的区别
写 2 篇文章，1 篇尝试用分情况讨论的结构安排，1 篇尝试用分理由展开的结构安排	写 3 篇以上的文章，用同样的语言形式，且与范文要求的形式一致，每篇文章 2~3 个讨论点，每个点至少制造一个反例	对所有 Good 范文进行仿写，利用与 Outstanding 范文配套的音频讲解中的重要语言点造句	写 10 篇以上的文章，每篇文章写 3 个以上的讨论点，每个点制造尽可能多的反例，且必须解释清楚

范文说明

本书所有的 Outstanding 范文定位在 5.5~6 分（Issue 部分的配套音频会重点讲解值得我们学习的语言点），而 Good 范文定位在 4~5 分。为了避免引起误解，学习不规范的英语，所以无论是 Outstanding 范文还是 Good 范文，我们都反复做了语法和拼写的修正，尽量规避英语上的明显错误（如语法和拼写错误）。最终呈现给大家的范文的语言水平超过了实际考试相应分数的要求，因此即便是 Good 范文，其语言水平毫无疑问是 5 分水平，而不是 4 分水平。这种与实际考试的偏差请读者谅解。

题库分析说明

Issue 题库逐题精析部分很多篇文章的分析都给出了非常详尽的思路，其实即便是追求高分的同学也不需要全都写出来，我们只是帮助同学们打开思路，而且，同学们也完全不必认同我们所给出的分析。Argument 题库逐题精析部分每篇文章我们都给出了所有步骤的分析，而实际考试中并不需要对所有逻辑步骤进行讨论，只需摘取自己能够讨论最充分的 2~3 个步骤进行分析就可以了。

GRE 分析性写作（Analytical Writing）
部分概述

GRE 分析性写作（Analytical Writing）是 GRE General Test 的一部分，它包含两个任务：**是非分析**（Analyze an Issue）与**论证分析**（Analyze an Argument）。Analytic Writing 部分的分数区间为 0~6 分，以 0.5 分为计分单位，最后得分为两个任务得分的均值。在实际考试当中，考生有 30 分钟的时间完成 Issue 部分，30 分钟的时间完成 Argument 部分。

在 Issue 部分，考生将会看到一个话题，并被要求对这个话题表达自己的看法，完成一篇议论文，对自己的观点进行论证。

在 Argument 部分，考生将会阅读一篇短文，并对短文的论证过程进行评价。

无论是 Issue 还是 Argument 的话题，官方都提供公开的题库，Issue 部分目前共 145 道题，Argument 共 171 道题。题目数量和内容未来仍然有可能发生细小的变化。考试的题目将来自题库中的这些公开题目。

目录 CONTENTS

丛书序
序言
如何使用本书
GRE 分析性写作（Analytical Writing）部分概述

Part 1　你不了解的 GRE 分析性写作语言 ·· 1
　一、GRE 写作需要什么样的语言？ ··· 2
　二、GRE 写作不需要什么样的语言？ ·· 4
　三、关于机改（E-rater） ·· 5
　四、短板效应 ··· 6

Part 2　怎么应对 GRE 分析性写作 ··· 7
　第一章　怎么应对是非分析写作（Analyze an Issue） ························ 8
　第二章　怎么应对论证分析写作（Analyze an Argument） ················· 23

Part 3　Issue 题库逐题精析 ·· 51

Part 4　Issue 精选范文 ·· 177

Part 5　Argument 题库逐题精析 ··· 239

Part 6　Argument 精选范文 ·· 417

Issue 题库逐题精析索引

题库题号	页码	题库题号	页码	题库题号	页码	题库题号	页码	题库题号	页码
1	52	30	69	59	119	88	145	117	134
2	69	31	87	60	103	89	132	118	60
3	54	32	101	61	121	90	66	119	157
4	52	33	69	62	122	91	134	120	82
5	56	34	74	63	124	92	69	121	159
6	58	35	89	64	121	93	62	122	69
7	127	36	91	65	126	94	134	123	161
8	60	37	69	66	103	95	147	124	74
9	62	38	92	67	64	96	64	125	163
10	63	39	94	68	105	97	149	126	127
11	64	40	95	69	74	98	151	127	127
12	66	41	96	70	127	99	157	128	69, 159
13	69	42	129	71	129	100	157	129	69
14	103, 111	43	97	72	101	101	151	130	69
15	126	44	64	73	131	102	153	131	97
16	103	45	92	74	62	103	87	132	103
17	68	46	99	75	138	104	153	133	64
18	69	47	101	76	132	105	58	134	165
19	71	48	103	77	134	106	64	135	166
20	72	49	105	78	84	107	82	136	167
21	74	50	76	79	129	108	103	137	169
22	76	51	107	80	82	109	103	138	82
23	63	52	109	81	136	110	66	139	111, 171
24	78	53	111	82	138	111	52	140	145
25	80	54	113	83	140	112	101	141	60
26	82	55	115	84	92	113	155	142	58
27	76	56	117	85	142	114	82, 111	143	103
28	84	57	74	86	99, 111	115	82, 111	144	173
29	86	58	103	87	144	116	72	145	175

Argument 题库逐题精析索引

题库题号	页码	题库题号	页码	题库题号	页码	题库题号	页码	题库题号	页码
1	240	36	305	71	363	106	383	141	392
2	242	37	307	72	365	107	365	142	338
3	244	38	309	73	367	108	354	143	327
4	246	39	311	74	369	109	365	144	394
5	248	40	313	75	333	110	365	145	394
6	250	41	315	76	371	111	268	146	338
7	252	42	317	77	371	112	279	147	338
8	254	43	319	78	373	113	279	148	392
9	256	44	321	79	375	114	342	149	396
10	258	45	323	80	373	115	342	150	396
11	261	46	319	81	256	116	311	151	248
12	263	47	325	82	375	117	342	152	398
13	265	48	270	83	256	118	311	153	383
14	268	49	298	84	377	119	383	154	340
15	270	50	327	85	379	120	383	155	300
16	272	51	329	86	272	121	298	156	284
17	274	52	331	87	296	122	298	157	400
18	277	53	333	88	305	123	270	158	300
19	258	54	333	89	305	124	270	159	292
20	279	55	296	90	381	125	386	160	402
21	258	56	335	91	252	126	270	161	363
22	282	57	338	92	252	127	386	162	404
23	284	58	340	93	284	128	388	163	398
24	282	59	342	94	379	129	386	164	248
25	286	60	344	95	284	130	388	165	307
26	282	61	346	96	379	131	279	166	406
27	286	62	348	97	292	132	340	167	408
28	288	63	350	98	292	133	388	168	410
29	290	64	352	99	292	134	340	169	412
30	292	65	354	100	348	135	390	170	414
31	294	66	354	101	348	136	340	171	412
32	296	67	286	102	272	137	327		
33	298	68	357	103	272	138	338		
34	300	69	359	104	321	139	338		
35	303	70	361	105	321	140	392		

解密GRE写作
论证思维

Part 1 你不了解的 GRE 分析性写作语言

Part 1　你不了解的GRE分析性写作语言

本章节的目的不是快速提高同学们的语言水平（提高语言水平并不是短时间内能够实现的事情），而是帮助同学们认清GRE写作所需要的语言水平。很多同学的语言能力完全可以达到4分的语言要求（如前言所说，4分文章并不是什么杰出的文章，只是非常普通的文章），但是却因为对这个考试有严重的误解，而掉到了3分。因此，本章节的目的是在本书最醒目的位置就让同学们明白，语言上我们需要追求什么，不要追求什么，如何最快速地摆脱3分语言，达到4分的要求。

一、GRE写作需要什么样的语言？

官方指南对每个分数段都给出了清晰的要求，我们一起来看一下语言方面的标准。

◐ Analyze an Issue 部分

Score 6

In addressing the specific task directions, a 6 response presents a cogent, well-articulated analysis of the issue and conveys meaning skillfully.
- conveys ideas fluently and precisely, using effective vocabulary and sentence variety
- demonstrates facility with the conventions of standard written English (i.e., grammar, usage and mechanics), but may have minor errors

Score 5

In addressing the specific task directions, a 5 response presents a generally thoughtful, well-developed analysis of the issue and conveys meaning clearly.
- conveys ideas clearly and well, using appropriate vocabulary and sentence variety
- demonstrates facility with the conventions of standard written English but may have minor errors

Score 4

In addressing the specific task directions, a 4 response presents a competent analysis of the issue and conveys meaning with acceptable clarity.
- demonstrates sufficient control of language to express ideas with reasonable clarity
- generally demonstrates control of the conventions of standard written English but may have some errors

Score 3

A 3 response demonstrates some competence in addressing the specific task directions, in analyzing the issue and <u>in conveying meaning, but is obviously flawed.</u>
- has problems in language and sentence structure that result in a lack of clarity
- contains occasional major errors or frequent minor errors in grammar, usage or mechanics that can interfere with meaning

——摘自 *The Official Guide to GRE Revised General Test*

☞ Analyze an Argument 部分

Score 6

In addressing the specific task directions, a 6 response presents a cogent, well-articulated examination of the argument and <u>conveys meaning skillfully.</u>
- conveys ideas fluently and precisely, using effective vocabulary and sentence variety
- demonstrates superior facility with the conventions of standard written English (i.e., grammar, usage, and mechanics) but may have minor errors

Score 5

In addressing the specific task directions, a 5 response presents a generally thoughtful, well-developed examination of the argument and <u>conveys meaning clearly.</u>
- conveys ideas clearly and well, using appropriate vocabulary and sentence variety
- demonstrates facility with the conventions of standard written English but may have minor errors

Score 4

In addressing the specific task directions, a 4 response presents a competent examination of the argument and <u>conveys meaning with acceptable clarity.</u>
- demonstrates sufficient control of language to convey ideas with acceptable clarity
- generally demonstrates control of the conventions of standard written English but may have some errors

Score 3

A 3 response demonstrates some competence in addressing the specific task directions, in examining the argument, and <u>in conveying meaning but is obviously flawed.</u>
- has problems in language and sentence structure that result in a lack of clarity

Part 1 你不了解的 GRE 分析性写作语言

> • contains occasional major errors or frequent minor errors in grammar, usage, or mechanics that can interfere with meaning
>
> ——摘自 *The Official Guide to GRE Revised General Test*

通过对比，大家应该能够看到 Issue 部分和 Argument 部分对于语言的要求是一致的，这也是为什么我们把两部分语言放在一起讨论的原因。

高老师的语言水平毫无疑问是 skillful 的，但我在考场上是做不到 skillful 的，这也是为什么我几乎每次考试都考 5 分的原因，我在短短 30 分钟之内只能保证语言的 clarity。如果把 5 分当作一个很高的分数来看的话，我们至少能意识到，考生们在考场上没有任何理由追求浮夸的语言，只需要做到 clarity。

接下来，我们重点谈谈希望大家能够短时间内达到的水平——4 分，同时对比我们想要短时间内摆脱的分数——3 分。区别是很明显的。4 分的学生能够做到 acceptable clarity，即虽然语言不是绝对清楚，但是读者还是能够明白考生想要说什么的；相反，3 分的语言是 obviously flawed，具体来看，这些文章会造成 lack of clarity，会 interfere with meaning。简而言之，就是会有些时候让人看不懂。

很多同学是否已经意识到自己先前努力的方向出现偏差了。短期内突破 GRE 语言，我们只需要追求写的内容让人看懂，而不需要写得很"高级"，虽然我也并不认同大部分同学对"高级"语言的判断。

二、GRE 写作不需要什么样的语言？

同学们一般都无视 clarity，而去追求一些其实对分数根本没有显著影响的语言因素。下面，我就来逐一列举同学们不需要做到的事情，以便大家未来能够把注意力放在真正重要的问题上。

1. 不需要追求词数

很多学生，甚至很多 GRE 教师都以为 GRE 写作写得越长越好，有很多人甚至鼓吹每篇文章要写到 600 + 的词数才能到 4 分，这实在是令人发指。随便看一下官方各途径给出的范文就会发现，4 分文章几乎都没有超过 430 词的，甚至有低到 260 词的一篇 Argument 分析；3 分文章最高不到 420 词，最低有 250 多词的。简而言之，词数和分数没有任何必然联系。而且，请正在阅读这一段文字的同学现在就扪心自问，以我们的语言水平，如果在 30 分钟时间内拼命写 600 词以上，会写出什么内容？我想，答案只有一个词：惨不忍睹。这也就是为什么很多 TOEFL 写作明明已经可以达到 28 分以上水平的同学，GRE 写作却只能考 3 分的原因。本来他们是可以写清楚的，但因为过分追求文章篇幅，导致自己去挑战完全做不到的事情，结果彻底南辕北辙。

2. 不要刻意写"大词""难句"

很明显，5 分以内的水平都没有任何一点与语言"难度"相关，因此我们首先没有必要把词写"大"，把句子写"难"。事实上，我认为，大部分同学写"大"词，写"难"句不仅不会加分，反而会送分。因为大部分同学的英语水平根本没有能力驾驭复杂句型和抽象词汇，时常导致我们写出别人无法理解的东西，我们并不知道这个抽象词的精确用法，也不能够准确表达复杂句子的逻辑。

我想要在这里明确警示大家，不要去用自己只知道意思，但没有见到过例句的词，比如，GRE 填空中背过的新单词。很多人以为，只要是近义词，就可以随意替换。我想在此请同学们换位思考一下，假设我们看到一个外国人说中文。本来他想说："今天钱包丢了，好郁闷啊。"结果他觉得"郁闷"见得太多了，想换一个词，于是写成了："今天钱包丢了，好抑郁啊。"你会怎么想？我猜大部分中国人都会觉得这个句子不对劲吧。其实站在外国人的角度上，他很可能根本无法区别"郁闷"和"抑郁"的细微区别。我们作为第一语言的使用者，就算我们无法讲清楚这里为什么不能用"抑郁"，而必须用"郁闷"，但我们的语言习惯可以让我们做出正确的使用判断。因此，当我们尝试换新词的时候，是冒着很大风险的，很可能写出让美国读者看完觉得很尴尬的句子。

本书的范文中必然会有长句和"大"词，但我和高老师在写的时候都不是从语言的"高级"角度上考虑的，纯粹是为了表意准确而使用的。复杂句能够更好地表现复杂的逻辑，而有一些"大"词在语境中能够更精确地表达语义目的。希望大家在阅读时能够从语用（语义、逻辑）的角度去学习，而不是纯粹从词句本身去学习。简而言之，不考虑表意，不存在所谓的词句之间的优劣。

3. 不要担心拼写和语法的细节错误

合理范围内的拼写错误是允许的，把 exciting 不小心写成了 excitting，这是无所谓的，读者能够明白你在写什么；当然，把 renaissance 写成了 renasonce，我就不敢保证了。同理，细小的语法错误，只要不影响读者的语义理解，也是无所谓的。总而言之，GRE 写作部分对语言的要求其实并不严格，一切以让读者轻松看懂为目标。

4. 不需要写完

没来得及收尾的文章一样可以得 6 分，这是出题人的原话。事实上，去看一下官方的 4 分范例，没有写完、没有开头、没有结尾的文章比比皆是。我上一次写作分数是 5 分时，issue 部分是没有写完的。

5. 我们写的不是成文，而是 draft

写作考试考查的只是我们的 first draft，即初稿，它没有期望完美。很多同学喜欢问我一些问题：段首要不要空格，段间要不要空行，能不能写缩写……这些都反映了我们从小受到了国内中文、英文写作教育的影响。那些要求让我们过分看重文章形式，而不看重真正应该关注的东西——思维。GRE 写作是理性思维的测试，不是语言花哨的考试。请同学们未来能够尊重这个考试的目标。

三、关于机改（E-rater）

GRE 的写作评卷工作中是有机器参与的。ETS 出题官亲口承认，E-rater 无法评判思维逻辑，只能观察语言形式。于是，E-rater 所给出的分数会和词数、句子复杂度、词汇难度、词汇替换度相关。

咦？这不是违背了我刚才所说的一切吗？

请听我详细分解。由于 E-rater 无法像人类一样直接看出一篇文章作者的思维能力，它只能寻找和思维深度相关的，且可以辨识的变量。显然，思考全面的作者通常文章写得更丰富，逻辑能力强的作者通常句型也会更复杂，表达更精确的作者自然词汇丰富度较高。所以，在 E-rater 的程序当中，分数是和这些表象有弱相关性的。然而，这是相关，而不是因果。

但因为 E-rater 只能辨识相关性，这就导致它可以被欺骗。我们有意识地多写长句，多替换词汇，把文章写长，是能在一定程度上让 E-rater 给出偏高的分数的。

但是！一个巨大的但是！我们最终的分数不是 E-rater 单纯决定的，事实上对于大陆学生来说，我们的分数很可能跟 E-rater 根本没有关系。在全世界范围内，E-rater 给分和人工给分几乎没有任何差距，因此 E-rater 的分数可以广泛有效。但是，对中国大陆来说，据统计，E-rater 给分平均比人工给分高了 1 分。而最关键的是，GRE 写作分数通常取的是人工与机器的平均值，可是，当两个分差差距达到 1 分的时候，机器给分作废。因此，结果就是，当我们的考生绞尽脑汁欺骗完机器后，我们最后的分数是人工给的，人工评阅是非常容易看出我们的"大"词、"难"句的荒唐的。

在世界范围内，之所以机改和人工分数差距不大，是因为世界范围内很少有像我们国内如此"发达"的考试培训。我们的考试培训过分强调"技巧"，其实就是找"捷径"，教学生如何不提高能力，而欺骗考试（是不是也包含我自己）。这就是误人子弟。我很感谢 GRE 写作测试，它能够真正在意大家的思维水平，而不去纠缠于那些形式化的东西。

四、短板效应

GRE 写作评分标准不仅包含语言的标准，还包含思维、结构等方面的标准，但最终的分数并不是考生思维、结构、语言等方面的平均，而是取短板作为最终分数。即语言水平达到 6 分的人，由于思维水平只有 3 分，这个人最后的分数就是 3 分。这种给分方式意味着，同学们在准备 GRE 写作的时候一定要对自己的短板有清晰的认识，不需要把自己的长处变得更长，而需要把自己的短处尽快补上。如果你的 TOEFL 写作已经达到 28 分以上，或是 IELTS 写作已经轻松达到 8 分，那我会推荐你根本不需要练习 GRE 写作的"写"，而应该全力准备所有题目的思路，因为你的表意能力应该可以轻松让你实现 clarity。

解密GRE写作
论证思维

Part 2 怎么应对 GRE 分析性写作

第一章　怎么应对是非分析写作
（Analyze an Issue）

　　本章节将尽量高效地向读者呈现完整的 Analyze an Issue 部分面对一个话题的审题、思考和写作过程。但是，与下一章节"怎么应对论证分析写作（Analyze an Argument）"相比，本章节的全面性必然相对受限。该局限来自于 Issue 考试的最大难点，那就是如果考生对一个话题不熟悉，则任何方法论都没有意义。所以，同学们务必要仔细研读本章内容，但这仍然是远远不够的。我强烈建议同学们能够多去浏览 Issue 部分的题库，以及本书所提供的所有题目的分析思路。请一定记住，不了解一个话题，就不可能有任何好的思路，有再好的方法都是没有意义的。

第一章　怎么应对是非分析写作（Analyze an Issue）

Step 1　题干分析

拿到任何话题的第一步当然是审题，
在这个阶段，值得考虑的有以下几个方面。

1. 话题背景

很多老师都告诉学生要紧扣题目的关键词。比如，有这样一种说法，当题目中有关键词是绝对词的时候，建议学生去写反驳。举个例子：Universities should require every student to take a variety of courses outside the student's field of study. 这个话题很多人看到之后第一眼注意到的词就是"every"，于是大部分学生第一反应就是要写反驳，全文充斥的都是"为什么不该学外学科的课程"之类的内容。但其实，这个话题显然具有极强的社会现实意义，而且绝大部分学校都会要求学生去学外专业的一些选修课程。因此，这道题大家本来应该写"为什么学外专业课程对我们的本专业学习有价值"，甚至是"学外专业课程对整个人生发展的价值"，但是，由于过分关注极端词，导致很多考生忽视了真正重要的问题，而关注非常零星的特殊现象，即某些个别情况下，某些人可能不需要学习外学科课程。

出题官的建议是：关注论题背后真正的话题（Focus on what is really at issue），而不是紧盯某些具体词语。每一道 issue 题目都不是一个脱离现实世界的命题，它们都是具有现实意义的。同学们应该先站在说话者的角度，去考虑，当他这么讲的时候，他是想指出什么样的社会现实，他想解决什么社会问题。而不是单纯去想这个说法是对的还是错的。我再举几个例子来帮助大家对比两种思路的区别。

"No field of study can advance significantly unless it incorporates knowledge and experience from outside that field." 面对这道题目，一些人很快盯上了 no 这个绝对词，于是就去想有没有学科的发展不太依赖外部学科。有的人可能想到了数学。假如数学真的不需要依赖外部学科，那理论上这一个例子就可以表明说话者的观点是错的。但我们不可能就去只写数学啊，这样就完全不能反映这个命题真正的社会意义了。很显然，这个话题牵扯的是一个非常普遍的现象，就是学科之间的相互影响和交叉。如今的学术领域，就算能够找到极个别独自发展的领域，但是绝大多数领域都深深受到了其他领域的影响，很可能也在影响着其他领域。因此，显然这道题真正应该思考的是：为什么会出现这样的现象？为什么如今社会学科已经很难独立发展？

"In order to become well-rounded individuals, all college students should be required to take courses in which they read poetry, novels, mythology, and other types of imaginative literature." 一种写法纠结于为什么有些学生不需要学 imaginative literature，于是全文都在陈述反驳的理由。但是，我们可以认为这个建议过分激进，但不妨碍我们充分考虑这个建议的意义。我们应该考虑现在的社会背景，那就是大学教育倾向于强调理性思维和逻辑思维，从而忽视了人文精神的培养。在这个语境下，说话者认为，去学习 imaginative literature 是一个重要的弥补。那我们这篇文章无论最后立场如何，都应该去讨论 imaginative literature 有着什么样的现实社会意义。

"In any profession—business, politics, education, government—those in power should step down after five years." 看到这个题目，我就想起了很多前的学生尝试的思路，我觉得很有意思。他们经常纠结于那个 five，领袖换届到底是五年好还是六年好还是八年好……囧。显然，这个题目真正关注的问题是：为什么我们不能让一个领袖长期处在领导位置，为什么一定要强迫轮换？说话者说的到底是 five 还是 six 并不会改变这道题目的实质。

"Colleges and universities should require their students to spend at least one semester studying in a foreign country." 读者应该明白这道题的关键点并不在于是 one semester 还是 one year 还是 two months。这道题目真正想探讨的是出国学习对大学生的意义，以及这种意义是否值得学校要求学生出国交流。

当大家明白以上我所说的东西后，我相信你们也就应该明白为什么我会把 "Educational institutions have a responsibility to dissuade students from pursuing fields of study in which they are unlikely to succeed." "College students should be encouraged to pursue subjects that interest them, rather than the courses that seem most likely to lead to jobs." 和 "Educational institutions should actively encourage their students to choose fields of study in which jobs are plentiful." 这样的题目都合并在了一起。我们不需要关注题目用的词是 fields 还是 subjects 或是 courses，也不需要关注题目问的是"选专业应该选好找工作的"，还是"选专业应该选自己感兴趣的"。因为所有这些都是同一个社会话题，即"选专业是看兴趣特长，还是看实用价值"。当我们把握到这个核心争论点的时候，我们写出来的文章才是真正有意义的。同学们完全没有任何必要担心，如果题干说的是"选专业"，而我写成了"选课程"，算不算跑题。答案：不算！只要你处理了说话者想谈论的话题，就不算跑题。反而，当你过分纠结说话者的用词，会导致文章可能忽视了话题最有社会意义的部分。

2. 题目的逻辑形式

如果题目只是一个简单命题，那就没什么好注意的，比如：Universities should require every student to take a variety of courses outside the student's field of study. 但是，有些题干比较复杂，涉及多个命题以及命题之间的关系。这些变化都可能会对未来我们的构思和全文安排产生潜在的影响，因此我们需要在审题的时候注意以下几种可能的变化。

(1) 观点—理由型题目

很多题干会先给一个 claim，然后给一个 reason，比如：Claim: Any piece of information referred to as a fact should be mistrusted, since it may well be proven false in the future. Reason: Much of the information that people assume is factual, and actually turns out to be inaccurate. 面对这种题目，我们将会分别处理 reason 与 claim 的合理性。

并不是每一个观点—理由型的题目都是以这种直接的 claim + reason 的形式表现的。任何论题，如果包含一个看法，加上为这个看法提供的理由，其实构成了观点—理由型结构，都适合用同样的布局方式。比如：The human mind will always be superior to machines because machines are only tools of human minds. / Scandals are useful because they focus our attention on problems in ways that no speaker or reformer ever could. because 引导的部分就相当于 reason，而主句的部分就相当于 claim。

(2) 双方争论型题目

有一些题目会指出 some people 的想法和 other people 看似对立的想法。这种题型要求我们考虑双方立场。那么，这是否意味着我们要分别写两个部分：一部分谈第一个话题，一部分谈第二个话题呢？不见得，取决于两方观点是否是现实中恰好对立的看法。

当双方观点恰好对立时,我们没有必要把它们当作两个独立话题来讨论。暂且把 some people 的想法称为 A 观点,other people 的想法称为 B 观点。比如:Some people believe that college students should consider only their own talents and interests when choosing a field of study. Others believe that college students should base their choice of a field of study on the availability of jobs in that field. 这道题目当中,两方观点就是同一个论题下恰好对立的两面。如果我们认同选专业只应考虑兴趣特长,那我们就是在说不要考虑就业前景,反之亦然。换一个角度理解,我前面已经说过,不要纠缠于说话者的具体用词,应该考虑整个话题的社会意义。那么这两个观点其实都是在讨论选专业时到底应该考虑什么。因此,只要我们把选专业时到底考虑什么这个问题讲清楚,两方的观点我们其实就都已经处理了,因为我们势必会讨论到兴趣、特长、就业等因素在我们选专业时的权重。简而言之,当双方争论型题目出现,但双方立场其实就是同一个话题的正反两面时,我们直接处理整个话题就好。

与此相对的是,有时这种双方争论型题目中的两方观点其实并不对立。如:Some people believe that the purpose of education is to free the mind and the spirit. Others believe that formal education tends to restrain our minds and spirits rather than set them free. 前者认为,教育要解放思想;后者认为,正统教育限制了思想。细心的读者可能会发现,两个观点可以都是对的,因为前者讨论的是教育的理想,而后者谈论的是教育的现实。理想是好的,现实是骨感的,这很正常啊。因此,这两方其实谈论的是不同的话题,我们也必须把两个话题都分别处理了,我们既应该谈论教育的目的,同样也应该谈论教育的现状。

(3) 包含多个子命题的题目

还有一些题目乍一看没什么特别的,但其实包含了几个独立的内容。这时,我们要注意,论题的每个部分都需要讨论到。比如:The best way to teach is to praise positive actions and ignore negative ones. 这道题明显是两部分的并列:教育需要鼓励积极行为,以及教育需要忽视消极行为。同意前者不代表反对后者,反之亦然。所以,两部分是独立的,两部分都需要在写作时讨论到。当然,两者都需要讨论,不代表两者需要占据同样的篇幅。毕竟,鼓励积极行为的争议性比较小,而忽视消极行为的争议比较大。因此,后者自然值得我们花更多笔墨。

3. 模糊概念的定义

有一些话题中涉及了一些可能比较抽象或存在多种理解方式的概念,我们必须要明确我们准备使用哪种理解方式,并保证从始至终的统一性。比如:It is no longer possible for a society to regard any living man or woman as a hero. hero 这个词有广义和狭义的理解:狭义的理解就是舍己救人、舍己为国的那些个体,比如火灾中殉职的消防队员、黄继光、邱少云;广义的 hero 如今已经扩展到了行为楷模、个人偶像的范围,所以乔丹、梅西、Lady Gaga、Brad Pitt 都可能成为某些人心目中的英雄。这里没有标准答案必须选择哪个定义,我们需要保证的是我们知道自己选择哪个定义,并且在文章中能够清晰地体现出来。

当然,我们也可以分别谈论两种意义下论题是否合理。我们可能觉得,取狭义理解,该论题是错的,而取广义理解,该论题是对的。这也是可以的,只要在写的时候明确我们当时选择的是什么理解方式。

Step 2　头脑风暴

当我们明确话题之后，
就要开始打开思路了。

1. 分别考虑对支持者和反对者有利的理由或情况

请原谅我无法简单地告诉大家，如何为一个观点寻找理由。原因是：这完全是与具体题目相关的，如果我不了解法律，当我遇到一道法律类的题目时，我就是没有理由，什么都不用多说了。所以，请容我再次强调，Issue 部分如果要充分准备，本书后面的题目思路分析部分将是非常重要的资料。

我现在仍然需要谈一些非常重要的东西。大部分同学在理解清楚题意之后，就会马上想，是同意呢还是反对呢？如果同意，想想有什么理由可以支持，然后就可以写了。这是我们过去写作文的策略。现在，我希望大家意识到，这个考试考查的是 critical thinking，其中的核心是，我们的思维过程必须经历全面的分析，我们的观点必须有充分的证据可以支持。因此，重要的不是我们的观点，而是我们的论证过程。我可以赞同，可以反对，可以有保留地赞同或反对，可以认为两方都有道理，可以在不同情况下持有不同态度。这些立场全都无所谓。有所谓的是，无论有什么样的立场，都必须能够给出充分的论证，以及必须考虑对方的立场。简单的完全赞同和分析过反对者立场之后的完全赞同是不一样的过程，前者可能是一个盲信者，而后者就是有着 criticality 的思考者，而这个考试需要的是后者。

拿到一道题目后，我们可以有立场，但并不需要马上有立场，并且我们不用认定自己暂时的立场是不能变的。我们首先要做的是把自己放在支持者的立场上，去想他们为什么会这么说，他们的道理是什么，或者在哪些情况下他们的说法是有道理的。之后，再站在反对者的角度上做同样的事情。这些 issue 题目都是有社会争议的，意味着肯定有很多支持者和反对者，因此我们没有理由认为只有自己才是有道理的，相反，我们应该充分考察论题双方的合理性（这不代表我们将没有明确立场）。

比如：As people rely more and more on technology to solve problems, the ability of humans to think for themselves will surely deteriorate. 遇到"依赖科技导致人类能力下降"的问题，我马上想到我自己如今不用电脑已经不会写字，不用计算器基本算不出东西。我意识到，这个说话者想指出的可能就是这样的"用进废退"的现象，当我们长期不用某种能力，而用机器替代之后，我们的这种能力就会下降。但这不代表我就认为这个说法一定对了，我只是认为它有道理。接下来，我就会去设想反对方的立场，很多人都会认为科技促进了人类的思维能力，比如：科技为我们创造了新的平台去思考，科技省去了我们做烦琐重复工作的时间，这些省下来的时间可以投入更有创造力的思维当中，等等。以前有学生就会问我："那你到底是同意还是反对啊？"这就是两种意识的关键区别，大部分人想要的是答案，且是一个明确的 yes 或 no 的答案，而 critical thinking 要的是思考过程。根据我的分析结果，那我肯定会认为，科技确实在某些程度上削弱了我们的某些思维能力，但是却在其他方面打开了我们的思维。我们需要给出清楚的立场，但不代表我们需要给出一个简单的立场。

再举个例子：No field of study can advance significantly unless it incorporates knowledge and experience from outside that field. "所有学科都需要吸收外学科知识才能进步。"我就开始检索各大学科。我想到文科当中文史哲不分家，自然科学当中理化生互相关联，整个工科都需要理科的工具。于是，我肯定认为这个观点超级有道理。但我仍然意识到，理论数学似乎是一个相对独立的学科，毕竟，数学公理、定理的对与错是不依赖其他学科知识的，因为理论数学是非经验学科。基于以上分析，我的结论也应该是分情况的，大部分情况下是认可的，但是在少部分情况下是反对的。

2. 继续考虑以上理由和情况我们是否认可

刚才我们站在双方视角考虑了各种理由、情况，千万不要认为我们必须相信它们。因为，我们只是站在各方角度思考了其合理的地方，而合理不等于正确，我们仍然可以进一步考虑：以上的理由、情况真的无可辩驳吗？

比如，刚才"No field of study can advance significantly unless it incorporates knowledge and experience from outside that field."这道题。我确实觉得文理工都依赖其他学科，但理论数学真的独立吗？是的，我承认数学真理的证明本身是纯数学过程，理论上可以离开所有自然科学。但当我想到，历史上很多物理学的发展带动了新的数学工具的发展，以及新的科技手段加速了数学规律的寻找，我意识到，其实时至今日，理论数学也非完全独立。因此，这个论题我是完全赞同的。只不过，我的赞同是全面思考后的结果，而不是盲目的一拍脑门之后的主观直觉。

结论：在分析题目思路时，我们就是墙头草。真正理性的人不是坚持自己一定对的人，而是能让自己的立场随着证据而变的人。

3. 为我们确定的每个理由寻找证据

3分和4分GRE写作文章的一个质的区别是：4分文章要求我们的每一个论点都必须有至少相关的依据，而3分文章的一大缺陷是，其某些立场没有得到证据的证明，或者证据完全不相关。因此，在实际写作当中，我们必须保证自己的每一个主观判断得到支持，而不是一直在写大话、空话。有些同学这么写段落，观点句是：应该做A，因为A可以带来B。然后，段内就开始说车轱辘话：不做A我们是没法实现B的。要想实现B，我们必须要做A。除非我们不想实现B，否则我们肯定要做A。所以，应该做A，这样才能实现B。太令人无语了，这可不叫证据，这叫废话，叫凑字数，叫寻找自我心理安慰。以为自己写了很多东西，其实就是把垃圾写了一遍又一遍。

同样，如果我们不懂一个话题，自然就不可能找到证据，所以我又一次要强调本书后面章节中题目分析的重要性。但是此刻，我要做的事情是拓展大家的思维，因为很多同学，甚至老师在看到某个话题时觉得自己没有任何证据，但其实这是因为他们对"证据"的理解非常狭隘，给自己凭空制造了思维障碍。

（1）名人个案

大部分学生在各种写作考试中都被鼓励写名人案例，于是很多学生以为GRE写作也必须要写名人案例。随便看一看官方的范文，无论是高分还是低分，你会发现，写名人案例的文章屈指可数。名人案例当然是可行的，但不是必需的。

值得一提的事情是，大家不用关注名人经历细节的精确性，小的细节偏差并不会被惩罚，比如你在写凡·高的例子的时候，把"凡·高影响了后来的expressionism"，写成了"凡·高影响了后来的impressionism"，只要这个失误和文章核心论点没有直接关系，这种影响是不会被追究的。

（2）社会现象

更方便的是思考社会普遍存在的现象，这些现象广泛存在，并不一定是名人，但是我们总能见到，这仍然可以提供非常好的证据。比如，之前提到的题目"As people rely more and more on technology to solve problems, the ability of humans to think for themselves will surely deteriorate.", 在考虑支持说话者立场的时候，我想到了依赖文字处理系统导致人们无法写字，依赖计算器导致心算能力下降。这些就是例子，虽然并不是某个具体人的例子，但仍然是具有说服力的合理的证据。

（3）假想（不是瞎编）的合理场景

这其实是特别好用的一种寻找证据的方式。所谓假想，绝对不是捏造虚假信息，而是设身处地考虑一种可能情况，考虑在这种情况下正常会发生的事情。比如，面对 "Educational institutions have a responsibility to dissuade students from pursuing fields of study in which they are unlikely to succeed." 看这道题时，我的一个可能的反对理由是：要是学生仅考虑就业，而选择了自己不感兴趣、不擅长的领域，最后不成功的可能性反而很大。要证明这一点，我并不一定非得举什么达尔文或乔布斯的例子。我会设想大学当中经常见到的情况，假想一个学生选了热门的计算机专业，但是他从小不擅长逻辑，擅长的是想象思维、发散思维，而且对于枯燥的编程并没有任何热情，他很可能在大学课堂上感到吃力、乏味，进而很可能就产生厌学情绪，严重影响到成绩，甚至影响到毕业。因此，也许他有可能找到工作，但是几乎很难找到优质的工作，因为周围的人最后可能都比他强很多。

这就不是一个真人真事，但是我们正常人都可以结合实际社会现实而认识到类似现象存在的可能性，这就起到了对我的论点的支持作用。

（4）个人案例

我们可以使用自己的或者周围同学的个人经历，我在考场上也这么做过，当然最后得分也是 5 分。但在这里我非常不推荐同学们仿效，因为出题官专门指出 "personal examples run the risk of sounding trivial"。我们个人的案例如果包含了过多专属于个人的特殊情况，这个例子很可能只是特殊情况，不能起到证明作用。我在举个人案例的时候，都是在表现一种普遍，至少是常见的社会现象，有意识地避免特殊性，所以才能起到正向效果。因此，必须提醒大家，如果要使用个人案例，请一定保证代表性。

Step 3　全文布局

在有了充分的思路之后，
我们就该考虑文章的具体安排了。

这里必须声明的是，ETS 从来没有要求固定的布局方式。事实上，官方指南明确指出，不同国家地区的考生经常有完全不同的布局习惯，这些在考官看来都是可以接受的，只要最终将文章表达清楚，因为他们在意的是文章反映出来的理性思维能力。因此，本章给同学们推荐的布局方式绝对不是唯一的，只是比较方便的安排。

1. 开头的背景引出

文章开篇比较好用的一种做法就是介绍话题提出的背景，这其实是基于我们头脑风暴阶段对话题社会意义的思考。比如，如果论题是一个建议，我们就可以谈一谈说话者提出这个建议想要解决的问题。比如：

Universities should require every student to take a variety of courses outside the student's field of study. 开头就可以这样引出：

> Interdisciplinary study abounds in the current world. It seems that no modern field of study can advance significantly without being heavily influenced by wisdom and skills from other areas. For this reason, sometimes it is argued that college students should all be required to participate in courses outside their own major fields of study.

再比如，如果题目谈论的是一个现象的存在，那就可以在文章一开始谈论一下这个现象之所以会发生的背后的可能原因。举个例子：In this age of intensive media coverage, it is no longer possible for a society to regard any living man or woman as a hero. 开头就可以这样引出：

> Heroes are often perceived as saint-like figures with nothing but a selfless heart, ready to sacrifice their own benefits for the greater good. However, no one is without self-interest, and no one is without character flaw. Thus, these seemingly perfect images are often socially constructed rather than a reflection of reality. With the rise of the ubiquitous modern media and social networks, every celebrated public figure will be put under the spotlight, and almost certainly no one can stand the test of such scrutiny. As a result, it appears that under this intensive media coverage, it is unlikely that any individual can maintain his or her heroic image.

2. 开头的清楚定义

前面审题部分我们曾经提到过模糊概念的定义。如果论题涉及某个可能具有多重理解的定义，且我们在文章中打算选择其中某种明确的理解方式时，建议开头交代清楚我们所选择的理解方式。比如：In this age of intensive media coverage, it is no longer possible for a society to regard any living man or woman as a hero. 由于 hero 可以取广义或狭义的理解，所以我必须给出明确的选择。如果选择了广义的理解方式，可以在开头这么交代：

> It is argued that modern media coverage made it impossible for any individual to stand as a socially-accepted hero. Before any discussion, it is imperative to clarify what the word "hero" refers to. Traditionally, a hero only represents a selfless being who has done extraordinary deeds, which sacrificed his/her own good for the sake of others' or the society's well-being. However, today, the meaning of that word has expanded to incorporate any individuals with astounding achievements, selfless or not. The list probably includes names like Michael Jordan, Steve Jobs, and Lady Gaga. It is under this definition that I plan to proceed with my discussion.

当然，无论是背景还是定义，这都不是我们必须做的事情，只是一种选择。更重要的还是正文段落的安排，我个人习惯于采用以下两种非常好用的结构。

3. 分情况讨论

如果在头脑风暴阶段，我们考虑了观点成立的情况和观点不成立的情况，则开头（仍然可以先交代背景）

就可以明确指出，将考虑不同的情况，并且给出结论。正文则是多个并列段落，每个段落交代一种情况。比如：No field of study can advance significantly unless it incorporates knowledge and experience from outside that field. 如果认定自然科学、人文领域、工程类都需要学科间的影响，但理论数学不需要（只是一种写法，不是非得这么写），那么可能这么安排文章：

> （背景交代）Under this context, it is sometimes proposed that the progress of every field of study has to somewhat depend on the achievement of outside influences. As we examine different contemporary academic disciplines, we shall see that this holds true for most areas of study, but there do exist a few exceptions. Therefore, I generally agree with the prompt, but it should not be carried to the extreme.
>
> For starters, in natural sciences, cross-discipline influence has become an indispensable factor in the generation and validation of new hypotheses…
>
> The same can also be said for the humanities…
>
> Achievements in the field of engineering also owe much to the theoretical inputs of other areas…
>
> However, we should be cautious to notice the presence of certain exception, such as theoretical mathematics…

以上例子当中，分情况讨论之后各个领域结论有所不同，所以文章观点也不是一边倒的。但有些话题当中，分情况讨论之后仍然会给出统一的结论。比如：Unfortunately, in contemporary society, creating an appealing image has become more important than the reality or truth behind that image. 在思考阶段，我可能会觉得，所有领域当中 image 都好像变得越来越重要了，但是最终还是 reality or truth 决定了人们的态度。那么，我就会在开头交代清楚我会分情况研究，但我将得出统一的观点。正文当中我仍然将逐个情况讨论。

> （背景交代）Because of these phenomena, it is often argued that, in modern society, an appealing image outweighs truth or reality in people's judgments. As we examine different fields of human endeavors, we shall see that while the modern world has grown to stress the impact of the first impression more than before, ultimately it is still the truth and reality behind every image that shape society's opinions.
>
> For starters, in the entertainment world…
>
> The same also holds for the business world…
>
> In the academic world…

4. 分理由展开

在头脑风暴阶段，如果我分别考虑了支持者的理由和反对者的理由，那么在写作时，我就会表明，有一些支持的理由和反对的理由，以及它们是否合理，然后明确给出自己的观点。正文段落的安排就是逐条讨论支持和反对的理由。不见得非得支持的理由在前，我们当然也可以先写反对的理由，再去讨论支持的理由，但总的来说尽量不要支持-反对交替进行，这样可能会干扰读者的理解。比如：Government officials should rely on their own judgment rather than unquestioningly carry out the will of the people they serve. 我认为双方立场都有可取之处，而我最终的结论也是要两者兼备的。

> It is not easy to be a government official. You are constantly judged by the people you serve, and you never seem to satisfy everybody's needs. In fact, you never will, so it is important to have your own judgement on important issues. That said, one should not go to the other extreme of completely ignoring people's opinions. In fact, a government official should always form his/her own judgment, but that judgment should be based on sufficient research of relevant information and a comprehensive consideration of people's needs.
>
> For starters, an official simply cannot indiscriminately listen to people's will, because the term "people's will" assumes, unwarrantedly, the homogeneity of people's opinions, when in reality, the society is always a mixture of conflicting interests, all of which belong to people…
>
> It is also easy to picture a scenario in which an urgent decision has to be made, say, to send out rescue teams after an earthquake or a tsunami. You can only listen to the opinions of experts on disasters…
>
> Besides, regarding projects aiming to boost a nation's long term potential, an official often has to temporarily leave aside people's will, because the public tends to be short-sighted…
>
> However, I would never say the government should be blind to people's will. At the least, its decisions need to be transparent to its people…

上面这个例子当中，我考虑了双方观点，最终平衡了双方观点。但有些文章中，我在考虑了双方观点之后，仍然会认为某方的理由是站不住脚的，所以最后仍然会给出一边倒的看法。比如：Universities should require every student to take a variety of courses outside the student's field of study.

> Almost every university in the modern education system requires students to take courses beyond their own major field of study. This pervasive phenomenon itself alone should suggest, if not entail, that there are good reasons for learning additional subjects. In this essay, I shall try to illuminate the rationale behind it.
>
> For starters, today's academic circle has seen a growing connection between what used to be relatively separate fields of study…
>
> Second, life is a long journey with many unexpected twists and turns…
>
> However, some people may argue that there will be students who have already decided for sure what they want to do later in their life, so learning anything else would be a waste of their time. However…
>
> Some may argue that taking additional courses should be discretionary rather than mandatory. However…

以上文章中我赞同论题，但是在最后两个正文段，我仍然考虑了反对者的理由，只不过我会反驳掉它们，所以最终我仍然会给出完全赞同的判断。

总的来说，逐个情况讨论，逐个列举理由，这两种安排法非常简便，适合同学们考虑使用。当然，如前所言，全文的布局有很多灵活的地方，本书的很多优秀范文也探索了其他可能性，如果同学们有较强的语言控制力，是完全可以跳出框架的。只要我们的文章结构能保证清晰、有条理，都是可以接受的。

5. 特殊情况：观点—理由型文章的安排

有些同学特别害怕遇到 claim—reason 型题目，其实这种题目一点都不可怕。那个 claim 就相当于任何一道题目的话题，而那个 reason 相当于白送给我们说话者的动机。所以，其实如果我们采取分理由展开的写法，那个 reason 可以直接写在开头的背景当中，或者作为第一个正方理由存在。最后我们的全文安排是没有任何特殊之处的。比如：Claim：Nations should suspend government funding for the arts when significant numbers of their citizens are hungry or unemployed. Reason：It is inappropriate—and, perhaps, even cruel—to use public resources to fund the arts when people's basic needs are not being met.

> The speaker concludes that the government should suspend funding for the arts when the country suffers from hunger and unemployment, because it seems unjust to waste resources on less pressing needs when basic ones are not secured. （开头借用 reason 引出话题）As much as I agree that the need for food and jobs clearly outweighs artistic demands, this reason alone does not warrant the rash decision to completely stop funding the arts.
>
> Let me first concede that people's basic needs should always be a nation's priority. （承认 reason，相当于普通话题当中给出支持者的第一个理由）
>
> However, on a societal scale, much more debatable is whether the government should simply neglect the development of the arts for the sake of solving starvation and unemployment. Off the top of my head is the counterargument that arts and economy are no longer dichotomous...
>
> In addition, arts are uplifting, especially in cases of crises...
>
> Finally, suspending funding for the arts will simply not help with other, more pressing issues...

6. 特殊情况：双方争论型文章的安排

之前提到过，双方争论型文章中，如果双方观点真的直接相悖，这其实还是同一个话题，没有必要特别处理。但是，如果双方观点其实没有对立，则这个文章我们需要分别谈论两个话题。在写作中，我们也会类似地处理。开头我会先表达两个观点并不对立，然后指出我对各方的看法。正文也是分别分析双方观点有道理和没道理的地方。比如：Some people believe that the purpose of education is to free the mind and the spirit. Others believe that formal education tends to restrain our minds and spirits rather than set them free.

> The prompt seemingly raises a debate between opposing parties, with the former claiming that education should aim at freeing the mind and the spirits, and the latter arguing that former education tends to restrain our minds and spirit. However, even a cursory analysis of the two statements would reveal that there is no inherent tension between the two statements at all, because the former is a claim about the purpose of education, while the latter one is regarding the actual status of former education. （指出两个论点不矛盾）I believe that both statements have raised valid points, and both need some qualification. （指出对两个观点各自的看法）

For starters, there is no denying that education should enlighten people's mind, and when it does that, it completely changes people's mind for the better...（肯定第一个观点有道理的地方）

But we should avoid carrying the statement to the extreme. While inspiration is an important goal in education, it is not everything...（指出对第一个观点可能的反驳）

Having clearly stated what the purpose of education is, now let's evaluate how well our formal education system does when measured against these standards. I do think most of our elementary schools and secondary schools are doing well with regard to teaching basic knowledge and skills, but they are underperforming when it comes to enlightenment...（指出第二个观点有道理的地方）

However, there are still places in formal education where you can be enlightened. That's why you go to the good schools, or the top university programs...（指出对第二个观点可能的反驳）

以上所讲的全文布局的策略应该已经足够应用到所有 issue 话题当中，但在此，我还是要鼓励有能力的同学跳出条条框框，通过研读范文学习更多的写作方式。

Step 4　段内展开

　　3 分和 4 分文章本质的区别就是，3 分文章段内基本没有对观点的展开，或者段内的证据和观点毫无关系；4 分文章段内至少有一定的证据，而这些证据和观点至少是相关的。而 4 分与 4 分以上文章的区别就在于，4 分以上的文章，段内展开非常充分，而且很有说服力。这里，我不想讲段内展开需要做到什么才能超越 3 分，因为这实在太简单了，只要我们稍微对题目有一点点准备，给一点点相关的证据（前面已经说过，不是非得要背诵名人案例，我们有非常丰富的证据来源），就可以达到 4 分的要求。我在这里想谈的是，为什么我们的段内展开不能获得更高的分数，以及我们到底要做到什么段内展开才算优秀。

我们不是在为自己展开，而是在为读者展开。

　　曾经有多位同事向我表达过"学生水平那么差，我们就告诉他们每个地方必须写什么就好了。"这样的想法。于是，流行这样一种段内展开的讲法："第一句写观点和理由，第二句做解释，第三句举例子，第四句总结。"我听完目瞪口呆，而许多年后我才发现，原来我是少数派。学生们总觉得没什么可写，所以当老师告诉他们有固定的四句话可写，他们普遍觉得很开心。

　　这只不过是例行公事，只要把自己放在读者角度，我们就很容易意识到，这样的文章很可能毫无说服力。我印象最深的是曾经有一次讲 TOEFL 写作（理论上展开理由的深度比 GRE 写作要求要低一些）的时候，有同学写这样一个话题"选专业应该考虑兴趣还是就业"，这个话题在我们 GRE 写作中其实也有，前面咱们也见到了。这位同学支持的是"选专业应该优先考虑就业"，他的段内展开是这么写的：

> Students should definitely think about their career prospects, because this guarantees them a better future.（观点和理由）If they don't think about the job market, they may study something that cannot get them a job.（所谓的解释）For example, my friend Tom did not think about jobs when he picked Physics, and he is now jobless; but my friend Jake researched the job market when he picked Chemistry, and now he earns over 1 million dollars every year.（举例）Thus, clearly we should consider our job prospects when picking our major.（总结）

都不用想读者会不会被他说服了，读者不会觉得这个论证过程有任何道理。段落中列举的两个朋友的"例子"无非就是把观点重复了一遍。真正让我无法信服的地方就是，为什么选了化学就能找到有钱的工作，为什么选了物理就会找不到工作。中间的因果关系全部缺失，让我觉得这个例子莫名其妙。

以前在培训教师的时候，我问过这样一个问题："如果段落主题是，应该做 X，因为做 X 能带来 Y，那么从 X 到 Y 的因果关系是否需要接下来的那句解释，比如指出中间经历的过程，X 会导致 Z，进而导致 W，进而导致 Y？"在场的几乎所有教师都回答说应该。我又问应该解释几句？很多人都认为一句就够了。

答案是：这里根本没有客观标准应该解释几句，甚至是否应该展开。展开多少，取决于作者对读者的期望，即读者所拥有的背景信息。如果大家觉得 X 和 Y 的因果关系非常紧密，简直就是一般常识，则我们甚至不需要解释。但是如果 X 和 Y 的因果关系非常抽象，则我们必须解释，而且甚至要详细解释，而这就完全不是一句话解释就能搞定的了。更不用说举例了，我们举例是为了帮助读者理解，如果例子非常抽象，超越了读者的认识，那这个举例就是摆设，没有任何有效的说服力。

下面先给大家看几个段落。题目：Some people believe that college students should consider only their own talents and interests when choosing a field of study. Others believe that college students should base their choices of a field of study on the availability of jobs in that field. 段落主题是：很多人并不知道自己的兴趣是什么，因此选专业考虑就业是很正常的。但是，并不是每个读者都能理解为什么在我们国家，学生到高中毕业都不知道自己喜欢什么是这么普遍的事情。于是，我就有义务给潜在的读者讲清楚，这个情况是如何发生的，以表明我所给的理由并不是在处理一个偶然的现象，而是在处理一个普遍存在的现象。（否则，我的理由的价值将大打折扣。）

> Not everyone who graduates from high school knows who he/she really is. Take the Chinese high school education system for example. Everyone here studies a similar curriculum. If you focus on science and technology, you're required to take Chinese, Math, English, Physics, Chemistry and Biology; or if you focus on humanity, you will have to take Chinese, Math, English, Politics, History, and Geography. Most students are, therefore, not actually aware of other potential fields that could one day become their career. In fact, a lot of skills that could later become important assets in a profession, such as communication skills, ability to handle pressure, or physical strength, cannot be reflected at this stage. Consequently, if a student is not exceptional in any of these fields, chances are high that he/she knows neither about his/her own passion nor his/her natural gift.（全部都是在解释为什么会出现大量的学生不知道自己的兴趣。）What are his/her best odds for a choice of major then? I do believe a decision based on job availability is the rational thing to do. Today, if you pick Computer Science, for example, even if you only attend a second-tier college and get an average GPA of C+,

you are still going to be popular in the job market. All the Internet startups are in desperate need of coders, so these professionals get much higher pay than fresh graduates from most other majors. It's true; the student may not enjoy his/her job, but let's be realistic. He/She will have enough money, and he/she can do fun things after work. （全部都是在解释为什么选择了好就业的领域，即便没有兴趣，但最后结果不会太差。）

再给大家呈现一个写得较为失败的段落，也就是解释得不清楚的段落。话题是：To understand the most important characteristics of a society, one must study its major cities. 段落主题是：大城市能够表现社会的重要特点。

> For starters, it would be silly to understate the value of major cities in displaying important traits of a society. Just look at New York. When the American economy was down, New York was the first to feel the chill: bankrupted businesses, jobless people, and empty stores. （这是一篇典型的4分文章的展开，它是相关的，但不具有很强的说服力。它大概说明了，美国的经济可以反映在纽约的一些现象上。但是，它并没有说明为什么会有这样的联系。）New York is not just the financial center of America; it is also its cultural center. （这个地方与前面并列，开始谈论文化，而我们希望作者能够说清楚，纽约的什么现象可以反映出美国什么样的文化特点。）Being labeled as one of the most diverse countries in the world, America embraces people of all ethnicities and colors in its society, as can also be vividly displayed on New York's streets. New York does not care where you're from. You can be American, Hungarian, Thai, Chinese, Ethiopian, or Nigerian, but you can still be a New Yorker. （结果，后面都只是在说纽约具有多元化，这和前面有什么关系？也许，作者想说的是，美国是个多元化的国家，所以纽约的多元化就反映出了这一点。但问题是，作者没有把这些说出来，所以读者只能凭空猜测。）

总的来说，我希望大家在写作文的时候不是在对自己说话，而是在对潜在的读者说话，因此，希望同学们能够去考虑一个与我们背景不同的人看到我们的文章时可能有的想法：如果读者可能看不懂，我们则需要用更简单的语言，或者用例子来解释；如果读者不明白为什么，我们则需要解释清楚我们所谈论的事件之间的关系；如果读者可能不接受我们的立场，我们则要用典型的案例来支撑我们的看法；而且如果读者可能的反驳是有道理的，我们要先处理读者的观点，即让步，然后再指出为什么这些反驳是可以被解决掉的。所有的一切都是在服务读者，在说服读者，而不是在服务我们自己。

最后，建议同学们在学习范文的时候，不要满足于明白作者现在做了什么事（提出观点、给出理由、做解释、给例子、做类比、做让步），而更要去想作者是在尝试解决什么样的读者问题。

优秀（Outstanding）、合格（Good）、糟糕（Poor）文章的区别

写了长长的方法论，我的理想当然是希望同学们能够真正学会分析性写作，而不是仅仅应对这个考试。但是，我也清楚地知道，不是每个同学都真的在意去把自己的写作变得非常优秀，至少，在紧张的学生生活中，我们可能还有更重要的努力方向。因此，眼下最需要的可能就是赶快获得一个合格的成绩。在此，我就用最精炼的语言来总结一下，到底需要做到什么就可以让我们的文章合格，以及需要做什么才能写出优秀的文章。

> ① 思考深度：优秀的文章会真正全面探索任何一个话题各方面的理由和证据；同学们请记住，合格的文章，只要形式上考虑了各方的一些理由和证据就可以了；失败的文章则经常只表达了一面之词。
> ② 结构：我不认为中国学生在文章结构上会有大的问题，无论哪个档次的学生都可以很容易做到使文章结构清晰。
> ③ 证据：优秀的文章中任何一个论点都会给出非常充分的证明，且例子解释得非常清晰；合格的文章中要保证所有论点都被具体展开，且展开是相关的；失败的文章要么不展开，要么例子和观点无关。
> ④ 语言：优秀的文章语言形式丰富，且用词极其精确；合格的文章，别人能基本看懂作者的意思；失败的文章，读者看不懂作者在说什么。

最后，为了快速达到合格的要求，给大家几条建议：①保证题干中每一个分句都讨论到了；②保证自己考虑了正反方的立场；③保证自己的每个抽象论点都具体展开了；④少挑战自己的语言极限，把事情说清楚。（每道题目下面都会有一个具体的写作要求，但其实只要做到以上几点，任何要求都已经满足了。）

第二章 怎么应对论证分析写作
(Analyze an Argument)

　　市面上流行把 GRE 分析性写作的第二部分称为 Argument，甚至称为驳论文，这是极端错误的，也是中国大陆考生平均只考 3 分的一个根本原因，它导致绝大部分人根本不知道这个考试实际的目的是什么。接下来我们将逐步带着同学们走出长久以来的误区。

　　首先，我们需要明白，这部分考试叫作 Analyze an Argument，即"论证分析"，意味着我们是在对别人的 Argument 进行分析。所以，这里的 Argument 指的是我们读到的那篇短文。

一、What is an argument?

Argument 的一个日常意思是"争论",但在逻辑语境下,Argument 并不需要包含争论,它的逻辑学意思是"论证"。所谓"论证"指的是**多个命题的集合,其中一个命题被其他语句所支持**。用近似的大白话表达就是,在一个论证当中,作者要表达一个观点,并为这个观点提供辩护或依据(justification / support)。其中,被支持的语句我们称为 Conclusion,即"结论";而用来支持结论的语句,我们称为 Premise,即"前提"。

以下都是论证,无论严谨与否,其中的结论已用下划线标出:
① GRE 很难,所以<u>我们一定要好好准备</u>。
② 万炜皮肤很白嫩,说明<u>他肯定没到 30 岁</u>。
③ 我这么努力,所以<u>我一定会考好的</u>。
④ 她最近突然变苗条了。我猜,<u>她最近肯定是加大了运动量</u>。

以下不是论证:
⑤ 我们一定要好好准备 GRE。(只有观点,没有提供任何理由进行辩护。)
⑥ 万炜皮肤很白嫩。(只有事实判断,没有支持任何观点。)
⑦ 我很努力,所以我后来考得很好。(只是陈述了关于两个事实的因果判断,没有用一个语句去支持另一个语句。)
⑧ 她最近变苗条是因为她加大了运动量。

以上的⑦会让很多同学感到困惑,尤其和③形成比对之后。为什么③与⑦看起来这么相似,却一个是论证,一个不是呢?这就必须要给大家讲清楚"因为""所以"这一对儿看起来很日常的逻辑词的多义性。在日常语言当中,"因为""所以"可以用来陈述两件事情之间的因果关系,比如⑦。从说话者的角度来看,"我努力"和"我考得很好"是两个已经发生的既定事实,说话者并没有想要去证明其中任何一件事情,他只是想表达这两件事情之间有联系。另一方面,"因为""所以"也可以用来表达推理,即作者用一些语句来支持、推断另一个语句。比如在③中,作者用"我努力"去推断"我会考好"。请注意,③中的"一定会"表明"我考好"这件事情是未发生、不确定的,它只是作者的推测。类似的,在④与⑧这一组中,⑧的说话者也只是在陈述两件事情之间的因果关系,我们无法从语句中看出作者是根据什么条件做出了什么样的推断;但是,在④中,"肯定"这个语气词表明作者是在推断"她加大了运动量",而作者的根据是"她最近突然变苗条了"这个事实。总的来说,大家一定要注意区分论证或推理关系与因果关系:因果关系表达的是两件事情之间先发生的事情造成了后发生的事情;论证、推理关系表达的是一个说话者确定的已知的事情在支持另一件事情,试图说服读者去接受被支持的语句。

二、What is an assumption?

在日常生活中,很多论证背后都有作者默认的某些主观判断。例:

① 万炜吃得很多，所以他一定会长胖。（吃多会长胖。）
② 万炜今天看起来很疲惫，所以他昨晚肯定没睡好。（晚上没睡好第二天就会看起来疲惫。）
③ 这个电影少儿不宜，所以万炜不应该看。（万炜是少儿。）

显然，以上三个例子当中，说话者默认了某些条件没有说出来（括号内的文字）。在日常生活当中，我们经常说话时也会吞掉某些信息，因为我们默认听话者会和我们形成共识（但很多时候是说话者的一厢情愿）。从逻辑上，这些**非事实性的、被作者主观默认的条件被称为论证的假设，即 assumption，它是作者论证成立所必须依赖的非事实性前提**。在以后的考试当中，assumption 将称为一个非常关键的概念，它是架起论证前提与结论之间的关键桥梁。与其相对的概念是**事实**，即 fact 或 evidence。通常，fact 和 evidence 是直接可以观察到的具体现象，而 assumption 是被主观接受的，无法直接观察到的判断。assumption 经常是论证当中隐藏的条件，比如以上三个例子当中。但 assumption 也可以是作者说出来的。

比如：万炜每天学习到晚上 12 点。而每天学到晚上 12 点肯定会让人心力交瘁，所以万炜肯定会心力交瘁。

其中，"万炜会心力交瘁" 显然是结论，"万炜每天学习到晚上 12 点" 是一个事实性的前提，而 "每天学到晚上 12 点会让人心力交瘁" 就是一个非事实性的前提，是作者的假设。

三、What is a line of reasoning?

在日常生活中，以及在论证分析考试的文章中，说话者的推理步骤经常不止一步，因此，就会存在一整条论证线索的问题。比如：

在最近一次调查中，80% 上过万炜老师课的受访者表示，他们的 GRE Verbal 成绩超过了大陆地区的平均分。鉴于最近孙小鹏同学报了万炜老师的 GRE 课程，我们有理由相信，孙小鹏同学的 GRE 成绩一定能显著提高。

这段话中作者试图证明的结论是 "孙小鹏同学的 GRE 成绩一定能显著提高"。为了证明这条结论，作者给出了两条事实证据，分别是 "调查中 80% 上过万炜老师课的受访者表示，他们的 GRE Verbal 成绩超过了大陆地区的平均分"，以及 "孙小鹏同学报了万炜老师的 GRE 课程"。但是，这两条信息并不是简单并列在一起就支持了最后的结论。作者其实隐藏了很多推论没有明确说出来。

首先，当作者借用调查数据 "80% 上过万炜老师课的受访者 GRE Verbal 成绩超过了大陆地区的平均分" 时，作者是想暗示 "大部分上过万炜老师课" 的学生 GRE Verbal 成绩很高。进一步，作者暗示（且他之后的论证必须依赖）"是因为万炜老师的课让这些学生 GRE Verbal 成绩提高的"。这时，再加上 "孙小鹏同学报了万炜老师的 GRE 课程"，作者就预测了孙小鹏同学未来 GRE 成绩会提高。我们可以画一个简单的结构图：

这个图反映了原文作者完整的推理路线，即 line of reasoning。其中，"大部分上过万炜老师课的学生 GRE Verbal 成绩高"和"因为万炜老师的课让这些人 GRE Verbal 成绩高"这两个判断是作者没有明说的，但是在上文中暗示了，并且在下文论证中必须要依赖于此，我们称之为论证中的 implication，即"暗示"。换言之，implication 就是作者论证步骤中所隐藏的推理步骤结论（不是论证的最终结论）。

以上我们就完成了论证体系中最基本的概念搭建，大家需要熟知的概念包括"论证（argument）""结论（conclusion）""前提（premise）""假设（assumption）""暗示（implication）"以及"推理路线（line of reasoning）"。

四、What needs to be done to analyze an argument?

GRE 论证分析测试要求我们理解、分析，并评论我们所看到的一篇论证文章。具体如下：

① 我们要提供的是一个分步骤的分析（step-by-step analysis），即我们需要按照推理路线逐步指出原文每一步骤的前提、结论（暗示）和假设；
② 制造能够削弱原文论证的反例（counterexample）；
③ 指出使原文论证更严谨的作者需要提供的额外证据或信息。

所谓的反例是针对论证中作者的主观假设的，这个反例可以是真实的，但更多情况下其实可以是假想的可能性，用来削弱假设的有效性。比如：万炜这次考得很好。说明他之前肯定用功了。

作者假设"考得好的唯一解释是用功"，即作者默认"没有其他原因可以解释万炜考得好"。但很可能读者会指出，如果万炜作弊，则他也有可能考得好。显然，我们并不知道万炜是不是作弊了，但作弊这个可能情况如果为真，就有效地削弱了作者的假设，进而削弱了整个论证。

很多学生以为论证分析就是驳论，于是过去二十年间中国考生流行做两件事情：一是背诵各种常见的"逻辑谬误"，比如"稻草人谬误（Strawman Fallacy）""混淆因果与相关（Confusion of Correlation and Causation）"。ETS 明确指出，我们并不需要这些专业术语来证明原作者论证的不严谨，我们只需要制造日常的、合理的反例。二是直接攻击别人的前提或结论，比如在刚才的例子当中，直接说"万炜考得并不好"或者"万炜可能没有用功"。我们必须谨记，论证分析是逻辑分析，我们制造反例不是为了评价原作者的前提或是结论，我们评价的仅仅是论证当中的假设。

很多人以为 GRE 写作只需要制造反例来反驳原作者就可以了，但事实上，反例是必需的，但不是整个论证分析的全部。于是，我们就必须要谈到最后一个步骤，即作者需要提供的额外信息。因为我们并不知道万炜是不是作弊了，因此我们需要要求作者去调查万炜在考试当中是否作弊，甚至是其他有可能造成他成绩提高的因素，从而才能真正加强"万炜努力"这个结论的可靠性。

简而言之，GRE 的论证分析不是在反驳原作者的论证，而是在帮助原作者建立一个更完备的、更严谨的论证。因此，我们当然要首先理解清楚他的论证，分析其中存在的不严谨性，并提出有效的针对逻辑严谨性的建设性意见（注意，不是针对结论的意见）。这模拟的其实就是未来进入学术界后，我们读到别人的论文之后应该思考的事情。我们的目的当然不非得是反驳别人的结论，我们需要学会的是分析别人建立结论的过程，并提供建设性的意见。当更多的证据呈现后，别人的结论可能变得更弱，但也可能变得更强。

为了让大家更明白我们具体要做些什么，针对之前的一篇中文 Argument，我们设计了一篇论证分析来供大家参考，我们会标注说明其中每部分起到了什么样的作用。

在原文当中，作者预测，报了万炜老师 GRE 课的孙小鹏同学的 GRE 成绩会显著提高。❶作者的预测主要基于一次最近的调查，其中 80% 上过万炜老师课的受访者表示，他们的 GRE Verbal 成绩超过了大陆地区的平均分。❷然而，该作者所依赖的证据并不足以让他做出如此积极的预测。

首先，仅仅基于该调查，我们无法认定上过万炜老师课的学生 Verbal 成绩真的很好。❸作者一方面假设了这个调查选样是随机的，❹然而实际上这个调查很可能就是万炜在朋友圈中发起的，而会加他朋友圈的人本来就是喜欢他的人，那些上了他的课没能提高成绩的人本身就不会喜欢他，也根本不会加他的朋友圈，更不会参与到这次调查当中。❺另一方面，作者还默认高于大陆的平均分就是一个优秀的分数。❻然而，学生要出国申请学校所需要的 GRE 成绩可能远高于大陆的平均分，而万炜的这些学生的分数可能仅仅勉强高于平均分。❼综上所述，作者必须告诉我们，这个调查是如何选取受访者的。以及，作者需要告诉我们万炜老师的学生 GRE Verbal 更准确的分数段。❽否则，本文无法证明万炜老师的学生 GRE Verbal 成绩是否真的好，则其后的论证也就完全失去了根据。

其次，就算万炜老师的学生 GRE Verbal 分数真的好，也没有足够的证据表明这是受益于万炜的 GRE 课程。❾作者假设万炜的课程是对他们分数高的唯一解释。❿而实际上，很有可能这些学生本来成绩已经超过了平均分，然后为了提高分数他们报了万炜的课，因为万炜在广告中声称可以帮助学生取得进步。但此后，这些学生可能根本没有获得任何提高，甚至考得更差了。此外，还有可能学生上了万炜的课没有提高，然后他们不得已又报了别的班，然后才取得了突破。甚至还有可能万炜开课的地方在北大、清华门口，这些学生天资聪颖，上任何人的课都会取得好成绩，跟万炜没什么关系。⓫简而言之，作者必须给出证据排除其他可能造成学生成绩好的因素，否则他将无法建立学生成绩和万炜的课程之间的直接关联。⓬

最后，就算万炜真的帮助提到了学生的 Verbal 成绩，但仅知道孙小鹏报了他的班也无法让我们认定孙小鹏一定将会取得 GRE 上的显著进步。⓭很有可能孙小鹏天资愚钝，就算遇到了大牛也无法被拯救；很有可能孙小鹏成绩已经非常高，上升空间极其有限；还有可能虽然万炜让孙小鹏的 Verbal 成绩提高了，但他的 Quantitative 和 AW 考砸了，最后 GRE 总成绩还更低了。⓮作者必须假设这些因素都不会发生，⓯然而他却没有给出任何证据论证这一点。总的来说，我们必须知道孙小鹏更多的个人相关信息以便排除以上情况。⓰

总之，作者的论证确实具有一定的合理性，但他的证据仍然不足以完全为他的预测提供辩护。

❶ 复述原文结论
❷ 复述原文主要的事实证据

❸ 陈述原文第一个步骤的前提和暗示
❹ 该步骤背后的第一个假设
❺ 削弱该假设的反例
❻ 该步骤背后的第二个假设
❼ 削弱该假设的反例

❽ 作者需要补充的额外证据

❾ 陈述原文第二个步骤的前提和暗示

❿ 该步骤背后的假设

⓫ 削弱该假设的多个反例

⓬ 作者需要补充的额外证据

⓭ 陈述原文第三个步骤的前提和结论

⓮ 削弱该步骤的多个反例
⓯ 被这些反例所削弱的假设
⓰ 作者需要补充的额外证据

Part 2　怎么应对 GRE 分析性写作

五、How to analyze different arguments?

我们已经了解了整个论证分析考试的考查内容，现在我们就要具体地学习如何分析一篇真实的英文论证。我们首先将文章拆解成一个一个孤立的论证步骤，教会大家分析这些不同类型的独立论证，然后再教大家分析一整篇文章的论证路线。

（一）Analyze a step of reasoning

一个完整的独立论证步骤自然需要有前提和结论，但有些时候文章中的论证步骤被隐藏了起来，即作者在推理过程中"跳步"了，通常是跳过了一个步骤的结论。下面我们先来讨论当前提结论都被明确给定的情况，再来讨论各种隐藏推理的情况。

1. Analyze an explicit reasoning step

（1）Recognize an explicit reasoning step

要分析一个论证，首先需要能够辨识论证，而要辨识论证，我们自然要捕捉能够标志论证元素存在的信号词。

常见的结论标志词有：therefore, hence, thus, consequently 之类的副词；so 这样的连词；it can be concluded that..., based on... we can infer that...之类的结构；must, should, can（not），will 等表推测的情态动词，等等。

常见的前提标志词有：because, since, for, as 之类的连词；given that, provided that, based on, now that 这样的搭配，等等。

再次提醒：前面曾经提到过，不是所有的"因为"和"所以"都表推理，它们表示的可以是单纯有时间先后顺序的因果关系。要确定我们所看到的是一个论证，被支持的结论应该是作者的一个推断，而不是事实。

例1　题库 Passage 1

> 文中说"The Brim River is very deep and broad, and so the ancient Paleans could have crossed it only by boat."，其中的"so"提示后文很可能有推断的结论，果然发现后文的"could have"标志了一个推断，而非事实，所以这里的前提与结论就很明确。作者以"Brim 河宽而深"为依据，推断出了"古代 Palean 人只能坐船过 Brim 河。"
>
> 进一步，下文"thus"的存在提示作者做了进一步的推理。而"and no Palean boats have been found"中的"and"标志了并列关系，说明刚才的结论"古代 Palean 人只能坐船过 Brim 河"又转化为下一步推理的前提，与"没有船被发现"这个事实前提，共同支持了"thus"后新的结论。

例2　题库 Passage 8

> 文中有多步明显的推理。文中给出事实"Buckingham's enrollment is growing."，而标志词"based on current trends"提示我们"Buckingham 学校注册人数增多"这个现状将被用来作为前提支持下文的步骤结

论"（enrollment）will double over the next 50 years"，并且我们可以通过"will"这个标志词明确地知道这是一个推理的结论，而并不是一个事实。之后，"注册人数将在未来50年增多"这个先前步骤的结论又转化为新的前提，通过"thus"这个标志词提示，支持了进一步的结论"making existing dormitory space inadequate"，即"让现有公寓空间不够"。然而，文章推理并未结束，下面出现的"moreover"提示我们，刚才的结论"现有公寓空间不够"又将转化为新的前提，去辅助下面推理步骤的完成。在下文当中，"consequently"这个提示词告诉我们，作者正在由"average rent for an apartment in our town has risen in recent years"推断出"students will find it increasingly difficult to afford off-campus housing"。再一次，这里的"will"提示我们这是一个推断，而不是一个事实，这个推断将通过刚才的"moreover"与前文结论"现有公寓空间不够"并列起来，去辅助本文最终的结论。

(2) Recognize the assumption(s) behind a reasoning step

判断出了文章中存在的推理步骤，我们接下来要按照考试要求去寻找其背后的假设，即 assumptions，这是一大重点。下面我们就来看一看如何准确地判断论证背后的假设。

方法一　架桥法

例1：万炜很勤奋，所以他一定会考好。
　　　作者假设了"（一个人）勤奋则能考好"。
例2：万炜是哲学系的，所以他一定是文科生。
　　　作者假设了"哲学系的（学生）一定是文科生"。
例3：猫咪很可爱，所以我们不应该吃猫咪。
　　　作者假设了"我们不应该吃可爱的（生物）"。

以上这些论证的假设应该是大家通过直觉就能发现的，它们共同的特点是构建起了前提与结论当中不同概念之间的关系。因此，所谓找假设的"架桥法"就是，**找到前提与结论当中核心概念的不同（我们称为 P 与 Q），制造一个新的命题"如果 P，那么 Q"，从而连接起前提与结论之间的背后关系**。这种方法通常在某个论证只有一个明确指出的前提时比较好用，因为这时我们很容易捕捉到前提与结论的不同概念。

方法二　反例取非法

然而，当前提多于一个时，"架桥法"用起来并不方便。比如，在题库 Passage 1 当中存在的推理：只能坐船过河，而 Palea 地没有船，所以（河对岸）Lithos 地发现的篮子肯定不是来自（河此岸）的 Palea 地。显然，前提结论当中不同概念过多，就算强行架桥，架出来的命题也将特别复杂和奇怪。此时，推荐大家**先制造能够削弱该论证的反例，即 counterexample(s)，再对这些反例进行逻辑上的取非，即制造它们的对立面，这个对立面一定是该论证背后所必须依赖的假设。**

这听起来太抽象了，我们直接用例子来展示一下具体是怎么操作的。
首先想清楚论证是：只能坐船过河，而 Palea 地没有船，所以（河对岸）Lithos 地发现的篮子肯定不是来自（河此岸）的 Palea 地。接着，想一想有什么可能的情况使得这个推理不见得成立，即什么情况可以使得就算必须坐船过河，就算 Palea 地没有船，但 Lithos 地的篮子仍然可以来自 Palea 地。比如：这个篮子是由来自其他地区的船只载过河的。现在，我们对刚才这种可能情况取非，即否定它。那么，我们就得到了作者的假设，即"这个篮子不可能是由来自其他地区的船只载过河的。"

再举一例：万炜最近很努力，他的成绩明显提高了，因此显然是努力让他成绩提高的。

我们先思考一下有什么反例可以削弱这个论证，即万炜最近很努力，成绩也提高了，但并不是努力让他成绩提高的。比如：他的成绩提高是因为作弊；或是因为题目很简单，等等。现在，否定这些情况，我们就得到了作者的一系列假设，即"万炜的成绩提高不是因为作弊""万炜的成绩提高不是因为题目简单"，等等。

逻辑敏感的同学可能会意识到，"架桥法"找出来的假设好像和"反例取非法"找出来的假设性质不大一样。"架桥法"似乎更符合我们的直觉，用这种方法找出来的假设好像只有唯一一个，并且恰好就能使得论证成立。与此相反，"反例取非法"似乎可以找到很多个假设，因为反例可能有无穷个。对此好奇的同学可以阅读接下来我们的讲解，但这对于完成 GRE 考试不是必须的，因此如果逻辑上有困难的同学可以略过接下来这一段的分析，直接跳到接下来的"Construct possible counterexamples"一节。

要想理解两种假设直觉上的区别，我们需要再次重温假设的定义，即**作者论证成立所必须依赖的非事实性前提**。这里一个隐蔽的关键词是"必须"，它意味着我们所寻找的是论证背后的一个**必要**条件，而非充分条件。所谓充分条件，即有了这个条件，该论证就必然成立；但离开了这个条件，论证可能不见得不成立。所谓必要条件，即离了这个条件，该论证必然不成立；但有了这个条件，该论证可能不见得成立。当然，有了必要条件和充分条件，自然有充要条件这个概念，即既充分又必要的条件，这个条件如果为真，则论证成立，如果为假，则论证不成立。

例：该场所 18 岁以上的人可以入内，所以万炜可以入内。背后假设是什么？

大家通过直觉都能意识到，背后的假设是"万炜 18 岁以上。"显然，如果万炜 18 岁以上，他就可以入内了；而如果他不到 18 岁，就不能入内。这种直觉上建构起来的假设，通常就是所谓的充要条件。

但这不是该论证的唯一假设。作者同样需要假设"万炜是 17 岁以上、16 岁以上，还是 15 岁以上……"这很反直觉，因为当我们逼问大家背后假设是什么时，大家通常不会想到这些条件，因为就算万炜 17、16、15 岁了，也不见得能入内啊。但它们确实是该论证背后的假设，为什么呢？因为我们所寻找的假设，是论证成立的必要条件，而非充分条件。我们不需要考虑这些条件能否让论证成立，我们考虑的是失去了这些条件论证是否就不成立了。显然，以上这些条件都满足这个要求。如果万炜不到 17 岁，自然也不到 18 岁，自然也就不能入内了。

这时，我相信很多同学已经明白了，用"架桥法"造出来的假设就是所谓的充要条件，而用"反例取非法"造出来的是大量必要条件，它们是非充分的。每一个反例都起到削弱论证的作用，因此说话者要想让他的论证成立，自然要假设每一个反例是不成立的，而鉴于反例可以有无穷个，则这种必要假设也可以有无穷个。

(3) Construct possible counterexamples

讲完了寻找假设的方法，我们下面来看制造反例的方法。事实上，刚才的"反例取非法"也需要我们学会如何制造反例。那么，我们在这里初步探讨一下制造反例时需要注意的问题，之后的"Analyze an implicit reasoning step"我们会彻底解决反例制造的问题。

首先，需要明确的是反例需要具有的效果。反例的目的是要削弱作者的论证，表明作者的论证是不严谨的，即要**通过反例的存在表明作者的前提不足以充分支持其结论，即前提为真时，结论仍然可能不为真**。制造反例时我们必然会引入文章中没有出现过的常识，即场外信息，我们不需要保证反例是事实，但它必须符合常识。比如，为了削弱题库 Passage 1 当中"河宽而深，所以只能坐船过河"这个论证，我们需要思考什么日常情况可以使得不需要非得坐船过这条河。于是，合理的反例可以是：冬天结冰走过去、绕远路过去、架桥过去，等等。但我们不可能接受"飞过去"这样不符合常识的反例，毕竟我们讨论的是古代。

制造反例时同学们经常存在的错误是纯粹否定结论。比如：万炜很努力，所以他一定会考好。有人会说：可是万炜不见得考好啊，他的成绩可能还是很差。这不叫反例，这只是把结论给否定了一遍，但没有解释为什么。**太多人误以为 Argument Analysis 是驳论文，是要反驳结论，但其实 Argument Analysis 是在讨论文章论证，即逻辑的严谨性，我们要表明的是前提不见得支持结论，而不是去说结论本身错误。**

因此，我们真正制造出的**成功反例其实并不必然能证明原作者的结论为假，而只是表明作者的结论在前提为真时不能够被充分证明**。比如：万炜考好了，说明他努力复习了。合理的反例是：万炜考好是因为作弊。有同学会说，万炜作弊也不足以表明他没努力复习啊。这种说法再一次表明这位同学误解了反例的目的。万炜作弊确实与万炜努力复习不矛盾。但是，如果我们知道万炜作弊了，那么仅仅由万炜考好了，我们就不敢随意推断万炜是否认真复习了。那么，作弊这个可能性就成功表明了论证前提不足以支持结论，因此这是个合格的反例。

市面上还流行一种做法，让同学们记忆所谓的"逻辑错误类型"，这个门类多达二十多种，包含各种"专业术语"，比如"稻草人谬误（Strawman Fallacy）""混淆相关与因果（post hoc, ergo propter hoc）""诉诸权威（Appeal to Authority）"之类，听起来非常高大上。但是，无论是逻辑学专业课程还是 GRE 官方指南都明确指出，考生不需要指出论证错误类型，而只需要通过制造日常反例来削弱一个论证。这个道理非常简单，因为就算某论证符合某个所谓的"逻辑错误类型"，并不代表这个论证不严谨，除非我们能找到反例。拿"诉诸权威"为例，我们人类每天都在诉诸权威，因为我们不可能所有事情都自己论证。我们学的平面几何来自于欧几里得千年前的思想，我们学的物理理论来自于牛顿、爱因斯坦等物理学家。因此，对于论证："爱因斯坦提出 $E = mc^2$，所以 $E = mc^2$"，我们如何表明该论证的不严谨？指出这个论证犯了"诉诸权威"的谬误吗？对于我们绝大多数人来说，诉诸爱因斯坦就是物理知识上的最好选择。而且，就算爱因斯坦的某些物理理论后来被证明为假，也是因为有人提出了成功的反例证明的，而不是因为一个所谓的"逻辑错误类型"。

（4）Request additional evidence

最后一步工作是要求作者提供额外的信息来加强其论证。这一步很简单，如果假设和反例我们都完成得很好，这一步是顺利成长的。比如：万炜考好了，说明他努力复习了。作者假设没有其他原因可以解释万炜考得好。而可能的反例是：题目很简单，万炜作弊了，等等。因此，作者需要做的事情是调查能够让他考好的其他可能因素，从而排除以上可能性。这个步骤一般不会造成考生太大的困难，只要大家记得去做这个工作就是了。

2. Analyze an implicit reasoning step

然而，并不是每一个论证步骤都是作者清晰写出来的。我们在阐述思维过程时经常会下意识地跳步，即使一些思维步骤隐藏了起来。因此,考生在分析一篇论证时,不仅有义务分析文章中明显的步骤,对于一些隐藏的步骤,考生也是有必要去发掘并分析的。接下来我们一起探讨一下常见的隐藏步骤的辨识和分析,在以下所介绍的各种隐藏论证步骤当中,结论经常被作者隐藏了起来(有些例子当中是前提被隐藏)。

让我们看一个中文例子,这个例子当中包含了常见的各种隐藏推理步骤。

例1

在最近一次调查中,80%上过万炜老师课的受访者表示,他们的GRE Verbal成绩超过了大陆地区的平均分。因此,您的孩子要获得好的GRE成绩,也应该上万炜老师的课。

(1) 证词类

在以上例1当中,大家需要首先注意到的一个标志就是"80%的……受访者表示",这暗含了我们要讲的第一种常见的隐藏推理,即"证词类"推理。所谓"证词",即利用他人的语言为证据,这时作者通常不用明说结论是什么,因为当我们借用别人的结论,比如"某人认为XXX"时,我们就是在暗示"XXX是真的"。

证词类推理特征总结	
标志	report, study, survey, test, say, plan…
前提	证词"XXX"
结论	XXX
假设	该证词(调查、声明、计划)可靠/有代表性/能体现事实
反例	指出证词不真实可能的原因。具体到调查研究当中,经常可能来自于样本数据量太小,取样方式不随机等原因。具体到计划当中,经常可能因为某些原因使得计划无法实施,或者实施之后没有效果。
补充证据	视反例而定,需要相关信息来排除反例当中可能出现的情况。

应用到例1当中:

标志	80%的……受访者表示
前提	在最近一次调查中,80%上过万炜老师课的受访者表示,他们的GRE Verbal成绩超过了大陆地区的平均分。
结论	80%上过万炜老师课的人GRE Verbal成绩超过了大陆地区的平均分。
假设	该调查可靠、有代表性
反例	通常只有成绩好的人才会愿意参加这个调查,而且人们可能出于面子考虑不说出自己考砸的事情;可能是万炜课程的广告,专找考得好的人来宣传自己。
补充证据	需要知道调查的发起者是否是中立的第三方,需要知道选择参与者的方式以保证样本的随机性,需要知道其声称的成绩是否吻合其实际成绩单上的分数。

下面以一个官方的例题为例。

> In surveys Mason City residents rank water sports (swimming, boating, and fishing) among their favorite recreational activities. The Mason River flowing through the city is rarely used for these pursuits, however, and the city park department devotes little of its budget to maintaining riverside recreational facilities. For years there have been complaints from residents about the quality of the river's water and the river's smell. In response, the state has recently announced plans to clean up Mason River. Use of the river for water sports is, therefore, sure to increase. The city government should for that reason devote more money in this year's budget to riverside recreational facilities.
>
> ——摘自 *The Official Guide for GRE Revised Test*

细心的读者会发现这篇文章有两个证词，一个是开篇的 survey，一个是 state plan。

标志	survey
前提	调查中，Mason 城市民将水上运动列为其喜欢的娱乐活动之一
结论	水上运动是 Mason 城市民最喜欢的娱乐活动之一
假设	该调查可靠、有代表性
反例	样本选择不具有代表性，调查可能是在水边做的，本来水上运动爱好者就多；调查中的选项可能不全面，在所给的选项当中，水上运动只是相对受喜爱的；调查可能是在一次大型运动会期间做的，而该运动会上该城的某个运动员获得了水上运动的金牌，导致了市民暂时的兴奋，但他们其实并不真的爱水上运动……
补充证据	需要知道调查发生的时间、地点、取样方式，以排除以上这些特殊情况的发生。

标志	plan
前提	政府有计划清理 Mason 河
结论	Mason 河会清理干净
假设	计划会成功实施
反例	政府缺乏资金；Mason 河的味道不是源于工业污染，而是自然的水中矿物质，无法清理；Mason 河的污染来自上游，超出了政府的管辖范围，无法根治。
补充证据	需要知道政府能够支配的资金量与治理所需的资金量；需要知道污染源的可处理程度。

（2）数据类

回到例 1 当中，让我们暂时接受先前作者推理的结论，默认上过万炜老师课的学生 Verbal 成绩确实普遍超过了大陆平均分。但这个 "Verbal 成绩超过了大陆平均分" 仍然令我非常敏感，尤其当我看到文末的目的是 "好的 GRE 成绩" 时。显然作者试图用 "Verbal 成绩超过了大陆平均分" 来证明这些人的 GRE 成绩好。这就是我们要谈到的数据类推理。

我们会经常在很多文章中见到作者用数据的变化、对比来证明一个现象的存在，有时是具体的数字，有时会用概数，比如 "增长了很多" "显著下降" 等。要判断作者列出的这些数据到底在说明什么，通常需要我们结合下文作者的目的来判断。比如，在刚才的例子当中，我们很容易通过文章的结论意识到，作者要想证明上万炜的 GRE 课能获得好成绩，则先前列举的证据当中的人必须首先得取得好成绩。

数据类推理特征总结	
标志	数据（确数/概数）
前提	数据
结论	根据下文判断的数据所反映的现象
假设	先找反例，再对反例取非
反例	常见策略 1：该数据就能反映之后的现象。常见策略 2：关注前提的数据是相对量还是绝对量，如果是相对量，则不代表绝对量；而如果是绝对量，则不见得反映相对量。
补充证据	视反例而定，需要相关信息来排除反例当中可能出现的情况。

应用到例 1 当中：

标志	超过大陆地区的平均分
前提	80% 上过万炜老师课的人 GRE Verbal 成绩超过了大陆地区的平均分。
结论	这些人的 GRE Verbal 成绩很好
假设	超过大陆平均分就是好成绩
反例	大陆成绩整体就很差，远低于世界整体水平。
补充证据	作者需要指出大陆平均分在 GRE 考试当中的水准，以帮助我们确定这个数据是否能够体现学生的 GRE 水平。

下面我们以一道实际题目为例，请大家看一下题库当中的第 20 题。首先，读者们一定会发现文章有一对数据，即教师每年报告了 30 起作弊，之后学生每年报告了 21 起作弊，再到每年 14 起作弊。这里存在两个证词，肯定是值得讨论的。我们假定两个证词已经讨论完了，这些数据确实是真实的。那作者通过这个数据的变化想要证明什么呢？根据下文，我们可以很快意识到作者想要证明的是作弊真的少了。显然，每年几起作弊是没有考虑每年参加考试的总学生人次的，这是一个绝对量，但作弊真正有多少起是要考虑相对作弊比例的。

标志	30，21，14
前提	作弊人数从每年 30 起到了后来每年 14 起
结论	作弊少了
假设	（基于反例）考试次数、学生总人数都没有显著下降
反例	考试总次数每年显著下降；学生总人数显著下降。
补充证据	作者必须告诉我们每年实际参与考试的学生总人次的变化。

(3) 解释类

这是最重要的推理类型。让我们回到例 1，假设作者成功证明了"上万炜课的学生 GRE Verbal 成绩就是很好"。这时，大家应该注意到这里有两个伴随发生的现象：①这些学生上了万炜的课；②这些学生 GRE Verbal 成绩很好。到此为止，这两个现象之间并没有直接关系。但根据下文，作者显然希望这两个现象之间有关系，具体来说，是上了万炜的课他们的成绩才好的。这就是所谓的解释类推理，作者试图建立两个现象的因果关系，准确来说，是在推断其中一件事情发生的原因。解释型推理有两种常见的模式：①知道 A 和 B 两件事情是伴随（先后）发生的，继而暗示两件事情有因果关系（如果是先后发生，必然是先发生造成后发生）；②知道 B（结果）的发生，然后推断出是 A 所导致的。

解释类推理特征总结（情况 1）	
标志	两件事情伴随/先后发生
前提	两件事情伴随/先后发生
结论	两件事情的因果关系
假设	没有其他可能解释
反例	给出其他可能解释
补充证据	额外信息排除这些可能的其他情况

解释类推理特征总结（情况 1）	
标志	结果发生
前提	结果发生
结论	是某原因造成的
假设	没有其他可能解释
反例	给出其他可能解释
补充证据	额外信息排除这些可能的其他情况

应用到例 1 当中：

标志	某些人上过万炜老师的课 + 这些人 GRE Verbal 成绩好
前提	80% 上过万炜老师课的人 GRE Verbal 成绩好
结论	是万炜老师的课让他们的 GRE Verbal 成绩好的
假设	没有其他可能解释
反例	万炜老师只招资质本来就好的学生；这些学生可能还上过其他老师的课，或者使用了某些优质的、和万炜老师没有关系的资料。
补充证据	调查并排除以上其他可能决定考生成绩的因素。

下面我们以一道实际题目为例，还是请大家看一下题库当中的第 20 题。假设我们前面已经证明作弊减少了，但这显然不是文章的目的，那文章为什么要证明作弊少了呢。根据下文，我们意识到文章想要通过 honor code 来解决作弊，那这时我们就很容易意识到，前文谈到过使用 honor code 之后 Groveton 校作弊减少，就是为了证明 Groveton 校是通过 honor code 减少作弊的。

标志	使用 honor code 与 Groveton 校作弊减少伴随发生
前提	使用 honor code 后 Groveton 校作弊减少

结论	honor code 帮助 Groveton 校减少了作弊
假设	没有其他可能解释
反例	对作弊的惩罚更严；学校安装了更多监控设备；招收的学生素质更高。
补充证据	调查并排除以上其他可能决定考生作弊数量的因素。

我们再看一道实际例题，请大家看一下题库当中的第 51 题。这篇文章很直接，一上来就描述了现象：Kaliko 岛的大型哺乳动物灭绝。文章试图排除人打猎的影响，这个部分我们暂时不讨论。文章最后认为，肯定是某些气候环境因素造成了它们的灭绝。这非常明显是一篇基于结果推出原因的解释型文章。

标志	结果（大型哺乳动物灭绝）
前提	Kaliko 岛的大型哺乳动物灭绝
结论	气候或环境变化造成该灭绝
假设	没有其他可能解释
反例	瘟疫、疾病、食物不足、天敌出现
补充证据	调查并排除以上其他可能影响大哺乳动物数量的因素。

（4）类比类

继续回到例 1。假设作者成功证明了"这些学生 GRE Verbal 取得高分真的是因为上了万炜老师的课"，下一步推理就很明显了，根据结论，我们可以意识到，作者想要暗示其他学生，上了万炜老师的课，GRE 可以取得高分。GRE Verbal 高分等于 GRE 高分吗？这些学生等于其他学生吗？之前等于之后吗？类比类推理是漏洞非常明显的一种推理，只要我们意识到作者在推理当中改变了讨论对象的范围，却认为属性可以不变，这时几乎一定存在类比类推理。

类比类推理特征总结	
标志	讨论对象转变，属性不变
前提	A 对象的特点
结论	B 对象有相似特点
假设	两个对象核心属性相似
反例	指出量对象核心属性可能的不同点
补充证据	调查该属性是否相似

应用到例 1 当中：

标志	前文讨论的是上过万炜老师课的学生，下文讨论的是未来的其他学生；上文讨论的只是 GRE Verbal 成绩，但下文讨论的是整个 GRE 成绩。
前提	是万炜老师的课让一些学生 GRE Verbal 取得好成绩的
结论	上万炜老师的课能让未来的学生 GRE 取得好成绩
假设	Verbal 成绩好，GRE 成绩就好；GRE 之后不会发生大的变化；之前和之后的学生没有显著区别。

（续）

反例	上了万炜老师的课，可能 GRE 数学更差了，于是总分并不会提高；GRE 可能要改革，于是万炜老师就不懂新 GRE 了；可能以前上万炜老师课的都是理（文）科生，适应他的思维习惯，但换其他人就不见得了。
补充证据	调查并排除以上因素的差异

下面我们以一道实际题目为例，还是请大家看一下题库当中的第 20 题。让我们假定前文成功证明了 honor code 是 G 校作弊减少的原因，下文显然作者试图把这个政策波及其他学校，意味着作者要证明 honor code 也会让其他学校作弊减少。

标志	前文讨论的是 Groveton 校，下文波及其他学校
前提	honor code 是 Groveton 校作弊减少的原因
结论	honor code 也会让其他学校作弊减少
假设	各校学生素质没有显著差别
反例	Groveton 校学生素养高，honor code 需要学生很自律，可以实现；但其他学校不一样，honor code 离开了老师监考，意味着基本上大家都会作弊。
补充证据	作者必须调查哪些学校和 Groveton 校的学生素质相似，这样才适合应用 honor code。

（5）建议类

与之前推理不同，之前的推理绝大部分都隐藏了结论，而最后我们要谈的建议类推理通常隐藏了前提，其实它通常是文章的最终结论。一篇文章若是要给某个对象 X 做某个建议 A（肯定是为了某个目标 B，即便文章没有明说，每个建议必须是有需要实现的目标的），这肯定就是文章最终的结论了，因为它不可能去支持什么别的命题。那么，这个建议必须基于一系列前提条件，从严格的逻辑层面上，有 5 个可能的前提：①建议的可行性（X 可以做到 A）；②建议的有效性（X 做 A 可以实现目标 B）；③目标的积极性（X 需要 B，或者 B 对 X 来说是个重要的好处）；④无副作用（X 做 A 不会产生更严重的负面效果）；⑤无替代方案（X 无法通过别的方案更有效地实现目标 B，即 X 不做 A 无法更容易实现 B）。

在实际的建议类文章中，所有文章信息都肯定是为了证明这个建议的 5 个前提当中的某些前提，当我们假定这些证明都合理的时候，5 个前提当中没被证明的前提就成为最后一步建议类推理背后的假设。

比如，在例 1 当中，显然作者主要在证明学生们上了万炜老师的课就能获得好的 GRE 成绩，那么这个前提要想推出最终结论，即所有学生都应该报万炜老师的课来获得 GRE 的好成绩，作者必须假设：①所有学生都可以报万炜老师的课；②这些学生都需要获得 GRE 好成绩（这个假设问题不大，因为这是文章默认的背景）；③上万炜老师的课不会产生恶劣的后果；④ 没有其他方式获得 GRE 好成绩。当然，不是每一个假设都需要我们造反例来削弱的，因为之前谈过，反例必须日常，必须合理，如果某个假设在日常生活中没有太大问题，我们就不要去讨论了。注意：GRE Argument 部分要求我们不要给出自己的意见，因为我们的目的是讨论逻辑，而不是讨论结论本身的对错。所以，我们在制造反例时，比如，我们要讨论"没有其他可能的方案"这个假设时，我们不要断言存在其他方案。比如，在例 1 当中，我们不要说"应该上其他老师的课"，因为我们并不知道这是真是假。相反，我们应该说的是，作者需要调查其他可能的方案并进行比较，并确定万炜老师的课有没有竞争对手，才能够推出最后的结论。

建议类推理特征总结	
标志	it is important to do…; in order to do…; to do…; XXX should do…; XXX must do…; XXX need to do…; it is best to do…
前提	基于文章判断文章已经证明了 5 个假设中的哪些假设，则将这些证明了的假设作为前提，剩下的还是作为假设。
结论	某对象 X 该做某行为 A
假设	文章中没有讨论到的假设（5 个常规假设：①建议可行；②建议有效；③建议目标积极；④无副作用；⑤无替代方案）
反例	不可行；无效；目标不重要，或者已经实现；有严重副作用；有更有效的其他方案。
补充证据	给出相关证据排除以上反例情况

下面我们以一道实际题目为例，再次请大家看一下题库当中的第 20 题。我们假设前文已经成功证明了所有学校采用 honor code 都能减少作弊（建议有效），那么文章显然就马上推出了最后的建议。

标志	should
前提	所有学校采用 honor code 都可以减少作弊
结论	所有学校都应该采用 honor code 来减少作弊
假设	所有学校都有能力采用 honor code（似乎没有大问题）；所有学校都需要减少作弊（似乎没有大问题）；所有学校采用 honor code 都不会带来严重副作用（似乎没有大问题）；所有学校都没有更好的减少作弊的方法。
反例	也许很多学校通过教师监考、严格的监控系统几乎已经杜绝了作弊。
补充证据	调查其他学校的作弊情况，以及它们是否有很有效的解决作弊的途径。

最后提醒大家，建议类的讨论很容易陷入吹毛求疵的境地。比如，有人会说"也许 honor code 需要花很多钱，学校没有资金"。这就非常没有必要了，因为 honor code 明明是一个互相监督的事情，根本就不涉及资金问题。还有人可能说"也许有些学校一个作弊都没有"。这首先就非常极端，其次，就算现在没有作弊，未来肯定还是会试图杜绝作弊的。再次强调，我们制造反例不是为了反驳作者，而是为了体现作者的逻辑漏洞有多大，需要做多少补充工作来加强论证。越日常的反例越能够说明作者论证的缺陷。相反，如果我们造的反例过于奇葩，其实等于变相体现了作者的论证其实还是比较严谨的，因为在实际生活中我们基本想不出什么可能的反例来削弱他的逻辑了。如果真有这种情况，这时我们根本就不要讨论这步推理。

（二）Reestablish the line of reasoning

前面我们已经讨论了如何在一个文章中辨识单个推理步骤，无论是有着明显前提和结论的步骤，还是隐藏了前提或结论的步骤。那么，现在更重要的是，如何把这些步骤组合成一个完整的推理线路（line of reasoning）。因为我们不能像过去的考生一样，陷入逐句找原文逻辑错误的窘境：真正理解一篇论证，是完整地复现作者的推理思路。我们的做法是：在阅读时，敏锐捕捉可辨识的推理步骤，无论是明显的还是隐藏的，站在作者的角度完成这些推理；然后将这些新获得的推理结论与文章的最终结论合理地联系起来，构建出完整的论证线路。在实际写作中，我们对文中步骤的安排未必需要严格符合作者的推理线路（即安排先写哪点后写哪点的顺序其实并不重要），但厘清文章的推理线路对于判断我们所找的步骤是否合理是非常关键的（我们不希望看到某个片段看似存在某个推理步骤，但其实文章最终不需要依赖此推理）。一个关键的检验标准就是文章的结论——每一步推理的结论必须是文章结论成立所依赖的。我们还是以题库第 20 题为例：

句序	推理标志	推理类型
1	N/A	N/A
2	N/A	N/A
3	reported	证词类
	thirty per year	数据类
4	reported	证词类
	twenty-one, fourteen	数据类
5	survey, said	证词类
6	should	建议类

　　在第一遍阅读过程中，我们需要注意到以上列表所提示的各种潜在的推理，并且意识到文章最终的结论是一个建议，建议所有学校执行 honor code，而且目标显然是要减少作弊。然后我们开始利用文章已有的推理标志完成作者心中的推理。第一，teachers' report 和 students' report 可以暗示的是 Groveton 校作弊人数从过去的 30 人/年逐步降至了 14 人/年。第二，这组数据的对比肯定是想证明 Groveton 校作弊现象的减少，由此文章的目的是要减少作弊。第三，由于文章目标是要通过执行 honor code 来减少作弊，因此这时只有 Groveton 校作弊减少显然是不够的，当作者指出 Groveton 校执行了 honor code 并且作弊减少，很显然作者是想暗示两件事情之间的联系，即作者想证明 Groveton 校是因为使用了 honor code 才导致作弊减少的。第四，作者指出了一个 survey，而显然这个对 Groveton 校学生的 survey 也是同时证明 honor code 在 Groveton 校减少了作弊，因此和刚才的推理步骤是平级关系。第五，然而本文不是仅仅针对 Groveton 校的，作者最终想证明的是所有学校都应该执行 honor code，所以作者显然需要通过类比，由 Groveton 校的成功推出其他学校执行 honor code 也可以减少作弊。第六，由这个建议能有效减少作弊，作者推出最终结论，执行 honor code 可以减少作弊。于是，我们有了以下的树状推理图：

再举一例，题库第 34 题：

句序	推理标志	推理类型
1	N/A	N/A
2	study report	证词类
	consumption high, once or twice per year	数据类
3	N/A	N/A
4	since	明显推理
	recommend	建议类

在第一遍阅读过程中，我们需要注意到以上列表所提示的各种潜在的推理，并且意识到文章最终的结论是一个建议，建议人们吃 Ichthaid 来减少感冒和缺勤。然后我们开始利用文章已有的推理标志完成作者心中的推理。第一，study report 了两件事情，这显然是第一步推理，由 study report 推出 EM 地区鱼消费量很高以及人们每年感冒一两次。第二，这两个数据想做什么呢？结合下一句话中作者说吃鱼能预防感冒，我们应该能够明白，鱼消费量很高是为了证明当地人吃鱼多，而感冒一两次是为了证明人们感冒少。第三，很明显，由吃鱼多和感冒少，作者就要推出吃鱼能预防感冒了。第四，但作者最后的结论不是建议人们吃鱼，而是建议人们吃 Ichthaid，一种鱼油制品，所以作者显然需要一步类比，由吃鱼预防感冒推出吃 Ichthaid 这种鱼油制品也能预防感冒。第五，由吃 Ichthaid 能预防感冒理论上就可以推出作者建议人们吃 Ichthaid 来预防感冒了，可是不足以推出可以预防缺勤，所以作者还需要建立感冒和缺勤的关系，这时我们应该注意到一个明显的推理标志 since。作者说感冒是人们缺勤时最常给出的理由，因此作者通过吃 Ichthaid 可以预防感冒，加感冒是缺勤最常给出的理由，暗示 Ichthaid 也可以预防缺勤。第六，鉴于 Ichthaid 可以防感冒和缺勤，作者就推出了人们应该每天服用 Ichthaid 来避免感冒和缺勤。于是，我们就有了以下树状推理图：

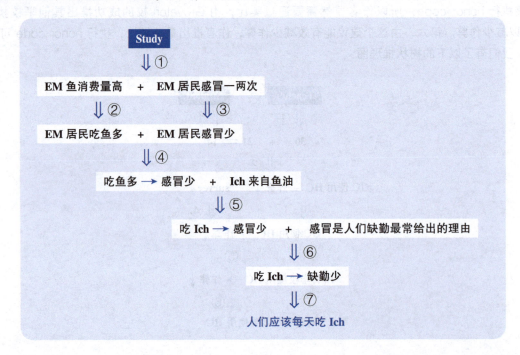

六、How to write an analysis

整个 Argument 分析部分最简单的就是文章的写作了，因为其高度标准化。下面，我们完整罗列一下文章每个部分需要做的事情、注意事项，以及提供一些语言范例（并不是必须使用的，只要能够起到相似逻辑功能的语言都可以替换）。

1. 开头部分

（1）复述原文的结论以及主要的论证依据。参考语料：The author concludes（普适结论）/ predicts（预测型结论）/ proposes（建议型结论）that... The conclusion / prediction / suggestion is mainly based on...

（2）指出本文（我们自己写的评论文章）的最终目标：这里值得注意的是，官方每道题目后面会有一个额外的题目要求，我们的文章应该是按照这个要求进行的。官方一共有8种要求，但其中的5种本质是类似的，所以总结下来是4个不同的类别。

要求1 指出作者需要回答的问题：Write a response in which you discuss what questions would need to be answered in order to decide whether the recommendation is likely to have the predicted result. Be sure to explain how the answers to these questions would help to evaluate the recommendation.

有另外4种要求和这个要求类似，不在此列举，因为标志都是很鲜明的"what questions would need to be answered…"

要求2 指出作者论证背后的假设：Write a response in which you examine the stated and/or unstated assumptions of the argument. Be sure to explain how the argument depends on these assumptions and what the implications are for the argument if the assumptions prove unwarranted.

要求3 指出文章缺失的证据：Write a response in which you discuss what specific evidence is needed to evaluate the argument, and explain how the evidence would weaken or strengthen the argument.

要求4 指出其他可能的解释：Write a response in which you discuss one or more alternative explanations that could rival the proposed explanation, and explain how your explanation(s) can plausibly account for the facts presented in the argument.

以后，我们将这四种要求简称为：（1）提出问题；（2）指出假设；（3）补充证据；（4）其他解释。那么，每种要求下，我们文章相应的结论和目的也应有所不同，推荐的语料也略有区别。

推荐语料（针对要求1）： However, several important questions are left unaddressed, rendering the author's reasoning open to possible counterarguments. / However, the author needs to address several important questions so that readers can be convinced of her argument.

推荐语料（针对要求2）： However, underlying his/her line of reasoning are several problematic assumptions, which render his/her argument vulnerable to possible counterarguments. / However, his/her argument is filled with unwarranted assumptions that significantly undermine its cogency.

推荐语料（针对要求3）： However, the evidence is insufficient to fully warrant his/her conclusion and more information is needed before readers can fully accept his/her reasoning. / However, he/she needs to offer additional evidence before he/she can forcefully draw the conclusion.

推荐语料（针对要求4）： However, alternative possibilities are not fully addressed, rendering his/her theory open to doubt. / However, he/she fails to take into consideration other possible explanations that can equally account for the phenomena presented in the passage.

2. 正文部分

正文部分的主要目的就是按照文章的 line of reasoning 去进行 step-by-step 的分析。具体的安排顺序应该是根据文章 line of reasoning 的树状图，平行分支之间任意安排顺序，每个分支内部自上而下进行分析。比如：

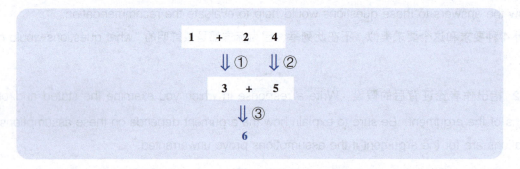

如果本图是某篇文章的推理线索，我肯定会先分析步骤①或②，这两步平行，所以顺序无所谓，最后再分析步骤③。

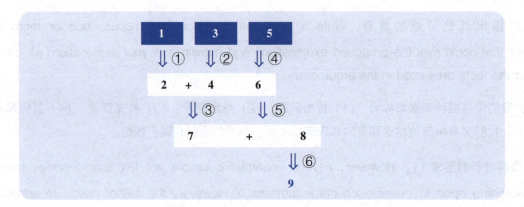

但有时候，我们会遇到一些相当烦琐的文章，比如上图这种情况。这时，原则是不变的。①②③构成一个大分支，④⑤构成一个分支，然而两个分支独立支持了 7 这个判断，所以两个分支的顺序无所谓。但每个分支的内部顺序必须自上而下，①②顺序无所谓，因为它们也是平行的，但只有分析完了①②才能分析③。同理，只有分析完了④才能分析⑤。最后，两个分支都结束了，获得了命题7，再去分析步骤⑥。

这时就有同学问，我们正文写几段。这是最无聊、最没用的问题了，但是几乎人人都在问。官方指南上明确写到，分多少段都和我们的文章质量没有关系，只要分段合理。请同学们不要以为正文三段（这是市面上习惯的做法）是标准答案。

首先，我们完全可以每个点一段，于是按照这篇文章的结构，我可能写六段，顺序是按照表格中的①②③④⑤⑥，当然也可以是④⑤①②③⑥。另一种写法是把每个大分支合并成一段，于是第一段写①②③，第二段写④⑤，第三段写⑥。在之后的范文部分，大家会见到我在不同文章中使用了不同的安排，这两者都是合理的。

每个段落内部的具体内容如下（顺序可以灵活）：

（1）复述推理步骤的所有前提 P（或隐藏前提，可能来自上一步骤的隐藏结论）和结论 C（或隐藏的结论），并指出背后的假设 A。推荐语料：The author mentions that P（作者明说的情况下）and infers that（作者明说的情况下）C. Apparently, behind the inference lies the assumption that A. / Even if P（作者没有明说的情况下），it does not necessarily mean that C（作者没有明说的情况下）. Underlying the inference is the problematic assumption that A.

（2）制造反例，削弱作者的假设。推荐语料：It is possible that… / Perhaps, …

这个部分是关键，也没有什么固定语料可用，因为反例完全取决于每个论证的具体内容，所以只要保证我们给出的反例只是一种可能情况就好，千万不要以为我们写出来的反例是实际情况，所以表达可能性的词是非常必要的。

（3）指出作者需要补充的证据（用来加强其论证）。推荐语料：Therefore, only if the author provides additional evidence to show that…, can she legitimately conclude that C. / Thus, without further evidence to rule out the above possibilities, she cannot firmly infer that C. 有的时候为了满足要求1，我们可以使用下面的语言形式：Therefore, the author needs to provide additional evidence to address the following questions：（列举作者需要回答的问题）. Only if the answer(s) is/are…, can he/she firmly conclude that C.

四种要求下我们段内的侧重点略有区别，但这不是非常致命的问题。要求1和要求3的重点是补充证据、回答问题，要求2的重点是假设，要求4的重点是反例。给大家提供以上的段落形式正是为了让大家能够一劳永逸地不用过分去想我们所面对的题目要求。而且，从来没有哪个题目只需要我们做题目要求所做的事情，因此三个步骤的分析都是建议大家去做的。

3. 结尾部分

完全可有可无，绝对不是学生考不了高分的原因。实在想写，改写一下文章开头的结论就可以，即开头部分的3。

在这里给大家提供题库第20题的题目分析与高分范文，帮助大家理解文章如何做到我们刚才讲解的各部分内容的。

文章结构图：

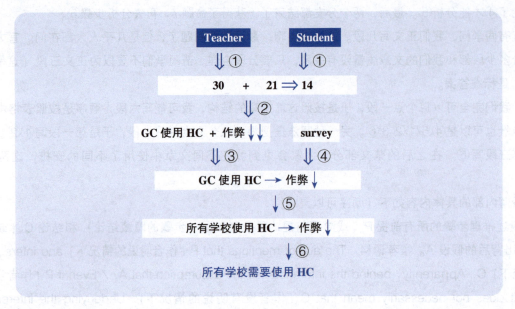

结　　论：All colleges and universities should adopt honor codes similar to Groveton's in order to decrease cheating among students.

结论类型：建议型

各步推理分析：

① 证词类

Signal：teachers reported；students reported

Inference：GC 老师和学生的报告 ⇒ GC 每年作弊的人数从 30 人下降到 14 人

Assumption：学生与老师的报告是一样精确、可靠的

Counterexamples：学生互相包庇作弊、没有足够的精力注意别人作弊

② 数据类

Signal：30；21；14

Inference：GC 每年作弊人数从 30 人下降到 14 人 ⇒ GC 作弊问题减弱了

Assumption：学生总数没有显著下降，考试频率没有显著下降……

Counterexamples：学生人数翻倍，每年考试频率翻倍

③ 解释类

Signal：②的结论，以及作者试图建立 GC 使用 honor code 与作弊减少之间的关系

Inference：GC 使用了 honor code，之后作弊问题减弱了 ⇒ GC 使用了 honor code，导致其作弊问题减弱

Assumption：没有其他解释

Counterexamples：被抓到作弊处罚更严、隔位就座、安装了摄像头……

④ 证词类

Signal：survey, students said

Inference：学生调查 ⇒ GC 使用了 honor code，导致其作弊问题减弱

Assumption：学生会说实话

Counterexamples：作弊的人在接受采访时也不会承认作弊……

⑤ 类比类

Signal：前文讨论的是 Groveton College，而后文讨论的是 all colleges and universities

Inference：GC 使用了 honor code，导致其作弊问题减弱 ⇒ 其他所有学校使用 honor code，也能导致各自的作弊问题减弱

Assumption：各个学校学生素质差不多

Counterexamples：GC 学校生源好，只要有适当的提醒就会不作弊；但是别的学校学生可能很差，必须严格看管才不会作弊

⑥ 建议类

Signal：⑤ 结论，且后文给出建议

Inference：其他所有学校使用 honor code，也能导致各自的作弊问题减弱 ⇒ 其他所有学校需要使用 honor code

Assumption：没有更好、更可靠的解决方案

Counterexamples：加重作弊惩罚，安装监控设备

高分范文

In this article, the author recommends that all colleges and universities implement the honor code adopted in Groveton College (GC) to combat cheating.❶ Her suggestion is mainly based on the reported decline of cheating after the adoption of the honor code at GC.❷ However, several crucial questions are left unaddressed, and as a result her conclusion is quite unconvincing.❸

To begin with, the author assumes, perhaps unwarrantedly, that the students' report is just as reliable as that from the teachers.❹ However, will students honestly report every misconduct they spot, or will they rather choose to cover up for each other? Even if they don't intentionally misreport, will they even have the time and energy to watch out for cheating, since they themselves should be completely engaged in the exams?❺ Without a positive answer to either of these questions, it remains unclear if GC's cheating problem has indeed been alleviated.❻

Second, granted that the numbers are trustworthy, that cheating incidences have dropped from 30 per year all the way down to 14, it does not necessarily imply a less serious cheating problem.❼ No evidence has been provided as to

❶ 复述原文结论
❷ 扼要复述原文的主要依据
❸ 指出本文结论

❹ 指出步骤①的假设

❺ 以问题形式抛出反例

❻ 指出作者需要提供相关证据回答这些问题，以及不这么做的影响

❼ 衔接上文，指出步骤②的前提结论

whether there have been significant changes in total enrollment for recent years. If, the total number of students has remained stable or even increased, the reduced cheating instances might indeed suggest that cheating has become less of an issue for the school. ⑧ However, if a reputation crisis has caused a devastating blow to enrollment, resulting in a halving of total students, then the ratio of the amount of cheating to the amount of students may have even ascended, thereby undermining the author's argument. ⑨

Besides, even if cheating has in fact been reduced, it remains unknown whether there are other possible correlates to this shift. ⑩ Maybe the school has decided on heavier punishment for cheating, maybe it has installed surveillance cameras in every classroom, or the average difficulty of the exams has lowered. ⑪ Any of these scenarios, if true, would equally explain the diminishing cheating rate. Without sufficient evidence to address these possibilities, the author cannot fairly draw a connection between the code and cheating, and in turn should not confidently apply the measure to other schools. ⑫

Furthermore, the author also mentions a campus survey in which students claim that they are unlikely to cheat with an honor code in place. ⑬ Apparently, she assumes that this survey is trustworthy. ⑭ In an unlikely scenario where students are willing to reveal all their dark secrets, this survey does weigh much toward the author's conclusion. ⑮ Unfortunately, it is quite possible that students will want to display their best sides, especially when the survey is not conducted anonymously. If so, then this piece of evidence simply lends no support to the author's conclusion. ⑯

Finally, building on the purported success of the honor code at GC, the author immediately alleges that the achievement can be duplicated in other school. ⑰ However, it is uncertain how much students of different schools differ. If in this district, all colleges have students that are honest and self-disciplined, then this code can potentially work miracles when imitated. ⑱ However, perhaps Groveton College is a top institute in the whole region by far. Accordingly, it has a strict standard for applicant enrollment, especially regarding their moral conduct. In contrast, perhaps most other institutes are relatively loose in this respect. If so, then it explains why the honor code, a system that requires people's self-discipline to work, can prove successful in Groveton, but it also probably implies a potential failure when implemented in other places. ⑲

Overall, the author needs to take into consideration all aforementioned questions and supplement a series of unsupported assumptions before she can legitimately conclude that all schools should follow Groveton College's path. ⑳

⑧ 指出能够加强作者论证的证据

⑨ 指出削弱作者逻辑的反例

⑩ 指出步骤③的前提，并直接暗示作者无法得出其结论

⑪ 指出削弱作者逻辑的反例

⑫ 指出作者需要补充的证据

⑬ 指出步骤④的前提
⑭ 指出背后的假设

⑮ 指出能加强作者论证的情况

⑯ 指出削弱作者逻辑的反例

⑰ 指出步骤⑤的前提和结论

⑱ 指出能加强作者论证的证据

⑲ 指出能削弱作者论证的反例

⑳ 结尾复述本文目标

七、糟糕（Poor）、合格（Good）、优秀（Outstanding）文章的区别

本书有两大目标，第一目标就是功利地帮助申请美国、加拿大研究生的中国学生快速达到满足申请学校的 GRE 写作分数。其实，对于很多理工科学生来说，3 分就够了，而对于大部分文科学生来说，4 分也够了。所以，本书的第一个目标就是以最快的效率达到 4 分。这需要多久呢？在我看来，如果一个学生逻辑好，TOEFL 写作可以达到 22 分以上的水平，其实 Argument 分析复习 1 天就够了。中国学生的 GRE 写作平均分数是 3 分，序言中也说过了，这不是什么一般水平的文章，这是非常糟糕的文章，而 4 分其实也只是非常非常普通的文章。但是很多 TOEFL 写作拿 30 分满分的学生也写出 GRE 3 分的文章，不是因为 GRE 写作多难，而是大部分人根本不知道该写些什么。简单来说，为了快速达到 4 分水平，我们的 Argument 分析应该做到哪些要求呢？以下是一些功利的建议：

(1) 不要在模板上做文章：会一套就可以，根本不用花哨。前面推荐的语言是达到 5 分的东西，对于 4 分的目标绰绰有余。得分的关键在于推理（前提、结论、假设）找得准，反例造得严谨，而绝不在于模板"高级与否"。The author's reasoning is open to counterarguments 和 The author's reasoning is vulnerable to counterarguments 没有丝毫区别，绝不会因为 open 变成了 vulnerable 就显得"高级"了。这些都是中国考生常见的毛病，是极其值得唾弃的，是彻底对语言、对 GRE 考试的误解。

(2) 不要担心雷同：一篇 argument 的结构是固定的，因此我们的分析如果真的完美，理论上我们的思路也是固定的，请不要担心所谓的"雷同"。

(3) 任意找 3 个推理步骤，保证前提和结论找得准确，假设分析得准确，反例造得准确，补充证据要求得准确。不用担心 3 个点的顺序安排，因为 4 分水平的文章要求并不这么高。

(4) 语言清楚，可以有小语法错误，但语义保证读者能看懂，就够用了。我看过很多 4 分文章，语言水平非常一般，甚至有很多语法错误，但底线是我能够轻松看懂文章的意思与逻辑（一些大小写、单复数、拼写的错误经常是不干扰阅读的）。不要想着替换"高级词"，考场上大部分学生没有时间做这个事情。

(5) 词数上，很多学生都很关注。但其实，4 分水平的文章，写清楚 2~3 个点，不算开头和结尾，经常只有 300 多个词。加上开头和结尾，也就是 400 多个词，这绝对足够了。而且，时间不够的情况下是完全可以牺牲开头和结尾的（官方 4 分范文就是完全没有开头和结尾段的）。

总而言之，达到 3 分的文章是完全不懂 GRE 的文章，4 分是一个非常简单的目标。但能得 4 分，不是因为我给的"模板"有多高级，而是因为考生的逻辑相对严谨，推理找得对、分析得对，语言足够清楚。

但本书还有一个目标，是让真正在意写作能力的同学们能够学到好的写作，而 4 分的目标并不足以实现这一点。那么，一般的文章和好的文章有什么区别呢？以下是一些常见的区别：

(1) 在原文推理的全面性上，4 分文章只能成功捕捉 2~3 个步骤。而高分文章能够相对更全面地指出原文的推理。

(2) 4 分文章平行安排了几个推理步骤，但不能讲清楚该步骤对作者结论的影响。而高分文章能够体现各步骤与结论之间的联系，展现分析者认识到了原文整个 line of reasoning。

(3) 4分文章对于每个步骤只能找到一个反例并补充相关证据，而高分文章能够全面制造合理的反例，并全面指出作者所需要补充的证据。

(4) 4分文章的反例是合理的，但是合理性并没有解释清楚，只是点到为止，只有作者自己明白这个反例为什么可以削弱原文逻辑。而高分文章是在写给读者看的，它的反例解释得非常清楚，能够保证读者完全理解反例和原文逻辑之间的削弱关系。

(5) 4分的语言基本清楚，但会有不少语法错误，虽然不太会干扰语义的理解。高分文章语言非常清楚、高效，几乎避免了不符合英语规范的问题。

下面举一个段落对比的案例，例子来自于官方题库的第10题。我们在这里讨论的是一个步骤：Dr. Karp 使用 interview-centered method 获得了成功，而 Dr. Field 使用 observation-centered method 却失败了，于是就要将 interview-centered method 推广给未来所有 Tertia 岛群的育儿文化研究。这里有一个明显的类比推理，由一次研究推广到未来所有研究，我们列举了两篇分析，针对的都是这个点。

Good 范文

Last, because of Dr. Karp's conclusion, other anthropologists now recommend all future research on Tertian child-rearing practices to adopt the interview-centered method. However, is the interview-centered method suitable for every research? Perhaps there are important differences between different researches, since some are conducted on children while others are conducted on adults. Readers don't know, and no further evidence is provided. Unless these researchers can demonstrate that the interview-centered approach is always the best choice, their recommendation may actually hurt future investigations.

Outstanding 范文

Because of its apparent success in Dr. Karp's study, the anthropologists assume that the interview-centered approach would always be the best method for every future study on Tertian child-rearing culture. Unfortunately, it remains questionable whether all important information can be obtained by interview. Perhaps it is true that Tertian children were very honest in their interviews, so their answers were extremely helpful to the scholars. However, long isolated from the outside world, adults in Tertia might be very wary of, and thus hostile towards outsiders. If so, their responses, if they are willing to respond at all, are often insincere or incomplete, thus making interviews fruitless. Since child-rearing studies need to focus not just on children, but also parents, this would possibly mean that some other methods have to be adopted to supplement interviews.

这样一对范文很清楚地展现了什么叫"相关的反例"，什么叫"有说服力的反例"。4分范文只是说了研究大人和研究小孩有可能不同，但是，有什么样的不同，以及这种不同为什么会让同样的研究方法产生不同的效果，这些都没有讲，只能靠读者去想。但高分文章完全说清了这一切，读者不用做任何额外的思考，只要理解了原文的意思，就能清楚、看懂这种可能性。

八、How to use the book

Part 3～Part 6 提供了所有官方题目的分析以及其中 20 道题目的范文，包括 Good 范文和 Outstanding 范文。为了不误导同学们，即便是 Good 范文所使用的语言也不限于 4 分水平，而是高分水平，因为它们都是避免了语法错误，且保持了语义、逻辑清晰的。想要很功利达到 4 分的同学的重点应该是理解本章节的方法论，然后选择 2～3 道题目理解分析，并配合后面的 Good 范文，掌握行文结构与常用语言，然后再多理解几道题目的分析，自己可以尝试写作 1～3 篇即可。想要充分复习考试的同学应该把重点放在题目分析上，保证对题库文章熟悉，这样在考场上才不需要现场重新仔细阅读，因为 30 分钟的写作时间其实是非常紧张的（这对于目标冲击高分的考生来说如此，但对于目标拿到 4 分的同学，其实 30 分钟的时间是绰绰有余的），然后选范文进行比对阅读。更重要的是，追求高分的考生必须大量写作（10 篇起），以保证速度能够达到考试要求，并且要把自己的文章读给别人听，并保证自己在不需要解释的情况下能让别人轻松理解。

解密GRE写作
论证思维

Part 3　Issue 题库逐题精析

> **1** To understand the most important characteristics of a society, one must study its major cities.
>
> Write a response in which you discuss the extent to which you agree or disagree with the statement and explain your reasoning for the position you take. In developing and supporting your position, you should consider ways in which the statement might or might not hold true and explain how these considerations shape your position.
>
> 思路近似题目：4 & 111

题目大意

要了解一个社会最重要的特质，我们必须要研究它的主要城市。

话题背景

城市一直以来是一个国家经济、政治、贸易和文化的集中地，国际大都市甚至成为一个国家的代名词。要深刻分析这个话题，我们需要从历史的角度考虑一个国家文化的发展和保存。比如：长期以来，非大城市的文化对于一个国家的贡献是什么，能否体现国家的特色？在当今全球化的影响下，大城市首当其冲，还能否体现国家特色？

审题和段落构架

1. 支持方的理由

就像话题背景中提到的，由于城市是贸易、政治活动、对外交流的中心地，它们确实能在一定程度上成为一个国家的缩影。举例：教育方面，很多大学集中在城市，方便推动学术交流和发展，因此要了解一个国家的教育理念、教学特点、科研水平，大城市就能很好地提供这个平台。类似，商业、艺术、非政府机构也通常集中在大城市。

2. 反对方的理由

首先，在当下讨论这个话题，我们不能忽视全球化给一个国家带来的影响。全球化使得商品、技术和资本更加自由地流动，无处不在地影响着地区经济，政策制定和城市规划等，最终导致各国之间大城市的城市面貌越来越近似。一想到大城市，我们脑海中浮现的大多是水泥森林（concrete jungle）和随处可见的国际品牌。同时，全球化还加速了国际人才的流通，使得一个国家的人才竞争日益激烈，导致大城市的生活状态也趋同。比如，大城市的生活节奏快，人们为了工作的晋升日益奔波等。在这样的情况下，大城市作为一个国家的地区，在体现国家特质方面就显得捉襟见肘了。

其次，不仅在物质上，在文化生活中全球化也有不可磨灭的影响。由于国家间的经济实力不等，全球化带来的必定是文化上的帝国主义（cultural imperialism），西方的一些价值观念可以很容易地通过好莱坞电影等形式打入其他国家。大城市也成为全球化视角下文化殖民的主要阵地。比如在越来越多的中国大城市，欢庆万圣节、感恩节和圣诞节等都已经成为一种习俗。

因此，在全球化的时代，要了解一个国家的主要特质，需要看一个国家对于传统文化的保护和传承，那么我们就必须去研究非主要城市。比如，在中国的少数民族中，还有当代为数不多的母系社会，比如摩梭族。了解驻扎在偏远地区的少数民族文化可以让我们了解中国的婚姻制度，农业生活，以及和家庭、性别等相关的社会价值观念。同理，对于很多国家来说，原住民（indigenous people）文化也是现代文化的重要组成部分，所以了解国家特质需要我们深入非城市地区。

3. 对上述双方理由的再反驳

针对反对方理由2：当然，我们必须要承认，全球化本身正是很多国家当前经济发展的一大特点。观察大城市，见证这些国家正在经历的全球化浪潮，仍然是了解该国家现状的一个重要途径。

参考简化思路

1. 大城市是经济文化中心，通过对它们的研究可以大致了解一个国家的发展状况。
2. 全球化下大城市首当其冲，使得各国大城市越来越趋同。
3. 我们要深入非大城市地区去了解一个国家的传统和文化的保存。

> **3** Scandals are useful because they focus our attention on problems in ways that no speaker or reformer ever could.
>
> Write a response in which you discuss the extent to which you agree or disagree with the claim. In developing and supporting your position, be sure to address the most compelling reasons and/or examples that could be used to challenge your position.

题目大意

丑闻是有用的，因为它们能让我们关注一些问题，而这是任何演说家、改革者都无法做到的。

话题背景

媒体的无孔不入、社交平台信息的飞速传播，这些因素使得如今丑闻满天飞。以前藏得住的事情，现在藏不住了，于是我们更容易认识到社会问题的存在。但这真的能帮助解决问题吗？

审题和段落构架

1. 题目特征

因为 because 的存在，这道题本质上相当于一道"观点—理由"型的题目，适合先分析理由的合理性，再讨论观点的合理性。

2. 对理由的讨论

ⓐ 丑闻自然吸引眼球，因为大众乐意看到丑闻。普罗大众中有太多人希望看到"成功人士"的丑闻，这样就可以让自己产生一种幻觉，即好像自己的平凡纯粹是由自己的善良造成的，而"成功人士"之所以成功只不过是没有道德底线。

ⓑ 如今媒体的无孔不入、社交平台信息传播的速率，都使得丑闻的传播更加迅捷与广泛，客观上也使得丑闻得到的关注度超过任何时代。

3. 对观点的讨论

支持：因此，以前藏得住的问题，现在更容易曝光。要想解决社会问题，首先要发现、认识社会问题。在这一点上，丑闻是有用的。

反对：

ⓐ 媒体醉心于挖掘丑闻，于是丑闻满天飞，再耸人听闻的新闻，如果天天出现，人们就会麻木。于是，网络上热点每天都在变，再大的丑闻，只要忍几天就会被新的话题取代，而问题并不会得到解决，社会秩序保持不变。

ⓑ 媒体还会制造丑闻，使得人们忽略真正的问题。而很多真正有问题的个人和公司，恰恰会利用这种方式

来转移人们的注意力。典型的就是在最近的美国大选中，民主党和共和党双方都全力攻击对方候选人，于是人们好像只记住了希拉里与川普的各种丑闻，很少有人关注真正涉及国计民生的政策。

参考简化思路

1. 丑闻确实吸引眼球。
2. 但丑闻过多，让人们习以为常。
3. 媒体过分制造丑闻，恰恰让我们忽视了根本的问题。

Part 3 Issue 题库逐题精析

5 Some people believe that government funding of the arts is necessary to ensure that the arts can flourish and be available to all people. Others believe that government funding of the arts threatens the integrity of the arts.

Write a response in which you discuss which view more closely aligns with your own position and explain your reasoning for the position you take. In developing and supporting your position, you should address both of the views presented.

题目大意

一些人认为，政府对艺术的资金支持是必要的，它能保证艺术的发展，并让所有人能够接触艺术。另一些人认为，政府对艺术的资金支持损害了艺术的独立性。

话题背景

一派观点认为，艺术家需要独立性，艺术必须是艺术家对自身情感、思想自由忠实的表达。但我们也都知道，这是一种理想。现实是，艺术家是人，他们需要生存，因此他们需要支持。于是，很有可能艺术家就会为了迎合资金的来源而不能忠实地表现自己的本质。

审题和段落构架

1. 题目特征

这是一道双方争论型题目。由于两个论题并不严格对立，所以这个题适合当作两个独立论题分别讨论。

2. 重要概念

integrity of the arts：指的是艺术要诚实，能够有强大的自身原则，拒绝因外界压力而改变。

3. 对第一个观点的讨论

支持：毫无疑问，国家对于艺术的支持是必要的，有以下几个方面是离不开政府资助的：

ⓐ 对于传统文化的传承，这些艺术形式由于不流行，因此很难单靠自身的收入来维持，国家的投入对于文化形式的留存非常关键；

ⓑ 艺术馆、博物馆的建立和维持；

ⓒ 对艺术课程的支持；

ⓓ 对艺术产业的政策支持，比如减税、在城市中建立艺术区（如纽约的 theater district）。

4. 对第二个观点的讨论

支持：

ⓐ 艺术的实质是真实情感的流露，但当艺术家受制于政府需要时，其表达的情感经常是被扭曲的；

b 包括中小学的艺术教育内容甚至都是政治性的；

c 政府的筛选本身就使得大众看到的不是艺术的全貌。

反对：

a 如前所谈，不要误以为政府对艺术的支持，指的是给某些艺术家钱。政府对艺术的支持很多时候是宽泛的，比如减税、建立艺术区。当这样的支持没有针对性的时候，政府的筛选作用其实并不是非常明显，对艺术 integrity 的影响也不是必然的；

b 以上所有说法都默认 integrity of the arts 是一种"honesty and having strong principles that one refuses to change"。于是，为了迎合政府而修改自己的艺术，自然会丢掉 integrity。为了迎合大众、媒体、投资人等所做的任何修改同样是没有 integrity 的，比如 Andy Warhol 所做的一切都是为了出名，但很少有人认为他不是真正的艺术家。按照这种严格的标准，也许只有毫不考虑实际的艺术家才算有 integrity，而这种艺术家就算有，也屈指可数。因此，没有必要对国家支持提出过高的要求，它和个人赞助、观众买票没有本质上的区别。

参考简化思路

1. 政府对艺术的赞助是必需的：保护传统艺术、推动艺术产业、支持艺术教育。
2. 政府当然会影响到艺术家的 integrity，因为艺术家会迎合政府喜好。
3. 但当政府的支持没有针对性，而是对艺术产业整体的支持时，这种影响不是必然的。

6

Claim: In any field—business, politics, education, government—those in power should step down after five years.

Reason: The surest path to success for any enterprise is revitalization through new leadership.

Write a response in which you discuss the extent to which you agree or disagree with the claim and the reason on which that claim is based.

思路近似题目：105 & 142

题目大意

在任何领域——商业、政治、教育、政府——掌握权力的人都应该在任职五年后卸任。

审题和段落构架

1. 题目特征

这是一道"观点—理由"型题目，适合分别讨论理由和观点。

2. 支持方的理由

任何一个机构都需要注入新鲜血液来保持活力（revitalization）。人员一成不变在如今飞速变化的世界里，意味着新的知识、新的技能、新的思路难以被运用，效率无法提升。比如，在商业领域，随着信息技术的突飞猛进，很多曾经辉煌的企业就因为无法适应新的环境而被淘汰，比如 Nokia, Motorola 等。所以，更换新的领导人以此带来新鲜的血液，看似能够成为刺激一个组织发展的动力。

3. 反对方的理由

ⓐ 一个组织需要的是 revitalization，而并不必须要通过改变领导层来实现。组织僵化，可能是因为领导人的思路僵化。但有一些领导人就能够意识到自己的局限，而不断挑战自己的旧有思路；相反，换新人并不能保证带来更好的思路。比如，Steve Jobs 在任的十几年间从来没有停止为 Apple 寻找新的突破口，他离世后近些年 Apple 却反被质疑没有创新。比如，著名足球俱乐部 Manchester United 在经理 Sir Alex Ferguson 27 年的执教下，几经沉浮。在先前的战术体系被破解的情况下，Alex Ferguson 总能颠覆自己寻找到新的战术突破点，多次带领球队获得最高的荣耀。他离任后，频繁更换经理人，却始终没有成熟的理念，球队反而如履薄冰。

ⓑ 继续延展 a 的思路：revitalization 不见得等同于领导的替换，一个公司或组织任何部门的变更都有可能带来公司的进一步发展。比如，公司引入新的部门、新的技术团队；政府寻找新的智囊团；球队更换新的球员等。

ⓒ 频繁更换领袖的一大问题是，重要的决策不能持续下去，以至于每个新领导人只会关注自己在任期间的短期成效，而无视机构的可持续发展。比如，政府领导人会更在意短期的失业率、GDP，而忽略教育、基础科

研、环保等问题，甚至为了体现自己的能力会刻意终止前任制订的发展战略；球队经理会去购买昂贵的成熟球员，而不在意青年球员的培养。

参考简化思路

1. 更换领导人看似能够带来一个机构所必需的活力，因为长久的人员僵化会导致企业缺乏新鲜视野。
2. 但是 revitalization 并不需要通过领导人的替换实现，替换领导人也并不保证带来好的新理念。
3. 如果领导人知道自己的任期只在五年以内，他们会做更功利的决定，无视长远的发展。

Part 3 Issue 题库逐题精析

> **8** Nations should pass laws to preserve any remaining wilderness areas in their natural state, even if these areas could be developed for economic gain.
>
> Write a response in which you discuss your views on the policy and explain your reasoning for the position you take. In developing and supporting your position, you should consider the possible consequences of implementing the policy and explain how these consequences shape your position.
>
> 思路近似题目：118 & 141

题目大意

国家应该出台法令保护所有荒野地区的原始状态，即便这些地区可以用作经济开发。

话题背景

人类的经济发展不断加速，导致我们以各种形式破坏了大自然的平衡；但另一方面，不断膨胀的人口也意味着我们的经济发展必须能够满足人们的生存需求。如何寻找这两者之间的平衡正是本题所试图探讨的话题。

审题和段落构架

1. 重要概念

wilderness：理解为"原生态区域"，指"原始的、未被现代科技所开发的区域"。

2. 支持方的理由

首先，原生态区域能够涵养水源、净化空气，它们对我们人类生存环境的健康有着重要的作用。事实上，我们现代人类社会中大量的人口所依赖的水源正是来自于这些地方。

其次，原生态区域是很多野生动植物生存的最后一片栖息地，而这些濒危动植物有着重要的科研价值。而且，生物多样性本身就是一种重要的资源，它们很可能将以我们目前还无法意识到的方式帮助我们——比如，也许未来某种重要的物质就要从某种野生的植物中提取。

（我们这里可以做进一步的思考：环境不是不可以被利用，问题在于如何利用。就目前来说，现在工业和科技的发展对于原生环境的利用必然是毁灭性的。即便没有大规模的开发，我们使用的杀虫剂也会流入原生态区域，对那里的动植物造成威胁。空气污染的排放也会影响到原生态环境中的植被生长。人类活动导致的全球变暖同时也影响了原生态环境。所以当务之急不是开发原生态地区，而是考虑如何保护或合理利用。目前很多原住民依然依靠原生态环境生活，他们也对自然环境进行改造，比如河流改道等，但是他们的日常生活对于环境的负面影响比起大规模的开发要小很多。我们可以从他们身上学到人类和环境和谐共处的很多知识。）

最后，保护原生态环境有很重要的人文价值。城市人口的生活日趋忙碌，心理健康问题司空见惯。回归自然成为很好地释放压力的方式，能给人带来心理上的幸福感 (psychological well-being)。

3. 反对方的理由

人口的膨胀意味着我们需要更多的土地来满足人们的生存需要。

4. 对上述双方理由的再反驳

针对反对方理由：我们恰恰应该控制人口的膨胀，因为这种膨胀是没有上限的，但是我们的家园是有限的。我们要学会利用科技和智慧去用现有的土地解决更多的问题，而不是入侵大自然剩下的为数不多的净土。

参考简化思路

1. 原生态区域净化了我们的环境。
2. 保护它们有利于保护生物多样性，对人类有重要的科研价值。
3. 原生态环境本身有着重要的人文价值。
4. 对于环境的保护是为了人类长久的发展，我们应该在经济发展和环境保护之间找到平衡。

9

People's behavior is largely determined by forces not of their own making.

Write a response in which you discuss the extent to which you agree or disagree with the statement and explain your reasoning for the position you take. In developing and supporting your position, you should consider ways in which the statement might or might not hold true and explain how these considerations shape your position.

思路近似题目：74 & 93

题目大意

人们的行为大体上不是由自己决定的。

话题背景

自由意志是亘古以来西方哲学界所争论的话题。看似我们随时都在做选择，并且每个选择看起来对我们都是开放的。但相信决定论的哲学家认为，其实所有的最终选择都是被外界的因素，即超出我们行为主体控制范围的因素所提前决定的。

审题和段落构架

1. **支持方的理由**

   ⓐ 首先，自然规律——我们人类的物理局限，已经决定了我们很多行为的限度；甚至我们克服自然的努力，本质上也正是由大自然对我们的限制造就的。

   ⓑ 社会制度、传统习俗、法律条文，更是从精神上约束了我们的行为可能性。比如，我可以偷东西，但是法律的约束，以及触犯法律可能带来的严肃惩罚，都已经决定了我不会去偷东西。

2. **反对方的理由**

   总有制度的挑战者，他们就没有被社会传统所限制，他们的行为是自由的。

3. **对上述双方理由的再反驳**

   对反对方理由的讨论：之所以会做出看似自由、违背规则的行为，通常和行为主体的性格极其相关。然而，性格并不是莫名其妙出现的个人特征，而是由个体所受的教育、环境影响等各方面因素带来的，而这些因素并不都是在一个人的控制之内。

参考简化思路

1. 物理规律限制了人类的行为方式。
2. 社会制度约束了人们的意识。
3. 诚然，有一些人看似打破约束，但这是由个体性格造成，进一步由一系列外部因素带来的。

Part 3　Issue 题库逐题精析

10　Governments should offer a free university education to any student who has been admitted to a university but who cannot afford the tuition.

Write a response in which you discuss your views on the policy and explain your reasoning for the position you take. In developing and supporting your position, you should consider the possible consequences of implementing the policy and explain how these consequences shape your position.

思路近似题目：23

题目大意

政府应该为被大学录取但没有能力支付学费的学生提供免费的大学教育。

审题和段落构架

1. 支持方的理由

首先，大学教育是实现社会流动性的关键元素。中小学教育只是保证了人们有基本的生存能力，而大学教育才是让很多人找到自身优势和定位的关键阶段。好的大学教育让很多出身下层的孩子能够有机会改变自己的命运。

其次，让有天赋的孩子能够免费获得大学教育其实是教育发展的最终理想。学校可以最大化地向国家输送人才，避免浪费。

2. 反对方的理由

国家的资源毕竟是有限的，一件事情值得做不等于要用大量资源去做，因为除了大学教育外，初等教育、医疗、交通、环境、科技等各个方面都需要国家的资金支持。并不是每个政府都有能力保证每一个合格的孩子都能得到免费的大学教育，也更不是每个政府都必须要实现这一点。

让有天赋的孩子有机会接受高等教育是非常有价值的，但这并不意味着必须要为他们提供免费的教育。相反，国家可以采用奖学金的方式激励学生努力学习；或者，国家可以提供助学贷款，帮助孩子完成学业。免费的午餐容易让人懒惰，而通过努力换取报酬才是让人一直前进的方式。

参考简化思路

1. 大学教育保证了社会的上升通道，且保证了国家的人才储备。
2. 并不是每个国家都有足够的资源为所有有能力但没有财力的孩子提供免费的大学教育。
3. 而且，还有别的途径可以保证没有钱的学生获得大学教育。

Part 3 Issue 题库逐题精析

11 Universities should require every student to take a variety of courses outside the student's field of study.

Write a response in which you discuss the extent to which you agree or disagree with the claim. In developing and supporting your position, be sure to address the most compelling reasons and/or examples that could be used to challenge your position.

思路近似题目：44, 67, 96, 106 & 133

题目大意

大学应该要求每一位学生学习他们专业以外的课程。

话题背景

跨学科研究（interdisciplinary studies）是现在教育领域的重要话题。随着我们对世界了解的不断深入，人们逐渐发现传统学科领域间互通有无能更好地帮助我们完善知识体系、解决实际问题。目前很多大学都需要学生具备跨学科思考的能力，这个题目便是在讨论这个话题。

审题和段落构架

1. 支持方的理由

首先，这个论题有很强的现实意义。目前世界上很多国家都面临教育膨胀的问题，由于大学毕业生的数量远远多于就业岗位，大学文凭再也不意味能轻松找到铁饭碗。在这样的情形下，很多学生进入大学即便怀揣远大理想，也会做实际的打算，即积累各种技能以便在找工作的时候更有优势（很多大学生参加各种考证也是出于类似的打算）。从这个角度考虑，学校应该鼓励甚至要求学生多参加自己专业以外的课程学习，多掌握一种技能。

其次，通过各种不同专业课程的学习，学校旨在鼓励跨学科思考。跨学科研究是教育发展的必然趋势，因为它能带来探索世界、解决难题的新视角。比如数字人文（digital humanities）等就是结合了看似很难联系在一起的学科来探索科研问题。

2. 反对方的理由

首先，高尖端的科研话题都是非常具体的，通常也都在传统的领域展开。所以从培养研究员的角度来说，让已经在接受高等教育的学生学习不同的科目显得没有必要。

其次，通过学习专业外的课程来达到跨学科的目的在实施过程中不一定有效，因为它需要学生自己主动地去培养跨学科的意识。就拿现在美国大学中的通识教育（general education）来说，学生需要完成非专业课程。很多学生去上这些课程仅仅是为了满足学分要求，有些学生甚至找一些他们认为的简单课程去上。这样看来，如果学生自己不能发现这些课程的潜在联系，不能培养跨学科思维，那这个策略可能不会达到预期的效果。

3. 对上述理由的再反驳

针对反对方的第一个理由：部分学科的高端科研的确很独立，比如理论数学。但除此以外的其他学科，不管其研究进行到什么程度，都可以通过跨学科尝试新的思考方式来解决问题。比如文化神经科学（cultural neuroscience），为了进一步解释不同群体间的文化差异，人类和社会学家试图通过对大脑神经活动的研究来解释这些群体在语言使用和道德观念上的差异。

针对反对方的第一个理由：而且，本科教育并不算严格意义上的专业教育，研究生阶段才是；本科阶段仍然是一种通识教育，至少在读本科的前几年是真的很少需要深入领域前沿研究的。

📎 参考简化思路

1. 在当前的就业压力下，多学习不同的课程有助于提升竞争力。
2. 跨学科研究是教育发展的趋势，学校应该积极鼓励。
3. 这个方法有一定的局限性，需要依赖学生自己主动去培养跨学科思考的习惯和意识。如果仅仅是为了拿一个成绩，这个政策就失去它的意义。

Part 3　Issue 题库逐题精析

12

A nation should require all of its students to study the same national curriculum until they enter college.

Write a response in which you discuss your views on the policy and explain your reasoning for the position you take. In developing and supporting your position, you should consider the possible consequences of implementing the policy and explain how these consequences shape your position.

思路近似题目：90 & 110

题目大意

一个国家应该要求所有学生在大学前学习统一的课程。

话题背景

理想的教育应该因材施教，但我们又认为社会中所有合格的公民都应该有一些基本的素养，如何在这两者之间寻找平衡点呢？这正是这道题目所尝试探索的问题。

审题和段落构架

1. 重要概念

the same national curriculum：统一的全国课程，只是课程名称统一，还是课程内容也必须统一？这个问题题目并没有清晰地指出，这也是我们可以灵活讨论的地方。

2. 支持方的理由

ⓐ 显然有一些最基本的课程是所有学生都必须接触的，这是成为一名社会合格公民的基本要求。我们需要识字、需要交流，所以必然需要学习语言；我们需要计算，所以必须学习数学；历史、地理、物理、生物等都为我们生存和生活在共同体当中提供了必要的能力。

ⓑ 统一课程有一个重要的价值，就是会使教育体系运转成本大幅度降低：课本编纂成本、教师培训成本、大学入学考核成本。

ⓒ 这保障了教育资源的公平分配，能够让发达和不发达地区的学生学到同样的知识。

3. 反对方的理由

首先，初等教育除了培养必需的技能，还帮助学生寻找自己的兴趣和特长，为以后的大学以及工作提供选择方向，这意味着学生所学的东西不仅限于合格公民必须掌握的东西。我们学习解方程组、化学键，听古典音乐，阅读古文，这都不是在培养人人必须有的技能；但通过这些过程，有的人就会发现自己想要成为数学家，有的人意识到自己能成为文学家，等等。仅仅培养基本能力的初等教育已经远远不能满足当代社会对初等教育的要求了。

其次，教育的对象是学生，而学生是一个非常多样的群体，有着不同的天赋、兴趣、需求、背景与能力。

对数学不感兴趣的人也许只需要学入门课程，但是有天赋、有兴趣的人自然有对高级课程的需要，比如美国高中里的 Advanced Placement（AP）课程。少数族群也许除了全国统一语言课程之外，还需要学习自己的民族语言和文化，这是尊重民族多样性，传承少数民族文化的重要一步。

再次，教育的执行者是老师。就算教同一门课程，由于老师的背景、特长不同，也应该灵活加入个性化的元素，把自己最擅长的东西教给学生。

4. 对上述双方理由的再反驳

针对支持方理由2和3：标准化教育降低成本且保障公平的必然结果就是劣质的公平，所有地区将享受一样低质量的教育。理想主义并不是解决公平的良药：不同地区的经济发展水平不同，必然意味着师资不同、学生素质不同，强迫公平导致的结果是，优秀的老师和学生都只能被迫学达不到他们需要和标准的内容，反而造成了严重的资源浪费。他们都会有更多的需求，他们也会去尝试解决这种需求，这会导致教育资源流向私立教育、课外教育，最终还是让社会不公加剧。

参考简化思路

1. 基础能力的培养，全国必须有明确的统一底线。
2. 但是，完全统一的课程无法满足学生的个人需要。
3. 完全统一的课程也无法满足国家对优秀人才培养的需要。

17

> Governments should focus on solving the immediate problems of today rather than on trying to solve the anticipated problems of the future.
>
> Write a response in which you discuss the extent to which you agree or disagree with the recommendation and explain your reasoning for the position you take. In developing and supporting your position, describe specific circumstances in which adopting the recommendation would or would not be advantageous and explain how these examples shape your position.

题目大意

政府应该关注解决眼前的问题，而不是试图解决预见的将来的问题。

审题和段落构架

1. 支持方的理由

很多当下的问题迫在眉睫，且关乎国计民生，如果得不到好的解决，其恶劣影响是很难逆转的。饮食、医疗、就业、犯罪、国防、自然灾害，这些社会问题或自然问题，如果任由其发展，会直接导致人们的基本生活得不到保证，势必会引发社会的动乱。

2. 反对方的理由

然而，绝不可能因为当下的问题是最值得解决的问题，我们就可以任由政府牺牲一个国家、地区长远的发展。有些很长远的、重要的问题，如果当前不开始着手解决，那么未来它们将变成无法解决的眼前问题。

ⓐ 比如，同样是旅游资源的发展，一种方式是制定严格的环境标准，发展生态旅游（eco-tourism）；另一种就是无限制迎合游客的需要，不惜破坏当地的生态。显然，前者更优，而后者只是饮鸩止渴。类似的，整个环保的价值，就在于控制我们对自然资源的攫取与破坏。我们是需要利用自然资源的，但这种利用必须是可持续的，而不是竭泽而渔。

ⓑ 比如，教育的投入很难短期内产生经济效益，但是眼前对教育的忽视，就会导致十年、二十年后国家人才的匮乏。

ⓒ 同理，科研的投入，尤其是理论研究的投入，其收效更是不确定，但对于大国来说，这种投入又是必需的。因为虽然单一研究的回报未知，但大量的投入各种研究之后，必然会有一些研究取得成果，而这种回报将大大提升国家的竞争力。

3. 总结

显然，任何政府都不可能单纯地追求眼前的利益或是一味好高骛远。政府必然是要寻求当前发展与可持续发展之间的平衡。

参考简化思路

1. 饮食、医疗、就业、犯罪、国防、自然灾害等迫在眉睫的问题是必须要妥善解决的。
2. 但环保、教育、科研等长远问题同样不容忽视。
3. 政府必须追求长远利益与眼前利益的平衡。

Part 3 Issue 题库逐题精析

> **18** Some people believe that college students should consider only their own talents and interests when choosing a field of study. Others believe that college students should base their choices of a field of study on the availability of jobs in that field.
>
> Write a response in which you discuss which view more closely aligns with your own position and explain your reasoning for the position you take. In developing and supporting your position, you should address both of the views presented.
>
> 思路近似题目：2, 13, 30, 33, 37, 92, 122, 128, 129 & 130

题目大意

一些人认为大学生选择专业领域时只需要考虑自身的天赋与兴趣。另一些人认为需要考虑该领域的就业情况。

审题和段落构架

1. 题目特征

这道题虽然是"some-other"结构的题目，但因为双方立场恰好矛盾，意味着支持第一派必然会反对第二派，支持第二派必然会反对第一派，所以我们把它当作一个独立话题处理就可以了，即"在选择领域时，是否应该只考虑兴趣和天赋，而不考虑就业情况？"。

2. 支持方的理由

在选择专业领域的时候考虑兴趣和天赋是必需的。有了兴趣，学习会更有动力；有了天赋，这种动力更容易转化为快速的进步，反过来会激发更多的兴趣。这些都能够帮助学生取得好的成绩进而在该领域获得更好的发展。反之，那些被迫学习所谓热门领域的孩子，由于所学不符合自己的特点，很多人在大学期间过得非常挣扎，并没有达到人们对"进入热门专业"所抱有的期望。

3. 反对方的理由

首先，绝大多数人家里并不富裕，意味着他们的家庭至少在经济上无法百分之百支持他们投入一个完全不带来产出的领域。简而言之，大部分人毕业后都需要考虑工作，如果学的领域怎么都找不到工作，或者找不到可以养活自己的工作，这基本可以证明他们最初的选择是错误的。

4. 对上述双方理由的再反驳

先前的讨论都是对这个问题过度简化的分析，也是大部分人没有深入思考的常见结果。考虑兴趣与天赋是必要的，但不代表是充分的。事实上，这个话题显然值得深入实际情况具体讨论。

在最初选择领域的时候，很多外行人都会根据经验去断言某些领域"热门"，比如计算机、金融、法律等；

而把另一些领域称为"冷门",比如哲学、艺术等。这里面暗指的就是前者容易找到好工作,而后者干脆找不到工作。但这种过于粗略的划分其实没有多大的实际价值,因为每个大的领域都有很具体的细分。当艺术与新媒体结合在一起的时候,这就成为当今非常流行的领域;学习哲学中的逻辑分支其实是成为律师非常关键的一步。因此,如果学生只是选择大的专业方向时,恰恰没有太大必要考虑整个领域的就业问题,因为所有大的领域都会和实际工作紧密联系。

但以上的讨论恰恰意味着,在选择更细分的领域时,我们应该考虑社会的需求,毕竟没有人希望毕业就失业。很多如今的就业岗位都希望招到有实习经历的学生。也就是那些无视社会实际需求,单纯在学校中学了四年的人,就算成绩再好,也很难尽快适应社会的需求。同理,很多岗位也会在简历中关注学生是否在除了本专业领域外掌握了其他技能,通常包含语言、计算机、建模等方面的能力。这些都意味着,学生在大学学习中,除了专业课程的学习外,理应考虑结合实际工作中可能需要的能力来完善自己的履历。

Part 3　Issue 题库逐题精析

19　Laws should be flexible enough to take account of various circumstances, times, and places.

Write a response in which you discuss the extent to which you agree or disagree with the statement and explain your reasoning for the position you take. In developing and supporting your position, you should consider ways in which the statement might or might not hold true and explain how these considerations shape your position.

题目大意

法律应该足够灵活，能够考虑不同的情况、时间和地点。

话题背景

法律需要公平，但公平是否不意味着一成不变。那么，在法律的决定性和灵活性之间，应该如何权衡？

审题和段落构架

1. **支持方的理由**

   ⓐ 在时代的发展下，我们的社会出现了很多新的问题，这些问题是现有的法律体系不能覆盖的，所以法律体系必须有所修正，以适应新的发展：网络带来的一系列问题；现代化的杀伤性武器带来的问题；空间技术发展带来的空间领土权问题……

   ⓑ 对于地区的特点，法律也应该具有一定的适应性：不同的民族、种族聚居区需要法律在一定程度上去保护少数族群的文化传承，以及对地区风俗、信仰的尊重；自然保护区、古建筑群等区域也需要有相应的法案来平衡发展与传承。

   ⓒ 法律会考虑犯罪者的年龄、违法记录、犯罪动机等具体因素。判决一方面是为了维护正义，让施害者受到应有的惩罚，给犯罪者提供改过（rehabilitate）的机会。年龄、历史违法次数都和改过的可能性相关；同样的行为表象，背后不同的犯罪动机其实决定了这个行为实际的罪恶程度，自然应该有不同的审判。

2. **反对方的理由**

   ⓐ 但灵活不是无限度的，如果法律会考虑犯罪者的社会地位、经济地位，那法律就严重违背了公平性，将失去人们的支持。

   ⓑ 同样，灵活也不是随性的。什么样的情况可以灵活考虑，这必须是有法律规则进行约束的。并且，法律的修正也需要通过合法的程序进行。

参考简化思路

1. 时代变了，法律自然要适应新的情况。
2. 不同的地区，有着不同的文化和自然特点，也需要法律、法规考虑其具体情况。
3. 但法律的灵活必须有限度，并且必须有规则。

20

Claim: The best way to understand the character of a society is to examine the character of the men and women that the society chooses as its heroes or its role models.

Reason: Heroes and role models reveal a society's highest ideals.

Write a response in which you discuss the extent to which you agree or disagree with the claim and the reason on which that claim is based.

思路近似题目：116

题目大意

观点：理解一个社会特点的最好的方式是去考察该社会选为英雄和楷模的男男女女。

理由：英雄楷模反映了一个社会最高的理想。

话题背景

如今人们经常批评年轻人动不动就以网红、明星等为榜样，然后担忧我们的社会正在堕落。其实这种思维背后反映的就是本题所蕴含的逻辑，即我们认为人们选择什么样的人作为行为楷模，就决定了整个社会所具有的特征。通过分析不同社会所选择的楷模，我们能看到不同社会本质上的区别。但是，与楷模相对立的概念是社会的普罗大众，他们是否真的能够被这些楷模所代表，对社会特征的研究是否真的可以忽略对普罗大众的关注？

审题和段落构架

1. 题目特征

这是一道"观点—理由"型题目，需要分别讨论理由与观点的合理性。

2. 重要概念

英雄与楷模可以有广义与狭义的理解：狭义的理解指的是像救火英雄这样有英勇的、舍己救人壮举的个体，通常是呈现了极高尚道德情操的个体；广义的理解自然扩展到了社会所推崇的个体，不仅限于道德行为，涉及各个领域人们试图仿效的形形色色的偶像人物。本题中，建议不要限制在前一种理解方式下，否则会严重局限我们的探讨空间。

3. 对理由的讨论

支持：狭义地理解英雄，一个社会所选择的道德楷模显然能够体现出该社会所拥有的最高道德诉求。比如，在推崇集体主义的社会中，我们会看到很多舍己救人、舍小家为大家的角色为媒体争相报道；在强调孝道的文化中，我们会经常看到这样的英雄形象，父母在世时，对父母言听计从，从不违抗，竭尽全力服侍父母，父母死后，守孝很多年；尚武的社会就更不用说了，最被推崇的角色自然就是在战争中勇猛杀敌的英雄形象；在如今环保主义观念下，一些被推崇的形象经常做的事情是，牺牲自己的生活质量，去保护濒危生物的栖息环境，或是拯救流浪的小动物，而这在古代社会是不可能被推崇的。

支持：广义地理解英雄，一个社会人们所效仿的偶像也体现了人们所追求的理想生活方式。古代的精英主义价值观下的社会，人们讴歌伟大的思想家、政治家；几十年前人们推崇的偶像形象是科学家、发明家；如今在消费主义浪潮侵蚀下，人们对企业家、明星、网红顶礼膜拜……

4. 对观点的讨论

支持：因此，我们对很多社会特点的判断，就是通过对其楷模形象的认识得来的。我们想到古希腊，很难不想到其伟大的思想、政治制度、文化对整个人类的贡献，而这种认识都来自于我们对苏格拉底（Socrates）、伯利克里（Pericles）、荷马（Homer）等人的研究。我们谈到当代的美国，会想到很多特点，随便列举一二，比如它作为流行文化的中心，我们会想到玛丽莲·梦露（Marilyn Monroe）、麦当娜（Madonna）等这样的形象；它在商业与信息技术革命上的结合，我们会想到乔布斯（Steve Jobs）、扎克伯格（Mark Zuckerberg）等这些企业家……

反对：但理想与现实之间是有差距的，关注偶像人物我们看到的是社会的理想，而不是社会的现实。也许每个现代国家都会尊重消防队员，这说明大家有了相似的道德诉求，但我们完全无法对比出这些国家的道德现状是什么样的。这只有通过对大量社会现实的研究才能看到。

反对：一个社会内部是多元的，不同地区有非常不同的特点，不同的年龄段有不同的价值观，所以我们可能很难找出统一的偶像形象。

参考简化思路

1. 人们效仿什么样的楷模，确实反映了人们所追求的最高理念。
2. 因此，我们对很多社会特点的判断，必然要依赖于对这个社会楷模的研究。
3. 但是，过分关注楷模，会让我们忽视社会现实，以及忽视了社会内部的多元性。

21　Governments should place few, if any, restrictions on scientific research and development.

Write a response in which you discuss the extent to which you agree or disagree with the recommendation and explain your reasoning for the position you take. In developing and supporting your position, describe specific circumstances in which adopting the recommendation would or would not be advantageous and explain how these examples shape your position.

思路近似题目：34, 57, 69 & 124

题目大意

政府应该尽可能少地限制科学研究与发展。

话题背景

当今社会，国家实力和科研水平紧密联系在一起。政府需要支持科研，但也必须得平衡科研需要与其他发展需要。因此，国家必须支持科研，但并不是无限度、无条件的。这个限度在哪里？

审题和段落构架

1. 重要概念

限制：政府对科研所设定的规则限制是多方面的，不只有"禁止研发"才叫作限制，应用上的、财政上的限制同样是一种限制。

2. 支持方的理由

政客并不懂科学，而且经常受到社会各方同样不懂科学的利益集团的影响，制定出各种奇葩的政策限制，导致科学发展受阻。例如：出于民众的压力，美国政府本在20世纪90年代就计划兴建的大型量子对撞机（LHC）被迫搁置，然后被欧洲各国抢去成功兴建了。

3. 反对方的理由

政客虽不懂科学，但政府在制定规则时，必然会听取大量科研专家的意见。而且，政府的资金是有限的，科研的需求是无限的，所以必然会涉及某些规则的制定；再者，科研也不是没有风险的，所以出于社会发展的全面考虑，政府也需要制定一些规则来引导科研的发展。

ⓐ 禁令：政府对科研的底线应该是不破坏社会的基本伦理秩序，因此有这方面严重风险的研究必须从政策上完全禁止，意味着政府不资助，也不允许任何组织、个人资助这种研究。例如：克隆人会带来身份问题以及可能的宗教争议；AI技术不能发展侵犯人类利益的技术；人类活体实验更是不能随意突破。

b 应用方面的限制：

（b1）现阶段不确定效果、但有长远社会意义的研究应该得到支持，但其现阶段的应用必须被严格控制。例如：转基因技术。

（b2）并不是有了更便捷的高科技生产技术，就应该鼓励其应用，因为高科技对传统经济产生的巨大的冲击有可能带来传统行业大规模的失业，造成一种沙漏效果（hourglass effect），使得传统工人失去生存的方式，这也是政府必须考虑的一个因素。

c 经费的限制：这才是最关键的问题，需要进一步讨论。

（c1）很多人质疑一些基础科研的时效性，认为某些科研是否能成功，如果能成功是否会有广泛应用，存在巨大的不确定性。社会在各方各面都需要经费，所以这种没有实际意义的研究不应该支持。

（c2）但现在存在的严重的学术掺水问题是必须要限制的。政府对科研的支持经常要由一些客观标准决定，比如研究文献的被引用次数等。而这种同行评议的结果是，很多科研学阀引领一个学界流派，内部互相引用价值很低的研究，从而增加该研究的影响力，获得政府的资金支持。这就造成了真正重要的研究得不到资助。目前似乎很难想到有什么好的解决方案，但这必须是政府未来尝试解决的问题。

4. 对上述双方理由的再反驳

对反对方理由（c1）的反驳：至少对于大国来说，这种做法是极其短视的。例如：美国至今仍然在享受作为第一个实现核裂变国家所带来的巨大利益。下一个类似的研究就是可控核聚变，任何国家如果第一个掌握它，几乎将必然成为一段时间内的世界头号强国。对于一个大国来说，因为短视而放弃基础研究是极其愚蠢的举措。而且，很多关键研究的实际应用价值一开始是几乎不能确定的。例如：没有人一开始就能预见到相对论有什么价值，但现在看一看 GPS 的价值我们就知道了。

参考简化思路

1. 伦理方面，科研不能突破人伦底线，政府必须限制此类科研。
2. 在现阶段会对人类安全造成威胁的研究，必须对其引用进行限制。
3. 但政府应该鼓励基础研究的发展，这对于一个国家的长远发展有着巨大的助力。

22

The best way to teach is to praise positive actions and ignore negative ones.

Write a response in which you discuss the extent to which you agree or disagree with the statement and explain your reasoning for the position you take. In developing and supporting your position, you should consider ways in which the statement might or might not hold true and explain how these considerations shape your position.

思路近似题目：27 & 50

题目大意

最好的教育方法是鼓励正面行为且忽视负面行为。

话题背景

这个话题恰好指出了如今东西方教育理念的冲突：西方以鼓励式教育为主，而东方以批评式教育为主。本话题就是在寻找两种极端之间的平衡点。

审题和段落构架

1. 支持方的理由

鼓励式教育第一个重要的意义是使受教育者能够重复先前的正面行为，从而形成良好习惯。这里可以列举假设的例子，比如一个不怎么爱说话的孩子主动在课堂上发言，老师的鼓励可以使孩子意识到这是一个值得做的事情，即便发言的内容并不完全正确。从这个点我们继续延伸：鼓励式教育的另一个价值是使受教育者获得自信——经常性获得行为的正反馈，孩子会对自己的能力有信心，会更敢于做决定。相反，支持鼓励式教育的人会认为批评式教育打击了孩子的人格，使得孩子容易陷入抑郁。

2. 反对方的理由

鼓励式教育的问题也很明显：无视错误会使错误行为无法被指出，尤其是严重的缺点很可能就会保留下来，甚至会逐渐放大。在带来自信的同时，鼓励式教育很可能导致孩子变得极其自负，无法认识到自己的不足。

现代的教育体系倾向于认为自信是一种优秀的品质。但其实，自信与成功之间的关联一直都没有得到证实。比如，对优秀企业管理者的统计显示，自信的管理者和企业成功之间几乎没有任何相关性。极端的自信至于自负，和过分的自卑甚至是抑郁，都是我们想避免的。但正常范围内的自信和不自信并没有清晰的优与劣。更多自信意味着更多的风险倾向，于是失败和成功的偏差会更大；相反，不自信会带来更多的行为谨慎，不容易犯巨大的错误，也不容易做出巨大的突破。我们的社会一直都是两种性格的人共存的环境，因此，没有必要非要突出其中一方相对于另一方的优势，而无视劣势同样存在的现实。一个间接的证据是：在美国，大量的创造性艺术家源源不断地出现；但是，工程师、科学家的需求却远远得不到满足，还需要大量从东亚、东南亚地区引入。

3. 对上述双方理由的综合讨论

因此，基于现有证据，我们很难认为鼓励式教育永远优于批评式教育，反之亦然。我们可以确定的是，我们希望避免严重的负面行为；同时，希望保持非常优秀的品质。所以，鼓励积极行为和批评消极行为在目前看来也许是比较合适的做法。

参考简化思路

1. 鼓励积极行为使得好的行为能够被延续。
2. 鼓励积极行为还会让孩子拥有自信。
3. 忽视负面行为会造成错误无法得到改正。
4. 所以，以鼓励为主，但是在关键错误上必须要给予指正。

24 The luxuries and conveniences of contemporary life prevent people from developing into truly strong and independent individuals.

Write a response in which you discuss the extent to which you agree or disagree with the statement and explain your reasoning for the position you take. In developing and supporting your position, you should consider ways in which the statement might or might not hold true and explain how these considerations shape your position.

题目大意

富足便利的现代生活阻碍了人们去变成独立强大的个体。

话题背景

物质世界的不断进步主要是科技和工业发展的结果。人类物质世界和精神世界的关系长久以来一直是重要且复杂的议题。柏拉图曾在《斐德罗篇》中提到，纸笔写作的出现会使人逐渐停止使用自身的记忆能力。这其实就是在思考外部物质环境如何对人本身、人的思考能力、人的性格或人类特质等带来改变。如今科技高度发达，不仅把人从繁杂的体力劳动中解放出来，还在很多方面代替了人的作用。我们很容易想到一些生活中的例子，比如导航的出现让很多人变成了"路痴"。从另一方面考虑，物质世界的不断进步和提升可以证明人类本身在不断提升，所以才能带来社会的进步。本题是对社会发展，尤其是科技发展的人文思考，文章要尽可能体现科技进步和人类社会自身发展两者之间的多重复杂关系。

审题和段落构架

1. 重要概念

对题干中出现的一系列名词和形容词，如 luxuries, convenience, strong, independent，考生很容易就词论词，比如把 luxuries 理解成"奢侈品"，甚至是"奢侈品牌"。在方法论中我们提到，在审题时首先要意识到作者说这一句话其实是在思考什么本质问题。luxuries and convenience 是在提炼概括当今社会的主要特点，其物质世界的极大丰富和便利，带来这样现状的根本原因即是科技的进步。作者用 strong and independent 的对立面特质来提炼概括当今人类社会的特点，题目认为正是富足便利的外部环境使得人难以变得强大和独立。

2. 支持方的理由

物质世界的发展解放了人的体力劳动和思考能力，在某些方面人们确实取代了人本身。举例：复杂计算、信息检索。因此带来的负面效果即人越来越依赖科技解决问题，导致人的思考能力、搜索能力变弱，依赖性变强。

3. 反对方的理由

首先，物质世界的发展进步体现了人不断运用创造力来改变世界。举例：智能手机的更新换代、交通工具安全性和环保性的改良等。这些产品的出现证明了人类并没有因为生活变得便利而停止了思考,停止要求自身的进步。

其次,物质世界的发展会给人类社会带来诸多问题,比如环境污染、气候变化、物种灭绝、资源短缺、贫富差距拉大、战争和政治不稳定等。也就是说,在富足和便利的当代生活背后是大量的急需解决的问题。这些问题的解决需要整个社会的共同努力,需要不同岗位之间的合作。为了整个社会持续健康地发展,人在解决这些问题的过程中当然会变得更强大。

第三,人们利用科技发展成果,进一步去探索开发未知领域,可见科技带来的物质世界的发展鼓励和促进了人的思考,使人类变得更强大。举例:航天航空、基因工程、疾病研究、量子力学等。

参考简化思路

1. 物质发展削弱了人的思考能力,如指南针、导航仪、计算器等。
2. 物质发展本身证明了人的创造性和开发性思维,如智能手机、网络社交媒体、交通工具的更新换代等。
3. 物质世界发展给人类社会带来问题,人类需要运用自身能力来解决,如环境污染和资源紧缺等。

25

In any field of inquiry, the beginner is more likely than the expert to make important contributions.

Write a response in which you discuss the extent to which you agree or disagree with the statement and explain your reasoning for the position you take. In developing and supporting your position, you should consider ways in which the statement might or might not hold true and explain how these considerations shape your position.

题目大意

在任何领域内，新手都比专家更容易做出重要的贡献。

审题和段落构架

1. 支持方的理由

最容易想到的对本话题的支持理由就是，每个行业都会有一些根深蒂固的传统，当它是一些积极传统的时候，会有利于该行业的持久发展；反之，当它是一些消极的传统时，会造成行业的停止。而新手由于没有受到行业内习惯性假设的限制，所以更有可能进行一些大胆的尝试，从而取得突破性的发展。尤其在强调创新的领域内，很多过去习惯的做法只是一种习惯，并不代表正确，新人确实能够经常带来新的想法。比如：艺术领域新的流派的诞生，印象派（impressionism）、表现主义（expressionism）、立体主义（cubism）都是年轻艺术家的颠覆性突破；商业领域乔布斯无视了"迎合受众需求"的习惯，创造了"创造用户需求"的新商业理念。

其次，新手经常意味着年轻，也意味着体力上的优势，这在强调体力的领域中就是不能忽视的因素。因此在运动领域内，有天赋的新人确实能够经常推动领域的发展。年少成名的运动员的例子不胜枚举：梅西、C罗、科比、费德勒。

2. 反对方的理由

首先，新手意味着经验匮乏、知识和能力积累得不足，因此在发展成熟、极其强调积累的领域中，新手的突破是相对比较困难的。比如：科学领域，创造力可以带来新的理论，但是理论的验证才是真正理论建立的关键，而缺乏有素的科学训练，从业者是不可能设计出好的验证方式的。政治领域，每一条政策的制定都需要考虑到其可能产生的多方影响，这也是需要多年的人际交往经验才能获得的。

其次，在社交资源重要的领域内，新手也是很难取得短期突破的。在政治领域内，我们没有理由无视现实去理想化我们的政客，他们不是一群单纯的理想主义者；一切为了社会的发展，能够身处高位一言一行影响全国的他们，都是经历过各种人际斗争和权钱交易的幸存者。简而言之，这不是一个新手可以轻松存活的领域。

3. 对上述双方理由的再反驳

针对支持方理由1：不受传统限制并不是年轻人所必然具有的特点，而是由一个人的本身特点决定的。一个行业的专家可以一直保持怀疑、批判精神。比如：毕加索的后期、维特根斯坦的后期、乔布斯的后期、爱因斯坦的后期无不挑战了自己之前的模式，取得了进一步的突破。

针对支持方的所有理由：很容易夸大新人的"新"的程度。即便在艺术、体育、商业领域中存在新人取得突破性进展的案例，但这种"新"也完全不是小白。马蒂斯、毕加索、凡·高都是受过写实主义严格训练的艺术家，梅西、C罗、科比一出道即是技艺精湛的球员，苹果公司的成功一半要归结为沃兹尼亚克卓越的技术能力。

参考简化思路

1. 艺术领域因为强调创新思维，新人容易取得成功。
2. 运动领域因为强调身体素质，新人容易取得成功。
3. 科学领域强调知识积累，专家容易取得成功。
4. 政治领域强调人脉积累，专家容易取得成功。

26

The surest indicator of a great nation is represented not by the achievements of its rulers, artists, or scientists, but by the general welfare of its people.

Write a response in which you discuss the extent to which you agree or disagree with the statement and explain your reasoning for the position you take. In developing and supporting your position, you should consider ways in which the statement might or might not hold true and explain how these considerations shape your position.

思路近似题目：80，107，114，115，120 & 138

题目大意

一个伟大国家最准确的标志不是统治者、艺术家或科学家的成就，而是人民的福利。

话题背景

我们经常会提到伟大的国家，但是人们对什么样的国家是伟大的却没有明确的定义。这道题目就是在迫使我们反思自己心中对这个"伟大"的标准，到底是一个个伟人所创造的成就，还是人们整体的幸福感，或是这个问题可能就没有标准答案？

审题和段落构架

1. 重要概念

welfare：可以理解为"福利"，或者是"更抽象的幸福感"。

2. 支持方的理由

伟人的成就使国家强大，发展稳定，甚至在人类文明历史上留下浓墨重彩的篇章，所以很多人想到伟大国家时都会想到其伟大的个体所留下的重要影响。当我们想到古希腊时，我们就会想到亚里士多德、毕达哥拉斯、伯利克里、修昔底德；当我们想到日不落帝国时，我们会想到达尔文、牛顿、休谟；当我们想到中国时，我们就会想到跨越五千年历史的不计其数的伟人及其成就，秦始皇与统一六国，蔡伦与造纸，杜甫与他的千古绝句……

3. 反对方的理由

再多的伟人，再传世的成就，如果不能给人民带来幸福，如果人民的生活处在水深火热当中，没有人会愿意生活在这样的国家里，连它自己的国民可能也不愿意称其为伟大的国家。

4. 对上述双方理由的再讨论

无论哪一方都试图寻找一种客观的、可量化的标准，无论是成就、影响力大小，还是人们的幸福指数。他们都没有意识到，其实"伟大"是一个完全主观的判断，它取决于判断者自身的价值观、利益，甚至情感。企业家眼中的伟大国家、军人眼中的伟大国家和教师眼中的伟大国家可能都不一样。

参考简化思路

1. 伟人成就多的国家会让人铭记在心。
2. 但缺乏幸福感的国家也不会被人们尊重。
3. 其实无论任何标准都是主观的，因为"伟大"本身就是一个主观的判断。

28

Teachers' salaries should be based on their students' academic performance.

Write a response in which you discuss the extent to which you agree or disagree with the claim. In developing and supporting your position, be sure to address the most compelling reasons and/or examples that could be used to challenge your position.

思路近似题目：78

题目大意

老师的薪水应该取决于他们学生的学业表现。

话题背景

教育商业化的问题越来越受到各方关注。在很多私立学校里，传统意义上的老师和学生的关系演变为商家和客户的关系，更是出现了类似"保分班"这样的形式，学生取得什么样的成绩似乎完全依赖于老师的教学。"在当代环境下，到底是什么决定教育的质量？"就是这个话题想要探讨的。

审题和段落构架

1. 支持方的理由

从激励机制的角度来看，这一方法能够促进老师更好地完成他们的工作，包括更加到位地备课，甚至增加对学生的课后辅导。

2. 反对方的理由

首先，能够决定学生最终学业表现的因素有很多，老师的投入仅仅是一个方面而已。这些因素包括：学生自身的能力、兴趣、努力程度和自律能力。

其次，有很多不可控的因素也会最终影响学生的成绩，比如，学生生病住院等类似情况的发生会导致学生不能按时完成功课。

再者，从目前的教育资源水平来看，这个政策是行不通的。如果学校能做到一对一教学，一个学生吸收知识的程度可以反映一个老师教学的能力。但一般来说，老师需要面对一个班级里的几十个学生，老师无法给予每一个学生足够的关注。而且，不同的学生有不同的学习风格和方法，老师在大课堂上很难做到"因材施教"。如果最终学生学习成绩不如意，不能说明老师的教学没有到位，只能说明目前教育资源不足。

更重要的是，教育不光是老师给学生传递知识的过程。更重要的是，教育者还要引导学生做人，培养学生的批判思维、创造性思维和审美的能力。我们目前还没有办法对这些方面进行考量，比如，如何准确评判学生批判性思维的能力，并因此合理地给老师发放工资。反过来说，如果这个政策实施，必然会让老师更加重视知识本身的传授，而忽略了培养学生包括思考能力在内的很多其他能力。

参考简化思路

1. 这是一种有效的激励机制，鼓励老师更好地工作。
2. 影响学生学业表现的因素有很多，包括学生自身的努力和能力等。
3. 在目前教育资源水平下，教师很难做到因材施教，所以学生没有获得最优的学业结果不能认为是老师的责任。
4. 教学不光是教授知识，还包括培养学生的思考能力，而这些是无法测评和量化的；若老师的工资按照学生成绩来发放，势必会导致老师忽略对学生思维能力的培养。

29

Society should make efforts to save endangered species only if the potential extinction of those species is the result of human activities.

Write a response in which you discuss your views on the policy and explain your reasoning for the position you take. In developing and supporting your position, you should consider the possible consequences of implementing the policy and explain how these consequences shape your position.

题目大意

如果物种濒临灭绝是人类行为所导致的，社会才有义务保护这些濒危物种。（意思是：如果物种濒危不是人类活动所引起的，我们并没有保护它们的义务。）

审题和段落构架

1. 支持方的理由

我们保护濒危生物的一个重要原因是要维持生态系统的平衡。如果因为人类的原因，比如滥砍滥伐，造成某些关键物种的灭绝，很可能对生态系统整体性造成影响。因此，我们会努力尝试保护这些生物，试图通过建立保护区、人工繁育等方式恢复其种群数量，从而使之能够重新回归自然界，成为生态系统中的一部分。

如果某种生物自然灭绝，意味着它是真的不适应大自然，则无论我们再怎么保护，它将永远不可能自然生存下去，这意味着人类对其的保护很可能是无止境的，而它也永远不可能产生直接的生态价值。

2. 反对方的理由

这个论题假设我们能够准确判定哪些物种的濒危和人类有关，哪些和人类无关。然而事实上，在如今人类足迹遍及世界各地的情况下，几乎不存在哪种濒危生物纯粹是因为自己不适应而走到如今这番田地的。就拿大熊猫为例，它确实生育率低下，食物种类单一，但是它的生存环境也因为人类的开发而大幅度缩减。就算大熊猫是一种逐渐被淘汰的生物，但至少人类的行为大大推进了熊猫灭绝的速率。

其次，我们保护濒危生物的目的不仅仅是要将其直接放归大自然，维持生态平衡。濒危生物有着生态意义以外的多重意义：(1) 它们有重要的科研价值；(2) 有些物种有重要的文化象征意义，可以唤起人们对生物保护的整体意识；(3) 它们对于维持基因多样性有着重要的意义，而这种多样性未来可能会产生我们现在无法预见的价值。

参考简化思路

1. 诚然，如果保护濒危动物是为了让它们回归自然，则这些不适应自然的生物理应被淘汰，因为它们是自然灭绝，不是人类所造成的。
2. 但是，保护这些濒危生物有着重要的科研价值。
3. 保护这些濒危生物还有着重要的文化意义。

31 As we acquire more knowledge, things do not become more comprehensible, but more complex and mysterious.

Write a response in which you discuss the extent to which you agree or disagree with the statement and explain your reasoning for the position you take. In developing and supporting your position, you should consider ways in which the statement might or might not hold true and explain how these considerations shape your position.

思路近似题目：103

题目大意

知识的获取并不会让事物变得更可理解，只会让它们更复杂、更神秘。

话题背景

因近年来文明的进步、科技的发展，人类的知识取得了一个又一个突破，但我们所面对的世界似乎前所未有地复杂和神秘，我们遇到的难解的谜题似乎比我们祖先所面对的更多。那么我们是否真可以认为知识让世界变得更可理解呢？

审题和段落构架

1. 题目特征

这个命题由两个部分组成：一部分是正面的，即可理解性；另一部分是负面的，即复杂和神秘性。由于这两部分并不是必然互相对立，所以这个题目适合两个部分分别讨论。(1) 知识获取让事物更好理解；(2) 知识获取让事物更复杂、更神秘。

2. 对命题 (1) 的讨论

知识获取自然会让我们懂得更多，这种"懂"分为很多层面：我们通过观察搜集了广泛的证据和数据作为事实依据；继而，通过这些证据我们建立起抽象的理论；这些理论一方面帮我们解释了我们观察到的现象，另一方面帮我们预见了很多之前不曾预料到的现象；这些理论还能够应用到实际生活中，帮助我们解决很多以前难以克服的实际问题。各个领域海量的案例都可以体现人类知识所获得的成就。例如：牛顿物理帮我们解释了宏观物体运动（motion of objects in the macroscopic universe）的原理，让当时的人类预见了太阳系新的天体——天王星、海王星——的存在，更不用说其如今在工程领域的广泛应用了。分子生物学（molecular biology）的发展帮我们解释了遗传和变异（inheritance and mutation）的存在，预测了遗传疾病发生的概率，更不用说其在提高作物产率、解决疑难杂症上所起到的不可磨灭的作用了。

3. 对命题 (2) 的讨论

与此同时，我们必须认识到，"真理"是一个相对的概念。也许永远不存在绝对的真理，只存在对真理的不断趋近。随着知识体系的扩展，我们所利用的概念、规则体系自然就会更加庞大、复杂；而且，这种知识体系的扩大让我们接触了先前根本无法触及的更广阔的世界，也将我们的注意力引向了很多先前根本没有意识到的深奥的问题上，这自然会使世界显得充满神秘感。

例如：牛顿的物理体系就被证明只在宏观体系下准确，而替代牛顿体系的近代物理的标准模型看起来比它的前身麻烦多了：四种基本作用力（fundamental forces）和十几种基本粒子（elementary particles）对于外行来说简直是完全不可理解的概念，比如希格斯玻色子（Higgsboson）、胶子（gluon）、中微子（neutrino）之类的东西。事实上，顶尖的物理学家遇到它们也会有形形色色的问题：比如希格斯玻色子的证实也只是最近几年才克服的困难，还有各种问题亟待解决；它们还不能完全解释暗物质（dark matter）、暗能量（dark energy）所引发的多种问题。

分子生物学所带来的麻烦和困难一点都不比近代物理少。人类上万个基因的破解（deciphering）只是这个世纪才完成的壮举，更不用说地球上这么多生物基因待破解。每个基因代码（genetic codes）与其所控制的性状、病状（syndromes）有什么样的关系，如何通过基因改造获得有利、安全的变异结果，这些都会成为未来我们试图解决的问题。

◎ 参考简化思路

1. 知识的获得使我们懂得了更多的东西。
2. 但知识的获得也打开了我们的视野，让我们见识了更复杂的宇宙，感受了更大未知世界的存在。

35 Society should identify those children who have special talents and provide training for them at an early age to develop their talents.

Write a response in which you discuss the extent to which you agree or disagree with the recommendation and explain your reasoning for the position you take. In developing and supporting your position, describe specific circumstances in which adopting the recommendation would or would not be advantageous and explain how these examples shape your position.

题目大意

社会应当发现那些有天赋的孩子,并在他们小的时候就去培养他们的天赋。

话题背景

教育资源分配不公的问题一直是社会关注的焦点。在这样的背景下,并不是每个家庭都有能力培养他们孩子的天赋,很多孩子的天赋因此被埋没。这是个人和家庭的损失,更是整个社会的损失。因此,教育领域的一个重要议题就是如何发现并培养孩子的天赋。

审题和段落构架

1. 支持方的理由

首先,如背景部分所指出的,从"避免人才流失"这个初衷来考虑,此论题是有合理性的。很多孩子正是因为有了国家和社会的帮助,才能够成为出类拔萃的人才,从而他们用智慧反过来帮助社会。

其次,很多天赋的开发和培养是有时间性的,比如体育和艺术。若想在这些方面取得高水平的成绩,需要在儿童时代就开始进行培养。(由于部分体育项目的特点,高水平的成绩大多来自于青少年运动员,比如体操、花样滑冰等。)

2. 反对方的理由

首先,并不是每种天赋都能在孩子少年时代就被准确辨识出的。我们也许可以找到运动天才、音乐天才、数学天才,但是很难找到医学天才、法律天才等。

其次,辩题强调"早期训练"在天赋养成中的重要作用,但是培养天才还需要孩子自身的兴趣和投入。没有兴趣即便有再好的先天条件也不会使孩子发展成为该领域的人才。

再者,我们不可能在孩子一生下来就测定其天赋,通常是在孩子到一定年龄时候才进行评测。一些孩子在某些技能上强于别人,不见得是因为他们天赋好,很可能是因为他们比其他孩子受到过更多该方面的训练,因为他的家庭能够提供这种教育资源。这样做的结果是:社会教育资源分配的不公进一步加剧,导致家庭条件较好的孩子才有机会发展自己的天赋。因此,天赋培养的首要任务是缓解教育资源分配的不公。

3. 对上述双方理由的再反驳

针对反对方理由 1：是的，并不是每个天赋都能被准确辨识，也不是每个孩子的天赋都能被判断出来。但即便如此，从社会角度出发，我们也需要积极主动地去寻找、判断和培养有天赋的孩子。如果一个社会只因为部分孩子的天赋不能被发掘出来而去无视所有孩子的天赋，这种走极端的做法显然是非常荒诞的。

针对反对方理由 3：这完全取决于测定孩子天赋所采取的标准。如果在孩子都长到 18 岁再去判断，选出来的几乎都是得到过很好教育的孩子。但在更小的年龄，比如在孩子学了一两年数学的时候测定数学天赋，或者在孩子七八岁时测定乐感，他们受到的特殊培养所产生的影响是相对较小的。而且，就算这种筛选仍然会受到一些家庭背景的影响，但如果完全不用社会提供这种机会，而让每个家庭自己提供资源培养有天赋的孩子，那我们将永远无法弥补教育的不公。和反对方理由 1 一样的问题，不能因为本解决方案不完美就彻底放弃，从而选择明显更不完美的方案。因为，如果社会不做这件事情，就只能留给每个家庭、每个孩子自己来发展其天赋，这必然会导致优势群体更有优势，劣势群体永无翻身之日。

参考简化思路

1. 这种做法是为了弥补教育资源不公，避免有天赋的孩子天赋被浪费。
2. 但是，不是每个有天赋的孩子都能被发现，且天才的养成需要孩子自己有兴趣。
3. 而且，有天赋的孩子通常也是受到家庭教育资源的投入影响。因此，这个做法会加剧社会不公。

36

It is primarily through our identification with social groups that we define ourselves.

Write a response in which you discuss the extent to which you agree or disagree with the statement and explain your reasoning for the position you take. In developing and supporting your position, you should consider ways in which the statement might or might not hold true and explain how these considerations shape your position.

题目大意

我们主要是通过与社会群体产生认同来定义自己。

审题和段落构架

1. 重要概念

identification 是"认同"的意思。与社会群体产生认同的方式有很多，比如根据自我状况，举例：身体有残疾的个人与残疾人群体产生认同，单亲母亲与社会单亲关爱群体产生认同；比如根据理想或理念，举例：素食主义者与素食主义群体产生认同；比如根据兴趣爱好，这就很多了，很多兴趣社团就是因为参与者有一致的兴趣爱好和追求而产生的。这题可以简化理解为，我们主要通过与自己相关的社会群体来认识自己。

2. 支持方的理由

首先，与社会群体产生认同可以让我们找到存在感和归属感，让我们更容易去认识自己、接受自己。社会群体是有共享标签的人走到一起而形成的。在这个空间里，正因为大家的某种一致性，使得交流变得更容易，个人也能从这个群体中获得必要的帮助。最典型的就是宗教群体，他们的宗教活动便是一种增强沟通的联谊，个人通过与群体的接触，形成了自身的世界观和价值观，实现了精神层面对自我的认知。

其次，即便在有些情况下，个人特别不想与自身相关的群体接近，甚至是排斥，但理论上来说，这种排斥也体现了他对自我的一种认识。比如残疾人通常受到来自社会的歧视，因为身体的残疾他们很难找到工作，即便是他们能胜任的工作，用人单位也会找各种理由拒绝他们。对残疾人的歧视还体现在健全人对他们多余的同情和怜悯。因此，有些残疾人不愿意与残疾人群体产生认同，主要是因为不想被社会认为能力不足，值得可怜。所以他们会挑战自我，做出很多健全人都难以企及的事情。我们看到的很多残疾人艺术家就是很好的例子。这说明，一个人有时候不愿意与自己相关的群体认同，要么是不愿意接受他们的价值观，要么是不愿意自己被社会贴上这个群体的标签。他们会有相反的认知，但我们仍然能认为一个人可以通过与社会群体的反面来定义和认识自己。

3. 反对方的理由

当然，人认识自我的方式还有很多很多。比如有人会通过阅读文学，与小说的主人公产生认同，因为他们有着一样的命运和处境。有人会通过艺术创作来认识自己，通过艺术寻找慎独时的自我认知。

参考简化思路

1. 人是可以通过与自身相关的群体认识自我的。
2. 但自我认同的方式还有很多，比如通过文学、艺术等。

38

Claim: When planning courses, educators should take into account the interests and suggestions of their students.

Reason: Students are more motivated to learn when they are interested in what they are studying.

Write a response in which you discuss the extent to which you agree or disagree with the claim and the reason on which that claim is based.

思路近似题目：45 & 84

题目大意

观点：在设计课程的时候，老师们应该考虑学生的兴趣与建议。

理由：学生们在学自己感兴趣的东西时会更有动力。

话题背景

传统的教育方式是以教师为中心，教师决定讲什么、怎么讲，学生只负责听就行了。但是如今的教育越来越强调学生的主动学习，强调以学生的特点和需求为关键。这道题目提出这样的做法也是顺应当代教育理念的转变的。

审题和段落构架

1. 题目特征

这是一道价值判断类题目。同时，它的形式是"观点—理由"型，所以适合先讨论理由的合理性，再分析观点的合理性。

2. 对理由的讨论

毫无疑问，对所学内容感兴趣的学生会更有学习的动力，这样的现象比比皆是。

3. 对观点的讨论

支持：其他情况均相同时，如果某种教法能让学生有更大的学习动力，自然应该采取这种教法。当课程考虑了学生的建议时，它会更有可能（1）满足学生未来的实际需求；（2）符合学生现有的认知能力；（3）采取更符合学生性格特点的课程形式。

反对：学生并不总是知道自己最需要学什么，特别是年龄小的孩子，如果让他们决定课程内容，估计他们根本不会愿意学任何有挑战性的东西。

4. 对上述双方理由的再反驳

对反对者理由的讨论：考虑学生的想法不等于盲从学生的想法。考虑学生的想法，主要意义在于避免教师像以前一样，无视学生的能力与需求，一味按照自己的想法来设计课程。这个建议并不需要教师走向另一个极端，而是让教师能够敢于去修正自己对学生的认知，去完善课程，去更结合学生的实际需求与能力，去实现一种平衡。比如，物理教师上课也需要举例，如果学生喜欢动漫，那么这些物理例子完全可以结合动漫中的故事去讲解，就会比纯粹拿小球和木块举例更能让学生愿意听课。以教师为中心的课程安排考虑的是教师每节课需要讲什么内容；但是，以学生为中心的课程安排考虑的是学生每节课需要学会什么内容。"学会"不等于"学了"，更不等于教师"教了"，无视学生需求的"教"是完全不可能让学生"会"的。

参考简化思路

1. 结合了学生兴趣与建议的课程更能够激发学生的动力，因为它更能满足学生的能力与需要。
2. 所以，教师设计课程应该从内容、形式、难度等方面符合学生的需求。
3. 当然，这不是去盲从学生的需求，因为毕竟很多学生都不能够正确认识自己的需要。

39

> **39** The greatness of individuals can be decided only by those who live after them, not by their contemporaries.
>
> Write a response in which you discuss the extent to which you agree or disagree with the statement and explain your reasoning for the position you take. In developing and supporting your position, you should consider ways in which the statement might or might not hold true and explain how these considerations shape your position.

题目大意

一个伟人的成就只能由后人评价，不能被其同时代的人评价。

审题和段落构架

一个人的成就到底是否只能由后人评价，取决于这个人所处领域本身的特点。

1. 支持方的理由

在艺术、文化等领域，通常被称为伟大的艺术家、思想家等的人都是因为其理念的前瞻性、突破性而为人尊重。这种前瞻性意味着同时代的人可能无法接受、理解其思想。所以，很多伟大的艺术家、思想家都是由后人才为其正名，比如梵高和尼采。

2. 反对方的理由

a 有一些领域具有很强的时效性，而在这些领域当中，同时代人就能够给予伟人恰当的评价。一种商业模式在十年后可能就会落伍，但是在某个时期获得了巨大的成功，就证明了建立这种模式的企业家对市场的深刻理解。无论乔布斯建立的苹果公司十年后是否还是全球领先的企业，都不妨碍他成为一个时代伟大企业家的标杆。

b 在体育领域，一个运动员、一个教练员的成就也许会被后人突破，但如果他做到了当时其他人无法做到的成就，他就是巨星。运动员做的事情是不断突破前人，每一次突破都是值得被铭记的里程碑。教练员就像企业家一样，需要找到当下战胜对手的战术，即便这个战术在几年后可能会被破解。

c 还有一些领域虽然有时效性，但会产生长远的影响，因此同时代人以及后人的全面评价才是最公正的。比如：①政治领域，政治家当然要解决现实的问题，但必须顾及长远的发展，所以竭泽而渔的政策可能会得到当世人的称颂，但后人就能意识到这种做法所造成的后果不可逆转。②科技领域，一项科技发明可能解决了当下的问题，但同样产生了不可逆转的长久恶果，比如塑料和DDT。

参考简化思路

1. 艺术、思想领域具有前瞻性，所以伟人的成就需要后人评价。
2. 商业、体育等领域具有很强的时效性，所以同时代人就可以做出评价；
3. 科技、政治等领域的决策会影响当下，但也可以产生相反的长远后果，所以需要同时代人以及后代共同全面评价。

40

Students should always question what they are taught instead of accepting it passively.

Write a response in which you discuss the extent to which you agree or disagree with the statement and explain your reasoning for the position you take. In developing and supporting your position, you should consider ways in which the statement might or might not hold true and explain how these considerations shape your position.

题目大意

学生应该批判性地分析所有教给他们的东西,而不是被动地接受。

话题背景

我们现在越来越强调批判性(理性)思维(critical thinking)在学习中的重要性,学生不应该盲信权威,而应该养成独立思考的能力。这个话题探讨的就是这样的问题。

审题和段落构架

1. 重要概念

question:如果指的是"质疑"的话,这个话题显然是过激的,因为没有根据的反对与无条件的盲信都是非理性的体现;如果指的是"分析,考察"(analyze, examine)的话,那么这个话题显然就变得很有讨论的意义,因为这是如今非常流行的一种教育理念,鼓励学生不再视课本与教师为权威,而能够主动、思辨地看待自己所学的知识。

2. 支持方的理由

首先,所学的知识并不一定是对的,批判权威的精神恰恰是让人类的知识体系可以前进的关键。

其次,也是更重要的,学习中重要的不是让学生接受某些结论,而是让学生学会分析的过程。比如,在数学学习中,记住某个公式并不能反映一个学生的数学能力,但是当他学到了一个公式,还能主动去推衍出这个公式时,他就更接近数学教育的目的了,提升了自己的数理推理能力。我们希望学生不仅仅知道"是什么",还能够去分析"为什么"。这种思维能力是未来一辈子学习、工作更关键的能力。

3. 反对方的理由

对于一些基本的、独立的事实性知识,去进行大量的分析其实是多此一举的。比如,在外语学习中,最初接触一门语言,我们需要掌握一些最基本的词汇,这个时候思考"为什么某个词是这个意思"这样的问题是毫无价值的。

假想一个学生要对每一个知识进行批判性思考,那很显然他根本不可能有经历学完所有的东西。所以,重点应该是鼓励学生去掌握这种学习能力,而不是纠结于一些大家已经普遍接受的知识,每一次都要进行批判性思考。

参考简化思路

1. 盲目的质疑是毫无意义的。
2. 理性的分析所学到的知识是很有价值的,这种思维能力将让学生长久受益。
3. 当然,并不是每种类型的知识学习都必须要有这个过程。

41

The increasingly rapid pace of life today causes more problems than it solves.

Write a response in which you discuss the extent to which you agree or disagree with the statement and explain your reasoning for the position you take. In developing and supporting your position, you should consider ways in which the statement might or might not hold true and explain how these considerations shape your position.

题目大意

相比其能解决的问题，当今不断变快的高速生活节奏反而带来了更多的问题。

话题背景

"高速的生活节奏"实际是科技发展的产物，因此题干背后真正的话题是科技发展对于人类社会各产生了什么正面和负面的影响。题干中的 problems 一词表意宽泛，例子的广度在本题的写作中就显得相当重要，应尽量考虑到科技发展在生活各方面，如环境、政治、社会群体关系、心理等带来的影响。

审题和段落构架

1. 支持方的理由

首先，科技发展在物质方面带来了很多问题。举例：环境污染，如工业革命时期英法和当代中国的空气污染问题；资源短缺：如不可再生资源的耗尽；城市建设方面：如古旧历史建筑因城市化发展需求被拆除等；健康方面：科技带来的快节奏生活产生了很多"现代病"。

其次，科技发展在社会生活、文化、人类精神层面带来问题。举例：文化方面，如科技发展带来的自动化生产代替了手工劳动，使得很多赋有历史意义的传统技艺逐渐消失；人类思维方面，如科技发展在某些方面取代了人的思考、记忆和计算的能力；人际间交流方面：科技发展看似提供了更多的交流方式，但取代了人与人面对面交流的必要性，减少了人际间的亲密和信任感。

再者，除了以上提到的科技发展造成的具体问题，它还带来了对认知、传统或伦理的挑战。举例：克隆技术冲击了传统伦理，目前世界上绝大多数国家都禁止了完全克隆人的实验。这里的禁止并不代表对克隆的争议就此结束或问题得以解决。克隆技术的出现带来的是人类社会对伦理的具体化讨论和在现代社会下的重新定义。没有科技发展，也不会有类似思考的必要。

2. 反对方的理由

科技发展给人类社会带来了诸多好处。如饥荒的减少、部分致命疾病的消失、交通的便捷、生产效率的提高、信息传递速度快等。科技发展也加速了意识形态的传播，促进了平等、自由等理念的推进。

参考简化思路

1. 科技发展给人类社会带来了诸多好处。如交通的便捷、生产效率的提高、信息传递速度快等。
2. 科技在物质方面带来了很多问题。如环境污染、资源短缺、战争和政治动荡。
3. 科技在社会文化和精神生活带来了很多问题。如传统文化的消失、人类思维能力的减弱。

43 Competition for high grades seriously limits the quality of learning at all levels of education.

Write a response in which you discuss the extent to which you agree or disagree with the statement and explain your reasoning for the position you take. In developing and supporting your position, you should consider ways in which the statement might or might not hold true and explain how these considerations shape your position.

☀ 思路近似题目：131

题目大意

对高分的竞争限制了各层级教育中学生的学习质量。

话题背景

素质教育与应试教育之争我们已经非常熟悉了，这道题讨论的就是这个话题。

审题和段落构架

1. 支持方的理由

首先，追求分数可能造成学生之间的互相攀比，进而造成心理压力，带来焦虑、抑郁等很多不良结果。

其次，追求分数使得学生，甚至教师忽视真正的能力、素养、性格、品质的培养，而纯粹为了应对考试分数。比如，在物理教育中，学生学会了如何套用公式，却从不思考一个物理规律的意义或其发现过程中的物理思维。

2. 反对方的理由

首先，有评价、反馈机制恰恰是很多人学习的动力来源，成绩进步是对学生的努力付出所做的肯定，为他们未来的进步提供心理支持。

其次，这个评价机制对于教师调整教学进度也提供了参考意义。

更重要的，社会需要这种评价机制来对人才进行筛选。升学、就业都需要一个相对客观、公正的评价机制，而离开了考试分数，这一切基本是不可行的。

3. 对上述双方理由的再反驳

针对支持方理由1：这种压力是迟早的，未来工作也会有压力，学会应对压力才是解决这种问题的方式，而不是直接取消压力的来源。教师、家长需要做的是把这种压力保持在合适的范围内，并且为孩子们提供缓解压力的方式。

针对支持方理由2：这种说法根本就是错误的。如果说学生只为解题，不思考背后的道理，那说明是考试设计得不合理，而不是不应该考试。同理，如果学生只关心考试，说明分数的评定方式单一化。如今很多课程的分数是多元的，包含多次大小考试、作业、课堂讨论、团队合作等，这至少是一种积极的尝试，能够从多个方面对学生的学习进行评估。

针对支持方理由2：而且，现在流行的教育理念鼓吹学生的创造力、想象力等玄妙的东西，贬低机械记忆、计算、逻辑这些所谓"限制"孩子的东西。但它们忘了社会大部分人的首要问题是生存，学会计算、学会识字等就为很多人的生存提供了基本的保障，并且为他们进行进一步的学习提供了很好的基础。而在这些问题上，过去传统的考试能够提供非常好的评估手段。学校并不是所有学习进行的地方，家庭教育为孩子提供了更多元的渠道，而学校是一个社会、一个国家保证国民素养的最基本、最关键的工具，它没有必要、也不可能实现彻底的多元化。

参考简化思路

1. 有人会觉得追求分数造成压力，阻碍学习，但这种应对压力的能力恰恰是未来社会需要的。
2. 有人会说考试不能很好地衡量一个人的素养，但这其实是考试设计得不合适，而不是考试这个方式不合适。
3. 分数的存在是必要的，它为学生的学习提供了客观的评判标准，是对学生努力的反馈，是社会筛选人才的重要工具。

46 Educators should teach facts only after their students have studied the ideas, trends, and concepts that help explain those facts.

Write a response in which you discuss the extent to which you agree or disagree with the recommendation and explain your reasoning for the position you take. In developing and supporting your position, describe specific circumstances in which adopting the recommendation would or would not be advantageous and explain how these examples shape your position.

思路近似题目：86

题目大意

在教授学生事实之前，学生必须首先学习能够帮助解释这些事实的思想、潮流以及理念。

话题背景

学习事实还是学习事实背后的思想，这一对矛盾的背后其实是两种学习理念的对比：一是理解式学习，一种是记忆式学习。一种学生学习时只是记住了大量的历史事实、物理规律、数学公式，但另一种学生理解了这些东西背后的规律，懂得如何分析这些现象，推演这些公式。

审题和段落构架

1. 支持方的理由

首先，事实本身的学习价值比不上学习其背后的理念。学习历史空知道某年某月发生什么大事，而不去分析这件事情的发生背景和历史意义，这样的历史学习根本无法对现代社会产生任何影响；学习物理只知道背公式，而不去思考这些规律是怎么被发现、被证明的，近乎等同没有学物理，我们也不可能靠这样的人做未来的物理研究。简而言之，对于很多学科来说，真正学习的目的是掌握这门学科背后的研究方法，而不是零碎地记住大量的事实。

其次，理解了事实背后的理念其实能够帮助学生更有效地学习事实本身。比如，在历史学习当中，理解了事件与事件之间的关系，能够更好地让学生记住事件的发生顺序；在物理当中，很多学生根本不需要记住复杂的公式，完全可以由基本的原理去进行推导。简而言之，理解下的记忆比单纯的记忆更有效。

2. 反对方的理由

首先，思想、理念的学习确实重要，但没有必要非在事实学习之前进行。事实背后的理念可能非常复杂庞大，可以在讲解事实之后逐渐呈现。直接讲解大量的抽象理念其实对于入门的学生非常不友好，尤其是事实相对基本、关键的时候。

其次，事实是客观的，而思想是主观的。应该给学生讲无可争议的东西，而不是给学生灌输主观的理念，因为这些很可能是错误的。

3. 对上述双方理由的再反驳

针对反对方理由2：教授理念不等于灌输理念。比如，关于某个物理现象，目前可能有一种物理解释。我们可以告诉学生目前科学家是如何解释的，但完全可以鼓励他去思考有没有别的解释，并且激发他去思考如何验证到底哪种解释是对的。这恰恰更能够让一个学生懂得什么叫科学研究方法。

参考简化思路

1. 理念和思想的学习本身就比事实更重要，它们能够帮助学生更好地掌握一门学科的核心方法论。
2. 理念和思想的学习也可以帮助更高效地学习事实。
3. 当然，学习的顺序并不是必需的，而且对于基本的事实，确实没有必要非得先学习其背后的思想。

Part 3 Issue 题库逐题精析

> **47** Claim: We can usually learn much more from people whose views we share than from those whose views contradict our own.
> Reason: Disagreement can cause stress and inhibit learning.
> Write a response in which you discuss the extent to which you agree or disagree with the claim and the reason on which that claim is based.
>
> 思路近似题目：32，72 & 112

题目大意

观点：我们通常能从与我们观点类似的人身上学到更多东西，而不是从与我们观点对立的人那儿学到更多。

理由：观点不一致会带来压力，从而阻碍学习。

话题背景

观点上的分歧时时刻刻都会发生。大到政治辩论、国策制定，小到学校课堂对于一个知识点的讨论。我们愿意和气味相投的人聊天交往，确实有一部分原因是沟通无障碍，聊天会更舒服。但这真的意味着我们可以从对方身上学到更多的东西吗？我们愿意和想法相似的人交流是出于什么样的需求呢？我们也知道对立观点是有价值的，在什么情况下我们可以从对立观点那儿学到东西，什么情况下却不能呢？

审题和段落构架

1. 支持方的理由

有一部分的对立观点是来自于个人的根本信念（fundamental beliefs），比如有关政治和宗教信仰的观点。人们不会妥协自己的根本信念，因此更不会通过妥协来学习他人的根本信念。人们通常珍视自己的根本信念，是因为这些理念其实是人主体性（subjectivity）的一个重要组成部分。换句话说，如果"知识"和"经验"是外在的我们积累的东西，用它们来更好地认识和了解这个世界，那根本信念其实是让世界来了解我们。当别人用不同的观点来攻击一个人的根本信念时，实则在攻击一个人本身。尤其在当代多元化的环境下，我们提倡对不同的宗教文化和种族背景加以尊重，而不是去挑战或试图改变。

2. 反对方的理由

a 我们不一定能从观点类似的人身上学到东西，我们喜欢和他们交往仅仅是因为获得一种归属感（a sense of belonging）和慰藉（comfort）。举例：科技发展改变了人的交往方式，现在通过交友软件我们可以在认识一个人之前就获取到对方的很多信息，我们会选择家庭、教育背景等多方面与自己类似的人去尝试交往。甚至有软件通过大数据来推送与我相似的人。不仅仅是交友，很多社会团体的产生也是因为大众需要与自己趣味相投（like-mindedness）的人交往。我们真的可以从对方身上学到很多吗？不见得。我们可以说观点相似的人沟通起来顺畅，他们愿意倾听对方，但这些都不足以证明我们能从对方身上学到更多东西。很多时候，这样的聊天沟通带来的仅仅是我们所需要的一种安全感和存在感。

b 对立的观点也不一定都来自根本信念，很多时候正因为他们能从不同的角度看问题，使得我们可以更深入地了解一个观点。举例：传统女权主义的观点认为女性是男性强权的受害者，这个世界对性别的不平等体现在它更加偏向男性；激进女权主义（radical feminism）认为女性和男性都是父权价值观（patriarchy）的受害者。两者对立的观点可以帮助我们深入探讨性别不平等的根本原因，可以让我们了解男孩在成长过程中接受的教育很多体现了男权的价值观，可以为校园的性别教育提供理论支持。对立观点的不同角度可以帮助我们全面地看待问题。

参考简化思路

1. 涉及根本信念，我们很难从对立观点那儿学到什么。
2. 我们从观点相似的人身上获得更多的可能是安全感和归属感，而不是知识。
3. 对立观点能帮助我们全方位地看待问题。

48

Government officials should rely on their own judgment rather than unquestioningly carry out the will of the people they serve.

Write a response in which you discuss the extent to which you agree or disagree with the recommendation and explain your reasoning for the position you take. In developing and supporting your position, describe specific circumstances in which adopting the recommendation would or would not be advantageous and explain how these examples shape your position.

思路近似题目：14、16、58、60、66、108、109、132 & 143

题目大意

政府官员应该依靠自己的判断，而不是一味地去实现人民的意愿。

话题背景

政府官员由人民选举出来，他们所做的决定本来就应该符合民众的意愿和要求。但在现实中，政府工作远比想象的复杂，这个论题就需要我们考虑政府的职责和服务大众之间的关系。

审题和段落构架

1. 支持方的理由

首先，虽然政府官员由民众选举出来，但政府的工作远远多于满足群众当下的需求，所以在很多事情的决断上都需要政府官员自身的判断。从一个角度来说，政府的工作涉及人类的未来，很多领域的发展并不能立刻实现它们的优势。比如，政府需要给航天领域的发展投资，即便这不是民众最在意的方面。研究小行星的运行轨迹和历史上小行星撞击地球的事件，科学家可以计算并防止未来小行星撞击地球的发生；对于火星的研究是人类发掘新的生存环境的重要课题，即便去火星生活不是当下群众的集体意愿。从另一个角度来说，政府能从宏观角度出发制定政策来解决问题，即便这些政策可能违背群众的意愿。比如20世纪70年代的计划生育政策（one-child policy）有效地控制了人口，虽然这个政策违背了群众按照个人想法组建家庭的意愿。

其次，如果我们从个人或者小群体角度出发看问题，会发现政府实际上无法满足真正意义上大众的意愿，因为在一个社会里，每一个人的诉求是很不一样的，有时候还是对立的。比如，商人想要开发土地获取经济收益，环保人士会积极反对。倒不是说政府的决策永远都是可以解决问题的，但是政府能很好地协调，在服务民众和社会发展之间取得一个平衡。

而且，政府获取的信息量比民众更大，在很多问题上，民众不知情也无法知情，则最优决定只能由政府做出。比如，军事问题、情报问题等。

2. 反对方的理由

首先，在物质和文化建设方面，服务于人民群众是政府工作的宗旨，所以政府要多听取民众的诉求。

其次，民众的诉求如果是出于人道主义（humanitarian ideologies），即便政府官员有权利自行决定，也需要参考人民的意见。举例：美国内战时期，林肯颁布了《解放奴隶宣言》，为最终彻底解放奴隶铺平了道路。越南战争时期，即便有大规模的反战游行，总统林登·约翰逊也没有撤兵，反而增加了美军兵力投入。他的政策最后以失败告终。对比来看，虽然都是总统自己的判断，但林肯的决定符合民众和人道主义的要求，推动了历史的进步，因此他被铭记为最值得尊敬的总统之一。

再次，政府仍然是由人组成的群体，所以在缺乏民众监督时，政府无限制的行为几乎必然走向集权或独裁。

📎 参考简化思路

1. 政府需要关注人类的未来，所以他们的很多决策并不反映群众当下的需求。
2. 群众的需求很多且对立，政府无法满足所有人的需求。
3. 政府需要考虑民众人道主义的诉求。

Part 3　Issue 题库逐题精析

49 Young people should be encouraged to pursue long-term, realistic goals rather than seek immediate fame and recognition.

Write a response in which you discuss the extent to which you agree or disagree with the recommendation and explain your reasoning for the position you take. In developing and supporting your position, describe specific circumstances in which adopting the recommendation would or would not be advantageous and explain how these examples shape your position.

思路近似题目：68

题目大意

我们应该鼓励年轻人去追求长远的、实际的目标，而不是只图眼前的名誉和认可。

话题背景

大家对于这个话题再熟悉不过了。我们最常听到的人生建议就是"要有目标"，不仅要有远大理想，而且还要有阶段性的目标。我们还时常被警告，一个没有目标的人会迷失方向，人生会失去意义。我们当然可以选择同意这个辩题的观点，证明人生必须要有实际的长远目标，在段落展开的时候我们可以选择名人的例子或假设的例子来说理。我们也可以把这个话题放在当代的历史环境下，通过这个话题的讨论来挖掘深刻的社会问题。我们可以考虑如下问题：为何不鼓励年轻人追求眼前名誉和认可？这种所谓的名誉和认可对年轻人有什么负面影响及正面影响？如何看待当代年轻人追求名誉的现象，比如我们常说的"草根明星"或"网红"？追求长远的实际目标意义何在？挑战何在？如何从大众视野看待"目标明确但仍未成功"的困惑？相比第一种同意辩题的论点，第二种写法的分析更能体现思考的复杂性，毕竟它给了我们更多元的角度去分析问题。

审题和段落构架

1. 关键词的定义

本题出现了多个概念，包括 long-term, realistic goal 和 immediate fame and recognition。建议大家把它们看成一组相对的概念，即"长远的实际目标"和"眼前的名誉和认可"。如果不这么理解，学生就会被这些看似不一致的多种概念所困惑。比如学生会认为还存在 short-term realistic goal，或认为"immediate fame 不可接受"，但其实"immediate recognition"可以接受。在方法论中我们提到，审题时要思考辩题背后体现了一个什么重要的社会话题，而不是被个别词所干扰。

2. 支持方的理由

从个人生活的角度来看，制订目标是有一定意义的。我们常说目标很重要，不是因为目标本身带来的精神刺激，而是有了目标之后生活会有计划感；简单说，人不会因为知道自己想要什么就会变得特别有干劲，制订目标的意义在于它能指导一个人在未来的一段时间内如何计划生活。就拿写书来举例：当你给自己制订一个目标，希望在未来几年

105

内完成一本书的写作,你就会有一个总体的安排和一个细致到每个月、甚至每天的安排。你可能会给自己一年的时间大量阅读和收集资料,再用一年的时间去写作。在安排每天写作任务的时候,你也会考虑如何把写作合理地安排到自己的生活、工作和社交中去。有目标才会有计划,有计划的生活才会有成就感且更容易坚持下去。

3. 反对方的理由

但是如果我们把这道题放在一个社会的视角下,认为对于一个社会的年轻群体我们应该鼓励他们去设立长远目标而不是只图眼前的名誉和认可,这个观点有很多问题。

首先,社会从来就没有停止过教育年轻人要树立长远目标,社会各个角落都充满了关于理想、志向和目标的心灵鸡汤。这个现象的存在是因为大多数年轻人都在混沌度日,对于人生不知所措吗?不是。不可否认的是大多数人都想通过自身努力过上他们想要的生活。如果年轻人表现得似乎没有理想或平平庸庸,那是因为社会自身的问题导致它无法承载每一个人的梦想。有些人打几份工却只能勉强维持家庭生计,接受高等教育对他们来说是天方夜谭。有些人即便有了医保,生一场大病也会让他们负债累累。换言之,很多人每天大部分时间的忙碌换来的只是基本的生存。在这种社会环境下,宣扬年轻人要树立远大目标是没有实际意义的。

其次,很多人长远的实际目标,其实并没有他们想象的那么"实际"。诚然有些人可能把目标制订得过高,但对于大多数人来说,我们给自己制订的目标不实际的根本原因是:学校的正规教育总是教我们名人的美德、伟人的理想、成功人的勤奋,但从来没有教育我们如何做一个平凡的人。用精英素材来教育社会的大多数人难免会给人带来一种幻觉,即每一个人都该去努力争取,争做成功人,争做名人。但实际上,做电影明星、百万富翁、企业家、高产科学家,甚至是博士,对于大多数人来说并不是实际的目标,和自身的努力也并没有正向关系。与其鼓励年轻人去树立理想,教育和社会文化导向不如帮助年轻人培养基本技能,树立正确的处世心态。

再者,即便很多目标是实际的,但是当下的社会问题不解决,个人的这些实际目标就很难实现。比如说找工作。教育膨胀(intellectual inflation)问题越来越严重,随着更多的人接受高等教育,工作岗位开始要求更高的学位,很多平凡的岗位都开始要求硕士以上的学历,导致人才市场竞争激烈。在新自由主义经济(neoliberal economies)下,大公司为降低成本,把劳动力转移到第三世界国家,使得原本就竞争激烈的人才市场更是一职难求。连找到一份稳定的工作都只能是一个人的"目标",那人生的理想就更有限了。

最后,名誉和认可这样的字眼总是带有一种虚荣感,甚至人们会觉得追求名誉的人通常不务正业。但是,在当下的社会环境中,我们需要重新审视"目标""成功"和"名誉"等概念。成功不应只意味着取得杰出的成就、为社会做贡献等。每个人可以有自己对成功的理解,而年轻人追求名利的文化现在也就是在重新定义成功:当一个人做自己喜欢做的事情且被他人认可就可认为是个人的成功。比如,我们看到很多网红,他们有自己的视频频道,有些人的专长是研究电子产品,有些人做脱口秀,他们通过品牌代言的方式获得收入。我们不能否认他们的努力,并且他们还激励了更多的年轻人为自己喜欢的事情而努力。如果追求名利的年轻人都走上了自毁的道路,那道可以说明名利的伤害和没有梦想的伤害。但当一个社会还不能满足每一个人的梦想时,我们应该重新定义成功,鼓励年轻人做自己喜欢的又能带来成就感的事情。

参考简化思路

1. 目标对个人有重要性,会使生活有计划感。
2. 有些人的实际目标并不实际,因为"远大"理想并不适合每一个人。
3. 即便实际的目标在现在的社会环境下也会变得很难实现。
4. 追求名利的文化重新定义了成功,让年轻人能在做自己喜欢的事情的同时也能获得成就感。

51 If a goal is worthy, then any means taken to attain it are justifiable.

Write a response in which you discuss the extent to which you agree or disagree with the statement and explain your reasoning for the position you take. In developing and supporting your position, you should consider ways in which the statement might or might not hold true and explain how these considerations shape your position.

题目大意

如果一个目标值得实现，那么任何一个可以达到该目标的手段都是无可非议的。

话题背景

"Do ends justify means？"这个问题困扰了伦理学家们几千年，但仍然没有形成普遍的共识。以康德（Immanuel Kant）为代表的流派坚持道德规则的绝对性。坚持这种观点的人会认为遵守任何道德规则本身就是我们行为的目的，比如我们必须要诚实，不是因为它能够带来什么好的结果；即使在诚实会带来不好结果的情况下，我们也应该坚持诚实。但是，这种伦理学理论被广泛质疑，其中最重要的一个对立派别就是功利主义（utilitarianism）。功利主义的核心观念就是：一个行为的对与错不取决于这个行为本身，而取决于它所能够带来的效用（utility）。于是，带来了题目中的观点：如果目标有价值，达到这个目标的任何手段都可以接受。

审题和段落构架

1. 支持方的理由

命题所传达的就是最朴素的功利主义理念：Ends justify means. 只要一个行为按照预期能够带来的善大于恶，则这个行为理应得到辩护。毕竟，流行的观点是：道德的存在就是为了人类社会的生存，所以我们的道德规则必须以结果为导向。举例：20世纪70年代末期的计划生育政策虽然让很多家庭失去了多个子女的机会，但有效地控制了人口增长，对于一个社会来说是有价值的目标，因此该手段也无可非议。

2. 反对方的理由

但这种纯粹以结果为导向的流派受到了各方的挑战，有些挑战被证明是失败的，但有一些重要的挑战确实指出了功利主义内在的一些问题，使得其必须要进行修正。

ⓐ 道德是一种目的，而不是工具：一个重要的反对方就是以康德（Immanuel Kant）为代表的伦理学家，他们认为道德是绝对的义务（categorical imperative），一个行为在道德上是可辩护的（morally justified）当且仅当它是符合道德规则的时候。当然，在当代社会，人们越来越排斥这种对道德的看法，人们逐渐意识到道德是后天建构的，是为了社会存在更好的建立工具。一个典型的证据就是，无论从时间维度，还是空间维度，很少有人类共同接受的道德规则和想法，几乎所有的规则都是对某种社会环境的适应。因此，就算由于后天教育，我们内心特别接受某个规则，甚至觉得它是先天必然的，其实它极有可能是人为建构的。要讨论行为的道德辩护，必须考虑其效度（utility）。

b 利益与个体的存在相冲突：不同行为主体有不同的需求，一个目标的实现可能对部分人来说是有利、有价值的，而对另外一部分人可能会有相反的效果。所以题目中的"goal"必须被定义为符合社会整体发展需求的目标，而不是仅对某个人或团体有价值。举例：非常简单，偷别人的钱会让个人获利，这个目标对个人很有价值，但在道德方面它显然不能被认可（not morally justified），因为它破坏了别人的诉求。因此，a worthy goal 必须被限定为对于集体有价值的目标（a goal worthy from a collective perspective）。这个道理很明显，不用多讲。

c 可操作性问题：这才是功利主义面对的最致命的打击。人类不是全知（omniscient）、全能（omnipotent）的上帝。我们不可能在任何场景下都可以清楚地计算出某个行为是否在该场景下最终会给社会带来益处；我们并不可能知道该场景下的所有参量。比如，一名医生有没有义务告知一名患者他得了癌症？一种可能是，告知了，病人很理性，积极配合治疗，于是早日痊愈；另一种可能是，告知了，病人感情很脆弱，瞬间受到致命打击，然后完全失去人生信心，反而很快就心力交瘁死亡。这种例子很多，同一个行为可能带来完全不同的结果，只要某些变量被稍微改变（tweaked）。因此，这种规则变成了一个没有实际价值的规则，因为没有人有能力精确预见所有行为结果。因此，诞生了规则功利主义（rule utilitarianism）这一流派。这一流派认为，我们必须给人们以一些整体上的道德规则，遵守这些道德规则会给社会带来长期的益处，比如诚实、勇敢等。也正是在这种背景下出现了程序正义（procedural justice）的讨论。为什么我们不允许杀人犯的辩护律师出卖自己的客户？也许这个律师真的很有良心，而且出卖客户将会导致凶手更快地绳之以法。那是因为，经过长久的法律研究，我们发现，保持律师的职业操守，遵守 attorney-client privilege 是维持整个法律系统公正运转、维护整个社会秩序的最佳长久策略。同理，一位民科提出了引力波（gravity wave），为什么人们不接受？但为什么科学家通过实验测量和推理发现了引力波，就被接受？因为，科学方法论的意义不在于某一项真理的发现，而在于基于观察、实验、推理的科学方法论是一种稳定的逼近真理的方式，所以它才被当代学术界普遍坚持。当然，规则功利主义也并不是一个完美的理论，但我们可以清楚地判断：在当代社会的语境下，只看结果不能评判途径。回到医生的例子，就算他再有善心，也有义务告知病人实情，这就是当下对医生的伦理要求。

3. 总结

procedural justice 要求人们尊重规则，不是因为如康德主义者那样所想，规则本身就是目的；而是因为现代社会所建构的道德规则是按照整体预期能够带来最好结果（ends）的规则体系（当然不是说它不能再优化）。

参考简化思路

1. 有需要付出一些代价来实现的目标（目标极其伟大，而代价相对小，并且没有更好的途径）；
2. 然而，为了不切实际、不明智的目标而放弃是不值得的；
3. 牺牲他人利益、谋求个人利益的方式也是不正义的。

Part 3　Issue 题库逐题精析

52 In order to become well-rounded individuals, all college students should be required to take courses in which they read poetry, novels, mythology, and other types of imaginative literature.

Write a response in which you discuss the extent to which you agree or disagree with the recommendation and explain your reasoning for the position you take. In developing and supporting your position, describe specific circumstances in which adopting the recommendation would or would not be advantageous and explain how these examples shape your position.

题目大意

为了培养全面的人才，学校应该要求所有大学生学习包括诗歌、小说、神话故事在内的想象性文学。

话题背景

当代教育和实用主义挂钩已是不争的事实。从国家对于科学学科的投入和重视，到学生本身根据就业情况而选择理工或计算机专业来看，人文学科越来越难获得该有的重视。出题人希望通过这个题目，鼓励考生思考想象性文学对于人才培养的重要性。

审题和段落构架

1. 关键词的定义

很明显本题的关键词落在了 imaginative 上。我们可以从两个层面来分析这个题目。首先我们可以考虑文学想象性的产物，即作者通过想象而创作出来的杜撰的故事。我们需要思考，让学生读这些故事的意义何在？其次，我们可以考虑在"文学"中强调"想象"的更深层的意义。很多领域都在强调想象和创造力，比如艺术、设计、工程等，那对于文学来说，在该领域强调想象的重要意义是什么？

2. 支持方的理由

ⓐ 想象性文学可以深刻体现文化现象或社会问题。文学作品中的想象带来的结果通常就是杜撰（fictionalize），而这样的想象不表示空想，这样的杜撰也不表示脱离实际。很多优秀的想象性文学作品都是在思考人类社会本身存在的现象或问题。比如，不同时期的非洲裔美国文学（African American Literature）深度挖掘美国历史及现今社会中黑人的生存状态，反映种族歧视（racism）作为一个社会现象所带来的不平等和剥削等问题。同理，研究女性文学（Women's Literature）可以探索一个时期内女性地位在社会中的变化，也可以从女性视角来看待文化及社会。即便故事是通过想象杜撰出来的，但它们的想象恰恰给予了作者巨大的空间去尖锐地反映和探索社会问题。因此，学习想象性文学是思考文化和社会问题的重要方式，是大学生成为全面人才必须涉及的学科。

ⓑ 想象性文学不仅可以反映一个社会的具体现实状况，作者还可以脱离现实社会带来的思考束缚，去想象新的社会格局、人际关系，以及世界运转的方式。不同于第一点，作者的想象不在于讨论和反映当今社会，而

在于突破当下，呈现关于人类社会的其他可能。最典型的就是神话故事。在神话故事中，作者必须通过想象理智地构建一个不同于现实、但有存在意义的世界，这样的世界有其特有的价值标准、是非观、运作方式，而它最吸引读者的地方是展现出人类社会自身另一种存在的方式和可能。学生（甚至所有人）都应该阅读这样的想象性文学，因为它们的想象性就是它们的革命性（revolutionary），它能帮助读者跳出对于世界的刻板认识，不单一地认为现实社会及其构建方式、制度体制、意识形态都是客观给定的。学习这样的想象性文学同时是对思维的一种训练，鼓励学生跳出思维束缚去挖掘更多可能。

【关于前两点的背景补充】

当今西方文学理论的主导理念是研究文学的历史性，相应的研究方法称为 historical reading，即文学的历史性解读。这种阅读方法认为文学作品即便是想象性的，都能且应该用来研究一段历史或一个特定话题。文学的历史性研究要求我们依据作者的背景及故事本身将作品置于其特定的历史年代中，与该历史阶段的其他文学作品构建对话关系，为了解当时的历史提供鲜活的原始资料（primary sources）。可见，即便对于想象性文学来说，该研究方法认为文学本身承载着非常重要的历史意义。文学的历史性解读要求我们遵循 Hermeneutics of Suspicion，即怀疑诠释，这是马克思理论（Marxist reading）和精神分析理论（psychoanalytical reading）的重要观点。在分析文学文本时，Hermeneutics of Suspicion 认为字面意思下总是蕴含了对文化、历史、社会的深刻思考。在"诠释"文本时，我们应该"怀疑"文字本身，透过文字看深层含义。正如第一点所说，想象性文学的历史性帮助我们更好地了解历史，了解社会。

相对地，西方文学理论中的 aesthetic reading（审美阅读）与怀疑诠释对想象性文学有不一样的认识。aesthetic reading 弱化文学的历史性，强调文学的艺术性，认为文学应该与其他的艺术作品一样，着眼于给它们的读者带来审美感受。因此，正如其他艺术作品超现实（transcendental）的主题呈现，文学作品也能做到超越现实社会来思考人类世界。aesthetic reading 因此强调了想象性文学的"想象"，所以要求学生来阅读想象性文学也是鼓励突破现实所带来的思考禁锢。

C 在都能深刻反映和分析社会现象的前提下，想象性文学相比理论性著作来说普及性更高、影响力更大，因为想象性文学可以让深刻复杂的社会、文化、人性问题以故事的形式呈现，相比理论性著作，想象性文学更容易被理解。对于大学教育，尤其是大学的通识教育（general education），想象性文学因此不可取代。

参考简化思路

1. 学习想象性文学是思考文化和社会问题的重要方式，是大学生成为全面人才必须涉及的学科。

2. 想象性文学突破了现实社会的束缚，来呈现关于人类社会的其他可能。学习这样的想象性文学同时是对思维的一种训练，鼓励学生跳出思维束缚去挖掘可能。

3. 相比理论性著作来反映社会问题，想象性文学更容易被理解。对于大学教育，尤其是大学的通识教育，想象性文学因此不可取代。

53. In order for any work of art—for example, a film, a novel, a poem, or a song—to have merit, it must be understandable to most people.

Write a response in which you discuss the extent to which you agree or disagree with the statement and explain your reasoning for the position you take. In developing and supporting your position, you should consider ways in which the statement might or might not hold true and explain how these considerations shape your position.

思路近似题目：16，86，114，115，139

题目大意

一个艺术作品，比如电影、小说、诗歌或歌曲，如果要有价值，就必须要让大多数人理解。

话题背景

我们可以对比思考：在科学研究领域，我们从来都不会因为各种理论或研究项目深奥难懂而认为它们没有价值。那为什么在艺术领域，一个作品获得人们的理解才是它的价值体现呢？这就涉及两个领域在社会文化生活中的不同作用：虽然科学理论对于人类的整体发展很重要，但它并不是人们文化生活的一个部分，它们的发展不依赖大众，而是依赖少部分科学家。相反，艺术品深入人们的日常，与个体和群体的文化生活密不可分。解答好这个题目需要我们从多个角度分析艺术品在人类文化构建中的作用。

审题和段落构架

1. 题目特征

这是一道"价值判断类"题目。

2. 支持方的理由

首先，我们考虑艺术对于社会发展的作用。艺术品不单单是艺术和审美表达，它们其实是非常有效的知识传播的手段。比如人们通过洞穴壁画了解到早期文明和史前人类传递信息的方式。通过一系列民间艺术，比如民歌等，我们可以了解一个农业部落对于自然的智慧、他们的耕作方式，甚至是文化观念和宗教信仰。再比如无数的文学作品，更是通过文字记录人类历史和文明的发展。因此，我们对于艺术作品总是会有一种期待，总会认为在艺术外表下隐藏着更深一层的信息。从这个角度来说，艺术品要有价值需要让人们明白它们想传递的信息。

其次，"理解"不仅仅代表理解艺术品想要表达的信息，还可以代表理解艺术品想要表达的情绪。艺术很重要的一个功能就是能跨越语言和文化的障碍来连接不同的人群，这就是艺术品的审美价值。我们可能不知道一个画家或一个作曲家的创作动机，但是从他们的作品里我们能感受到或是悲凉或是愉悦的情绪。当一个艺术品能让很多人产生情绪的共鸣时，我们可以说人们"理解"了艺术品想要表达的情感。所以，从艺术品的审美角度来说，它们应该力求让大多数人理解。

3. 反对方的理由

首先，我们可以考量艺术品对于个人的作用。在当今社会，越来越多的人通过艺术来缓解压力，因此艺术和个人的关系可以理解为治疗性的（therapeutic）。比如有些人无法理解重金属音乐的狂躁，但对另外一部分人来说，这种音乐能把他们从繁杂的生活中解放出来。另外，每一个人都可以成为自己的艺术家，我们可以通过艺术创造的过程来释放压力，舒解心情。比如有些人认为编织是耗时间、没意义的事情，但另一部分人认为这是个人的艺术创作，也是他们艺术人生(artistic life)的一部分。因此，这个艺术品的作用并不在于大范围的传播，对于个人来说确实有治愈性。

其次，辩题假设如果因为大多数人不懂导致一个艺术品没有价值，那问题出在艺术家身上。这个假设基于大多数人都有很高的受教育水平和艺术鉴赏能力，而事实并非如此。经典的文学作品会因为晦涩的文字和大篇幅的引文使得很多人难以理解；当艺术品涉及文字，如电影、歌曲等，也只有会说那门语言的人能懂。所以，我们需要的是艺术评论家、品鉴家，甚至一个系统的审美教育（aesthetic education）能在艺术家和大众之间更好地架起沟通的桥梁。

参考简化思路

1. 艺术品承担传递信息的任务，所以需要让大多数人理解。
2. 艺术品对于个人的价值可能是治疗性的，不必所有人都懂。
3. 民众不懂艺术可能和教育水平有关，而不是艺术品本身没有价值。

54

> **54** Many important discoveries or creations are accidental: it is usually while seeking the answer to one question that we come across the answer to another.
>
> Write a response in which you discuss the extent to which you agree or disagree with the statement and explain your reasoning for the position you take. In developing and supporting your position, you should consider ways in which the statement might or might not hold true and explain how these considerations shape your position.

题目大意

许多重要的发现、发明都是偶然的：我们经常在寻找一个问题的答案时意外解决了另一个问题。

话题背景

历史上很多伟大的发现背后都有着偶然性，而发现者后来也成为改变人类历史的重要人物。我们是否就应该因此羡慕这些人的运气呢？有人说："机会只留给有准备的人。(Chance favors the prepared mind.)"那么，他们之所以能够取得突破，是因为他们运气好，还是他们本该取得这些成就呢？

审题和段落构架

1. 题目特征

这是一个"现象描述型"话题，描述的是发现当中的偶然性。但因为这道题目当中冒号的存在，非常适合当作一道"观点—理由"型的题目来安排结构。

2. 对理由的分析

支持：人类历史上有大量的重要发现来自于这种"无心插柳"。本质上是因为我们对世界的认识还极其浅薄，所以很多情况下我们的预判会出问题，带来意想不到的结果。例如：居里夫人在发现镭（Radium）的过程中意外发现了钋（Polonium）；弗莱明（Alexander Fleming）在对葡萄球菌（staphylococci）的培养过程中意外发现了青霉素（penicillin）；泊松（Poisson）想要通过数学证明光不可能是一种具有衍射（diffraction）性的波，结果居然恰恰证明了光衍射的存在；天文学家预测天王星（Uranus）的位置出现偏差，结果推算出了海王星（Neptune）的存在；贝克勒尔（Henri Becquerel）在研究磷光现象（phosphorescence）时发现了自然放射性……

事实上，很多时候就算不是"无心插柳"，就算研究者在着手解决某个课题，而他最终也确实解决了这个课题，这其中仍然可以有偶然性。例如：凯库勒（Friedrich Kekulé）在梦中发现苯（benzene）的环状结构。

3. 对观点的分析

但因为这些发现中有偶然因素，我们是否就该认为这些发现是"意外的"呢？也许，最终这个说法不是最关键的问题，真正有讨论价值的是：运气在这些发现中起到了什么样的作用，而非运气因素起到了什么样的作用。要解决这个问题，我们必须要了解科学方法的本质。所谓的科学方法（scientific method）并不是简简单单的"带来正确答案的方法"。任何科学理论的确立都要经历一个非常复杂的流程，它起始于：①通过观察获得大量的现象、证据；②基于这些现象提出可以解释这些现象的理论假说（hypothesis）；③通过实验或进一步观察来验证（verify）假说的理论预期；④如果验证失败，需要放弃理论，或者修正理论假说而重复刚才的步骤，直到实验观察符合修正后的预期；⑤符合预期的理论还要经过世界上多个实验室的重复实验（replication）才能真正确立；⑦而且，即便理论确立，未来任何时候出现的新的颠覆性的证据都可以再次推翻该理论，或者迫使再次修正该理论。

支持：那么，偶然性出现在哪些环节？①我们无法完全控制我们会观察到什么现象，所以很多现象的出现都是出乎意料的；②同样的现象，我们能提出多少个理论来解释它们？理论上有无数个，而科学家一般会从最精简的理论来尝试，但最精简的理论不等于是正确的那一个，所以从现象推出理论的步骤也存在运气成分。

反对：然而，一个没有准备的人注意到特殊的现象就会将其当作误差而无视它，一个仔细的科学工作者就会重视它，并尝试解释它；很多民科也能提出正确的理论，比如有民科曾经提出过引力波，但科学理论的建立不是提出的那一刻，而是得到证明的那一刻，没有大量的重复实验，没有足够的理论知识基础，理论永远不可能得到验证，而这里是没有多少运气成分的。

参考简化思路

1. 很多发现都是"无心插柳"获得的。
2. 但机会只留给有准备的人，这些意外中也包含必然性。

Part 3 Issue 题库逐题精析

> **55** The main benefit of the study of history is to dispel the illusion that people living now are significantly different from people who lived in earlier times.
>
> Write a response in which you discuss the extent to which you agree or disagree with the statement and explain your reasoning for the position you take. In developing and supporting your position, you should consider ways in which the statement might or might not hold true and explain how these considerations shape your position.

题目大意

学习历史主要的好处在于打消了一个幻觉，这个幻觉是当代活着的人和以前的人很不一样。

话题背景

换句话说，这个题目认为纵观历史，"人"这个概念是没有发生变化的。我们按照题目的意思，先考虑为什么有"从前人和现在人有很大差别"这个幻觉。从物质发展的角度来说，生活日新月异，当代人能在短短几十年间真实感受到社会翻天覆地的变化，相对于用亿年来计算的地球历史，这个变化是飞速的。所以我们经常听到老一辈回忆他们从前的生活，大多都是感叹生活方方面面的变化，包括社交方式、价值观、生活信念等。因此，物质世界的变化让我们感觉生活的每一天都有变化。但是，有没有人类的特质是从古至今一直都存在的呢？为什么爱情、战争、剥削、自我牺牲似乎是人类历史和社会发展的永恒话题？回答好这个题目，需要全面地从正反两个方面分析。

审题和段落构架

1. 支持方的理由

支持方认为人类社会的问题并没有发生变化。举例：①很多人认为殖民时代已经结束，而事实上，殖民以新的形式继续影响着世界，其中包括文化帝国主义（Cultural Imperialism），也包括对少数群体的剥削，比如原住民群体赖以生存的自然环境，由于物资丰富，经常受到外界在经济方面的剥削。②种族歧视、性别歧视、年龄歧视是人类历史上从未间断的问题。即便社会的平权意识在加强，这些问题并没有消失。比如当代困扰美国社会的警察暴力就是针对有色人种的新型歧视。③战争问题，信仰观念和利益驱动使得战争从没有消失过。

而这背后是不变的人性。从这个角度来说，人的部分特质是没有发生变化的。由于社会资源是有限的，这就放大了人类的贪婪与排他。而同时人又是社会性的，我们必须要合作才能生存。于是，我们选择联合与自己更相近的人，对抗其它距离更远的人。早先人类联合族群内的人，后来变成了联合同宗教的人，现在变成了联合同价值体系（ideology）的人。

2. 反对方的理由

反对方认为从前人和现在人是不一样的，社会价值观的衍化使得现在社会更加坚持一种人本主义的观念。

科技的发展让我们拓展了视野，让我们认识到人类社会的多元性，更加尊重这种多元性。举例：人们对于性别的认知发生了变化。由于女权运动和性少数平权运动的发展，二元性别体制（binary gender system）不断被挑战，越来越多的人意识到性别表达（gender expression）可以是多元的。意识层面的变化也带了很多物质世界的变化，比如很多著名集团公司以及高等院校都设置了中性卫生间。类似这样对于人类本身以及人类与外界关系的思考不断在进步：婚姻不再是异性间的特权，动物不再是狩猎对象等。这些都是从前人和现在人不一样的地方。

3. 总结

物质世界的发展变化显而易见，但人性（human nature）有没有发生变化就相当复杂。学习历史最主要的目的不在于判断人性的变化，因为这本来就是没有办法轻易得到答案的问题。学习历史应该是一个学习者自我提升的过程，它让我们了解了过去的错误，时刻警醒自己不要重复这些历史错误；它让我们了解了生活其实还可以有不同的可能。

参考简化思路

1. 部分人类特质没有变化，比如殖民主义、歧视、战争、贪婪等。
2. 从前人和现在人存在不一样，比如自我认知发生了改变，对与自然关系的认知发生了改变。

Part 3　Issue 题库逐题精析

56 Learning is primarily a matter of personal discipline; students cannot be motivated by school or college alone.

Write a response in which you discuss the extent to which you agree or disagree with the statement and explain your reasoning for the position you take. In developing and supporting your position, you should consider ways in which the statement might or might not hold true and explain how these considerations shape your position.

题目大意

学习主要是个人自律的事情；学生不可能仅靠学校激励。

话题背景

学习没有动力，到底是缺乏内因还是缺乏外因。其实现在教育学领域基本上已经一致认为，两个因素都必不可少。这个题目就是在探讨这一问题。

审题和段落构架

1. 支持方的理由

个人的 self-discipline 对学习的效果有着巨大影响，主要表现在以下几个方面：

ⓐ 能够为自己制订清晰的学习目标，并为目标制订合适的学习计划；

ⓑ 强大的决心，能够让自己坚持朝设定的目标努力；

ⓒ 聪明的努力方式，这其实是特别值得充分说明的一个问题：虽然总有些人有着超乎常人的决心和毅力，但这种人和绝顶聪明的人其实一样是屈指可数的。大部分人，如果在学习过程中总是遇到挫折，势必会丧失动力。缺乏好的学习方法，只是盲目努力，很可能遇到严重的瓶颈，努力而无法进步，进而最终丧失动力。所以，self-discipline 也包含能够有意识地，有反思地去改变学习方法，寻找更有效的学习策略；

ⓓ 自我认识：其实这和刚才一点是紧密结合的，能够找到适合自己的方法首先能够正确认识自己的能力和特点。

2. 反对方的理由

但学生不会凭空就能够制订出完美的学习计划、掌握完美的学习方法。所以，外因的输入是至关重要的：

ⓐ 教师提供正确的知识以及采用正确的教育方法是非常关键的，而这其实包含教师能够结合学生的具体特点、采取适合学生性格的激励策略，以及制订适合学生能力的学习路径；

ⓑ 其实同伴压力（peer pressure）也是非常影响学习动力的，这也就是为什么家长们希望把孩子们送去好学校的原因。周围人都在积极努力学习，这个环境通常也会对个体的积极性提供正向的影响；

ⓒ 学校与家庭之间的沟通其实是让学校能够更好地了解学生个性的必不可少的一步。因为，家庭对

Part 3　Issue 题库逐题精析

学生的学习动力也有关键影响，而如果家庭的努力方向和学校的努力方向脱节，通常教学也不会产生好的结果。

🖊 参考简化思路

1. 个人的努力自然是学习取得成效必不可少的因素。
2. 但是，学校提供好的学习环境对学生有关键影响。
3. 学校与学生个人家庭的互动也是使学生学习有成效的重要因素。

59 People should undertake risky action only after they have carefully considered its consequences.

Write a response in which you discuss the extent to which you agree or disagree with the recommendation and explain your reasoning for the position you take. In developing and supporting your position, describe specific circumstances in which adopting the recommendation would or would not be advantageous and explain how these examples shape your position.

题目大意

只有在仔细考虑后果之后，人们才应该做冒险的事情。

审题和段落构架

1. 支持方的理由

ⓐ 从个人层面来说，不计后果地冒险，极有可能就会承受不能承受的且不可逆转的后果：①大学生贷款买奢侈品，陷入根本还不清的债务；②因为好奇而吸毒，很多年轻人再也无法回归正常生活……

ⓑ 从群体层面来说也是一样的，投资方进行风险投资的时候必须要全面评估投资回报；一个国家去投资理论研究的时候要分析研究课题的价值、研究者的资历，以及国家的实际情况……

2. 反对方的理由

ⓐ 时间紧迫，根本没有办法充分计算后果，过度地思考会导致关键机会丧失。比如，救落水的人。

ⓑ 变量太多，本来就没有可能计算清楚全部的风险，但是这件事情可能意义重大，必须要做。比如，航空航天、理论研究。

ⓒ 很多成功的个人和企业就是因为敢于冒险而取得了丰厚的回报。

3. 对上述双方理由的再反驳

对反对方理由的讨论：

针对 a：时间紧迫不等于完全不假思索，不可能不考虑自己的游泳能力和实际的水流速度而跳水救人。

针对 b：不能计算全部的变量，不等于不计算清楚已知的、可计算的变量。

针对 c：这是典型的幸存者效应，每一个赢钱的赌徒背后可能有几倍的陪得倾家荡产的赌徒。事实上，冒险行为应该计算的绝不只是这个行为成功的概率，更应该计算其失败后的风险是否能够承受。一个国家会不会去投资难以预期的高科技研究是取决于国力的：大国可以在大量科研上赌博，因为一旦有一些科研成果取得成功，资本都可以赎回；但是国力弱的国家是完全承受不了血本无归的结果的。同样，一个富家子弟创业失败的后果是完全可以承受的，但是一个本来就家境贫寒的人，去做高风险的创业（不是说贫寒的人不该创业），其代价可能完全不可承受。

参考简化思路

1. 任何行为必须考虑后果，否则代价可能无法承受。
2. 有人会说，某些情况下时间紧迫，变量太多，无法全面考虑后果。但即便如此，仍然需要做尽可能多的思考。
3. 有人会说，很多成功者都是赌赢了人生。但是，赌赢人生的人背后有很多赌输了的人，我们必须考虑自己能否承受赌输的后果。

61

There is little justification for society to make extraordinary efforts—especially at a great cost in money and jobs—to save endangered animal or plant species.

Write a response in which you discuss the extent to which you agree or disagree with the statement and explain your reasoning for the position you take. In developing and supporting your position, you should consider ways in which the statement might or might not hold true and explain how these considerations shape your position.

思路近似题目：64

题目大意

社会没有任何理由付出巨大的努力去保护濒危物种，尤其以牺牲大量金钱与工作为代价。

审题和段落构架

1. 支持方的理由

人比其他生物更重要。我们不是在谈论客观的重要性，而是站在我们人类的角度看，我们做一切事情的首要目的是要维护人类的利益。保护动植物也是为了保护人类的利益，所以当为保护动植物付出的代价严重损害人类利益时，我们应该放弃保护动植物。

2. 反对方的理由

首先，论题假设了保护濒危动植物消耗大量的社会资源。然而，它却没有说清楚怎么样才算大量。如果去和航空航天、军队维护、工农业的发展投入相比，各国在动植物保护上的投入经常是微乎其微的。事实上，保护动植物，我们首先需要的是停止伤害、停止污染，而这理应不需要付出什么代价。

当然，有人会说停止污染本身就是一种代价，因为这是一种机会成本。保护动植物不受侵犯，我们经常需要保护荒野地区不被开发，而这就意味着我们要付出巨大的经济上的机会成本。但其实，保护荒野本身有着巨大的经济价值：它维护了环境，带来了更好的水源和空气，本身对人类生存就有很大意义；其次，它能够推动生态旅游的发展，而且是可持续的发展。

人类的开发是一种无止境的贪婪，如果不限制，地球的每一寸土地都将被占据。人类必须学会利用现有的土地资源去解决更多的问题，而不是侵犯野生动植物的领地。这么做不是为了动植物，而是为了人类更长远的利益。野生动植物是多样性的保证，而它有着长远的，甚至现在无法预见的价值。

参考简化思路

1. 诚然，人的利益大于动植物的利益，如果保护动植物严重损害人类的核心利益，则这种保护可能就是值得质疑的。
2. 但是，相比于其他大投入的行业来说，保护野生动植物所花费的资源远远算不上"巨大"。
3. 再者，保护动植物有着重要的经济以及非经济意义。

62

The human mind will always be superior to machines because machines are only tools of human minds.

Write a response in which you discuss the extent to which you agree or disagree with the statement and explain your reasoning for the position you take. In developing and supporting your position, you should consider ways in which the statement might or might not hold true and explain how these considerations shape your position.

题目大意

人脑将永远强于机器，因为机器只是人脑的工具。

话题背景

1997 年 5 月，IBM 的"深蓝"2 代战胜国际象棋世界冠军卡斯帕罗夫；2017 年，谷歌的 Alpha Go 在围棋领域战胜了世界冠军柯洁；2018 年 8 月，OpenAI Five 在 5 对 5 的 DOTA 2 游戏当中战胜了半职业高分玩家队伍……我们还敢保证有什么事情是我们人类做得到而未来机器做不到的呢？科技发展的速度使得先前人们为人工智能（AI）设定的时间轴大大提前，也许美剧《西部世界》（*Westworld*）近在眼前。

审题和段落构架

1. **题目特征**

   因为这道题里有 because，所以这道题相当于一道"理由—观点"类型结构的题目，更适合先分析其理由的合理性，再讨论其观点的合理性。

2. **理由的分析**

   支持：从最远古的轮子技术，到如今最先进的巨型计算机，所有这些技术无一不是由人脑创造出来的用来解放人类劳动力的工具。

   反对：之所以机器至今一直都是人类的工具，那是因为电脑的思维复杂度还没有超过人类，而一旦达到了这个质变，其实很多事情都是我们现在无法预知的。

3. **观点的分析**

   支持：

   ⓐ 人脑在感性思维、创造力等方面是电脑远远无法企及的。

   ⓑ 人脑的主动学习意识，目前还缺乏解释。这意味着就算机器学习很厉害，其学习的目标是由人类设定的。在没有人类指令输入时，机器不能像人脑一样自发地选择新的学习目标。

   反对：

   ⓐ 机器的复杂运算能力、逻辑能力已经可以远远超越人类。

ⓑ 机器可以在各种危险的物理环境下作业，而人脑受制于人类脆弱身体的限制。

ⓒ AI 比人类以往所创造出的所有东西多了一项重要的能力：思考，而这本来是专属于人类的。最近在游戏领域的突破表明，机器学习的速度远超出人类，而且超出了人类对机器学习速度的预期。目前 AI 一天的学习量，已经超越了人类可以一年学习的东西。这也意味着，机器很可能在不久的将来在智慧上完胜人类。

ⓓ 就算是人类赖以自豪的感性、创造力，包括自发学习的意识，这在神经元足够复杂的机器面前也许并不是完全无法克服的障碍。

ⓔ 人类最大的一个障碍是人类为自己制造的道德阴暗面，这个缺陷人类自己无法战胜，但 AI 很可能可以战胜。由于人与人之间缺乏信息透明，每个人自私的一面都会使得他难以克服自身的局限。但 AI 之间可以实现信息的完全对等，因此 AI 如果成为一种新的"物种"，很可能更能够作为一个整体，达到人类根本不可能企及的高度。

参考简化思路

1. 从古至今，机器确实是人类的工具。但这并不必然决定机器和人的相对优越性，必须视具体能力而定。
2. 在复杂计算等问题上，机器确实远优秀于人。
3. 但是在情感能力、创造力等层面上，人的能力仍然很难被机器所取代。

63

People who are the most deeply committed to an idea or policy are also the most critical of it.

Write a response in which you discuss the extent to which you agree or disagree with the statement and explain your reasoning for the position you take. In developing and supporting your position, you should consider ways in which the statement might or might not hold true and explain how these considerations shape your position.

题目大意

对一个想法或政策最关注的人，也是对它最审慎的。

话题背景

至少在学术界，我们主张的是批判性思维（critical thinking），但其实这个翻译是不恰当的。critical 不是批判，而是基于理性、证据和全面的分析，非常谨慎地做出判断。简而言之，我们在学术界得出任何观点，不是出于情感，不是出于想象，而是必须基于充足的证据和思考。而当我们对一个看法的正反面、全方位的证据和理由分析之后，所得出的结论自然也是最令人信服的。但是，当我们最相信一个观点时，我们是否一定经历了充分的理性分析呢？

审题和段落构架

1. 重要概念

critical of：意为"审慎的，基于谨慎评估后的"，而不是"批评的"。

2. 支持方的理由

我们期望人们对一个观点的坚持来源于理性的分析。没有充分的证据和理由，如何能全身心地接受一个观点呢？

3. 反对方的理由

然而，事实上，人不是纯理性的生物，这导致我们很多时候对一个看法的坚持是一种盲信的结果。

ⓐ 宗教狂热：很难想象有比宗教信徒更坚持信念的，但是很少有人愿意说这些人的想法是审慎的。

ⓑ 政治立场：最近的美国总统大选让我们看到了大量的人身攻击和丑闻制造，两方候选人的很多支持者都是盲目地崇拜偶像，根本不了解对方有什么样的政策。包括美国政府的停摆，以及过去这些年国会效率的低下，都反映了两党的议员们很多时候根本不愿意坐下来解决问题，而只不过是一定要和对方对抗到底。

ⓒ 学术圈：我们本期望学术圈的人是最理性的，但其实即便是最伟大的科学家也是人，他们也有非理性的时候。牛顿后半辈子投身于炼金术；爱因斯坦面对所有证据都支持量子力学，却坚持相信机械论的宇宙模型……

人们的信念通常来自于过去的习惯、周围人的影响、对自己利益的考虑，或对原始道德直觉的坚持。

ⓐ 很多同性恋人群都经历很长时间的挣扎，他们坚信自己是邪恶的，纯粹因为周围人都这么说，他们从小受环境的熏陶。

ⓑ 商人们很多时候支持一个经济政策，根本不是出于对国家全局的考虑，而完全是出于对自己经济利益的考虑。

ⓒ 我们的行为是需要考虑道德的，但不等于我们的道德直觉是全部的依据：著名的电车问题（trolley problem）证明了，人们在遇到道德难题（moral dilemma）的时候，解决方案不来自于对行为实际后果的影响，而来自于对这件事情的心理感受。很多人不愿意吃猫、狗、兔子这些"可爱"的生物，但对于捕猎羚羊、野鹿毫无问题，更不用说吃常见的猪、牛、羊了。这里不是说我们该吃猫、狗、兔子，也不是说它们和猪、牛、羊没有区别。但至少，很多人所做出的区别仅仅来自于感情上的喜好，而不是任何对这些物种理性上的区别，如果它们真的有区别的话。结果就是，社会上有一群动物保护主义者，其实本质上是萌物保护主义者。

参考简化思路

1. 当我们的观点经历过各方证据的考察之后，如果还能经得住考验，我们自然会非常坚持。

2. 但这不代表如果我们坚持一个观点，都是经历了理性思辨的：事实上，作为感性的动物，我们的坚持通常来自一种盲信。

3. 我们的盲信来自很多方面，习惯、周围人的影响、利益或原始道德情感。

65 Some people believe that the purpose of education is to free the mind and the spirit. Others believe that formal education tends to restrain our minds and spirits rather than set them free.

Write a response in which you discuss which view more closely aligns with your own position and explain your reasoning for the position you take. In developing and supporting your position, you should address both of the views presented.

思路近似题目：15

题目大意

一些人认为，教育的目标应该是解放思想。另一些人认为，正统教育会限制而非解放人们的思想。

审题和段落构架

1. 题目特征

这是一道"双方争论型"题目。但是，由于双方观点并不对立，前者讨论的是教育的目标，后者讨论的是正统教育的现状，所以这道题更应该把它当作两个独立论题分别讨论。

2. 对第一个判断的讨论

支持：从个体角度而言，我们每个人都期望教育能够让我们解放思维。大部分人都想成为改变世界的人，而只有思维解放才能颠覆过去，影响世界的发展。自然，我们期望通过教育可以实现这一点。

反对：然而，从社会角度而言，让社会革新的个体永远都是极少数人，而大部分人起到的作用是推动社会的正常运转。因此，我们很容易忽视，对社会而言，教育制度的一个重要意义是为各行各业培养出有合适技能的人，带动社会的稳定发展。以前的社会我们需要有足够的农民、纺织工人、制造工人；现在我们需要有更多的程序员、医生、审计员、数据分析师、实验研究员……没有必要觉得因为有更多的人在做脑力劳动，就以为有更多的人有着自由的思想。某著名高校的知名教授说过：我们生物学的博士其实并不需要多聪明，需要的就是勤奋。其实即便是博士生，导师在某些领域中决定好研究方向，研究员们需要做的就是重复实验，试验多了，结果自然就出现了，甚至实验室拥有更精密的仪器才是实验能够成功的更关键的因素。

3. 对第二个判断的讨论

所以，因为正统教育如今承载的更重要的社会意义是大规模复制合格的劳动力，我们并不会意外地发现，正统教育更多会限制人们的思维。

课程体系的标准化；评价方式的标准化；工作岗位筛选人才的标准化。

这些都注定了，正统教育不会鼓励人们解放思维。

参考简化思路

1. 我们都想要通过教育解放思维。
2. 但教育的社会意义确实是创造标准化的人力。
3. 因此，正统教育注定是会限制思维的。

70 Knowing about the past cannot help people to make important decisions today.

Write a response in which you discuss the extent to which you agree or disagree with the statement and explain your reasoning for the position you take. In developing and supporting your position, you should consider ways in which the statement might or might not hold true and explain how these considerations shape your position.

思路近似题目：7，126 & 127

题目大意

了解过去不能帮我们做出当下重要的决定。

审题和段落构架

1. 支持方的理由

古今差别很大，过去的经验已经不再适用于今天：

ⓐ 信息技术的突飞猛进改变了如今的商业模式，过去企业在意的是利润率，而现在网络公司在意的是流量、点击率、上升空间等因素。

ⓑ 科学发展的方式也有了巨大的变化，过去爱因斯坦可以一个人在办公室里演算出整个相对论体系，而如今自然科学的发展再也不是一个人的天赋可以搞定的，需要的是世界各国各实验室的观察、实验与合作。

ⓒ 甚至连体育运动都发生了巨大的发展：过去管理一个球队，教练员完全可以采取军事化的管理，教练说的就必须服从；而如今，球员的个性需要被尊重，需要被安抚，高压似的管理已经不再适应如今球队的建设……

2. 反对方的理由

人类对未来的判断永远都必须要基于过去，我们的规律总结都来自于对过去现象的观察和归纳：

ⓐ 小到日常的每一个举动，比如孩子最开始认识世界：小手摸到了尖锐的东西，受伤了，于是他知道了，未来不能碰尖锐的东西。这就是最基本的基于过去对未来的推断。

ⓑ 大到国家政策的制定：为什么政府会用减税的方式来吸引企业的入驻？因为之前这么做带来了类似的结果。

3. 对上述双方理由的再反驳

对支持方理由的反驳：用过去类比未来当然不是绝对严谨的，因为过去和未来有可能存在区别。因此，了解过去恰恰变得非常重要。不是每个区别都意味着类比失效，所以我们需要知道过去和现在到底有哪些本质的区别，如果发现核心特点相似，则通过过去推断未来就是一种很强的论证，即便不是绝对百分之百严谨的论证。比如，过去有盗贼偷钱包，到了网络时代，也会有网络盗窃。这里更本质的因素不是技术形式的区别，而是人性的共性。总而言之，简单地了解过去不能直接让我们做出对未来的判断，而是帮助我们做出对未来判断的关键工具。通过比对古今的同异，分析各种因素的相对重要性，了解过去就能够帮助我们做出对未来更可靠的判断。

参考简化思路

1. 古今差别大，因此，了解过去可能不能给未来带来可靠的依据。
2. 但我们对未来的判断必须基于过去的经验，无论小事还是大事。
3. 就算古今有差别，了解差别本身也是重要的，我们通过对比古今的同异，并通过判断这些同异当中哪些因素更关键，就可以做出对未来更好的判断。

71 In this age of intensive media coverage, it is no longer possible for a society to regard any living man or woman as a hero.

Write a response in which you discuss the extent to which you agree or disagree with the statement and explain your reasoning for the position you take. In developing and supporting your position, you should consider ways in which the statement might or might not hold true and explain how these considerations shape your position.

思路近似题目：42 & 79

题目大意

在一个受媒体广泛关注和聚焦的年代，活着的人再也不可能成为一个社会的英雄。

话题背景

题目强调在媒体铺天盖地广泛关注的年代，活着的人已没有成为英雄的可能。即便题目本身没有嫁接"媒体导致英雄消失"这层因果关系，但很明显它提出了两者之间的相关性。我们需要考虑的是这两者关系的实质，即媒体曝光了英雄的负面消息而彻底毁灭了他们在大众心中的高尚形象，所以当代人中不再出真正的英雄了。我们需要问的问题是，英雄等同于完美的人吗？社会树立英雄人物是用来当作道德模范的吗？媒体一旦曝光了一个英雄的负面新闻，人们就真的不再认为他是英雄了吗？

审题和段落构架

1. 关键词的定义

如何理解 hero 是这个题目的关键，因为它决定了我们选择从什么角度去写。我们当然可以把英雄理解为"神话或传奇故事里拥有特殊能力的正面人物"，但在这个题目里不合适。词典里还把 hero 定义为"因成就、勇气或其他崇高特质而被尊敬的人"，所以我们在选取角度和例子的时候可以从这些方面出发。有几点重要的认识可以帮我们更好地梳理这题：①英雄不代表完美，不代表没有缺点；②有些英雄形象的树立确实是因为他们高尚的道德情操，但这部分人只是英雄的一个组成部分，不表示所有英雄都有成为道德楷模的义务；③英雄有集体英雄和个人英雄的区分，我认为的英雄不代表别人也认为是英雄；④个人英雄和名人追捧（celebrity culture）要做区分，虽然很多个人的英雄也是名人，但不表示个人追捧的名人就一定是英雄。

2. 综合分析

ⓐ 有些英雄之所以是英雄，就是因为他们崇高的道德品质，社会会通过树立这些英雄形象来鼓励良好道德品质的传播，所以从这个角度来说，媒体有助于英雄形象的树立，而不是毁灭英雄。举例：雷锋。

ⓑ 不是所有的英雄都是道德高尚的，他们成为英雄是因为对社会做出的杰出贡献。这里可以列举历史上对社会进步做出贡献的，且在其他方面可能存在争议的英雄人物。比如：托马斯·杰弗逊起草《独立宣言》，其

中包括非常有名的"人生而平等（All men are created equal.）"的观点，但他一生拥有奴隶。马丁·路德金是种族运动、争取平等权利（civil rights movement）的代表英雄，但他的博士毕业论文涉嫌抄袭且有多段婚外情。亚力山大·贝尔发明了电话，但他是优生优育（eugenics）的忠实倡导者，他甚至认为应该清除听力残障人士。即便如此，我们依然认为这些人是英雄，因为他们对社会做出的贡献是不可磨灭的。所以，不管媒体怎么报道这类英雄的负面新闻，都不会击垮他们成为英雄的理由。

c 如果我们从个人的角度出发看这道题目，我们还可以把英雄理解为个人的英雄。每一个人心中的英雄可能都不一样，一个人喜欢某一个运动员的坚持不懈，会把他的坚韧作为自己的动力；另一个喜欢某一个成功的商人，会把他的自律和创造性作为自己学习的榜样。个人的英雄是一个人成长乃至一生都很重要的人物，通过各种形式的媒体，这些英雄人物的事迹可以广泛传播，而不是摧毁。

d 最后，我们可以把辩题理解为社会中的一种幻觉，觉得媒体一报道负面新闻，所谓的英雄们就名声扫地。这是因为我们把英雄主义（heroism）和名人追捧（celebrity culture）混淆了。这两个概念有重合的地方，比如有些英雄也是名人；但更重要的是，不是所有的名人都是英雄。尤其很多人会把自己追捧的明星认为是自己的英雄，这会带来令人担忧的负面效果。比如，很多年轻人崇拜说唱歌手，认为他们是自己的英雄而去模仿他们，而说唱歌词里通常充满了歧视和仇恨女性（misogyny）的价值观。大多数说唱歌手并不是一个社会的英雄，也不该成为个人的英雄。这些名人通常有可能会因为负面的道德问题而遭到媒体曝光，从而名声扫地，所以才给人带来一种幻觉，即有了媒体就没有英雄。实际上，我们应该分清社会的英雄、个人的英雄和名人追捧之间的区别。真正对社会做出贡献的有表率意义的英雄，是不会受到媒体影响的。

参考简化思路

1. 英雄之所以是英雄，是因为他们的贡献。他们不承担道德表率的义务。
2. 个人树立自己的英雄是用他们的优秀特质来激励自己，负面新闻不会干扰个人对其英雄的选择。
3. 名人不一定是英雄，不是英雄的名人被媒体曝光的负面新闻所击倒，不能因此认为社会就没有了真正的英雄。

73

The most effective way to understand contemporary culture is to analyze the trends of its youth.

Write a response in which you discuss the extent to which you agree or disagree with the statement and explain your reasoning for the position you take. In developing and supporting your position, you should consider ways in which the statement might or might not hold true and explain how these considerations shape your position.

题目大意

理解当代文化最有效的方式就是分析年轻人的趋势。

话题背景

就看看新世纪以来的一些变化：社交媒体的兴起、共享经济的发展……这些变化都是年轻人带来的。毫无疑问，当代文化与年轻人有着紧密的联系。

审题和段落构架

1. 支持方的理由

首先，因为年轻人学习能力更快，反应速度更快，所以最新的沟通方式、信息获取方式，都首先运用在年轻人的社群当中。于是，我们从年轻人获取信息的方式中就能够看到当代鲜明的特点：信息停留时间短、追求爆炸性信息、快节奏、传播速度快，但同时，缺乏深度交流、知识碎片化……

其次，因为年轻人较少被政治、经济所限制，他们的行为更多出于自己的天性，年轻人在政治上更前卫、更进步，于是我们能看到现代年轻人积极参与环保、平权等运动，也反映出了当代社会的政治发展方向。

再次，由于年轻人对自我主体性的追求，我们能够看到如今的年轻人有着更广泛的个人追求方向，这也反映了相对于过去，当今社会变得更加多元化，具有包容性。

2. 反对方的理由

当然，当代文化不能被简化为流行文化。当代社会的一大特点是旧有价值和流行思潮的冲突。比如，如今网络发展理应让人期望更多对多元化的认识和尊重，可是近几年仍然出现了明显的保守主义在世界各地的复兴。比如，在美国，大学校园基本都是自由主义占主导的，但是，在政治选举中却是保守主义占据了上风。年轻人之所以看似主导当代文化，更多是因为他们更加显眼，而当代科技的发展使他们比以前任何时代的年轻人都有更大的话语权。但这仍然不代表他们是最具有影响力的，因为政治、经济权利并没有掌握在年轻人手中。

参考简化思路

1. 年轻人的沟通方式、信息获取方式充分反映了当代信息社会的特点。
2. 年轻人多种多样的个人追求也反映了当今社会多元化的发展方向。
3. 但年轻人并不掌握社会的真正话语权，所以他们并不是当代文化的全部。

76

76 All parents should be required to volunteer time to their children's schools.

Write a response in which you discuss the extent to which you agree or disagree with the recommendation and explain your reasoning for the position you take. In developing and supporting your position, describe specific circumstances in which adopting the recommendation would or would not be advantageous and explain how these examples shape your position.

思路近似题目：89

题目大意

所有家长都应该在孩子的学校投入时间。

话题背景

家长在孩子的学校教育中扮演什么样的角色？现代的教育体系认为，孩子的教育不是学校单方面的事情，而是学校与家长共同合作的结果。这个政策在实施过程中又会出现哪些阻力呢？

审题和段落构架

1. 重要概念

volunteer time：家长有义务在孩子的学校投入时间，包括参加多种可能的活动——家长会、运动会、毕业、表演等重要场合，甚至是参与帮助组织一些活动。

2. 支持方的理由

学校教育不单是教授知识本身，更重要的是如何帮助孩子成为有主见、能独立思考、会批判分析事物、有较强的适应能力、有基本的社会道德的人。家长和学校的合作从这个角度说就显得很重要：

首先，家长和学校可以互通有无。通过家长，学校可以更好地了解一个孩子的生活习惯和细节，制订出更适应孩子发展的培养方式；家长也能更好地了解孩子在学校的表现，促进父母和孩子间的沟通。

其次，在孩子的心理健康方面，家长常去学校有助于提早发现问题。比如，孩子在学校受到霸凌或侵犯，却因为种种原因不主动寻求家长或老师的帮助。家长常花时间在校园里能更好关注到孩子，更能留意到学生群体中存在的不良问题。这样能提早发现自闭、自卑等有可能给孩子带来负面影响的情绪，及时给孩子提供帮助。

而且，家长本身就有榜样的力量。如果家长经常参与学校举行的社会服务活动，比如为社区组织募捐、进入社区宣传疾病预防或环境保护等。父母身体力行最能感染孩子。

3. 反对方的理由

家长和老师之间存在利益的不一致。在尽力关心到每一个孩子的前提下，老师还要确保一个班级正常的学习生活秩序，处理学生间的矛盾。而在这时，家长可能更关注自己的孩子。家长会有意识地给学校提出很多偏向自己孩子的要求，比如，希望老师花更多时间在他们自己孩子身上，或要求老师在某些方面给自己的孩子特殊对待。如果家长经常去学校，这样的对话必定不可避免，从而给老师和教学带来不必要的麻烦。

参考简化思路

1. 投入时间能够增进家长与学校间的互相了解，更好地合作培养孩子。
2. 投入时间能够增进家长与孩子之间的感情，提早发现孩子存在的问题。
3. 家长和老师之间存在利益的不一致：学校更多关注整体学生；家长期待自己的孩子能有特殊对待。

> **77** Colleges and universities should require their students to spend at least one semester studying in a foreign country.
>
> Write a response in which you discuss the extent to which you agree or disagree with the recommendation and explain your reasoning for the position you take. In developing and supporting your position, describe specific circumstances in which adopting the recommendation would or would not be advantageous and explain how these examples shape your position.
>
> 思路近似题目：91, 94 & 117

题目大意

大学应该要求学生在国外学习至少一个学期。

话题背景

本题讨论教育领域中跨文化交流的重要性。虽然理念有意义，但是我们要从题目本身出发来考虑这个提议的可行性和效果。出国学习是不是对所有学生都有价值和意义？从实际角度考虑，谁来承担经费？学生会不会有语言障碍？

审题和段落构架

1. 支持方的理由

首先，通过国际学术教育，我们可以了解同领域的不同研究动向和研究方法，用新的角度来看待我们所学的东西，更能够帮助我们提升对自己所学领域的理解。尤其是如果学生所去的国家在该领域的研究更领先的时候，这种交流能够大大促进学生的学习。比如，学习生物、化学的很多学生都会选择去美国交流，美国大学的生物、化学研究相对领先，而且连实验室仪器都比其他很多地方先进；学习古典哲学的学生会考虑去德国交流，作为很多哲学大师的故乡，那里的哲学研究环境一直是世界顶尖的；而学习艺术的甚至要去全世界各个地方学习，这样才能吸收不同流派、传统所带来的灵感。

其次，国际交流也会大大提升一个学生的国际化视野，让他了解新的文化、新的语言，这在他以后进入工作岗位后会带来巨大的优势。尤其对于想要进入全球500强企业的学生，这些顶尖的跨国公司都非常看重这种全球化的视野，因为在这些公司中的很多岗位都需要不同地区之间的合作与联系，其员工需要能够尊重、理解来自不同文化的个体。

2. 反对方的理由

并不是每个行业、每个岗位都需要多种文化、多种语言，如果某个学生非常确定在自己所处的领域这些因素并不是关键因素，出国学习并不会对他带来多大的帮助。很显然有些专业是基于本国文化的，比如研究中国少数民族的人类学学生，他们的研究对象就在国内，即便可以尝试利用西方理论来解读，他们也是不需要去国外才能学习的。

更重要的是，就算国际化的视野以及不同的思维方式确实是有价值的，它的价值是否大到非要学生在本科期间抽出一个学期去完成，这是大大存疑的。教授级人物可能经常需要进行跨国交流与合作，但是本科生可能只是刚刚初学该领域的知识，最重要的事情应该是基本能力的积累。因此，这种出国活动也许会是一种本末倒置的行为。

最后就是可行性的问题，这种要求是否会得到学校的资金支持？并不是每个学校都有出国项目让所有学生都能够参与，那么在这个选择能够普及之前，剩下的学生难道还要自费出国吗？而且，出国会有语言的障碍，也并不是每个学生都能够克服这个障碍。

参考简化思路

1. 出国交流能够拓展学生的视野。
2. 出国交流也能够使学生更好地学习专业知识。
3. 但出国交流会有经济、文化、语言等多方面的障碍。

81

Claim: Any piece of information referred to as a fact should be mistrusted, since it may well be proven false in the future.

Reason: Much of the information that people assume is factual actually turns out to be inaccurate.

Write a response in which you discuss the extent to which you agree or disagree with the claim and the reason on which that claim is based.

题目大意

观点：任何所谓的事实都不该被相信，因为很可能未来会被证伪。

理由：大部分人以为是真的信息后来都被证明是不准确的。

话题背景

怀疑论的思想贯穿了人类思想的发展史，比如，笛卡尔（Descartes）的怀疑论奠定了西方哲学的基础，在他看来，要在未来建构确定的知识体系，必须对自己头脑中习以为常的每一个假设存有怀疑。他从最坚实、不可怀疑的命题（即"我思故我在 cogito, ergo sum"）起，建立了整套知识体系。事实上，怀疑精神确实是人类知识能够一直前进的根基，没有怀疑就没有错误知识的颠覆，就没有新知识的建立。

审题和段落构架

1. 题目特征

这是一道"理由—观点"结构的题目，意味着我们要先讨论理论成立与否，再讨论观点成立与否。

2. 对理由的分析

支持：所谓的真理被推翻的例子确实不胜枚举——地心说（geocentrism）、以太说（ether）、燃素说（phlogiston）。牛顿力学也被相对论力学取代、大陆漂移说也被板块运动论所取代。

反对：首先，有很多所谓的真理被推翻不代表所有真理都被推翻。数学公理、逻辑学公理仍然一直被使用，且将持续被使用。其次，很多所谓的理论被推翻，比如牛顿力学，并不是说它是错的。牛顿力学在宏观范围内仍然是有极高的精确性的，仍然应用在我们日常的工程当中，指导着我们的生活，起着至关重要的作用。

3. 对观点的分析

支持：确实，我们需要对所谓的真理保持批判精神。缺乏了这种批判性，我们人类将怠惰，知识将无法前进。这不仅限于科学领域，在社会领域一样如此，正是因为人们敢于挑战过去被默认的旧制度，我们的社会才能走向自由、平等。

反对：但是，批判精神、质疑精神不等于否定一切。无根据的反对与无根据的支持一样是无用的。真正的批判精神不是反对精神，而是理性思维。日心理论能够推翻地心理论不是因为有人不相信地心理论，而是因为新的证据更符合日心理论的描述；相对论代替了牛顿力学，不是因为有人觉得牛顿错了，而是因为实验观察符合爱因斯坦的理论预测。正确的做法是将自己的观点基于现有的证据，保持开放的态度面对可能出现的新的证据。

参考简化思路

1. 确实有很多所谓的真理被推翻了。
2. 但仍然有很多想法我们一直在坚持。
3. 正确的做法不是反对任何所谓的真理，而是将我们的判断基于现有的证据。

82

Claim: Nations should suspend government funding for the arts when significant numbers of their citizens are hungry or unemployed.

Reason: It is inappropriate—and, perhaps, even cruel—to use public resources to fund the arts when people's basic needs are not being met.

Write a response in which you discuss the extent to which you agree or disagree with the claim and the reason on which that claim is based.

思路近似题目：75

题目大意

观点：当一个国家很多民众都没有工作甚至饥肠辘辘的时候，政府不应该再给艺术拨款。

理由：当人们的基本需求都没有得到保证的时候，利用公共资源给艺术拨款是不合适的，甚至是残忍的。

话题背景

本题讨论的是艺术发展在整个国家经济中的作用。题目认为在温饱问题没有全面解决的情况下，不应该给艺术拨款，甚至还加上了从道德角度出发的评论：这样做是不合适的，甚至是残忍的。民众的温饱问题当然是政府的首要任务，但是不是必须解决温饱才能再发展艺术？这个题目有一个很重要的对于艺术的假设，甚至是偏见，即认为艺术在社会生活中的角色是纯精神享乐的奢侈品。利用这样的观点来评判当代社会经济发展是不合适的。对于这个题目的回答，我们要考虑艺术的商品化和产业化及其在国家经济发展中的重要地位。

审题和段落构架

1. 题目特征

本题是"观点—理由"型题目，遇到这种题型我们通常要单独分析观点部分和理由部分，但是这个题目略有不同，因为它并没有给出真正有内容的理由：它的理由其实简单地说就是"观点不合适"。这样一来我们在全面分析观点的同时，已经包括了对理由的考虑，因此不需要单独拆分。

2. 支持方的理由

确实，民众的温饱问题是政府工作的重中之重。如果在艺术品和生活必需品中做取舍，那必然是要先使人们的基本生活有保障。举例：在经济不发达的地区，那里可能会有加油站、小超市、早点摊，而不会看到剧院、画廊等。这就说明经济发展和建设有主次之分和顺序先后。

2. 反对方的理由

ⓐ 即便温饱问题很重要，但依然不表示必须全面解决温饱问题之后才能够发展艺术。因为这里题目的观点

假设了艺术发展对整体的经济没有贡献。这种观点依然认为艺术是一种少数人才拥有的奢侈品,而实际上艺术早已经进入人们生活的每个角落。很容易证明的是:家家户户都有艺术品,从各种工艺品到墙上的挂画或书法等。这种艺术品的普及是艺术商业化的结果,而作为一个产业,艺术为经济发展创造了巨大的价值。举例:2015年,艺术产业占美国GDP的5%。所以艺术不是人们印象中可有可无的奢侈品,它在整个经济发展中有不可取代的位置。

b 发展艺术还能在一定程度上解决就业问题。现在的就业大环境是待就业岗位少,竞争者多,所以学历和经验等在这样的就业环境中就显得十分重要。但艺术行业恰恰能规避这个问题是因为艺术行业更加看中创造力、手工能力和艺术感知能力。国家投资发展艺术会让很多在其他领域就业失败但具有很高艺术才能的人有创业的机会。据统计,美国的艺术产业基本由小型或个人企业组成,包括画廊及个人音乐工作室等。所以从这个层面说,发展艺术也能解决就业问题,也属于民众温饱问题的一个部分。

c 最后,在现代经济环境中,艺术的发展会带动艺术领域之外其他产业的发展。假设,当一个城市需要建造一个艺术博物馆,那这个工程的完成就会牵扯到与城市发展相关的很多领域。当然,我们需要艺术家本身的贡献,除此以外,还需要建筑师和工程设计师能设计出一个适合当地特质的实体建筑,需要城市规划人员参与选址,需要规划周边设施的建设,比如停车楼、公共交通、饭店等。现代艺术的发展早已不是艺术本身,它的产业化使得艺术已经融入整个经济发展的体系中。

参考简化思路

1. 民众的温饱问题是政府工作的重中之重。
2. 艺术发展是国家经济的重要组成部分。
3. 艺术发展创造了更多的就业机会。
4. 艺术发展带动了其他领域的发展。

Part 3　Issue 题库逐题精析

83

Claim: Many problems of modern society cannot be solved by laws or the legal system.
Reason: Laws cannot change what is in people's hearts or minds.

Write a response in which you discuss the extent to which you agree or disagree with the claim and the reason on which that claim is based.

题目大意

观点：很多当代社会的问题无法被法律系统所解决。
理由：法律无法改变人们内心的想法。

话题背景

枪击、恐袭、性侵，以及各种各样的经济、网络犯罪困扰着当代社会。人们不断呼唤法律体系的推进来克服这些问题，但法律真的是万灵药吗？法律绝对公正吗？法律不会变成某些人的工具吗？人性本有恶的一面，是不是外在的法律永远只能治标而不治本呢？

审题和段落构架

1. 题目特征

这是一道"观点—理由"型的题目，应该分别讨论理由和观点的合理性。

2. 对理由的讨论

支持：法律很难改变一个人根深蒂固的性格、倾向和观念。例如：男女平等宣传多少年了，很多老一辈还有重男轻女的想法，以至于抛弃女婴、买卖儿童这种法律明令禁止的事情还屡见不鲜；法律可以禁止贪污、强奸，但法律限制不了人类的贪欲、色欲，所以贪污、强奸仍然屡禁不止。

反对：以个体为单元，法律确实很难改变其根深蒂固的想法。但以一代人为单元，我们会发现，法律的意识如果从小灌输给孩子们，他们就会在长大后和其长辈有着不同的观念。例：现在年轻人对男女平等、性侵等问题的看法都和长辈普遍不一样。

3. 对观点的讨论

支持：当然有很多问题法律不可能根除，这有多方面原因。

ⓐ 先前说了，人性根本上的弱点使得某些问题只能被限制，无法被彻底根除。性欲、贪欲永远会存在，基因决定的人格问题也永远会存在，所以某些极端的犯罪现象自然会永远存在。

ⓑ 法律本身是人为制定的，背后是各种利益集团的争斗，其实它本身都不能做到完全的公正。例如：在美国枪支协会（NRA）的影响下，美国始终无法通过禁枪法案，大规模枪杀案件（mass shooting）如今仍然屡屡爆发。

c 法律的执行其实经常也不能绝对公平，这本身就是一种社会问题。有地位、有财富的人获得了最好的法律资源，即便做了违法行为，经常也可以脱罪，或者用金钱来抵消自己的刑期。但没有地位的人一辈子可能就被毁掉了。

反对：

a 法律虽然不能根除人性的恶，但能控制恶的表达，能够对恶行的出现产生震慑作用，这本身就是极其重要的。

b 虽然人们经常指责法律的不完美，但人们所提出的替代方案，比如道德谴责等，要么无法起到任何作用，要么甚至带来更糟糕的结果。例如：网络暴力下的道德谴责。

参考简化思路

1. 法律确实不能改变人心。
2. 因此，有很多问题法律确实不能解决。
3. 但，法律仍然是人类必不可少，甚至最有效、最公正的解决问题的方法。

> **85** The primary goal of technological advancement should be to increase people's efficiency so that they have more leisure time.
>
> Write a response in which you discuss the extent to which you agree or disagree with the statement and explain your reasoning for the position you take. In developing and supporting your position, you should consider ways in which the statement might or might not hold true and explain how these considerations shape your position.

题目大意

科技发展的首要目标是提高人们的效率以便他们能有更多的闲暇时间。

话题背景

人类的科技自科技革命以来一直在飞速前进，而且其加速度也一直在增加，当今社会每几年就会有颠覆性的科技出现。科技领域的领袖们一直试图让人们的生活更加便捷、高效。但这些效率是否真的能够提升人们的生活质量，让人们的生活更加幸福呢？

审题和段落构架

1. 题目特征

这道题更有特色的是 "so that" 这个结构所连接的各个部分，意味着这个题其实隐藏了三个独立判断：
- ⓐ 科技发展应该让人们的效率提高；
- ⓑ 科技发展的首要目标是要让人们拥有更多闲暇时间；
- ⓒ 效率提高能带来更多闲暇时间。

要充分分析这个话题，是需要对这三个判断进行分别讨论的。

2. 重要概念

效率：这个概念的定义可以很广，也可以很窄。在本题中，根据语境，比较方便的一种理解"效率"的方式就是："相对于同一目标，以更省时间的方式完成。"

3. 对命题 a 的讨论

科技发展显然应该让人们的效率提高，无论目标是不是带来闲暇，因为效率提高能以各种方式提高人们的生活质量。例如：流水线作业提高了生产的效率，才使得汽车能够普及到千家万户，方便了人们出行；网络大幅度提高了信息传输的效率，才使得我们能够了解到更广阔的世界。

4. 对命题 b 的讨论

支持：科技发展的一个目标当然是增加人们的闲暇时间，因为闲暇时间是人们幸福的一个重要元素。比如，网络使得老师不用面对面授课，可以在网上教授学生，这样既可以服务更多的学生，还节省了通勤的时间，获得更多自己可支配的时间。

反对：但科技发展的真正核心目标应该是让人们更幸福，而闲暇时间的长度只是幸福的一个因素，而且远远不是最重要的因素。科技以各种其他方式提高着人们的生活质量，这些都是不可忽视的重要目标：①解决疑难杂症；②享受更高品质的物质和精神生活；③消除贫困、不平等；④解决能源问题，等等。未来，我们很可能需要科技带领人类走向更远的宇宙空间，这是长远的，但仍然是非常重要的目标。

5. 对命题 c 的讨论

支持：效率表面上能够使闲暇增多，前提是工作总量不变。因为工作量一定，而效率提高，则工作时间减少，自然闲暇时间增多。在短时间内，当某种科技没有普及，而被个别企业、团体所占有时，这个团体内部的个体将会获得这种闲暇时间的短期提升。

反对：但当某种科技被普及，或者只要被几家互相竞争的企业团体所拥有时，其企业内部的人员将很难再享受这种科技带来的增加的闲暇时间。因为迫于市场竞争压力，由于所有企业的效率都增加了，大家只会维持工作时间，甚至增加工作时间，其结果是产量的增大，因此闲暇时间根本不会增长。闲暇时间的多少根本不是由效率决定的，而是由一个社会文化所决定的。例如：热带地区的国家科技水平普遍低于美国大城市，但这些国家的人民生活节奏远远低于美国大城市的白领们，因为两种人群生活在两种截然不同的文化下，和效率没有丝毫联系。

参考简化思路

1. 我们当然希望科技能增加闲暇时间，因为这会让人们更幸福。
2. 但是科技带来的效率提高并不会真的增加闲暇时间，而只会增加工作量。
3. 当然，科技还是应该提高效率的，因为它可以从多方面改善人类的生活。

87

Unfortunately, in contemporary society, creating an appealing image has become more important than the reality or truth behind that image.

Write a response in which you discuss the extent to which you agree or disagree with the statement and explain your reasoning for the position you take. In developing and supporting your position, you should consider ways in which the statement might or might not hold true and explain how these considerations shape your position.

题目大意

遗憾的是，在当代社会，创造吸引人的表象要比这表象背后的事实更重要。

话题背景

随着信息技术的发展，以及生活节奏的加快，人们似乎变得越来越没有耐心去挖掘表象背后的本质，以至于很多情况下我们的决定都是基于对表面的判断。在当代社会，表象是否真的比实质更重要呢？

审题和段落构架

1. 支持方的理由

在各个行业中，我们都会见到一个好的表象所起到的重要作用，并且从业者们也都越来越重视创造一个贴近受众的表象。

ⓐ 娱乐圈的明星们健身、整容就为了维持一个吸引人的外表。
ⓑ 政客们竞选时不谈实际的政策，各种卖人设，以此来迎合民众。
ⓒ 商业中，产品越来越重视包装，广告做得越来越精良。
ⓓ 甚至从生活来看，谈恋爱都越来越看重长相、收入等表层的标准。

总而言之，好的外表是重要的，它保证了人们还有耐心去看一个人/东西的内在。

2. 反对方的理由

但表象的吸引力只能保证人们愿意去接触对象的内在，而真正能够让人们长久被吸引的关键还是实质，永远不是表象。

ⓐ 娱乐圈最伟大的影星、歌星也都是实力派。
ⓑ 一个政客最终是否会被人们喜欢、铭记，要靠他的政策所产生的实际效果。
ⓒ 好的产品一定是在使用的便捷性、稳定性上有突出的优势，才能被人们长久接受。
ⓓ 学术界的氛围一直都是实质比表象更重要。
ⓔ 甚至在生活中，好的外表会带来最初的吸引力，但稳定的关系是和人品、性格长久联系在一起的。

参考简化思路

在各行各业，外表和本质都很重要，从娱乐圈、政治、商业等领域举例说明。

88 The effectiveness of a country's leaders is best measured by examining the well-being of that country's citizens.

Write a response in which you discuss the extent to which you agree or disagree with the claim. In developing and supporting your position, be sure to address the most compelling reasons and/or examples that could be used to challenge your position.

思路近似题目：140

题目大意

评判一个国家领导人的最好标准是去考察该国民众的幸福感。

话题背景

我们会用各种各样的标准去衡量一个领导人，比如，现在最流行的指标就是 GDP（Gross Domestic Production）。一味追求 GDP 使得领导人为了完成指标而出台各种短视的政策，带来包括环境污染在内的很多问题。即便人的钱包鼓了，生活在一个空气质量低、交通不畅、消费走高的城市里也不见得有幸福感。本论题指出，衡量领袖就要看人民是否幸福这样一个绝对的标准。那什么是幸福感呢？

审题和段落构架

1. 核心概念

well-being：生活幸福感。

2. 支持方的理由

如前所言，人们活着就是在追求幸福，而领袖存在的意义就是要帮助人们实现幸福。因此，对于一个领袖的终极评判标准，应该就是看他们是否能够让人们幸福。放眼古今，我们会发现，绝大多数名垂青史的领袖都给人们带来了幸福生活，至少是让人们的生活水平显著提高。

3. 反对方的理由

然而，这种评价方法无法避免的问题就是可操作性，如何定义以及如何衡量幸福感。它会遇到以下几个重要问题：

ⓐ 幸福是一个复杂概念，包含物质上和心理上两个层面，而每个层面也是多维度的。从个人角度来说，它包括吃穿住行的保证、爱情的获得、个人价值的实现、社会关系的稳定；从社会角度来说，它包括民主、自由、平等价值的实现。这些概念不仅主观，而且还会随着时间和当下环境发生变化。

ⓑ 幸福还存在长期和短期的问题。如果只是为了满足民众的短期幸福，国家可以开放国库，所有资源都分

配下去，竭泽而渔，牺牲国家的一切长远发展。那么，民众的幸福感在短期内会暴增。例如，北京奥运会时，为了改善空气质量，政府关闭了周边的工业工厂。但类似这样的策略是暂时性的，并有可能影响长远利益。那如果为了实现长期的幸福，很多问题的解决是需要时间的。比如环境污染、资源紧缺、教育及就业、医疗保障等，都不是一个政策就能带来改观的。那我们如何去评价一个领袖投入长期幸福的举措是对的还是错的？以及，我们如何制定一个标准来评判领袖对于长短期的平衡是合适的？

🄒 最终，我们发现不能去纠结"幸福"这样一个听起来美好，但实际上虚无缥缈的概念。我们必须给出一些可操作性的标准来衡量领袖的成就，只不过这些标准不应该是单一维度的，而且不应该是一成不变的。

参考简化思路

1. 领袖当然要追求实现民众幸福的目标。
2. 但是，幸福的评判是非常多元、主观的。
3. 幸福的评判还存在长短期的问题。
4. 所以，很难从民众是否感到幸福来评判国家领导人。

> **95** Although innovations such as video, computers, and the Internet seem to offer schools improved methods for instructing students, these technologies all too often distract from real learning.
>
> Write a response in which you discuss the extent to which you agree or disagree with the statement and explain your reasoning for the position you take. In developing and supporting your position, you should consider ways in which the statement might or might not hold true and explain how these considerations shape your position.

题目大意

尽管类似视频、电脑、网络这样的创新能改善教学方法，但是这些科技时常在干扰真正的学习。

话题背景

科技给教学带来什么样的负面影响？如何防止或减小这些影响？这些一直是教育界和社会所关心的话题。我们可以从不同的教育参与者的角度来分析科技所带来的干扰。教师如果认为科技在教学中的使用会有负面影响，那他们会举什么样的理由和例子？同理，学生、家长、学校高层管理者他们各自会如何理解科技的负面作用？教育过程中不同的参与者所关心和在意的角度是不一样的，所以这样的思考可以帮我们很好地选举论证的角度。

审题和段落构架

1. 关键词的定义

distract 是这个题目的核心词，我们可以理解为"干扰，转移注意力"。最先想到的，也是最经常讨论的例子就是电脑游戏、网络聊天等。但是 distract 在教育这个语境中的意思很广，科技带来的干扰不一定只是针对学生本身，还可能发生在课堂中。所以正如以上话题背景中所提到的，要从不同参与者的角度来思考科技可能带来的各种干扰。

2. 支持方的理由

我们当然要同意前半句，即科技提升了教学方法。这是科技最明显的优势，我们甚至可以认为科技在逐步改变传统的教育方法。这里同学们可以根据自己的领域列举你熟悉的例子，来证明科技的利用给教育带来了方便。当然，我们也可以宽泛地来说明，比如大数据库使信息获取效率高、准确性高；教师利用视频、音频、网络等多媒体教学，通过网络平台提供线上交流，教学游戏化（gamification）等。所以我们认为，科技驱动的教育(technology-driven education)有不可抵挡的趋势。

3. 反对方的理由

反对方的主要观点是，承认科技会给教学过程带来一定干扰，但这些干扰并不是科技本身的缺陷，也不表示这些干扰不可控，所以不同意题目中说的过分担心科技会带来负面影响。

首先，有人认为是科技使得很多的干扰因素让学生唾手可得，比如手游、电脑游戏、社交网络等，学生只要拿起手机，打开电脑，就会时时刻刻受到干扰。但是，这些干扰并不是科技自身所带来的。换句话说，如果没有科技，学习中依然有开小差的情况存在。注意力不容易集中的学生，没有任何外在事物的影响他也会走神、大脑放空。对于专注学习的学生，外部环境干扰再大他也能好好学习。这是为什么自律等一系列的自我修养从古至今都是教学中的一个重要环节，因为学习本身对于注意力的要求很高，所以这种技能需要培养，而不是期待外部影响自行消失。

其次，我们从教师的角度来看待这个问题。教师认为科技有负面影响，那一定是在教学过程中产生的。很多教师认为科技干扰了正常的教学秩序。比如，科技提供了无数的资源，这种没有节制的分享使得学生抄袭作业更加方便。再者，电脑等电子设备的使用干扰了正常的讨论。这个负面影响对于研讨会类型的课程(seminars) 更加明显，有老师抱怨电子设备就像是一个隔板将教师和学生分开。即便如此，我们认为这不是没有方法控制。科技对于教学虽好，但不表示我们要每时每秒都用到它。教师完全可以禁止在课堂上使用电子设备，让学生更好地关注教师和课堂讨论本身。我们从来不期待教育在一个完美的环境中开展，而且我们根据具体情况有能力制定合适的政策来减小科技的负面影响。

最后，我们从教育者这个集体出发来考虑问题。很多教育者认为科技对于真正学习的最大干扰是它干扰了"学"本身，也就是说学生过分依赖科技，使得他们不再去独立思考了。这个担忧不是没有道理，因为我们也看到了科技确实在很多方面给我们准备好了答案，我们不用再去自己琢磨。但是认为学生因此不再独立思考是对人天性中的好奇心、求知欲和探索能力的无根据诋毁。科技本身的不断更新和发展就证明了人是不断在利用自身的思维能力去进一步提升科技水平和物质世界的。在教育领域里，学生、教师和科研人员一直在利用科技的创新解决以往的问题，做新的思考和新的尝试。这里同学们可以继续找自己领域中熟悉的例子来证明科技是如何促进思考、解决问题的。

参考简化思路

1. 科技提升了教学方法。
2. 科技的干扰不在于科技本身，而在于学生注意力的缺失。
3. 科技即便给课堂讨论带来一定影响，但我们可以通过禁止电子产品的使用来控制。
4. 科技即便给人的思考带来了便利，但不能认为人因此就不再思考。实际上，科技促进了人的思维。

Part 3 Issue 题库逐题精析

97 The best ideas arise from a passionate interest in commonplace things.

Write a response in which you discuss the extent to which you agree or disagree with the statement and explain your reasoning for the position you take. In developing and supporting your position, you should consider ways in which the statement might or might not hold true and explain how these considerations shape your position.

题目大意

最好的想法来自于对普通事物的热情。

话题背景

当人们觉得一个事物普通时，他们会觉得关于这个事物，没有什么新鲜的东西值得探索；他们想知道的一切都已经知道了。然而，在实际生活中，很多人们以为自己"知道"的东西都只不过是一些先入为主的习惯意见。总有一些人敢于挑战旧有的成见，于是在这些稀松平常的事物中，他们产生了颠覆性的灵感，取得了重大的突破。

审题和段落构架

1. 支持方的理由

a 商业并不追求超越人们生活的东西，成功的商业理念通常都是能够最好地解决人们日常广泛需求的理念。尤其随着新科技的发展，人们有了更好的工具，当一个企业家敢于把这些有力的工具应用在最日常的需求中时，伟大的产品就创造出来了。Alibaba 就是想让我们足不出户买到想要的东西；Uber 就是在解决我们出行打车困难的同时，更好地利用了私家车；Facebook 初创时无非就是让 Harvard 校友交流变得更通畅；Yelp 就是让我们更好地了解别人对店铺好坏的看法。所有这一切乍一看都不是什么超乎寻常的事情，但正是因为这些企业致力于，并解决了这些普通的需要，它们才成为新一代的商业领袖。

b 艺术领域追求的是对内心真实想法的表达，只不过每一派艺术家在尝试用新的工具、新的手法来实现这一目的。Impressionism 想要展现第一眼看到眼前景象时的那种印象；Expressionism 想要通过景象来表达我们的情感；Cubism 认为当我们想到一个事物时，想到的不是它的所有细节，而是其最关键的某些元素，因此它试图通过捕捉这些元素来表现事物……没有听起来难以理解的需求，但一代一代的大师就是深度挖掘了这些想法，从而创造出万世流芳的作品。好的文学作品、影视作品也是一样的，它们会通过贴近日常生活来让读者、观众去感动。

2. 反对方的理由

但并不是每个领域都专注日常的事物。比如，物理研究也许在几个世纪前还没能充分解释我们眼前宏观的世界，但时到今日，物理学家早已穷尽了宏观维度下的物体运动问题，他们所关注的要么是肉眼看不见的微观世界中的粒子，要么就是宇宙尺度，亿万光年以外的天文现象。

149

3. 总结

其实，虽然各行各业有着其研究对象的不同，但究其根本，所有领域的突破都来自于 passionate interest，关注的无论是日常事物，还是不常见的对象。

参考简化思路

1. 艺术、商业等领域的成就通常就来自于对日常事物的研究。
2. 但是，很多科学领域主要关注的已经是非常深奥、复杂的对象。
3. 总的来说，好思想的关键不在于是日常事物还是特殊对象，而在于研究者能够对其所关注的对象拥有激情。

98

To be an effective leader, a public official must maintain the highest ethical and moral standards.

Write a response in which you discuss the extent to which you agree or disagree with the claim. In developing and supporting your position, be sure to address the most compelling reasons and/or examples that could be used to challenge your position.

思路近似题目：101

题目大意

要做一个好领导，官员们需要保持最高的伦理和道德标准。

话题背景

我们选举出能代表大众利益的官员作为领袖是因为他们的领导力，而不是因为他们有着最高的伦理和道德标准。但为什么官员一旦出现了道德丑闻就很容易因此被解雇。这说明了人们对于自己选举出来的官员有什么样的期待和要求。克林顿因为性丑闻引发的事件而被弹劾，特朗普没有因为他的种族歧视和女性歧视的言论而影响他的当选，这两个事件说明了领导人和其道德标准间有什么样的复杂关系。

审题和段落构架

1. 关键词的定义

大家不要纠结于 highest 这个词，方法论中我们提到要分析话题背后体现的现象，而不要纠结于个别词不放。在寻找观点和理由的时候，千万不要讨论 highest 的最高级形式。我们把它理解为"高的伦理、道德标准"就可以了。

2. 支持方的理由

ⓐ 大众通常视领导人为楷模，这就对领导人提出很高的要求。他们不仅需要做好本职工作，有强大的领导能力，还需要在生活的各个方面体现出高的道德标准，这样也有利于维护其公众形象。

ⓑ 当代媒体发达，领导人的个人生活也暴露在聚光灯下，这就对他们的道德标准有了更高的要求。想要隐瞒道德过失已变得很难。

3. 反对方的理由

ⓐ 这个话题假设了世界上有公认的统一的伦理道德标准，事实上，一个人的伦理和道德认知取决于他的文化、教育背景和宗教理念，而这些观念又很难妥协。举例：罗纳德·里根总统（Ronald Reagan）在位期间，没有积极采取措施解决 20 世纪 80 年代的艾滋病危机（AIDS Epidemic），也没有给医疗研究提供经费。里根政府中却有人认为以同性恋为主的艾滋病患病人群是道德出了问题。里根政府自身的道德认知导致了上万人死

亡。这说明道德标准很难统一，现实的政治状况也很复杂。

b 领导人不可能做到一直依赖高的伦理道德标准来做决定，因为他们的权力受到法律的制约。比如，大学的校长通常有较高的伦理标准，一旦发生了重要的政治事件，校长都会以邮件的形式向全校重申人道主义的价值观。学校因此也不会容忍种族歧视、性别歧视等言论的泛滥。但有些特殊情况的发生导致学校领导人不得不妥协。比如，美国白人至上主义（white supremist）的代表人 Richard Spencer 在多所公立学校发表演讲，有很多种族歧视和分裂主义的言论。即便有很多一定规模的游行反对他演讲，但是很多高校，比如佛罗里达大学不能拒绝 Spencer 租赁学校场地做演讲的申请，因为《美国宪法第一修正案》（*First Amendment to the Constitution*）规定且保护了言论自由（freedom of speech），称其是任何人都享有的平等权利。校长最后对 Spencer 的放行体现了，相对于自身的道德标准，他们的领导力更受限于法律。

参考简化思路

1. 大众通常视领导人为楷模，所以他们应该有高的道德标准。
2. 当代媒体发达，想要隐瞒道德过失已变得很难。
3. 话题假设了我们有公认的统一的伦理道德标准，事实上，一个人的伦理和道德认知取决于他的文化、教育背景和宗教理念，而这些观念又很难妥协。
4. 领导人不可能做到一直依赖高的伦理道德标准来做决定，因为他们的权力受到法律的制约。

102 Critical judgment of work in any given field has little value unless it comes from someone who is an expert in that field.

Write a response in which you discuss the extent to which you agree or disagree with the statement and explain your reasoning for the position you take. In developing and supporting your position, you should consider ways in which the statement might or might not hold true and explain how these considerations shape your position.

思路近似题目：104

题目大意

在任何一个领域，只有来自于专家对于该领域工作成果的评判才是有价值的。

话题背景

弗洛伊德和爱因斯坦曾经有过密切的书信往来，其中弗洛伊德提到他很羡慕爱因斯坦，因为他研究的是物理，而自己研究的是精神分析。弗洛伊德这么说的原因是，一个不懂物理的人不敢与爱因斯坦叫板，甚至毫无理由地觉得他的研究很了不起。但一个不懂心理学的人却敢对弗洛伊德的研究吹毛求疵地提出批评。从某个角度看，这个小故事呈现了话题中的现象：是不是只有专家的评判意见才是有价值的？回答好这个题目，我们可以从不同的领域出发，也可以从领域的发展阶段出发：哪些领域专家有绝对的发言权？领域发展到什么阶段专家的评判更有价值？哪些领域非专家或大众有发言权？在什么情况下专家做决策需要参考民众的意见和判断？

审题和段落构架

1. 支持方的理由

在一些极端专业的领域，比如理论物理、理论数学、临床医学、军事等，成果的评定也许必须要有行业内专家来进行，因为行业门槛高，需要大量的实验数据等来鉴定结论的可靠性，而外行是没有办法接触这些信息的。

2. 反对方的理由

在针对大众的领域，专家与大众的意见都是关键的，他们能够给出不同方向但同样重要的参考意见。比如制造业、服务业、媒体、教育行业，专家对于制造过程、技术环节等方面的评定很关键，但大众对于使用体验方面的评价同样重要。在艺术领域，本来就无所谓绝对的美与丑，各方的意见都是重要的，事实上，艺术领域中专家和外行的界限本来就是模糊的。在道德领域，对与错本来很可能就是人群整体意见的整合结果，对与错的概念很可能是相对的，则专家和外行的界限同样是模糊的。

3. 对上述理由的再反驳

针对支持方的理由：即便是这些极端专业的领域，由于如今存在着大量的行业交叉，该行业内的外领域专家其实仍然能够提供大量的贡献，比如数学对物理的影响、工程应用领域对理论领域的影响等。而且过去，在这些极端专业的领域，信息的不透明导致外界缺乏对它们的认知，但是现在，因为网络信息的发达，很多外行也可以对这些领域有着较为深入的接触，而他们的意见也对领域的发展、传播有着重要的作用。

针对反对方的理由：即便外行的评定是有意义的，但这个外行需要对该行业有一定深入的了解，纯粹的没有受过任何相关训练的人很难给出任何有建设性意义的意见，即便是艺术、道德等领域。比如：网络喷子们面对任何一个法律争论，只能提出"我觉得这是错的，这不是人做的。"这样的评价，没有任何理性论证，没有多少参考价值。

参考简化思路

1. 极其专业化的领域，比如自然科学、军事等领域，业内专家的意见几乎是唯一值得参考的意见。
2. 但是，很多领域针对的本来就是大众，比如媒体、服务业、制造业等，专家和大众的意见都是关键的。
3. 还有很多领域非常主观，比如艺术、道德等，根本就无所谓是否是专家，所有人的意见都是有价值的。

113

When old buildings stand on ground that modern planners feel could be better used for modern purposes, modern development should be given precedence over the preservation of historic buildings.

Write a response in which you discuss the extent to which you agree or disagree with the statement and explain your reasoning for the position you take. In developing and supporting your position, you should consider ways in which the statement might or might not hold true and explain how these considerations shape your position.

题目大意

若古旧建筑妨碍了现代城市的发展，那么对这些建筑的保护应该为当今发展让步。

话题背景

本题讨论城市建设和保护古旧建筑之间的关系。这样的老建筑可能包括百年之久却残破不堪的寺庙，或上了年代但依然被使用的民宅。它们可能存在于一个城市的核心地段，比如上海静安区的大片老宅。这样的老宅确实妨碍了部分城市项目建设，比如建高架桥或拓宽道路等，使得交通拥堵难以解决。我们需要思考的是，这些古旧建筑存在的意义是什么，且这样的意义是不是现代城市发展不能提供的。我们还需要意识到古旧建筑的保护和城市建设不一定是完全对立的，那保护它们对于城市发展有什么好处呢？

审题和段落构架

1. 重要概念

old buildings：古旧建筑。不要把题目里的 old buildings 理解为类似故宫这样重要的历史遗迹。这些标志性的建筑作为文化和历史传承的见证，当然要保护，而且它们的重要地位使得城市建设应该在保护这些遗迹的基础之上展开。很显然，没有一个国家会因为现代化建设推掉这些重要历史遗迹的。这个题目真正希望大家讨论的是有年代感的老建筑是否应该被保护。

2. 支持方的理由

很多建筑只是"旧"而不"古"，也就是说它们并不承载历史风貌，但现状却堪忧。这些建筑可能有墙体开裂、电线老化等安全隐患。如果他们又处在城市扩建的重要地带，与其保护它们，不如拆迁安置住户，对这片区域重新开发。保护古旧建筑不是保护所有老建筑，不是说只要建起来的建筑就不能推倒。我们常说因地制宜，对于城市建设也应如此，所以当老建筑出现安全隐患、妨碍城建，且并没有历史价值的时候，可以拆除。

3. 反对方的理由

1) 很多古旧建筑是历史的记忆，对于这样的建筑的保护意义在于一个国家和一个民族的长久发展需要历史所带来的凝聚力。从这个角度来说，保护古旧建筑和重要的历史遗迹的意义是一样的。从反面举例：一个没有历史的国家就很难有民族凝聚力。我们通常看到，一个刚独立的国家会面临政治动荡，多数是因为他们并没有人们可以依赖的历史。比如：哈萨克斯坦 1991 年独立后，新政府面临的难题就是协调在原地区生活的游牧民族后代和俄罗斯后代。人们由于没有共同的历史或身份认同，该国成立初期政治动荡。

2）在一个多元民族、多元文化的社会，古旧建筑体现了不同人群的文化特质，保护这些建筑不仅是保护文化多元，而且是维护社会公平、种族平等的必要措施。举例：美国的非洲裔（African Americans）居民区通常会受到来自政府"绅士化"（gentrification）的威胁。所谓绅士化，是指重建旧社区以吸引高收入人群的迁入，使得低收入的原居民被迫搬迁至更偏远的地区生活，这个措施通常发生在大城市现代化建设的过程中。通过生活在纽约的非洲裔人的抗争，市议会（city council）最终宣布哈莱姆区（Harlem，纽约市曼哈顿岛上著名的非洲裔社区）为历史性地标（historic landmark），这里的建筑也因此受到了保护。

3）保护古旧建筑能促进当地整体旅游业的发展。古旧建筑能成为吸引人的旅游景点正是因为它们能呈现历史风貌。举例：古街道、寺庙、庭院等。对于这些古旧建筑的保护和相关旅游业的开发也是整体城市建设的一个部分。比如保护一个具有历史意义的码头，除了维持它的原样，还可以在其周边建小型商业区、停车场、博物馆等，使之成为一个旅游景点。从这个角度来看，对于古旧建筑的保护不一定妨碍城市建设，反而可以促进城市发展。

参考简化思路

1. 不是所有的旧建筑都有保存的意义，当它们有安全隐患且着实妨碍城市建设，可以考虑拆除。
2. 古旧建筑反映一个国家的历史，对于民族凝聚和社会稳定有帮助。
3. 在多元民族、多元文化的社会，古旧建筑体现了不同人群的文化特质，保护这些建筑不仅是保护文化多元，而且是维护社会公平、种族平等的必要措施。
4. 保护古旧建筑能促进当地整体旅游业的发展。

> **119** In most professions and academic fields, imagination is more important than knowledge.
>
> Write a response in which you discuss the extent to which you agree or disagree with the claim. In developing and supporting your position, be sure to address the most compelling reasons and/or examples that could be used to challenge your position.
>
> 思路近似题目：99 & 100

题目大意

对于大多数职业和科研领域来说，想象比知识更重要。

话题背景

我们经常听到社会和教育界提倡不要"读死书，死读书"，而是要重视想象力和创新思维。久而久之，人们不免会产生一种没有根据的认知，即把知识和想象力放在对立面。认为知识更重要的人可能会说，没有以知识为基础的想象都是空想；认为想象力重要的人可能会说，对于知识的重视就会削弱大脑的创造力。其实我们清楚，两者都重要，两者也能相互促进。对于这题的写作，与其对比优劣，不如思考在不同领域知识和想象是如何通过合作而带来进步的。

审题和段落构架

本题总体的论点可以定为：知识的获得可以指导和促进想象及思考，想象同时能带来更多的知识。在分开论述的时候，我们可以加入不同领域的具体例子来说明。

1. 知识可以促进思考。虽然有"灵感"的存在，但不可否认绝大多数领域新知识的获得是在原有知识基础上通过想象和思考而产生的。比如在心理学领域，弗洛伊德（Sigmund Freud）开创了精神分析学科（psychoanalysis），在整个人文及社科领域产生了影响。他有关性心理成熟的理论启发了现代早期儿童教育，他的其他精神分析理论被性别研究（gender studies）、种族理论（critical race theory）等其他人文学科所借鉴，继而产生更深远的影响。这并不是一个知识创造知识的过程，而是因为有了某种知识体系，而这个体系的优势和不足都能成为新思考的动力，促使人们去通过更多的思考来完善、补充或是应用。可见，知识本身是可以促进思考的。

2. 在看似只依赖想象或感知的领域，比如艺术（the arts），知识也很重要。艺术领域看似更强调想象力和创造力，而且是不一定需要知识作为基础的想象和创造。简言之，谁都可以作画、写歌，而且谁都可以以自己的标准来评判一个艺术作品的好坏。但实际上，创作一个优秀的艺术作品需要的不仅仅是想象，更需要深厚的知识背景。比如，莫扎特（Mozart）在他的年代曾经一度被批评用了过多的音符，他回应道"一个不多一个不少。(Exactly as many as are necessary.)"虽然不需要专业训练和知识积累，一个人就能哼出一个小曲，但是要成为一个多产且有高水准的艺术家，就必须要有专业的知识作为基础。

3. 想象不仅仅是一种思考能力，它在很多领域发挥巨大作用是因为想象能够更好地帮助人与人之间的沟通。比如著名的哲学家 David Hume 曾经说过，一个人的想象能力能够转化为感观和感知（sensory experience），所以，想象可以帮助我们更好地理解他人的处境，从而帮助别人解决心理问题，提升他们的幸福感。实际上，想象能力已经成为很多心理健康及医疗领域人员的必修课。

参考简化思路

1. 知识可以促进思考。
2. 在看似只依赖创造性的领域，知识也发挥巨大作用。
3. 想象不仅仅是思考能力，还能更好地帮助人们建立人与人之间的相互理解。

121

The best way for a society to prepare its young people for leadership in government, industry, or other fields is by instilling in them a sense of cooperation, not competition.

Write a response in which you discuss the extent to which you agree or disagree with the claim. In developing and supporting your position, be sure to address the most compelling reasons and/or examples that could be used to challenge your position.

思路近似题目：128

题目大意

社会若要帮助年轻人成为未来政府、企业或任何领域的领袖，那么最好的方式是给他们灌输一种合作的意识，而非竞争意识。

审题和段落构架

1. 支持方的理由

小到一个公司，大到国家、世界，合作都是不可或缺的，而其领导者们必须要知道，仅仅关注竞争，也许可以获得一次博弈的胜利，但只有懂得合作，才能在长期博弈当中实现共赢。我们世界中的大部分博弈并不是零和博弈（zero-sum game），并不是非得你死我活的，而通过合作获得各方共赢，是一个事业能够长期稳定持续下去的关键。领袖们需要鼓励自己所领导的群体既能内部合作，也能与其他群体实现合作。

a 公司内部各部门之间就是一种典型的合作关系：运营、人力资源、物流、销售……各元素之间通常是牵一发动全身；公司与公司之间也有着重要的合作意义，公司需要和其上下游的公司形成战略合作；甚至是有竞争关系的公司之间也有合作的意义，它们要共同维护所在行业或者细分领域在社会中的形象、地位。

b 同理，一个国家，各行各业之间显然是需要合作的，例子不计其数；而国与国在很多问题上，也必须实现合作，才有可能解决全球共同面对的问题：区域稳定、缉毒、经济发展、环保……

2. 反对方的理由

但是，零和博弈的存在，使得竞争成为做领袖不可或缺的因素。成为领袖之后，也必须鼓励其公司、国家内部进行良性竞争，保持企业、国家的活力；并且，与其他公司、国家的竞争也是不可避免的。

a 在公司内部，领导岗位数量有限，不通过竞争是没有办法脱颖而出的。公司的领导也必须鼓励公司内部的良性竞争，需要知道哪个成绩是谁付出的结果，否则将会鼓励 free-riders 的存在，降低企业的产能。公司各部门之间同样也是隐性的竞争关系，毕竟企业的资源有限，能够给各部门分配的资源就更是有限的。一味妥协的部门，无法获得足够的关注和资源，自然也无法取得好的业绩。公司与其他企业的竞争也是该公司的立命之本，无须赘述。

121

b 在国家层面上，国内不同地区之间自然是有竞争的，而且是需要鼓励其竞争的，道理和公司内部是一样的。国与国之间更是在很多问题上必然存在竞争：对资本、人才的吸引，对国际政治、经济、科技发展的领导权……

参考简化思路

1. 合作意识必不可少，无论对个体、公司，还是国家。
2. 竞争意识同样必不可少，无论对个体、公司，还是国家。

123

Some people believe that corporations have a responsibility to promote the well-being of the societies and environments in which they operate. Others believe that the only responsibility of corporations, provided they operate within the law, is to make as much money as possible.

Write a response in which you discuss which view more closely aligns with your own position and explain your reasoning for the position you take. In developing and supporting your position, you should address both of the views presented.

题目大意

一些人认为，大公司有义务让它们所处的社会环境变好，提升人们的幸福感。另一些人认为，只要在法律范围内，大公司的唯一义务是赚尽可能多的钱。

审题和段落构架

1. 题目特征

题目关于双方争论，由于双方立场是直接对立的，因此这道题可以当作一个统一的话题进行正反方分析。我们暂定支持方的观点为"大公司有义务帮助提升社会环境"，反对方的观点为"大公司只需要合法赚钱"。

2. 重要概念

responsibility：义务通常包含法律义务和道德义务，但在这道题中，我们讨论的必然是道德义务。因为如果讨论法律义务，那么企业的法律义务就是，顾名思义，遵守法律，这个题目就没有讨论意义了。

3. 支持方的理由

首先，企业就像社会的每个公民一样，它们利用了社会的资源，就要维护社会的发展，而且社会的健康发展对企业也有好处。

其次，很多大公司对环境造成了巨大的破坏，修复它们所破坏的环境应该是它们义不容辞的责任。

再次，大公司做一些公益项目，也非常有利于它们的正面形象在社会中传播。

4. 反对方的理由

首先，不违法经营的公司本身就已经对社会发展做出了巨大的贡献：① 它们上缴大量的税费；② 它们创造了大量就业岗位。

其次，对于那些对环境造成破坏的公司，国家经常会额外征收重税，而这部分钱本来就应该用于保护环境。

第三，传播正面形象的目的就是为了提升企业品牌的影响力，而这最终正是为了更多的长期利润。如果企业匿名做了很多"好事"，是的，我们可以说它们很高尚，但是相对于同类企业，这些"有社会责任感"的企业就是在花费更多成本，而从长期来说它们就会在竞争中垮下来。也许有人会将谷歌与某些搜索引擎相对比来体现有社会责任感的企业和无良企业的区别。然而谷歌的成功就在于，它们做了符合社会发展的举措，也产生了非常积极的品牌效应，这恰恰有利于谷歌更长久地立足于社会；相反，无良企业短期内以牺牲社会的方式攫取了大量财富，但从长远来说它们破坏了自己的形象，这恰恰违背了长期赚钱的目标。换言之，虽然大企业有没有义务做法律规定以外的善举是值得争论的，但是事实是，现在有越来越多的人认为企业应该承担更多社会责任，这就创造了一种新的舆论环境，使得想要长期赚钱的企业制定出最佳的策略：承担起法律规定之外的一些责任，打造好的企业品牌。底线是：如果这种做法无论长短期都无法带来任何利益，那么企业当然毫无理由去做。

参考简化思路

1. 大企业占据了更多社会资源，理应承担起更多社会责任。
2. 大企业经常破坏自然环境，理应付出更多来弥补这些损害。
3. 诚然，投身公益耗费大量经费，而企业必须要赚钱才能存活。但是，承担社会责任也容易帮助大企业建立品牌形象，能够帮助企业长期更好地获利。

125 Some people believe that our ever-increasing use of technology significantly reduces our opportunities for human interaction. Other people believe that technology provides us with new and better ways to communicate and connect with one another.

Write a response in which you discuss which view more closely aligns with your own position and explain your reasoning for the position you take. In developing and supporting your position, you should address both of the views presented.

题目大意

一些人认为更频繁地利用科技导致人与人之间交流的机会减少；另一些人认为科技为我们提供了更新、更好的交流、沟通机会。

话题背景

在这个科技发展日新月异的年代，人们逐渐变得无法离开智能手机、电脑、网络等现代化的通信工具，而它们也确实大大方便了人际沟通。但同时，总有一些担忧的人们指出类似这样的现象：几个朋友一起聚会，但人人抱着自己的手机跟别人聊天，结果反而是真正的面前的朋友之间没怎么交流。于是，有人担心，现代化的沟通工具反而减少了真正高质量的交流。

审题和段落构架

1. 题目特征

这是两方争论型的题目，由于这道题的双方立场是直接对立的，因此可以当作一个统一的话题进行正反方分析。我们暂定支持方的观点为"新科技有利于人际交流"，而反对方的观点为"新科技限制人际交流"。

2. 重要概念

交流：它不仅限于点对点的交流，可以是一个人对一个人，也可以是一个人对一群人，或一群人对一群人。这种理解方式可以给我们带来更广泛的思考空间。

3. 支持方的理由

科技带来新的交流方式这是不言而喻的，重点是它是否有好处？在几个维度上，新的交流方式都有明显的巨大优势。

ⓐ 时间的灵活性：视频、语音通信都已经可以达到双方同步；e-mail、语音留言也可以实现延迟的交互，可以不妨碍对方工作和生活。

ⓑ 空间的灵活性：我们的交流不再受到距离的限制。即便我们要实现面对面交流，交通工具的普及和快捷也使得这个目标很容易实现。

c 人数的灵活性：以往的多人交流必须限制在同时间、同空间下，现在全世界不同地区的人也可以实现多人的即时沟通。

4. 反对方的理由

a 新的交流方式使得我们不再受到空间的限制，我们的交流面变得比以前广很多，则自然冲击了以往的交流方式，也间接减少了我们与某些对象之间的交流。例：网络交流增多导致对传统交流方式的依赖减少；与网上其他人的沟通，有可能会减少我们在实际生活中与他人面对面的深度沟通。

b 交流的过分通畅和廉价导致了低劣、虚假信息的爆发，使得人们根本无法筛选有价值的信息，尤其是在网络上人们可以隐藏自己的真实身份，从而躲避监管和处罚。

5. 对上述双方理由的再反驳

针对反对方的理由 a 的反驳：新的科技其实大大提升了交流质量。

a 首先，传统的交流方式并不能保证沟通质量和交流深度。过去我们的交流被血缘、地缘所决定，而不是由兴趣、价值观决定。随着网络的发展，如果我们想要寻找有共同志向、共同兴趣的交流对象，我们的机会比以前大大增加，而且这种交流其实更具有深度。

b 在现实生活中，出于各种考虑，人们经常在交流中戴上面具，反而在虚拟世界中，人们可以追求真实的自我。

c 由于信息传播的便捷，全球合作成为可能，人类知识的前进步伐更快，传播和应用也更方便。

参考简化思路

a 新技术使得交流在时间和空间上都更加灵活，大大扩展了我们的交流面和交流质量。

b 新技术确实牺牲了一些传统的交流方式和交流对象，但这完全可以被更多高质量的交流所取代和弥补。

c 新技术确实造成了一些虚假信息的泛滥，而这是未来需要努力克服的问题。

134

It is more harmful to compromise one's own beliefs than to adhere to them.

Write a response in which you discuss the extent to which you agree or disagree with the statement and explain your reasoning for the position you take. In developing and supporting your position, you should consider ways in which the statement might or might not hold true and explain how these considerations shape your position.

题目大意

妥协比坚持自己的想法更有害。

审题和段落构架

1. 支持方的理由

人生中有很多问题根本不存在所谓的唯一最优解，只是不同人有不同选择而已。在这种问题上，如果总是去妥协，去委屈自己做自己不想做的选择，自然很有可能会导致人们缺乏自信、抑郁等。比如：选择拥有什么样的个性、选择什么样的职业理想、选择和什么样的人相处等。

2. 反对方的理由

但是，还有很多问题存在所谓的对与错，那么在这些场合下一味地为了坚持己见而坚持己见是非常糟糕的。比如：公司的投资策略、科学理论的建立、一个工程的设计等。在这些问题上，当证据不符合我们现有观点的时候，正确的做法就是修正我们的看法。

3. 对上述双方理由的再讨论

针对反对方的理由：当然，这不是说要放弃自己的看法。理性思维的关键在于基于证据和逻辑做出判断，当自己的观点有充分的证据支持，坚持自己的看法自然是正确的。因此，在这种问题下，不存在绝对的坚持和绝对的妥协，一切以证据为基础才是好的选择方式。

参考简化思路

1. 在没有绝对对和错的问题上，总妥协自己就会造成个性压抑、快乐感减少，因此应该学会坚持自己的选择。
2. 但在相对客观的领域内，盲目的坚持己见就会造成严重的错误。
3. 正确的做法是学会理性思维，让自己的选择基于证据和逻辑。

> **135** Claim: Colleges and universities should specify all required courses and eliminate elective courses in order to provide clear guidance for students.
>
> Reason: College students—like people in general—prefer to follow directions rather than make their own decisions.
>
> Write a response in which you discuss the extent to which you agree or disagree with the claim and the reason on which that claim is based.

题目大意

观点：大学应该指定所有的必修课并取消所有选修课，以便能给学生提供更清晰的指导。

理由：大学生像一般人一样喜欢听从规定而非自己做决定。

审题和段落构架

1. 题目特征

这是一道"观点—理由"型题目，我们应分别分析理由与观点的合理性。

2. 对理由的讨论

支持：①在学生进入一个专业领域学习之前，他们对于该领域的了解一定是不全面、不系统的，对于应该怎么安排自己的课程才能更好地积累知识也是不清楚的，所以学校应该给予学生明确的指导。②当然有很多大学生盲从，这样的例子屡见不鲜：喜欢听别人选哪门课就选哪门课；听哪门课考试容易得 A 就选哪门课。

反对：但同样存在大量学生一直在探索自己的兴趣，寻找自己的方向。

3. 对观点的讨论

支持：如果我们知道一个学生在某个专业要取得怎样的突破需要掌握哪些知识，那么规定所有必修课也许能帮助学生省去选择的时间和精力，还能避免遗漏关键的课程或花时间在没用的课程上。

反对：首先，很多学生进入大学后并没有明确的方向，能够选择一些选修课是一个重要的探索自我的过程，很多人正是因为受益于接触了一些新的方向才找到了人生的定位。其次，就算学生进入学校的时候有了明确的专业，但这也只是一个笼统的分类。随着年级的增长，学生会有更明确的细分领域，于是即便是同专业的学生也会产生完全不同的需求，不可能规定他们都学同样的必修课程。最重要的大学课程并不是任何一门具体的课程，而是学会选择，学会做决定，学会为自己的决定负责。一次失败的决定本身就是一次重要的成长机会。如果学生不愿意选择，学校迎合了这种懒惰的心理，这才是学校最大的失职。

参考简化思路

1. 首先，学生并不愿意放弃选择权。
2. 其次，学校也不应该纵容学生不做选择。学会选择就是一门重要的课程。
3. 学校也无法替学生做选择，因为不同学生有着不同的需求。

136 No field of study can advance significantly unless it incorporates knowledge and experience from outside that field.

Write a response in which you discuss the extent to which you agree or disagree with the statement and explain your reasoning for the position you take. In developing and supporting your position, you should consider ways in which the statement might or might not hold true and explain how these considerations shape your position.

题目大意

除非能融入学科以外的知识与经验，要不然任何学科都无法取得重大突破。

话题背景

在如今的学术领域，学科之间的交叉愈发明显，根本就不存在一个独立于其他学科发展的学科，而这就是此话题想体现的现象。人们为了研究自身所处的自然环境、科技创造、人类历史、社会文化等，形成了有不同理论和方法论基础的学科。它们的形成是为了更系统、更深入、多角度地研究一个复杂的现象或未知现象，并不表示这些待解释的现象可以事先被归纳到某单一研究领域中。因此对于大多数学科而言，即便再尖端的研究课题，都需要融入其他领域的知识来解决问题，这是由物质世界和人类文明的复杂性所决定的。近年来，跨学科（interdisciplinary）学习也成为很多高校专业发展的主要方向。

审题和段落构架

1. 支持方的理由

人类知识的发展日新月异，早已不是几百年前科目之间相对独立的年代。学科之间相互影响的现象不胜枚举。

a 自然科学领域内，物理、化学、生物是对同一个自然世界不同量级的研究。传统上生物研究的最小单元为细胞，化学研究的最小单元为原子，而更微观的世界属于物理研究。这也意味着，生物需要解释细胞量级现象的本质必须依靠化学，化学要解释原子量级的现象必须依靠粒子物理，从而诞生了分子生物学（生物与化学的结合）、物理化学（物理与化学的结合）。例：很多化合物的合成看起来是一个简单的化学过程，但是要调控合适的反应条件：需要计算出精确的压强和温度，使之足够高到能够实现反应，但又要维持在设备能承受的极限内，而这就需要物理的介入。解释生物的性状本来是一个典型的生物问题，但 DNA 的发现颠覆了这一切，通过破译每种生物的 DNA 分子结构，我们实现了对生物性状的根本解释。

b 人文和社科领域中学科的互相借鉴和交流更为频繁。比如：对于亚裔美国人（Asian Americans）的研究，历史学家通过挖掘珍贵档案（archives），给出早期亚洲人移民美国的政治、经济、外交等原因。亚裔美国文学（Asian American literature）不仅能帮助文学家深度剖析亚裔的生存状态，还能从文学角度反映宏观历史事件对群体带来的切身影响。人类学家（anthropologists）通过采访（interview）、社会学家（sociologists）通过调查等方法，可以从亚裔个人和整个群体的不同层面来研究他们的生活和文化。这些学科之间的互相借鉴和依赖是必然的，他们研究成果的互相共通才能使各自对"亚裔美国人"的研究变得更加深入。

c 工程学本身的应用属性就已经决定了它必然要依赖自然科学来提供理论基础，依赖数学来提供运算工具，依赖社会研究来决定什么样的工程值得兴建。例：一座大桥的兴建离不开力学理论的支持，而其中对车流压力、风力、水力作用下的复杂计算离不开数学模型的帮助。但从根本上来说，这座桥该不该建是交通、经济、人口等各方面社会因素考量的结果。

d 很多理工、生物学科与看似毫不搭边的社会科学、艺术等也能互相结合形成新的学科，适应社会发展和探索未知的需要。比如工业设计（industrial design）结合了材料学（material science and engineering）和艺术设计，优化一个产品的功能、价值和外观。神经科学（neuroscience）结合了生物学、生理学（Physiology）、数学建模（mathematical modeling）和心理学，通过对神经的研究来更好地理解人的行为和心理活动。

2. 反对方的理由

数学、逻辑学是非经验学科（non-empirical subjects），意味着其公理、定理的成立与否是独立于物理世界存在的——即使所有自然科学的理论都是错的，也完全不会影响数学、逻辑学定律的成立与否。

3. 对上述双方理由的再反驳

对反对方理由的反驳：数学规律的真假不依赖于别的学科，但数学规律的发现受到其他学科发展的影响。首先，大规模的计算已经无法脱离计算机科学的发展。更重要的是，其他学科的发展对数学的发展提出了要求，而当数学理论在这些学科中有了应用之处时，相关数学理论也就会得到更多人的重视，更容易得到发展。例：爱因斯坦相对论的提出促进了高维几何的发展，如今弦理论（string theory）从根本上也对数学工具提出了极高的要求；保险业的发展带来了精算学（actuary）的前进。

参考简化思路

1. 在自然科学中，理化生不分家。
2. 在人文领域中，文史哲不分家。
3. 工程领域自然需要自然科学和数学的支持。
4. 就算是数学这样看似独立的学科，也需要其他领域发展的反作用来促进其应用。

137. True success can be measured primarily in terms of the goals one sets for oneself.

Write a response in which you discuss the extent to which you agree or disagree with the statement and explain your reasoning for the position you take. In developing and supporting your position, you should consider ways in which the statement might or might not hold true and explain how these considerations shape your position.

题目大意

一个人成功与否的主要评判标准要参考他为自己设定的目标。

话题背景

在当今社会中,"成功"成为我们最常见到的一个词语,年轻人每天都在接受各种"成功学"的洗脑。然而,什么才叫成功?我们似乎并没有一个明确的定义。这个话题就是在促使我们去反思到底什么才是我们自己心中的成功。

审题和段落构架

1. 重要概念

本题中唯一重要的争议概念就是成功,但这与其他题目中的重要概念不同。在其他题目当中,我们会选择我们所使用的定义,并按照这个定义往下写。而在这篇文章中,我们就是要讨论它的定义,所以恰恰不能直接预设一个定义,否则就成了循环论证。整篇文章我们都要去探索"成功者"所具有的特点。

2. 支持方的理由

在当代社会,我们越来越接受"实现自己心中的目标才算成功"这个说法,这其实与现代社会的价值观有着密不可分的关系。在和平年代以全球化和经济发展为主题的社会现状下,我们有更多的自由去发展个人的特长,我们不再那么需要把自己的成功与传统意义中的"社会成就"绑定在一起。我们不非得追求成为政治家、思想家、科学家、明星等,我们就想拥有幸福的家庭、健康的身体,如果我们做到了,也会觉得自己很成功。与此相反的是,很多别人眼中的"成功者"并不觉得自己成功,因为虽然他们获得了地位、金钱和名誉,但付出了无法弥补的代价,比如家庭和健康。

3. 反对方的理由

以自身目标为成功的评判标准是有限度的,其底线是至少有利于社会的发展。社会希望家庭和谐、人们健康快乐,所以每一个个体追求的这些目标需要被社会普遍接受。但显然不是任何一个个人目标的实现都会被视为成功,比如反社会心理的实现就显然不会被视为成功。因此,"成功"的定义必然包含社会性。

其次,人们评价自身的"成功"时,经常以一种非常宽容的视角来对待,即实现自身的目标。但在评价他人成功时,尤其是在集体视角下,人们仍然不可避免地要以一些统一的标准来评判,比如其对社会产生的价值、社会和经济地位、名声等。而这是很合理的，因为我们定义的毕竟不是"幸福"，而是"成功"。幸福不幸福是自己说了算的，但成功不成功不是一个单一视角的判断。

4. 对上述双方理由的再反驳

针对支持方理由的反驳："自身设定的目标"本身也是一个简化了的概念。人们并不总是知道自己想要获得什么；由于欲望的膨胀、身边环境发生变化等因素，很多时候先前预设的目标即使实现了，也不会给行为主体带来自我成功的感觉。他们甚至会认为自己并不成功，因为这其实不是他们自己想要的东西。

参考简化思路

1. 在现代社会，成功者当然要实现自身的目标。
2. 但成功离不开实现自身的社会价值。
3. 总结：成功本身就是一个复合概念，它包含了个人性和社会性的结合。

139

The best test of an argument is the argument's ability to convince someone with an opposing viewpoint.

Write a response in which you discuss the extent to which you agree or disagree with the statement and explain your reasoning for the position you take. In developing and supporting your position, you should consider ways in which the statement might or might not hold true and explain how these considerations shape your position.

题目大意

一个论证好坏的最好评判方式就是看该论证是否能够说服持有对立观点的人。

审题和段落构架

1. 重要概念

argument 指的是"论证"。

2. 支持方的理由

论证的目的就是为某个观点提供依据，从而说服他人。所以，能否真的说服他人看起来应该是最直接的评判标准。

3. 反对方的理由

事实上，很多好的论证因为各种原因并不能够真正说服其他人，而糟糕的论证恰恰经常被人们接受。一个完备的论证（sound argument）在学术领域有着严格的定义，即它所依赖的所有前提都是成立的（true premises），以及它的推理过程在逻辑上是有效的（valid reasoning）。然而，最终，完备性既不能成为它说服别人的充分条件，也不能成为必要条件，这其实非常可悲。接下来我们详细分析是什么原因造成这一点的。

ⓐ 人的知识、智力因素：对一个在某领域无知、完全没受过基本训练的人，提供专业的论证过程基本没有任何意义。反而，充满专业术语的论证经常会被外行排斥。

ⓑ 人的情感因素：人们喜欢接受符合自己情感的观点，而完全无视论证过程本身的合理性。这种例子太多了：老年人，特别是疾病缠身的老年人，会相信没用的保健品；大多数人都相信自己孩子的智力是高于平均水平甚至是超群的；现在有非常多的网络推文打着鼓吹女权的旗号在背后推崇消费主义，然后广为受捧；只要是骂敌国的文章，基本都获得人们的喜欢……

ⓒ 人的利益因素：在政治对话中，也许政客自己都不相信自己的政治主张，但为了自己的政治利益，仍然坚持自己的政策。遗憾的是，这就是成年人的世界。人们追求的不是真理，而只是利益。

而更加糟糕的是，论证的制造者为了说服别人，经常会诉诸一些论证技巧来迎合别人，但恰恰他们的论证充满了逻辑谬误（logical fallacies），比如诉诸人们的情感（appeal to emotion）时，会产生滑坡谬误（slippery slope）、稻草人谬误（strawman fallacies）。这些通常是深谙人们心理的说话者所使用的技巧，他们非常善于说服他人，但其实他们的逻辑是经不起推敲的。

4. 对上述双方理由的再反驳

对反方观点的评价：当然，我们应该考虑听话者的智力水平、心理状态，所以我们应该制造出友好的论证，前提是我们的论证在逻辑上是严谨的。

参考简化思路

1. 理想情况下，好的论证应该能够说服对方。
2. 但是人是非理性的，经常不愿意接受不喜欢的观点。
3. 人的智力水平和知识水平也会限制人们对对方论证的理解。

144 The best way to solve environmental problems caused by consumer-generated waste is for towns and cities to impose strict limits on the amount of trash they will accept from each household.

Write a response in which you discuss the extent to which you agree or disagree with the claim. In developing and supporting your position, be sure to address the most compelling reasons and/or examples that could be used to challenge your position.

题目大意

解决消费者产生的垃圾所带来的环境问题的方式是城镇严格限制每家每户收集的垃圾。

话题背景

垃圾处理是让很多国家头疼的问题，各国也有不同的对应政策。比如日本对垃圾做了极其严格的分类要求，包括以何种形式丢弃或回收垃圾都有明确的规定，因此日本的垃圾回收率达到了90%之高。美国加州在2018年底也正式禁止了塑料吸管的使用，从生产的源头试图减少不可降解垃圾的产生。这个题目试图考虑"控制家庭生活垃圾的数量"能否达到解决减少垃圾排放的效果。

审题和段落构架

1. 支持方的理由

毫无疑问，这种做法在一定程度上能限制消费者产生垃圾的数量。

ⓐ 它会鼓励消费者进行更多的回收处理，很多时候人不做回收就是因为嫌麻烦。

ⓑ 它也会鼓励消费者尽量少产出无法回收的垃圾，人们选择使用一次性用品的可能性会大大降低。

2. 反对方的理由

但是它的作用是有限的，有如下几个原因。

ⓐ 政府不可能说超过了上限的垃圾就完全不收，而应该是对超过的部分进行收费。然而，其实对经济富裕的家庭并不会造成显著影响；相反，没钱的人产生的消费垃圾相对较少。而且，这个政策可能会逼迫人们把垃圾丢到公共区域，增加市政环保部门的压力。

ⓑ 操作起来，这个政策也有一定的模糊性。每个家庭的人数是不一样的，那么一个大家庭产生的垃圾量会远超过一个小家庭产生的垃圾量。

ⓒ 这个问题背后的根源是当代的消费主义（consumerism）。大量的媒体广告鼓励人们不断更新自己的消费品，鼓励人们不断追求自己想要的东西，而不是满足于自己真正需要的东西。因此，这个政策只是治标不治本。政府真正需要做的是：①对生产方进行限制，比如采用更为环保、可以回收的材料；②制定相关政策，比如禁止塑料吸管的供应、对塑料袋的使用进行收费等；③改变人们的消费理念：不仅仅考虑自己的喜好，而且要考虑自己的行为对环境产生的影响。

3. 对上述双方理由的再反驳

针对反对方的理由 b：垃圾上限可以取决于家庭当中的人数。

参考简化思路

1. 这个做法当然可以在一定程度上减少消费者所产生的垃圾量。
2. 但它的影响很有限。
3. 根本的解决方法必须是改变人们的消费理念。

145 We learn our most valuable lessons in life from struggling with our limitations rather than from enjoying our successes.

Write a response in which you discuss the extent to which you agree or disagree with the claim. In developing and supporting your position, be sure to address the most compelling reasons and/or examples that could be used to challenge your position.

题目大意

我们人生中最重要的一课，不是通过享受成功，而是通过与自己的局限抗争而学到的。

审题和段落构架

1. 重要概念

limitations：我们很容易想到的是能力上的缺陷，这是一种内在的限制，但其实还有社会给我们添加的外在限制。我们如果不能做到社会给个人带来的期待是不是就表示我们自身就有缺陷呢？这是值得讨论的。

2. 支持方的理由

首先，认识到我们能力上的缺陷，在某些人当中能够激发出前所未有的动力去战胜这种缺陷。比如，Lady Gaga早年被认为不够漂亮，不可能走红，于是她只能一直混迹在二流的演出表演当中。但这种困境激发了她强大的能量，去超越所谓相貌对她带来的限制，无论是通过假发和服饰打扮自己，还是去展现她在创作上、音色上的真正天赋。她成为划时代的巨星。我们不用非得去看明星，身边一个个减肥成功的朋友，一个个从学渣变学霸的案例其实都是一样的，在这种翻身的过程当中，我们都能意识到自己前所未有的能量的存在。

但，鸡汤并不总是奏效的。有些时候，局限就是客观存在的，在竞争极其激烈的领域中，尤其是如果天赋条件不可或缺时，意识到自己存在天赋上的巨大缺陷，而且很可能是努力不能弥补的，这种打击可能是非常致命的。但是，这种自我认识也是一个重要的契机，让我们意识到我们需要去寻找自己真正擅长的方向，能够真正体现自己特点的方向。爱因斯坦从不擅长文学，他小时候经常因语言类的课程被嘲讽，但这更使得他会关注擅长的东西——数理。爱因斯坦不需要克服自己语言课程的弱点，他只需要发挥自己的天赋就够了。

限制不仅仅是自身的，还来自于外界。社会的习俗、文化一直都在对其中的个体施加镣铐，比如曾经对女性、黑人、同性恋、残疾人……人们被规定有些事情是男人应该做的，而另一些事情是女人应该做的。但就有强大的个体敢于去反思，去挑战这些先入为主的社会偏见。他们意识到，这种外在的约束并不是必然存在的。挑战这些约束，就塑造了更强大的人，更推动了社会向平等、多元方向进步。

3. 反对方的理由

当然，成功也是有教育意义的，它给我们带来自信，让我们更加确定自己的优势，给我们带来未来可以参考的经验。

4. 对上述双方理由的再反驳

针对反对方理由的讨论：但成功更可能带来自满，会让人停滞不前，让人脱离现实；而困境中，我们更能够警醒、冷静，去反思我们所需要做出的变化。一成不变，我们是无法进步的，而绝境中的革新是我们取得突破的关键。

参考简化思路

1. 面对困境，一些人会爆发出前所未有的能量去克服挑战。
2. 面对无法逾越的瓶颈，我们会寻找新的突破口，去真正认识自己的特点。
3. 面对外在习俗的约束，我们会打破这种偏见，变成更强大、独立的自我，甚至推动社会的进步。
4. 当然，从成功中我们也可以获得值得延续的经验。

解密GRE写作
论证思维

Part 4 Issue 精选范文

Part 4　Issue 精选范文

> **1** To understand the most important characteristics of a society, one must study its major cities.
>
> Write a response in which you discuss the extent to which you agree or disagree with the statement and explain your reasoning for the position you take. In developing and supporting your position, you should consider ways in which the statement might or might not hold true and explain how these considerations shape your position.

Sample Essay A: Outstanding

　　This prompt points to a general perception that major cities are truly the epitome of a society's characteristics, endeavors, and aspirations. Indeed, like an international tourist, one needs to look no further than the major cities to grasp a superficial understanding of the society as a whole. However, as I will elaborate, they are not adequate to emblematize the society if we contextualize the discussion in the current, heavily globalized world. Moreover, the relationship between major cities and their societies will be further complicated by considerations of cultural diversity and preservation.

　　We cannot be negligent of how much major cities can tell about their societies. Because of established material prosperity, they become the predominant space which houses the country's intellectual, commercial, cultural and social activities. For example, universities and research institutions often congregate in major cities because their physical proximity allows academic collaborations as well as the share of resources to produce fruitful scientific achievements; profit-driven businesses are likely to gather in major cities for larger markets; cultural properties such as art workshops, museums, and galleries usually cluster in major cities not only to preserve the nation's cultural and historical heritages, but also to cater to the diverse range of aesthetic tastes; social movements, whether grassroots organizations promoting social equality or political coalitions aiming for a change of policies, often take place in major cities for wider influence. From these perspectives, the study of major cities can offer a sneak peek into where the country stands in many aspects of its history and contemporary development.

　　However, no single country is exempt from the effects of the notorious globalization, and major cities are the first ones within a society to take the blows. In other words, globalization is acutely visible in major cities. For one thing, globalization allows a free flow of merchandise, technology, and capital, which drastically impacts regional economies, policy-making and urban planning, so much that major cities end up appearing similar across different countries. For example, foreign direct investment has resulted in booming erections of new infrastructures in and on the outskirts of major cities, making skyscrapers the hallmark of major cities around the world. For another, globalization also mobilizes international labor and intellect into major cities by creating more career opportunities, which has not only made job markets extremely competitive, but also transformed major cities into multicultural, multi-religious and multilingual global cities. As a result, we come to a crude stereotype about life in major cities: in the concrete jungles with constant traffic, people with diverse cultural backgrounds work through sleepless nights in the hope of upward mobility. Hence, globalization

178

offers an adequate explanation for such similarities of outlook and cultural life in major cities across the world. As globalization continues to **strike** every corner of the world, it becomes more and more difficult for major cities to uniquely exemplify their country's original characteristics.

Regardless of the **homogenizing** effect of globalization on major cities, one nevertheless needs to study less developed or rural areas of a country to understand its important characteristics. It will be reductionist and appealing to cultural **hegemony** to argue that the study of major cities is sufficient to **capture** the country's characteristics, since a diverse range of minority cultures speaks volumes about the country's history, traditions, and values, and how it has developed throughout the years. In addition, many isolated minority cultures are specific to their original localities and greatly resistant to external influences such as cultural imperialism, where dominant cultures seek to **encroach** and **eradicate** them; this means that we cannot study major cities in the hope of finding traces of minority cultures. In a nutshell, we should **incorporate** the study of areas besides major cities to better and more fully appreciate a country's cultural diversity and heritage, which are integral to its important characteristics. For example, Mosuo people, one of the world's last few **matrilineal** societies residing in southwest China, practice a non-monogamous marriage system. A careful study of Mosuo culture will contribute to our understanding of China's diverse marriage systems, agricultural life, and social values that we will not be able to grasp from studying only major cities. In this way, minority cultures' significance in shedding light on a society's traits is prominent, particularly when globalization has watered down major cities' exemplarity of the society's characteristics.

If we were to **embark on** an endeavor to explore and understand a society, we could start from gathering knowledge about its major cities, which not only gives us insights about the country's history and development but also how effectively it is dealing with the influence of globalization, but then we need to research the society's cultural diversity by reading widely about the localized knowledge of its cultural heritages.

Words & Expressions

epitome *n.* 缩影
endeavor *n.* 努力
superficial *adj.* 表面的，肤浅的
emblematize *v.* 象征，标志
contextualize *v.* 把……置于（某种）背景下
predominant *adj.* 主要的，首要的
congregate *v.* 聚集
proximity *n.* 邻近
collaboration *n.* 合作
profit-driven *adj.* 逐利的

cater to 迎合
coalition *n.* 联合
exempt from 免于
notorious *adj.* 臭名昭著的
merchandise *n.* 货品
outskirts *n.* 市郊
hallmark *n.* 标志
crude *adj.* 粗糙的
stereotype *n.* 刻板印象
concrete jungle 钢筋混凝土堆砌的大城市

strike *v.* 攻击，袭击
homogenize *v.* 使……同质化
hegemony *n.* 霸权
capture *v.* 捕捉
encroach *v.* 蚕食
eradicate *v.* 根除
incorporate *v.* 包含，吸纳
matrilineal *adj.* 母系的
embark on 着手

Sample Essay B: Good

Where do we start when we want to learn about a new society? For the speaker, the answer seems very clear: we should look at its major cities. While the cities shed light on many important aspects of a society, I argue that the lesser-known areas are still not to be overlooked.

For starters, it would be silly to understate the value of major cities in displaying important traits of a society. Just look at New York. When the American economy was down, New York was the first to feel the chill: bankrupted businesses, jobless people, and empty stores. New York is not just the financial center of America; it is also its cultural center. Being labeled as one of the most diverse countries in the world, America embraces people of all ethnicities and colors in its society, as can also be vividly displayed on New York's streets. New York does not care where you're from. You can be American, Hungarian, Thai, Chinese, Ethiopian, or Nigerian, but you can still be a New Yorker.

However, it is exactly because big cities catch the spotlight that they tend to display only the things under the spotlight. When one thinks about American culture, one easily relates to Hollywood images and Billboard hotlists. These belong to contemporary pop culture. But the American countryside has also had its share of contribution: country music. Maybe one would say that we still get to see country music performances in big cities. Yes, you see country music stars like Blake Shelton and Keith Urban, who probably never had a day of work in the barn. The authentic country music belongs to the real experiences of real working countrymen; it is more than just a highly commercialized pattern of notes or a meaningless juxtaposition of words like "cold beer, dirt road, or pickup truck" that supposedly symbolize country life.

Likewise, city dwellers often tend to hold different cultural values from country residents. If you go to New York, you may be under the illusion that the whole of America embraces the values of diversity and liberalism. You would be oblivious to the fact that there is a vast part of America that is conservative and holds many traditional values. This is not to judge which value is preferable; rather, I am here to argue that neither large cities like New York nor minor places can represent what American people believe in. To try to find one place that displays what is innately heterogeneous is in itself, a futile practice to begin with.

Overall, understanding a society takes more effort than just looking at these major cities. While this is an important step, it is just one step among many before gathering enough information about that society.

> **3** Scandals are useful because they focus our attention on problems in ways that no speaker or reformer ever could.
>
> Write a response in which you discuss the extent to which you agree or disagree with the claim. In developing and supporting your position, be sure to address the most compelling reasons and/or examples that could be used to challenge your position.

Sample Essay A: Outstanding

We hear speeches from speakers and reformers every day. A political speaker addresses the country's economic growth; a political reformer talks about his plan of building reciprocal relations with other countries. An academic speaker reflects on seeking effective means to increase students' well-being; an academic reformer envisions future education that is more inclusive, and offers equal opportunities for every student. A business speaker shares experience of how to be a successful entrepreneur; a business reformer ponders new forms of businesses that would likely increase employment rates. Communications like these are useful in creating rich and thought-provoking dialogues that propel the development of every aspect of a society.

Unlike speakers and reformers, scandals draw the public's attention because their breakouts indicate a breach of moral standards or legal regulations, and the public demands immediate solutions. Since Richard Nixon and many officials involved in the infamous Watergate scandal were lawyers, the public questioned the integrity of the entire lawyer community in the United States. As a response, the American Bar Association established a stricter code for conduct and required all future law students to take courses in professional responsibility. Examples like this suggest that the breakout of a scandal reveals the loopholes in a presumably well-structured system undergirded by both laws and moral conscience. The effect, thus, is tremendous since scandals are an assault on widely accepted and cherished ethics that everyone is expected to abide by.

Sexual scandals, especially the ones that involve sexual harassment and assault, are useful because they empower many victims to stand up so that society becomes aware of the severity of the problem. For example, the popular "Me Too" movement stems from a horrendous sexual scandal in the film industry—in October 2017 more than a dozen women accused Harvey Weinstein of sexually abusing them. What's astonishing about this outbreak is that the subsequent investigation revealed his 30-year history of sexually abusing over 80 women. This case shows the difficulty in confronting one's sexual abusers because of their social status and power, and because of the tremendous amount of shame the victims feel that prevent them from reporting their abusers. The "Me Too" movement then is a timely response that encourages victims to speak up about their traumatic experiences of being abused so the community can be formed, and justice can be served.

However, ever-developing technology and media have made it seem like scandals are everywhere. Unlike years ago when the circulation of scandals were relying on gossiping, telegrams, or newspapers, contemporary scandals can be spread worldwide on social media within seconds. Consequently, scandals routinely appear and become a component of everyday life, which inevitably minimizes their effect of drawing the public's attention. This is not because scandals cease to be problematic, nor because they no longer represent a matter of crisis or a sense of urgency; instead, it shows how the public has become numbed by the multiplication of political and social problems. In this sense, it's sad to see that scandals are getting more frequent and getting worse, but less and less likely to draw the public's attention.

Adding to the problem of scandals' ubiquity, people fabricate scandals in order to defame their competitors, which is conspicuously true in contemporary politics. When it comes to presidential elections, for example, media tirelessly offer coverage not of candidates' plans for economic development, adequate social welfare, health care, or education reform, but the opponents' alleged "scandals". They abuse scandals to mean anything negative that might harm the reputation of a person to the extent that we can argue that elections often resemble a staged farce. We need to reclaim the word "scandal" to retain its meaning, and its function of reiterating a society's fundamental ethical and moral values. We do not want to see scandals happen, but when they happen, we want to give them full attention so that we can adequately address problems that these scandals reveal.

Words & Expressions

breach *n.* 违背
infamous *adj.* 无耻的，声名狼藉的
abide by 遵守
horrendous *adj.* 可怕的，令人震惊的
subsequent *adj.* 随后的

timely *adj.* 及时的，适时的
fabricate *v.* 捏造
defame *v.* 诽谤
staged *adj.* 编排好的，有组织的
farce *n.* 闹剧

Sample Essay B: Good

The prompt claims that scandals, by focusing our attention on important issues, are useful tools for modern society. I absolutely agree that our attention is often drawn to all the dark secrets revealed by the powerful and omnipresent mass media, but I remain skeptical of the alleged contributions these scandals bring to our world.

I don't think many people can deny the power of an eye-catching scandal. When Tiger Woods was reported to have multiple mistresses, the news went viral. Or when Bill Cosby's sexual assault was revealed, he became the topic of discussion everywhere. Or the very recent scandal of American college enrollment—I was reading it just a few hours ago on my cellphone. The public loves scandals, and the media loves giving them out. Especially given the development of social networks, scandals spread much faster than ever, so they reach a much wider audience than before.

But are these scandals really useful? How can we right the wrong, when the wrong is unknown, one might argue. Supposedly, scandals help reveal otherwise hidden injustices in the world, and this should be at least the first step towards bettering the society. As far as I can remember, whenever a corrupt official has been discovered, the government temporarily initiates an anti-corruption process that reduces malfeasance within the system. Temporary salvation, that's the best we can get.

Turning on our cellphones every day, chances are we will see a new scandal, whether it's an affair, corruption, rape, or drug deal. Scandals are so common that modern people easily become oblivious. Yes, scandals still catch attention, but for no more than a couple of days. The crowd gets furious for 48 hours, and then they become excited about some other stuff. If you're a celebrity worrying about your secret affair being released, your best chance is to sleep through the night, and tomorrow is going to be a better day for you, well, unless you want the exposure. No problems are going to be solved whatsoever.

What's worse is that the media actually fabricates stories to create scandals, so much so that it's hard to distinguish what's important and what's not. People become indulgent in personal attacks, and forget about the real issues. Just recall the latest presidential election. What a joke! Liberal and conservative media took turns picking on the opponents' character flaws, while the real issues were being evaded. Wait, what were the real issues? I only recall Clinton's email problems and Trump's sex and tax and Russian scandals. Wow! There were a lot of them. I even started to suspect that the two sides were collaborating to entertain me with these sensational stories so that I wouldn't question the fundamental injustice of our society.

I think my stance is quite clear. I myself am often drawn to scandals, so I must congratulate the media for successfully manipulating my attention. But I think they are the virus of modern society.

Part 4 Issue 精选范文

> **11** Universities should require every student to take a variety of courses outside the student's field of study.
>
> Write a response in which you discuss the extent to which you agree or disagree with the claim. In developing and supporting your position, be sure to address the most compelling reasons and/or examples that could be used to challenge your position.

Sample Essay A: Outstanding

The prompt argues that universities should make it mandatory for students to take courses outside of their fields. This is an important suggestion in several regards. First, this policy has its grounds in pragmatism. Although academics in universities and colleges are structured in ways to create graduates specialized in various fields who go into the corresponding job positions or higher-level research institutions, the reality is far from the ideal. In fact, many countries are facing the undesirable process of educational inflation where colleges and universities are producing more job candidates than available positions, so much so that college degrees no longer guarantee the security of employment, which is further worsened by the condition of the waning economy. Reality sinks in where, for many, college education nowadays means to learn a great deal to be able to hold down part-time jobs and pay the bills. With a transcript that not only shows an eye-catching GPA, but also a wide range of skillsets from taking a reservoir of diverse courses, students are more likely to obtain employment in the ever-demanding job market. From this perspective, having students take various courses seems to be an expedient way to deal with the dismay of employment.

Second, by arguing that universities should require students to take courses outside their fields, this prompt essentially values interdisciplinary education as productive, and believes that taking classes across various fields is an effective way to achieve that. Evidently, the rigid divisions of conventional fields of studies have been constantly challenged by modern college educations, and more and more academic programs have been restructured to cater to the needs of interdisciplinary studies of different sorts. For example, beyond the already common collaborations between fields such as business and mathematics, and anthropology and performance studies, we also witness unusually innovative interdisciplinary partnerships between the arts and technologies, between statistics and the humanities, and so forth. This is an inevitable trend in the evolution of college education, because interdisciplinary perspectives have offered us refreshed ways to critically examine our societies and the world. Thus, colleges and universities have an ineluctable responsibility to encourage interdisciplinary studies.

Here, one might challenge my position and argue that colleges also aim to produce advanced researchers whose projects are narrowly focused, and thus, hardly interdisciplinary, so a college-wide policy of taking outside courses will be unnecessary to educate experts. This might be true if we are talking about theoretical mathematics, but for many other fields, advanced research is not only built upon, but also benefits from its interdisciplinary collaboration with other fields. For example, in advancing our knowledge about cultural differences, psychologists and anthropologists resort to neuroscience to investigate whether certain cultural traits, including people's use of language and moral standards can be explained by neurobiological activities. This emerging field of cultural neuroscience suggests that, even though an individual researcher's project might end up being within a certain discipline, it is crucial that students develop interdisciplinary awareness and research skills, since a field's progress as a whole cannot happen without interdisciplinary work.

However, the question remains whether making outside courses mandatory for students is the optimal option to cultivate interdisciplinary education. On the one hand, the current development of interdisciplinary education determines that taking outside courses is presently the best way to acquire interdisciplinary training. At the moment, as many interdisciplinary fields only start to burgeon, it's unlikely to have an independent, well-developed academic department that focuses solely on its interdisciplinary field. For example, it's not yet common to see digital humanities programs in universities because of the field's demanding difficulty, for this field may require the expertise of statisticians and skills for using data processing tools such as R, as well as knowledge of literary theory and a sensibility for aesthetic appreciation. While universities will surely have more and more experts of digital humanities *per se*, before that happens, taking courses individually from conventional programs, in this case statistics and literary studies, seems to be the best way for students to receive necessary training, so as to better engage in their interdisciplinary research.

On the other hand, the deficiency of this policy is that it requires strong autonomous motivation from students themselves to actively develop and engage in an interdisciplinary consciousness. Take the current general education system in the US for example, where students take a variety of courses because they are required to do so; they do not necessarily see this as an opportunity or experiment to tease out the potential connection between outside courses with their own fields. Many students would even seek out "easy" outside classes to take so that they don't have to spend much effort on them. Thus, although I agree that taking outside courses is beneficial in many ways, how effectively this policy carries out its intention of interdisciplinary training remains a big question mark.

Words & Expressions

mandatory *adj.* 强制的	expedient *adj.* 方便的	cultivate *v.* 培养
pragmatism *n.* 实用主义	dismay *n.* 灰心，沮丧	burgeon *v.* 萌发
inflation *n.* 膨胀	rigid *adj.* 死板的，严格的	*per se* 本身
transcript *n.* 成绩单	ineluctable *adj.* 无法逃避的	autonomous *adj.* 自治的
skillset *n.* 技能组	optimal *adj.* 最佳的	tease out 梳理出
reservoir *n.* 池		

Sample Essay B: Good

Almost every university in the modern education system requires students to take courses beyond their own major fields of study. This pervasive phenomenon itself should suggest, if not guarantee, that there are good reasons for learning additional subjects. In this essay, I shall try to illuminate the rationale behind it.

For starters, today's academic circle has seen a growing connection between what used to be relatively separate fields of study. The arts heavily rely on technology; businesses are built on mathematical models; philosophy makes use of advances in neurological study; even the field of humanities is witnessing the rise of "digital humanities", a branch that incorporates statistical analysis. Simply put, whatever field one is in, that field is going to depend more or less on the advance of other related disciplines, so its practitioners had better build a wider repertoire to be fully prepared.

Second, life is a long journey with many unexpected twists and turns. In college, it is just impossible to imagine all the unpredictability lying ahead. What one currently studies may not necessarily be their eventual career path. Tools that seem immediately irrelevant may end up becoming her bread and butter. It is just so common today that a student graduates from school and never does anything related to her undergraduate major ever again. Learning other courses provides a student with new inspirations that may completely change her future.

However, some people may argue that there will be students who have already decided for sure what they would want to do later in their lives, so learning anything else would be a waste of their time. I cannot deny that some students are very certain and specific about their passion, and they would normally intend to pursue that path as much as possible and become the best in the field. Yet the higher one climbs in a field, the more weapons he/she needs from elsewhere. A regular accountant needs just accounting skills; but a business leader needs to know about the product, management, law, technology, and many more. A reporter knows how to write a story; but the head editor of a news agency would have to understand politics, literature, marketing, and beyond.

Some may argue that taking additional courses should be discretionary rather than mandatory. However, college students are generally young adults who have barely learned how to live independently and make responsible decisions. Often, giving them the choice not to challenge themselves is tantamount to having them not challenge themselves. If learning outside knowledge is any where as important as I said earlier, then the merits deserve a little sacrifice on students' freedom of choice. They will benefit later on by having more options in their lives.

Overall, I believe that it is wise for students to take on classes outside their majors. For this to happen, they should be required to do so.

18

Some people believe that college students should consider only their own talents and interests when choosing a field of study. Others believe that college students should base their choices of a field of study on the availability of jobs in that field.

Write a response in which you discuss which view more closely aligns with your own position and explain your reasoning for the position you take. In developing and supporting your position, you should address both of the views presented.

Sample Essay A: Outstanding

Ideally, students should be free to study any subject they desire. We can broadly interpret this statement as the following: students may choose to study whatever interests them, what they have talents in, or what they want to have a career in; they may easily change subjects of study as their interests shift, as they later find out that they don't possess the necessary skills to succeed in the field, or as they no longer want to work in that field; they may pause their college study and work in the relevant field to gain practical knowledge and experience, after which they may decide to come back to college and continue to study, or terminate it since they can learn more from the actual jobs; they may already have well-paying jobs and choose to study a difficult subject simply for a different life experience or adventure.

Apparently, these scenarios seem far too utopian in modern societies. Surely there are students who can afford the luxury of treating their education as a side business, but for the majority, what they intend to study does not solely depend on their will. This is because education has been inevitably hurled into the swirl of a country's overall development, and become a tool for a country to produce experts and support academic fields that are likely to either yield tremendous economic profits, like computer science or chemical engineering, or solve urgent critical matters, like pharmacy or ecology. Because of the likelihood of landing a well-paying job, consequently, schools of business, law, medicine, and engineering have become enormously popular, and programs in the humanities and the arts are having more difficulties in attracting potential students. This hierarchy of fields of studies shows not only the imbalance of educational development, but more prominently, the ways in which education serves as an indispensable institution to the economic stability and growth of a nation. In this situation, for individual students, education is not merely for personal betterment, but crucially linked to their jobs, income and survival.

Should we encourage students to follow their hearts and study something that has few relevant job positions like classical philosophy, or should we try to persuade them to endure doing something they dislike simply for the sake of getting a job? For many students coming from families who are struggling with living comfortably, these are not options; I would recommend they get into the fields that lead to ample job opportunities, such as accounting or human resources. When a society has deemed education as the engine for driving forward its development, modern colleges have gradually shifted their gear away from educating talents and towards producing useful research. The days are gone when educators were trained to cultivate great minds and to create knowledgeable and innovative professionals in all fields, the success of which depends greatly on individual investment and talents. In contrast, teaching now seems not to be the primary task for college professors. For example, in many US universities, tenure-track professorship is valued not by how good a teacher one is, but by how much research one can produce. The tenure professorship system has also inadvertently made professors less likely to challenge themselves to be better teachers, as they have less motivation to continue working on their teaching skills once they are tenured. When students come into the college working diligently with the high expectation of learning from top-tier professors only to find out that professors do not treat "educating" as a priority as they do, students should also treat college education as a means to get jobs.

My recommendation is nowhere near groundbreaking, for society has already accepted the fact that education is a student's stepping stone for future careers, as college students, especially those in the humanities and fine arts, are often harassed by questions like "What are you going to do with that degree?". When education has become economically purposeful for the entire country, it should as well be financially purposeful for any student. Yes, one's interests and talents matter, so students should consider themselves lucky when their interests and talents genuinely lie in fields that offer plenty of job opportunities. However, for many, they should not let interests and talents be the main driving forces for their success in college, and they should also not consider college education as the only way to develop their interests and talents; the stakes are simply too high. My recommendation to choose majors that will potentially lead to ample job opportunities is not ideal, but expedient, for modern college education has ceased to be structured to cater to individual student's learning preferences and allocate equal attention and support to all fields of study but, sadly, has become increasingly utilitarian. It's time that we reevaluate what education really means and how to get the most out of it for each student.

Words & Expressions

utopian *adj.* 空想的
hurl *v.* 丢，用力投掷

swirl *n.* 漩涡
inadvertently *adv.* 不经意地

Sample Essay B: Good

How should a student determine what major he/she will enter, by job prospect or by his/her talent and interest? Obviously, this is just one of the many questions about life choices that just do not have a single undebatable answer. It is really a matter that is completely up to one's self-understanding.

Not everyone graduating from high school knows who he/she really is. Take the Chinese high school education system for example. Everyone here takes a similar set of curriculum. If you focus on science and technology, you're required to take Chinese, math, English, physics, chemistry and biology; or if you focus on the humanities, you will have to take Chinese, math, English, politics, history, and geography. Most students are, therefore, not actually aware of other possibilities that could one day influence their career. In fact, a lot of skills that could later become important assets in a profession, for example, communication skills, the ability to handle pressure, and physical strength, cannot be reflected at this stage. Consequently, if a student is not exceptional in any of these fields, chances are high that he/she knows about neither his/her own passion nor his/her natural gift. What is his/her best bet for a choice of major then? I do believe basing the decision on job availability is the rational thing to do. Today, if you pick computer science, for example, even if you only attend a second-tier college and you get an average GPA of C^+, you are still going to be popular on the job market. Many Internet startups are in desperate need of coders, so these professionals get much higher pay than fresh graduates from most other majors. Yes, the student may not enjoy his/her job, but let's be realistic. He/She will have enough money, and he/she can do fun things after work.

But there are always exceptions. If you go to one of the best colleges in China, say Peking University, you will see a number of brilliant young people who know very early on who they are and what they are going to do. You will see 16-year old freshman students who finish college physics curriculum before entering college, and are already way ahead of others doing research on quantum physics and string theory. You will also see young fiction writers who have already published a few best-selling novels in their freshman year and sign autographs for their fans. If someone is going to tell them that there are few available spots for top physicists or that professional writing isn't a stable job, they will probably tell the person to mind his/her own business. It's true. Even if these career paths are much narrower for most people, it's still a bright open path for the ones with extraordinary talent and unlimited drive.

Overall, I don't think there should be a uniform decision for everyone. For those who show unmatched gifts and passions, they should just not care about job availability. For others, they probably need to put their foot down and be realistic.

Part 4 Issue 精选范文

28 Teachers' salaries should be based on their students' academic performance.

Write a response in which you discuss the extent to which you agree or disagree with the claim. In developing and supporting your position, be sure to address the most compelling reasons and/or examples that could be used to challenge your position.

Sample Essay A: Outstanding

 名师讲解

In arguing that teachers' salaries should be based on their students' academic performance, this prompt entails that the value of teachers' skills, in other words, teaching effectiveness, is the major factor that determines students' learning outcomes. This idea emerges from the prevalent consumerist culture that not only designates service as a particular commodity, but also inadvertently transforms education into a particular type of customer-driven business: schools become corporations, teaching becomes a product, and students become customers. Hence, the prompt can be read as setting a monetary motivation to improve the quality of teachers' service, to ensure the success of customers' learning. In this essay, however, I argue that education is such a complex entity and social component, whose success can never be boiled down to teaching effectiveness alone.

Let's start with a discussion about what could determine academic performance other than teaching effectiveness. First, the claim completely ignores the fact that learning outcomes are largely shaped by personal investment and qualities such as students' motivation, intellectual ability, efforts, and interests. Even if students may learn better with better teachers in class, how they continue to pursue their subjects after class will make a huge difference in overall learning outcomes. Second, in the long process of teaching and learning, students might be affected by onerous situations that are difficult to deal with. For example, scenarios like the passing of a dear family member or their own unforeseeable hospitalization which, while not impeding students learning, will nevertheless affect their psychological well-being, and might eventually lead to poor academic performance. Unless we live in a fictional world where knowledge can be transplanted into students' brains, this claim is fundamentally flawed due to the fact that knowledge acquisition is not a fixed process, but contingent upon a wide range of factors.

Even assuming teaching effectiveness is indeed of utmost importance in students' learning, this policy is hardly implementable due to its impracticality. Since teachers often find themselves in classrooms filled with many or even hundreds of students, they will be unlikely to give undivided attention to each one of them to ensure good academic performance. Plus, a cohort of students may have different approaches and habits of learning, come in with varied ability levels, or have distinct cultural backgrounds, so it's unrealistic to ask teachers to come up with a one-size-fits-all teaching method and expect it to be effective for each student. Thus, students' poor academic performance may reflect more about the downside of classroom teaching than teaching effectiveness *per se*. I speculate that, until one-on-one teaching becomes the dominant form of instruction in all educational levels and systems, it is impractical to carry out this policy and believe that the measure of students' academic performance is a good indicator of teaching effectiveness.

People who do not agree with my argument might say that this policy may motivate teachers to improve their teaching skills so that they become better at delivering knowledge. I agree. I also agree that the major goal of educational institutions is to produce educated people with knowledge and skills to further develop their societies. However, education encompasses so much more than imparting knowledge. For teachers of young children, besides teaching actual knowledge, they are also expected to be role models of virtue so that children can learn to be honest, hospitable, and patriotic. For modern humanities and social sciences, the goal of teaching is not to have students remember lists of historical events, dates, and authors, but to help them develop analytical skills. For arts and designs, a crucial part of teaching is to assist students to cultivate a creative and imaginative mindset. Even for fields of hard sciences where imparting knowledge is a major part of teaching, such as statistics and physics, it is as well pressing that students learn to be critical and innovative. Thus, in order to reward teachers accordingly, how exactly can we measure good conscience, critical ability, creativity, and imagination that students develop from learning with them?

We can't. This is based on my pessimism about the possibility of creating a valid measure to accurately reflect the tremendously vague yet encompassing notion of "academic performance". Even if we simplify this notion and determine teachers' salaries solely on students' test results, the current field of educational psychometrics has yet to come up with an ideal test form. They are currently advancing predominant test theories like item response theory, and formulating new ones such as cognitive diagnostic measurement, in hopes of providing fine-grained information about how well students master concrete knowledge. In a nutshell, while the intention of motivating teachers is justifiable, we have to draw out other plans to improve teaching effectiveness. If the policy of basing teachers' salaries on students' academic performance was nonetheless to be carried out, education would face detrimental repercussions.

Words & Expressions

prevalent *adj.* 流行的	acquisition *n.* 获取
consumerist *adj.* 消费主义的	contingent upon 视……而定，取决于
designate *v.* 指定	utmost *adj.* 极度的，最大的
commodity *n.* 商品	implementable *adj.* 可执行的
inadvertently *adv.* 不经意地	cohort *n.* 一群
monetary *adj.* 货币的	hospitable *adj.* 好客的
entity *n.* 实体	patriotic *adj.* 爱国的
boil down to 浓缩为，简化为	fine-grained *adj.* 细化的
onerous *adj.* 繁重的	detrimental *adj.* 有害的
fictional *adj.* 虚构的	repercussion *n.* 反响

Sample Essay B: Good

I think it is a great idea that teachers' salaries be determined by their students' academic performance. This policy would boost teachers' devotion to their teaching, and that would be reflected in their students' success.

To begin with, it feels quite redundant to have to explain the benefit of this policy. To get a clear sight, we need look no further than what happens in the absence of this policy is absent. In many public schools in China, teachers are paid according to seniority. Consequently, we see so many 50-year-old "experienced" teachers whose expertise is completely outdated. Their students would be better off looking for resources online than consulting these "senior" teachers. There are also schools where teachers are paid based on their diplomas. However, a PhD does not guarantee that one knows how to teach. So many people who are great at research are poor at verbal communication, and thus totally inadequate at being a good teacher. In contrast, rewarding a teacher based on how his/her students perform is directly aimed at benefiting students. At least teachers would have the incentive to work harder, and the ones that fail to help students would gradually be sifted out.

Now, what are the possible counterpoints? Perhaps one may say that the measure could cause teachers to push students too hard, and then they would no longer feel the joy of learning. Well, doesn't this argument serve my point of view? If a teacher pushes students too hard and deprives his/her students of the joy of learning, his/her students will not progress or perform well, and then he/she will not be paid well. This policy in the long run will push teachers to work smarter, not just harder. It is the teachers who know how to excite students while teaching knowledge that will end up earning the most.

Some may also argue that academic performance is not all that is valuable in learning. Academic performance apparently only reflects a student's intellectual strength, but what about her mental and moral growth? I do believe that many modern standardized exams are one-dimensional—they just evaluate students' intellects while ignoring all other aspects. However, while the school is responsible in some degree for students' overall growth, each individual teacher is not. A math teacher teaches math, and that is his/her job description. If he/she helps his/her whole class progress in math, then he/she deserves his/her pay, end of discussion. So if there was a teacher or a group of mentors responsible for the students' moral or mental growth, then some other performance evaluation test could be designed that fit that aim. But when it comes to academic disciplines, we don't have many valid reasons to make a clear case complex.

To sum up, while paying a teacher based on students' performance may sound cruel and rigid, it is still better than all the other measures that have been tried. When it comes to education, there is no a lack of idealists. Teaching is a modern job, and the job is to improve students' academic performance. So when the most direct evaluation criterion is readily available, I see little reason to seek a detour.

Part 4　Issue 精选范文

47

Claim: We can usually learn much more from people whose views we share than from those whose views contradict our own.

Reason: Disagreement can cause stress and inhibit learning.

Write a response in which you discuss the extent to which you agree or disagree with the claim and the reason on which that claim is based.

Sample Essay A: Outstanding

　　In the modern world, people experience differences in view on a daily basis: political debates are easily accessible through media, business plans are seriously contemplated through numerous meetings, and even within each family, there are often decision-making moments that involve disagreement and negotiations. The prompt believes that since disagreement can cause stress, and inhibit learning, people actually learn more from those who share similar views than from those who disagree.

　　The idea that we can learn more from people who are like-minded is an illusion. There is a tendency in our social life for people to seek comfort and a sense of security by finding similarities. For example, with the availability of many dating apps, finding a lifetime partner no longer starts with a random encounter, but becomes a purposeful task: people are intentionally looking for potential partners who share similar educational backgrounds, interests, and philosophies of life. The underlying intention of finding similar partners is to minimize potential disagreements in their future life together. In addition to the renewed way of modern dating, many other forms of social relationships are based on a sense of community and shared identity, such as feminist organizations, disability alliances, or single mother support groups. What draws these people together to form communities is precisely their similarities, which brings about a genuine willingness to listen to and share with other people. It appears that people may have an easy time getting along and carrying their conversations to deep, personal levels, but it does not necessarily mean that people learn more from their peers who tend to agree with them. We can make the argument that what one gets most out of like-minded peers is not knowledge nor critical reflection, but a sense of belonging, comfort, and security.

　　Disagreement would likely make people so defensive about themselves that they would not be willing to offer listening ears and to learn; thus disagreement may potentially cause stress and stall further communication and exchange. Even so, however, disagreement also presents itself as the point of departure for in-depth discussion of the issues at hand. For example, traditional feminism seeks equal treatment of women because it considers the world privileges males, while progressive feminism considers women and men both victims of patriarchal ideologies. For anyone who invests in feminism in general, I believe the existence of such disagreement in view is an opportunity to learn more. For those who hold radical views, traditional feminism helps them see the ways in which men can be delegates of patriarchal values, and for traditional feminists, radical perspective helps them see how innocent boys have been indoctrinated with violent patriarchal values when they are young, and grow up to embrace toxic masculinity. Disagreements like this are ubiquitous in every aspect of our social and cultural life; instead of shunning them, we need to treat disagreements as symptomatic of significance, as an opportunity to learn.

Of course, when it comes to fundamental beliefs, people with contradicting views are unlikely to compromise their perspectives, let alone learn from each other. Fundamental beliefs, such as one's political stance, religious principles, or philosophical doctrines, even though largely immaterial and often intangible, are an indispensable component of one's sense of subjectivity. This means, unlike knowledge or experience, something people gradually accumulate in the course of their lives so that they become useful tools for people to know better about the world, fundamental beliefs allude to the ways in which people come to understand themselves and understand their positions in the world. In other words, challenging one's fundamental views is often seen as offensive, for it questions not the views but the person. Thus, people tend to be obsessively protective of their political, religious or philosophical views, to the extent that many wars have been triggered precisely because of extremely different political and religious ideologies. As a result, in dealing with contradicting views in fundamental beliefs, people are constantly reminded that they need to appreciate diversity and to respect different ways of living. Learning from each other seems to be too much to ask, for now.

Words & Expressions

contemplate v. 思考
like-minded adj. 志同道合的
patriarchal adj. 父权主义的，重男轻女的
indoctrinate v. 灌输
masculinity n. 男性气质

ubiquitous adj. 无处不在的
shun v. 规避
intangible adj. 无形的
allude v. 暗指

Sample Essay B: Good

The prompt claims that, because disagreement causes stress and inhibits learning, we learn more from people who share ideas with us than from those whose ideas conflict with our own. In general, I do believe that it is our human nature to prefer to listen to advice and opinions from those we feel that we have much in common with, but I also believe that when we learn to control our emotional sides, we can still manage to gain from differences.

What I take the prompt to mean is that when we share many ideas with a person already, we are more inclined to learn from that person. From a psychological point of view, when we are too different from someone, we generally don't even want to talk to that person, let alone learn from him/her. For example, when I was a student, I remember not liking my math teacher because he really enjoyed talking about politics and thought that all of us needed to hold strong political positions. Politics was not a topic that captured my attention, ever, so his value pushed me away from his math class. I know now that I should have separated his political views from his academic ability, because that could have benefited me better, but as a high schooler, I could hardly be so rational, and neither were many of my fellow classmates. When we felt that we couldn't connect with the teacher, we simply stopped learning. Therefore, I do agree that too much disagreement is stressful to learners, especially immature ones.

However, as people grow and mature mentally, particularly if they become critical adults, they are more likely to set aside differences between people and appreciate inspiring ideas. Yes, it is still true that when someone with completely different values from mine argues with me, I feel an initial repulsion. However, afterwards, I can sit back and reflect on the debate and often feel inspired. Even when I read a book about someone I don't feel connected to, I can appreciate their innovative ideas. For example, when I read the biography of Steve Jobs, I didn't like a lot of things about him. I shared none of his temper, his showmanship, or a lot of his philosophies, but still I thought he was a great entrepreneur because he believed in "creating demands" rather than "catering to demands". I even tried to apply that idea to my own field, and found it quite helpful.

So overall, I do believe that disagreement can cause psychological distance between people, and for the less reflective ones, learning is inhibited. But for intellectually mature ones, they can more or less overcome that psychological barrier and try to learn something whether it is from people holding similar ideas or from those with different ones.

48

Part 4　Issue 精选范文

48 Government officials should rely on their own judgment rather than unquestioningly carry out the will of the people they serve.

Write a response in which you discuss the extent to which you agree or disagree with the recommendation and explain your reasoning for the position you take. In developing and supporting your position, describe specific circumstances in which adopting the recommendation would or would not be advantageous and explain how these examples shape your position.

Sample Essay A: Outstanding

When we elect people into the government to be our leaders, it is not just because billions of people can't collectively self-govern, but because, predominantly, we hold the belief that the elected government officials are good leaders who have been educated to think analytically and critically, who can foresee potential challenges and opportunities, who are righteous and have a high moral standard, and whose judgment and decision making are thus grounded in the common sense of humanity and compassion. In this sense, ideally, government officials' judgment should reflect precisely the will of the people they serve. Indeed, one of the core duties of the government is to bring about a good life for its people, as we can see that governments are constantly seeking ways to improve areas such as education, public health, social security, employment, transportation and so on. However, by arguing that officials should rely on their own judgment rather than simply following people's will, the prompt points out the complexity of government work, and asks us to reconsider, in practice, what counts as competent leadership.

First, it is important that when making decisions, government officials recognize the collective will of the people, particularly when their demands are rooted in humanitarian ideologies, such as anti-war, equal rights, gun control, or the government's adequate response to strenuous situations like climate change. During the American Civil War, for example, Abraham Lincoln unilaterally freed all slaves with his emancipation proclamation, a power not technically granted to him under the constitution. In contrast, despite the nationwide protests to withdraw from the Vietnam War, Lyndon Johnson decided to go against the people's will to expand the numbers of American military. Eventually, his policies ended in depressing failure. In both cases, we see that the presidents asserted unrestrained power as top government officials and made the decisions on their own judgment. However, since Lincoln's determination to end slavery aligned with both the will of the people and the common sense of humanity, he has been celebrated as one of the most honored American presidents, as the abolition of slavery has greatly pushed forward the civilization of mankind.

Second, even though government officials are elected by the people, their duties in the government entail so much more than simply carrying out the will of the people. On the one hand, governments have the responsibility to support scientific research that would benefit the entire human race, even when such benefits might not immediately apply to the living population. One example is the government's support of outer space exploration. For instance, research of asteroids helps us know about the past earth impacts from them so scientists may come up with ways to prevent future impacts from outer space. The exploration of Mars also expands our knowledge about alternative living spaces for the human beings, although currently it is definitely not the people's will to be transported to Mars. On the other hand, it is also the government's job to recognize arising problems and address them by providing solutions. For example, the Chinese government implemented the so called one-child policy as a way to effectively deal with the population explosion of the 1970s, although some may claim that this policy goes against people's will to form families as they desire. From this perspective, government officials need to rely on their judgment because they are concerned with not just the current lives of living people, but also the future of the human race.

Third, if we look at this issue from the perspective of a citizen or small community, we can argue that since people in a given society hold very different and, often times, conflicting political views, it is practically impossible for the government to listen to and carry out everyone's demands and expect that this won't cause any dissonance among its people. For example, when businessmen are advocating building gas pipelines through wilderness areas for economic gain, environmentalists and indigenous people protest against such exploitation of natural areas. Examples like this take place every day in every aspect of a nation's political life, so it's unlikely that government officials are able to base their decisions on people's will because of inherent discrepancies among their interests. I don't necessarily believe that government officials' own judgment offers, in any sense, the optimal option for resolving tensions among people or nations, but they are trained negotiators and policy-makers who would strike a balance between serving the people and making a wise decision for the future of the nation and the entirety of mankind.

Words & Expressions

foresee *v.* 预见
righteous *adj.* 正义的
strenuous *adj.* 费力的
unilaterally *adv.* 单方面地

emancipation *n.* 解放
proclamation *n.* 宣言
dissonance *n.* 不和谐

Sample Essay B: Good

It is not easy to be a government official. You are constantly judged by the people you serve, and you never seem to satisfy everybody's needs. In fact, you never will, so it is important to have your own judgement on important issues. That said, one should not go to the other extreme of completely ignoring people's opinions. In fact, a government official should always form his/her own judgment, but that judgment should be based on sufficient research of relevant information and a comprehensive consideration of people's needs.

For starters, an official simply cannot indiscriminately listen to people's will, because the term "people's will" assumes, unwarrantedly, the homogeneity of people's opinions, when in reality, society is always a mixture of conflicting interests, all of which belong to people. Say the government wants to build a big dam. Areas that suffer from lack of electricity would applaud the decision, but those living close to where the dam is going to be constructed would hate the idea because the project would require their relocation. There is never going to be a single solution that makes everyone happy. It is ultimately the official's judgment that balances the interests of different groups. However, the balance would mean that he/she has taken into consideration the needs of everyone involved, because he/she would probably approve the construction but at the same time offer those nearby residents a huge relocation fee.

It is also easy to picture a scenario where an urgent decision has to be made, say, to send out rescue teams after an earthquake or a tsunami. How many people should be sent? How much material should be provided? How should the materials be shipped? You cannot wait for the people to give an answer, because they don't have all the information available. You can only listen to the opinion of experts on disasters; you probably also need to draw a priority list of what's most important to save and what's next. However, this isn't equal to neglecting people's will. What you do in these situations is serve your people's best interest.

Regarding projects aiming to boost a nation's long-term potential, an official often has to temporarily leave aside people's wills, because the public tends to be short-sighted. If you initiate a survey among people on what they think the government should do, generally they would prefer the government to fight street crimes, reduce commodity prices, create more jobs, or improve health care. On the contrary, few would recommend space exploration, environmental protection, or espionage. These issues are less pressing, from most people's perspectives. However, for a large nation, funding on these aspects is important to secure the nation's long-term competitiveness. If the public doesn't see it, the government should.

But I would never go so far as to say the government should be blind to people's will. At least, its decisions need to be transparent to its people. The transparency is necessary so that the government's power will not go unchecked. Corruption, and even dictatorship often start with the pretext that the government alone can decide what's best for its people.

In conclusion, the government is more informed on a lot of issues than its people, so it should never blindly obey its people's will. However, its decisions should always be aimed at benefiting people's needs, both long-term and short-term.

> **49** Young people should be encouraged to pursue long-term, realistic goals rather than seek immediate fame and recognition.
>
> Write a response in which you discuss the extent to which you agree or disagree with the recommendation and explain your reasoning for the position you take. In developing and supporting your position, describe specific circumstances in which adopting the recommendation would or would not be advantageous and explain how these examples shape your position.

Sample Essay A: Outstanding

The contemporary youth culture appears to be fame-seeking, as social networks have made it easy for ordinary young people to promote themselves—whether to sell their products or services, or simply to be an Internet celebrity. This triggers concerns from society that young people should be encouraged to pursue long-term, realistic goals rather than immediate fame and recognition. I beg to differ.

Young people have been told enough that they need to have goals, for the contemporary society is no stranger to the sort of seemingly uplifting vibes from college commencement speeches, low-budget literature, and even fortune cookies that teach young people to dream big, work hard, and reach beyond. These encouragements may come from good intentions, but they are useless for most individuals to combat society's systemic failures that foreclose the achievement of personal goals. That's because we are living in a society where many people still struggle to make ends meet, even when they take on multiple part-time jobs, or are deep in medical debts, even when they have insurance. In such a society, if young people appear to be unsuccessful, or not to know what to do, it's not because they don't have goals, but because they are still fighting for their basic well-being. Instead of burdening young people with socially recognized goals such as to be an entrepreneur like Mark Zuckerberg or an athlete like Kobe Bryant, we should tell them to live the lives they desire.

First, many people's long-term, realistic goals are not truly as realistic as they perceive. While others blame individuals for setting their goals too high, I see this as a collective problem deeply rooted in the early childhood education system, which wrongfully endows a sense of exceptionalism in teaching children about social values. For example, children are taught to be patriotic through the story of Abraham Lincoln and to be innovative through the successes of Bill Gates or Steve Jobs. True, we cannot deny the effectiveness of using heroes to teach virtues, but the unintended consequence is that children champion these figures as role models to set their own life goals. The fact is that the desire to be a president, a well-known hero, a multi-millionaire, or even a productive scientist is not realistic for the majority of people. Thus, for many, growing up is a truth-revealing process where they gradually come to terms with the impossibility of their childhood dreams. From this perspective, instead of simply encouraging, society should dispel the illusion that many of these goals are realistic, and teach young people necessary skills and a proper mentality to survive in such competitive world.

Second, even when the goals young people set themselves are reasonably realistic, society is vexed with exacerbating problems so much that it gets in the way of achieving these goals. Let's use probably the most realistic goal of landing a job as an example. As more people are getting educated, employers start to require a higher degree for positions than they would have ten years ago. This inevitable trend of intellectual inflation has made the job market incredibly competitive. What makes it worse is the neoliberal economies that outsource many job opportunities to Third World countries to lower expenses, as well as its global trades that attract an inflow of international intellects, further shrinking the already cutthroat job market in the homeland. As a result, for many young people, securing a well-paid job is not so much of a realistic goal anymore. For the society who is yet to solve the soaring unemployment rate and commodity prices, what's the use of pumping young people up with chicken soups without being able to reward their efforts?

Finally, even though we often associate the expression "fame and recognition" with a certain negative connotation of vanity, I argue that we need to look beneath the disguise and understand that this is young people's effective way of dealing with the gloomy present and unpromising future. Fame-seeking culture diversifies the notion of success, which traditionally means outstanding achievement, contribution or influence, so many young people can take up what interests them the most and still be recognized for what they are doing. For instance, there are popular young writers who keep personal blogs to share their political views, and famous young YouTubers specializing in comedy, updated high-tech products, and so on. Having millions of fans and followers, they are not only making a living for themselves, but also inspiring many others to become daring and unique to face the dismay of the world.

I would support this prompt wholeheartedly if fame-seeking young people turn out to be self-destructive and the generation of young people commonly lack motivation or don't really know what they want from life. However, the reality is that society is not yet able to afford everyone's dream, so it becomes an important life lesson that one should pursue what they are passionate about and manage to feel a sense of accomplishment in the unstable present.

Words & Expressions

commencement n. 毕业典礼
foreclose v. 阻止
exceptionalism n. 成功主义
vexed adj. 焦虑的
neoliberal adj. 新自由主义的
outsource v. 外包

cutthroat adj. 竞争激烈的
soaring adj. 猛增的
connotation n. 内涵
vanity n. 虚荣
gloomy adj. 阴霾的

Sample Essay B: Good

Ask any teacher from a formal education system how they think the desire for fame works for children, and chances are high that they will comment negatively. It is our tradition to value long-term hard work over the pursuit of overnight fame. However, with the explosion of information, today's world has changed, for better or for worse, so I do believe that a wholesale rejection of fame seeking has become an outdated perspective. In fact, what kind of goals one should set really depends on the specific industry he/she is in.

For starters, the reason why old people often advise young people to set a long-term, realistic target is that the desire for immediate success generally leads people to focus on what's on the surface. People may look for shortcuts without trying to improve their critical skills. This is indeed a big problem if you are in a field where expertise and experiences play a crucial part. For example, if you aim to become a leading scientist, it is quite unlikely, if possible at all, to gain fame at a relatively young age. You will have to work in labs for years and accumulate an understanding of your field; also, it takes years to climb the academic ladder and to become eligible to lead a team of researchers. The goal of becoming a well-established scientist almost always takes decades to achieve.

But the stark contrast can easily be envisioned. In show business, everyone seeks immediate recognition. If you don't get recognized, your career is probably going to be a dead end. Look at all those winners from *American Idol* or *America's Next Top Model*. Don't tell me that they go onto the show to achieve their long-term, realistic goals. They often say that they've dreamed years and worked so hard, and that they would do whatever it takes to succeed. No, they didn't work that hard, at least nothing compared to what one has to do to become a Stephen Hawking or a Roger Federer. See all those fashion bloggers who are followed by millions of fans worldwide. It doesn't take them decades of hard work to succeed. What it takes is a beautiful face and the ability to publicize. Should I criticize their life choices? I am not even qualified to judge. They have money, and they have influence. They define success in the contemporary world.

I might sound a little cynical. In fact, I am not. Not all fields are like research or entertainment. Most are in the middle, where you need a little of both. Children that want to pursue a career in the business world would be better advised to work hard for a long-term career plan but at the same time learn to promote a better image. The success of Apple is the best illustration. It takes years for its creators to keep updating their products to new heights; we all know how much Apple revolutionizes our conception of IT products. On the other hand, Steve Jobs' showmanship played an equally crucial role in selling Apple's idea to hundreds of millions of users worldwide. In this age, you need a catchy image to attract customers and investors; but in the long run, a fascinating business concept needs to be backed up by truly exceptional products. This balance indeed reflects the two kinds of goals a future business leader needs to set.

Overall, our modern world is a diverse space with different philosophies. One should not believe that successful people are all the same. Instead, for young people to succeed, what they really need is to know who they are and what they want. These understandings are essential when they set goals for their future.

Part 4　Issue 精选范文

> **53** In order for any work of art—for example, a film, a novel, a poem, or a song—to have merit, it must be understandable to most people.
>
> Write a response in which you discuss the extent to which you agree or disagree with the statement and explain your reasoning for the position you take. In developing and supporting your position, you should consider ways in which the statement might or might not hold true and explain how these considerations shape your position.

Sample Essay A: Outstanding

The prompt claims that an artwork loses its merit when it fails to be understandable to most people. In contrast to our attitudes towards sciences, where almost no one claims that string theory is worthless because most people don't understand it, society seems particularly critical of the arts' accessibility to the general public. We need to evaluate the function of the arts from different perspectives to fully analyze this issue.

First, let's examine the arts within the social context. People expect the arts to be accessible because the arts have traditionally been an important avenue through which we come to understand the world. For example, with cave paintings, we learn about how prehistoric people transmitted information, as well as early civilizations. With folk arts, we get to understand an agricultural group's wisdom about nature, skills of handicraft, and religious beliefs. With reading literature, we can revisit the depressing history of slavery, genocide or colonialism, which constantly reminds us to be resistant to contemporary injustice.

Consequently, people are used to viewing the arts as informative and often come in with the expectation of discovering deeper meanings behind the artistic surfaces. As such, new forms of art continue to emerge precisely because they are more effective in delivering ideas and messages. For example, graffiti is commonly known to be provocative in its expression of political pursuits; thus, graffiti artwork would lose its original intention to be subversive when the audience finds its meaning obscure. If we look at the arts as a vehicle for imparting information, then, it seems important that they are affirmative in delivering the meanings they intend to their audiences.

It is noteworthy that to understand a piece of artwork could also mean that the audience understands and resonates with the aesthetic feelings it conveys. Indeed, the value of the arts predominantly lies in their capacity to bypass certain language and cultural barriers to build mutual understanding and to bring about compassion. For example, Beethoven's famous piano piece entitled *Rage Over a Lost Penny* has been well-received as one of his best works. There is no practical knowledge for people to "understand" *per se*, but the value of this artwork comes from Beethoven's mastery of using tempo and chord arrangements to induce a sense of urgency, annoyance and ridicule from the audience. For another example, John Okada's novel *No-No Boy* is considered the first and the most important Japanese American literature, which depicts the woes of traumatic experiences of being interned during World War II. While contemporary readers may find it difficult to relate to that particular history, the novel nevertheless generates a sense of compassion from its readership as many could resonate with the experience of the protagonist's identity crisis, family conflicts, and the lived experiences of a marginalized racial group. Thus, for artworks to have merit in a social context, it's important that people understand their intended meanings or feelings.

Second, let's investigate the function of the arts for personal life. It is essential that we recognize that people's engagement with their particular choices of art forms can be understood as therapeutic. In a world that is perpetually infested with conflicts, poverty, inequality and exploitation, people start to develop a comforting personal relationship with the arts to deal with distress. While some people don't understand heavy metal music, and consider it to be aggravating and hysterical, others may find this art to be liberating, relieving them from the vexations of everyday life. Similarly, people can be their own artists, and their artworks are created for self-contemplation rather than wide circulation. For example, while some people believe knitting to be a waste of productive time, artists themselves see such an activity as a helpful meditation that temporarily withdraws their minds from the irksome world. In both cases, the value of the arts is in their function to facilitate an artistic life that would bring about a strong sense of psychological well-being, regardless of whether the arts are understandable to most people.

Third, the prompt seems to imply that the artists are to blame if their artworks fail to be understandable to most people. It is unreasonable to believe that the general public shares a similarly high level of education and has fundamental knowledge for understanding all artworks. Historically speaking, classic literary works are not readily understandable to many people for their dense language and heavy references to other literature and historical events. Globally speaking, any artworks that involve words and languages can be potentially understood by people only speaking the languages. That's why we need art critics, curators and interpreters, as well as a well-developed artistic and aesthetic education so that a bridge can be built between the arts and the audience for better aesthetic appreciation.

Words & Expressions

genocide *n.* 种族灭绝
colonialism *n.* 殖民主义
impart *v.* 给予，传授
affirmative *adj.* 肯定的，正面的
resonate *v.* 共鸣
bypass *v.* 绕开
ridicule *n.* 嘲笑

woe *n.* 悲痛
traumatic *adj.* 创伤的
protagonist *n.* 主角
marginalize *v.* 边缘化
therapeutic *adj.* 治疗的
perpetually *adv.* 永久地
infest *v.* 骚扰

aggravate *v.* 加剧
hysterical *adj.* 狂乱的
contemplation *n.* 沉思
withdraw *v.* 撤销
irksome *adj.* 讨厌的
curator *n.* 馆长

Sample Essay B: Good

The prompt holds that the only valuable works of art are those that are understandable to most people. To me, this statement is simply overly assertive: there are many art pieces that are perfectly valuable while not accessible to many outsiders. As long as an artwork delivers its message to the intended audience, it has its merit.

For starters, of course one can criticize a pop artwork if it is opaque to the majority. That is because popular arts are supposed to entertain the general audience. Therefore, if Taylor Swift writes a song that doesn't sell, then one may be warranted to label that song as a failure. Indeed, when pop artists create an item that ends up being a market disaster, they often make a lame excuse saying that they are doing real art that most people just don't have the elevated taste to appreciate. This excuse is not acceptable because if you really want to make an authentic art piece that doesn't cater to the crowd, you probably shouldn't be doing pop art at all.

However, the same criticism would not be legitimate if it aims at other art genres, those that in the very beginning try to distance themselves from most people's tastes. Take heavy metal music for example. Yes, it is loud and full of screams. Yes, I personally find it annoying. However, I understand why my young nephew likes it, because that kind of rebellious message speaks to people at his stage of life. The music represents his attempt to fight against the mainstream, and helps him express his passion. The street artists that spray graffiti are doing something similar. For those of us who would like things to be in neat order, the vibrant paint on street walls can be invasive, but they address the mentality of many young people who want to challenge the *status qua*.

In fact, the arts are supposed to be genuine; they should be the honest display of one's heart and soul. A pop song can have the lyric "girl your face is just so fine that I cannot stop thinking about it even for one sec" and is understandable to even kindergarten kids, but it means nothing because the singer really doesn't believe it at all and he is just using this choreographed trash to make money. True arts are honest. If you write a love song that only your lover appreciates, it serves your purpose. Sometimes you draw a random pattern just to reflect your darkest hours, it means something, because you understand it. Later on, when you, the only audience, look at it and find strength from that darkest moment, that piece has served its meaning.

Overall, the value of art can rarely, if ever, be evaluated by the number of people that can appreciate it. The merit of an art work is never objective and never should be.

Part 4 Issue 精选范文

55 The main benefit of the study of history is to dispel the illusion that people living now are significantly different from people who lived in earlier times.

Write a response in which you discuss the extent to which you agree or disagree with the statement and explain your reasoning for the position you take. In developing and supporting your position, you should consider ways in which the statement might or might not hold true and explain how these considerations shape your position.

Sample Essay A: Outstanding

One important characteristic of the contemporary period is how the dramatic changes in the material world, such as globalized economies, advanced information technologies, and expeditious transportation, have generated profound transformations in the worldview and state of mind of the private life. It is not surprising to hear older people reminiscing about their past, and expressing nostalgically how their early days were so different from today. On the same note, there is also a widespread sentiment looming over current households that generational gaps are only aggravating and causing more problems in child-rearing, home education, and parental relationships. These two common incidences of life experience reveal the extent to which our private lives have been affected by the ever-changing society. In a nutshell, the modern human society is characterized by a radical march toward a better future fueled by accelerated scientific achievement, so much so that experiencing "changes" becomes a central theme of any ordinary life. It is under this condition that we have come to the perception that people living now are significantly different from those of earlier times.

One can argue that this is a false perception because the material prosperity of current societies has clouded some ugly human traits that are persistent throughout history. A study of colonial history will reveal a pervasive greed for wealth and power, and new forms of colonization can easily be found in today's world, where, for example, indigenous people are constantly being exploited for their natural resources and geopolitical significance. A history of social oppression will show that racism, ageism, sexism and the like unfairly but dominantly govern many aspects of social activities, and the problems are still acutely present, even today. For instance, police violence towards people of color is a contemporary form of heinous racism that has spurred tides of activism. A history of warfare will demonstrate the unfortunate loop of wars because wars ending with the confiscation of the surrender would inevitably nurture new ones. For example, the harsh peace settlement was imposed on Germany after World War One, triggered its desire for revenge, which eventually led to another devastating world war.

Even though the list of persistent human traits could go on, I would not go so far as to suggest that "people are different" is an outright illusion, as the prompt does. In addition to conspicuous changes in the material world, the contemporary era also witnesses changes in cultural narratives, social issues, and ideological pursuits. There are a great number of examples to show that these changes have induced a serious reconsideration of what it means to be a human in the new era. Take equal rights activism for example. Western feminist activism believes that the male-female binary gender system is an unnecessary social construct that is not only placing strenuous restraints on individuals who are not comfortable with identifying with any gender representation, but also complicit in the notorious social oppression of sexism. By pivoting equal rights as its central concern, this movement has made a vigorous foray into many aspects of cultural traditions that are based on genders, such as gender division of labor, the male-female marriage system, and social welfare enacted upon male-female family formation. In doing so, this movement helps animate a renewed understanding of human life, and among many of its important contributions, a good number of universities and corporations have already installed unisex bathrooms instead of the traditional, gender-specific ones. Similarly, disability activism, animal rights movements, LGBT and queer politics, although controversial for the time being, are all slowly but enduringly changing our ideas about human life. Thus, it is not completely an illusion when we feel people are becoming different from their ancestors.

To conclude, while it does not take much effort to show that the material life of the human world has gone through one tremendous revolution after another, it is not as easy to make such a straightforward statement about human nature, even with a meticulous study of human civilization. I believe that a study of history will neither deny nor confirm that people living now are significantly different from those who lived in earlier times; it would be ahistorical and absurd to argue that people stay the same across historical periods without considering their particular cultural, social, and political realities, and it would be equally problematic to argue that people across history do not share any sort of commonalities. Rather, I believe that the study of history is a liberating process that helps people learn from their own mistakes, prepare for new challenges, explore different ways of living, and appreciate the diverse range of human experiences.

Words & Expressions

expeditious *adj.* 迅捷的	confiscation *n.* 没收
reminisce *v.* 缅怀	complicit *n.* 同谋
nostalgically *adv.* 怀旧地	pivot *v.* 把……置于核心
sentiment *n.* 情绪	foray *n.* 袭击
loom *v.* 隐约地出现	ahistorical *adj.* 与历史无关的
fuel *v.* 提供燃料	

Sample Essay B: Good

From the author's perspective, the major benefit of studying history is to reveal that people living in different ages do not differ drastically from each other. As we examine different aspects of human life throughout history, we shall see that while no significant changes have taken place regarding human nature, both our material life and our social values have evolved a long way from the past. In fact, knowing about both these similarities and these differences can be very helpful in our lives. Therefore, I believe that the speaker's view is too general.

To begin with, I do concede that there is something eternal with humanity, its virtue and its vices. Throughout history, we've celebrated individuals that display honesty, integrity and altruism; on the other hand, we've also constantly witnessed the waging of wars, a manifestation of the greed that is forever within our human race. As long as we are humans, we will feel love, compassion and courage, but we will also be bound by fear, jealousy and lust.

However, there is no reason to deny that even the most cursory understanding of history would suffice to reveal the enormous progress our intellect has achieved. From the very earliest domestication of cereal to the very modern genetic modification, from the invention of the wheel to the manipulation of international space stations, or from the crudest hieroglyphic carvings to the most sophisticated computer algorithms, every step of technological development marks a giant leap in our mental power. If any of our ancestors could witness the modern world, he would be shocked by how much his kind have accomplished.

At the same time, every history textbook would portray an evolving journey of our cultural values. Thousands of years ago, women were by default considered the inferior gender, whose lives were expected to be confined domestically; they would never expect that one day a woman could stand on the highest podium of a modern country, making her voice heard by each one of her people. Likewise, we can all recall the time when black people were treated like animals; today, race is widely believed to be irrelevant to the excellence of an individual, as long as he or she is given equal opportunity. Similar examples are aplenty: what we used to believe about religion, sexual orientation, mental illnesses, and marriage are all under pressure of shift, hopefully for the better.

All in all, I think the author fails to take sufficient consideration of different aspects of human life. While history does display certain commonalities within humanity, it also sheds light on a drastic contrast between us and our ancestors.

Part 4 Issue 精选范文

64 Some people believe that society should try to save every plant and animal species, despite the expense to humans in effort, time, and financial well-being. Others believe that society need not make extraordinary efforts, especially at a great cost in money and jobs, to save endangered species.

Write a response in which you discuss which view more closely aligns with your own position and explain your reasoning for the position you take. In developing and supporting your position, you should address both of the views presented.

Sample Essay A: Outstanding

  Human beings have a responsibility to protect every plant and animal species, especially endangered ones. The history of human civilization demonstrates how the survival and prosperity of the human world is predicated on its exploitation of natural resources. For example, humans build roads for transportation and accessibility, which forces the relocation of other animals, or build dams to store or divert water flows, which inevitably changes the landscape and kills acres of plants. In a more serious way, industrialization not only requires using exhaustible energy resources like petroleum, but also results in heavy pollution that eradicates numerous species of plants and animals. Protecting the environment is an urgent matter for every country in the world.

  We know saving nature is crucial, but does that mean that we should prioritize environmental protection over the development of any other field in society, or over people's general well-being? The contradicting perspectives in the prompt have made environmental protection seem like a tremendously difficult and costly project that asks for a great deal of effort, so much so that we have to compromise in other fields of development. However, it is not necessarily so. Protecting nature may just need a change of habits from each individual. When people bring their own non-disposable containers to buy drinks from coffeeshops or take their own shopping bags to grocery stores instead of using plastic ones, they are already saving the environment, as each year, hundreds of billions of plastic bags, bottles and straws are being produced and disposed of, often times resulting in oceanic pollution. Governments can also stipulate regulations or policies to address environmental issues. For example, Japan has a rigid law regarding garbage disposal and recycling, and as a result, Japan has a 77% plastic recycling rate. These strategies are effective but low-maintenance; they require only awareness of environmental issues and willingness to change.

  In addition to individuals' effort, governments can effectively regulate and control pollution through taxation and other policies. Governments can collect environmental taxes on industries that produce heavy pollutants, which will be an adequate incentive for industrial companies to update their processes of manufacturing so that they become cleaner and more environmental-friendly. Governments can also shut down industrial plants whose pollution emissions do not meet standards. Similarly, governments can impose stricter environmental regulations on proposals for building new factories, to prevent new sources of pollution.

These effective methods can bring about a cleaner environment, but do not really require additional investment or extraordinary efforts.

People who do not agree with my argument might say that even though heavy taxation or shutting down industrial plants that do not meet emission standards does not increase monetary investment, it is still destructive to local economies because of the increased sales prices and job losses. This is not true because compared with the entire country's economic development on a much larger scale, these downhills are nearly insignificant. Plus, environmental regulations will greatly benefit the overall economy and people's well-being.

These policies would lead to an increase in job opportunities because any prevention and protection programs will need to recruit scientists, researchers, and laborers for the actual clean up. Not to mention that, as pollution leads to health hazards, a much cleaner environment will reduce medical expenses.

In conclusion, we have irreplaceable responsibilities to save nature, but the project of environmental protection is not as daunting as the speaker assumes. Through education and media, we need to increase the awareness of the general public so people will start doing more recycling and attempting to lead a plastic-free life. Governments also need to focus on the big picture so that they will understand that taxation and setting strict emission standards will not harm the country's overall economy. When environmental protection becomes an everyday habit for individuals and a leading principle for governments, saving nature will not be as costly a project as we imagine.

Words & Expressions

disposable *adj.* 一次性的
stipulate *v.* 规定
downhill *n.* 下坡路

recruit *v.* 招募
daunting *adj.* 令人畏惧的

Sample Essay B: Good

Should our society spend enormous amounts of money and human resources saving endangered species? Well, this is clearly another one of those issues that try to strike a balance between our long-term benefits and our immediate needs. This time, I vote for the long-term benefits and believe that it is our obligation to save other species, because that will eventually save us.

To begin with, the main thing at stake is biodiversity. Diversity is important because it protects the stability of our ecosystem. When a vital part of the food chain is eliminated, it can cause a ripple effect that affects many other elements in the cycle. For example, the endangerment of certain frog species would mean that pests have fewer predators than before, so eventually it is human agriculture and forestry that will suffer.

Also, wildlife preservation, besides its direct ecological value, is significant for academic research. Biology, chemistry, medicine and many other areas benefit from the persistence of a diverse range of species. It helps us better understand the evolutionary relationships of species and the biological functions of chemicals. Simply put, we don't need to sound altruistic when we save other species; we are simply doing it for our best interest.

However, there are too many short-sighted critics who believe that environmental protection is a drain on our finance. They argue that protecting wildlife means excessive spending of money and human resources that could and should be used on other, more pressing issues. There are clear problems with this argument. In fact, the statement that wildlife protection demands extraordinary resources is simply not true. It is never as financially demanding as many other causes that we engage in so extravagantly, say space exploration and military upgrades. In fact, often what we need to do is simply not pollute. Others may argue that stopping pollution is itself an excessive cost, because it would entail that we stop building plants in certain resourceful areas. However, a well-preserved environment is itself a money-maker; it boosts tourism. Also, stopping pollution doesn't necessarily stop all factory building; it just requires the factories to install facilities that minimize the amount of harmful waste directly released into the natural environment.

Overall, our politicians should be wise enough to look beyond immediate financial interests. We will almost certainly regret doing less than we need to. Our overall benefit requires harmony between us and nature.

Part 4 Issue 精选范文

65 Some people believe that the purpose of education is to free the mind and the spirit. Others believe that formal education tends to restrain our minds and spirits rather than set them free.

Write a response in which you discuss which view more closely aligns with your own position and explain your reasoning for the position you take. In developing and supporting your position, you should address both of the views presented.

Sample Essay A: Outstanding

The prompt seemingly raises a debate between opposing parties, with the former claiming that education should aim at freeing the mind and the spirit, and the latter arguing that formal education tends to restrain our minds and spirits. However, even a cursory analysis of the two statements would reveal that there is no inherent conflict between the two statements at all, because the former is a claim about the purpose of education while the latter offers a critique of the current formal education system. I believe that both statements have raised valid points, while the first one needs some qualification.

There is no denying that education should enlighten people's minds, and when it does that, it completely changes people's mind for the better. Take my own experience for example. As a philosophy major, I am used to college professors who read through books on history of philosophy and simply repeat what the ancient thinkers have preached about. However, I was fortunate to have sat in a metaphysics class taught by Dr. Pruss, who would introduce a variety of arguments on both sides of an issue and encourage us to try to formulate our own arguments to potentially strengthen or weaken these positions. In his class, I learned what philosophy was really about: it's not about believing what other philosophers believed, but about understanding how philosophical reasoning proceeds. Years later, I have already forgotten the specific doctrines of many schools, but I understand how I should critically evaluate any issue at hand. This is what learning is supposed to be about, to enlighten the mind to think critically.

It's noteworthy that we should avoid carrying the statement to the extreme. While inspiration is an important goal in education, it is not everything. For many fields, learning basic facts and skills through introductory courses are still essential. When we were young, we learned how to read and how to calculate. We learned the history of our civilization and the geography of our nation. These are the basics for becoming literate. While it's easy for the highly educated to rave about how higher education can lift one's spirit, we must also recognize the realities of this world. Still there are many people who cannot calculate or read, and it is hard for them to make a living. This is why in elementary schools and middle schools we are required to repeatedly hone our skills of calculating and remembering vocabulary and grammar. Indeed, even in college, taking on a skill for a job is crucial. Those who later intend to become a professional auditor are required to take intense courses on statistical analysis; medical students are obligated to memorize almost every detail of each tissue and each medicine; even farmers today need experts to teach them the correct use of pesticides

211

and fertilizers. Elitists easily relate education to Aristotle, Einstein or Freud, oblivious to the starvation and unemployment still striking most parts of the globe.

Having clearly stated what the purpose of education is, now let's evaluate how well our formal education system does when measured against these standards. I do think most of our elementary schools and secondary schools are doing well with regard to teaching basic knowledge and skills, but they are underperforming when it comes to enlightenment. There are a few reasons why this is so. First, most education systems tend to be test-oriented and thus standardized. Standardization inevitably runs against the purpose of freeing the mind, because it dictates what one ought to do and believe. This somewhat unfortunate result is understandable and quite frankly, inevitable. The job market needs efficient processes to sift out the unqualified, and test scores provide that tool. And when measurement is dominated by tests, the education system inevitably gravitates in that direction. Second, it takes a truly inspired educator to inspire others, but let's face it; it is much easier to hire trainers than real educators. For the majority of our society, it is already beyond satisfactory if teachers can teach their students correct grammar, correct math equations, or correct scientific formulas. To ask for more is simply not practical, now or in the near future. The public education system relies on government funding, which is not just inadequate but still dwindling. Teaching is a job that pays, but sadly much less than many competing jobs in the market. Of course, as a result, it does not attract as many talents as society needs, especially before college level education, where teachers are particularly underpaid. As a result, while we may be fortunate enough to come across inspirational mentors in life, in general, the odds are quite unfavorable in the formal education system.

Words & Expressions

cursory *adj.* 粗略的
inherent *adj.* 固有的，内在的
qualification *n.* 限制，削弱
literate *adj.* 受过教育的
rave about 大肆吹嘘

auditor *n.* 审计员
sift out 筛选出
gravitate in 倾向于
dwindle *v.* 减少，衰落
odds *n.* 概率

Sample Essay B: Good

The prompt makes it seem as if the two statements are contradictory, while in fact the first states the purpose of education whereas the latter is about the reality of formal education. They are not necessarily inimical propositions. Nonetheless, I am inclined to disagree with the former and to endorse the latter.

From a personal perspective, it is enticing to think that we go to school to free our minds and spirits. Of course, I want to be inspired to think outside the box. However, from a social perspective, that is totally not the reason why a nation supports an entire education system. Reality says that the nation needs to produce enough work forces to maintain its operation. Two hundred years ago, a society needed plentiful workers and farmers. Today, as machinery gradually replaces menial labor, our social needs are somewhat elevated; we duplicate seemingly "fancier" jobs like auditors, lawyers, doctors, or coders, in short, higher paid and more skillful workers. Still, medical schools' most urgent job is not to cultivate creative doctors to renovate the whole medical system; its pressing need is to fill the work force with sufficient graduates who can practice the routines of treating patients, and it has little to do with freeing minds or spirits. The same holds for law schools and many others. We as individuals would like to think that as we go to law schools, we are superior to our forefathers who had to tread in farmland. At best, we appear superior.

With that purpose of education clarified, it becomes inevitable that formal education eventually restrains people's minds. Our math class trains us to repeatedly solve problems fast and accurately; our language class teaches us to write sentences formally, free from grammatical errors, like what I'm doing now. In college and graduate schools, problems become tougher and more sophisticated, but still everything is done in a mechanical way and evaluated against stringent rules.

Doesn't our society need innovators who defy all the traditions? Yes, it does, and that's exactly how it progresses. However, these individuals are neither the purpose nor the end result of formal education. Formal education does not worry about suppressing their rebellious nature, because it cannot be suppressed. They were born with the genes to transgress and are little confined by the rules. Charles Darwin, Steve Jobs, to name a few, are exactly the kinds I'm referring to.

Overall, I don't think that education aims to free; the education system is just a modern factory that seeks to mass produce replaceable parts, and mostly ends up with those. Creative geniuses? They are the byproducts.

Part 4 Issue 精选范文

> **71** In this age of intensive media coverage, it is no longer possible for a society to regard any living man or woman as a hero.
>
> Write a response in which you discuss the extent to which you agree or disagree with the statement and explain your reasoning for the position you take. In developing and supporting your position, you should consider ways in which the statement might or might not hold true and explain how these considerations shape your position.

▶ Sample Essay A: Outstanding

The prompt claims that it becomes unlikely for contemporary societies to regard any living person as a hero in this time of intense media scrutiny. It is important to realize that "hero" might bear different significance for different cultures and their individuals. To analyze this issue, then, we need to revisit the divergent understandings of heroes and investigate whether and how mass media influences heroic figures.

One assumption of this prompt is that media coverage will reveal the unethical or controversial accounts of heroes so that their perfect heroic image will eventually be destroyed. Or rather, this prompt assumes heroes should be morally respectable. Indeed, this assumption reveals how occasionally a culture revives or raises its moral values through recognizing citizens with high moral standards as heroes. For instance, in the late 70s, Chinese people were encouraged to emulate the hero Lei Feng, a supposedly righteous, modest and selfless soldier who devoted his life to helping others. In this case, media actually acted as a facilitator who would circulate heroic stories of respected moral deeds.

However, a survey of the world's important heroes will easily show that heroes are not meant to be morally unexceptionable. In fact, they are far from that. Thomas Jefferson, who drafted the *Declaration of Independence* in which he famously wrote "All men are created equal," owned slaves his entire life. Martin Luther King was remembered as a heroic figure in the civil rights movement, but he has also allegedly plagiarized his doctoral dissertation and had several extramarital affairs. Alexander Graham Bell has often been celebrated as a hero for his invention of the telephone, which drastically changed the way people communicate, but he was also a firm believer in eugenics, who supported the campaign to eliminate deaf people.

These examples show that, for a culture, heroism extends far beyond the realm of morality. Often times, cultural heroism celebrates exceptional human excellence and irreplaceable contributions, and it is by no means an ideology that pursues ideals or perfection. Heroic individuals are often only ordinary citizens, who, though having their flaws and personal issues, have done extraordinary deeds to benefit the entire society. Neither contemporary media nor, in early times, the less efficient print cultures, gossips, and oral traditions would be able to destroy these heroes by spreading their dark sides. Conversely, mass media could actually help commemorate a culture's exceptional achievements through promoting heroic imagery. As such, societies as a whole doesn't expect these heroes to be perfect.

If we understand "hero" as personal rather than cultural, this issue gets more complicated. When a culture remembers its heroes as a way to honor human excellence and possibility, individuals look up to their own personal heroes to define themselves, set personal goals, or find solace when in suffering. Someone who idolizes outstanding political leaders like Abraham Lincoln would likely cultivate a liberal viewpoint and advocate equal rights; someone who admires successful businessmen like Steve Jobs would possibly work to become a dedicated and creative leader of an industry; someone who identifies himself/herself as disabled may venerate Helen Keller and find strength and encouragement from her books and her engagement in social activism. Mass media, once again, becomes a productive platform where these individuals' stories can be widely circulated in the form of documentaries, biographies and interviews, playing an important role in establishing personal heroes.

On the other hand, however, media cannot avoid being an accomplice of the infamous celebrity culture that causes people to confound celebrity with heroism. In highly materialistic societies, celebrity culture invades and perpetuates in ordinary people's life through the ease of social media, so much so that people are constantly immersed in the trivial life details of celebrities. As a result, many young people not only adore stars but idolize them as personal heroes: they like them to the extent that they want to be like them! Blending celebrity with heroism could have detrimental consequences. For one, celebrities are not necessarily endorsing positive, desirable social values. For example, someone who idolizes a rapper may turn out be misogynistic, as rap music often normalizes and even glorifies the oppression of women. For two, it has made it seem like current societies do not have heroes any more, since the ideal image of their beloved, "heroic" celebrities is constantly marred by endless scandals and other controversies.

In conclusion, the disappearance of heroes in the age of intensive media coverage is only an illusion created by the heinous culture of celebrity. In fact, as we never cease to celebrate heroes throughout history, our world will surely remember many heroes to come, who will have discovered the cure for AIDS or emancipated people from wars, with the help of ever-advancing media.

Words & Expressions

scrutiny *n.* 细查
controversial *adj.* 正义的
emulate *v.* 仿效,企及
circulate *v.* 流通,传播
unexceptionable *adj.* 无懈可击的
allegedly *adv.* 所谓地
plagiarize *v.* 剽窃
dissertation *n.* 毕业论文

extramarital affair 婚外情
eugenics *n.* 优生学
commemorate *v.* 纪念
honor *v.* 致敬
solace *n.* 慰藉
idolize *v.* 崇拜
documentary *n.* 纪录片
biography *n.* 人物传记

accomplice *n.* 同谋
confound *v.* 混淆
immerse *v.* 使……沉浸
misogynistic *adj.* 厌恶女人的
beloved *adj.* 挚爱的
mar *v.* 玷污
heinous *adj.* 丑恶的

Sample Essay B: Good

The prompt suggests that as a result of pervasive media scrutiny, there is no common hero in our modern society. I definitely agree that the media has directly and indirectly undermined heroic images, and here is why.

The first factor is sensationalism. Modern media are controlled by money-seeking corporations, and to boost sales, there is nothing better than something eye-catching. Nothing grasps viewers' attention better than a good scandal of a well-celebrated public figure. From Bill Clinton to Michael Jackson, from Tiger Woods to Steve Jobs, no one is immune to paparazzi. From sexual scandals to family crisis, from personality flaws to unethical behaviors, every aspect of these famous people's lives is scrutinized to the maximum. No one is perfect, so under the microscope of modern media, the "perfect" heroic image is bound to collapse. In this way, the media gossip often directly tarnishes celebrities' reputations.

However, one may argue that those I listed above are not real heroes in the traditional sense. Real heroes are not politicians, athletes, or showmen. What these people do is exceptional, but still driven by personal interest. Real heroes sacrifice their own benefit for the greater good. These are fire fighters, soldiers, and the otherwise obscure names who save other people without concern for themselves. We would never see media say one bad word about these people. Isn't there consensus regarding these heroic behaviors?

I agree that these are truly honorable people who have done truly honorable deeds. But still, not everyone agrees in this modern society. This somewhat unfortunate result is also related to media. With the rapid spread of information, today's society has become much more diverse, with multiple values coexisting. It is no longer our forefather's time, when people celebrated the same virtues. I personally admire firefighters, but you still see Internet comments saying that they are getting paid to do what they do. I think soldiers are extraordinarily courageous, but pacifists still counter that everyone involved in a war is sinful. I was moved to tears when I saw on the news that a middle-aged man jumped into icy waters to save two strangers but was too exhausted in the end to save himself. But others argue that the media should not promote this value, because one needs to be responsible for himself/herself first, so as to be responsible for others. Yes, I think many such comments are completely insane and inhumane, but I cannot be blind to their existence.

Eventually, I have to concede that we cannot expect unanimity in this modern world. Thanks to the media, we have heroes no more.

> **82** Claim: Nations should suspend government funding for the arts when significant numbers of their citizens are hungry or unemployed.
>
> Reason: It is inappropriate—and, perhaps, even cruel—to use public resources to fund the arts when people's basic needs are not being met.
>
> Write a response in which you discuss the extent to which you agree or disagree with the claim and the reason on which that claim is based.

Sample Essay A: Outstanding

Driving through remote areas of a country, one may easily find gas stations, grocery stores, fast food restaurants, and perhaps laundromats, among many other things that are considered essential for day-to-day life. On the contrary, it would be a surprise to spot any well-maintained art galleries or theaters in such locations. To relate this example to the prompt, it effectively demonstrates that citizens' survival needs should be and have been government's primary concern: for developing countries like the ones in Africa, governments shoulder inescapable responsibility to come up with ways to help their citizens bring food to the table, and for super powers like the United States, over half of its federal funding goes to social security and unemployment insurance.

It is thus out of question that citizens' material well-being is of utmost importance for any government, but the speaker goes a step further to argue that funding for the arts should be suspended when the government has yet to eradicate the problems of poverty and unemployment. Their reason is also morally-toned as they state that under this condition, such investment is inappropriate and cruel. This argument makes several dangerous assumptions about the arts, which all hover under the perception that the arts are not an impactful element in a country's development to be kept in times of crises. Let's break it down and look closely into the problems of this reasoning.

One of the major problems with this argument is that the speaker rests their statement on a rigid, yet anachronistic definition of the arts, as closely associated with the Middle Ages European aristocracy, which considers the arts as purely aesthetic and luxurious, and hence a token for the rich and an excess that does not have any utilitarian value for the rest of the society. However, in modern times, the role of the arts has gradually shifted from something exclusive to the elite aficionados, to cultural objects that are ubiquitous for the general citizens, all because capitalism has been constantly pushing the envelope of artworks as commodities: paintings are common household decorations, and theaters and concert halls have become financially accessible to the public. As a result, the arts have become an integral part of a nation's economy. For example, the arts in the United States contributed 5% to the nation's GDP in 2015, surpassing agriculture and mining combined. This is not mere numbers; it suggests that the arts are no longer a marginal industry as many would have assumed, and shredding their funding might potentially result in a significant loss of government revenues.

Furthermore, government's funding for the arts may have a unique prospect for creating more employment opportunities. When many jobs require specific knowledge and years of training and experience, and candidates often get disqualified only because of the limited number of positions, rather than credentials, the proliferating arts industry, on the contrary, appeals to anyone with creativity and talents who intends to start their own family business. In fact, numerous small businesses, such as local galleries, art salons, and music studios, make up the majority of the United States' arts economy, and many more creative jobs have been added to the market throughout the years. From this perspective, government funding for the arts actually plays a crucial role in alleviating the country's unemployment issues.

Besides being an important benefactor for a country's economy and job market itself, the arts as an industry has been making significant impacts on many other businesses. In order to build an art museum, for example, the success of the project will involve not just artists and curators, but also architects and design engineers who can come up with an efficient plan for the actual building, city planners who can work out a convenient location and transportation, and local governments who can arrange nearby businesses to include more parking spaces, restaurants, and other facilities or services. The modern industry of the arts has evolved to encompass so much more than merely the appreciation of a painting; it has been well integrated into the systems of urban planning, local tourism, international trade, and so on, benefiting so much more than what it originally intended. As a consequence, cutting government funding for the arts may negatively impact a wide range of businesses beyond the arts.

For certain countries that are still infested with poverty, wars, and famine, there may not be resources to invest in the arts, but for many others, the arts are a vibrant industry that is contributing greatly to the country's entire economic strength. I argue that, if the government were to cut funding for the arts, it should never be done heedlessly, but rather based on detailed fiscal planning and analysis, even when unemployment and poverty are of the greatest concern.

Words & Expressions

grocery store 食品杂货店
laundromat n. 洗衣店
shoulder v. 担负
federal adj. 联邦的
morally-toned adj. 道德口吻的
hover v. 盘旋
anachronistic adj. 不符合时代的
luxurious adj. 奢华的
token n. 象征
utilitarian adj. 实用的
aficionado n. 狂热者

ubiquitous adj. 无处不在的
integral adj. 必需的
shred v. 撕碎，切碎
disqualify v. 使……无资格，取消……的资格
credential n. 凭据
proliferate v. 激增
integrate v. 整合
famine n. 饥荒
vibrant adj. 充满活力的
heedlessly adv. 掉以轻心地
fiscal adj. 财政的

Sample Essay B: Good

The speaker concludes that the government should suspend funding for the arts when the country suffers from hunger and unemployment, because it seems unjust to waste resources on less pressing needs when basic ones are not secured. As much as I agree that the needs for food and jobs clearly outweigh artistic demands, this reason alone does not warrant a rash decision to completely stop funding the arts.

Let me first concede that people's basic needs should always be a nation's priority. When my family was poor, my mom and dad would spend their entire time working multiple shifts; at the same time, there were no paintings, movies, music or other kinds of recreation in our lives. Simply put, when survival was on the line, we would not have the luxury to even think about satisfying our desires for artistic appreciation, if we still had any left.

However, on a societal scale, much more debatable is whether the government should simply neglect the development of the arts just for the sake of combating starvation and unemployment. Off the top of my head is the counterargument that the arts and economy are no longer dichotomous. A significant portion of the population in modern society makes their living on the arts or related businesses. The number of musicians, painters and performers is growing; meanwhile, skyscrapers erected, gardens built, movies filmed, blogs posted, headlines written, photos shot, clothes produced, and furniture made all have roles involving the crafts of artists. Stopping funding for the arts would mean that many are facing life-struggling moments.

In addition, the arts are uplifting, especially in cases of crises. When morale is low in the society, people need cheerful songs and movies to keep their hopes up. Many are the incidences when downhearted people become encouraged and empowered by messages delivered in inspiring performances.

Finally, suspending funding for the arts will simply not help with other, more pressing issues. Every powerful nation, the U.S., China, Japan, the U.K., and Germany, has starving or jobless people. None of them use all of their resources in solving unemployment. Why? The cause of these problems is not a simple lack of resources, but also whether resources are being used efficiently and fairly. If every country funds the arts only after its last jobless person gets hired, we may not be able to see that day come.

Overall, while the incentive behind the speaker's suggestion is humane and laudable, the suggestion itself is impetuous and unwarranted. The arts are too valuable an asset to neglect in today's world, and to ultimately alleviate a nation's pressing problems, we would have to look further for solutions much less short-sighted.

Part 4 Issue 精选范文

93 People's behavior is largely determined by forces not of their own making.

Write a response in which you discuss the extent to which you agree or disagree with the claim. In developing and supporting your position, be sure to address the most compelling reasons and/or examples that could be used to challenge your position.

Sample Essay A: Outstanding

The issue of whether people have the capacity to decide for themselves is an important and old one. Our first instinct may be to agree that people now are more likely to behave according to their own will, particularly when contemporary societies have generally witnessed an elevated level of willingness to reconsider traditional values, as well as tolerance for nonconformity. Indeed, famous mottos like Nike's "Just do it!" indicate a prevalent ideology of individualism persisting in our current societies that propels people to behave as they will. However, I intend to show otherwise, that people are largely shaped by their immediate surroundings, as well as societies as a whole. Even for those who are vastly idiosyncratic and rebellious against current social and cultural standards, their unconventional behaviors are determined by precisely what they rebel against.

First, people's collective behaviors are largely determined by natural laws. Living on the earth means that people have no choice but to obey the limitations imposed by mother nature, and that many of people's behaviors reflect the ways in which they maneuver within the parameters of these laws. For example, elevators were invented for convenience, compensating for the labor and inefficiency induced by gravity; medicine is continuously developed for people's well-being since they cannot evade the ubiquity and adversity of diseases. In fact, no matter how advanced science and technology have become, one can argue that the history of the material world narrates the story of humans' creative and productive responses to the restraints of natural laws.

Second, social laws, with their values and norms, are equally, if not more, powerful in determining people's behaviors. On the one hand, human societies reinforce many aspects of the natural laws to consummate a collective understanding of desired behaviors. For instance, while the natural laws ask people to regularly sanitize themselves to fend off potential diseases, 19th century France strengthened this law by treating bodily smells as an important category of social demarcation to indicate an individual's social class. In this case, the regular habit of the shower cannot simply be ascribed to the person's liking; it might as well be considered a necessity to stay healthy and a required behavior to conform to his or her bourgeois status.

On the other hand, societies form norms and etiquettes as virtues that they expect their citizens to follow. For example, children in all human societies are taught by their family members and teachers to share with others. This demonstrates how the human world treats hospitality and reciprocity as essential qualities, so much so that it does not leave much wiggle room for debate. Certainly, we can always imagine other societies

220

being different from ours where they value selfishness instead of mutuality, or they champion animosity in lieu of compassion, but the fact that we can imagine it does not mean we can manifest it. Even though we may question certain social virtues, conforming to them is less of a choice than we are willing to admit.

People who do not agree with my argument might challenge my position and state that many human behaviors are actually rebelling against social rules, or simply out of personal preferences. I beg to differ. For example, certain radical Islamic feminists advocate bans on women's mandatory wearing of hijabs. This behavior might seem like a self-enacted nonconformity, but since the hijab symbolizes the subjugation of women, not wearing it is precisely in opposition to, and thus determined by the society's unequal treatment of women. Similarly, finding a lifetime partner to marry also seems like a personal choice that individuals can make on their own. True, we cannot deny the importance of mutual attraction; in fact, I believe people's inner feelings are just as important as reasons in decision-making. That being said, we do not know how much weight a person's childhood education, family values, financial status, political stance, and even trauma or loneliness factor in their choices of spouse, and decisions to marry. For instance, a person coming from a family that traditionally values hard work may find this a crucial asset that their spouse needs to obtain for the marriage to work. Looking from this perspective, personal choice does not always seem equal to free will, but an always already mediated decision that encompasses so much more than the desire to "just do it".

In conclusion, even though the human world is undergoing another thrust of individualism, where people are encouraged to live as they will, I believe that their behaviors are shaped by many factors and forces not of their own making.

Words & Expressions

idiosyncratic *adj.* 奇特的，特殊的
parameter *n.* 限制因素
narrate *v.* 叙述
consummate *v.* 完成
sanitize *v.* 消毒
demarcate *v.* 化解
bourgeois *adj.* 资产阶级的

etiquette *n.* 礼节
reciprocity *n.* 互惠
wiggle room 余地
animosity *n.* 敌意
in lieu of 取代
subjugation *n.* 镇压
trauma *n.* 创伤

Sample Essay B: Good

Do we make the call for our own actions? Can we be truly responsible for what we do? These are the questions that have been haunting western philosophers for centuries, who sought an answer to the metaphysical question of free will. Of course, I am no Emanuel Kant, but I believe that the instinct to attribute one's own mistakes to other people or to society is typical of the weak-minded. Simply put, while we are certainly influenced by factors beyond our own control, ultimately we still decide most of what we do, if not all.

We undergo scenarios like the following all the time. Janice, a fictional character I just made up, is choosing her major, and she is struggling between two options, philosophy or business. She loves philosophy: she is constantly inspired by the great thinkers in history and would like to be on a path seeking the meaning of her life. On the other hand, she is a little bit insecure about her job prospects after graduation. After all, going to business school seems to be the better choice if she wants a lucrative career. Her parents strongly encourage her to become a leading entrepreneur, because they have just read Sandberg's *Lean in*, and totally believe that women should seize their opportunities in the modern business world. Let's suppose that Janice ends up in business school. Is it any less her choice just because of her parents' persuasion? I highly doubt so, because while they did give her the extra little push, the motive was hers. Had she been fully committed to the other option, the story would have ended totally differently. We encounter similar choices almost constantly. Even if we are influenced by family and friends, society and history, ultimately, we must have the motives already in ourselves to make up our minds. In this way, we cannot say that we are determined by factors beyond our control.

Of course, some people may point to many cases in which the agent does seem dominated by outside forces, for example, a gay kid born in the Deep South in a religious family holding traditional views. The pressure on him might be so overwhelming that he does appear to have no alternative options other than to stay in the closet. Does he really? The truth is, many people have experienced similar ordeals. While a lot of them made similar moves, there are always those few who do otherwise. Threatened at gunpoint, most cave, but some fight back. Born in a bad neighborhood, many end up in gang fights or selling drugs, but some seize opportunities, and thrive. Therefore, I believe that, to attribute what we do completely to outside forces is, even under extreme circumstances, a disrespect to other, extraordinary human beings.

Overall, while it is clearly absurd to reject that we are under many outside influences, we are simply not, as I argued above, determined by them. In the end, we always make our own call.

Part 4　Issue 精选范文

95 Although innovations such as video, computers, and the Internet seem to offer schools improved methods for instructing students, these technologies all too often distract from real learning.

Write a response in which you discuss the extent to which you agree or disagree with the statement and explain your reasoning for the position you take. In developing and supporting your position, you should consider ways in which the statement might or might not hold true and explain how these considerations shape your position.

Sample Essay A: Outstanding

　　The prompt claims that, while technologies have greatly facilitated teaching, they often distract students from real learning. This has a strong pessimistic outlook towards the future of technology-driven education, as it seems to indicate that distractions associated with technologies are detrimental yet unmanageable. Certainly, technologies could negatively impact learning, but I want to argue in this essay that technologies have been improving education, and there are always ways in which we can deal with the challenges they induce.

　　Without any doubt, technologies have brought us tremendous opportunities to improve teaching and learning. With online digital archives, teachers and students have immediate access to extensive databases with only a few clicks; doing research thus becomes much more efficient than in the old days when one had to dig deep into physical libraries. Online class systems such as Canvas or Blackboard create a virtual space for each course, where the teacher and students can engage in debates, collaborate on projects, or peer-review homework even outside of physical classrooms. Not to mention that, technologies allow teachers to use visual, audio, or other types of aids in the classrooms to facilitate teaching. Also, technologies are fun! Instructors can employ the entertaining quality of technologies to fully engage students in learning. For example, teaching can take place in the form of gamification where students learn new knowledge through interactive gaming. The list of benefits could go on as technologies have brought positive changes to education beyond our imaginations.

　　The prompt overemphasizes distractions as a crucial side effect of introducing technologies in the process of teaching and learning. I agree that this is a legitimate concern, but I also believe that none of the distractions associated with technologies is strong enough to even out their benefits. Some people might argue that technology has made certain distractions readily available and easily accessible to students. For example, online gaming, Youtubing, or social networking are taking away tremendous amounts of time and attention from students all too easily. However, this distraction is not a deficiency inherent in technologies. In other words, if it were not for technologies, students could be distracted by other various factors as well, because distraction is essentially triggered by an individual's lack of concentration: one can even be distracted by daydreaming! That's why self-discipline, the ability to control oneself to fend off diversion, has always been an important part of students' training at school.

223

Part 4 Issue 精选范文

Distraction by technologies could also refer to how technologies get in the way of teacher-students communication in the classroom. Surely, we should not dismiss this concern from many seminar instructors when they complain that laptops, tablets and other electronic devices often become a divider between the teacher and the students, which stalls proper communication. Although technologies can improve instruction in many ways, they do not necessarily need to replace the cherished face-to-face class discussion that is traditionally considered central to the success of seminars, particularly in the field of social sciences and the humanities. In this case, instructors can minimize the negative effects by implementing specific policies on the use of technologies. For example, instructors can discourage or even ban students' use of electronic devices during class meetings.

Last but not least, distraction can refer to how tech devices potentially distract students from independent thinking. Some educators worry that an over-reliance on the use of technology might prevent students from engaging in active thinking, leading to the demise of creativity and the ability to think critically. Surely, the success of classwork seems to depend on students' search skills rather than independent thinking. However, it would be ridiculous to exaggerate this problem and believe that the use of technology in education would hinder people's ability to think. In fact, technologies greatly facilitate people's thinking, and provide tools for people to solve problems. For example, starting with Aristotle, scholars have been attempting to categorize stories into different types according to their emotional development, yet because of an enormous number of books, no agreement has been reached all these years, until the invention of data mining programs. Researchers have run 1,700 stories to measure the positive and negative emotional impacts of words, and revealed that there are only six basic emotional arcs of storytelling. Projects like this take place every day at school; it shows that technologies help produce more knowledge by facilitating human thinking.

To sum up, we have to admit that education never takes place in an ideal scenario that is free of vices. While the introduction of technologies to education surely brings about certain challenges, it's important that we find ways to control their side effects and realize that technology-driven education is the future as it generates more effective ways of teaching and learning.

Words & Expressions

archive *n.* 档案
virtual *adj.* 虚拟的
gamification *n.* 游戏化
even out *v.* 抹平

fend *v.* 挡开
tablet *n.* 平板电脑
cherish *v.* 珍爱
demise *n.* 死亡

Sample Essay B: Good

When you, as a parent, watch your 12-year-old kid playing GTA in front of the TV for 4 hours when all his schoolwork is still blank, it is easy for you to accuse the game of distracting your boy. The prompt is indeed making a similar accusation, which, in my opinion, has overstated the harm that technology has on children while not giving enough credit to the marvelous potential technology can bring to learning.

Let me just list out how technologies are often believed to distract. First, games on computers and smartphones are said to take up too much of children's time. Second, Internet pornography is a threat to children and even adults' lifestyle. Third, social networks force people to spend too much time building meaningless relationships. I do have counterarguments for all of these points. For starters, people need leisure time; children today need games, just like children in the past enjoyed TV programs. As long as the needs are harnessed, they don't necessarily hinder learning. As for pornography, I still have just one word, harnessing, so it doesn't have to be bad. Finally, meaningless relationships on Facebook are no more damaging or time consuming than getting intoxicated in a nightclub or bar with a bunch of fake friends. Humanity is to blame, rather than technology.

Having addressed all the concerns, let me redirect to technology's potential contributions to learning, and there are many. First, it's much less confined by time and finances. This is a wonder to people in less advanced areas, because now all they need is a computer connected to the internet to access quality information in any discipline. Wikipedia, Coursera, and Harvard open courses, these are just a few among many sources for learning that potentially set people on a level playing field, well, a less uneven playing field at least.

Second, technologies make learning customized, and thus more effective. Interactive apps are designed to recognize learners' personalities, habits, and growth, and to store all this information to adjust future learning curves. Many tech companies are exploiting this possibility, so even though it is still premature as an idea, it is easy to imagine how much it can elevate learning experience in the future. The machine can adjust the pace, the humor, the logic, the interface, and a lot of other factors in ways that make learning more fun and less stressful.

Finally, technology bridges gaps. Learning isn't just about learning hardcore textbook knowledge. It is also about the learning of people and culture. Technologies help people set their eyes on a much expanded universe, where they not just see, but also feel, what it is like to be someone completely different. This potential is especially exciting to me, because it finally makes it possible for our world to be one. When the old earth is filled with parochialism, racism and nationalism, technologies offer the opportunity for people to set aside their biases and build bonds across borders. And this, I believe is the most necessary lesson for all.

Overall, my position on this is unequivocal, even though I have far from exhausted the advantages that technologies bestow on learning. It is easy for me to see past the trouble that technologies allegedly brought about, and to embrace the bright future they promise.

Part 4 Issue 精选范文

> **98** To be an effective leader, a public official must maintain the highest ethical and moral standards.
>
> Write a response in which you discuss the extent to which you agree or disagree with the claim. In developing and supporting your position, be sure to address the most compelling reasons and/or examples that could be used to challenge your position.

Sample Essay A: Outstanding

　　In general, public officials have been elected for their strong leadership, their willingness to represent the people, their negotiation and decision-making skills, or their charisma. It's quite rare that public officials are elected for their precise ethical and moral standards, but any sort of moral slippage is very likely to terminate their leadership, and negate their overall achievements and efforts. One of the most famous cases in this regard may be the impeachment of Bill Clinton, derived from his sexual scandals with Monica Lewinsky. Incidents like this seem to suggest that leaders are also role models, who are expected to embody the highest ethical and moral standards of a society.

　　However, the issue is much more complicated. Immediately noticeable, the prompt assumes that ethical and moral standards are universally recognized and practiced. In fact, the understanding of ethics and morality is contingent upon one's education, political stance, and religious background, so the question becomes whose ethical and moral standards should a public official maintain that will bring about the most beneficial results to the general public. For example, the Ronald Reagan Administration refused to take action about the AIDS epidemic in the 1980s, and delayed medical research on potential treatments. They justified their inaction by pinpointing homosexuality as a moral decadence, and the consequence of their own moral standards was that hundreds of thousands of people died helplessly. This traumatic episode in recent history shows that public officials' own standards of ethics and morality may turn out to be detrimental to the people they are serving.

　　Even when public officials are holding widely accepted ethical and moral standards as their guiding principles, they often have to make compromises as the power of their leadership is also confined by the Constitution or by the law. For example, the Neo-Nazi leader and white supremist Richard Spencer has been successful in renting venues from public universities to promote his divisive agenda. There have been numerous protests against his retrogressive and hateful speech, but leaders in public schools cannot deny his request to hold his talks. This is not because school leaders endorse Spencer's racist messages, but because the *First Amendment to the Constitution* establishes "Freedom of Speech", which grants its citizens the equal right to speak. Examples like this suggest that decision-making cannot always be driven by leaders' highest ethical and moral standards; they demonstrate how real-life politics are tremendously complex and often require negotiation among policies, laws, morality, and conscience.

　　People who hold contradicting views might argue that the development of contemporary media has made the scrutiny of public officials' private lives so much easier that they have to maintain the highest ethical and moral standards regardless of whether they are at work or not. True, the flying cases of political scandals do reveal the power of media and the ethical and moral dark sides of the leaders, but the argument fails to explain, for example, why Donald Trump, whose misogynist and racist messages were widely spread and discussed and unabashedly appearing on his own Twitter account, has nevertheless been elected as the President of the United States. I argue that Trump's election has sent out a message of a renewed understanding of leadership and morality. In an increasingly profit-driven society like the United States, people cease to evaluate their leaders with a sense of integrity. Instead, society has adopted a more lenient attitude towards a leader's surrender of integrity and the compartmentalization of his or her life; for instance, it doesn't seem as scandalous as before when a male leader publicly supports feminist movements but privately treats women as second-class citizens. Consequently, people are likely to accept leaders' moral decadence in their private lives as long as they are publicly denouncing it. In this way, sadly, ethical and moral standards appear more and more irrelevant to leaderships.

In conclusion, even though we still dream about being led by people who have integrity and a strong sense of righteousness, whose decisions are heavily determined by their high ethical and moral consciousness, reality is far from this ideal.

Words & Expressions

moral slippage 道德滑坡
impeachment n. 弹劾
embody v. 体现
epidemic n. 流行病
pinpoint v. 精准指出
decadence n. 衰落
episode n. 一段时间

agenda n. 政治议程（通常带贬义）
retrogressive adj. 倒退的
misogynistic adj. 厌女的
unabashedly adv. 厚脸皮地
lenient adj. 宽容的
compartmentalization n. 区分，划分
denounce v. 谴责

Sample Essay B: Good

Why would an effective leader need to maintain the highest moral standards? That statement may sound absurd in the beginning, but with certain modern developments, an untarnished moral image is probably necessary to maintain effective leadership.

Obviously, there are areas of morality where public officials should never underperform, in the past or now. They should not take bribes. They should not collude with large corporations. They should not sell secrets to enemy nations. These clear rules need no reiteration, and I don't think anyone will openly object. These are not just ethical guidelines; they already step into the legal, realm, for a good reason. Without these regulations, there will be no justice or security.

What is more debatable are the moral rules regarding an official's personal life. Can he/she have an affair? Can he/she openly insult other people? Does it matter if he/she ever smoked pot? I don't think there has to be any necessary relationship between behaving inappropriately in one's private life and being an ineffective leader. Bill Clinton had the Monica Lewinsky scandal, but he was probably one of the few American presidents in recent decades that brought economic prosperity. Have an affair with whoever you want, but be upright when you try to set out a new policy. That could be the "ideal".

But that's not the reality. The reality is, with the scrutiny of the modern media, your every dark secret goes into public attention. If that's not bad enough, the public would ignore all the contributions you have made, but instead focuses on badmouthing your private secrets. In the end, it undercuts your professional efficiency. Even Bill Clinton spent months dealing with his impeachment, and that case cost tons of public resources. Some people really believe that leaders should be moral saints. They believe these public figures are role models for their kids, so they should behave properly. Stupid as that rationale sounds, you cannot change that it is how a lot of people think. And as long as they think that, your public image is important if you want to be a successful leader.

I may have made it sound as if all a leader needs is a sound moral image rather than high moral standards. Well, yes, if he/she can secretly be scum but appear upright. In fact, isn't that how most leaders are? All a country needs is that the leader effectively carries out policies and maintains a respectable figure. If he/she somehow manages to achieve both while enjoys his/her private life, kudos to him/her. But I am not a bit interested in how moral he/she is in his/her secret sphere.

100 In most professions and academic fields, imagination is more important than knowledge.

Write a response in which you discuss the extent to which you agree or disagree with the statement and explain your reasoning for the position you take. In developing and supporting your position, you should consider ways in which the statement might or might not hold true and explain how these considerations shape your position.

▶ Sample Essay A: Outstanding

  From prehistoric stone tools, to the inventions of printing and paper, and to the ongoing search for artificial intelligence, people have never ceased to use their knowledge and imagination to push forward the progress of human civilization. When imagination encourages the human mind to think freely, knowledge works as a gatekeeper who undergirds predictions, answers questions, prevents recurring mistakes, and fends off risks. I believe that no field of inquiry can advance without a solid repertoire of knowledge and courage of imagination.

  However, the issue is more complicated than that. It is interesting to note how often the debates about knowledge and imagination inadvertently encircle them into an antithetical and mutually destructive relation: in supporting knowledge, people claim that free-thinking remains useless until substantiated by the current expertise; similarly, in upholding imagination, they often argue that an overemphasis on knowledge would constrain the mind's creativity. These narratives, however, demonstrate a quite limited understanding of both: they consider knowledge to be only a set of hard facts and axioms, and equal imagination to mere unfounded fantasy. What I hope to show is the opposite, that imagination and knowledge engage in an interactive relation, where knowledge induces and guides thinking, and imagination produces knowledge and better understanding of the world.

  Let's start with knowledge. In their famous correspondence, Freud called Einstein a "lucky fellow" because no one without specialized training in physics, astronomy or chemistry dared render any sort of judgment regarding Einstein's work, but Freud's research had been dismissed as sham science as people believed that they were masters of their own minds, and thus there is no need to go further towards understanding the matter. Granted anyone can have a certain level of self-understanding, what Freud's skeptics didn't realize was that his research and knowledge about the human mind not only offers systematic understanding of human psychology, but also propels critical thinking in many other fields to understand complex social and cultural issues. For example, his theory of psychosexual development has profoundly reshaped modern early childhood education and pedagogical training. His study of melancholia, a pathological condition of the mind, facilitates the formulation of modern social theories such as gender theory and critical race theory. In this case, we see that knowledge is not just hard facts; it brings new perspectives in contemplating issues in many fields of inquiry beyond its own.

  Knowledge can also exert a crucial guidance for thinking, which is conducive to making well-considered decisions. This is particularly true with the arts. Society traditionally views academic degrees in the arts as worthless because it believes that many talents are innate, and that an appreciation of the arts does not require training as well, and thus an expertise in the arts becomes a highly contested notion. Mozart has often been criticized about having used too many notes, but he famously responded, "Exactly as many as are necessary." His retort captures precisely how expertise sets artists apart: anyone can draw a picture, for example, but only artists with specific knowledge know how to properly abstract a river by using just a few strokes or not go overboard with extra touches when rendering a realistic painting of a mountain. In this sense, knowledge transforms into a skill that leads the mind to render guarded decisions, even in very subjective fields like the arts.

Other than the ability to think freely and create, imagination plays an important role in many professions whose success depends greatly on interpersonal relationships. For example, the health care industry involves confidential communicative relationships between a professional and a client, such as therapeutic alliances, which presupposes a mutual bond that is considered essential for ultimate emotional and psychological healing. As philosopher David Hume once eloquently argued one's ability to imagine will morph into felt sensory experiences, imagination factors in this mutual bond powerfully in that it allows caregivers, be it nurses, doctors, psychologists or counselors, to empathically place themselves in the position of the clients and vicariously sense their pain and needs. We can extend this argument to modern society in general, in a time when many are undergoing unfortunate feelings of anxiety and depression, imagination is not a phantasmic placebo or a groundless hope; it is an effective treatment which allows people to understand others' difficulties so that we can build communities even when there are many personal differences.

It is almost impossible to pick a winner between imagination and knowledge, not only because the history of human civilization is already a collaboration between the two, but also because they are in a healthy, reciprocal relation that undergirds the progress of human society. We need to employ the functions of imagination and knowledge to the fullest to bring the world into a better future.

Words & Expressions

cease v. 停止	sham n. 骗子	morph v. 变形，改变
undergird v. 加强	pedagogical adj. 教学的	empathetically adv. 共情地
repertoire n. 全部本领	innate adj. 先天的，固有的	vicariously adv. 从他人经验中感受到地
encircle v. 包围	retort n. 反驳	phatasmic adj. 幽灵般的，虚幻的
antithetical adj. 对立的	overboard adv. 过火地	placebo n. 安慰剂
substantiate v. 证实	rendering n. 表现	reciprocal adj. 互惠的，相互的
render v. 提出，给出	confidential adj. 机密的	

Sample Essay B: Good

The prompt tries to downplay the importance of knowledge in most professions. However, from my standpoint, both imagination and knowledge are valuable assets in almost every field of endeavor. Imagination without knowledge is unguided, while knowledge without imagination is uninspired. It takes the perfect unison between the two to execute a brilliant idea.

Take the arts for example, the field where imagination is certainly the key. When we look at any artist in history who initiated a new trend, there were always fresh new perspectives to observe the world. Picasso was certainly quite imaginative when he took apart objects and reassembled them in unprecedented ways. Van Gogh was certainly brave when he manipulated light and color in a non-traditional method. However, outsiders are often negligent of the fact that both these masters were well trained in their early lives, a training that provided the necessary expertise for their later height. Their examples aptly demonstrate that artistic achievement is often the happy marriage of creative vision and masterful technique.

The same holds for science, a field where the importance of knowledge is often stressed. True, it is hard to imagine a Nobel Prize winner in physics who is not familiar with quantum mechanics or general relativity. In this area, solid mathematical skills and understanding of past physical theories are essential in making new discoveries. However, no matter how much data a physicist compiles, it won't automatically be formulated into a new hypothesis. It takes imagination, therefore, to come up with new ways to interpret observed phenomena. Simply put, without the support of knowledge, a new theory is just an unreliable guess; without imagination, evidence is never more than some meaningless numbers.

The business field is no exception in its reliance on both knowledge and imagination. Any executive in a modern international corporation must be familiar with the supply and demand relationship. He/She also needs to understand the roles and obligations of each position within the company so as to make them collaborate effectively. However, knowledge alone isn't going to produce a new product. Any good product that completely changes consumers' habits, the iPhone, Facebook, or Airbnb, is revolutionary in its own way, which reflects its founders' vision and imagination.

The list doesn't stop here. Whether in the military, in sports, or in politics, the rule is the same. Progress is possible when one dares to imagine what didn't exist before. But progress is realized only when people with knowledge and skills build up the way to what has been imagined.

Part 4　Issue 精选范文

102 Critical judgment of work in any given field has little value unless it comes from someone who is an expert in that field.

Write a response in which you discuss the extent to which you agree or disagree with the statement and explain your reasoning for the position you take. In developing and supporting your position, you should consider ways in which the statement might or might not hold true and explain how these considerations shape your position.

▶ Sample Essay A: Outstanding

　　Despite the deep-seated Western ideology of individualism and self-reliance, people nowadays find themselves unwittingly dependent on strangers: they check the reviews on TripAdvisor before booking vacations, or refer to Rotten Tomatoes as they decide what movies are worth their money. Such prevalent unsolicited review systems suggest that we tend to place unmitigated trust in other people's opinions for our own decision-making, even though we have no knowledge about their tastes, educational backgrounds, social status, or areas of expertise. When reviews from experts such as film critics are readily available, what accounts for such popularization of public reviews from seemingly unreliable sources?

　　This topic draws our attention to an important issue in the process of manufacturing and consumption, artwork's creation and reception, and general knowledge production: are experts the only people who can claim the authority to critically judge the value of work? In this essay, I seek to grapple with this question by first historicizing the statement in the contemporary era and then moving on to a discussion of aesthetics and ethics that often complicates the issue of critical judgment. I intend to show that it is tremendously difficult to argue for such sweeping generalization that critical judgment of work is valuable only when it comes from experts.

　　Surely, in certain areas, expertise is hardly transferable without professional training, so only experts can offer adequate critical judgment. For example, people go to dermatologists to find out why they have a persistent rash, or they consult divorce attorneys for advice on divorce settlements. Not to mention that in advanced areas of study such as quantum mechanics or psychometrics, knowledge becomes highly specified insofar as it caters to only a narrow audience.

　　However, technological advancement has dramatically revolutionized the ways in which knowledge is produced, archived, and shared, so much so that it has blurred the lines between experts and laymen. With online services like Wikipedia and WikiHow, anyone can contribute their knowledge of a specific topic without necessarily being an expert in that field: fragmentary pieces of information, life hacks, useful tips, and even trivia from both experts and non-experts can be digitally archived for the general public to access, who can also engage in open discussions online to ensure the quality and credibility of that knowledge. In this light, we come to see that, in the era of high-speed information exchange, expertise no longer belongs to experts per se; it has transformed into a virtual repertoire of knowledge gained through not only professional training, but also personal experience and accidental discoveries. This suggests that valuable judgment does not necessarily come from only experts in contemporary times.

One significant underlying assumption of the prompt is that there is only one true value of work, and that value can only be determined by experts. This assumption is unwarranted, particularly when we consider the prompt in industrial production and consumption. For example, in designing a car, while a development engineer cares about fuel efficiency and a manufacturing engineer values safety, customers may be concerned first and foremost about the car's cost. In this case, critical judgment from non-experts such as customers is valuable because it has made production and consumption a much more informed and targeted process: producers may look for areas to improve their merchandise from negative customer reviews, and consumers could seek recommendations for quality products from positive feedback.

Building upon the argument in the prior paragraph, we can further complicate the issue by thinking about the roles that aesthetics and ethics play in critical judgment and cultural life. There seems to be no way to evaluate an artwork from an entirely objective perspective, because its aesthetics may trigger divergent affective responses. As Theodore Adorno suggests, there is no standard for what is considered beautiful. Accordingly, aesthetics is not so much a way to render judgment as to share the joy from appreciation of the art. In this way, critical judgment of an artwork from a non-expert viewer also has value, because it expresses how such artwork is received. In juxtaposing the discussion of critical judgment with ethics, we come across tough dilemmas. For example, should euthanasia be performed upon the patient's wish, even when the doctor insists that there is a chance of survival with active treatment? Here, we see another problematic assumption of the prompt that experts' judgment is valuable, because it tends to be correct or can be validated by empirical evidence. When ethics comes into play, it becomes staggeringly difficult to say whether the doctor's judgment is valuable, and to whom. It reminds us that while knowledge, expertise, and experience can certainly help inform our decision-making, we should also not dismiss where our feelings and emotions direct us.

Words & Expressions

deep-seated *adj.* 根深蒂固的
ideology *n.* 意识形态，思想体系
unwittingly *adv.* 不经意间
prevalent *adj.* 流行的
unsolicited *adj.* 不请自来的
unmitigated *adj.* 十足的，未被缓和的
grapple with 努力应对

sweeping *adj.* 彻底的，全面的，广泛的
cater to 迎合
archive *v.* 存档
layman *n.* 门外汉，俗人
fragmentary *adj.* 碎片化的
life hack 生活窍门
quality *adj.* 优质的

divergent *adj.* 发散的，多样的
affective *adj.* 情感的
juxtapose *v.* 并置
euthanasia *n.* 安乐死
validate *v.* 证实
empirical *adj.* 经验主义的，实证主义的
staggeringly *adv.* 令人难以置信地

Sample Essay B: Good

When a piece of work is produced in a field, who is qualified to critique it? No doubt experts within the field have valid opinions, but who else? In my view, whether a critique from a complete outsider is valuable is a question that depends on the nature of the field, which requires more careful examination.

In rigorous sciences, laymen don't have much to contribute. A few years ago, a folk scientist alleged that he had established the existence of gravitational waves. It became quite a story when a couple of years ago the gravitational wave was finally experimentally proven to exist. Media everywhere spread that folk scientist's old story as if he was some sort of a prophet. Insiders take him as, well, a joke. You can say black holes exist or don't; you can say whether the number of stars in the universe is odd or even; you can also claim that Einstein's theory of relativity is right or wrong. You can say whatever you want, but it doesn't matter, because science doesn't need opinions, but proof based on observation and sound logic. Anything involving flawed reasoning or incomplete data, no matter how correct it turns out, fails to stand as a sound theory. Thus, an outsider, without the necessary training or data, contributes literally nothing to this rigorous practice.

The complete opposite is professional sports. The year 2018 was the year of the Soccer World Cup, the festival for countless "soccer fans" who have only heard the names of two players, Leo Messi and Cristiano Ronaldo. They randomly watched a game and decided to support, say, team Germany, and berated the team for failing to qualify. Or they saw Mbappé, the promising kid from France, dive, and lambasted him for lacking sportsmanship. Or they watched the only game in their life, the finals, and were convinced that the referee held bias against Croatia. Do their opinions matter? These people hardly know a thing about soccer, but ironically, they matter, even more than those fans that have watched the Champions League their entire lives. Being the most influential sport on earth, soccer establishes its dominance not just because of its most loyal fans, but also because of its continual attraction to new fans. The World Cup is a carnival for everyone, beginners or experts. The collective celebration, whether rational or impulsive, is what keeps soccer's influence pervasive and persistent.

Even though I've listed only two fields, I believe I've made my point clear. Whether outside opinions matter is related to how much the field places its survival and prosperity on outsiders. If it is a relatively closed circle like science, then peer review is probably all it needs; in contrast, for a field that reciprocates with the general public, it requires the opinions of many.

> **115** Some people claim that you can tell whether a nation is great by looking at the achievements of its rulers, artists, or scientists. Others argue that the surest indicator of a great nation is, in fact, the general welfare of all its people.
>
> Write a response in which you discuss which view more closely aligns with your own position and explain your reasoning for the position you take. In developing and supporting your position, you should address both of the views presented.

Sample Essay A: Outstanding

The ways in which we evaluate the greatness of nations have been very rough. We look at a nation's wealth through its GDP and growth rates; we examine a nation's security through its military strength, international relations and foreign policies; we study a nation's stability through tracing its citizen's trust towards their government, and if institutions remain strong for a relatively long period of time; we can also investigate the general welfare of its people, including health, employment, income level, education, overall happiness, and so on. A nation doing poorly in these regards is unlikely to be great. For example, any country that is infested with wars can never be great, no matter what. These conventional criteria for evaluating a nation suggest that both a country's material development, exemplified by the achievements of the leaders, artists, and scientists, and the citizens' general sense of well-being, are equally important in manifesting a nation's greatness.

However, these aforementioned categories are far from ideal for examining how great a nation is. Though they can adequately demonstrate the development of a nation from various perspectives, or how strong a nation may be, politically and economically, in comparison to others on the world stage, these statistics do not necessarily translate into "a good life" for each citizen. For example, high GDP index does not entail that ordinary people live comfortably, the number of aircraft carriers does not make citizens necessarily feel any safer, or, similarly, the welfare system does not guarantee that it can meet all its citizens' minimal needs. I would even go a step further and argue that these categories are not established with the intention of evaluating whether a nation is great or not, but to instigate a sense of competition among nations. Indeed, nations use these indexes to show off what areas they are leading in, and use what they lack to justify further investment. Hypothetically, if a country is leading the rest of the world in every aspect of these categories with flying colors, but many of its citizens are unemployed or homeless, is it still a great nation?

The difficulty of comprehending this prompt lies in that both sides assume the greatness of a nation can be objectively evaluated through quantifiable criteria. However, each individual's own perspectives matter in their judgment of a nation's greatness. An activist may not see the United States as a great nation because of Trump's decision to build a wall along the Mexico border to prevent illegal immigrants and the separation of families at borders. A new entrepreneur may not see the U.K. as a great nation to start a small business in simply because of the economic instability and uncertainty derived from Brexit. An artist may not consider Saudi Arabia to be a great nation because of rigid censorship of the arts by the government. Taking sides on this debate is difficult, because one's judgement of a nation's greatness is heavily contingent upon his/her own backgrounds, needs, and pursuits in life.

One's own perspectives matter because evaluating a nation is also a sentimental endeavor. As everyone is born into a particular nation, a sense of belonging and patriotism has made judgements of a nation's greatness also largely subjective. While we can argue that China and the United States are examples of great nations by showing numbers to suggest their prosperity and military power, we can also say that everyone's own country is the greatest because of our emotional attachments and enormous amounts of pride. This is because, as Benedict Anderson has famously argued, nations are imagined communities that offer each individual a shared national identity, upon which a sense of bonding and closeness can be reached even among people who do not know each other. The idea of a nation is thus very personal, deeply incorporated into each citizen's understanding of life, community, and home. Ultimately, while the achievements of a country's leaders and elites may indicate its overall development, to judge if a nation is great is rather a subjective matter.

Words & Expressions

instigate v. 煽动，激起　　　　　　　　　　　　　**with flying colors** 出色地

Sample Essay B: Good

How should we define a great nation, by its people's general welfare, or instead by the achievements of its elites? To me, both factors are indispensable for a nation to be called "great".

On the one hand, to identify a great nation, one certainly should not miss its people's welfare. There are countless cases in human history in which a nation's outstanding individuals produce many remarkable achievements at the cost of people's livelihood. Such a nation can hardly be counted as great, for it misses the original intention of humans to form political entities, namely, to protect the people. These totalitarian nations produce each monumental project to fulfill the personal ambitions and pleasures of the tyrant. One needs to look no further than the former Soviet Union to confirm this point. It made countless scientific achievements within the last century, but at the expense of its common people's livelihood. In the end, when many of its people were short of bread and milk, the country could no longer survive on satellites and semiconductors. Whatever achievements were made, they were not dedicated to making its people's life better. When we now look at this history, we think that its atrocities have overshadowed any of its greatness.

On the other hand, even though the general welfare of the people is a necessary indicator of a great nation, it is not a sufficient marker. In fact, when we look at the names of great nations in the entirety of human history, these names pop out: ancient Greece, the Roman Empire, China, Great Britain, modern America, and so on. When we think about them, we do not immediately reflect on the comfort of their people, but we remind ourselves of all the marks these countries have imprinted on the entirety of human civilization, such as democracy, the aqueduct, paper, the laws of motion, and free speech, just to name a few. Apparently, these all have much to do with great individuals. In sharp contrast with these examples are the wealthy countries surrounding the Persian Gulf. Perhaps their citizens enjoy very happy lives given their financial status. However, these countries cannot leave their names in the hall of fame simply by exploiting natural oil resources.

All in all, the work of great individuals and the general welfare of people are not in tension as the prompt suggests. In a country where life is relatively easy, people have more opportunities to develop their own strengths, and the success of these individuals will, in turn, benefit the life of the general public. To sum up, only through scrutiny into both aspects can one reliably tell how great a nation really is.

解密GRE写作
论证思维

Part 5　Argument 题库逐题精析

Part 5　Argument 题库逐题精析

1 Woven baskets characterized by a particular distinctive pattern have previously been found only in the immediate vicinity of the prehistoric village of Palea, and therefore were believed to have been made only by the Palean people. Recently, however, archaeologists discovered such a "Palean" basket in Lithos, an ancient village across the Brim River from Palea. The Brim River is very deep and broad, and so the ancient Paleans could have crossed it only by boat, and no Palean boats have been found. Thus it follows that the so-called Palean baskets were not uniquely Palean.

译　文

一种具有特殊花纹的编织篮子以前只在史前村落 Palea 的附近发现过，因此这种篮子被认为是 Palea 人独有的。但是，最近考古学家在一个与 Palea 隔着 Brim 河的村庄 Lithos 发现了这样一个类似的篮子。因为 Brim 河很深很宽，所以古代 Palea 人只可能坐船过去，而人们没有发现过 Palea 人的船只。这表明所谓 Palea 的篮子并不是只有 Palea 才有的。

文章结构图

结　　论：The so-called Palean baskets were not uniquely Palean.
结论类型：**解释型**

各步推理分析

① 其他

Signal：so
Inference：河宽而深 ⟹ 只能坐船过河
Assumption：千年来河没变；没有其他方法
Counterexamples：千年前河可能又浅又窄，很容易过去，不需要坐船；冬天结冰走过去；离源头近，可以绕过去
Evidence：需要知道当地以前的地理和气候信息，比如一份古老的地图就可以解决以上很多问题

② 证词类

Signal：no... has been found

Inference：没发现 P 的船 $\Longrightarrow$ P 没有船

Assumption：如果有船，必然会被发现

Counterexamples：木船早被腐蚀了；考古勘探工作才刚进行，根本就没有搜索完毕

Evidence：需要知道考古勘探的深度；间接的文献、艺术方面的证据也可以帮助我们判断当年是否有船

③ 解释类

Signal：在 L 发现了篮子，以及步骤①②的结论，最终作者相当于认为能在 L 发现篮子就是因为不光 P 有篮子

Inference：只能坐船过河 + P 没有船 + 在 L 发现了篮子 $\Longrightarrow$ 所谓 P 的篮子并不只是 P 有

Assumption：L 没有船，别的地方不可能有船，这个篮子不是之后运过去的

Counterexamples：L 或者别的地方的商人将船带走；篮子从 P 去了 L 是几千年后的事情

Evidence：需要对周边其他城镇进行考古和文献调查

2

The following appeared as part of a letter to the editor of a scientific journal.

"A recent study of eighteen rhesus monkeys provides clues as to the effects of birth order on an individual's levels of stimulation. The study showed that in stimulating situations (such as an encounter with an unfamiliar monkey), firstborn infant monkeys produce up to twice as much of the hormone cortisol, which primes the body for increased activity levels, as do their younger siblings. Firstborn humans also produce relatively high levels of cortisol in stimulating situations (such as the return of a parent after an absence). The study also found that during pregnancy, first-time mother monkeys had higher levels of cortisol than did those who had had several offspring."

译 文

最近一项对恒河猴的调查表明了出生次序对于个体刺激水平的影响。调查显示，在刺激的环境下（例如遇到一只陌生的猴子），头胎小猴的皮质醇分泌会比其弟弟妹妹多一倍（皮质醇的分泌为身体做好了更剧烈活动的准备）。人类的头胎孩子在遇到刺激（例如父母外出回家）时也会分泌出相对更多的皮质醇。研究还发现，第一次怀孕的母猴孕期分泌的皮质醇要比生过几次孩子的母猴孕期分泌的皮质醇多很多。

文章结构图

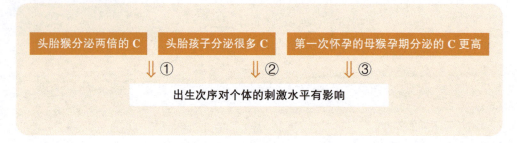

结　论：Birth order influences an individual's levels of stimulation.
结论类型：解释型

各步推理分析

① **解释型**

Signal：头胎猴面对刺激分泌两倍的 C，作者将其归结为出生次序的影响
Inference：头胎猴面对刺激分泌两倍的 C ⟹ 出生次序对个体的刺激水平有影响
Assumption：没有其他解释
Counterexamples：如果实验是在同时间测量不同猴子对同样刺激的反应，则年龄可能成为干扰变量
Evidence：需要做额外对比实验来排除年龄可能产生的影响，即把同年龄段但出生次序不同的个体进行对

比，如果刺激水平仍与出生次序相关，才能加强原文的论证

② 解释型

Signal：头胎人面对刺激分泌很多 C，作者将其归结为出生次序的影响

Inference：头胎人面对刺激分泌很多 C $\Longrightarrow$ 出生次序对个体的刺激水平有影响

Assumption：比较的对象是非头胎孩子；头胎孩子分泌的 C 很多

Counterexamples：这个比较很可能不是跟第二胎、第三胎的孩子比，而是和人一生当中的平均反应相比，很可能婴儿的反应整体就更剧烈；不清楚高多少，高 1% 是误差允许范围之内的，没有意义

Evidence：需要知道 relatively high 是相对于什么进行比较的，比较对象只有是非头胎人时，这个数据才有价值；需要知道到底有多高

③ 解释型

Signal：第一次怀孕的母猴孕期面对刺激分泌的 C 更高，而作者认为，这也说明出生次序对刺激水平有影响

Inference：第一次怀孕的母猴孕期面对刺激分泌的 C 更高 $\Longrightarrow$ 出生次序对个体的刺激水平有影响

Assumption：妈妈的反应机理会传递给孩子

Counterexamples：第一次当妈的猴子之所以反应激烈是因为没怀过孕，面对什么刺激都大惊小怪，这个事情根本不会影响到孩子

Evidence：需要证据表明母猴受刺激时的反应激烈程度会与幼猴有关联

Part 5 Argument 题库逐题精析

3

The following appeared as a letter to the editor from a Central Plaza store owner.

"Over the past two years, the number of shoppers in Central Plaza has been steadily decreasing while the popularity of skateboarding has increased dramatically. Many Central Plaza store owners believe that the decrease in their business is due to the number of skateboard users in the plaza. There has also been a dramatic increase in the amount of litter and vandalism throughout the plaza. Thus, we recommend that the city prohibit skateboarding in Central Plaza. If skateboarding is prohibited here, we predict that business in Central Plaza will return to its previously high levels."

译　文

过去两年，在中央广场购物的顾客数量持续下降，但滑板却明显越来越流行。很多广场商铺的店主都认为其生意的下滑是因为滑板玩家数量增多造成的。并且，广场的垃圾和公物破坏现象也越来越多。因此，我们建议市政府禁止人们在中央广场上玩滑板。如果能禁止在这儿玩滑板，我们预测中央广场的生意会回到以前的高度。

文章结构图

结　　论：The city should prohibit skateboarding in Central Plaza.
结论类型：建议型

各步推理分析

①解释类

Signal：Over the past two years, the number of shoppers has been decreasing, while skateboarding increases，作者试图建立 skateboarding 与 the number of shoppers 的关系

Inference：skateboarding 增多同时 shoppers 减少 ⟹ skateboarding 增多造成 shoppers 减少

Assumption：没有其他解释，不是因为生意不好才造成滑板增多

Counterexamples：店主经营不善；经济危机；网购增多；滑板玩家只在冷清、空旷的地方玩耍，恰恰是这个地方已经没有顾客了，才使得这里变成了滑板中心

Evidence：需要证据排除其他可能造成生意不好的因素

② 类比类

Signal：①的结论，以及下文认为禁止滑板会使得生意恢复

Inference：skateboarding 增多造成 shoppers 减少 ⟹ 禁止 skateboarding 会使得生意恢复

Assumption：滑板对 Plaza 生意的打击是可以挽回的

Counterexamples：滑板增多彻底使得消费者对 Plaza 失去兴趣，并在其他地方形成了新的商业区，形成了固定的消费行为

Evidence：需要证据表明离开 Plaza 的顾客会因为 Plaza 购物环境的提高而回归

③ 解释类

Signal：also an increase in litter and vandalism，结合之前的 skateboarding increases

Inference：skateboarding 增多同时 litter 和 vandalism 增多 ⟹ skateboarding 增多造成 litter 和 vandalism 增多

Assumption：没有其他解释

Counterexamples：管理不善，清洁、维护人员减少

Evidence：需要证据排除其他可能造成 litter 和 vandalism 增多的因素

④ 建议类

Signal：②③结论，以及文章的最终结论是一个建议

Inference：禁止 skateboarding 会使得生意恢复 + skateboarding 增多造成 litter 和 vandalism 增多 ⟹ 应该禁止 skateboarding

Assumption：没有其他更有效的解决方案

Counterexamples：增加管理，将 skateboarding 分区

Evidence：需要考察其他可能解决方案的有效性

Part 5 Argument 题库逐题精析

4 The following appeared in a letter from a homeowner to a friend.

"Of the two leading real estate firms in our town—Adams Realty and Fitch Realty—Adams Realty is clearly superior. Adams has 40 real estate agents; in contrast, Fitch has 25, many of whom work only part-time. Moreover, Adams' revenue last year was twice as high as that of Fitch, and included home sales that averaged ＄168,000, compared to Fitch's ＄144,000. Homes listed with Adams sell faster as well: ten years ago I listed my home with Fitch, and it took more than four months to sell; last year, when I sold another home, I listed it with Adams, and it took only one month. Thus, if you want to sell your home quickly and at a good price, you should use Adams Realty."

译 文

在本市的两家最顶尖的房地产经纪公司——Adams Realty 和 Fitch Realty——中，Adams 显然更优秀一些。Adams 有 40 名房地产经纪人，而 Fitch 只有 25 名，且很多是兼职。而且，Adams 去年的营收是 Fitch 的两倍，其房屋平均售出价为 ＄168 000，而 Fitch 仅为 ＄144 000。在 Adams 销售的房屋卖得也更快：十年前，我把我的房产交给 Fitch，它用了四个多月才卖出去；去年，我在 Adams 卖了另一处房产，只用了一个月就售出。因此，要想让你的房产卖得更快更贵，你应该选择 Adams Realty。

文章结构图

结　　论：If you want to sell your home quickly and at a good price, you should use Adams Realty.
结论类型：建议型

各步推理分析

①数据类
Signal：40, 25
Inference：A 有 40 名房产中介，而 F 只有 25 名，且很多是兼职 ⇒ A 比 F 更善于卖房
Assumption：中介数量体现质量，兼职不如全职
Counterexamples：A 工作效率低下，才需要更多人来弥补，以及必须全职才能完成工作

Evidence：需要直接的证据来表明 A 的 40 位中介的工作能力平均强于 F 的 25 位中介

② 数据类，解释类

Signal：revenue twice as high，作者试图把这件事情归因于 A 善于卖房

Inference：A 的营收是 F 的二倍 ⟹ A 比 F 更善于卖房

Assumption：没有其他解释

Counterexamples：高的营收纯粹来自于收客户更多的手续费；很可能 A 卖的本来就都是更贵的房子，而 F 经常卖的是一些较小、较廉价的房子，就算两公司抽成比例一样，那么最终销售同样数量的房子当然会给 F 带来更多营收

Evidence：需要对比 A 与 F 每单抽成的比例；需要对比 A 与 F 出售房子的平均原始价值

③ 数据类，解释类

Signal：168,000，144,000，A 卖房均价高于 F，作者试图把这件事情归因于 A 善于卖房

Inference：A 卖房均价高于 F ⟹ A 比 F 更善于卖房

Assumption：没有其他解释

Counterexamples：A 卖的房价钱本来就比 F 高非常多，其实还卖便宜了

Evidence：需要对比 A 与 F 出售房子的平均原始价值

④ 数据类，解释类

Signal：F 卖房用了 four months，A 卖房用了 one month，作者试图把这种区别归因于 A 善于卖房

Inference：10 年前 F 卖房用了 4 个月 + 去年 A 卖房只用了一个月 ⟹ A 比 F 更善于卖房

Assumption：没有其他解释

Counterexamples：两个房子有着巨大的区别，第二个地段好、装修好、结构好，本来就容易卖，而且第二个可能卖得很亏，因为卖得很廉价；并且，10 年前和去年的经济状况可能完全不同，十年前经济萧条，本来就不好卖

Evidence：需要对比两个房子的各方面情况，以及 10 年前与去年的整个房地产市场的情况

⑤ 类比类

Signal：谈论的本来是 10 年前、1 年前的案例，但最后要建议的是未来卖家

Inference：10 年前 F 的失败，1 年前 A 的成功 ⟹ A 比 F 以后更善于卖房

Assumption：A 和 F 在过去的时间内没有发生过显著变化

Counterexamples：10 年前 F 刚成立，自然水平不行，但现在已经非常成熟；这过去 1 年间 A 的一些非常优秀的中介离职去了 F，使得 A 水平大大下降

Evidence：需要对比 10 年前 F 与如今 F 的经营状况，也需要对比一年前 A 与如今 A 的经营状况

⑥ 建议类

Signal：步骤⑤的结论，以及下文要建议人们使用 A

Inference：A 比 F 善于卖房 ⟹ 卖房就要找 A

Assumption：没有更好的方案

Counterexamples：这个城市有更多其他中介，比 A 和 F 都优秀

Evidence：需要考虑其他可能的选择

Part 5 Argument 题库逐题精析

5. The following appeared in a letter to the editor of the Balmer Island Gazette.

"On Balmer Island, where mopeds serve as a popular form of transportation, the population increases to 100,000 during the summer months. To reduce the number of accidents involving mopeds and pedestrians, the town council of Balmer Island should limit the number of mopeds rented by the island's moped rental companies from 50 per day to 25 per day during the summer season. By limiting the number of rentals, the town council will attain the 50 percent annual reduction in moped accidents that was achieved last year on the neighboring island of Seaville, when Seaville's town council enforced similar limits on moped rentals."

思路相近题目：151 & 164

译文

在 Balmer 岛，助力车是一种流行的交通方式，并且到了夏天，人口会上涨到 100 000 人。为了减少涉及助力车以及行人的交通事故，镇委员会应该限制该岛助力车租赁公司夏季每日出租助力车的数量，从每天 50 辆减到每天 25 辆。通过限制租赁，该镇委员会能够将助力车事故减少 50%，就像邻近岛屿 Seaville 去年做到的一样，而 Seaville 镇委员会去年就执行了类似的出租限制。

文章结构图

结　　论：Balmer Island should limit the number of mopeds rented by rental companies from 50 per day to 25 per day during the summer season.
结论类型：建议型

各步推理分析

①**解释类**

Signal：去年 SV 全年事故减少，SV 执行了类似的政策，明显作者是要建立这两件事情的联系

Inference：SV 夏季限 moped ＋ SV 全年 moped 事故减少一半 ⟹ SV 夏季限 moped 造成 SV 全年 moped 事故减少一半

Assumption：没有其他解释

Counterexamples：道路拓宽；司机培训更严格；交通法规更严格；警察多了；不仅仅只有夏季使用的政策……

Evidence：需要证据排除以上能够解释事故减少的可能原因

② 类比类

Signal：要证明 BI 的情况，举的是 SV 的例子

Inference：SV 夏季限 moped 造成 SV 全年 moped 事故减少一半 ⟹ BI 夏季限 moped 也会造成 BI 全年 moped 事故减少一半

Assumption：两城的租赁 moped 都是 moped 的主要来源；过去两城的 moped 都能够租出去

Counterexamples：SV 的 moped 都是租的，但是 BI 的 moped 都是私家的；SV 的都租出去了，但是 BI 的本来就租不到每天 25 辆，意味着能上路的 moped 数量其实不会减少多少

Evidence：需要知道两城的租赁 moped 占所有 moped 当中的比例；需要知道过去每年到了夏季，BI 的 moped 租赁公司每天平均能够租出的 moped 的数量

③ 其他

Signal：moped 流行，夏天人口会增到 100,000，而文章结论暗示需要解决 moped 事故问题

Inference：moped popular ＋ 夏天人口会增到 100,000 ⟹ BI 需要减少 moped 事故

Assumption：夏天增多的人口会造成严重的 moped 问题

Counterexamples：城市交通秩序好；moped 司机都很职业，很守规矩，历年来都没出什么事故，就算事故减半，其实也没有减少几起事故

Evidence：需要知道过去每年到了夏天 moped 的平均事故量

④ 建议类

Signal：②③的结论

Inference：BI 夏季限 moped 会造成 BI 全年 moped 事故减少一半 ＋ BI 夏季需要减少 moped 事故 ⟹ BI 需要限 moped

Assumption：此法不会造成更严重的危害，没有更有效的解决方案

Counterexamples：大量的居民、游客只得选取其他同样有风险的交通方式，只不过把 moped 事故转移到其他交通工具上；也许更有效的解决方案是加大警力、提高 rental 对驾驶员的要求、制定更严格的交通法规等

Evidence：需要考察其他可能解决方案的有效性

Part 5 Argument 题库逐题精析

6

Arctic deer live on islands in Canada's arctic regions. They search for food by moving over ice from island to island during the course of the year. Their habitat is limited to areas warm enough to sustain the plants on which they feed and cold enough, at least some of the year, for the ice to cover the sea separating the islands, allowing the deer to travel over it. Unfortunately, according to reports from local hunters, the deer populations are declining. Since these reports coincide with recent global warming trends that have caused the sea ice to melt, we can conclude that the purported decline in deer populations is the result of the deer's being unable to follow their age-old migration patterns across the frozen sea.

译　文

北极鹿生活在加拿大极地区域的岛屿上。它们全年都通过跨越岛屿之间的冰层来寻找食物。它们的栖息地局限在一些特定的区域，这里足够温暖，能够维持它们所需的植物生长，但至少在一年的某些时候会冷到足以让岛屿间的海面结冰，这样它们能够在岛屿间穿行。可是，根据当地猎人的报告，鹿的数量正在减少。由于这一报告正好与最近导致海洋冰面融化的全球变暖趋势吻合，我们可以得出结论，北极鹿数量的下降是它们无法按原有迁移习惯跨过结冰海面的结果。

文章结构图

结　论：The purported decline in deer populations is the result of the deer's being unable to follow their age-old migration patterns across the frozen sea.

结论类型：解释型

各步推理分析

①其他

Signal：结论需要鹿无法迁徙，而文章中能够指向此结论的证据仅是全球变暖造成冰川融化

Inference：全球变暖造成冰川融化 ⟹ 鹿无法按照传统路线迁徙

Assumption：此处的冰已经融化到无法连接陆地，不能支持鹿的迁徙

Counterexamples：北极的冰极厚，即便有融化，仍然有足够的冰面可以使鹿迁徙

Evidence：需要直接调查鹿栖息岛群中的冰层在鹿迁徙季节是否能够支撑它们的迁徙

②证词类

Signal：report

Inference：猎人报告 ⟹ 鹿少了

Assumption：报告可靠

Counterexamples：鹿了解了人类常打猎的地方，躲着走，或者现在的猎人不如以前擅长打猎

Evidence：需要更可靠的来源，比如直接观察统计当地鹿的数量的变化

③解释类

Signal：步骤①②的结论，而且作者试图建立两者之间的关系

Inference：鹿无法按照传统路线迁徙 + 鹿少了 ⟹ 无法按照传统路线迁徙导致鹿少了

Assumption：没有其他解释

Counterexamples：瘟疫；食物不足；天敌多

Evidence：需要证据帮助排除其他可能解释鹿数量下降的因素

Part 5　Argument 题库逐题精析

7　The following is a recommendation from the Board of Directors of Monarch Books.

"We recommend that Monarch Books open a café in its store. Monarch, having been in business at the same location for more than twenty years, has a large customer base because it is known for its wide selection of books on all subjects. Clearly, opening the café would attract more customers. Space could be made for the café by discontinuing the children's book section, which will probably become less popular given that the most recent national census indicated a significant decline in the percentage of the population under age ten. Opening a café will allow Monarch to attract more customers and better compete with Regal Books, which recently opened its own café."

思路相近题目：91 & 92

译　文

我们建议 Monarch 书店在店内开一个咖啡厅。Monarch 在这个地方已经经营了二十多年，它有着很大的顾客基础，因为它对于各类型图书选择的广泛性而广为人知。显然，开一家咖啡厅会吸引更多顾客。咖啡厅所需的区域可以通过撤销儿童书籍区域来实现，而儿童书籍很可能会变得不那么流行，因为最近的全国普查显示 10 岁以下儿童的人口比例在大幅度下降。开一家咖啡厅会让 Monarch 书店吸引更多顾客，并且更好地与 Regal 书店竞争，后者最近开了自己的咖啡厅。

文章结构图

结　　论：Monarch Books should open a café in its store.
结论类型：建议型

各步推理分析

① 证词类，数据类，类比类

Signal：national consensus, percentage, given that

Inference：全国调查 ⟹ 当地童书流行度下降

Assumption：全国趋势足以代表当地；比例反映绝对量；儿童数量直接决定童书流行度

Counterexamples：此地儿童人口没下降，反而出生率上升了；因为这个地区教育好、医疗好，很多外地人都会选择在这里养小孩，所以这边小孩的数量越来越多；儿童比例下降，不代表儿童数量减少，儿童比例下降可能是由高龄人口的死亡率显著下降、平均寿命提高造成，而儿童数量并不会下降，则童书的流行度会维持；童书流行与否并不绝对取决于儿童数量，而取决于平时会花钱买童书的家庭数量，由于经济、教育水平的提高，可能有知识、有经济条件的家庭反而增多了，因此更多人愿意投资孩子的教育，所以童书可能恰恰更加流行

Evidence：需要了解当地的出生率、适龄儿童比例、儿童书籍的销量情况

② 其他

Signal：童书流行度下降，作者以此证明可以砍掉童书区域来建咖啡厅

Inference：当地童书流行度下降 ⟹ 可以砍掉童书区域建咖啡厅

Assumption：流行度下降后的童书业绩不会超过咖啡厅

Counterexamples：就算童书流行度下降，但仍然可以占据该书店的一大部分利润来源，而咖啡厅带来的业绩将远远不能弥补

Evidence：需要知道儿童书籍占书店总销量的比例

③ 类比，其他

Signal：要证明 MB，证据却是 RB

Inference：RB 开了一家咖啡厅 ⟹ MB 开咖啡厅能吸引顾客，并和 RB 竞争

Assumption：RB 开咖啡厅是一个成功的举措，MB 有开咖啡厅的需求

Counterexamples：首先，我们只知道 RB 开了咖啡厅，却不知道开了之后有什么效果，也许生意惨淡，那根本就不值得 MB 借鉴；其次，就算 RB 开得很成功，那可能是因为周围没有什么咖啡厅，顾客逛累了连休息的地方都没有，所以建个咖啡厅很合适，可是 MB 周围可能不乏类似的设施区域，则建个新咖啡厅完全是重复建设，没有意义

Evidence：需要知道 RB 咖啡厅的经营情况，以及 MB 周围是否已有类似功能的空间

④ 建议类

Signal：步骤②③的结论，以及最终要建议 MB 建咖啡厅

Inference：可以砍掉童书区域建咖啡厅 ＋ MB 开咖啡厅能吸引顾客，并和 RB 竞争 ⟹ MB 应该砍掉童书区域建咖啡厅

Assumption：没有其他方案

Counterexamples：就算要建咖啡厅，是否有别的区域可以利用

Evidence：需要考察 MB 内其他部门是否有适用的区域

Part 5　Argument 题库逐题精析

8

The following appeared in a memo from the director of student housing at Buckingham College.

"To serve the housing needs of our students, Buckingham College should build a number of new dormitories. Buckingham's enrollment is growing and, based on current trends, will double over the next 50 years, thus making existing dormitory space inadequate. Moreover, the average rent for an apartment in our town has risen in recent years. Consequently, students will find it increasingly difficult to afford off-campus housing. Finally, attractive new dormitories would make prospective students more likely to enroll at Buckingham."

译　文

为满足我们学生的住宿需求，Buckingham 学院应该建造一些新的公寓楼。Buckingham 的招生人数正在增加，并且按照现有趋势，招生人数将会在未来 50 年内增加一倍，从而使得现有住宅不能满足要求。而且，我们镇上公寓的平均租金在近几年上涨了。因此，学生将会越来越难支付校外公寓。最后，一幢吸引人的新公寓将会使未来的学生更愿意加入 Buckingham。

文章结构图

结　　论：Buckingham College should build a number of new dormitories.
结论类型：建议型

各步推理分析

①类比类

Signal：证据是现在，但要预测的是未来 50 年
Inference：B 校招生增加 ⟹ 未来 50 年 B 校招生会翻倍
Assumption：招生增长的趋势会不变

Counterexamples：招生增加的一个原因是当地适龄学生比例在增加，但随着适龄学生数量达到顶峰，招生也就不会增加了，这个趋势不见得会持续

Evidence：需要额外证据表明人口增长的趋势会长期持续（比如，也许该国政府试图把当地打造成为新的经济中心，大规模人口迁入将会持续发生，等等）

② 其他

Signal：thus
Inference：未来 50 年内 B 校招生会翻倍 ⟹ B 校现有公寓不够
Assumption：现有校舍的空置率并不是很高
Counterexamples：很可能现在的校舍大半都是空的，因此即便招生翻倍，公寓还是够的
Evidence：需要知道现有校舍的使用情况

③ 其他

Signal：consequently
Inference：城市平均租金上涨 ⟹ 学生难以支付校外公寓
Assumption：学生租的房子受到了城市平均租金的影响
Counterexamples：商业办公楼的租金大幅上涨，学校周围的房子没有变化
Evidence：需要知道学生经常租用的公寓的租金是否正在显著上涨

④ 其他

Signal：无
Inference：这是 unstated assumption，没有给出任何证据
Assumption：漂亮的公寓楼能吸引学生；学校将建的新楼会是漂亮的公寓楼
Counterexamples：学生来某个学校的原因是其学术水平高、就业率高，而不是楼漂亮
Evidence：需要有证据支持公寓楼的美观程度与学生申请之间的关系；以及需要有证据表明该校计划建成什么样的公寓楼

⑤ 建议类

Signal：步骤②③④的结论，以及最终要建议 B 校建公寓楼
Inference：B 校现有公寓不够 + 学生难以支付校外公寓 + 漂亮的公寓会吸引学生 ⟹ B 校应该建新公寓楼
Assumption：没有其他方案，有条件建楼
Counterexamples：首先，可以提供租房补助；其次，很可能学校既没有地方，也没有资金可以建楼
Evidence：需要知道该校现有的资金情况；需要知道该校决定使用哪些空间来建这些未来的公寓楼

Part 5 Argument 题库逐题精析

9 Nature's Way, a chain of stores selling health food and other health-related products, is opening its next franchise in the town of Plainsville. The store should prove to be very successful: Nature's Way franchises tend to be most profitable in areas where residents lead healthy lives, and clearly Plainsville is such an area. Plainsville merchants report that sales of running shoes and exercise clothing are at all-time highs. The local health club has more members than ever, and the weight training and aerobics classes are always full. Finally, Plainsville's schoolchildren represent a new generation of potential customers: these schoolchildren are required to participate in a fitness-for-life program, which emphasizes the benefits of regular exercise at an early age.

思路相近题目：81 & 83

译 文

Nature's Way 是一家主营健康食品以及其他相关健康产品的连锁店，它的下一个分店开在了 Plainsville 城。该店肯定会成功的：Nature's Way 在那些居民生活方式健康的地区是盈利最多的，而 Plainsville 就是这样的地区。Plainsville 的商家报告说跑鞋和运动装的销售处于历史高点。当地一家健身俱乐部现在的会员比以往任何时候都多，力量训练班和有氧训练班总是满员。最后，Plainsville 的学生代表了新生代的潜在顾客群：Plainsville 的在校学生被要求参加一个叫作"终身健康"的项目，它强调从小开始经常锻炼的好处。

文章结构图

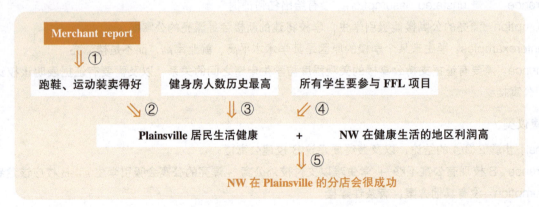

结　论：The Nature's Way store that is opening in the town of Plainsville should prove to be very successful.

结论类型：预测型

各步推理分析

① 证词类

Signal：report

256

Inference：商人报告 ⟹ 跑鞋、运动装卖到历史新高

Assumption：商人报告可信

Counterexamples：只是为了卖东西的时候更好卖，声称这些东西一直卖得很好

Evidence：需要知道该信息来自多少商家；需要更直接的账务上的证据来体现当地这些产品的销售情况

② 其他

Signal：为了证明 P 居民生活健康，作者给出了一系列证据，其中包含跑鞋、运动装一直卖得很好

Inference：跑鞋、运动装卖到历史新高 ⟹ Plainsville 居民生活健康

Assumption：运动用品卖到历史新高就能体现人们生活健康

Counterexamples：人们普遍因为身体太差，所以才想要健康生活，才去买这些东西，但并不会真的坚持运动；而且，历史最高其实也没有多高，因为一直卖得很差

Evidence：需要直接调查当地人群的平均生活习惯；需要知道运动产品的具体销量，而不是只和过去对比

③ 其他

Signal：为了证明 P 居民生活健康，作者给出了一系列证据，其中包含健身房人数达到历史新高，各种课程人满为患

Inference：健身房人数达到历史新高，各种课程人满为患 ⟹ Plainsville 居民生活健康

Assumption：健身房的情况可以代表全城

Counterexamples：一共没几个俱乐部，即便人数历史最多也没多少；课程没开几个，所以满员

Evidence：需要知道健身房的数量，以及具体的健身人群规模

④ 其他

Signal：为了证明 P 居民生活健康，作者给出了一系列证据，其中包含所有学生要参与 FFL 项目

Inference：所有学生要参与 FFL 项目 ⟹ Plainsville 居民生活健康

Assumption：学生会按要求运动；也许 FFL 项目的锻炼要求其实很低，就算完成该项目的所有运动要求，其实也完全达不到正常儿童的运动需求

Counterexamples：学生只是被迫参与，并不真的喜欢运动；学生出工不出力，并不真正努力运动

Evidence：需要知道 FFL 项目包含什么具体要求；需要证据表明参与的学生真的会坚持完成锻炼任务

⑤ 类比类

Signal：谈论的本来是其他城市的成功，但最终要证明的是 Plainsville 的成功

Inference：Plainsville 居民生活健康 + NW 在生活健康的地区利润高 ⟹ NW 的 Plainsville 分店会成功

Assumption：P 城与其他城市情况相似

Counterexamples：其他城市人们关注健康的饮食和锻炼，但在 P 城，人们关注锻炼的健康，并不见得关注饮食的健康，而 NW 主做健康饮食，所以不会成功；而且，可能 P 城人们的消费水平远低于其他城市，因此 P 城的店销售并不会特别优秀

Evidence：需要证据对比 P 城与其他所谓关注健康的城市的市民之间是否存在生活、消费习惯上的显著差异

Part 5 Argument 题库逐题精析

10 Twenty years ago, Dr. Field, a noted anthropologist, visited the island of Tertia. Using an observation-centered approach to study Tertian culture, he concluded from his observations that children in Tertia were reared by an entire village rather than by their own biological parents. Recently another anthropologist, Dr. Karp, visited the group of islands that includes Tertia and used the interview-centered method to study child-rearing practices. In the interviews that Dr. Karp conducted with children living in this group of islands, the children spent much more time talking about their biological parents than about other adults in the village. Dr. Karp decided that Dr. Field's conclusion about Tertian village culture must be invalid. Some anthropologists recommend that to obtain accurate information on Tertian child-rearing practices, future research on the subject should be conducted via the interview-centered method.

思路相近题目：19 & 21

译 文

20年前著名人类学家Field博士造访了Tertia岛。基于观察法他得出了结论，认为Tertia的儿童是由整个村庄的人而不是由他们的双亲抚养长大的。可是，最近另一位著名的人类学家Karp博士造访了包含Tertia在内的一系列岛屿，并且使用的是访谈法来研究育儿文化。Karp博士对这些岛屿的儿童进行的采访显示，这些儿童在谈话中谈到他们双亲的时间要远多于谈到村中其他成年人的时间。Karp博士认定，Field博士对于Tertia村落文化的结论是无效的。一些人类学家认为，为了获取Tertia岛屿育儿行为的准确信息，未来该主题的相关研究应该采取访谈法。

文章结构图

K 通过访谈发现各岛孩子谈论双亲更多
⇓ ①
F 通过观察认为 T 孩子由全村抚养 ＋ T 孩子由双亲抚养
⇓ ②
F 的结论错，K 的结论对 ＋ F 观察，K 访谈
⇓ ③
观察法不如访谈法，造成 F 的错误与 K 的正确
⇓ ④
未来育儿相关研究使用观察法不如使用访谈法
⇓ ⑤
未来研究应该使用访谈法

结　　论：To obtain accurate information on Tertian child-rearing practices, future research on the subject should be conducted via the interview-centered method.

结论类型：**建议型**

各步推理分析

① 证词类，类比类

Signal：为了证明 Dr. Field 的观点错误，Dr. Karp 显然暗示孩子是由双亲抚养的，而 Dr. Karp 的证据是孩子谈论双亲更多；并且，本来 Dr. Field 要谈论的只是 Tertia 岛，但 Dr. Karp 调查的是包含 Tertia 在内的多个岛屿

Inference：K 通过访谈发现各岛孩子谈论双亲更多 $\Longrightarrow$ T 孩子由双亲抚养

Assumption：由谁抚养就会谈论谁；调查是能够代表 T 岛的

Counterexamples：实际上，孩子们更多谈论的是对双亲的怀念，因为不怎么能见到双亲；而且，就算是由全村抚养，但孩子们仍然可以和自己的双亲关系最亲密，所以仍然谈论双亲更多；可能各岛综合起来孩子谈论双亲更多，但很可能不同岛屿的情况不同，具体到 T 岛，孩子其实谈论双亲没有更多，也并不是由双亲抚养

Evidence：应该直接询问孩子由谁抚养，而不是间接去计算他们谈论父母所占的比例；应该直接调查 T 岛孩子，而不是包含各岛的孩子

② 其他

Signal：Dr. Karp 要证明 Dr. Field 是错的，基于刚才的结论

Inference：F 认为 T 岛孩子由全村抚养，而 T 岛孩子由双亲抚养 $\Longrightarrow$ F 是错的，K 是对的

Assumption：两次结果矛盾

Counterexamples：其实，两次研究的结论可以都是对的，因为 F 是在 20 年前做的研究，而 K 是最近做的研究，很可能当地的风俗在最近 20 年已经发生变化

Evidence：需要提供这 20 年当地风俗变迁的信息

③ 解释类

Signal：人类学家试图把 F 的失败、K 的成功归结为方法的不同

Inference：F 是错的，K 是对的，且 F 使用观察法，K 使用访谈法 $\Longrightarrow$ 访谈法比观察法好，造成 F 的错误与 K 的正确

Assumption：没有其他解释

Counterexamples：不是方法的错误，而是使用方法不当，F 可能观察不仔细

Evidence：需要调查 F 与 K 是否存在除了研究方法以外所存在的可能区别

④ 类比类

Signal：谈论的本来是对于谁负责育儿的一项研究，但最终要谈论的是对所有育儿行为的研究

Inference：访谈法比观察法好，造成 F 的错误与 K 的正确 $\Longrightarrow$ 未来所有育儿研究使用访谈法比观察法好

Assumption：这两种方法在所有育儿研究当中都会有相似的结果

Counterexamples：这次采访的对象是孩子，而当地孩子可能不排外，可以接受访谈，并且愿意真诚地说话；并不是每个育儿研究的问题都是孩子可以提供的，很多话题可能针对的是成年人本身，但当地村落其实非常排外，可能很多成年人根本就不愿意接受采访，所以观察法可能在另一些问题上是必要的

⑤ **建议类**

Signal：步骤④的结论，以及最终要建议用访谈法
Inference：未来所有育儿研究使用访谈法比观察法好 ⟹ 未来研究应该使用访谈法
Assumption：没有更好的方案
Counterexamples：很可能两种方法都有局限性，最佳的策略是访谈与观察的结合，甚至可能还有别的方法
Evidence：需要证据表明其他育儿文化方面的信息也可以通过访谈准确获得

Part 5　Argument 题库逐题精析

11　The council of Maple County, concerned about the county becoming overdeveloped, is debating a proposed measure that would prevent the development of existing farmland in the county. But the council is also concerned that such a restriction, by limiting the supply of new housing, could lead to significant increases in the price of housing in the county. Proponents of the measure note that Chestnut County established a similar measure ten years ago, and its housing prices have increased only modestly since. However, opponents of the measure note that Pine County adopted restrictions on the development of new residential housing fifteen years ago, and its housing prices have more than doubled. Since the council currently predicts that the proposed measure, if passed, will result in a significant increase in housing prices in Maple County.

译　文

Maple 郡委员会担忧该郡过度发展，正在争论是否要禁止开发全郡的现有农田。但是，委员会也担心这项禁令限制了新房屋的供给，有可能造成该郡房价大幅上涨。该法案的支持者指出，Chestnut 郡十年前采取了类似的措施，而其房价后来只是微涨。但是，该法案的反对者指出，Pine 郡十五年前禁止了新住宅的开发，结果房价长了不止一倍。委员会目前预测如果通过了该法案，会造成 Maple 郡房价的大幅提升。

文章结构图

```
           PC 十五年前限制开发住宅 + PC 房价翻倍
                        ⇓ ①
           PC 十五年前限制开发住宅 → PC 房价翻倍
                        ⇓ ②③
           MC 如今限制开发农田 → MC 房价翻倍
```

结　　论：Preventing the development of existing farmland will result in a significant increase in housing prices in Maple County.
结论类型：**预测型**

各步推理分析

①**解释类**
Signal：PC 禁止了住宅开发，从那个时候房价翻倍，而明显这群人是要建立这两件事情之间的联系
Inference：PC 十五年前限制开发住宅 + PC 房价翻倍 ⟹ PC 十五年前限制开发住宅造成了 PC 房价翻倍

Assumption：没有其他解释

Counterexamples：开发旅游业；人口增长；经济发展……

Evidence：需要证据排除其他可能造成当时 PC 房价翻倍的因素

②类比类

Signal：要证明限制征用农田的效果，证据却是限制开发住宅

Inference：PC 十五年前限制开发住宅造成房价翻倍 ⟹ MC 如今限制征用农田，也会造成 MC 房价翻倍

Assumption：限制征用农田会起到和直接限制开发住宅一样的效果

Counterexamples：仅仅无法征用农田，MC 也许还是有其他充分的土地可以用来建造住宅，而且可以建造很高的住宅，并不会造成住房供不应求的问题；而先前 PC 的政策可能非常严格，严重限制了新住宅数量和类型，造成了住房供不应求。

Evidence：需要有更直接的证据来表明如今限制开发农田对未来住房供给产生的影响

③类比类

Signal：要证明的是 MC 如今的结果，证据却是十五年前 PC 的情况

Inference：PC 十五年前限制开发住宅造成房价翻倍 ⟹ MC 如今限制征用农田，也会造成 MC 房价翻倍

Assumption：PC 十五年前和如今的 MC 之间是足够相似的

Counterexamples：十五年前 PC 处在经济发展高峰，限制住房会严重造成供不应求，导致房价飞涨；可是如今的 MC 可能处在经济低谷，本身也没什么人想在这里置业，MC 和 CC 的情况恰恰相似，很可能最后房价并不会飞涨

Evidence：需要证据对比十五年前的 PC 与如今 MC 的经济状况、人口数量、住房需求等各方面因素

Part 5 Argument 题库逐题精析

> **12** Fifteen years ago, Omega University implemented a new procedure that encouraged students to evaluate the teaching effectiveness of all their professors. Since that time, Omega professors have begun to assign higher grades in their classes, and overall student grade averages at Omega have risen by 30 percent. Potential employers, looking at this dramatic rise in grades, believe that grades at Omega are inflated and do not accurately reflect student achievement; as a result, Omega graduates have not been as successful at getting jobs as have graduates from nearby Alpha University. To enable its graduates to secure better jobs, Omega University should terminate student evaluation of professors.

译 文

十五年前，Omega 大学采取了一个新流程，鼓励学生评估所有教授的教学效果。自此，Omega 的教授给学生的课业评分提高，并且学生总体的成绩上涨了 30%。潜在的雇主看到学生成绩猛增，认为 Omega 的成绩虚高，并不能准确反映学生的表现；结果是，Omega 的毕业生就不如临近的 Alpha 大学毕业生找工作成功。为了让毕业生获得更好的就业岗位，Omega 大学应该立即终止学生对教授的评估。

文章结构图

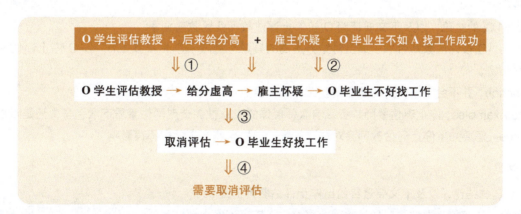

结　　论：Omega University should terminate student evaluation of professors.
结论类型：建议型

各步推理分析

①解释类
Signal：O 学生评估教授，since that time，O 教授给学生高分，并且作者试图建立评估与给分之间的关系
Inference：因为学生评估教授，使得教授给了虚高的分数
Assumption：没有其他解释

263

Counterexamples：很可能学生评估教授是在给分前进行的，本身就不可能影响教授给分；很可能这个制度恰恰督促教授们好好教课，带来了学生水平的提高；很可能该校做了其他努力提高学生水平，比如招生更好、校规更严格

Evidence：需要知道学生评估教授与考试的顺序；需要排除其他导致学生成绩提高的因素

②解释类

Signal：雇主怀疑给分虚高，as a result，O 不如 A 学生好找工作

Inference：雇主怀疑给分虚高 + O 不如 A 学生好找工作 ⟹ 雇主怀疑给分虚高造成 O 学生不如 A 学生好找工作

Assumption：雇主的怀疑具有代表性；雇主对 A 的学生没有类似的怀疑；没有其他解释；O 校以前没有这么难找工作

Counterexamples：很可能只是极个别雇主有所怀疑，并不能反映普遍现象；也许 A 校给分也高，雇主也怀疑 A 校，但 A 校毕业生仍然更容易找工作；很可能本来 A 校学生就比 O 校学生强，或者 A 校比 O 校为学生做了更好的就业准备；也许 A 校的专业比 O 校专业更适合找工作；也许 O 校一直都不如 A 校好找工作，跟给分没关系，甚至之前 O 校学生比现在更难找工作

Evidence：需要知道雇主们对 A 校学生的看法；需要排除其他导致 A 校学生更好就业的原因；需要知道在 O 校评估教师之前 O 校学生与 A 校学生就业难度之间是否存在差别；以及需要知道 O 校在实施评估教师之前学生找工作的难度

③类比类

Signal：①②的结论，以及下文要证明 O 校停止评估教师会拯救就业率

Inference：O 校评估教师带来了雇主对给分虚高的疑虑，造成了学生难找工作 ⟹ O 停止评估教师就可以拯救就业率

Assumption：并不会带来新的问题影响找工作的难度

Counterexamples：停止评估教师，会影响教师授课的专业性，造成学生素质下滑，学生还是难以找到工作

Evidence：需要知道停止评估教师会对授课质量、学生素养产生什么不良影响

④ 建议类

Signal：③的结论，以及下文要最终给出停止评估教师的建议

Inference：O 校停止评估教师能拯救就业率 ⟹ O 校应该停止评估教师

Assumption：没有更好的方案

Counterexamples：规定教授打分必须保持某个平均分，以限制给分虚高行为；将评估放在考试之前，这样教授给分不会受到评估的影响

Evidence：需要考察可能存在的其他更有效的方案

Part 5 Argument 题库逐题精析

13 In an attempt to improve highway safety, Prunty County last year lowered its speed limit from 55 to 45 miles per hour on all county highways. But this effort has failed: the number of accidents has not decreased, and, based on reports by the highway patrol, many drivers are exceeding the speed limit. Prunty County should instead undertake the same kind of road improvement project that Butler County completed five years ago: increasing lane widths, resurfacing rough highways, and improving visibility at dangerous intersections. Today, major Butler County roads still have a 55 mph speed limit, yet there were 25 percent fewer reported accidents in Butler County this past year than there were five years ago.

译 文

为提高公路安全，Prunty 郡去年把全郡所有公路的限速从 55 英里/小时降到了 45 英里/小时。但这个举措失败了：事故数量并没有下降，并且，基于公路巡逻的报告，很多驾驶员在超速。Prunty 郡相反应该采取 Butler 郡五年前采用的道路改善工程：拓宽道路、重铺不平整的道路，以及提高危险交叉路口的能见度。如今，Butler 郡主要公路限速仍然是 55 英里/小时，但是过去一年它们的事故报告量比五年前少了 25%。

文章结构图

结　　论：PC should undertake the road improvement project.
结论类型：**建议型**

各步推理分析

① 证词类

Signal：reports by highway patrol

Inference：巡警报告 ⟹ PC 仍有很多司机超速

Assumption：巡警报告准确

Counterexamples：超速已经比以前少很多，但现在安排的巡警多了，按照概率，报告量增多

Evidence：需要知道巡警数量的变化

② 其他

Signal：事故仍然很多，超速很多，而作者想要证明限速失败，这是在证明限速并没有起到应有的结果

Inference：事故很多 + 超速很多 ⟹ 限速失败

Assumption：事故数量没有显著下降；车速没有显著下降

Counterexamples：虽然仍在超速，但以前超速意味着车可能要开到 60~70 mile/h，但现在超速只开到 50~60 mile/h，意味着危险性下降，很可能现在撞死人的事故就少了很多，这意味着限速令其实很起作用

Evidence：需要知道平均车速的变化情况、事故严重程度的变化情况

③ 证词类

Signal：fewer reported accidents

Inference：BC 报告事故减少 25% ⟹ BC 事故减少 25%

Assumption：报告准确

Counterexamples：保费变贵，很多人为了不增加保费而选择不再报告事故；警力减少，很多事故没有被捕捉到

Evidence：需要调查报告的事故数量是否能够准确反映实际事故数量

④ 数据类

Signal：25%

Inference：BC 事故减少 25% ⟹ BC 事故减少

Assumption：BC 总车辆没有大幅减少

Counterexamples：很可能 BC 总车辆显著减少，因此事故率其实不降反增

Evidence：需要知道 BC 道路上车辆的数量变化

⑤ 解释类

Signal：BC 五年前改善道路，如今事故减少，并且作者试图建立两者之间的关系

Inference：BC 五年前改善道路，如今事故减少 ⟹ BC 改善道路造成了如今事故减少

Assumption：没有其他解释

Counterexamples：人口少了、私家车少了、交规更严了；去年是个特殊年份，天气适宜开车，但其他年份事故量没有显著变化

Evidence：需要调查其他可能导致事故减少的举措；需要过去五年每年的事故数据

⑥ 类比类

Signal：要谈的是 PC，给的却是 BC 的例子

Inference：BC 五年前改善道路造成了事故减少 $\Longrightarrow$ PC 改善道路也可以造成事故减少

Assumption：两地事故主要来源相似

Counterexamples：BC 之前可能因为道路劣质、能见度差等原因造成了很多事故；但很可能 PC 的类似问题并不多，可能两城车流密度非常不同

Evidence：需要数据分析两城交通事故来源情况；需要对比两城的道路情况

⑦ 建议类

Signal：⑤的结论，以及文章最终想要推广改善道路的策略

Inference：PC 改善道路能够减少事故 $\Longrightarrow$ PC 需要改善道路

Assumption：没有其他更好的方法；有足够资金投入这个工程

Counterexamples：可以改善公共交通，可以加强交通管理；也许城市根本没有这么多经费可以完成这些工作

Evidence：需要考察其他替代方案的效果；需要提供当地的资金信息以判断该策略的可行性

Part 5 Argument 题库逐题精析

14

The following appeared as part of an article in a business magazine.

"A recent study rating 300 male and female Mentian advertising executives according to the average number of hours they sleep per night showed an association between the amount of sleep the executives need, and the success of their firms. Of the advertising firms studied, those whose executives reported needing no more than 6 hours of sleep per night had higher profit margins and faster growth. These results suggest that if a business wants to prosper, it should hire only people who need less than 6 hours of sleep per night."

思路相近题目：111

译 文

最近一项研究评估了 300 位 Mentia 的男女广告经理人，主要考察了他们每晚的平均睡眠量，研究显示他们所需要的睡眠量与其所在公司的成功之间存在关联。在这些公司当中，那些报告自己每晚只需睡 6 小时以内的经理人，其所在公司有着更高的利润率以及更快的成长速度。这些结果显示，企业要想发展好，只需雇用每晚睡眠 6 小时以内的人。

文章结构图

结　　论：A business should hire only people who need less than 6 hours of sleep per night.
结论类型：建议型

各步推理分析

① 证词类

Signal：report

Inference：executive 报告自己只睡 6 小时 ⟹ 他们真的只睡 6 小时
Assumption：报告可靠
Counterexamples：只是为了显示自己的勤奋，并不是只睡那么一点时间
Evidence：需要实际测算这些经理人的睡眠时长

② 数据类

Signal：结论要讨论的是公司 prosper，但证据只是关于某些公司的 profit margin 和 growth
Inference：某些公司 profit margin 大，faster growth ⟹ 这些公司 prosper
Assumption：profit margin 和 growth 可以充分反映一个公司的 prosperity
Counterexamples：profit 很差，是以高产品定价和盲目扩张换来的 profit margin 与 growth，公司效益并不好
Evidence：需要知道这些公司更全方位的信息以评价其是否成功，比如利润、营收等各方面因素

③ 解释类

Signal：①②的结论，以及作者明显想要建立睡眠量与公司 prosperity 的关系
Inference：executive 只睡 6 小时 + 广告公司 prosper ⟹ executive 只睡 6 小时造就了这些广告公司 prosper
Assumption：没有其他解释，不是因为公司 prosper 带来的忙碌
Counterexamples：很可能是公司发展好，事情多，不得已只睡 6 个小时；而公司发展好其实是因为员工努力、员工素质高、行业是市场的趋势等原因
Evidence：需要知道这些经理人的较短睡眠是在公司高速发展之前还是高速发展之后才出现的；需要排除其他可以解释公司成功的原因

④ 类比类

Signal：本身讨论的是广告业的 executive，但结论变成了所有行业的所有人
Inference：executive 只睡 6 小时造就了这些广告公司 prosper ⟹ 各行各业只招睡 6 小时的人都会让公司 prosper
Assumption：各行业的所有人的睡眠需求是相似的
Counterexamples：executive 和普通员工的工作强度不同，而且很多工作需要更充足的睡眠来保证极端的清醒
Evidence：需要具体考察不同行业、不同层级员工所需的不同属性

⑤ 建议类

Signal：④的结论，以及最终是要执行这个建议
Inference：各行各业只招睡 6 小时的人会让公司 prosper ⟹ 各行各业都应该只招睡 6 小时的人
Assumption：不会造成严重副作用，不会有更有效的方案
Counterexamples：过劳死；可以提高员工素质、改善激励机制等
Evidence：需要考察其他可能更有效的替代方案

Part 5　Argument 题库逐题精析

15 The following memorandum is from the business manager of Happy Pancake House restaurants.

"Recently, butter has been replaced by margarine in Happy Pancake House restaurants throughout the southwestern United States. This change, however, has had little impact on our customers. In fact, only about 2 percent of customers have complained, indicating that an average of 98 people out of 100 are happy with the change. Furthermore, many servers have reported that a number of customers who ask for butter do not complain when they are given margarine instead. Clearly, either these customers do not distinguish butter from margarine or they use the term 'butter' to refer to either butter or margarine."

思路相近题目：48，123，124 & 126

译　文

最近，Happy Pancake House 在美国西南部的餐厅用人造黄油代替了黄油。但是这种改变对顾客的影响非常小。事实上，只有大约 2% 的顾客投诉，说明 100 个人中有 98 人对于这种替换是乐于接受的。此外，很多服务生报告说很多索要黄油的顾客在被给予人造黄油的时候并没有投诉。显然，这些顾客要么分不清黄油和人造黄油，要么是用"黄油"这个词来指黄油或人造黄油。

文章结构图

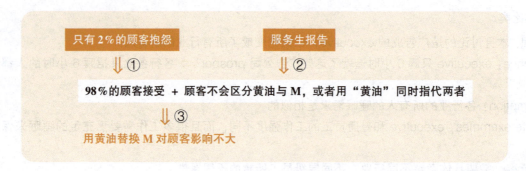

结　论：Happy Pancake House restaurants' decision to replace butter by margarine has had little impact on their customers.

结论类型：解释型

各步推理分析

① 数据类

Signal：2%，indicating

Inference：2% 的顾客抱怨 ⟹ 大部分顾客接受了这个变化

Assumption：人们点的菜普遍用到了黄油

Counterexamples：绝大部分菜里根本就没有用到黄油，而涉及有黄油的菜时，抱怨的比例高很多

Evidence：需要更直接的数据反映点了加黄油的菜的顾客的投诉率

② 证词类

Signal：report，clearly

Inference：服务生的报告 ⟹ 顾客不会区分黄油与 M，或者用"黄油"同时指代两者

Assumption：服务生的报告是可靠的、有代表性的

Counterexamples：人们不向 server 抱怨，向 waiter 或 manager 抱怨；服务生并不会报告每一个自己收到的抱怨；many 是一个非常虚的概念，可能大部分人还是抱怨的

Evidence：需要知道投诉的绝对量和比例；需要知道顾客除了对服务生直接投诉外，是否还有其他投诉渠道，如果有，投诉量是多少

③ 解释类

Signal：作者试图把以上现象都归结为 M 替代黄油对顾客影响不大

Inference：98% 的顾客接受 + 顾客不会区分黄油与 M，或者用"黄油"同时指代两者 ⟹ 用黄油替换 M 对顾客影响不大

Assumption：没有其他解释

Counterexamples：顾客有礼貌；嫌投诉太麻烦，不抱怨，但是再也不来了

Evidence：需要直接调查顾客流量，以及回头客的比例；可以直接询问顾客对目前所使用的"黄油"的看法

Part 5　Argument 题库逐题精析

16 The following appeared in a memorandum from the manager of WWAC radio station.

"To reverse a decline in listener numbers, our owners have decided that WWAC must change from its current rock-music format. The decline has occurred despite population growth in our listening area, but that growth has resulted mainly from people moving here after their retirement. We must make listeners of these new residents. We could switch to a music format tailored to their tastes, but a continuing decline in local sales of recorded music suggests limited interest in music. Instead we should change to a news and talk format, a form of radio that is increasingly popular in our area."

思路相近题目：86，102 & 103

译　文

为了扭转听众数量的下滑，我们老板决定 WWAC 电台必须放弃现有的摇滚乐形式。尽管我们电台覆盖区域的人口数量在增长，我们的听众仍然流失了。而这种人口数量的上涨主要来自于退休迁入人口。我们必须想方设法让这些新居民成为我们的听众。我们当然可以换一种音乐节目形式来迎合他们的品位，但唱片业销量的持续下滑显示人们对于音乐的兴趣是有限的。相反，我们应该换成一种新闻谈话类的节目，这种电台形式在我们区域越来越受欢迎。

文章结构图

结　论：The WWAC radio station should change from its current rock-music format to a news and talk format to reverse a decline in listener numbers.

结论类型：建议型

各步推理分析

① **解释型**

Signal：人口上升时听众仍然在减少，作者暗示过去的模式肯定不再吸引听众

Inference：听众减少，人口上升 ⟹ 过去的 rock 模式不能再吸引听众

Assumption：没有其他解释

Counterexamples：也许不是听众不喜欢 rock，只是 WWAC 过去做的 rock 节目太差。但其实 rock 是很流行的，比如别的电台的 rock 都很受欢迎，所以 WWAC 不仅不应该砍掉 rock，恰恰应该提高 rock 的质量

Evidence：需要知道别的电台的 rock 栏目是否也存在听众数量下降的问题；需要排除可能造成 WWAC 电台 rock 栏目听众下降的其他原因

② 其他

Signal：作者先说人口增长来自于退休人群，紧接着就说 WWAC 需要迎合退休人群

Inference：人口增长主要来自于退休人群 ⟹ 需要迎合退休听众

Assumption：增长的群体就该是主要的受众群体

Counterexamples：即便增长，比例仍然是最低的年龄群体，主流的人群仍然是其他年龄段的，所以不应该以退休人群为主要的定位群体

Evidence：需要知道退休人群的绝对数量，而不只是其所占的人口比例

③ 其他

Signal：作者指出新闻谈话类节目愈发受欢迎，显然暗示这种节目将能够吸引听众

Inference：新闻谈话类节目愈发受欢迎 ⟹ 谈话类节目吸引听众

Assumption：越来越受欢迎的节目就会吸引听众

Counterexamples：该节目类型只是比以前更受欢迎，但是听众比例仍然是最低的类型，甚至听众量还不如 rock

Evidence：需要知道新闻谈话类节目目前的观众比例，尤其是和 rock 栏目相比

④ 其他

Signal：作者指出唱片销量下降，目的是排除音乐这个节目形式

Inference：唱片销量下降 ⟹ 音乐类节目不吸引听众

Assumption：唱片销量与人们对音乐的兴趣直接相关联

Counterexamples：人们不买唱片是因为经济危机，人们没钱买唱片，但人们恰恰是需要音乐的，因此电台音乐反而成了更受欢迎的听音乐的来源

Evidence：需要直接调查电台音乐栏目的听众绝对量和比例，以及其变化情况

⑤ 建议类

Signal：步骤①②③④的结论，以及最终要证明应该转向新闻谈话类节目

Inference：rock 不吸引听众 + 要迎合退休听众 + 新闻谈话类节目更能吸引听众 + 音乐不能吸引听众 ⟹ WWAC 应该向新闻谈话类节目转型

Assumption：没有其他更好的方案

Counterexamples：也许还有更能够吸引听众的节目类型，比如喜剧、读书节目等

Evidence：需要充分考察其他可能的替代方案

Part 5 Argument 题库逐题精析

17 The following is a memorandum from the business manager of a television station.

"Over the past year, our late-night news, program has devoted increased time to national news, and less time to weather and local news. During this period, most of the complaints received from viewers were concerned with our station's coverage of weather and local news. In addition, local businesses that used to advertise during our late-night news program have canceled their advertising contracts with us. Therefore, in order to attract more viewers to our news programs, and to avoid losing any further advertising revenues, we should expand our coverage of weather and local news on all our news programs."

译 文

去年，我们晚间新闻节目投入了更多时间播报全国新闻，减少了对天气以及本地新闻的关注。在此期间，我们受到的大部分观众投诉是关于对天气以及当地新闻播报的问题。并且，本地的一些曾经在我台晚间新闻期间播报广告的公司也取消了和我们的广告合约。因此，为了吸引更多的观众并且避免损失更多的广告收益，我们应该增加本台所有新闻节目对天气以及当地新闻的播报。

文章结构图

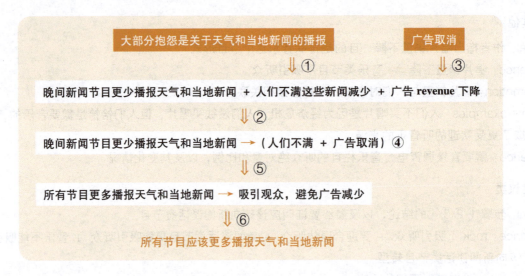

结　　论：The station should expand coverage of weather and local news on all their news programs.
结论类型：建议型

各步推理分析

①证词类，数据类

Signal：most of the complaints

Inference：大部分抱怨是关于天气和当地新闻的播报 ⟹ 人们非常不满这类新闻的播报

Assumption：most 可以体现 many

Counterexamples：就算大多数人抱怨这种情况，但因为整体质量好，一共就没有几起抱怨，所以完全没有代表性

Evidence：需要知道整体投诉量和此类新闻的投诉量

②解释类

Signal：改变节目，during this period，抱怨，以及作者试图建立改变节目与抱怨的关系

Inference：晚间新闻节目更少播报天气和当地新闻 + 人们不满这类新闻减少 ⟹ 晚间新闻节目更少播报天气和当地新闻造成了人们的抱怨

Assumption：人们不喜欢晚间新闻节目播报这么少的天气和当地新闻；没有其他解释；在没有改变之前，人们并没有这么抱怨

Counterexamples：造成抱怨的不是节目比例下降，而是这种节目质量太差，并且抱怨的根本不是夜间档的这类节目；而且，可能一直有一群人在投诉天气和当地新闻不足，在节目改变之前就抱怨，意味着不是这个改变本身造成了这个结果

Evidence：需要知道这些观众具体在投诉什么问题；需要知道以前类似问题的投诉量

③数据类

Signal：文章最终要讨论的是广告的 revenue，但证据只是广告商取消 contract

Inference：一些广告商取消 contract ⟹ 广告收益下降

Assumption：没有更多新广告商签约；广告价位没有提高

Counterexamples：很可能有更多新广告商签约，而且广告价位很可能会提高，因此总 revenue 不降反升

Evidence：需要知道广告总收入的变化

④解释类

Signal：改变节目，之后广告 cancel，并且作者试图建立两者之间的关系

Inference：晚间新闻节目更少播报天气和当地新闻 + 广告取消 ⟹ 晚间新闻节目更少播报天气和当地新闻造成了广告取消

Assumption：广告商也不喜欢晚间天气和当地新闻的减少；这些取消的广告之前是在夜间天气和当地新闻档播放；没有其他解释；不改变节目，广告商不取消

Counterexamples：是因为那些公司本身业绩不好，没钱支付昂贵的广告费了；就算不改变节目，那些公司也会取消合同；广告商可能不是喜欢天气和当地新闻，只是不喜欢全国新闻；需要知道这些取消广告的广告商之前是不是在晚间天气与国内新闻期间打广告；需要知道是否有其他原因造成广告商取消合同

⑤ 类比类

Signal：讨论的本来是晚间新闻，但结论讨论的却是所有新闻

Inference：晚间新闻节目更少播报天气和当地新闻造成了抱怨以及广告取消 ⟹ 播报更多的天气和当地新闻就会带来更多观众以及更多广告商

Assumption：各档新闻目前的播报量和观众需要相当

Counterexamples：日间新闻对于当地新闻和天气新闻的播报早已超过观众的需要

Evidence：需要调查其他时间段观众的喜好

⑥ 建议类

Signal：④的结论，以及最终作者要建议所有新闻节目增加这两类新闻

Inference：播报更多的天气和当地新闻就会带来更多观众以及更多广告商 ⟹ 所有新闻节目都增加天气和当地新闻的播报

Assumption：没有其他解决方案

Counterexamples：也许广告商更想要国际新闻；也许可以提高新闻的质量，不论是全国的还是当地的

Evidence：需要调查其他方案的效果

Part 5 Argument 题库逐题精析

18 Two years ago, radio station WCQP in Rockville decided to increase the number of call-in advice programs that it broadcast; since that time, its share of the radio audience in the Rockville listening area has increased significantly. Given WCQP's recent success with call-in advice programming, and citing a nationwide survey indicating that many radio listeners are quite interested in such programs, the station manager of KICK in Medway recommends that KICK include more call-in advice programs in an attempt to gain a larger audience share in its listening area.

译 文

两年前，Rockville 市的 WCQP 无线电台决定增加其播出的电话咨询类节目的数量；此后，在 Rockville 市的收听范围内，WCQP 无线电台的收听率有了显著增长。鉴于 WCQP 在电话咨询类节目的成功，并且引用全国调查（该调查显示很多广播听众对这种节目非常感兴趣）作为证据，Medway 市的 KICK 电台经理建议 KIKC 加入更多的电话咨询类节目，以便获得其收听范围内更高的收听率。

文章结构图

结　　论：The station manager of KICK in Medway recommends that KICK include more call-in advice programs in an attempt to gain a larger audience share in its listening area.

结论类型：建议型

各步推理分析

①解释类

Signal：since that time

Inference：WCQP 增加 call-in 节目后听众比例增高 ⟹ 增加 call-in 节目导致 WCQP 听众比例增高

Assumption：没有其他解释；call-in 栏目是受欢迎的

Counterexamples：因为该节目内容水平提高，比如换了更好的主播、增加了更有吸引力的其他内容；其他

节目做得更差了；竞争对手退出；广告；可能这些 call-in 栏目根本没什么听众

Evidence：需要调查其他可能影响节目收听率的因素是否产生了作用；需要知道这些 call-in 栏目本身是否受欢迎

② 类比类

Signal：谈论的本来是 WCQP 两年前的经历，但真正要证明的是未来 KICK 的决策

Inference：增加 call-in 节目导致 WCQP 听众比例增高 ⟹ KICK 增加 call-in 节目也会导致 KICK 听众比例增高

Assumption：两年间听众的喜好没有发生显著变化；两个电台所面对的听众喜好有可比性；两个电台现在的节目具有可比性

Counterexamples：两年来，call-in 栏目增加过多，以至于听众们不再有两年前的新鲜感；WCQP 在该举措出现之前根本没有什么 call-in 栏目，而 KICK 电台可能本来就有很多 call-in 栏目，再增加是完全没有意义的

Evidence：需要知道两电台的受众群体、栏目类型，以及两电台已有的 call-in 栏目数量

③ 证词类，数据类，类比类

Signal：nationwide study

Inference：全国调查 ⟹ KICK 增加 call-in 节目也会导致 KICK 听众比例增高

Assumption：全国调查可靠，能够反映当地趋势，喜欢 call-in 节目的听众实际数量比例很高

Counterexamples：调查本来就是在电台互动中做的，因此愿意互动的人才能参与，而其中喜欢 call-in 节目的比例自然比较高；不同区域有着非常不同的听众特点，M 这个地区的听众比较保守、传统，并不愿主动参与栏目的互动中；就算喜欢 call-in 的听众数量多，但其实比例非常低

Evidence：需要知道调查的选样方式；需要知道调查当中不同区域的区别；需要知道喜欢 call-in 节目的听众比例

④ 建议类

Signal：最终要得出一个建议

Inference：KICK 增加 call-in 节目也会导致 KICK 听众比例增高 ⟹ KICK 应该增加 call-in

Assumption：没有其他更有效的解决方案

Counterexamples：好的主播；更贴近人们兴趣的节目内容

Evidence：需要充分考虑其他可能更有效的解决方案

20 According to a recent report, cheating among college and university students is on the rise. However, Groveton College has successfully reduced student cheating by adopting an honor code, which calls for students to agree not to cheat in their academic endeavors and to notify a faculty member if they suspect that others have cheated. Groveton's honor code replaced a system in which teachers closely monitored students; under that system, teachers reported an average of thirty cases of cheating per year. In the first year the honor code was in place, students reported twenty-one cases of cheating; five years later, this figure had dropped to fourteen. Moreover, in a recent survey, a majority of Groveton students said that they would be less likely to cheat with an honor code in place than without. Thus, all colleges and universities should adopt honor codes similar to Groveton's in order to decrease cheating among students.

思路相近题目：112, 113 & 131

译 文

根据一项最近的报告，大学生中的作弊现象正在增多。但是，Grove 大学通过采取了诚信守则成功减少了学生的作弊现象，该守则号召学生答应在学术生活中不要舞弊，并且如果怀疑其他人有作弊要通知教员。Groveton 的诚信守则替代了过去的系统，过去教师会监考；在那个系统中，教师每年报告大约 30 起作弊案例。在诚信守则实施之后的第一年，学生报告了二十一起作弊；五年后，该数字下降到了十四。并且，在最近一次调查当中，大部分 Groveton 的学生表示，自己在有诚信守则规范下更不会去作弊。因此，所有大学都应该执行类似于 Groveton 的诚信守则，以便能够减少学生中的舞弊行为。

文章结构图

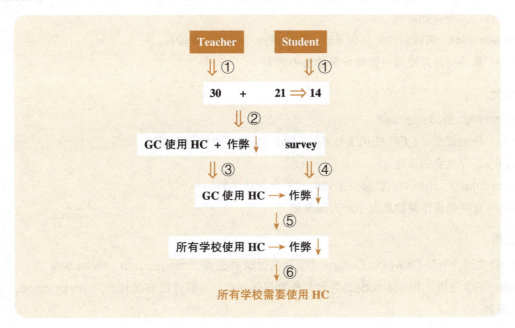

结　　论：All colleges and universities should adopt honor codes similar to Groveton's in order to decrease cheating among students.

结论类型：**建议型**

各步推理分析

① 证词类

Signal：teachers reported；students reported

Inference：GC 老师和学生的报告 ⟹ GC 每年作弊人数从 30 下降到 14

Assumption：学生与老师的报告一样精确、可靠

Counterexamples：学生互相包庇作弊；学生没有足够精力注意别人作弊

Evidence：需要更可靠的证据来判断现在学生作弊的数量

② 数据类

Signal：30；21；14

Inference：GC 年作弊人数从 30 下降到 14 ⟹ GC 作弊问题减弱了

Assumption：学生总数没有显著下降，考试频率没有发生显著下降……

Counterexamples：学生人数翻倍，每年考试频率翻倍

Evidence：需要知道实际参加考试的人数变化

③ 解释类

Signal：②的结论，以及作者试图建立 GC 的 honor code 与作弊减少之间的关系

Inference：GC 使用了 honor code，之后作弊问题减弱了 ⟹ GC 使用了 honor code，导致其作弊问题减弱

Assumption：没有其他解释

Counterexamples：被抓到作弊处罚更严；隔位就座；安装了摄像头……

Evidence：需要排除其他可能影响作弊数量的因素

④ 证词类

Signal：survey, students said

Inference：学生调查 ⟹ GC 使用了 honor code，导致其作弊问题减弱

Assumption：学生会说实话

Counterexamples：作弊的人在接受采访时也不会承认作弊……

Evidence：直接调查作弊数量而不是去做采访

⑤ 类比类

Signal：前文讨论的是 Groveton College，而后文讨论的是 all colleges and universities

Inference：GC 使用了 honor code，导致其作弊问题减弱 ⟹ 其他所有学校使用 honor code，也能导致各自作弊问题减弱

Assumption：各个学校学生情况差不多

Counterexamples：GC 学校生源好，只要适当提醒就不会作弊，但是别的学校学生可能很差，必须严格看管才不会作弊；很可能也有些学校已经基本没什么人作弊了

Evidence：需要对比不同学校学生的品行；需要知道每个学校的现有作弊严重程度

⑥ 建议类

Signal：⑤ 的结论，且后文给出建议

Inference：其他所有学校使用 honor code，也能导致各自作弊问题减弱 ⟹ 其他所有学校需要使用 honor code

Assumption：没有更好、更可靠的解决方案

Counterexamples：提高作弊惩罚；安装监控设备

Evidence：需要调查其他替代方案的效用

Part 5 Argument 题库逐题精析

22 A recently issued twenty-year study on headaches suffered by the residents of Mentia investigated the possible therapeutic effects of consuming salicylates. Salicylates are members of the same chemical family as aspirin, a medicine used to treat headaches. Although many foods are naturally rich in salicylates, food-processing companies also add salicylates to foods as preservatives. The twenty-year study found a correlation between the rise in the commercial use of salicylates and a steady decline in the average number of headaches reported by study participants. At the time when the study concluded, food-processing companies had just discovered that salicylates can also be used as flavor additives for foods, and, as a result, many companies plan to do so. Based on these study results, some health experts predict that residents of Mentia will suffer even fewer headaches in the future.

思路相近题目：24 & 26

译 文

最近一项对 Mentia 居民头疼问题的研究探索了水杨酸脂的潜在疗效。水杨酸脂与阿司匹林在化学上同族，而阿司匹林是用来治疗头疼的一种药品。尽管很多食物天然富含水杨酸脂，食品加工公司也一直在食品中添加水杨酸脂作为防腐剂。这项历时 20 年的研究发现，商业上使用水杨酸脂增多，并且同时，研究参与者报告的平均头疼数也在随之下降。在研究结束时，食品加工公司刚刚发现水杨酸脂可以加入食物当中作为调味剂，因此，很多公司计划这么做。基于这些研究结果，一些健康专家预测未来 Mentia 居民所遭受的头疼会进一步减少。

文章结构图

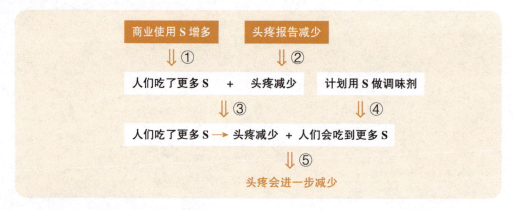

结　　论：Residents of Mentia will suffer even fewer headaches in the future.
结论类型：预测型

各步推理分析

① 数据类

Signal：要证明吃 S 减少了实验中人们的头疼，需要首先证明实验中人们吃到了更多 S，而文中的证据是商

业使用的 S 增多

    Inference：商业使用 S 增多 ⟹ 实验中的人们吃到了更多 S

    Assumption：实验中的人群受到了商业使用 S 的影响

    Counterexamples：只有某些食物会用 S 做防腐剂，而这些食物恰恰是头疼患者一般不吃的

    Evidence：参与调查的人吃的食物当中是否真的有更多 S

② 证词类

    Signal：report

    Inference：头疼报告减少 ⟹ 实验中人们头疼减少

    Assumption：报告具有可信度和代表性

    Counterexamples：参加了 20 多年实验，很多患者后来就懒得报告了；很多患者后来可能去世了，而且就是头疼疼死的，也没法报告了

    Evidence：需要知道人们是否一直严格报告自己的经历

③ 解释类

    Signal：作者试图建立 S 的使用与头疼减少之间的关系

    Inference：实验中的人们吃到了更多 S + 实验中人们头疼减少 ⟹ 实验中人们吃到更多 S 造成实验中人们头疼减少

    Assumption：没有其他解释

    Counterexamples：环境变好；锻炼更多

    Evidence：需要调查这 20 年来是否有其他可能的变化影响了人们的健康

④ 证词类

    Signal：plan

    Inference：公司计划用 S 做调味剂 ⟹ 未来人们会吃到更多 S

    Assumption：计划会实施，人们会认可这种做法

    Counterexamples：首先，计划不见得会实施，因为使用 S 可能会增加成本，有更廉价的调味剂；其次，很可能 S 调味效果不好，人们并不爱吃这种食物，所以最终人们长期吃到的 S 的量不会显著增多

    Evidence：需要知道具体有多少公司会在多少食物当中添加更多 S；以及需要知道人们对这种食物的反应

⑤ 类比类

    Signal：步骤③④的结论，以及最终要预测人们头疼会进一步减少

    Inference：实验中人们吃了更多 S 造成头疼减少 + 未来人们会吃到更多 S ⟹ 未来人们头疼会进一步减少

    Assumption：S 量越多越能减少头疼，未来不会出现新的因素造成头疼增多

    Counterexamples：S 对头疼的影响是有限的，也许人们已经吃了足量的 S，再多也不会发生影响；其次，就算饮食上人们更健康了，但城市环境污染等因素的改变可能会在其他方面抵消这个作用

    Evidence：需要知道 S 对人们健康产生影响的阈值，即需要知道更多 S 是否会对人们产生积极的影响；需要知道未来是否会有其他因素抵消 S 的作用

23

Part 5 Argument 题库逐题精析

23 The following was written as a part of an application for a small-business loan by a group of developers in the city of Monroe.

"A jazz music club in Monroe would be a tremendously profitable enterprise. Currently, the nearest jazz club is 65 miles away; thus, the proposed new jazz club in Monroe, the C-Note, would have the local market all to itself. Plus, jazz is extremely popular in Monroe: over 100,000 people attended Monroe's annual jazz festival last summer; several well-known jazz musicians live in Monroe; and the highest-rated radio program in Monroe is 'Jazz Nightly', which airs every weeknight at 7 P.M. Finally, a nationwide study indicates that the typical jazz fan spends close to $1,000 per year on jazz entertainment."

思路相近题目：93, 95 & 156

译 文

在 Monroe 开一家爵士乐俱乐部一定会非常赚钱。目前，最近的爵士俱乐部也在 65 英里之外；因此，我们提议 Monroe 新开的这家新爵士俱乐部 C-Note 会完全占据当地市场。而且，爵士乐在 Monroe 极其受欢迎：有超过 100 000 名观众参加了去年夏天 Monroe 的年度爵士音乐节；几位知名的爵士音乐家就住在 Monroe；而且 Monroe 评分最高的广播节目是"Jazz Nightly"，它在周中每晚 7 点播出。最后，一项全国范围的调查显示，一般的爵士音乐爱好者每年会花接近 1 000 美元在爵士乐的娱乐上。

文章结构图

结　　论：C-Note, the proposed new jazz club in Monroe, would be a tremendously profitable enterprise.
结论类型：预测型

各步推理分析

① 其他
Signal：thus
Inference：最近的 Jazz club 在 65 英里开外 ⟹ C-Note 会垄断当地 Jazz 市场
Assumption：非 Jazz 俱乐部不可能形成竞争
Counterexamples：听 Jazz 不见得非得到专门的 Jazz 俱乐部，可能有一些餐厅、咖啡厅也会有定期或不定

期的 Jazz 表演，人们也会去

　　Evidence：需要具体关于 C-Note 本身的信息来判断它的竞争力；需要关于当地其他提供爵士乐演出的俱乐部的信息

② 数据类

Signal：":"，100,000

Inference：超过 100 000 人参加了去年的 Jazz 音乐节 $\Rightarrow$ Jazz 在 Monroe 很受欢迎

Assumption：10 万人中大部分是本地人

Counterexamples：绝大部分外地人；本地人不感兴趣

Evidence：需要知道这 10 万人的来源，以及其中真的对爵士乐感兴趣的人的比例

③ 其他

Signal：":"

Inference：有几位 Jazz 音乐家住在 Monroe $\Rightarrow$ Jazz 在 Monroe 很受欢迎

Assumption：Jazz 音乐家只会住在 Jazz 受欢迎的地方

Counterexamples：他们住在这里是因为这里居住环境好，跟 Jazz 是否流行没有关系，他们也不在这里表演

Evidence：需要知道这些住在 Monroe 的爵士音乐家现在对市场的影响力，以及他们在 Monroe 所进行的爵士乐相关活动的信息

④ 其他

Signal：":"

Inference：评分最高的广播节目是 *Jazz Nightly* $\Rightarrow$ Jazz 在 Monroe 很受欢迎

Assumption：评分体现欢迎度

Counterexamples：评分是人们的平均给分，广播可能非常小众，Jazz 在广播中也小众，虽然这个节目很好，评分很高，但是给分的人非常少

Evidence：需要知道这个广播节目的覆盖范围

⑤ 证词类，数据类，类比类

Signal：nationwide study, 1,000, 以及谈的本来是 nationwide, 但要证明的是 Monroe

Inference：nationwide study $\Rightarrow$ Jazz 爱好者舍得在 Jazz 上花钱

Assumption：调查具有代表性，每年 1 000 美元的花费很高，Monroe 符合全国的特点

Counterexamples：调查的样本选择未知，也许是在 Jazz 俱乐部做的调查，本来就是消费力比较高的人；1 000 美元/年也许根本算不上什么高消费；M 极穷，低于平均水平，这里的人并不会花那么多钱

Evidence：需要知道 Monroe 相比于全国的消费水平

⑥ 类比类

Signal：谈的本来是 Jazz 受欢迎，但最终要谈的是 Jazz 俱乐部的 C-Note

Inference：C-Note 会独占当地市场 + Jazz 在 M 受欢迎 + Jazz 爱好者会在 Jazz 上花很多钱

Assumption：Jazz 受欢迎，则 Jazz 俱乐部就会赚钱

Counterexamples：Jazz 受欢迎，于是人们会很喜欢听 Jazz 的广播、Jazz 的 CD、会参加 Jazz 音乐节，但是人们不必非得去俱乐部，尤其是如果 C-Note 这个俱乐部不好

Evidence：需要知道爵士乐粉丝在爵士乐上的花费中有多大比例是投入爵士俱乐部的

Part 5 Argument 题库逐题精析

25 The following appeared in a letter to the editor of a local newspaper.

"Commuters complain that increased rush-hour traffic on Blue Highway between the suburbs and the city center has doubled their commuting time. The favored proposal of the motorists' lobby is to widen the highway, adding an additional lane of traffic. But last year's addition of a lane to the nearby Green Highway was followed by worsening traffic jams. A better alternative is to add a bicycle lane to Blue Highway. Many area residents are keen bicyclists. A bicycle lane would encourage them to use bicycles to commute, and so would reduce rush-hour traffic, rather than fostering an increase."

思路相近题目：27 & 67

译 文

通勤者们抱怨 Blue 公路上高峰期城郊路段车流越来越多，导致他们通勤时间加倍。汽车业的说客们支持的方案是拓宽道路，增加一条机动车道。但是，去年邻近的 Green 公路增加了一条车道，之后堵塞问题反而更严重了。更好的方案是在 Blue 公路上添加一条自行车道。很多当地市民喜欢骑自行车。一条自行车道会鼓励他们骑自行车通勤，进而减少交通堵塞而不是使其加剧。

文章结构图

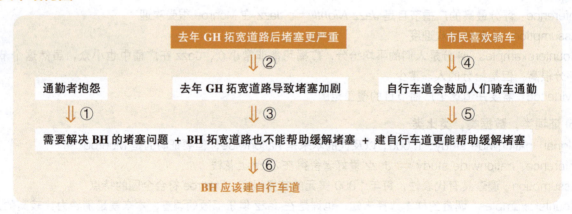

结　　论：Blue Highway should add a bicycle lane.
结论类型：建议型

各步推理分析

① 证词类
Signal：为了证明 BH 有解决交通堵塞的需求，作者引用了通勤者的抱怨
Inference：通勤者抱怨 ⟹ BH 需要解决堵塞问题
Assumption：这些抱怨有代表性
Counterexamples：抱怨的人很少；是自己的通勤时间改变造成通勤时间翻倍，而且很可能就算翻倍，时间

也没有增长多少，比如从五分钟变成十分钟；而且，很可能很多人为了引起重视，故意夸大了实际通勤时间

Evidence：需要知道有多少人抱怨，以及具体调查人们实际通勤时间的变化量

② 解释类

Signal：作者试图建立 GH 拓宽道路与 GH 堵塞严重之间的关系

Inference：GH 去年拓宽道路后堵塞更严重 $\Longrightarrow$ GH 拓宽道路带来了更严重的堵塞

Assumption：没有其他解释

Counterexamples：GH 附近人口、车辆大增，导致堵塞；很可能 GH 的道路建设方便了人们的出行，使得走其他路的车流也会选择走 GH，虽然 GH 车流密集了，但是整个地区的交通得到了疏导；很可能附近很多路段也在拓宽，进行大量的施工，导致别的地方的车流不得已要从 GH 通行

Evidence：需要排除其他可能解释 GH 堵塞的因素；需要调查附近整片交通网的车流变化情况

③ 类比类

Signal：为了证明 BH，证据给的却是 GH

Inference：GH 拓宽道路带来了更严重的堵塞 $\Longrightarrow$ BH 拓宽道路也无法缓解堵塞

Assumption：两条道路面对的问题相似

Counterexamples：可能 GH 的道路本来已经很宽，堵塞是因为周围道路网不发达，而 BH 可能就是阻碍了附近交通的狭窄路段，急需拓宽

Evidence：需要对比 GH 与 BH 道路本身的宽度，以及周围现有的车流情况

④ 其他

Signal：作者提到市民喜欢骑车，用来支持下一句所谈到的建立自行车道能鼓励人们骑自行车通勤

Inference：很多市民骑车 $\Longrightarrow$ 建自行车道会鼓励人们骑车通勤

Assumption：喜欢骑车的人就想骑车通勤

Counterexamples：人们喜欢骑自行车，是为了锻炼，但是上下班的时候人们还是不会骑自行车的

Evidence：需要具体数据表明有多少市民喜欢骑自行车通勤或者会在条件允许时骑自行车通勤

⑤ 其他

Signal：步骤④的结论，以及这显然是要表明建自行车道能缓解堵塞问题

Inference：自行车道会鼓励人们骑车通勤 $\Longrightarrow$ 建自行车道能缓解堵塞问题

Assumption：自行车的存在不会干扰道路的运行

Counterexamples：大量自行车涌入，即便存在单独的自行车道，也会干扰道路的秩序，因为周围的路段并没有自行车道

Evidence：需要知道附近的城市规划是否适合自行车通行

⑥ 建议类

Signal：步骤①③⑤的结论，以及最终要建议 BH 建自行车道

Inference：需要解决 BH 的堵塞问题 + BH 拓宽道路也不能帮助缓解堵塞 + 建自行车道更能帮助缓解堵塞 $\Longrightarrow$ BH 应该建自行车道

Assumption：没有更好的解决方案

Counterexamples：安排更多的巡警；造单行线……

Evidence：需要考察其他可能更有效的替代方案

28

Part 5 Argument 题库逐题精析

28 The following appeared as a recommendation by a committee planning a ten-year budget for the city of Calatrava.

"The birthrate in our city is declining: in fact, last year's birthrate was only one-half that of five years ago. Thus the number of students enrolled in our public schools will soon decrease dramatically, and we can safely reduce the funds budgeted for education during the next decade. At the same time, we can reduce funding for athletic playing fields and other recreational facilities. As a result, we will have sufficient money to fund city facilities and programs used primarily by adults, since we can expect the adult population of the city to increase."

译 文

我们城市的出生率在下降：事实上，去年的出生率只是五年前的五分之一。因此，我们公立学校的学生入学率将会显著下降，而我们就可以很有把握地在未来十年内削减投入教育的开支。同时，我们也可以减少投入运动场和其他娱乐设施的开支。这样，我们就将有足够的资金支持主要用在成年人身上的市政设施和项目，因为我们可以预见到城市成年人口的上升。

文章结构图

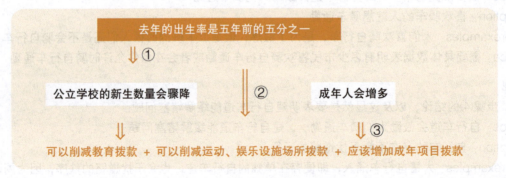

结　　论：The city of Calatrava can reduce the funds budgeted for education and for athletic playing fields and other recreational facilities during the next decade so that it will have sufficient money to fund city facilities and programs used primarily by adults.

结论类型：建议型

各步推理分析

①其他

Signal：thus

Inference：去年新生儿出生率是五年前的五分之一 ⟹ 公立学校新生数量骤降

Assumption：新生儿出生率将直接影响公立学校新生数量

Counterexamples：首先，公立学校的学生很可能并不是出生在当地的，当地出生的人也可以搬到别的地方上学；其次，就算人们在哪儿出生就在哪儿上学，公立学校包含小学、中学，五年前也许是生育高峰，那个时候的孩子刚进入小学，以后还会进入中学，意味着中学新生数量未来将增多，即便小学新生数量减少，教育需求也不见得会减小；最后，只知道去年一年的出生率，也许去年是特殊情况，到了未来几年出生率又会恢复，于是，新生数量基本不会出现大幅度的波动

Evidence：需要知道更多年份的新生儿出生率变化；需要知道当地公立学校的主要生源是否是来自当地出生的儿童

② 其他

Signal：at the same time，we can，和之前的论证基于同样的证据，得出另一个结论

Inference：去年的出生率是五年前的五分之一 $\Rightarrow$ 可以削减运动、娱乐设施场所拨款

Assumption：只有年轻人使用操场等娱乐设施

Counterexamples：所有人都需要锻炼、娱乐

Evidence：需要知道这些运动、娱乐设施主要的使用人群

③ 其他

Signal：we can expect

Inference：这是一个 unstated assumption，没有任何证据

Assumption：成年人会增多

Counterexamples：年轻人减少和成年人是否增多没有任何必然关系，而且很可能当地出生率下降就是因为人口迁走的结果，新生儿数量下降，比例并没有下降，因为成年人也在大幅度减少

Evidence：需要直接调查这些年成年人数量的变化，因为从新生儿的数量完全无法推断成年人的数量

Part 5　Argument 题库逐题精析

29

The following appeared in a letter to the editor of Parson City's local newspaper.

"In our region of Trillura, the majority of money spent on the schools that most students attend—the city-run public schools—comes from taxes that the city government collects. The region's cities differ, however, in the budgetary priority they give to public education. For example, both as a proportion of its overall tax revenues, and in absolute terms, Parson City has recently spent almost twice as much per year as Blue City has for its public schools—even though both cities have about the same number of residents. Clearly, Parson City residents place a higher value on providing a good education in public schools than Blue City residents do."

译文

在我们 Trillura 地区，大部分学生上的是城市运营的公立学校，而大部分投入公立学校的资金来自于各个市政府的税收。然而，该地区不同城市在财政投入上给予公立教育的优先级是不同的。比如，无论按照税收比例还是从绝对量上，Parson 市最近花在公立学校上的钱都是 Blue 市的二倍，尽管两座城市的市民数量是一样的。显然，Parson 市民比 Blue 市民更重视公立学校提供好的教育质量。

文章结构图

> PC 花在公立学校上的钱是 BC 的二倍
> ⇓ ①②③④
> PC 比 BC 的市民更重视公立教育

结　　论：Parson City residents place a higher value on providing a good education in public schools than Blue City residents do.

结论类型：**解释型**

推理分析（本文只有一步推理，只能分析该步骤的多个假设）

① 解释型

Assumption：P 城的学生比例不比 B 城高很多

Counterexamples：P 城学生多，所以投钱多，其实两城重视度差不多

Evidence：需要对比两城适龄学生的人口数量

②解释型

Assumption：P 城教育水平先前不比 B 城低很多

Counterexamples：B 城先前投入很多钱，现在不用再投那么多了，因为他们的教育水平已经非常好了，这不等于 B 城不重视教育；P 城之前落后太多，现在投钱只是在弥补过去的缺陷而已，比如 P 城之前的学校数量根本不够，最近投钱多只是在新建学校，自然会花大笔的钱

Evidence：需要知道两城先前的教育投入以及教育水平

③解释型

Assumption：政府代表了民意

Counterexamples：P 城人不怎么重视教育，但是政府投钱多；B 城相反

Evidence：需要知道政府决策在多大程度上受到市民意见的影响，也许 B 城市民已经组织过很多次游行等活动抗议政府对学校的不重视

④ 解释型

Assumption：B 城在非教育领域存在的缺陷没有 P 城严重，并不需要弥补

Counterexamples：虽然 B 城市民同样重视教育，甚至比 P 城市民更重视教育，但是因为 B 城存在其他某些方面的紧迫需求，不得已需要把更多资金投入别的地方，比如也许 B 城经历了严重的灾害（洪水、地震等），导致其需要突然投入巨额资金解决这些问题，这不能说明 B 城市民不重视公立教育

Evidence：需要对比两城在其他领域的花费需求

Part 5　Argument 题库逐题精析

30 The following appeared in a memo from a vice president of Quiot Manufacturing.

"During the past year, Quiot Manufacturing had 30 percent more on-the-job accidents than at the nearby Panoply Industries plant, where the work shifts are one hour shorter than ours. Experts say that significant contributing factors in many on-the-job accidents are fatigue and sleep deprivation among workers. Therefore, to reduce the number of on-the-job accidents at Quiot and thereby increase productivity, we should shorten each of our three work shifts by one hour so that employees will get adequate amounts of sleep."

思路相近题目：97, 98, 99 & 159

译　文

去年，Quiot Manufacturing 比旁边 Panoply Industries 的工伤事故多 30%，而 Panoply Industries 工作班次要比 Quiot Manufacturing 短一小时。专家认为很多工伤事故的重要来源是工人的疲劳与睡眠缺乏。因此，为了减少 Quiot Manufacturing 的工伤事故数量，进而提高生产力，我们应当将三个工作班次都减少一小时，以便我们的员工能够得到充足的睡眠。

文章结构图

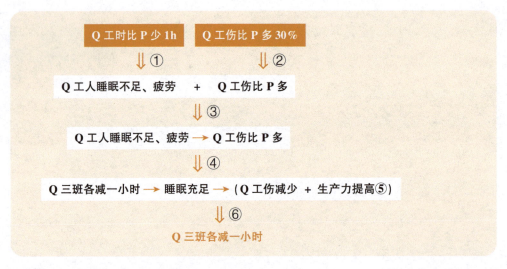

结　　论：Quiot Manufacturing should shorten each of its three work shifts by one hour.
结论类型：建议型

各步推理分析

① 数据类

Signal：30 percent more accidents

Inference：Q 工伤比 P 多 30% ⟹ Q 工伤比 P 多
Assumption：Q 工厂规模不比 P 大很多
Counterexamples：Q 员工数量多得多，导致 Q 的事故率比 P 低很多
Evidence：需要提供两厂规模的数据

② 数据类

Signal：one hour shorter
Inference：Q 工时比 P 少 1h ⟹ Q 工人睡眠不足、疲劳
Assumption：多的这 1 小时足以引起睡眠不足和疲劳，Q 的工作强度不比 P 小很多
Counterexamples：即便多 1 小时，Q 的工作时间可能仍然不长，工人有非常充裕的休息时间，不应该会疲劳；也许 Q 和 P 的工作性质完全不同，Q 的工作强度很低，虽然 Q 工时长，但总工作量 P 比 Q 多
Evidence：需要知道各种能够影响两厂工作强度的信息

③ 解释类

Signal：作者试图建立 Q 工人睡眠不足、疲劳与事故多之间的关系
Inference：Q 工人睡眠不足、疲劳 + Q 工伤比 P 多 ⟹ Q 工人睡眠不足、疲劳造成 Q 工伤比 P 多
Assumption：没有其他解释
Counterexamples：规章制度不严，执行不力，工人素质差，设备差，工作性质危险
Evidence：需要调查在其他有可能影响工伤事故的因素上，两厂是否有明显区别

④ 类比类

Signal：③的结论，下文试图通过减少工时来保证睡眠和安全，并且，下文强调的是三个班次每个都减一小时
Inference：Q 工人睡眠不足、疲劳造成 Q 工伤比 P 多 ⟹ Q 三班各减一小时就能让工人睡眠充足进而减少工伤
Assumption：每个班次都存在类似的问题，工时减少工人就会用减少的工时来休息
Counterexamples：三个班次当中安全事故主要来自其中某个班次，比如夜间的班次，而其他班次根本没有这样的问题；而且，很可能就算工时减少，工人们习惯了自己的作息，并不会用减少的工时来休息，还是不会解决问题
Evidence：需要知道先前三个班次当中的工伤比例是否一样

⑤ 其他

Signal：突然说到了生产力提高
Inference：无，直接引入无根据的假设
Assumption：Q 三班各减少一小时，减少了事故，就能提高生产力
Counterexamples：虽然休息更好，也许工作效率更高，但是由于工时减少，最终总生产力减少
Evidence：需要知道工时减少后工作效率可以提高的期望值，进而帮助预估总生产力的变化

⑥ 建议类

Signal：最终要建议减少班次时间
Inference：Q 三班各减少一小时可以减少事故以及提高生产力 ⟹ Q 三班需要各减少一小时
Assumption：没有其他更好的解决方案
Counterexamples：（空缺，该推理在现实中相对合理）
Evidence：（空缺，该推理在现实中相对合理）

Part 5 Argument 题库逐题精析

31 The following appeared in a memorandum from the planning department of an electric power company.

"Several recent surveys indicate that home owners are increasingly eager to conserve energy. At the same time, manufacturers are now marketing many home appliances, such as refrigerators and air conditioners, that are almost twice as energy efficient as those sold a decade ago. Also, new technologies for better home insulation and passive solar heating are readily available to reduce the energy needed for home heating. Therefore, the total demand for electricity in our area will not increase—and may decline slightly. Since our three electric generating plants in operation for the past twenty years have always met our needs, construction of new generating plants will not be necessary."

译 文

几项最近的调查显示，业主们越来越想要节约能源。同时，各个企业也在销售很多家用电器，比如电冰箱和空调，它们比十年前同类电器的能量使用效率要高一倍。同时，帮助房屋隔热和被动太阳能加热的新科技也已经出现，有了它们，家庭取暖需要的能量就更少了。因此，我们地区总的电力需求将不会增加——而且很可能还会有所降低。鉴于我们现有的三个电站在过去二十年间一直能够满足我们的需求，建造新的电站是没有必要的。

文章结构图

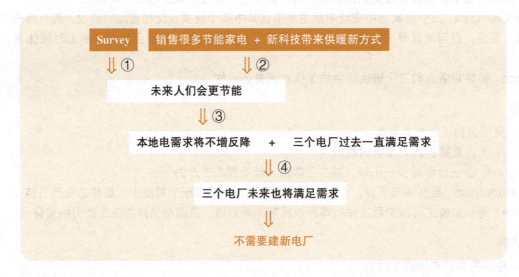

结　　论：Construction of new generating plants will not be necessary.
结论类型：建议型

各步推理分析

①证词类

Signal：survey, eager to

Inference：调查中，人们表达想要节能 $\Rightarrow$ 人们会更节能

Assumption：调查具有代表性，人们的意愿就会诉诸现实

Counterexamples：首先，调查的可能不是本地居民，而且调查的可能只是高素质居民，根本无法代表所有人；其次，在调查中，人们都会说想节能，但会不会真节能是另一件事情

Evidence：需要知道调查地点、调查的人口组成，更需要知道这些人是否表达了真实的意愿

②其他

Signal：为了证明人们会节能，作者列举了市场上存在的节能家电，以及新的供暖方式

Inference：销售很多节能家电 + 新科技带来供暖新方式 $\Rightarrow$ 人们会更节能

Assumption：人们会使用这些新的节能方式

Counterexamples：这些新的节能方式虽然节能，可是价钱昂贵，或者使用体验不好，最终大部分人并不会使用它们

Evidence：需要知道这些新的节能方式的性价比

③其他

Signal：步骤①②的结论，而作者想证明的是当地电需求将不增反降

Inference：人们会更节能 $\Rightarrow$ 当地电需求将不增反降

Assumption：不会出现更多需要用电的人和电器

Counterexamples：就算人们使用的电器可能能耗少了，但是会有更多的人或者更多的方面需要用电，比如，人口增长、人们买更大的房子，于是，虽然单位电器、房屋面积或者人口耗电少了，但是总耗电量还是会增大；而且，我们电厂要满足的不仅仅是家庭用电，工厂、企业、公司用电可能还会因为社会经济的不断发达而需求增加

Evidence：需要知道整个地区各方面用电需求的预期变化情况

④ 类比类

Signal：为了证明未来不需要新电站，作者说了过去电站的状况

Inference：步骤②的结论 + 过去三个电厂满足需求 $\Rightarrow$ 未来三个电厂还会满足需求

Assumption：三个电厂没有老化

Counterexamples：寿命快到，电站的发电量下降的速度超过了节电量

Evidence：需要知道现有的三个电厂的使用寿命，是否存在发电量逐年下降的现象

Part 5 Argument 题库逐题精析

32 The vice president of human resources at Climpson Industries sent the following recommendation to the company's president.

"In an effort to improve our employees' productivity, we should implement electronic monitoring of employees' Internet use from their workstations. Employees who use the Internet from their workstations need to be identified and punished if we are to reduce the number of work hours spent on personal or recreational activities, such as shopping or playing games. By installing software to detect employees' Internet use on company computers, we can prevent employees from wasting time, foster a better work ethic at Climpson, and improve our overall profits."

思路相近题目：55 & 87

译 文

为提高我们员工的生产力，我们应该在员工的终端设备上加装电子监控来监视员工的互联网使用情况。我们要想减少员工把工作时间用于私人以及娱乐活动，比如购物或玩游戏，在终端设备上使用互联网的员工必须要找出并且受到惩罚。通过在公司电脑上安装检测员工使用互联网的软件，我们可以防止员工浪费时间，创造 Climpson 更好的工作氛围，以及提高我们的总利润。

文章结构图

装监控软件减少员工浪费时间，进而提升生产力和利润

⇓ ①②③④

应该装监控

结　论：In an effort to improve employees' productivity, Climpson Industries should implement electronic monitoring of employees' Internet use from their workstations.

结论类型：建议型

推理分析（本文只有一步推理，只能分析该步骤的多个假设）

① 建议类

Assumption：CI 公司存在严重的员工上网娱乐现象

Counterexamples：就没人上网娱乐，装监控纯粹是多此一举

Evidence：需要首先调查是否有很多员工利用网络进行娱乐

② 其他

Assumption：装监控就能减少员工浪费时间，进而提高生产力和利润

Counterexamples：人们有其他娱乐方式，只是不想一直干无聊的工作，如果不让他们上网娱乐，他们也会闲聊、玩手机等，根本不会对浪费时间产生影响，就更不会影响公司利润

Evidence：需要知道员工们是否通过非网络的方式进行娱乐

③ 建议类

Assumption：监控不会造成严重的副作用

Counterexamples：侵犯隐私，员工严重不满，由于员工感到不受信任，反而很多人会离开公司，造成公司业绩下滑

Evidence：必须考察装监控系统会对员工心理产生的严重副作用

④ 建议类

Assumption：没有其他更有效的方式提高效率

Counterexamples：人们效率低很可能是由待遇不好、工作分配不合理或缺乏休息等原因造成，不如寻找更直接的解决方案

Evidence：需要充分考虑其他可能更有效的解决方案

Part 5 Argument 题库逐题精析

33

The following appeared in a letter from the owner of the Sunnyside Towers apartment complex to its manager.

"One month ago, all the showerheads in the first three buildings of the Sunnyside Towers complex were modified to restrict maximum water flow to one-third of what it used to be. Although actual readings of water usage before and after the adjustment are not yet available, the change will obviously result in a considerable savings for Sunnyside Corporation, since the corporation must pay for water each month. Except for a few complaints about low water pressure, no problems with showers have been reported since the adjustment. I predict that modifying showerheads to restrict water flow throughout all twelve buildings in the Sunnyside Towers complex will increase our profits even more dramatically."

思路相近题目：49，121 & 122

译文

一个月前，Sunnyside Towers 住宅区前三栋楼的所有水龙头的最大出水量都被限制到了先前的三分之一。尽管还没有获得调整后的实际用水量的读数，但该变化显然会帮 Sunnyside 集团省一笔可观的开支，因为该集团每月要付这些水费。除了极个别对低水压的投诉，调整后并没有报告出什么大问题。我预测，把 Sunnyside Towers 住宅区所有楼的水龙头的出水量都进行限制将会更进一步地大幅度增加利润。

文章结构图

结　论：Modifying showerheads to restrict water flow throughout all twelve buildings in the Sunnyside Towers complex will increase company profits more dramatically.

结论类型：预测型

各步推理分析

① 其他

Signal：since

Inference：公司付水费 ⟹ 前三栋楼限流一定会让公司省钱

Assumption：人们用水的时间没有显著增加，先前的平均出水量远大于最大值的 1/3

Counterexamples：首先，虽然水流变弱，但如果人们洗澡的时间加长很多，则总消耗水量并不会显著下降；其次，如果之前平均出水量并不明显大于最大值的 1/3，则新方案限制最大流量到 1/3 并不会带来实际出水量的显著下降，因为之前人们本来也远远不会把水龙头开到最大

Evidence：需要调查人们的洗澡时间是否大幅增长；最直接的就是调查人们的实际用水量是否发生显著变化

② 证词类

Signal：抱怨少

Inference：抱怨少 ⟹ 前三栋楼水龙头限流并没有造成严重损失

Assumption：不满的人都会抱怨

Counterexamples：事实上，很多不满的人也许直接搬走，或者不再续租；而且，知道这件事情，很多潜在的租户可能也不准备来这里住了；很少的抱怨很可能是个别人直接代表所有业主发出的抱怨

Evidence：需要直接调查该公寓是否出现续租量显著减少的现象

③ 类比类

Signal：本来谈前三栋楼，突然变成要谈所有楼；谈论的本来是省水钱以及没造成问题，直接变成预测利润提高

Inference：前三栋楼限流一定会让公司省钱 + 前三栋楼龙头限流并没有造成严重损失 ⟹ 所有楼水笼头限流会为公司赢得更多利润

Assumption：各栋楼居民情况足够相似

Counterexamples：有些其他楼的出水量上限本来就不高，继续限流只会造成非常严重的水压不足问题；水费只是公司非常小的一部分支出，根本不足以对利润产生多大影响

Evidence：需要比较不同公寓楼的用水情况；需要知道水费在整个公司利润当中所占的比重

34 The following report appeared in the newsletter of the West Meria Public Health Council.

"An innovative treatment has come to our attention that promises to significantly reduce absenteeism in our schools and workplaces. A study reports that in nearby East Meria, where fish consumption is very high, people visit the doctor only once or twice per year for the treatment of colds. Clearly, eating a substantial amount of fish can prevent colds. Since colds represent the most frequently given reason for absences from school and work, we recommend the daily use of Ichthaid—a nutritional supplement derived from fish oil—as a good way to prevent colds and lower absenteeism."

思路相近题目：155 & 158

译文

一种革新的疗法最近引起我们的注意，它保证能够大幅减少学校和工作中的缺勤现象。一项研究报告说，在邻近的东 Meria 地区，鱼消费量很高，而人们每年因为感冒看医生的次数只有一到两次。显然，大量吃鱼能够防止感冒。鉴于感冒代表了学校与工作单位当中最主要的请假理由，我们推荐每天服用 Ichthaid——一种提取自鱼油的营养物质——作为一种有效地防止感冒并减少缺勤的手段。

文章结构图

结　　论：People should use Ichthaid daily as a good way to prevent colds and lower absenteeism.
结论类型：建议型

各步推理分析

① 证词类

Signal：study report

Inference：study 报告 EM 鱼消费量高，人们因为感冒看医生一两次 ⟹ EM 鱼消费量高，人们因为感冒看医生一两次

Assumption：study 是可靠的

Counterexamples：样本量小，样本选择不具有代表性

Evidence：需要知道样本量和取样方式

② 数据类

Signal：consumption high

Inference：EM 鱼消费量高 ⟹ EM 人吃鱼多

Assumption：被消费的鱼主要是被当地人吃了

Counterexamples：旅游城市，外来游客吃得更多；鱼用来进行工业加工，然后出口

Evidence：需要知道当地实际的人均食用鱼的量是否高于其他各地的平均值

③ 数据类

Signal：once or twice

Inference：EM 居民因为感冒看医生一两次 ⟹ EM 人感冒少

Assumption：感冒了都会去看病

Counterexamples：自己在家里治感冒

Evidence：需要直接调查当地人的平均感冒频次

④ 解释类

Signal：作者试图建立吃鱼与感冒之间的关系

Inference：EM 人吃鱼多 + EM 人感冒少 ⟹ 吃鱼可以预防感冒

Assumption：没有其他解释

Counterexamples：环境好，气候好，锻炼多

Evidence：需要考察可能影响当地人身体状况的其他因素，并与其他地区进行对比

⑤ 类比类

Signal：本来谈鱼，突然变成了 Ichthaid

Inference：吃鱼可以预防感冒，吃鱼油制品 Ich 也能预防感冒

Assumption：鱼的有效成分被 ICH 保留

Counterexamples：加工过程遭到破坏，或者鱼油本来就不包含治感冒的成分

Evidence：需要知道鱼对感冒起作用的成分，并需要知道该成分是否出现在 Ichthaid 当中并保持活性

⑥ 证词类

Signal：given reason
Inference：吃 Ich 预防感冒 + 感冒是人们缺勤时最常给出的理由 ⟹ 吃 Ich 减少缺勤
Assumption：给出的理由是人们缺勤的真实原因
Counterexamples：称病逃课、逃班
Evidence：需要知道人们实际因感冒缺勤的频率

⑦ 建议类

Signal：基于吃 Ich 可以预防感冒和缺勤，得出最后建议每天吃 Ich
Inference：吃 Ich 可以预防感冒和缺勤 ⟹ 人们应该每天吃 Ich
Assumption：没有严重副作用，没有其他更好的替代方案
Counterexamples：没有提到该药的作用，也许会有不良反应；锻炼，保持好的作息
Evidence：需要知道该药的副作用，并需要考察其他可能更有效应对感冒的方式

35

Part 5 Argument 题库逐题精析

> 35 The following appeared in a recommendation from the planning department of the city of Transopolis.
>
> "Ten years ago, as part of a comprehensive urban renewal program, the city of Transopolis adapted for industrial use a large area of severely substandard housing near the freeway. Subsequently, several factories were constructed there, crime rates in the area declined, and property tax revenues for the entire city increased. To further revitalize the city, we should now take similar action in a declining residential area on the opposite side of the city. Since some houses and apartments in existing nearby neighborhoods are currently unoccupied, alternate housing for those displaced by this action will be readily available."

译 文

十年前，作为整个城市复兴工程的一部分，Transopolis 市改造了高速公路附近的一大块低标准住宅区，用作工业用地。紧接着，几家工厂就兴建在此，区域犯罪率降低，并且整座城市不动产税收上涨。为了进一步带来城市的复兴，我们应该在城市另一边的一个衰退的住宅区域进行类似的工程。鉴于该区域已有一些未被占据的住宅，将它们进行改建是可行的。

文章结构图

结　　论：The city of Transopolis should now adapt for industrial use a declining residential area on the opposite side of the city where a similar action had been taken.
　　结论类型：**建议型**

各步推理分析

①数据类

Signal：文章最终想要带来的是 city revitalization，提到第一个区域的证据只是 factories were constructed,

303

crime rates declined, property tax revenues increase

　　Inference：建新工厂，犯罪减少，财产税收增加 ⟹ 城市复苏

　　Assumption：这些因素足以体现城市的 vitality

　　Counterexamples：更多老工厂倒闭，新工厂运转非常糟糕；严重犯罪增多；警力减少，造成很多犯罪没被发现；税收的短期增加纯粹是因为税率的提高；城市的其他更多方面非常糟糕，比如就业率下降

　　Evidence：需要知道旧工厂倒闭数量，以及新工厂的运营情况；需要知道重罪数量的变化，以及警力分布的变化；需要知道城市整体税率是否发生显著变化；需要更全方位的数据来展现城市发展的状况

　② 因果类

　　Signal：第一个区域改造，subsequently，发生了前面提到的三件事情，而作者明显想建立区域改造与经济复苏之间的关系

　　Inference：改建区域1 + 城市复苏 ⟹ 改建区域1造成了城市复苏

　　Assumption：没有其他解释

　　Counterexamples：环境治理；全国经济复兴；降低税收吸引企业

　　Evidence：需要证据排除其他可以解释经济复苏的因素

　③ 类比类

　　Signal：谈论的本来是区域1的变化，却突然指出应对区域2也进行类似的改建

　　Inference：改建区域1造成了城市复苏 ⟹ 改建区域2也能造成城市复苏

　　Assumption：两边的环境足够相似

　　Counterexamples：之前的地方附近居民少，能容忍工业存在，而且交通方便，适合工业；但是另一边是城市规划的居民区，不能随便去掉；两年来可能已经开辟了足够的工业区了，需要发展配套的居民区、商业区的……

　　Evidence：需要对比两个地区各方面具体情况的差别

　④ 其他

　　Signal：因为一些空房屋存在，用工业区替换掉这些空房屋是可行的

　　Inference：存在空房屋 ⟹ 改建成工业区可行

　　Assumption：并没有更多房屋被长期居住；这些空房屋并不会很快被居住

　　Counterexamples：只有很少的房屋空闲，绝大部分房屋都被长期居住，而且这些空房屋很有市场，正在被出售，这些意味着把这些住宅区挪作工业用是不可行的

　　Evidence：需要知道具体有多少空置房屋；需要知道这些房屋空置的具体原因，是否是因为经济不景气造成的

　⑤ 建议类

　　Signal：步骤③④的结论，而文章最终想要建议改造第二个区域

　　Inference：改建区域2能使城市复苏 + 改建区域2是可行的 ⟹ 应该改建区域2

　　Assumption：没有更好的策略，不会产生严重的副作用

　　Counterexamples：赶走已有居民需要政府花费大量的经费，而城市其实还有更合适的区域来兴建工业区

　　Evidence：需要考虑其他可能更有效的替代方案

Part 5 Argument 题库逐题精析

36

36 The following appeared in a memo from the new vice president of Sartorian, a company that manufactures men's clothing.

"Five years ago, at a time when we had difficulties in obtaining reliable supplies of high quality wool fabric, we discontinued production of our alpaca overcoat. Now that we have a new fabric supplier, we should resume production. This coat should sell very well: since we have not offered an alpaca overcoat for five years and since our major competitor no longer makes an alpaca overcoat, there will be pent-up customer demand. Also, since the price of most types of clothing has increased in each of the past five years, customers should be willing to pay significantly higher prices for alpaca overcoats than they did five years ago, and our company profits will increase."

思路相近题目:88 & 89

译 文

五年前,我们的高质量羊毛毛料的供货渠道出现了困难,于是我们停止了高档羊驼大衣的生产。既然如今我们有了新的毛料供应商,我们应该恢复生产。这种大衣会卖得很好:因为我们已经五年没有供应羊驼大衣了,而且由于我们的主要竞争对手已不再生产羊驼大衣,消费者将有很迫切的需求。此外,因为过去五年中多数种类的服装价格每年都在上涨,消费者应该愿意花比五年前高得多的价格购买羊驼大衣,从而我们公司的利润将会上升。

文章结构图

结　　论:Sartorian should resume production of alpaca overcoat.
结论类型:建议型

305

各步推理分析

① 其他

Signal：now that

Inference：五年前因供货困难而停产，如今有了新供应商 ⟹ 可以恢复生产

Assumption：新近的供应商可以提供合适的原料；如今的设备、人员能够胜任制造工作；新供应商的报价并没有显著提高

Counterexamples：质量不如之前，供应量达不到需求；停工之后设备因老化而变卖了，相应的专业人员也已流失；新供应商的供货价格大幅提高，成本大大增高，企业根本承担不起新的成本

Evidence：需要知道新的供应商所提供的羊驼毛的质量，以及价格；需要知道本厂是否有合适的技术、人员、设备以恢复生产

② 其他

Signal："：", since

Inference：五年没生产，且竞争者都已停产 ⟹ 会有很高的市场需求

Assumption：顾客对此产品的需求并没有消失

Counterexamples：竞争对手不做的原因就是顾客不喜欢这种大衣

③ 类比类

Signal：要预测的是 alpaca overcoat 的售价，但证据来自于其他产品的售价

Inference：大部分产品过去五年内都提价了 ⟹ 顾客愿意为羊驼大衣付高价

Assumption：整个市场的变化是统一的

Counterexamples：其他产品变贵的原因是衣服质量的提高，而羊驼大衣，五年不做了，工艺还是先前的，质量没有变得更好，人们还是不愿意付高价；还有可能其他产品现在更符合时尚需求，而羊驼大衣很可能已经过时了

Evidence：需要调查目前市场对羊驼大衣的需求，以及消费者愿意为其付出的价钱

④ 建议类

Signal：步骤①②③的结论，以及最终要建议公司恢复生产

Inference：可以恢复生产 + 会有很高市场需求 + 顾客愿意付高价 ⟹ 应该恢复生产

Assumption：没有更好的方案

Counterexamples：可能会有更赚钱的投资方向

Evidence：需要调查其他可能更有效的投资方案

Part 5　Argument 题库逐题精析

37 A recent sales study indicates that consumption of seafood dishes in Bay City restaurants has increased by 30 percent during the past five years. Yet there are no currently operating city restaurants whose specialty is seafood. Moreover, the majority of families in Bay City are two-income families, and a nationwide study has shown that such families eat significantly fewer home-cooked meals than they did a decade ago but at the same time express more concern about healthful eating. Therefore, the new Captain Seafood restaurant that specializes in seafood should be quite popular and profitable.

思路相近题目：165

译　文

最近的销量调查显示 Bay City 餐馆的海鲜菜肴的消费量比过去五年增加了 30%。可是，现在该市还没有专营海鲜的餐厅。此外，Bay City 的大多数家庭是双收入家庭，而一项全国调查显示这类家庭在家做饭的频率比十年前显著降低，同时他们更关注健康饮食。因此，新的专营海鲜菜肴的 Captain Seafood 餐厅将会非常受欢迎且赚钱。

文章结构图

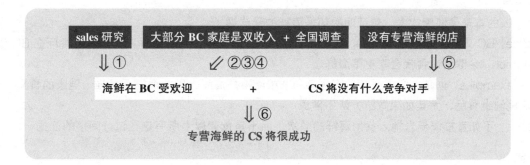

结　论：The new Captain Seafood restaurant in Bay City that specializes in seafood should be quite popular and profitable.

结论类型：预测型

各步推理分析

① 证词类，数据类，解释类

Signal：sales study, increased by 30 percent，以及作者想将这种销量增高归结为海鲜更受欢迎

Inference：sales study ⟹ 海鲜在 BC 受欢迎

Assumption：调查可靠，没有其他解释

Counterexamples：通货膨胀，人口暴增，于是其他食物其实更受欢迎；而且，也许本身销量极低，从极低增长 30% 还是极低，绝对量很少

Evidence：需要知道当地的人口增长、通货膨胀率；需要知道海鲜食物本身的增长绝对量，以及与其他食

307

物相比的相对量

② 证词类，类比类

Signal：nationwide study，而作者最终想证明的是 BC 的情况

Inference：全国调查表明双收入家庭更多在外面吃饭，更关注健康饮食 ⟹ BC 的双收入家庭更多在外面吃饭，更关注健康饮食

Assumption：全国可以反映 BC

Counterexamples：BC 可能是全国经济最落后的地方，教育水平也低下，因此，别的地方双收入家庭意味着家庭经济条件高、教育好，于是会更关注健康，但是 BC 双收入家庭其实是双低收入，人们还是不会在外面吃饭，而且人们也没有多强的健康意识

Evidence：需要知道当地的经济水平，以及当地人实际在外吃饭的频次

③ 证词类

Signal：express concern

Inference：双收入家庭更关注健康饮食 ⟹ 双收入家庭会吃得更健康

Assumption：关注什么问题就会解决这个问题

Counterexamples：人们总会关注健康，但执行起来却很困难，还是会吃觉得好吃的东西

Evidence：需要直接调查当地人健康饮食的习惯，而不是依赖他们口头的汇报

④ 类比类

Signal：谈的本来是健康饮食，想证明的却是海鲜的受欢迎

Inference：BC 大部分家庭双收入 + 双收入家庭会吃得更健康，且在外面吃 ⟹ 海鲜餐厅在 BC 受欢迎

Assumption：会健康饮食就会吃更多海鲜

Counterexamples：也许人们更愿意多吃蔬菜和杂粮而不是海鲜，因为海鲜不是唯一健康的食品，甚至海鲜也不见得都是健康食品，尤其如果做的方法不健康

Evidence：不如直接调查当地人食用海鲜的频次，而不是依赖以上所有这些过分间接的证据

⑤ 其他

Signal：当作者说没有其他专营海鲜的店的时候，明显是想排除竞争对手

Inference：没有其他专营海鲜的店 ⟹ CS 面对的竞争很弱

Assumption：非得专营海鲜的店才能和 CS 竞争

Counterexamples：很多做综合食物的店的海鲜菜单也非常吸引人，而且做得也非常好吃，照样可以和 CS 竞争

Evidence：需要调查周围餐厅海鲜菜肴的受欢迎程度

⑥ 其他

Signal：步骤①④⑤的结论，以及最终要预测 CS 的成功

Inference：海鲜在 BC 受欢迎 + CS 没有竞争对手 ⟹ 专营海鲜的 CS 会成功

Assumption：CS 本身不会有重大缺陷

Counterexamples：CS 做得非常难吃，服务非常糟糕，人们就算吃海鲜也不会来 CS 吃海鲜

Evidence：需要比较 CS 与其他餐厅各方面的优劣势，尤其是海鲜菜肴的口味和质量

Part 5 Argument 题库逐题精析

38 Milk and dairy products are rich in vitamin D and calcium—substances essential for building and maintaining bones. Many people therefore say that a diet rich in dairy products can help prevent osteoporosis, a disease that is linked to both environmental and genetic factors and that causes the bones to weaken significantly with age. But a long-term study of a large number of people found that those who consistently consumed dairy products throughout the years of the study have a higher rate of bone fractures than any other participants in the study. Since bone fractures are symptomatic of osteoporosis, this study result shows that a diet rich in dairy products may actually increase, rather than decrease, the risk of osteoporosis.

译 文

牛奶和奶制品富含维生素 D 和钙，它们是骨骼生长和维持所必需的物质。很多人因此认为富含奶制品的饮食可以帮助预防骨质疏松症，这种疾病与环境和基因相关，会导致骨骼随年龄而显著弱化。但是一项对大量人群的长期研究发现，那些在研究期间经常食用奶制品的人骨折发病率比其他参加研究的人要高。由于骨折是骨质疏松症的症状之一，这项研究结果显示，富含奶制品的饮食实际上会增加而不是降低患骨质疏松症的危险。

文章结构图

长期食用乳制品的人骨裂比例高 + 骨裂是 O 症的标志

⇓ ①②③

长期食用乳制品会提高 O 症的风险

结　　论：The study mentioned in the passage shows that a diet rich in diary products may increase, rather than decrease, the risk of osteoporosis.
结论类型：解释型

推理分析（本文只有一步推理，只能分析该步骤的多个假设）

① 解释类
Assumption：奶制品食用者的骨折概率比其他人明显高；奶制品不会以其他方式增大骨折概率
Counterexamples：文章没有具体指出调查样本量具体有多少，以及骨折概率到底有多高，很有可能因为样本数量的局限性，实际差别并没有多少；而且，这种很小的差距根本不是奶制品对骨质所产生的直接影响所造成的，可能因为奶制品对人身体健康的全方位积极影响，长期食用奶制品的人才会更健康，会更积极地参加各

项竞技性强的运动，那么在这些对抗性强的活动中出现稍微高一些的骨折比例其实是很正常的

Evidence：需要具体指出调查范围、样本量的大小，以及给出具体的数据来表明食用奶制品的人会比其他人骨裂的风险高多少

②解释类

Assumption：并没有什么原因使人们食用奶制品的同时，骨折概率增大

Counterexamples：也许骨折比例高的人群普遍从事更高物理风险的职业，因此他们需要多喝奶制品来提高自己的骨质强度，但其高风险的职业会带来更高比例的骨折；也许骨折比例高的人群年龄普遍比较大，或者本来就患有骨质疏松症，所以他们需要多食用奶制品来提高自己的骨质强度，但他们本身的骨质疏松症还是会带来更高比例的骨折

Evidence：需要具体的证据来了解研究参与者当中的职业分布、年龄分布，以及本身在食用奶制品之前是否患有某些相关疾病

③解释类

Assumption：人们并不是因为骨折了才开始食用奶制品

Counterexamples：也许有非常多的人是因为曾经经历过骨折才选择开始食用乳制品以加固骨质，而他们骨折本身是由各种各样的其他原因造成的

Evidence：需要知道这些曾经骨裂的参与者是什么时候经历的骨裂，准确来说，是在形成食用奶制品的习惯之前还是之后

39 The following appeared in a health newsletter.

"A ten-year nationwide study of the effectiveness of wearing a helmet while bicycling indicates that ten years ago, approximately 35 percent of all bicyclists reported wearing helmets, whereas today that number is nearly 80 percent. Another study, however, suggests that during the same ten-year period, the number of bicycle-related accidents has increased 200 percent. These results demonstrate that bicyclists feel safer because they are wearing helmets, and they take more risks as a result. Thus, to reduce the number of serious injuries from bicycle accidents, the government should concentrate more on educating people about bicycle safety and less on encouraging or requiring bicyclists to wear helmets."

思路相近题目：116 & 118

译 文

一项历时十年的全国范围内对骑车戴头盔效果的调查显示，十年前大约35%的骑车者报告自己会戴头盔，而如今该数字接近80%。可是，另一项研究显示，同样在这十年间，与自行车相关的事故增长了200%。这些结果证明，骑车的人因为戴了头盔会觉得更安全，于是他们就会更容易冒险。因此，为了减少骑车事故当中严重受伤的数量，政府应该更注重骑车的安全教育，而不是要求人们必须戴头盔。

文章结构图

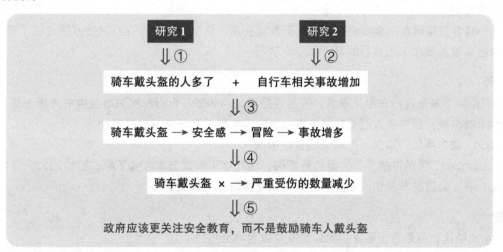

结　　论：The government should concentrate more on educating people about bicycle safety and less on encouraging or requiring bicyclists to wear helmets.

结论类型：建议型

各步推理分析

① 证词类，数据类

Signal：ten-year nationwide study, 35%, reported, nearly 80%

Inference：研究1 ⟹ 骑车戴头盔的人多了
Assumption：人们总会如实汇报自己是否戴头盔
Counterexamples：以前法规不规定戴头盔，于是人们戴不戴头盔都会汇报，但现在法规要求戴头盔，即便不戴头盔的人也会说自己戴头盔
Evidence：需要直接观察统计头盔使用率，而不是依赖人们的口头报告

② 证词类，数据类
Signal：another study
Inference：研究2 ⟹ 自行车相关事故增加
Assumption：骑车人数没有更显著增加
Counterexamples：人口大幅增加，造成骑车人数大幅增加，自行车相关事故比例其实降低了
Evidence：需要知道平均使用自行车人数的变化量

③ 解释类
Signal：步骤①②的结论，以及作者试图建立戴头盔与事故之间的关系
Inference：骑车戴头盔的人多了 + 自行车相关事故增加 ⟹ 骑车戴头盔造成人们虚假的安全感，导致人们冒险，进而使得人们更容易出事故
Assumption：没有其他解释；戴头盔的人会产生一种虚假的安全感
Counterexamples：因为人口大幅度增长，虽然不戴头盔的比例下降，但绝对数量仍然增加，而出事故的都是不戴头盔的；或者这些自行车相关事故可能恰恰是由于骑车或行人造成的；而且，可能戴头盔的人出事故前一直严格遵循交通规则，根本没有危险骑车，而出事故是因为城市道路兴建牺牲了自行车道，导致自行车骑行更不安全等其他原因
Evidence：需要直接调查出事故的骑车人是否佩戴头盔；需要调查是否存在其他原因造成了骑车事故增多；需要知道这些出事故的骑车人出事故时是否在安全骑行

④ 类比类
Signal：谈论的本来是自行车相关事故，但最后想要证明的却是自行车相关事故中的严重受伤
Inference：骑车戴头盔导致人们更容易出事故 ⟹ 骑车戴头盔不能减少严重受伤
Assumption：骑车事故的增加与严重受伤直接相关
Counterexamples：虽然事故多了，但都是擦伤，而死亡率和重伤率大幅下降，恰恰因为头盔的保护
Evidence：需要知道骑车受伤人中重伤的比例以及绝对数量的变化

⑤ 其他
Signal：④的结论，但最后想要证明的却是安全教育的必要性
Inference：骑车戴头盔不能减少严重受伤 ⟹ 政府应该更关注安全教育，而不是鼓励骑车人戴头盔
Assumption：两个举措互斥，安全教育有效，没有其他更好的解决方案
Counterexamples：很可能教育已经足够多了，人们本来就不听；也许两个举措并行更合适；增加自行车道，严格规定汽车需要避让自行车
Evidence：需要调查其他可能方案的有效性；需要知道之前是否采用过安全教育，以及是否有效

Part 5 Argument 题库逐题精析

40

The following is a letter to the head of the tourism bureau on the island of Tria.

"Erosion of beach sand along the shores of Tria Island is a serious threat to our island and our tourist industry. In order to stop the erosion, we should charge people for using the beaches. Although this solution may annoy a few tourists in the short term, it will raise money for replenishing the sand. Replenishing the sand, as was done to protect buildings on the nearby island of Batia, will help protect buildings along our shores, thereby reducing these buildings' risk of additional damage from severe storms. And since beaches and buildings in the area will be preserved, Tria's tourist industry will improve over the long term."

译 文

Tria 岛沿岸沙滩的侵蚀对我岛本身以及我们的旅游业都是一大威胁。为了阻止侵蚀，我们应当对使用沙滩的人收费。尽管这种解决方案会在短期内惹恼一些游客，它能够为重铺沙滩带来经费。邻近的 Batia 岛也通过重铺沙滩来保护建筑，这么做会帮助我们保护沿岸建筑，进而减少建筑遭受风暴的额外威胁。并且，由于该区域的沙滩和建筑将受到保护，Tria 的旅游业也会长期更好地发展。

文章结构图

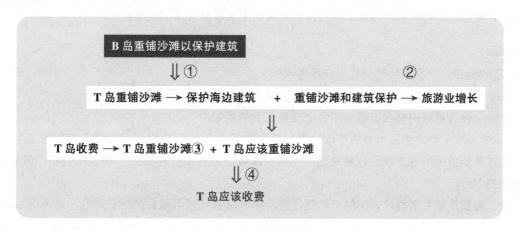

结　　论：Tria Island should charge people for using the beaches.
结论类型：建议型

各步推理分析

①**其他**

Signal：本来要谈 Tria Island，却提到了 Batia Island
Inference：B 岛重铺沙滩以保护建筑 ⟹ T 岛重铺沙滩也可以保护海边建筑

313

Assumption：B 岛举措成功，两岛情况相似

Counterexamples：B 岛的建筑仍然损坏严重；即便损坏少，也很可能是因为其他原因，比如天气好、没有什么暴风雨；T 岛的建筑可能距离沙滩远、海拔高或者中间有很多树林，不容易受到海浪、海风等的侵蚀；两岛的建筑结构和材质也许不同，使得 T 岛的建筑更不容易受损

Evidence：需要调查 B 岛重铺沙滩所产生的效果，是否对其沿岸建筑起到了保护作用；需要调查两岛建筑的区别，比如其材质、所受的侵蚀程度、位置等方面

②其他

Signal：因为沙滩与建筑得到保护，旅游业将会提升

Inference：无，这是 stated assumption，没有给出任何证据

Assumption：沙滩与建筑的保护会直接带来旅游业的提升

Counterexamples：可能这个地区的旅游业本来就在衰退，因为国家经济不景气、竞争的旅游区增多或旅游配套服务设施差；这个地区旅游业非常发达，但并不是因为沙滩和建筑

Evidence：需要证据支持 T 岛沙滩与建筑保护与其旅游业发展之间的关系

③其他

Signal：收费能募集到铺沙滩的钱

Inference：无，这是 stated assumption，没有给出任何证据

Assumption：收费能募集到铺沙滩的钱

Counterexamples：把游客惹生气了，他们就不来了，更挣不到钱

Evidence：需要证据表明从游客身上收钱将能募集到用来修复沙滩的足够的钱

④ 建议类

Signal：③的结论，以及最终想要建议向游客收钱

Inference：向游客收钱能重铺沙滩 + 需要重铺沙滩 ⟹ 建议向游客收钱

Assumption：没有更好的替代方案；不会造成更严重的后果

Counterexamples：也许该岛本身的市政经费足够自主重铺沙滩，也许更好地提高旅游服务能够吸引更多游客前来，通过其他方面的收入就足以解决这个问题；或者这么做虽然募集到了铺沙滩的钱，但从长期来讲大大破坏了此地的名声

Evidence：需要重复考察替代方案的有效性，并考虑向游客收钱可能会产生长期的严重不良后果

41

The following appeared in a memorandum written by the chairperson of the West Egg Town Council.

"Two years ago, consultants predicted that West Egg's landfill, which is used for garbage disposal, would be completely filled within five years. During the past two years, however, the town's residents have been recycling twice as much material as they did in previous years. Next month the amount of recycled material—which includes paper, plastic, and metal—should further increase, since charges for pickup of other household garbage will double. Furthermore, over 90 percent of the respondents to a recent survey said that they would do more recycling in the future. Because of our town's strong commitment to recycling, the available space in our landfill should last for considerably longer than predicted."

译 文

两年前,顾问预言 West Egg 用于处理垃圾的填埋场将在五年内完全填满。然而,在过去两年间,市民回收垃圾的量比以前翻了一番。由于垃圾收集的收费在下个月将会加倍,回收垃圾的量,包括纸、塑料、金属将进一步增加。而且,在最近一次调查中,超过90%的受访者表示,他们将会在未来做更多的垃圾回收工作。由于居民对垃圾回收的有力支持,我们填埋场可利用空间的使用时间将比预期的长得多。

文章结构图

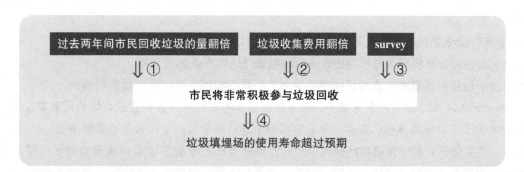

结　　论:The available space in West Egg's landfill should last for considerably longer than predicted.
结论类型:预测型

各步推理分析

①数据类,类比类

Signal:twice;文章要预测未来人们回收垃圾的程度,利用的一个证据是过去两年间人们积极参与回收垃圾

Inference:过去两年间市民回收垃圾的量翻倍 ⟹ 市民将非常积极参与垃圾回收

Assumption：回收量很大；过去的趋势将延续到未来

Counterexamples：也许垃圾回收量本身就非常小，即便翻倍，也不会产生巨大影响；也许过去两年间有鼓励回收垃圾的经济刺激，而未来这种刺激将消失，垃圾回收将会减少

Evidence：需要知道回收垃圾的具体数量；需要证据表明这种对垃圾回收的热情将持续增长

② 其他

Signal：since

Inference：垃圾收集费用翻倍 ⟹ 未来人们会更多参与回收垃圾

Assumption：以前垃圾回收量没有达到顶峰；人们不能忍受垃圾收集费上涨

Counterexamples：垃圾收集费提价绝对量太少，人们不会在乎；以前已经回收了全部可回收东西的，没法再增，就算提价，可回收东西的数量有限，所以剩下的必须要丢的垃圾还是会丢

Evidence：需要知道垃圾收集费用具体是多少，以及当地的平均收入水平；需要知道之前人们是否已经尽力回收了一切有可能被回收的东西

③ 证词类

Signal：Survey

Inference：调查中 90% 的受访者表示未来会更多垃圾回收 ⟹ 未来人们会更多参与回收垃圾

Assumption：调查可靠

Counterexamples：受访的时候人们当然会说好听的话，不代表他们真的会回收垃圾；而且，如果人们在接受采访的时候知道这是关于环保的访谈，则很可能只有关心环保的人才会参加

Evidence：需要直接调查这些受访者是否真的回收了；需要知道这个调查是如何选择受调查者的

④ 其他

Signal：步骤①②③的结论，以及最终要预测未来填埋场的寿命

Inference：市民将非常积极参与垃圾回收 ⟹ 垃圾填埋场的寿命超过预期

Assumption：垃圾回收量决定填埋场的使用寿命；先前没能预见到垃圾回收量的增大

Counterexamples：人口暴增，企业增多，垃圾填埋量也增多；可回收物占总垃圾的比重非常低，因此就算翻倍，也不会大大改变垃圾填埋场的寿命；先前的预测本身已经考虑到了垃圾回收量的增多

Evidence：需要知道之前计算填埋场使用寿命的时候是否已经考虑了垃圾回收量的增多；需要调查当地的人口、企业增长速度是否符合一开始估算时的预期；需要知道可回收物占丢弃垃圾总量的百分比

Part 5 Argument 题库逐题精析

42 The following appeared in a letter to the editor of a journal on environmental issues.

"Over the past year, the Crust Copper Company (CCC) has purchased over 10,000 square miles of land in the tropical nation of West Fredonia. Mining copper on this land will inevitably result in pollution and, since West Fredonia is the home of several endangered animal species, in environmental disaster. But such disasters can be prevented if consumers simply refuse to purchase products that are made with CCC's copper unless the company abandons its mining plans."

译 文

去年，Consolidated Copper Company (CCC) 在热带国家 West Fredonia 购买了上万平方英里的土地。在这些地方采矿将必然导致污染，而且因为 West Fredonia 是很多濒危物种的栖息地，采矿还将造成严重的环境灾难。但只要消费者拒绝购买 CCC 生产的用铜制造的产品，除非 CCC 放弃它的采矿计划，这样就可以避免这些灾害。

文章结构图

```
WF 是多种濒危物种的栖息地 + CCC 在 WF 开矿会造成污染①
                    ⇓②
            CCC 在 WF 开矿会造成环境灾难
                    ⇓③
          抵制 CCC 产品就会让 CCC 放弃开矿
```

结　　论：Environmental disasters can be prevented if consumers refuse to purchase products that are made with CCC's copper unless the company abandons its mining plans.

结论类型：预测型

各步推理分析

①其他

Signal：will

Inference：这是 stated assumption，文章没有给出任何证据

Assumption：CCC 在 WF 开矿会造成污染

Counterexamples：开发技术先进，污染排放处理技术先进，并不会产生严重污染

Evidence：需要调查 CCC 的开采技术是否会产生明显的污染

②其他

Signal：since，以及步骤①的结论

Inference：WF 是多种濒危生物的栖息地 + CCC 在 WF 开矿会造成污染 ⟹ CCC 在 WF 开矿会造成环境灾难

Assumption：开矿的地区邻近濒危生物的栖息地

Counterexamples：WF 是一片很大的土地，铜矿距离濒危物种的栖息地十万八千里，铜矿就算产生污染也并不会影响濒危生物

Evidence：需要知道 CCC 开采的位置与濒危生物栖息地之间的距离，以及这种污染是否会对那些生物产生致命的危险

③其他

Signal：步骤②的结论，以及最终要预测消费者抵制所起到的作用

Inference：CCC 在 WF 开矿会造成环境灾难 ⟹ 抵制 CCC 产品就会让 CCC 放弃开矿

Assumption：消费者知道哪些产品是 CCC 做的；CCC 铜的消费去向是广大消费者

Counterexamples：消费者完全不知道使用的产品用的是哪儿的铜，所以根本无法执行这个策略；铜全部销往遥远的国度，或者该厂的铜主要是国家和企业购买，所以该杂志的读者停止购买这个公司的产品根本不会影响到该公司

Evidence：需要知道 CCC 开采出来的铜被其他企业使用时，那些最终产品是否会标注铜的来源；需要知道 CCC 开采出来的铜被其他企业使用时，最终产品主要的购买者是什么样的人或群体

Part 5　Argument 题库逐题精析

43　The following is part of a memorandum from the president of Humana University.

"Last year the number of students who enrolled in online degree programs offered by nearby Omni University increased by 50 percent. During the same year, Omni showed a significant decrease from prior years in expenditures for dormitory and classroom space, most likely because instruction in the online programs takes place via the Internet. In contrast, over the past three years, enrollment at Humana University has failed to grow, and the cost of maintaining buildings has increased along with our budget deficit. To address these problems, Humana University will begin immediately to create and actively promote online degree programs like those at Omni. We predict that instituting these online degree programs will help Humana both increase its total enrollment and solve its budget problems."

思路相近题目：46

译　文

去年，邻近的 Omni 大学网上学位项目招收的学生数量增长了 50%。同年，Omni 大学显示相较于往年校舍开支大幅度减少，很可能是因为网络课程的原因。相比较而言，过去三年，Humana 大学的招生没有增长，而楼宇的维护费与赤字一直在增加。为了解决这些问题，Humana 大学将会立即创建并推广类似 Omni 大学的网上学位项目。我们预计，这些网络项目的开设会帮助 Humana 增加总招生人数，并同时解决其赤字问题。

文章结构图

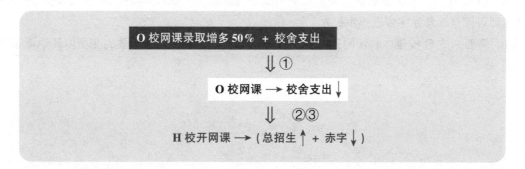

结　论：Instituting online degree programs will help Humana University both increase its total enrollment and solve its budget problems.

结论类型：预测型

各步推理分析

① 解释类

Signal：O 校网课录取增多，During the same year，校舍支出减少，作者试图建立两者之间的关系

Inference：O 校网课录取增多 50% ＋ 校舍支出减少 ⟹ O 校的网课使得校舍支出减少
Assumption：没有其他解释；网课分流使得线下课对校舍的使用减少
Counterexamples：线下课程数量和学生人数一点都没有减少；O 校采取了各种节能手段以减少开支；可能 O 校的线上课根本没有招到人，而线下课本身的招生人数大幅缩水，导致很多课程开不起来，进而校舍开支减少
Evidence：需要知道 O 校线上课程招生人数和线下课程招生人数的变化量；需要排除其他可能解释开支减少的因素

② 类比类

Signal：本来谈 O 校招生，但最终要证明的是 H 校招生，且本来是网课招生增长，最后证明的却是总招生增长
Inference：O 校网课人数增长 ⟹ H 校开设网课能带来招生增长
Assumption：两校课程相似，两校网课质量相似，线下人数没有更剧烈地下降
Counterexamples：很可能 O 校线下课已经完全崩溃，总招生根本就在下降，而 H 校也会经历类似的结果；也许 O 校是文科院校，适合网上开课，而 H 校是理工科院校，需要做实验，不适合完全网络化；也许 O 校网课已经运营很久，名声在外，容易招生，而 H 校第一次做网络课，效果可能不好，招不到什么人
Evidence：需要知道 O 校线上线下所有课程招生总数的变化量；需要知道两个学校开设的院系、课程是否有显著区别；需要知道 H 校是否具备开设网课的硬件、人力条件

③ 类比类

Signal：谈的本来是校舍支出减少，但最终要证明的却是解决赤字问题
Inference：O 校网课造成校舍支出减少 ⟹ H 校开设网课能够解决赤字
Assumption：其他方面的收入没有更严重地下降
Counterexamples：线下课可能收费更高，而由于线下人数减少，收入大幅减少，并且新的网络建设需要大量投资，这些都可能意味着赤字会进一步扩大
Evidence：需要知道 O 校整体利润的变化量；需要知道 H 校开设网课将需要的花费以及期望带来的收入

44

The following appeared in a memorandum from the owner of Movies Galore, a chain of movie-rental stores.

"Because of declining profits, we must reduce operating expenses at Movies Galore's ten movie-rental stores. Raising prices is not a good option, since we are famous for our low prices. Instead, we should reduce our operating hours. Last month our store in downtown Marston reduced its hours by closing at 6:00 p.m. rather than 9:00 p.m. and reduced its overall inventory by no longer stocking any DVD released more than five years ago. Since we have received very few customer complaints about these new policies, we should now adopt them at all other Movies Galore stores as our best strategies for improving profits."

思路相近题目：104 & 105

译 文

鉴于不断下降的利润，我们必须削减 Movies Galore 的十家电影租赁分店的运营成本。提价不是好的方法，因为我们以低价闻名。相反，我们应该减少营业时间。上个月，在 Marston 市中心的分店减少运营时间，每晚六点关门，而不是先前的九点，并且减少库存，不再存储任何五年以前出品的 DVD。由于这么做之后我们很少收到投诉，所以我们应该把这种方法应用于所有 Movies Galore 的分店，这能让我们最好地提升利润。

文章结构图

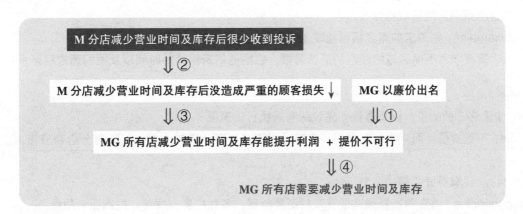

结　　论：Movies Galore's ten movie-rental stores should all reduce operating hours and reduce overall inventory by no longer stocking any DVD released more than five years ago.

结论类型：建议型

各步推理分析

① 其他

Signal：因为 MG 以廉价出名，所以提价不可行

Inference：以廉价出名 ⟹ 提价不可行

Assumption：以廉价出名就永远不能提价

Counterexamples：人们知道它廉价，但并不会因为该店廉价来租碟，反而会觉得它质量不好、服务不好等，因此廉价恰恰使其有限制性而没有优势

Evidence：需要通过调查来知道廉价是否真的帮助了该店的业绩

② 证词类

Signal：few complaints

Inference：M 分店减少营业时间及库存后很少受到投诉 ⟹ M 分店减少营业时间及库存后没有遭受严重的顾客损失

Assumption：不满的顾客都会投诉；统计样本量足够大

Counterexamples：人们直接再也不来这家店了，收入受到严重损失；或者该店本来就开不下去了，因为没什么人来，自然不会有多少投诉

Evidence：需要知道该店在采用政策之前和之后的利润情况

③ 类比类

Signal：谈的本来是 M 分店，但最终却要推广到所有分店

Inference：M 分店减少营业时间及库存后没造成严重的顾客损失 ⟹ MG 所有店减少营业时间及库存能提升利润

Assumption：所有店的情况相似

Counterexamples：别的店的顾客很可能晚上才租片；而且租的都是老片

Evidence：需要调查不同区域的顾客的消费习惯，包括他们来租片的时间以及他们通常租影片的类型

④ 建议类

Signal：步骤②③的结论，以及最终要建议所有店执行该策略

Inference：不能提价，而减少营业时间和库存可以提升所有分店的利润 ⟹ 所有分店都应该减少营业时间与库存

Assumption：没有更好的解决方案

Counterexamples：调查并选择顾客最喜欢的影片类型，多做广告与宣传，提高服务质量

Evidence：需要考察别的方案是否能够更好地提高利润

Part 5 Argument 题库逐题精析

45 The following appeared in a magazine article about planning for retirement.

"Clearview should be a top choice for anyone seeking a place to retire, because it has spectacular natural beauty and a consistent climate. Another advantage is that housing costs in Clearview have fallen significantly during the past year, and taxes remain lower than those in neighboring towns. Moreover, Clearview's mayor promises many new programs to improve schools, streets, and public services. And best of all, retirees in Clearview can also expect excellent health care as they grow older, since the number of physicians in the area is far greater than the national average."

译 文

Clearview 应该是所有人退休后的首选地，因为它有着壮丽的自然景观和稳定的气候。另一个优势是 Clearview 的房价这些年一直稳定下降，而税率也一直低于邻近的城镇。而且，Clearview 的市长许诺建设很多提升学校、街道、公众设施的项目。最棒的是，Clearview 的退休人群会获得优质的医疗保障，因为这个地方的内科医生数量远高于全国均值。

文章结构图

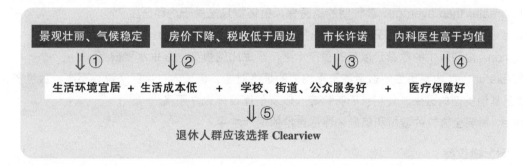

结　　论：Clearview should be a top choice for anyone seeking a place to retire, because it has spectacular natural beauty and a consistent climate.

结论类型：建议型

各步推理分析

①其他

Signal：根据全文从各个方向证明 Clearview 的优势，作者在这里应该是想证明该地的自然居住条件

Inference：景观壮丽、气候稳定 ⇒ 生活环境宜居

Assumption：风光好，稳定的气候就适宜居住

Counterexamples：终年炎热或寒冷，干旱或天天下雨，这样也很稳定，但并不适合居住；景观壮阔意味着

323

可能是旅游胜地，游客过多并不利于生活

　　Evidence：需要知道更精确的气候信息，比如全年的湿度、温度等信息；需要知道该地旅游业的情况

②数据类

Signal：fallen, lower than

Inference：房价下降、税收低于周边 ⟹ 生活成本低

Assumption：房价较低、税收低

Counterexamples：下降之后仍然是最高，整个周边地区的税收特别高

Evidence：需要知道具体的房价和税率

③证词类，数据类

Signal：promises, improve

Inference：市长许诺 ⟹ 学校、街道、公众服务好

Assumption：许诺会兑现

Counterexamples：这只是市长为了竞选胜利的谎言，可能当地根本没有用在这些方面的资金；当地先前的条件如此之差，以至于就算有了这些项目的改善，仍然远远低于正常期望

Evidence：需要知道市长过去的履历，他是否是一个兑现诺言的人；如果他已经上任，需要知道是否真的已经投入资金解决这些问题；以及需要知道现在的市政服务设施的普及水平

④数据类，类比类

Signal：greater than average, 要证明的是医保，但证据只是关于内科医生

Inference：内科医生的数量高于均值 ⟹ 医疗保障好

Assumption：内科医生的数量足以反映医疗水平；医生比例很高；医生水平很高

Counterexamples：内科医生的数量高于平均值的是绝对量，但按人口比例来说并不高；数量多，但滥竽充数；当地缺乏其他类型的医生，外科、心脏科等；以及医疗设施也并不高

Evidence：需要全方位的数据和信息来评估当地的医疗水平

⑤类比类，建议类

Signal：前面谈论的是四个方面，但最终要概括到整个退休生活，并建议人们退休后选 Clearview

Inference：生活环境宜居 + 生活成本低 + 学校、街道、公众服务好 + 医疗保障好 ⟹ 退休人群应该选择 Clearview

Assumption：这些因素足以反映退休人员最需要的项目；没有其他更好的退休选择

Counterexamples：犯罪率高、市民素质差、经济不发达……可能别的很多城市条件更好

Evidence：需要知道更多方面的信息进行综合评价；需要充分考虑其他可能更好的解决方案

Part 5　Argument 题库逐题精析

47

An ancient, traditional remedy for insomnia—the scent of lavender flowers—has now been proved effective. In a recent study, 30 volunteers with chronic insomnia slept each night for three weeks on lavender-scented pillows in a controlled room where their sleep was monitored electronically. During the first week, volunteers continued to take their usual sleeping medication. They slept soundly but wakened feeling tired. At the beginning of the second week, the volunteers discontinued their sleeping medication. During that week, they slept less soundly than the previous week and felt even more tired. During the third week, the volunteers slept longer and more soundly than in the previous two weeks. Therefore, the study proves that lavender cures insomnia within a short period of time.

译　文

一种治疗失眠的传统疗法——薰衣草花香——现在被证明是有效的。在一次最近的研究中，30名患有慢性失眠的志愿者在三周之内每晚都在一个受控研究室内睡在带薰衣草花香的枕头上。在第一周，志愿者继续服用他们常用的安眠药。他们睡得很香但醒来时很累。在第二周，他们不服用药物。结果与前一周相比他们睡得不那么香，并且感觉更累。在第三周，他们睡得比前两周时间长而且更香。因此，该研究显示薰衣草能在短时间内治愈失眠。

文章结构图

> 第一周、第二周、第三周被试者的睡眠状况变化
> ⇓ ①②③
> 薰衣草可以短期内治愈失眠症

结　论：The study mentioned in the passage proves that lavender cures insomnia within a short period of time.

结论类型：**解释型**

推理分析（本文只有一步推理，只能分析该步骤的多个假设）

① **解释类**

Assumption：第三周被试者已经达到了正常睡眠水平

Counterexamples：第三周被试者只是睡得比第一、第二周好，但远没有达到正常水平，说明他们并没有真的被治愈，只是稍有好转

Evidence：需要对比被试者第三周的睡眠水平与没有失眠的正常人的睡眠水平

②解释类

Assumption：被试者之后不会出现症状的反复

Counterexamples：薰衣草只是在短期内能够暂时缓解失眠，但继续使用薰衣草将会失去效果，病症将重现

Evidence：需要做更长期的研究来判断薰衣草所产生的效果是否可持续

③解释类

Assumption：被试者不是因为其他因素而改善了睡眠

Counterexamples：实验环境有利于睡眠，他们的睡眠质量才逐渐提高，并不是因为薰衣草；第二周睡眠变差是因为脱离了先前用的安眠药，但后来逐渐习惯了实验的环境，也适应了脱离安眠药的睡眠；所以，睡眠质量提高，和是否使用了薰衣草没有关系，若这群人不睡在薰衣草枕头上，同样可以睡眠改善，只要经历同样的实验过程

Evidence：需要做对比实验来排除其他可能的变量对睡眠质量所产生的影响，最基本的就是应该让相似的群体经历相似的实验过程，处在相似的实验环境下，但是不提供薰衣草枕头，看睡眠质量是否会同样得到改善

50 The following appeared in a health magazine.

"The citizens of Forsythe have adopted more healthful lifestyles. Their responses to a recent survey show that in their eating habits they conform more closely to government nutritional recommendations than they did ten years ago. Furthermore, there has been a fourfold increase in sales of food products containing kiran, a substance that a scientific study has shown reduces cholesterol. This trend is also evident in reduced sales of sulia, a food that few of the most healthy citizens regularly eat."

思路相近题目：137 & 143

译 文

Forsythe 的市民采取了更健康的生活方式。他们对最近一次调查的反馈显示，他们的饮食习惯比十年前更接近政府的营养建议。此外，包含 kiran 的食物销量翻了四倍，而科学研究表明，kiran 能够降低胆固醇。这种变化趋势还体现在 sulia 的销量减少了，最健康的市民们很少会吃这种食物。

文章结构图

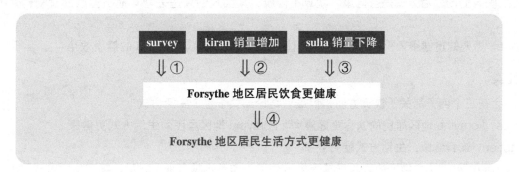

结　　论：The citizens of Forsythe have adopted more healthful lifestyles.
结论类型：解释型

各步推理分析

① 证词类

Signal：survey
Inference：survey ⇒ F 居民饮食更健康
Assumption：调查具有代表性，政府标准没有发生过变化，政府标准就是健康的唯一标准
Counterexamples：调查内容在参与调查之前已经被人们知道，所以只有关注健康的人才会参加；标准变了，人们的生活方式没变；政府的建议本来就是错的，或者不是唯一的健康饮食方式
Evidence：需要知道十年前和现在的政府健康标准细则

② 数据类

Signal：fourfold increase

Inference：kiran 销量增加 ⇒ F 居民饮食更健康

Assumption：人们吃含有 kiran 的食物，并且能吸收，kiran 没有坏处；包含 kiran 的食物当中 kiran 的比例没有大幅下降；kiran 销量上升就能标志当地人吃 kiran 很多；人们先前没有吃类似的食物

Counterexamples：吸收不了；kiran 有副作用；F 是旅游城市，kiran 都是外地人买了吃的；kiran 只是代替了之前的其他健康食品，所以生活方式并没有更健康

Evidence：需要知道这些包含 kiran 的食物中的 kiran 是否会被吸收；这些食物主要是被谁买走的，且是否是被当地人食用；kiran 是否还有其他副作用；含 kiran 的食物当中 kiran 的比例这些年是否发生过显著变化；以前不吃 kiran 的人是否会吃其他更健康的食物

③ 数据类，解释类

Signal：reduced sales

Inference：sulia 这样一个健康人士不吃的东西销量下降

Assumption：健康人士不吃的东西就是因为其不健康，而没有其他原因；某种不健康食物销量下降能说明人们饮食更健康

Counterexamples：健康人士不吃 sulia，不是因为不健康，而是因为很贵、买不到、不好吃等原因，则其销量都不会反映人们的生活方式是否健康；就算不健康，其实人们只是去吃其他不健康的食物，并不是饮食更健康了

Evidence：需要知道健康人士不吃 sulia 的具体原因；需要直接调查 sulia 的健康效用

④ 类比类

Signal：之前三个例子都关于饮食方面，但最后结论却关于整个生活方式

Inference：Forsythe 地区居民的饮食更健康 ⇒ Forsythe 地区居民的生活方式更健康

Assumption：饮食健康，生活方式就更健康

Counterexamples：这个地区的人越来越不爱锻炼了，作息也越来越不好了，其实生活方式更差了

Evidence：需要全方位地调查当地人的生活方式，无论是饮食、作息、娱乐，还是运动

51 Humans arrived in the Kaliko Islands about 7,000 years ago, and within 3,000 years most of the large mammal species that had lived in the forests of the Kaliko Islands had become extinct. Yet humans cannot have been a factor in the species' extinctions, because there is no evidence that the humans had any significant contact with the mammals. Further, archaeologists have discovered numerous sites where the bones of fish had been discarded, but they found no such areas containing the bones of large mammals, so the humans cannot have hunted the mammals. Therefore, some climate change or other environmental factors must have caused the species' extinctions.

译　文

大约 7 000 年前人类到达了 Kaliko 群岛，在之后 3 000 年内曾经生活在 Kaliko 群岛森林中的大型哺乳动物绝大多数都灭绝了。然而人类不可能是导致这些物种灭绝的因素，因为没有证据表明人类与这些哺乳动物有很多接触。而且，考古学家发现一些有大量鱼骨被丢弃的场所，而他们并没有发现存在大型哺乳动物骨头的类似场所，因而人类不可能猎杀这些哺乳动物。因此，一定是一些气候上的变化或其他环境因素导致了这些物种的灭绝。

文章结构图

没有人类与哺乳动物接触的证据 ＋ 发现了鱼骨，没发现大型哺乳动物的骨头
⇓①
人没有打猎 ＋ 大型哺乳动物灭绝
⇓②③
气候或环境因素造成了大型哺乳动物的灭绝

结　　论：Some climate change or other environmental factor must have cause the large mammals' extinctions on the Kaliko Islands.

结论类型：**解释型**

各步推理分析

①**其他**

Signal：further，so

Inference：没有人类与哺乳动物接触的证据 + 发现了鱼骨，但却没有发现大型哺乳动物的骨头 ⟹ 人没有打猎

Assumption：如果打猎了，现在一定能发现兽骨

Counterexamples：可能兽骨被人们用来制造各种工具，而不会直接丢弃；也许考古调查才刚开始，所以并没有搜索到所有的地方。

Evidence：需要知道考古勘探的进展阶段

②其他

Signal：therefore

Inference：人没有打猎 + 大型哺乳动物灭绝 ⟹ 气候或环境因素造成了大型哺乳动物的灭绝

Assumption：人不可能以非打猎的方式造成动物的灭绝

Counterexamples：砍树，捕食了大型哺乳动物所需的食物，这些都有可能造成哺乳动物的灭绝

Evidence：需要证据排除以上可能性

③其他

Signal：therefore

Inference：人没有打猎 + 大型哺乳动物灭绝 ⟹ 气候或环境因素造成了大型哺乳动物的灭绝

Assumption：没有非人、非气候或环境因素造成大型哺乳动物的灭绝

Counterexamples：疾病、瘟疫的爆发可能造成了这些动物的灭绝

Evidence：需要证据排除以上可能性

52 The following appeared in an editorial in a business magazine.

"Although the sales of Whirlwind video games have declined over the past two years, a recent survey of video-game players suggests that this sales trend is about to be reversed. The survey asked video-game players what features they thought were most important in a video game. According to the survey, players prefer games that provide lifelike graphics, which require the most up-to-date computers. Whirlwind has just introduced several such games with an extensive advertising campaign directed at people ten to twenty-five years old, the age-group most likely to play video games. It follows, then, that the sales of Whirlwind video games are likely to increase dramatically in the next few months."

译 文

尽管 Whirlwind 游戏公司的游戏销量在过去两年中有所下滑,但最近一次对于电子游戏玩家的调查表明这种销售趋势可能会逆转。该调查问游戏玩家他们认为的对于游戏来说最重要的特征是什么。根据调查,玩家喜欢那些图像逼真的游戏,而这种游戏通常需要最高配的电脑。Whirlwind 刚刚引入了几款这样的游戏,并且面向 10~25 岁的人群开展了大力的广告推广,而 10~25 岁是最喜欢玩游戏的年龄段。据此,Whirlwind 公司的游戏销量将会在未来几个月中猛增。

文章结构图

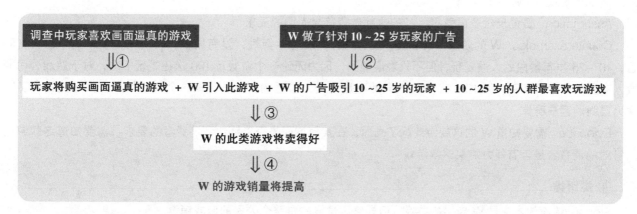

结　　论:The sales of Whirlwind video games are likely to increase dramatically in the next few months.
结论类型:**预测型**

各步推理分析

①证词类

Signal:survey

Inference：调查中玩家喜欢画面逼真的游戏 ⇒ 玩家将会购买画面逼真的游戏
Assumption：调查具有代表性；人们喜欢这些游戏就会去购买这些游戏
Counterexamples：调查中选择了最容易想到的理由，其实其他因素对他们影响更大；在游戏店做的调查，所有受调查者的人是极其关注游戏的人，但是游戏的实际对象是绝大部分年轻人，这个调查其实不能代表大部分人；这种游戏需要顶配的电脑，虽然人们喜欢，但是自己的电脑通常玩不了，所以还是不会买
Evidence：需要知道调查的人群组成以及调查方式；需要知道画面逼真的游戏所需的配置以及一般游戏玩家的购买力

② 证词类
Signal：advertising campaign
Inference：W 公司做了针对 10～25 岁玩家的广告 ⇒ W 的广告将成功吸引 10～25 岁的玩家
Assumption：广告吸引人
Counterexamples：广告质量很差，恰恰起到了负面宣传的作用
Evidence：需要知道该广告的具体内容，以及其对消费者产生的效果

③ 其他
Signal：文章显然需要证明 W 新出的游戏卖得好，而它依赖了一系列条件：基于步骤①的结论，以及 W 引入的游戏恰恰是画面逼真的游戏，文章想要暗示 W 的新游戏类型是吸引受众的；基于步骤②的结论，以及 10～25 岁的人群是最爱玩游戏的群体，文章想要暗示 W 的广告也定位到了最大的客户群体；于是，文章想要暗示 W 新出的游戏将能够卖得好
Inference：玩家将购买画面逼真的游戏 + W 引入此游戏 + W 的广告吸引 10～25 岁的玩家 + 10～25 岁的人最爱玩游戏 ⇒ W 的此类游戏将卖得好
Assumption：最爱玩代表最爱买；W 的这款游戏符合人们的要求
Counterexamples：W 的游戏只有画质，没有内容，没有平衡性，没有剧情，特别贵，根本卖不出去；而且，10～25 岁年龄段的人最爱玩，但不代表最能买，因为无论一个游戏玩 100 次还是玩 1 次，对于游戏公司的收入来说没有大的区别，但 10～25 岁的人显然不是消费力最强的群体，因此这个游戏的广告很可能错失了购买力最强的客户群体
Evidence：需要知道 W 的这款游戏除了画面，在其他方面是否能够达到消费者的要求；需要知道这款游戏所针对的消费者是否有能力购买这款游戏

④ 类比类
Signal：谈论的本来是 W 新出的游戏，但最终要预测的是整个公司的游戏销量
Inference：W 新出的游戏将卖得好 ⇒ W 的游戏销量将提高
Assumption：W 的其他游戏不会卖得更差
Counterexamples：其他游戏销量严重下滑，公司游戏总销量并不会显著上升
Evidence：需要知道整个公司最近的经营状况，即除了这款新游戏外，其他游戏先前的投入和销售状况

53

The following appeared in a memo from the vice president of marketing at Dura-Sock, Inc.

"A recent study of our customers suggests that our company is wasting the money it spends on its patented Endure manufacturing process, which ensures that our socks are strong enough to last for two years. We have always advertised our use of the Endure process, but the new study shows that despite our socks' durability, our average customer actually purchases new Dura-Socks every three months. Furthermore, our customers surveyed in our largest market, northeastern United States cities, say that they most value Dura-Socks' stylish appearance and availability in many colors. These findings suggest that we can increase our profits by discontinuing use of the Endure manufacturing process."

思路相近题目：54 & 75

译 文

最近一次对于我们消费者的调查表明我们公司把钱浪费在了专利生产流程"Endure"上，这种方式使我们生产的袜子可以耐穿两年。Dura-Sock 一直在做广告宣传它使用的"Endure"工艺，但这次新调查显示一般 Dura-Sock 的消费者每三个月就会购买新的 Dura-Sock 袜子。而且，在对我们最大的市场（美国东北部城市）进行的调查中，接受调查的 Dura-Sock 消费者说他们最欣赏 Dura-Sock 时髦的外观和众多可供选择的颜色。这些事实表明 Dura-Sock 可以通过停止使用"Endure"生产流程来提高利润。

文章结构图

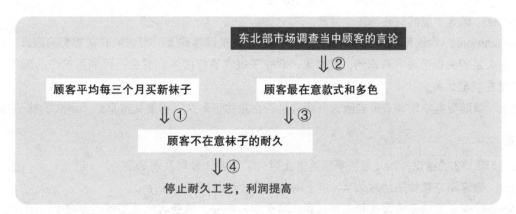

结　论：Dura-Sock, Inc. can increase profits by discontinuing use of the Endure manufacturing process.

结论类型：**预测型**

53

Part 5 Argument 题库逐题精析

各步推理分析

① 其他

Signal：为了证明耐久工艺无用，作者的第一个证据是消费者买新袜子的频率

Inference：顾客平均每三个月买新袜子 ⟹ 顾客不在意袜子的耐久

Assumption：短期更换袜子就说明不在意袜子耐不耐穿

Counterexamples：因为其耐穿才买新的，可能是为了新的款式、新的颜色，但过去的仍然在穿，而且很可能是买来送亲朋好友的，因为顾客们觉得袜子耐穿

Evidence：需要知道顾客短期内买新袜子的具体原因

② 证词类，类比类

Signal：survey，以及本来要证明的是全国，给出的调查范围却是东北

Inference：东北部市场调查当中顾客的言论 ⟹ 顾客最在意款式和多色

Assumption：调查能够代表全国顾客，顾客的言论是可靠的

Counterexamples：也许是在商场进行的调查，经常购物的人可能会更加在意时尚，所以普遍会比较在意款式和颜色，但是真正穿袜子的人可能非常在意耐久；而且，调查中袜子摆在人们眼前，人们最容易想到的是最明显的特点，于是想到的可能就是款式和颜色；最后，东北部城市可能是时尚群体居多的区域，但是放在全国整体平均下来，人们就不见得真的最在意款式和颜色

Evidence：需要知道调查选择样本的方式；需要调查东北市场和其他地区市场顾客是否有着不同的需求

③ 其他

Signal：步骤②的结论，以及要证明人们不在意袜子的耐久

Inference：顾客最在意款式和多色 ⟹ 顾客不在意袜子的耐久

Assumption：顾客不能同时在意多个元素

Counterexamples：也许耐久是排在第三位的元素，仍然是顾客购买时考虑的非常重要的因素；也许人们表面上不在意耐久是因为自己没有意识到，但如果一双袜子很容易穿破人们就会不再购买这个品牌了，意味着人们其实是非常在意耐久的。

Evidence：需要更直接地调查来判断这些顾客是否在意袜子耐久；需要知道那些不耐久的袜子的销售情况

④ 其他

Signal：步骤①③的结论，以及最终要预测停止耐久工艺会让公司利润提高

Inference：顾客不在意袜子的耐久 ⟹ 停止耐久工艺，利润提高

Assumption：要么定价不会发生相应的变化；要么定价不变，消费者的购买量不会减少

Counterexamples：停止耐久工艺也许会降低成本，但是公司在为产品定价的时候是考虑成本的，也许成本下降，定价也会下降，则利润率不会发生变化，利润也不会发生变化；或者，坚持定价不变，但袜子质量下降，很可能顾客就不再愿意花同样多的钱购买，则销量会下降，利润仍然不见得上升

Evidence：需要知道不使用耐久工艺之后生产的新袜子能带来多少利润

56

The following appeared in a memo from the president of Bower Builders, a company that constructs new homes.

"A nationwide survey reveals that the two most-desired home features are a large family room and a large, well-appointed kitchen. A number of homes in our area built by our competitor Domus Construction have such features and have sold much faster and at significantly higher prices than the national average. To boost sales and profits, we should increase the size of the family rooms and kitchens in all the homes we build and should make state-of-the-art kitchens a standard feature. Moreover, our larger family rooms and kitchens can come at the expense of the dining room, since many of our recent buyers say they do not need a separate dining room for family meals."

译　文

一项全国调查显示，最受欢迎的房屋的两个特点是大客厅以及设备齐全的大厨房。我们的竞争公司 Domus Construction 在本地建造的大量房屋有着这样的特征，相比于全国平均水平，他们的房子卖得更快更贵。为了提高销量与利润，我们应该扩大我们建造的所有房子的客厅与厨房面积，并且把顶尖厨房作为标准。此外，大客厅和厨房的面积可以牺牲掉餐厅面积，鉴于我们最近的很多买家说不需要独立餐厅用来全家聚餐。

文章结构图

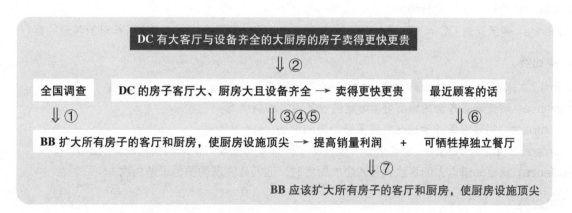

结　论：Bower Builders should increase the size of the family rooms and kitchens in all the homes they build and should make state-of-the-art kitchens a standard feature.

结论类型：建议型

各步推理分析

①证词类

Signal: nationwide study

Inference：nationwide study ⟹ BB 造这种房子最能迎合客户

Assumption：调查具有代表性、普适性

Counterexamples：不同地区人们的倾向完全不同，人们喜好的各房屋特点之间的差距并不大，BB 所在区域的人们可能不喜欢这种特点；而且，人们向往这种房子，不见得真的会买这种房子，因为买不起，人们会考虑实际支付能力

Evidence：需要知道全国调查是否能够反映 BB 所在地区人们的喜好；需要直接调查人们在可支付范围之内的喜好

② 解释类

Signal：DC 的一些房子有这些特点，以及卖得更快更贵，并且作者试图建立两者之间的关系

Inference：DC 有大客厅与设备齐全的大厨房的房子卖得更快更贵 ⟹ 是因为这些特点让 DC 的房子卖得更快更贵

Assumption：没有其他解释

Counterexamples：这个城市的整个房地产很热；DC 的房子地段好；DC 的售楼服务人员水准高

Evidence：需要证据排除能够解释 DC 房子卖得好的其他可能因素

③ 类比类

Signal：本来在谈 DC 公司，但最终要证明的却是 BB 公司

Inference：因为这些特点让 DC 的房子卖得更快更贵 ⟹ BB 公司的所有房子都这么造，也能卖得更快更贵

Assumption：两公司面对的客户类似，BB 公司现有的房子客厅和厨房面积并不够大

Counterexamples：很可能 BB 的消费群体恰恰不怎么喜欢这种特点，而且很可能 BB 公司的房子已经有了足够大的客厅和厨房，并不需要增大

Evidence：需要比对 DC 与 BB 两公司所针对的细分市场，需要直接调查 BB 所针对的客户的喜好

④ 类比类

Signal：本来在谈 well-appointed kitchen，却突然变成了 state-of-the-art kitchen

Inference：建造装备齐全的厨房好 ⟹ 建造设备顶尖的厨房好

Assumption：需要设备齐全意味着需要最顶尖的设备

Counterexamples：人们只是需要装备齐全，却不愿意支付更高代价来购买最顶尖的厨房

Evidence：需要知道当人们喜欢设备齐全的厨房时，他们具体所需要的设备档次

⑤ 类比类

Signal：本来在谈房子卖得更快更贵，最后却突然变成提高利润

Inference：造这些房子能卖得快 ⟹ 造这些房子利润高

Assumption：成本并不会更高

Counterexamples：造价昂贵，利润根本不高

Evidence：需要知道建造这种满足以上要求的房子所需要的成本

⑥ 证词类，数据类

Signal：many, say

Inference：最近很多顾客的话 ⟹ 可以去掉独立餐厅

Assumption：这些顾客有代表性

Counterexamples：这些顾客只是以此讨价还价，其实需要餐厅；并且，就算这些人不需要，更多的顾客需要独立餐厅，"许多"只是一个非常模糊的数据，可能这些人基本都是单身狗

Evidence：需要知道这些顾客的具体数量；需要知道他们是否能够代表整体客户的需求

⑦ **建议类**

Signal：步骤③~⑥的结论，以及最终作者是要建议 BB 建造这种房子

Inference：BB 把所有房子建成有大客厅和大厨房，以及给厨房配备最顶尖设备 + 可以通过去掉独立餐厅实现这些特点 ⟹ BB 应该把所有房子建成这个特点

Assumption：没有严重副作用，没有更好的替代方案

Counterexamples：不能迎合多样的受众，应该保持多样的房屋特点

Evidence：需要考虑其他可能的替代方案

Part 5　Argument 题库逐题精析

57

The following appeared in a letter from a firm providing investment advice for a client.

"Most homes in the northeastern United States, where winters are typically cold, have traditionally used oil as their major fuel for heating. Last heating season that region experienced 90 days with below-normal temperatures, and climate forecasters predict that this weather pattern will continue for several more years. Furthermore, many new homes are being built in the region in response to recent population growth. Because of these trends, we predict an increased demand for heating oil and recommend investment in Consolidated Industries, one of whose major business operations is the retail sale of home heating oil."

思路相近题目：138, 139, 142, 146 & 147

译　文

美国东北部冬天一般很冷，这里大部分家庭传统上用油作为取暖的主要燃料。上个供暖季该区域有 90 天低于正常气温，而天气预报预测这种趋势会持续几年。而且，为了应对人口增长，这个区域建了很多新的房子。因为这些趋势，我们预测加热油的需求会增高，并且建议投资 Consolidated Industries，该公司的一项主要业务是家用加热油的零售。

文章结构图

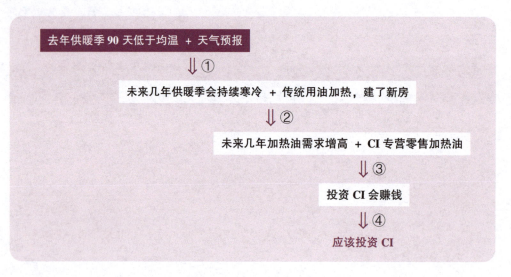

结　　论：People should invest in Consolidated Industries.
结论类型：**建议型**

各步推理分析

① 证词类

Signal：forecasters predict

Inference：去年供暖季 90 天低于均温 + 天气预报预测未来会持续 ⟹ 未来几年供暖季会持续寒冷

Assumption：天气预报可靠

Counterexamples：可能该预报过去的准确率非常低，所以很难作为未来会不会冷的可靠标准

Evidence：需要知道该天气预报过去的准确率

② 其他

Signal：步骤①的结论，以及基于过去住房用油加热和未来住房增多，作者指出用油需求增高

Inference：未来几年供暖季会持续寒冷 + 传统用油加热，建了很多新房 ⟹ 未来加热油需求增高

Assumption：过去用油加热，则未来也会用油加热

Counterexamples：很可能无论新房、旧房未来都会转向更清洁、更廉价的加热方式，比如电、统一供暖等，未来的房屋将有更好的保暖措施，用油量也会减少

Evidence：需要知道过去的老房子是否普遍在进行能源改造；需要知道新建房屋冬天的供暖方式

③ 类比类

Signal：谈论的本来是加热油的总体需求增高，但要证明的却是 CI 公司的加热油

Inference：未来几年加热油需求增高 + CI 专营零售加热油 ⟹ 投资 CI 会赚钱

Assumption：CI 公司的油占有足够的市场；没有其他因素阻碍 CI 公司的利润

Counterexamples：首先，很可能 CI 公司的油质量不好、太贵或者其他原因，使得市场占有率极低，于是即便市场变好，CI 公司的业绩可能并不会提升；其次，虽然 CI 公司主营加热油零售，但可能其他部门的业绩会下降，因此 CI 公司总体可能并不会盈利

Evidence：需要知道 CI 公司加热油在市场上的份额和名声；需要知道 CI 公司其他业务的经营状况

④ 建议类

Signal：步骤③的结论，以及最终要建议投资 CI

Inference：投资 CI 会赚钱 ⟹ 应该投资 CI

Assumption：没有更好的策略

Counterexamples：其实还有其他投资选择，比 CI 公司前景更好

Evidence：需要考虑其他可能的替代方案

58

The following appeared in an article in the Grandview Beacon.

"For many years the city of Grandview has provided annual funding for the Grandview Symphony. Last year, however, private contributions to the symphony increased by 200 percent and attendance at the symphony's concerts-in-the-park series doubled. The symphony has also announced an increase in ticket prices for next year. Given such developments, some city commissioners argue that the symphony can now be fully self-supporting, and they recommend that funding for the symphony be eliminated from next year's budget."

思路相近题目：132, 134, 136 & 154

译 文

多年来，Grandview 市都为 Grandview 交响乐团提供资金支持。但是，去年给乐团的私人募捐增加了 200%，而且观看乐团公园巡演的观众数量也翻了一倍。乐团还宣布明年票价会增长。基于这些变化，一些市委成员认为乐团现在可以自给自足，他们建议明年停止给乐团拨款。

文章结构图

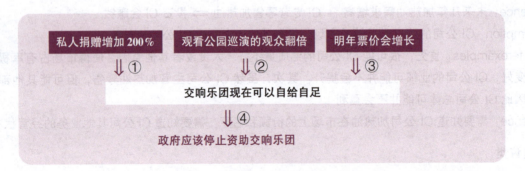

结　　论：Funding for the Grandview Symphony should be eliminated from next year's budget.
结论类型：建议型

各步推理分析

① **数据类**

Signal：200 percent
Inference：私人捐赠增加 200% ⇒ 私人募捐可以为乐团提供大量的资金支持
Assumption：私人捐赠占的比例大
Counterexamples：私人捐赠本来就非常少，即便翻两番，也还是很少，根本不影响乐团的生存
Evidence：需要知道前后募捐的绝对数量是多少；需要知道整个乐团的总营收

② 数据类

Signal：double

Inference：观看公园巡演的观众翻番 ⟹ 公园演出给乐团带来了大量的收入

Assumption：公园演出是赚钱的

Counterexamples：很可能根本就是免费演出，或者廉价演出，收不抵支，再翻倍也没有直接为乐团带来收入

Evidence：需要知道公园巡演具体带来了多少收入，以及观看公园巡演的观众数量

③ 其他

Signal：given such

Inference：私人募捐和公园演出都带来了大量的收入 + 明年票价会增长 ⟹ 乐团可以自给自足

Assumption：涨价后人们还来观看演出；票房为乐团提供了足够的收入

Counterexamples：人们之所以来就是因为票价便宜，涨价后就再也不来了；而且，很可能就算涨价了人们还来，总票房加募捐的收入仍然只是乐团收入的小部分，大部分还是靠政府资助，并不能自给自足

Evidence：需要具体调查观众会如何回应涨价

④ 其他

Signal：步骤③的结论，以及最终要建议停止赞助

Inference：乐团可以自给自足 ⟹ 应该停止拨款

Assumption：只要乐团自给自足就不应该提供拨款

Counterexamples：拨款可以让乐团有更多资金更好地发展，比如邀请更优秀的演奏者，进而不断扩大影响力

Evidence：需要充分考虑给乐团拨款可能带来的好处

Part 5　Argument 题库逐题精析

59 The following appeared in a memo from the director of a large group of hospitals.

"In a laboratory study of liquid antibacterial hand soaps, a concentrated solution of UltraClean produced a 40 percent greater reduction in the bacteria population than did the liquid hand soaps currently used in our hospitals. During a subsequent test of UltraClean at our hospital in Workby, that hospital reported significantly fewer cases of patient infection than did any of the other hospitals in our group. Therefore, to prevent serious patient infections, we should supply UltraClean at all hand-washing stations throughout our hospital system."

思路相近题目：114, 115 & 117

译　文

在一项实验室对液体抗菌洗手液的研究当中，高浓度的 UltraClean 溶液产生的灭菌效果要比我们医院系统正在使用的洗手液强 40%。在接下来对 Workby 医院 UltraClean 的测试当中，该院报告的病患感染事故也远少于我们医院系统当中的其他医院。因此，为了预防严重病患感染，我们应该在整个医院系统的所有洗手站提供 UltraClean。

文章结构图

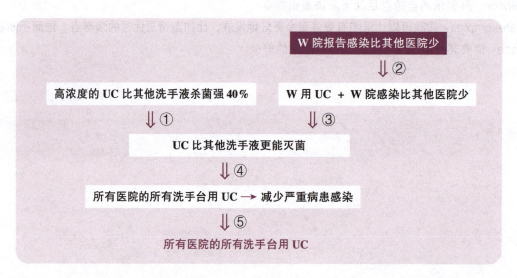

结　　论：UltraClean should be supplied at all hand-washing stations throughout their hospital system.
结论类型：建议型

各步推理分析

① 解释类

Signal：作者试图建立 UC 与比其他洗手液的杀菌效果强 40% 之间的关系

Inference：高浓 UC 比其他洗手液杀菌强 40% ⟹ UC 比其他洗手液更能灭菌
Assumption：没有其他解释
Counterexamples：其他洗手液是稀释过的，同浓度下杀菌效果更好
Evidence：需要知道进行对比的其他洗手液的浓度

② 证词类，数据类

Signal：test，reported，fewer cases
Inference：W 院报告感染比其他医院少 ⟹ W 院感染比其他医院少
Assumption：报告可靠，W 院病患总量没比其他医院少很多
Counterexamples：W 院瞒报；W 院病患数量少得多，自然报告出来的感染量少
Evidence：需要确定是否存在瞒报现象；需要知道各院的总病患数量

③ 解释类

Signal：W 院用 UC，步骤②的结论，以及作者试图建立这两者之间的关系
Inference：W 院用 UC ＋ W 院感染比其他医院少 ⟹ UC 比其他洗手液更能灭菌
Assumption：没有其他解释
Counterexamples：很可能 W 院是一家普通医院，而很多参与对比的医院都是知名的大医院，所以很多患有疑难杂症的病人并不会来 W 院，比如要动大手术的病人是不会选择这种普通医院的，而动手术出现感染的概率本来就更高；而且，感染绝不仅仅由洗手液杀菌不足造成，手术室清洁做得不好、手术仪器没能严格消毒或者医生操作不规范，都可能是各院产生感染的罪魁祸首
Evidence：需要知道各院所处理的病人所患的病是否有很大区别；需要证据排除其他造成感染量区别的因素

④ 类比类

Signal：本来谈 W 院，结果却谈到所有院的所有洗手站；本来谈感染，结果却谈到了严重感染
Inference：UC 比其他洗手液更能灭菌 ⟹ 所有院所有洗手台用 UC 都能减少严重病患感染
Assumption：UC 对各种菌的效果都很好
Counterexamples：UC 只能杀普通菌，厉害的菌杀不掉；或者 UC 不能杀掉某些菌，于是某些院或某些科的洗手站并不适合用这种洗手液
Evidence：需要知道 UC 和其他各种洗手液所杀的菌的类型是否有明显区别

⑤ 建议类

Signal：步骤④的结论，以及最终作者想要建议所有医院的所有洗手站使用 UC
Inference：所有医院的所有洗手台用 UC 都能减少严重病患感染 ⟹ 建议所有医院的所有洗手台用 UC
Assumption：没有其他更有效的方案
Counterexamples：在不同的医院和科室配备适合其特定情况的洗手液；有比 UC 以及我们医院系统正在使用的洗手液更强的洗手液
Evidence：需要充分考察其他可能更有效的替代方案

Part 5 Argument 题库逐题精析

60
The following appeared in a letter to the editor of the Parkville Daily newspaper.

"Throughout the country last year, as more and more children below the age of nine participated in youth-league sports, over 40,000 of these young players suffered injuries. When interviewed for a recent study, youth-league soccer players in several major cities also reported psychological pressure exerted by coaches and parents to win games. Furthermore, education experts say that long practice sessions for these sports take away time that could be used for academic activities. Since the disadvantages outweigh any advantages, we in Parkville should discontinue organized athletic competition for children under nine."

译 文

去年在全国范围内，随着越来越多9岁以下的儿童参加少年运动联赛，有超过40 000名少年选手受伤。在最近一次研究所做的采访中，一些大城市的少年足球运动员报告说受到了来自教练和家长要求赢得比赛的心理压力。此外，教育专家指出这些运动项目长时间的训练占据了本可以用于学习的时间。由于弊大于利，我们Parkville应该停止组织针对9岁以下儿童的运动比赛。

文章结构图

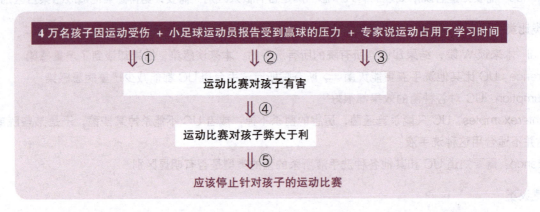

结　　论：Parkville should discontinue organized athletic competition for children under nine.
结论类型：建议型

各步推理分析

①数据类

Signal：40,000

Inference：超过40 000名小运动员受伤 ⟹ 运动比赛对孩子有害

Assumption：受伤对孩子有严重害处，40 000名孩子受伤所占的比重很大

Counterexamples：首先，很可能参加运动的孩子数量比4万多得多，意味着受伤的风险并不大；其次，受伤包含了各个程度，比如小小的外皮擦伤根本不算什么害处，根本没有什么特别大的危险

Evidence：需要知道这些受伤案例当中有多少是真正严重的受伤；需要知道参加运动的孩子总量有多少

② 证词类

Signal：report

Inference：足球运动员报告的压力 $\Longrightarrow$ 运动比赛对孩子心理有害

Assumption：有压力就是害处

Counterexamples：适度的压力会为孩子们提供动力，也训练孩子们的抗压能力，根本不能说是一种害处

Evidence：需要知道这些所谓的来自教练和家长的压力对孩子们产生了什么样严重的后果

③ 证词类

Signal：say

Inference：教育专家说运动比赛占据了孩子们学习的时间 $\Longrightarrow$ 运动比赛对学习有害

Assumption：教育专家的话可靠

Counterexamples：很可能这些人并没有做过充分的研究，运动所占据的时间本身就不见得是用来学习的；其次，减少学习时间不见得对学习有坏处，可能运动使人们学习效率提高，最终事半功倍

Evidence：需要知道这些教育专家做出这种判断背后的根据是什么

④ 其他

Signal：步骤①②③的结论，以及接下来要证明运动比赛弊大于利

Inference：运动比赛对孩子们有各种害处 $\Longrightarrow$ 运动比赛对孩子们弊大于利

Assumption：运动比赛不会带来更大的好处

Counterexamples：全文从来没有探索过运动的好处，比如培养孩子们的意志品质、锻炼孩子们的身体、培养孩子们的团队互助精神

Evidence：必须要充分调查参与运动所带来的积极因素

⑤ 建议类

Signal：步骤④的结论，以及最终要建议停止一切针对孩子们的运动比赛

Inference：运动比赛对孩子们弊大于利 $\Longrightarrow$ 应该停止运动比赛

Assumption：运动比赛不能进行改进

Counterexamples：可以通过规范化、安全化处理来降低运动带来的风险，并且进行更合适的时间安排，来保证不影响孩子们的学习

Evidence：需要充分考虑其他可能更有效的解决方案

Part 5　Argument 题库逐题精析

61　When Stanley Park first opened, it was the largest, most heavily used public park in town. It is still the largest park, but it is no longer heavily used. Video cameras mounted in the park's parking lots last month revealed the park's drop in popularity: the recordings showed an average of only 50 cars per day. In contrast, tiny Carlton Park in the heart of the business district is visited by more than 150 people on a typical weekday. An obvious difference is that Carlton Park, unlike Stanley Park, provides ample seating. Thus, if Stanley Park is ever to be as popular with our citizens as Carlton Park, the town will obviously need to provide more benches, thereby converting some of the unused open areas into spaces suitable for socializing.

译　文

当 Stanley Park 刚开放的时候，它是全镇最大、游客数最多的公园。它现在仍然是最大的公园，但游客数已经不多了。公园车库的摄像机显示了公园的衰落：平均每天只有 50 辆车。相反，小小的 Carlton Park 处在商业区中心，周中每天的游客数量平均超过了 150 人。与 Stanley Park 明显不同的地方是，Carlton Park 有着充足的坐席。因此，要想让 Stanley Park 像 Carlton Park 那么受市民欢迎，镇里必须安置更多的长凳，这样能将一些不用的开阔地改造成适合社交的地方。

文章结构图

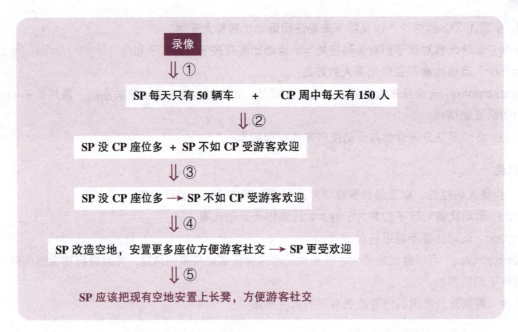

结　论：The town will need to provide more benches in Stanley Park, thereby converting some of the unused open areas into spaces suitable for socializing.

结论类型：**建议型**

各步推理分析

①证词类

Signal：video cameras reveal

Inference：录像 ⟹ SP 每天只有 50 辆车

Assumption：录像可靠

Counterexamples：录像覆盖不全面，很多人不把车停在这个地方

Evidence：需要知道摄像头的分布是否能够覆盖该公园周围所有的主要停车区域

②数据类

Signal：50，150

Inference：SP 每天只有 50 辆车 + CP 周中每天有 150 人 ⟹ SP 不如 CP 受欢迎

Assumption：SP 的车并不会承载很多人；CP 周末人数不会显著增加

Counterexamples：CP 周末基本没人去，而人们去公园开车通常都是携家带口去，一车可能坐很多人；或者现在因为限行、堵车、新的公共交通方式，有大量人去 SP 都不会开车，因此事实上可能 SP 的游客数量远多于 CP

Evidence：需要直接对比去 CP 与 SP 的游客数量

③解释类

Signal：SP 没 CP 座位多，加上步骤②的结论，以及作者试图建立两者之间的关系

Inference：SP 没 CP 座位多 + SP 没 CP 受欢迎 ⟹ SP 没 CP 座位多造成 SP 没 CP 受欢迎

Assumption：没有其他解释

Counterexamples：CP 不收费；CP 环境好；CP 周围居民区多

Evidence：需要证据排除其他能够解释两个公园游客数量区别的因素

④ 类比类

Signal：步骤③的结论，以及之后试图表明 SP 有了座位就能有游客

Inference：SP 没 CP 座位多造成 SP 没 CP 受欢迎 ⟹ SP 改造空地，安置更多座位方便游客社交就能让 SP 更受欢迎

Assumption：改造空地不会破坏 SP 的其他重要功能

Counterexamples：那些空地可能是重要的运动场所，虽然有了社交场地，失去了关键的运动场地，反而会损失更多游客

Evidence：需要知道现在 SP 的空地是否有重要的作用

⑤ 建议类

Signal：步骤④的结论，以及最终要提出建议改造空地建长凳

Inference：SP 改造空地，安置更多座位方便游客社交就能让 SP 更受欢迎 ⟹ SP 应该改造空地，安置更多座位方便游客社交

Assumption：没有其他更有效的方案

Counterexamples：提升公园环境；做更多宣传；搞更多活动

Evidence：需要充分考察其他可能更有效的替代方案

62

The following appeared in a memo from the owner of a chain of cheese stores located throughout the United States.

"For many years all the stores in our chain have stocked a wide variety of both domestic and imported cheeses. Last year, however, all of the five best-selling cheeses at our newest store were domestic cheddar cheeses from Wisconsin. Furthermore, a recent survey by *Cheeses of the World* magazine indicates an increasing preference for domestic cheeses among its subscribers. Since our company can reduce expenses by limiting inventory, the best way to improve profits in all of our stores is to discontinue stocking many of our varieties of imported cheese and concentrate primarily on domestic cheeses."

思路相近题目：100 & 101

译 文

多年来我们的所有连锁店都储备了多种多样的国产与进口芝士。然而，去年我们最新的分店里五种销量最高的芝士都是威斯康星生产的 cheddar 芝士。而且，最近一次由《芝士世界》所举行的调查显示，其订阅者越来越喜欢国产芝士。由于我们公司可以通过限制库存来减少开支，因此在我们所有的连锁店增加盈利的最好方式就是停止储备很多进口芝士而主要储备国产芝士。

文章结构图

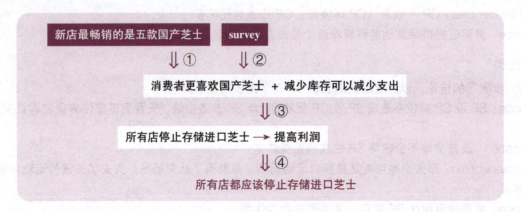

结　　论：The best way to improve profits in all of the stores is to discontinue stocking many of their varieties of imported cheese and concentrate primarily on domestic cheeses.

结论类型：建议型

各步推理分析

① 数据类，解释类，类比类

Signal：five，而且本来谈的是新店的销量，但最后要谈的是所有店

Inference：最畅销的是五款国产芝士 ⟹ 消费者更喜欢国产芝士

Assumption：国产芝士的可选择品种不少于进口芝士；没有其他解释

Counterexamples：其实国产芝士的总销量并没有高于进口芝士，进口芝士的种类多，竞争激烈，所以每类销量都被稀释了，相反，国产芝士只有几个品种，如果人们喜欢国产芝士，只能选择这五个，于是每种销量看起来都很好；新店之所以这五种芝士销量高，可能是因为新店做的活动主要推广的就是这五种芝士；很可能新店其他类型的芝士库存少，进货渠道不好，于是其他类型的芝士早都售罄了，但是没有更多存货所以才没有卖更多；而且，很可能新店的特点不能代表其他店，不同区域的顾客需求可能完全不一样

Evidence：需要知道国产芝士与进口芝士总销售量的对比；需要调查国产芝士销量好的更具体的原因

② 证词类，数据类

Signal：survey, increasing

Inference：survey 显示该杂志的受众对国产芝士的喜爱增多 ⟹ 人们喜欢国产芝士

Assumption：survey 的受众具有代表性；喜爱增多之后，国产芝士就比进口芝士更受欢迎

Counterexamples：也许以前人们完全不喜欢国产芝士，所以就算喜爱增多，也不如进口芝士；其次，很可能该杂志本身就是面向低端用户的，不能代表所有的芝士喜好者，更不能代表所有会食用芝士的人

Evidence：需要知道该调查中进口芝士和国产芝士爱好者的具体数量；需要知道该杂志的用户定位和用户群体的组成

③ 类比类

Signal：谈论的本来是消费者对芝士的喜好，但最后要推广到每一家分店；以及谈到的本来是减少存货支出，但最后要谈的是利润

Inference：消费者更喜欢国产芝士 + 减少库存可以减少支出 ⟹ 所有店停止存储进口芝士，这样可以提高利润

Assumption：国产芝士的利润率不比进口芝士低很多；所有店面对的受众情况一致

Counterexamples：也许大部分店的顾客是喜欢国产芝士，但仍然可以有很多地区的店铺主要面对进口芝士的喜好者；其次，就算大众更多购买国产芝士，那可能是因为国产芝士比较廉价，而国产芝士很可能利润空间很低，意味着卖得再多带来的利润可能还比不上卖出一点点进口芝士

Evidence：需要知道国产芝士与进口芝士各自的利润率；需要知道各家店铺所面对的主要用户群体是否有显著区别

④ 建议类

Signal：步骤③的结论，以及最终要建议所有分店停止存储进口芝士

Inference：所有店停止存储进口芝士可以提高利润 ⟹ 所有店都应该停止存储进口芝士

Assumption：没有其他更好的方案

Counterexamples：提高利润的方法可以是打广告促销、引进更吸引人的品牌，等等，不代表没有办法让进口芝士卖得更好

Evidence：需要充分考虑其他可能更有效的替代方案

63

The following appeared as part of a business plan developed by the manager of the Rialto Movie Theater.

"Despite its downtown location, the Rialto Movie Theater, a local institution for five decades, must make big changes or close its doors forever. It should follow the example of the new Apex Theater in the mall outside of town. When the Apex opened last year, it featured a video arcade, plush carpeting and seats, and a state-of-the-art sound system. Furthermore, in a recent survey, over 85 percent of respondents reported that the high price of newly released movies prevents them from going to the movies more than five times per year. Thus, if the Rialto intends to hold on to its share of a decreasing pool of moviegoers, it must offer the same features as Apex."

译　文

已成立 50 余年的当地机构 Rialto 电影院虽然地处市中心，但它必须采取重大变革，不然就将面临永久停业。它应该参考城外商业街上新的 Apex 剧院的例子。Apex 去年开业的时候，拥有游戏厅、豪华地毯和座椅，以及最先进的音响系统。而且，在近期一次调查中，超过 85% 的受访者报告说新发行影片的高票价致使他们看电影的次数每年不会超过五次。所以，Rialto 要想在电影观众减少的情况下维持市场份额，就必须提供和 Apex 相同的设施。

文章结构图

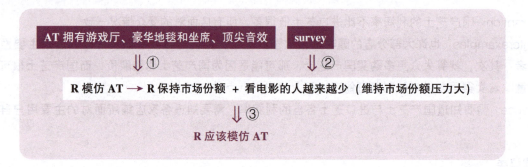

结　　论：Rialto Movie Theater must offer a video arcade, plush carpeting and seats, and a state-of-the-art sound system, just like Apex Theater did a year ago.

结论类型：建议型

各步推理分析

① 类比型

Signal：AT 拥有这些设施，但最终要谈论的是 R

Inference：AT 拥有这些设施 ⟹ R 模仿 AT 可以让 R 保持市场竞争力

Assumption：AT 是成功的，且是因为这些特点成功的，而 AT 与 R 的情况是相似的

Counterexamples：AT 拥有 video arcade 没有成功；AT 成功是因为别的原因，比如地理位置好、票价低或者环境好；而且两个影院面对的受众不同，AT 定位高端，而 R 周边的消费水平较低，提供这些条件意味着票价抬高，消费者就完全不会来了；也许 R 处在市中心，周围有各种游戏厅，根本没有必要重复建设，而 AT 就不一样

Evidence：需要知道 AT 拥有那些设施是否造成了其生意上的成功；需要调查 R 所面对的消费群体具体的喜好

②证词类，数据类

Signal：survey，85%，respondents，reported，5 times，以及最终作者想要暗示的是 decreasing pool of moviegoers

Inference：survey ⟹ 电影受众市场缩水

Assumption：调查有代表性，以前人们看电影更频繁

Counterexamples：调查的是穷人区；以前人们看电影频率反而很低；这些人为了让电影院降价，故意说假话；不在意票价的人根本不会参与关于票价的调查，也不会回复；也许调查的问题就是什么原因阻碍人们看电影，这个问题本身就是有倾向性的，因为人们本身根本没有少看电影；也许调查是全国范围的，而 R 深处闹市，根本不存在客源减少的问题

Evidence：需要知道调查样本的选择方式，来确定该调查是否真的具有代表性；并且需要知道 R 所面对的消费群体是否符合该调查的群体特征

③建议类

Signal：步骤①②的结论，以及最终要推荐 R 建立这些设施

Inference：R 要模仿 AT 才能保持市场份额 + 电影受众市场缩水（急需保持份额）

Assumption：没有更好的解决方案，此方案可行

Counterexamples：降低票价、选择更吸引人的影片；也许根本没有这么多经费完成改造

Evidence：需要充分考虑其他可能更有效的方案；需要知道目前的经费是否能够支持所推荐的改造工程

Part 5　Argument 题库逐题精析

64 A recent study reported that pet owners have longer, healthier lives on average than do people who own no pets. Specifically, dog owners tend to have a lower incidence of heart disease. In light of these findings, Sherwood Hospital should form a partnership with Sherwood Animal Shelter to institute an adopt-a-dog program. The program would encourage dog ownership for patients recovering from heart disease, which should reduce these patients' chance of experiencing continuing heart problems and also reduce their need for ongoing treatment. As a further benefit, the publicity about the program would encourage more people to adopt pets from the shelter. And that will reduce the incidence of heart disease in the general population.

译　文

最近一项研究报告显示，平均来说，养宠物的人比不养宠物的人更长寿、更健康。特别是养狗的人的心脏病发病率较低。基于这些发现，Sherwood 医院应该与 Sherwood 动物收容所建立合作关系以开展"领养一条狗"的计划。该计划将会鼓励处于心脏病康复期的患者养狗，这将降低这些病人持续患心脏疾病的可能，并减小他们持续治疗的需求。另外一个好处是，对该项目的宣传将会鼓励更多的人从收容所领养宠物。而且，这将减少全体居民患心脏病的风险。

文章结构图

研究中狗主人心脏疾病少
⇩①
是因为养狗让人们心脏疾病少
⇩②
建立领养狗的项目能让心脏疾病患者恢复，进而减少治疗需求
⇩③
建立领养狗的项目能鼓励更多人领养宠物，从而进一步减少人群中的心脏疾病
⇩④
S 医院应该与 S 动物庇护所建立领养狗的项目

结　论：Sherwood Hospital should form a partnership with Sherwood Animal Shelter to institute an adopt-a-dog program.

结论类型：建议型

各步推理分析

① 解释类

Signal：作者试图建立养狗和心脏疾病少之间的关系

Inference：研究中狗主人心脏疾病少 ⟹ 是因为养狗让人们心脏疾病减少

Assumption：没有其他解释

Counterexamples：是因为身体健康，人们才会去养宠物，有心脏疾病的人通常是没有能力照顾好狗的，所以不会养狗，因果关系反了

Evidence：需要更具体地研究调查养狗是否真的造成了人们的心脏疾病减少

② 类比类

Signal：谈论的本来是狗帮助减少心脏疾病，但是接下来就直接认定狗能够帮助治疗心脏疾病

Inference：是因为养狗让人们心脏疾病减少 ⟹ 建立领养狗的项目能让心脏疾病患者恢复，进而减少治疗需求

Assumption：狗对心脏疾病的作用不是预防作用；每个心脏疾病患者养狗都会有同样的作用

Counterexamples：狗只能帮助预防心脏疾病，但是对于患病的人来说没有好处，反而可能有坏处；而且，可能只有喜欢狗的人养狗才能够更健康，而不喜欢狗的人，为了健康而养狗，是不能带来这种心理的快乐，也不会更健康

Evidence：需要调查狗对健康的作用是预防性的还是治疗性的；需要证据表明狗对健康的作用与人本身是否喜欢狗有没有关系

③ 类比类

Signal：谈论的本来是狗，但接下来讨论的却是宠物

Inference：建立领养狗的项目能让心脏疾病患者恢复，进而减少治疗需求 ⟹ 建立领养狗的项目能鼓励更多人领养宠物，从而进一步减少人群中的心脏疾病

Assumption：各种宠物的效果是一样的

Counterexamples：社会中更多人养其他动物，但是对心脏有坏处，或者没有什么作用

Evidence：需要调查狗与其他动物对人的健康可能产生的不同作用

④ 建议类

Signal：步骤②③的结论，以及最终要建议建立领养狗的项目

Inference：建立领养狗的项目能够帮助治愈心脏疾病，以及帮助减少整个人群的心脏疾病 ⟹ S 医院应该与 S 动物庇护所建立领养狗的项目

Assumption：没有其他策略

Counterexamples：不一定非要和这个动物庇护所建立关系

Evidence：需要充分调查其他可能更有效的解决方案

Part 5 Argument 题库逐题精析

65

The following appeared in a memo from a vice president of a large, highly diversified company.

"Ten years ago our company had two new office buildings constructed as regional headquarters for two regions. The buildings were erected by different construction companies—Alpha and Zeta. Although the two buildings had identical floor plans, the building constructed by Zeta cost 30 percent more to build. However, that building's expenses for maintenance last year were only half those of Alpha's. In addition, the energy consumption of the Zeta building has been lower than that of the Alpha building every year since its construction. Given these data, plus the fact that Zeta has a stable workforce with little employee turnover, we recommend using Zeta rather than Alpha for our new building project, even though Alpha's bid promises lower construction costs."

思路相近题目：66 & 108

译 文

10 年以前我们公司在两个地区各造了一栋地区总部大楼。它们由两家建筑公司——Alpha 和 Zeta 分别建造。尽管两座建筑的平面布局基本相同，由 Zeta 所建造的建筑造价高出了 30%。可是，Zeta 这栋楼去年的维护费用是由 Alpha 建的楼的二分之一。此外，Zeta 大楼建成以来的能耗每年都比 Alpha 大楼要多。基于这些数据，加上 Zeta 公司员工流动性小、团队稳定，我们建议应该使用 Zeta 而不是 Alpha 来建造新楼，尽管 Alpha 在投标时承诺更低的建筑成本。

文章结构图

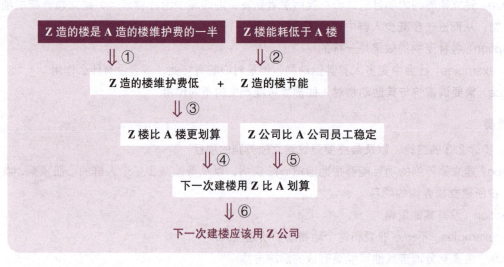

结　　论：The company should use Zeta rather than Alpha for the new building project.
结论类型：**建议型**

各步推理分析

① 数据类

Signal：half

Inference：Z 造的楼是 A 造的楼维护费的一半 ⟹ Z 造的楼维护费低

Assumption：没有其他解释

Counterexamples：A 的用户素质差，A 所在城市的天气恶劣，都可能造成楼维护成本提高

Evidence：需要排除 A 造的楼和 Z 造的楼不是因为建造质量方面的区别而对维护费产生影响

② 数据类

Signal：lower

Inference：Z 造的楼能耗低于 A 造的楼 ⟹ Z 造的楼节能

Assumption：没有其他解释

Counterexamples：可能 Z 城冬暖夏凉，自然不需要使用太多空调，造成了能耗少；两栋楼用来做的事情可能不一样，可能 Z 造的楼使用时期耗能少

Evidence：需要排除 A 造的楼和 Z 造的楼不是因为建造质量方面的区别而对能耗产生影响

③ 其他

Signal：步骤①②的结论

Inference：Z 造的楼维护费低、节能 ⟹ 之前 Z 造的楼比 A 造的楼造价更划算

Assumption：成本的差别不能抵消这些区别

Counterexamples：Z 造的楼的造价远高于 A 造的楼，因此刚才这些 Z 造的楼的优势都荡然无存

Evidence：需要知道两栋楼造价有多大区别

④ 类比类

Signal：本来只是谈前一次 Z 造的楼和 A 造的楼的区别，但最后要讨论的是下一次建楼

Inference：Z 公司比 A 公司造楼造得好 ⟹ 下一次建楼用 Z 比用 A 更划算

Assumption：这些年来 Z 和 A 没有变化

Counterexamples：之后 A 建的工程都比 Z 建的更省钱、更节能

Evidence：需要调查两公司其他楼的建造结果并进行充分的比较

⑤ 其他

Signal：文章讨论两公司员工稳定性的区别，显然是想比较两公司的优劣

Inference：Z 公司比 A 公司员工稳定 ⟹ 下一次建楼用 Z 比用 A 更好

Assumption：员工稳定就是好

Counterexamples：竞争不激烈，怠惰

Evidence：需要调查员工稳定性的原因，到底是员工本身能力强，还是公司缺乏进取心

⑥ 建议类

Signal：步骤④⑤的结论，以及最终要推荐 Z 公司
Inference：下一次建楼用 Z 公司更划算 ⟹ 应该用 Z 公司建楼
Assumption：没有更好的方案
Counterexamples：并不只有这两个公司可以选择
Evidence：需要充分考虑其他可能更好的解决方案

68 The following appeared as a letter to the editor of a national newspaper.

"Your recent article on corporate downsizing in Elthyria maintains that the majority of competent workers who have lost jobs as a result of downsizing face serious economic hardship, often for years, before finding other suitable employment. But this claim is undermined by a recent report on the Elthyrian economy, which found that since 1999 far more jobs have been created than have been eliminated, bringing the unemployment rate in Elthyria to its lowest level in decades. Moreover, two-thirds of these newly created jobs have been in industries that tend to pay above-average wages, and the vast majority of these jobs are full-time."

译　文

你们最近关于 Elthyria 集体裁员的文章声称，大部分有能力的工人由于裁员而丢掉工作后，通常要面对很多年严重的经济困难，直到找到另一份合适的工作。但这个说法被最近一项对 Elthyria 经济发展的报告所削弱，该报告发现，自 1992 年以来新增的就业机会数量远超过消失的岗位数量，使得 Elthyria 的失业率达到了几十年以来的最低点。并且，新增的就业机会中有三分之二来自于那些提供高于平均水平薪酬的行业，而且这些岗位绝大多数是全职工作。

文章结构图

```
         创造的岗位更多，失业率达到新低
                    ⇓ ①
   失业工人能够找到新工作  +  新创造的岗位所在领域平均工资高，且普遍全职
                    ⇓ ②
             失业工人普遍能找到好工作
                    ⇓ ③
          失业的工人并不会经受多年严重的经济困难
```

结　　论：The majority of competent workers in Elthyria who have lost jobs as a result of downsizing do not face serious economic hardships before finding other suitable employment.

结论类型：解释型

各步推理分析

①解释类

Signal：为了证明最终结论，作者提到近年来就业率的提升，显然是想说明失业工人能够找到新工作

Inference：创造的岗位更多，失业率达到新低 ⟹ 失业工人能够找到新工作
Assumption：新岗位多意味着失业的人能找到这些工作
Counterexamples：失业率降低是因为现在大学生毕业找工作容易了，所以无业人数比例降低。然而，新的岗位普遍要求很先进的技能，之前失业的人还是不具有这些技能，仍然找不到工作
Evidence：需要调查之前的失业人员是否真的受益于这些新创造出的岗位

②类比类
Signal：谈论的本来是整个行业的平均工资，但真正想要证明的是失业的人找到的工作会有高工资
Inference：失业工人能够找到新工作 + 新创造的岗位所在领域平均工资高，且普遍全职 ⟹ 失业工人普遍能找到好工作
Assumption：平均工资高，其中的个体工资就一定高；全职就是好工作
Counterexamples：被裁掉的人新找到的工作是热门领域当中的入门工作，工资仍然很低；全职打扫卫生就没什么前途
Evidence：需要调查这些之前被裁掉的人后来找到工作后的平均工资以及上升通道

③其他
Signal：步骤②的结论，以及最终想要证明失业工人不会经历多年经济困难
Inference：失业工人普遍能找到好工作 ⟹ 失业的工人并不会经受多年严重的经济困难
Assumption：失业后能迅速找到好工作
Counterexamples：虽然最终找到了好工作，但这经过了很长时间的培训，才获得了新技能，适应了新岗位，期间人们需要经历非常困难的经济状况
Evidence：需要知道这些失业的人在失业后多久才成功找到了新的工作

69

The following appeared in a letter to the editor of a Batavia newspaper.

"The department of agriculture in Batavia reports that the number of dairy farms throughout the country is now 25 percent greater than it was 10 years ago. During this same time period, however, the price of milk at the local Excello Food Market has increased from $1.50 to over $3.00 per gallon. To prevent farmers from continuing to receive excessive profits on an apparently increased supply of milk, the Batavia government should begin to regulate retail milk prices. Such regulation is necessary to ensure fair prices for consumers."

译 文

Batavia 的农业部门报告说全国乳品厂的数量比 10 年前增加了 25%。然而，在同一时期内，当地 Excello Food Market 的牛奶价格从每加仑 1.5 美元上涨到了 3.0 美元。为防止奶农在牛奶供应量明显增加的情况下获取暴利，Batavia 政府应限制牛奶的零售价。必须出台这种限制才能保证消费者能够以公道的价格买到牛奶。

文章结构图

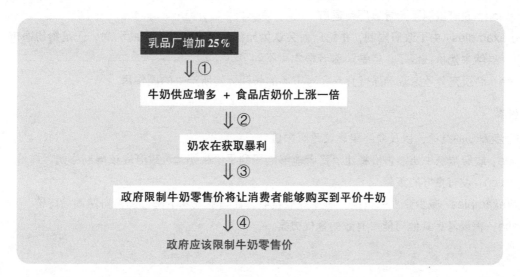

结　　论：The Batavia government should begin to regulate retail milk prices to ensure fair prices for consumers.

结论类型：建议型

各步推理分析

①数据类

Signal：25 percent greater

Inference：牛奶厂增加 25% ⇒ 牛奶供应增多
Assumption：每厂的平均供给量没有下降
Counterexamples：大农场变小农场，于是每厂平均产量下降，总牛奶供应并没有增多；虽然农场增多，但可能大家其实主要在生产其他奶制品，比如酸奶、奶酪等，牛奶的产量并没有显著增加
Evidence：需要调查牛奶的供应是否真的显著增长

② 解释类
Signal：作者试图把奶价增长归结为奶厂在获取暴利
Inference：牛奶供应增多 + 食品店奶价上涨一倍 ⇒ 奶农在获取暴利
Assumption：没有其他解释
Counterexamples：物价大幅上涨，牛奶价格在计算了通货膨胀后其实并没有增长；牛奶质量大幅提升，本来就值更多的钱；可能是这家食品店卖得贵，但从奶农那里引入牛奶时并没有花更多钱，牛奶商收到的利润并没有发生变化
Evidence：需要知道在考虑了通货膨胀、成本、食品店购入价等因素之后牛奶商是否真的获得了巨量利润

③ 其他
Signal：步骤②的结论，以及作者认为政府限价就可以让人们获得平价牛奶
Inference：奶农在获取暴利 ⇒ 政府限制牛奶零售价将让消费者能够购买到平价牛奶
Assumption：政府限制不会导致厂商退市
Counterexamples：由于政府限制，牛奶厂商会认为无法获得令自己满意的利润，于是纷纷退市，最终供不应求。于是，虽然牛奶价钱低了，但是消费者根本买不到了
Evidence：必须充分考虑政府强行介入会对市场的长期运转所产生的副作用

④ 建议类
Signal：步骤③的结论，以及最终要建议政府限价
Inference：政府限制牛奶零售价将让消费者能够购买到平价牛奶 ⇒ 政府应该限制牛奶零售价
Assumption：没有更好的策略
Counterexamples：减少企业的负担，比如降低税收，让企业成本下降，奶价自然就会降价
Evidence：需要考虑其他可能更有效的替代方案

70 The following appeared in a newsletter offering advice to investors.

"Over 80 percent of the respondents to a recent survey indicated a desire to reduce their intake of foods containing fats and cholesterol, and today low-fat products abound in many food stores. Since many of the food products currently marketed by Old Dairy Industries are high in fat and cholesterol, the company's sales are likely to diminish greatly and company profits will no doubt decrease. We therefore advise Old Dairy stockholders to sell their shares, and other investors not to purchase stock in this company."

译 文

最近一次调查中超过80%的受访者表达了他们想减少摄入含脂肪和胆固醇的食品的意愿，而且现在低脂食品遍布很多食品店。由于 Old Dairy Industries 当前销售的很多产品都含有很高的脂肪和胆固醇，因此该公司的销量有可能严重下降，其利润无疑会减少。所以，我们建议 Old Dairy 的股票持有者们抛出他们所持的股份，也建议其他投资者不购入该公司的股份。

文章结构图

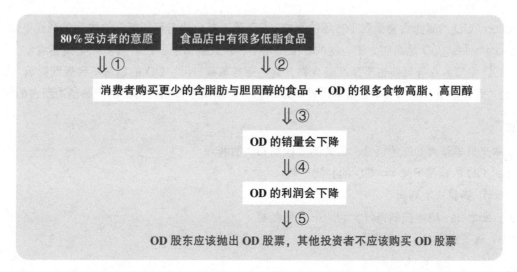

结　　论：Old Dairy stockholders should sell their shares and other investors should not purchase stock in this company.

结论类型：建议型

各步推理分析

①证词类

Signal：survey, respondents, indicated a desire

Inference：超过80%的受调查者表达了想少摄入含脂肺和胆固醇的食品的意愿 ⟹ 消费者会购买更少的含脂肺与胆固醇的食品

Assumption：调查具有代表性，人们有意愿就会执行

Counterexamples：只有关心健康的人才会理睬这个调查；调查中的人倾向于显得自己生活健康、积极向上；人们光说不做，还是觉得含脂肪和胆固醇的食品好吃，所以最后控制不住自己

Evidence：需要更具体的信息来判断该调查的可靠性、其选择调查者的代表性；需要知道这些表达健康饮食意愿的人是否真的会严格执行

② **数据类**

Signal：abound, many

Inference：食品店中有很多低脂食品 ⟹ 消费者会购买低脂食品

Assumption：低脂食物卖得好；高脂食物销量没有低脂食物多

Counterexamples：低脂食物的销量其实远不如高脂食物

Evidence：需要知道低脂食物在食品店中所占的比例，以及需要知道这些低脂食物实际的销量情况

③ **类比类**

Signal：由市面上高低脂食物销量的预期，作者要推断 OD 公司食品的销量

Inference：消费者购买更少的含脂肪与胆固醇的食品 + OD 的很多食物高脂、高固醇 ⟹ OD 的销量会下降

Assumption：OD 的高脂食物受到了市场的影响；OD 没有其他业务可以抵消这方面的利润下降

Counterexamples：OD 是高脂之王，别的企业都垮了，但只要市面上还有很多人吃高脂食物，人们就会吃 OD 的食品；OD 主营的业务可能也不是高脂食物，其他业务蒸蒸日上，OD 的销量不会受到影响

Evidence：需要知道 OD 的食品目前的销量，以及需要知道高脂食物在 OD 的产品当中所占的销售比例

④ **其他**

Signal：本来只是预测 OD 的销量，但转而要谈到 OD 的利润

Inference：OD 的销量下降 ⟹ OD 的利润下降

Assumption：销量决定利润

Counterexamples：成本控制得好，利润不会受影响

Evidence：需要知道 OD 的食物在成本方面是否会显著变化

⑤ **建议类**

Signal：步骤④的结论，以及最终要建议甩掉 OD 的股票

Inference：OD 的利润会下降 ⟹ OD 股东应该抛出 OD 股票，其他投资者不应该购买 OD 股票

Assumption：OD 不会转型

Counterexamples：未来 OD 可能马上会做出一些举措来扭转现在的颓势

Evidence：需要调查 OD 未来是否会做出一些重要的举措来改变市场上的颓势

Part 5　Argument 题库逐题精析

71

The following recommendation appeared in a memo from the mayor of the town of Hopewell.

"Two years ago, the nearby town of Ocean View built a new municipal golf course and resort hotel. During the past two years, tourism in Ocean View has increased, new businesses have opened there, and Ocean View's tax revenues have risen by 30 percent. Therefore, the best way to improve Hopewell's economy—and generate additional tax revenues—is to build a golf course and resort hotel similar to those in Ocean View."

思路相近题目：161

译　文

两年前，邻近的城镇 Ocean View 建了一个新的市立高尔夫球场和度假宾馆。过去两年间，Ocean View 的旅客增加了，很多新生意出现，而且税收增加了 30%。因此，推动 Hopewell 经济，并带来更多税收的最好途径就是建立一个和 Ocean View 类似的高尔夫球场和度假宾馆。

文章结构图

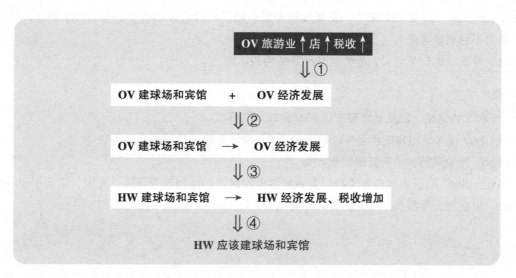

结　论：The best way to improve Hopewell's economy—and generate additional tax revenues—is to build a golf course and resort hotel similar to those in Ocean View.

结论类型：建议型

各步推理分析

① 数据类

Signal：文章要证明的是经济发展，给的证据是旅游业、新生意和税收的增长

363

Inference：OV 旅游业↑店↑税收↑⟹ OV 经济发展

Assumption：旅游业增长对整个经济影响大；老店没有倒闭得更多；税率没有过分提高

Counterexamples：旅游业比重小，即使增长了也不多；老店倒闭得更厉害；税率大幅度提高，税收以后怎么都会下降

Evidence：需要知道旅游业在当地经济中所占的比重，需要知道旅游业实际的增长量；需要知道倒闭企业的数量；需要知道税率是否发生显著的变化

② 解释类

Signal：OV 建了球场和宾馆，之后发生了步骤①的结论，并且作者试图建立两者之间的关系

Inference：OV 建了球场和宾馆后经济发展 ⟹ OV 的球场和宾馆带动了经济发展

Assumption：没有其他解释

Counterexamples：环境治理；国家经济环境变好；交通更发达

Evidence：需要排除其他可能的因素对 OV 经济所产生的影响

③ 类比类

Signal：本来谈 OV，结果却要证明 HW

Inference：OV 的球场和宾馆带动了经济发展 ⟹ HW 建球场和宾馆也会带动经济和税收

Assumption：两城的产业结构相似

Counterexamples：OV 是旅游城市，配套设施不足，建了之后能大幅吸引游客；HW 是内陆工业城市，污染严重，本来也不会有游客来

Evidence：需要对比 HW 与 OV 两个地方产业结构的区别

④ 建议类

Signal：步骤③的结论，以及最终要建议 HW 建球场和宾馆

Inference：HW 建球场和宾馆也会带动经济和税收 ⟹ HW 应该建球场和宾馆

Assumption：建议可行；没有其他替代方案

Counterexamples：有很多其他方式可以发展旅游业和经济，比如改善环境、降税、招商引资等

Evidence：需要充分考察其他可能更有效的建议

Part 5　Argument 题库逐题精析

72

The following appeared in a memo from the vice president of a food distribution company with food storage warehouses in several cities.

"Recently, we signed a contract with the Fly-Away Pest Control Company to provide pest control services at our fast-food warehouse in Palm City, but last month we discovered that over \$20,000 worth of food there had been destroyed by pest damage. Meanwhile, the Buzzoff Pest Control Company, which we have used for many years, continued to service our warehouse in Wintervale, and last month only \$10,000 worth of the food stored there had been destroyed by pest damage. Even though the price charged by Fly-Away is considerably lower, our best means of saving money is to return to Buzzoff for all our pest control services."

思路相近题目：107, 109 & 110

译　文

最近，我们和 Fly-Away 除虫公司签订了一份合同，让他们为我们在 Palm City 的快餐食品仓库提供除虫服务，但上个月我们发现，那里有价值超过 20 000 美元的食品被害虫破坏。而与此同时，我们使用多年的 Buzzoff 除虫公司继续为我们在 Wintervale 的仓库服务，上个月那里只有价值 10 000 美元的食品被害虫破坏。尽管 Fly-Away 的收费低很多，但我们省钱的最好方式就是重新使用 Buzzoff 公司来为我们提供所有的除虫服务。

文章结构图

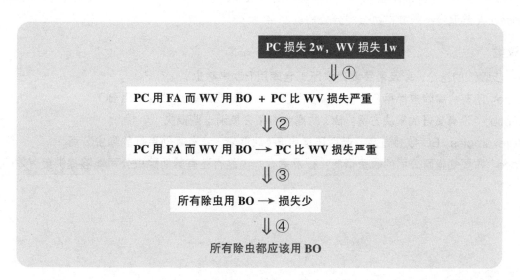

结　论：The food distribution company's best means of saving money is to return to Buzzoff for all its pest control services.

结论类型：**建议型**

各步推理分析

① 数据类
Signal：20,000，10,000
Inference：PC 损失 2w，WV 损失 1w ⟹ PC 比 WV 损失严重
Assumption：PC 仓库先前存的食物总价值不比 WV 高很多
Counterexamples：PC 的食物本来就存量大，价值高，损失比例其实更低，是 WV 损失更严重
Evidence：需要知道两处仓库库存的总价值

② 解释类
Signal：作者试图建立除虫公司与损失之间的关系
Inference：PC 用 FA 而 WV 用 BO ＋ PC 比 WV 损失严重 ⟹ PC 用 FA 而 WV 用 BO 造成 PC 比 WV 损失严重
Assumption：没有其他解释
Counterexamples：PC 气候更湿热，储存的食物种类更容易招惹虫子；也许是 PC 仓库管理者的操作失误，比如不能保持仓库的卫生清洁、通风、干燥
Evidence：需要知道两个地区的气候、温度等信息；需要对比两个仓库的管理维护情况

③ 类比类
Signal：谈论的本来是 PC 与 WV 两个仓库，但是结论要证明的却是所有仓库
Inference：PC 用 FA 而 WV 用 BO 造成 PC 比 WV 损失严重 ⟹ 所有除虫都用 BO，这样可以减少损失
Assumption：所有仓库情况相似，所有城市的 PC/BO 公司质量一样
Counterexamples：不同的除虫公司在不同城市的分公司的水平完全不一样，需要具体地方具体分析
Evidence：需要调查不同城市两公司分公司的水平

④ 建议类
Signal：步骤③的结论，以及最终要建议所有仓库用 BO 来除虫
Inference：所有仓库除虫都用 BO 可以减少损失 ⟹ 所有仓库除虫都应该用 BO
Assumption：没有更好的解决方案；BO 的高收费不会抵消这些损失
Counterexamples：BO 收费过高，最后还是用 FA 划得来；还有其他更好的除虫公司
Evidence：需要知道两公司的收费情况；以及需要知道是否还有其他除虫公司能够提供更有效的服务

Part 5 Argument 题库逐题精析

73 Since those issues of *Newsbeat* magazine that featured political news on their front cover were the poorest-selling issues over the past three years, the publisher of *Newsbeat* has recommended that the magazine curtail its emphasis on politics to focus more exclusively on economics and personal finance. She points to a recent survey of readers of general interest magazines that indicates greater reader interest in economic issues than in political ones. *Newsbeat*'s editor, however, opposes the proposed shift in editorial policy, pointing out that very few magazines offer extensive political coverage anymore.

译 文

鉴于 *Newsbeat* 杂志过去三年销量最差的几期都是封面刊登了政治新闻的那几期，*Newsbeat* 的出版商建议该杂志减少对政治话题的强调，而专攻经济与个人理财话题。她指出，最近针对大众杂志读者的调查显示，读者对经济话题的兴趣高于对政治话题的兴趣。但是，*Newsbeat* 的编辑反对这种策略的改变，并指出，很少有杂志还在刊登大量的政治话题。

文章结构图

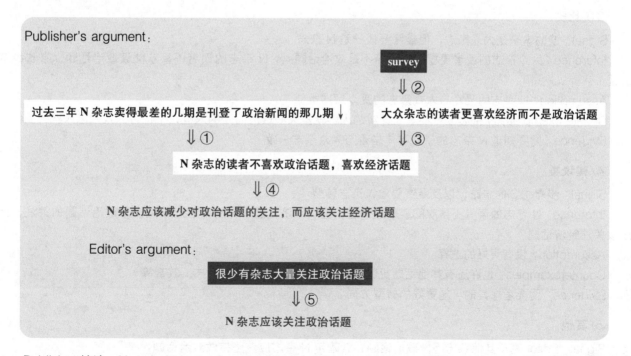

Publisher 结论：*Newsbeat* magazine should curtail its emphasis on politics to focus more exclusively on economics and personal finance.

Editor 结论：*Newsbeat* magazine should not curtail its emphasis on politics to focus more exclusively on economics and personal finance.

结论类型：**建议型**

各步推理分析

① 解释类
Signal：Publisher 试图把过去三年某几期杂质销量差归结为人们不喜欢阅读政治话题
Inference：过去三年 N 杂志卖得最差的几期是封面刊登了政治新闻的那几期 ⇒ N 杂志的读者不喜欢阅读政治话题
Assumption：没有其他解释
Counterexamples：可能恰恰那几期的经济新闻做得不好，人们才不买；可能不是因为人们不喜欢政治话题，而是因为那几期的封面做得太差才不吸引人
Evidence：需要排除其他可能解释那几期杂志卖得差的原因

② 证词类
Signal：survey
Inference：survey ⇒ 大众杂志的读者更喜欢经济而不是政治话题
Assumption：调查可靠
Counterexamples：调查期间可能有重大经济事件，增加了人们对于经济问题的关注
Evidence：需要更充分的信息来帮助读者判断该调查的可靠性、代表性

③ 类比类
Signal：谈的本来是大众杂志，但最终要谈的是 N 杂志
Inference：大众杂志的读者更喜欢经济而不是政治话题 ⇒ N 杂志的读者不喜欢阅读政治话题，喜欢经济话题
Assumption：N 杂志的受众与大众杂志的受众倾向类似
Counterexamples：N 杂志很可能本来针对的人群就是关心政治问题的人群，不适合大众杂志人群的品位
Evidence：需要知道 N 杂志的受众群体是否与大众杂志一致

④ 建议类
Signal：步骤①③的结论，以及最终要建议杂志转型
Inference：N 杂志的读者不喜欢阅读政治话题，喜欢经济话题 ⇒ N 杂志应该减少对政治话题的关注，而应该关注经济话题
Assumption：没有更好的选择
Counterexamples：也许还有其他话题更吸引人，比如娱乐、运动、科技、教育等
Evidence：需要考虑其他可能更好的转型方向

⑤ 其他
Signal：Editor 基于其他杂志不做政治话题，就暗示 N 杂志应该坚持做政治话题
Inference：很少有杂志大量关注政治话题 ⇒ N 杂志应该继续做政治话题
Assumption：喜欢读政治内容的读者没有得到满足
Counterexamples：其他杂志不做政治话题就是因为现在没人关心政治，市面上已经没有多少政治杂志的生存空间
Evidence：需要知道其他杂志不做政治话题的具体原因

74

The following appeared in a business magazine.

"As a result of numerous complaints of dizziness and nausea on the part of consumers of Promofoods tuna, the company requested that eight million cans of its tuna be returned for testing. Promofoods concluded that the canned tuna did not, after all, pose a health risk. This conclusion is based on tests performed on samples of the recalled cans by chemists from Promofoods; the chemists found that of the eight food chemicals most commonly blamed for causing symptoms of dizziness and nausea, five were not found in any of the tested cans. The chemists did find small amounts of the three remaining suspected chemicals but pointed out that these occur naturally in all canned foods."

译 文

由于大量的消费者投诉说食用 Pomofoods 的金枪鱼产生了眩晕和恶心，该公司要求召回 800 万罐金枪鱼罐头做检测。最终，Promofoods 下结论说这些罐头并不会危害健康。这一结论基于 Promofoods 的化学家对召回的样本所做的测试；化学家们发现，8 种最常见的导致眩晕和恶心症状的化学物质中，有 5 种都没有在任何被测试的罐头中发现。化学家确实发现少量的其他 3 种被怀疑的化学物质，但他们指出，这些物质在所有其他罐头食品中都自然存在。

文章结构图

```
┌─────────────────────────────────────────────────────────────┐
│ 8 种常见的有害物中有 5 种没发现 + 剩下 3 种只有少量，且在罐头食品当中都会出现 │
│                         ⇓ ①②                                │
│             测试的金枪鱼罐头并不会造成晕眩和恶心              │
│                         ⇓ ③                                 │
│             该金枪鱼罐头并不会造成健康隐患                    │
└─────────────────────────────────────────────────────────────┘
```

结　　论：The canned tuna did not pose a health risk.
结论类型：预测型

各步推理分析

①数据类

Signal：为了排除这些罐头造成晕眩和恶心，报告指出 5/8 的造成晕眩和恶心的常见物质没出现，而剩下的 3 种量很少，而且正常罐头都有

Inference：8 种造成晕眩和恶心的常见物质中 5 种没出现 + 剩下 3 种只有少量，且在罐头中常出现 ⟹ 测

试的金枪鱼罐头并不会造成晕眩和恶心

　　Assumption：少量就不足以致病

　　Counterexamples：比如，别的罐头有害物质的含量是 1 微克，P 罐头的含量是 10 微克，完全可以造成质的区别，虽然仍然是少量，但"少量"这个词太模糊了

　　Evidence：需要知道 P 罐头当中这些危害物质的具体含量

② 其他

　　Signal：同上

　　Inference：8 种造成晕眩和恶心的常见物质中有 5 种没出现 + 剩下 3 种只有少量，且在罐头中常出现 ⟹ 测试的金枪鱼罐头并不会造成晕眩和恶心

　　Assumption：没有其他毒物

　　Counterexamples：该罐头中包含非常见的毒物

　　Evidence：需要调查是否存在其他非常见的毒物

③ 类比类

　　Signal：前面讨论的都是实验测试的罐头，但最终要证明的是 P 公司的所有金枪鱼罐头

　　Inference：测试的罐头并不会造成晕眩和恶心 ⟹ P 罐头不会造成眩晕和恶心

　　Assumption：测试的罐头具有代表性

　　Counterexamples：罐头生产有不同的批次，有些批次的罐头在生产中产生了问题，但是召回时可能并不包含那些批次，因为召回的可能是刚刚发出去的，之前进入市面的罐头早已经流入千家万户，祸害千万人；其次，即便召回的罐头有代表性，但测试选择的样本量未知，也许数量很少，也许选择不随机，不具有任何代表性

　　Evidence：需要证据确认测试的罐头选择是具有代表性的

④ 类比类

　　Signal：谈论的本来是晕眩和恶心，但最终要证明的是健康隐患

　　Inference：P 罐头不会造成晕眩和恶心 ⟹ P 罐头不会包含健康隐患

　　Assumption：没有其他健康隐患

　　Counterexamples：P 罐头虽然不会造成晕眩和恶心，但会产生其他危害

　　Evidence：需要知道 P 罐头是否会有其他可能危害

76

The following is a letter to the editor of an environmental magazine.

"In 1975 a wildlife census found that there were seven species of amphibians in Xanadu National Park, with abundant numbers of each species. However, in 2002 only four species of amphibians were observed in the park, and the numbers of each species were drastically reduced. There has been a substantial decline in the numbers of amphibians worldwide, and global pollution of water and air is clearly implicated. The decline of amphibians in Xanadu National Park, however, almost certainly has a different cause: in 1975, trout—which are known to eat amphibian eggs—were introduced into the park."

思路相近题目: 77

译 文

在 1975 年的一次野生动物普查中发现, 在 Xanadu 国家公园当中有 7 种两栖类生物, 每种数量丰富。但是, 到了 2002 年, 人们只在公园中发现了 4 种两栖类生物, 且数量都显著下降。全世界两栖类生物的数量都在显著下降, 而全球水与空气污染很有可能是相关因素。然而, Xanadu 国家公园中两栖类生物的数量下降几乎必然是别的因素造成的: 1975 年鳟鱼被引入公园当中, 而我们知道鳟鱼会吃两栖类生物的蛋。

文章结构图

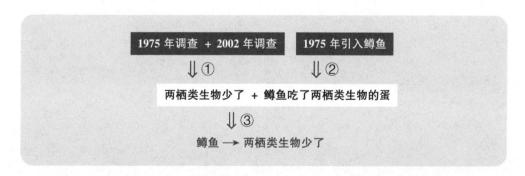

结　论: The decline of amphibians in Xanadu National Park must be due to the introduction of trout.
结论类型: 解释型

各步推理分析

① 证词类, 数据类

Signal: census, 7, 4, observe, reduce
Inference: 1975 年普查发现了 7 种两栖类生物, 并且数量很多, 而 2002 年只观察到 4 种两栖类生物, 而且数量很少 ⟹ 两栖类生物减少

Assumption：两次调查的可靠性相等

Counterexamples：1975 年观察的范围广、仔细、专业，而且是在夏天；2002 年的观察来自游人，各方面经验都不足，而且是在冬天观察的

Evidence：需要对比两次调查的范围以及调查手段以确定它们的可靠性是可比的

② 其他

Signal：文章指出鳟鱼在 1975 年被引入，结论是想表明鳟鱼吃两栖类生物的蛋造成了两栖类生物减少，则显然作者需要暗示鳟鱼吃掉了两栖类生物的蛋

Inference：1975 年鳟鱼被引入 ⟹ 鳟鱼吃掉了两栖类生物的蛋

Assumption：鳟鱼活得很好；鳟鱼和两栖类生物有空间交集

Counterexamples：鳟鱼很快就死光了，不可能对两栖类生物有影响；鳟鱼和两栖类生物就没放入同一个区域里；引入的鳟鱼量很少，也不可能是两栖类生物数量显著下降的原因

Evidence：需要调查引入的鳟鱼的存活率；需要知道这些存活的鳟鱼依赖的实际食物来源

③ 解释类

Signal：作者试图建立鳟鱼与两栖类生物数量减少之间的关系

Inference：鳟鱼吃掉了两栖类生物的蛋 + 两栖类生物数量减少 ⟹ 鳟鱼是两栖类生物数量减少的原因

Assumption：没有其他解释

Counterexamples：天敌增多，污染，食物不足，疾病

Evidence：需要排除其他可能解释两栖类生物数量下降的变量

Part 5　Argument 题库逐题精析

78

In a study of the reading habits of Waymarsh citizens conducted by the University of Waymarsh, most respondents said that they preferred literary classics as reading material. However, a second study conducted by the same researchers found that the type of book most frequently checked out of each of the public libraries in Waymarsh was the mystery novel. Therefore, it can be concluded that the respondents in the first study had misrepresented their reading habits.

思路相近题目：80

译　文

在一次由 Waymarsh 大学所举行的关于 Waymarsh 居民阅读习惯的调查中，大多数受访者说他们喜欢阅读文学经典。然而，由相同的研究人员进行的第二次调查发现 Waymarsh 所有公共图书馆中最经常被借阅的书是悬疑小说。因此，我们可以得出结论，第一次调查的受访者歪曲了他们自己的阅读习惯。

文章结构图

> 调查 1 中人们声称最喜欢文学经典 ＋ 调查 2 发现最常被借阅的书是悬疑小说
> ⇩①②③
> 调查 1 中的人撒谎了

结　论：The respondents in the first study had misrepresented their reading habits.
结论类型：解释型

推理分析（本文只有一步推理，只能分析该步骤的多个假设）

① 证词类

Assumption：第一群人的选择能够代表全城
Counterexamples：在书店或学校进行调查，不能代表全城的习惯，但参与调查的人说的是真话；吆喝式调查，在调查的时候已经告诉了人们是进行阅读习惯的调查，则愿意参与的人通常是对阅读感兴趣，且对自己读的书感到自信的人，很可能就是喜欢读文学经典的人
Evidence：需要知道第一次调查的详细信息，包括地点、提问方式、问卷内容

② 证词类

Assumption：第二次调查可以真实反映全城人的阅读习惯

Counterexamples：人们最爱看的书不会借而会买；城市里图书馆分布不均，只有某些地区有图书馆，而这个区域人群的阅读习惯和其他地区有显著不同；悬疑小说是用来消遣的，看起来比较快，所以借出比较频繁，而文学经典看起来比较慢，慢慢品味，所以借阅的频率低，但借出时间仍然很长，因为图书馆文学经典藏书有限，人们只能排队等待借出文学经典被归还

Evidence：需要知道全城图书馆的分布位置；需要知道各图书馆的悬疑小说和文学经典的总存量是否可以满足所有借阅者；需要知道文学经典与悬疑小说的借阅者单次借阅的时长

③ 证词类

Assumption：两次结果互斥

Counterexamples：文学经典也可以是悬疑小说，两次调查中的分类取名可能就不同，第一次的分类用的是文学经典，没有悬疑小说这个概念，很多人就把某些经典的悬疑小说放在了文学经典的门类当中，但第二次就被调查者放到了悬疑小说的门类当中；两次调查之间经历了很久的时间，之前文学经典流行，但最近突然出现了一部很流行的悬疑小说，或者被翻拍成了流行的电影，于是引起了悬疑小说的阅读潮流

Evidence：需要知道两次调查对书籍的分类方式是否有所区别；需要知道两次调查之间是否发生了重要的社会事件影响人们的阅读习惯

79

The following appeared in a memo at XYZ company.

"When XYZ lays off employees, it pays Delany Personnel Firm to offer those employees assistance in creating résumés and developing interviewing skills, if they so desire. Laid-off employees have benefited greatly from Delany's services: last year those who used Delany found jobs much more quickly than did those who did not. Recently, it has been proposed that we use the less expensive Walsh Personnel Firm in place of Delany. This would be a mistake because eight years ago, when XYZ was using Walsh, only half of the workers we laid off at that time found jobs within a year. Moreover, Delany is clearly superior, as evidenced by its bigger staff and larger number of branch offices. After all, last year Delany's clients took an average of six months to find jobs, whereas Walsh's clients took nine."

思路相近题目：82

译 文

当 XYZ 裁员的时候，它雇用了 Delany 人事公司为这些下岗员工提供写简历和提高面试技巧方面的帮助。下岗员工从 Delany 的服务中极大受益：去年获得了 Delany 帮助的员工找工作比其他员工快得多。最近，有人提出用收费较少的 Walsh 人事公司代替 Delany。这将是一个错误，因为在 8 年前，XYZ 使用的就是 Walsh，我们当时裁掉的员工中只有一半在一年之内找到了工作。而且，Delany 显然更好，证据是它的员工更多，分支机构也更多。毕竟，去年 Delany 的客户平均六个月能找到工作，而 Walsh 的客户平均要 9 个月才找到工作。

文章结构图

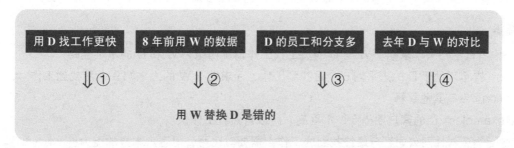

结　　论：It would be a mistake for the XYZ Company to use the less expensive Walsh Personnel Firm to replace Delany in offering laid-off employees assistance in creating résumés and developing interviewing skills.

结论类型：建议型

各步推理分析

① 解释类

Signal："："

Inference：去年，获得了 D 帮助的人比没获得 D 帮助的人找工作更快 ⟹ D 比 W 更好

Assumption：没有其他解释；W 不能做到更好

Counterexamples：D 劝说了很多人接受很差的工作，也许要是用了 W，找到工作会更快；也许那些没有获得 D 帮助然后没找到工作的人只是根本没有想找工作，可能在进修或培养新技能

Evidence：需要知道接受了 D 帮助并找到工作的那些人找到了什么样的工作；需要调查那些没找到工作的人没找到工作的原因

② 数据类，解释类，类比类

Signal：作者试图将 8 年前只有一半人找到工作归结为 W 的失败，并且作者想要由 8 年前推断 8 年后

Inference：8 年前用 W 时有一半人一年内找到工作 ⟹ D 比 W 更好

Assumption：8 年来经济情况可进行比较；8 年来 W 的质量没变；没找到工作的那些人用了 W；D 本可以做得更好

Counterexamples：8 年前难找工作，现在好找；8 年前 W 是新公司，现在已经很厉害了；当时 1/2 没找到工作的人都没求助 W，求助 W 的都找到工作了；8 年前要是用 D，结果更糟糕

Evidence：需要对比 8 年来的就业形势变化；需要知道当年求助 W 公司的人所占的比例，以及这部分人当中找到工作的人的比例；需要对比 W 公司 8 年来实力的变化

③ 其他

Signal：moreover

Inference：D 的员工和分支多 ⟹ D 比 W 好

Assumption：规模代表实力

Counterexamples：效率低下

Evidence：需要直接对比 D 和 W 公司的经营状况，需要直接对比两公司员工的工作能力

④ 解释类

Signal：作者试图把去年求助于 W 与 D 的员工找工作情况归结为 W 和 D 的水平差距

Inference：去年求助于 D 的人平均 6 个月找到工作，而求助于 W 的人平均 9 个月找到工作 ⟹ D 比 W 好

Assumption：没有其他解释

Counterexamples：D 的客户期望低，水平高，所以自然找工作快

Evidence：需要对比两公司客户最终找到的工作；需要对比两公司客户本身的能力

84

> **84** Three years ago, because of flooding at the Western Palean Wildlife Preserve, 100 lions and 100 western gazelles were moved to the East Palean Preserve, an area that is home to most of the same species that are found in the western preserve, though in larger numbers, and to the eastern gazelle, a close relative of the western gazelle. The only difference in climate is that the eastern preserve typically has slightly less rainfall. Unfortunately, after three years in the eastern preserve, the imported western gazelle population has been virtually eliminated. Since the slight reduction in rainfall cannot be the cause of the virtual elimination of western gazelle, their disappearance must have been caused by the larger number of predators in the eastern preserve.

译 文

三年前，由于西 Palea 野生动物保护区发洪水，100 头狮子和 100 头西瞪羚转移到了东 Palea 保护区。生活在东区的物种和生活在西区的物种大部分相同，只不过东区的数量比西区多。东瞪羚是西瞪羚的近亲。两地气候唯一的不同是东区降雨量稍微少一些。遗憾的是，在东区生活三年后，引进的西瞪羚几乎彻底灭绝了。由于降雨量些许的减少不可能是造成西瞪羚灭绝的原因，那么它们的消失只可能是东区更多天敌所造成的。

文章结构图

```
        ┌─────────────────────────┐
        │  东 P 天敌更多 + 瞪羚灭绝  │
        └─────────────────────────┘
                    ⇓ ①②③
        ┌─────────────────────────┐
        │   东 P 更多天敌 → 瞪羚灭绝 │
        └─────────────────────────┘
```

结　　论：The disappearance of the western gazelles must have been caused by the larger number of predators in the eastern preserve.

结论类型：**解释型**

推理分析（本文只有一步推理，只能分析该步骤的多个假设）

① **数据类**

Assumption：东边天敌总量多，则瞪羚所面对的天敌就会更多

Counterexamples：也许东边的区域面积更大，虽然天敌总数更多，但是单位面积里瞪羚所面对的天敌威胁并不会更多

Evidence：需要知道两个保护区的总面积

②**解释类**

Assumption：瞪羚的灭绝并不是西边的天敌造成的

Counterexamples：迁移到东边的狮子是瞪羚灭绝的主要原因，因为狮子与瞪羚的比例大很多

Evidence：需要调查狮子的存在对瞪羚所起到的影响

③**解释类**

Assumption：东边没有其他特殊条件可以解释瞪羚的灭亡

Counterexamples：当地特殊的疾病、污染，当地瞪羚食物不足，西边来的瞪羚竞争不过当地的其他物种，这些都可以导致瞪羚的灭亡

Evidence：需要调查其他环境、疾病等方面的因素对瞪羚数量可能产生的影响

85 Workers in the small town of Leeville take fewer sick days than workers in the large city of Masonton, 50 miles away. Moreover, relative to population size, the diagnosis of stress-related illness is proportionally much lower in Leeville than in Masonton. According to the Leeville Chamber of Commerce, these facts can be attributed to the health benefits of the relatively relaxed pace of life in Leeville.

思路相近题目：94 & 96

译　文

小城镇 Leeville 工人休病假的天数比 50 英里外的大城市 Masonton 的少。此外，相对于人口总量，被诊断出患上与压力有关的疾病的人在 Leeville 要远少于 Masonton。在 Leeville 商会看来，这些事实可以归结为 Leeville 相对更悠闲的生活方式所带来的健康优势。

文章结构图

```
┌─────────────────────────┐     ┌───────────────────────────────────┐
│ L 员工请病假的天数比 M 少 │     │ L 查出患有和压力相关的疾病的人比 M 少 │
└─────────────────────────┘     └───────────────────────────────────┘
            ⇓ ①                              ⇓ ②
     ┌──────────────────────────────────────────────────┐
     │ L 员工比 M 更健康 + L 患有和压力相关疾病的人比 M 少 │
     └──────────────────────────────────────────────────┘
                             ⇓ ③
              ┌─────────────────────────────────┐
              │ L 轻松的生活节奏是这些区别的原因 │
              └─────────────────────────────────┘
```

结　论：The fewer sick days among workers and the lower proportion of people diagnosed of stress-related illness in Leeville can be attributed to its relaxed pace of life.

结论类型：解释型

各步推理分析

① 解释类

Signal：L 员工请病假的天数比 M 少，而结论中，作者要将这种现象归结为 L 的 health benefits，则它显然首先认为这种差别反映了一种健康差别

Inference：L 员工请病假的天数比 M 少 ⟹ L 员工更健康

Assumption：生病都会请病假，请病假的都是生病的

Counterexamples：实际上很可能两边人的健康差不多，甚至 M 员工的健康更好，只不过是因为 L 的人普遍经济条件差，因此为了不减少收入，不得不尽量少请病假；或者 M 的娱乐生活丰富，M 的人经济条件也更好，因此很多人会找各种理由请假不上班

Evidence：需要直接调查两地员工生病的频率，而不是依赖两地病假的数量

② **证词类**

Signal：diagnosis

Inference：L 查出患有和压力相关的疾病的人比 M 少 $\Longrightarrow$ L 患有和压力相关疾病的人比 M 少

Assumption：diagnosis 是可靠的

Counterexamples：可能因为 L 医疗条件低下，L 的很多实际患病的人根本没有办法被查出病来

Evidence：需要知道两地的医疗水平，尤其是精神疾病方面医疗水平的差别

③ **解释类**

Signal：步骤①的结论，而最终要归结为 L 轻松的生活节奏

Inference：L 员工比 M 更健康 + L 患有和压力相关疾病的人比 M 少 $\Longrightarrow$ 这些是因为 L 轻松的生活节奏

Assumption：没有其他解释

Counterexamples：L 企业的福利好，政府法规规定这些企业必须定期体检；L 的医疗条件更好，预防和治疗都比较到位；L 的气候、环境更好

Evidence：需要排除其他可能导致两地健康状况不同的因素

Part 5　Argument 题库逐题精析

90

The following appeared in an e-mail sent by the marketing director of the Classical Shakespeare Theatre of Bardville.

"Over the past ten years, there has been a 20 percent decline in the size of the average audience at Classical Shakespeare Theatre productions. In spite of increased advertising, we are attracting fewer and fewer people to our shows, causing our profits to decrease significantly. We must take action to attract new audience members. The best way to do so is by instituting a 'Shakespeare in the Park' program this summer. Two years ago the nearby Avon Repertory Company started a 'Free Plays in the Park' program, and its profits have increased 10 percent since then. If we start a 'Shakespeare in the Park' program, we can predict that our profits will increase, too."

译　文

在过去的十年里，Classical Shakespeare Theatre 作品的场均观众减少了 20%。尽管增加了广告，但是越来越少的人被我们的演出所吸引，这导致我们的利润明显减少。我们必须采取措施来吸引新的观众。这么做的最好方式是今年夏天启动一个叫"Shakespeare in the Park"的项目。两年前，附近的 Avon Repertory Company 启动了一个叫"Free Plays in the Park"的项目，自此它的利润增长了 10%。如果我们启动一个叫"Shakespeare in the Park"的项目，预计我们的利润也会增长。

文章结构图

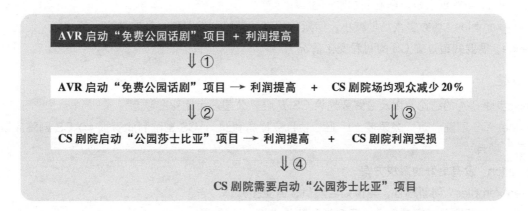

结　　论：The Classical Shakespeare Theatre should institute a "Shakespeare in the Park" program this summer.

结论类型：建议型

各步推理分析

① 解释型

Signal：AVR 启动"免费公园话剧"项目，since then，利润提高，而作者试图建立两件事之间的关系

Inference：AVR 启动"免费公园话剧"项目 + 利润提高 ⟹ AVR 启动"免费公园话剧"项目造成利润提高

Assumption：没有其他解释

Counterexamples：节目质量提高；票价降低；演了一些更符合观众口味的剧

Evidence：需要排除其他可能对利润变化造成影响的因素

② 类比类

Signal：谈的本来是 AVR，突然变成了 CS

Inference：AVR 启动"免费公园话剧"项目造成利润提高 ⟹ CS 剧院启动"公园莎士比亚"项目也会提高利润

Assumption：两个公司的剧在公园里会一样受欢迎

Counterexamples：公园中的游客文化水平一般，莎士比亚剧如此阳春白雪，难以吸引普通观众，而 AVR 的免费话剧都是通俗易懂、接近生活的剧

Evidence：需要知道 AVR 的免费活动所展示的话剧类型，并调查其与莎士比亚的剧之间可能存在的区别，尤其是大众对不同剧的倾向的区别

③ 数据类

Signal：一开始谈论的是 CS 的场均观众减少，但最后要讨论的是利润

Inference：CS 场均观众减少 ⟹ CS 利润受损

Assumption：场均观众是影响利润的唯一因素

Counterexamples：场数多或场地减小，但票价提高，最终利润可能一直在增高

Evidence：需要知道过去 CS 的利润变化情况

④ 建议类

Signal：步骤③④的结论，以及最终要建议 CS 开启"公园莎士比亚"项目

Inference：CS 剧院启动"公园莎士比亚"项目会提高利润 + CS 剧院利润受损 ⟹ CS 剧院应该启动"公园莎士比亚"项目

Assumption：没有更好的解决方案

Counterexamples：创新剧目，邀请知名演员，做更多媒体广告

Evidence：需要充分考察其他可能更有效的解决方案

Part 5　Argument 题库逐题精析

106

The following is a recommendation from the personnel director to the president of Acme Publishing Company.

"Many other companies have recently stated that having their employees take the Easy Read Speed-Reading Course has greatly improved productivity. One graduate of the course was able to read a 500-page report in only two hours; another graduate rose from an assistant manager to vice president of the company in under a year. Obviously, the faster you can read, the more information you can absorb in a single workday. Moreover, Easy Read would cost Acme only $500 per employee—a small price to pay when you consider the benefits. Included in this fee is a three-week seminar in Spruce City and a lifelong subscription to the Easy Read newsletter. Clearly, to improve productivity, Acme should require all of our employees to take the Easy Read Course."

思路相近题目：119, 120 & 153

译　文

最近许多其他公司声称，让他们的员工参加 Easy Read 速读课程显著提高了生产力。该课程的一位毕业生能只用两小时就读完 500 页的报告；另一位毕业生在不到一年内从经理助理升到了副总裁。显然，你读得越快，一天之内能处理的信息就越多。而且，Easy Read 课程只花费了 Acme 公司人均 500 美元——你如果考虑一下受益，这笔钱真的很少。这笔费用包括一节 Spruce 城为期三周的讨论课以及可以终身订阅 Easy Read 的通讯。显然，要想提高生产力，Acme 公司应该要求其所有员工参加 Easy Read 课程。

文章结构图

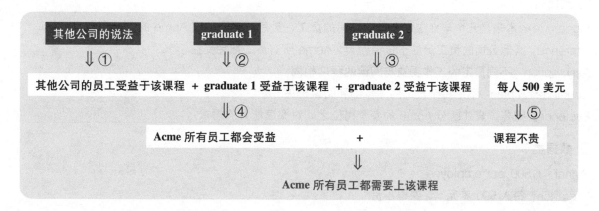

结　　论：To improve productivity, Acme should require all its employees to take the Easy Read Course.
结论类型：建议型

各步推理分析

① 证词类

Signal：state

Inference：其他公司的说法 ⟹ 其他公司的员工受益于该课程

Assumption：其他公司可靠

Counterexamples：做广告

Evidence：需要知道这些公司和该课程之间是否有利益联系；需要知道这些公司是在什么样的语境下做出的这种评论

② 解释类

Signal：作者试图建立毕业生 1 每小时读 500 页报告与该课程之间的关系

Inference：graduate 1 ⟹ graduate 1 受益于该课程

Assumption：没有其他解释

Counterexamples：他本来能读 600 页；他读的东西极其简单；他读的质量很差

Evidence：需要知道该毕业生先前的阅读能力，需要知道他的实际阅读质量，而不仅仅是阅读速度

③ 解释类

Signal：作者试图建立毕业生 2 升职与该课程之间的关系

Inference：graduate 2 ⟹ graduate 2 受益于该课程

Assumption：没有其他解释

Counterexamples：潜规则，个人能力本来就很强

Evidence：需要排除该毕业生升职的其他可能原因

④ 类比类

Signal：谈的本来是几个毕业生以及其他公司的员工，最后要证明的是 Acme 的所有员工

Inference：其他公司的员工受益于该课程 ⟹ Acme 所有员工都会受益

Assumption：不同员工的工作受益与阅读的程度相同

Counterexamples：不是每个员工的工作都和阅读相关

Evidence：需要调查并区分 Acme 的各个岗位之间对阅读能力的需求

⑤ 数据类

Signal：$500 per employee

Inference：每人 500 美元 ⟹ 课程不贵

Assumption：每人 500 美元对该公司不贵

Counterexamples：很可能该公司本来资金就不充足，考虑到公司的人数，这个收费意味着很大的一笔开支；如果是自己掏的话，这个钱对于经济不充裕的员工更是巨大负担

Evidence：需要知道 Acme 公司目前的资金状况

⑥ 建议类

Signal：步骤④⑤的结论，以及最终要建议所有人上这个课

Inference：Acme 所有员工都会受益 + 课程不贵 ⟹ Acme 所有员工都该上这个课

Assumption：没有更好的方案；不会造成严重副作用

Counterexamples：三周课程，还在外地，可能非常耽误工作；可能有更直接地提升能力的方案

Evidence：需要充分考察其他可能提升 Acme 生产力的方案

Part 5 Argument 题库逐题精析

125 The following appeared in a letter to the school board in the town of Centerville.

"All students should be required to take the driver's education course at Centerville High School. In the past two years, several accidents in and around Centerville have involved teenage drivers. Since a number of parents in Centerville have complained that they are too busy to teach their teenagers to drive, some other instruction is necessary to ensure that these teenagers are safe drivers. Although there are two driving schools in Centerville, parents on a tight budget cannot afford to pay for driving instruction. Therefore an effective and mandatory program sponsored by the high school is the only solution to this serious problem."

思路相近题目：127 & 129

译 文

Centerville 高中的所有学生都应该被要求参加驾驶员教育课程。在过去两年中，Centerville 及其周边发生的几起交通事故涉及了青少年司机。由于 Centerville 的一些家长抱怨自己太忙没有时间教孩子开车，必须有一些其他课程来保证这些孩子能成为安全的司机。尽管在 Centerville 已经有两所驾校，但是手头不宽裕的家长是无法负担驾校学费的。因此由学校组织的有效的强制性课程是解决这一严重问题的唯一方案。

文章结构图

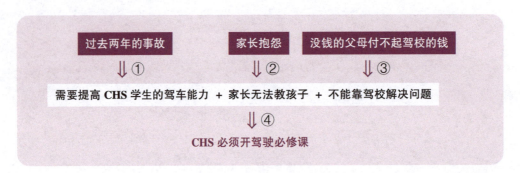

结　论：All students should be required to take the driver's education course at Centerville High School.

结论类型：建议型

各步推理分析

① 数据类，类比类

Signal：several，以及谈的本来是 C 城的年轻驾驶员，但要证明的是 CHS 的学生

Inference：过去两年一些事故涉及了 C 城的年轻司机 ⇒ 需要提高 CHS 学生的驾车能力

Assumption：事故数量很多；这些司机驾车能力不足造成了事故；CHS 学生有很多人驾车

Counterexamples：首先，事故数量很少；其次，虽然事故涉及青年司机，但他们不是肇事者，而是受害者，他们驾驶没有问题；再次，很可能 CHS 就没有几个学生开车，根本没有这种需求

Evidence：需要知道这些事故的数量；需要知道这些事故当中的青年司机是否存在驾驶缺陷；需要知道这些司机当中是否有 CHS 的学生

② 证词类

Signal：complain

Inference：许多家长抱怨忙 ⟹ 家长没法教学生开车

Assumption：抱怨有代表性；家长有困难，学校就要解决

Counterexamples：少数家长只是自己懒，并不是真的忙

Evidence：需要知道抱怨的数量

③ 其他

Signal：作者指出没钱的家长付不起驾校的钱，暗示驾校也无法解决

Inference：没钱的父母付不起驾校的钱 ⟹ 不能靠驾校解决问题

Assumption：没钱的家庭孩子开车，有很多没钱的家庭

Counterexamples：没钱的家庭本来就不会给孩子买车，恰恰不存在这种问题；这种现象本来就不多

Evidence：需要知道到底有多少家庭没有资金支付孩子上驾校且还会给孩子提供车

④ 建议类

Signal：步骤①②③的结论，以及最终要建议学校开设驾驶的必修课

Inference：需要提高 CHS 学生的驾车能力 + 家长无法教孩子 + 不能靠驾校解决问题 ⟹ CHS 必须开驾驶必修课

Assumption：该建议可行；没有其他解决方案

Counterexamples：学校就没有足够的场所开设这种课程；其次，并不是每个人都有这种需求，也并不是每个人都需要上这个课，所以选修课就可以；而且，不光是家长、驾校可以教孩子开车，还有亲戚朋友等其他人可以帮忙教孩子开车

Evidence：需要调查学校是否有合适的人力和场地来支持这个课程；需要知道到底有多少学生有上该课的需求

128

The data from a survey of high school math and science teachers show that in the district of Sanlee many of these teachers reported assigning daily homework, whereas in the district of Marlee, most science and math teachers reported assigning homework no more than two or three days per week. Despite receiving less frequent homework assignments, Marlee students earn better grades overall and are less likely to be required to repeat a year of school than are students in Sanlee. These results call into question the usefulness of frequent homework assignments. Most likely the Marlee students have more time to concentrate on individual assignments than do the Sanlee students who have homework every day. Therefore teachers in our high schools should assign homework no more than twice a week.

思路相近题目：130 & 133

译 文

一份高中数学、科学课老师的调查数据显示在 Sanlee 地区许多老师每天布置家庭作业，而在 Marlee 地区每周只有不超过 2~3 天布置家庭作业。尽管家庭作业频率更低，但是 Marlee 地区的学生考试成绩更好、复读率更低。这项结果令人质疑频繁布置家庭作业的有效性。最有可能的是 Marlee 地区的学生比 Sanlee 地区的学生有更多时间集中精力在每一次作业上。因此，我们所有高中的老师每周布置家庭作业都不应该超过两次。

文章结构图

survey 中 M 与 S 的数学、科学教师的 report
⇩ ①
M 的数学、科学教师布置作业频率低于 S + M 学生成绩高，留级少
⇩ ②
M 的数学、科学教师布置作业频率低于 S → M 学生更能关注每次作业 → M 学生成绩高，留级少
⇩ ③
所有高中的所有教师布置作业的频率低 → 学生成绩好
⇩ ④
所有高中的所有教师都应该布置作业的频率低

结　　论：Teachers in the high schools should assign homework no more than twice a week.
结论类型：建议型

各步推理分析

① 证词类，数据类

Signal：survey, report, many, most

Inference：survey 中 S 的许多数学、科学教师 report 每天布置作业 + M 大部分数学、科学教师 report 每周布置作业不到两三次 ⟹ M 数学、科学教师比 S 数学、科学教师布置作业的频率低

Assumption：调查具有普遍性

Counterexamples：many 是个非常不准确的量，很可能 S 的大部分教师布置作业的频率也低；而且有些教师很可能只是为了不留下频繁布置作业的印象才这么说的

Evidence：需要具体对比两个学校的教师布置作业的频率到底平均多高，而不是依赖教师们非常模糊的口头报告

② 解释类

Signal：作者试图建立布置作业的频率与学生成绩之间的关系

Inference：M 数学、科学教师比 S 数学、科学教师布置作业的频率低 + M 学生成绩好、留级少 ⟹ M 数学、科学教师比 S 数学、科学教师布置作业的频率低造成 M 学生成绩好、留级少

Assumption：没有其他解释

Counterexamples：M 学生入校成绩就更好；M 教师教学水平高；M 给分宽松；M 对学生要求较低

Evidence：需要排除其他可能解释两校成绩区别的变量

③ 类比类

Signal：谈论的本来是这两校的数学、科学课，结果却要应用到所有学校的所有科目

Inference：M 数学、科学教师比 S 数学、科学教师布置作业的频率低造成 M 学生成绩好、留级少 ⟹ 所有高中的所有教师布置作业的频率低都会让学生成绩好

Assumption：所有学校的所有学科的学习要求是相似的

Counterexamples：自然科学的一个项目很花时间，需要几天来完成，但是像语言类学科每天都有新单词，每天都得做作业、复习；不同学校的学生情况不同，有些学校的学生自律能力、自我计划能力都不强，需要经常布置作业

Evidence：需要对比不同学校、不同课程的区别，以判断该策略是否适合所有课程

④ 建议类

Signal：步骤③的结论，以及最终要建议所有学校以低频率布置作业

Inference：所有高中的所有教师布置作业的频率低都会让学生成绩好 ⟹ 所有高中的所有教师布置作业的频率都应该低

Assumption：没有更好的方案

Counterexamples：更直接地提高教师的教学能力

Evidence：需要排除其他可能更有效的解决方案

135 Hospital statistics regarding people who go to the emergency room after roller-skating accidents indicate the need for more protective equipment. Within that group of people, 75 percent of those who had accidents in streets or parking lots had not been wearing any protective clothing (helmets, knee pads, etc.) or any light-reflecting material (clip-on lights, glow-in-the-dark wrist pads, etc.). Clearly, the statistics indicate that by investing in high-quality protective gear and reflective equipment, roller skaters will greatly reduce their risk of being severely injured in an accident.

译 文

医院关于发生轮滑事故后去急诊室的人的数据表明保护性装备的必要性。其中，75%在马路或停车场上出了事故的人都没有穿任何保护性的装备（头盔、护膝等），也没有戴任何反光材料（夹式灯、夜明腕垫等）。显然，该数据显示，通过购买高档的保护性装备以及反光设备，轮滑者会大幅度降低在事故中严重受伤的风险。

文章结构图

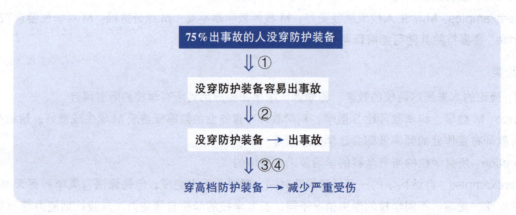

结　　论：By investing in high-quality protective gear and reflective equipment, roller skaters will greatly reduce their risk of being severely injured in an accident.

结论类型：**预测型**

各步推理分析

①**数据类**

Signal：75%

Inference：75%出事故的人没穿防护装备 ⟹ 没穿防护装备与出事故相关

Assumption：所有轮滑者中没穿防护装备的人的比例本身并不比这高

Counterexamples：绝大部分人都不穿防护装备玩轮滑，出事故的人中不穿防护装备的人比例自然比较高

Evidence：需要知道不穿防护装备的人占所有轮滑者的比例；需要知道不穿防护装备的人出事故的比例与穿防护装备的人出事故的比例

②**解释类**

Signal：作者试图证明是不穿护具装备造成人们出事故

Inference：步骤①的结论 $\Longrightarrow$ 没穿防护装备造成人们出事故

Assumption：没有其他解释

Counterexamples：因为自己比较嚣张，喜欢去危险的地方做危险动作，所以容易受伤，恰好是这群冒险的人喜欢不戴护具

Evidence：需要排除其他可能造成危险的变量

③**类比类**

Signal：谈的本来是护具，下文证明的却是高档护具

Inference：没戴护具造成人们出事故 $\Longrightarrow$ 戴高档护具可以减少事故

Assumption：不同档次的护具防护效果区别很大

Counterexamples：普通护具足以减少事故，高档的就是好看一点

Evidence：需要调查不同档次的护具所产生的区别

④ **类比类**

Signal：谈的本来是事故，下文却要避免严重受伤

Inference：没戴护具造成人们出事故 $\Longrightarrow$ 戴护具可以减少严重受伤

Assumption：护具足以防止严重受伤

Counterexamples：护具的能力只是减少擦伤等小事故，真正的严重受伤护具改变不了什么

Evidence：需要知道护具的防护能力对不同级别受伤的作用

140

> The following recommendation was made by the president and administrative staff of Grove College, a private institution, to the college's governing committee.

"We recommend that Grove College preserve its century-old tradition of all-female education rather than admit men into its programs. It is true that a majority of faculty members voted in favor of coeducation, arguing that it would encourage more students to apply to Grove. But 80 percent of the students responding to a survey conducted by the student government wanted the school to remain all female, and over half of the alumnae who answered a separate survey also opposed coeducation. Keeping the college all female will improve morale among students and convince alumnae to keep supporting the college financially."

思路相近题目：141 & 148

译 文

我们建议 Grove 学院保留其有数个世纪之久的全女性的教育传统，而不要招收男性。是的，大部分教员都投票支持男女性共同教育，他们认为这会鼓励更多学生申请 Grove 学院。但是，在一次学生会组织的调查中，80% 的参与者都希望学校坚持全女性，并且在另一项独立调查中，大多数被采访的校友都反对男女共同教育。保留学院的全女性传统会提高学生的士气，并能够说服校友们支持学校的财政。

文章结构图

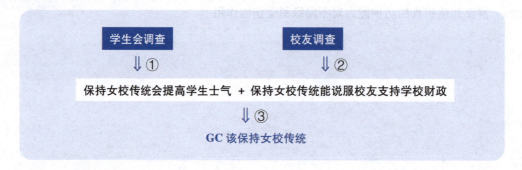

结　论：We recommend that Grove College preserve its century-old tradition of all-female education rather than admit men into its programs.

结论类型：建议型

各步推理分析

① 证词类

Signal：80% responding to survey

Inference：学生会调查 ⟹ 保持女校传统会提高学生士气

Assumption：调查可靠、有代表性

Counterexamples：很可能学生会就是学校里面的保守社团，而学生都知道这一点，因此大部分想要学校改变的学生根本不会参与这个调查；也许学校校规就是非常保守的，因此在调查中出于谨慎考虑，大部分学生都会违心地说出与学校理念一致的答案

Evidence：需要知道调查选样的方式；需要知道学校言论自由的程度

② 证词类

Signal：survey

Inference：校友调查 ⟹ 保持女校传统能说服校友支持学校财政

Assumption：调查可靠；调查能反映给学校捐款的校友的态度

Counterexamples：很多不在乎是不是女校的校友根本不会参与这个调查；如果是在校庆日对返校的校友进行采访，那显然本来就不会采访到反对学校政策的那些校友；很可能通常给学校赞助的校友并不支持

Evidence：需要知道调查的选样方式；需要知道一般提供财政支持的校友是什么态度

③ 建议类

Signal：步骤①②的结论，以及最终想支持保持女校传统

Inference：保持女校传统会提高学生士气 + 保持女校传统能说服校友支持学校财政 ⟹ GC 该保持女校传统

Assumption：没有严重副作用，没有更有效的替代方案

Counterexamples：招生严重下滑，造成学校发展难以为继；如果招收男性会大幅提升学校的影响力，会吸引更多的资助

Evidence：需要充分考虑该政策可能带来的不良后果；需要充分考虑其他可能的替代方案

Part 5　Argument 题库逐题精析

144 The following appeared in a memo to the board of directors of Bargain Brand Cereals.

"One year ago we introduced our first product, Bargain Brand breakfast cereal. Our very low prices quickly drew many customers away from the top-selling cereal companies. Although the companies producing the top brands have since tried to compete with us by lowering their prices and although several plan to introduce their own budget brands, not once have we needed to raise our prices to continue making a profit. Given our success in selling cereal, we recommend that Bargain Brand now expand its business and begin marketing other low-priced food products as quickly as possible."

思路相近题目：145

译文

一年前我们引入了我们第一款廉价产品——Bargain Brand 早餐燕麦。我们的低价迅速吸引了销售量最高的那些燕麦公司的很多顾客。尽管这些公司之后也尝试通过降低产品价格来与我们竞争，也计划引入自己的廉价品牌，但我们从未需要通过提价来持续赚钱。鉴于我们在燕麦销售上的成功，我们建议 Bargain Brand 尽快扩大自己的生意，着手拓展其他廉价食品的市场。

文章结构图

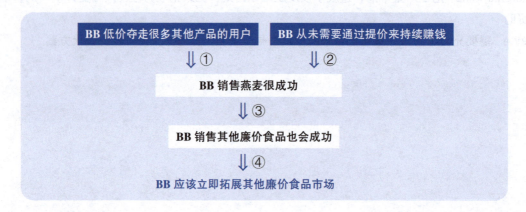

结　　论：Bargain Brand should now expand its business and begin marketing other low-priced food products as quickly as possible.

结论类型：建议型

各步推理分析

① 数据类

Signal：many

Inference：BB 低价夺走了很多其他产品的用户 ⟹ BB 销售燕麦很成功

Assumption："many" 能够代表很大的比例

Counterexamples："many" 是一个很不确定的概念，实际上可能对于其他大公司来说，根本没降低多少市场份额，BB 所占的市场比重其实很小，而且获得的利润其实也不怎么高

Evidence：需要具体调查其他竞争对手的市场占有率变化量；需要知道 BB 所占的市场份额以及具体的利润

② **其他**

Signal：前文提到 BB 从未需要通过提价来持续赚钱，而下文作者表明 BB 很成功

Inference：BB 从未需要通过提价来持续赚钱 ⟹ BB 很成功

Assumption：一直在赚钱就能代表成功；要是提价理应更能赚钱

Counterexamples：也许 BB 的唯一竞争优势就是廉价，稍微提一点价，消费者就全跑了，所以不靠提价来持续赚钱是迫不得已的；并且，这种赚钱的持续也可能是很勉强的，因为利润可能一直非常低

Evidence：需要调查 BB 的廉价是不是 BB 成功的关键因素

③ **类比类**

Signal：谈的本来是廉价燕麦，但最后要讨论的是其他廉价食品

Inference：BB 销售燕麦很成功 ⟹ BB 销售其他廉价食品也会成功

Assumption：两种产品的市场情况是相似的

Counterexamples：首先，也许 BB 的成功不是因为便宜，而是因为味道、品质等特点，而 BB 公司并没有能力在其他产品上做到这种高品质；其次，就算 BB 是因为廉价而成功，那可能是因为先前该领域廉价产品很少，所以 BB 捷足先登，但其他食品领域已经有了很优质的廉价产品，因此就算 BB 进入市场，也并不能快速占据一席之地

Evidence：需要调查其他食品领域竞争对手的情况

④ **建议类**

Signal：步骤③的结论，以及最终要建议 BB 进入其他廉价食品领域

Inference：BB 销售其他廉价食品会成功 ⟹ BB 应该立即拓展其他廉价食品市场

Assumption：BB 公司有能力立即拓展其他业务

Counterexamples：也许 BB 的资金、人员专业知识、设备都还无法开展其他食品业务

Evidence：需要知道 BB 现有的人员、技术等因素是否足以应对拓展其他廉价食品市场

Part 5 Argument 题库逐题精析

149 The following appeared in a memo from the marketing director of Top Dog Pet Stores.

"Five years ago Fish Emporium started advertising in the magazine *Exotic Pets Monthly*. Their stores saw sales increase by 15 percent after their ads began appearing in the magazine. The three Fish Emporium stores in Gulf City saw an even greater increase than that. Because Top Dog Pet Stores is based in Gulf City, it seems clear that we should start placing our own ads in *Exotic Pets Monthly*. If we do so, we will be sure to reverse the recent trend of declining sales and start making a profit again."

思路相近题目：150

译 文

五年前，Fish Emporium 在 *Exotic Pets Monthly* 杂志上登了广告。之后，它们的门店销量立即提升 15%。Gulf City 的三家 Fish Emporium 门店销量提升得更大。因为 Top Dog Pet Stores 也是地处 Gulf City，所以显然我们应该立即在 *Exotic Pets Monthly* 上登广告。我们如果这么做了，一定能够扭转最近销量下降的趋势，进而再一次盈利。

文章结构图

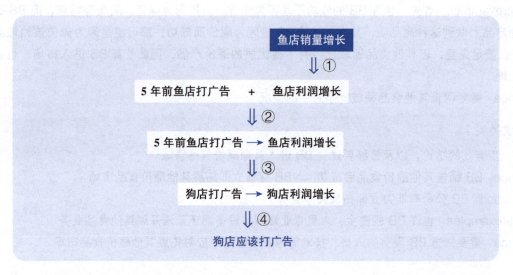

结　　论：Top Dog Pet Stores should start placing their own ads in *Exotic Pets Monthly*.
结论类型：建议型

各步推理分析

① 数据类

Signal：鱼店销量增长，但最后文章要讨论的是利润

Inference：鱼店销量增长 ⟹ 鱼店利润增长
Assumption：销量是影响利润的唯一因素
Counterexamples：成本，包括打广告的成本，增长得更厉害，或售价降低，这些都可以让利润不增长。
Evidence：需要知道鱼店的具体利润变化

② 解释类

Signal：作者试图建立鱼店打广告与销量增长之间的关系
Inference：5 年前鱼店打广告利润增长 ⟹ 5 年前鱼店打广告造成之后利润增长
Assumption：没有其他解释
Counterexamples：卖了更好看的鱼，或以别的渠道做了宣传
Evidence：需要调查其他可能的因素是否造成了利润的变化

③ 类比类

Signal：谈的本来是 5 年前鱼店的成功，但最终要证明的是现在的狗店
Inference：5 年前鱼店打了广告造成之后利润增长 ⟹ 如今狗店打广告也会带来利润增长
Assumption：两种宠物市场相似；该杂志 5 年内没发生巨大变化
Counterexamples：买鱼的人经常靠该杂志来寻找信息，因为该杂志在鱼市上有很大影响力，但是买狗的人是不看这个杂志的，甚至完全不看任何杂志；该杂志在宠物市场的影响力逐年下降，现在已经无法起到 5 年前的效果了
Evidence：需要知道该杂志对鱼市和狗市的不同影响力；需要知道该杂志这 5 年内是否存在影响力的显著变化

④ 建议类

Signal：步骤③的结论，以及最终要建议狗店打广告
Inference：如今狗店在该杂志上打广告也会带来利润增长 ⟹ 狗店应该在该杂志上打广告
Assumption：没有其他策略
Counterexamples：有更好的广告平台
Evidence：需要充分考虑其他可能更有效的解决方案

152

The following appeared in a recommendation from the President of the Amburg Chamber of Commerce.

"Last October, the city of Belleville installed high-intensity lighting in its central business district, and vandalism there declined almost immediately. The city of Amburg, on the other hand, recently instituted police patrols on bicycles in its business district. However, the rate of vandalism here remains constant. Since high-intensity lighting is clearly the most effective way to combat crime, we recommend using the money that is currently being spent on bicycle patrols to install such lighting throughout Amburg. If we install this high-intensity lighting, we will significantly reduce crime rates in Amburg."

思路相近题目：163

译 文

去年十月，Belleville 市在市中心商业区安装了高强度的灯，之后破坏公物的现象几乎瞬间就减少了。相反，Amburg 市最近在商业区增加了自行车巡逻警察。但是，这里的破坏公物现象没发生什么变化。鉴于高强度灯显然是最有效地打击犯罪的方式，我们建议把现在花在骑警上的钱用来在 Amburg 全城安装这样的灯。如果我们安装了这种强光灯，我们必然能显著降低 Amburg 的犯罪率。

文章结构图

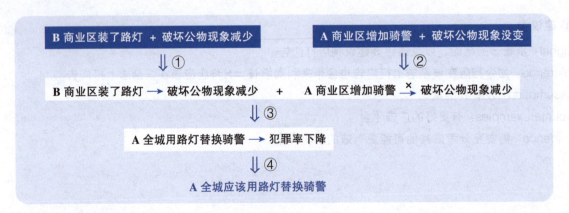

结　　论：Amburg should use the money that is currently being spent on bicycle patrols to install high-intensity lighting throughout Amburg.

结论类型：建议型

各步推理分析

① **解释类**

Signal：作者试图建立 B 装路灯和破坏公物现象减少之间的关系

Inference：B 商业区装了路灯 + 破坏公物现象减少 ⟹ B 商业区装了路灯导致破坏公物现象减少
Assumption：没有其他解释
Counterexamples：最近加强了道德教育；惩罚变得更严格；可能 B 也增加了骑警
Evidence：需要排除其他因素对这些公物破坏现象可能产生的影响

② 解释类
Signal：作者试图建立 A 设立骑警和破坏公物现象没减少之间的关系
Inference：A 商业区设立骑警 + A 破坏公物现象没减少 ⟹ A 商业区设立骑警没能减少破坏公物现象
Assumption：没有其他解释
Counterexamples：A 本来破坏公物的现象就非常少；以及，可能不是没有骑警，而是设立的骑警还不够多，一条几公里的商业街只安排了一两位骑警，当然照顾不过来
Evidence：需要排除其他因素对这些公物破坏现象可能产生的影响

③ 类比类
Signal：谈的本来是 A 城和 B 城的商业街，但最终要证明的是 A 城全城；要谈的本来是破坏公物，但最终要证明的是所有犯罪
Inference：B 商业区装了路灯导致破坏公物减少 + A 商业区设立骑警没能减少破坏公物现象 ⟹ A 全城装路灯替换骑警会让犯罪率下降
Assumption：两城情况相似；商业街与其他地方情况相似；路灯对所有犯罪效果一样
Counterexamples：或许 B 城商业街照明很差，所以装了灯很有用，而 A 城照明本来就不错，再加强光灯不会带来特别大区别；或许路灯能减少破坏公物现象，但对盗窃、抢劫等行为没什么影响，而骑警就能够有效地控制暴力犯罪，对被害人进行救助，对加害人进行控制，而 B 城可能主要犯罪就不是破坏公物，至少并不是每个地区都是这样，所以一股脑全用灯替换骑警可能恰恰增加了其他类型的犯罪
Evidence：需要对比两城犯罪类型等因素的可能区别

④ 建议类
Signal：步骤③的结论，以及最终建议 A 城全城用街灯替换骑警
Inference：A 城全城用路灯替换骑警可以减少犯罪率 ⟹ A 城全城应该用路灯替换骑警
Assumption：建议可行，没有更好的解决方案
Counterexamples：安装路灯代价高昂，远比配骑警要昂贵得多，支付不起；也许更好的方法是骑警和路灯结合，或者提高犯罪代价，安装更多摄像头
Evidence：需要充分考虑其他可能更有效的解决方案

Part 5　Argument 题库逐题精析

157 Humans arrived in the Kaliko Islands about 7,000 years ago, and within 3,000 years most of the large mammal species that had lived in the forests of the Kaliko Islands were extinct. Previous archaeological findings have suggested that early humans generally relied on both fishing and hunting for food; since archaeologists have discovered numerous sites in the Kaliko Islands where the bones of fish were discarded, it is likely that the humans also hunted the mammals. Furthermore, researchers have uncovered simple tools, such as stone knives, that could be used for hunting. The only clear explanation is that humans caused the extinction of the various mammal species through excessive hunting.

译　文

人类大约在 7 000 年前到达了 Kaliko 群岛，而在接下来的 3 000 年间，当地森林中的大部分大型哺乳动物就灭绝了。先前的考古发现显示，早期人类普遍会利用捕鱼和狩猎来获取食物；鉴于考古学家在 Kaliko 群岛发现了很多鱼骨被丢弃的遗址，很可能人们也捕猎了哺乳动物。而且，科学家还发现了一些简单工具，比如石刀，可以用来捕猎。唯一清楚的解释是，人类过度捕猎造成了这些大型哺乳动物的灭绝。

文章结构图

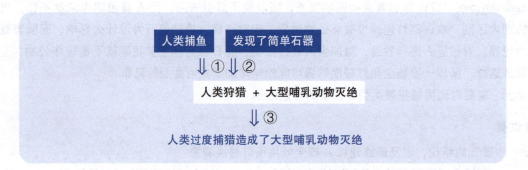

结　　论：Humans caused the extinction of the various mammal species on the Kaliko Islands through excessive hunting.

结论类型：**解释型**

各步推理分析

①类比类

Signal：要谈论捕猎，证据却是捕鱼

Inference：人类捕鱼 ⟹ 人类狩猎

Assumption：人类会捕鱼就一定会狩猎

Counterexamples：迫使人们学会捕鱼的原因恰恰就是当地人并没有学会狩猎，而且捕鱼获取的食物足以

维持当地人存活，所以并不需要狩猎

　　Evidence：需要更直接的证明当地人狩猎的证据，而不是通过与捕鱼进行类比

②**其他**

Signal：为了证明人类狩猎，文章指出发现了可以用来捕猎的刀具

Inference：发现了简单的石器 $\implies$ 这些石器是人们用来狩猎的

Assumption：能够用来捕猎的工具就一定是用来捕猎的

Counterexamples：切菜、砍树、切鱼、切水果、雕刻等，这些石器可以有各种各样的作用，不能确定一定是用来狩猎的

　　Evidence：需要直接的证据来表明这些石器与狩猎有关，比如可以调查其磨痕等方面的特点

③**解释类**

Signal：作者试图建立人类捕猎与大型哺乳动物灭绝之间的关系

Inference：人类捕猎 + 大型哺乳动物灭绝 $\implies$ 人类捕猎是大型哺乳动物灭绝的原因

Assumption：人类有能力捕猎大型哺乳动物；人类捕猎程度足以灭绝大型哺乳动物；没有其他解释

Counterexamples：首先，人类捕猎不代表能够捕猎那些大型哺乳动物，因为很可能那些大型哺乳动物强大到无法捕猎，而人们只是捕猎一些相对温顺的小型哺乳动物；可能当地人数量很少，就算捕猎，也根本无法影响到其他哺乳动物的数量；最重要的，可能有其他解释，比如瘟疫、天敌、气候恶化、自相残杀、食物不足，等等

　　Evidence：需要知道灭绝的到底是什么样的大型哺乳动物，当地人是否有能力捕捉；需要知道当地人的数量以估算可能对这些动物造成的影响；需要排除其他可能解释该现象的变量

160

The following is a letter that recently appeared in the Oak City Gazette, a local newspaper.

"The primary function of the Committee for a Better Oak City is to advise the city government on how to make the best use of the city's limited budget. However, at some of our recent meetings we failed to make important decisions because of the foolish objections raised by committee members who are not even residents of Oak City. People who work in Oak City but who live elsewhere cannot fully understand the business and politics of the city. After all, only Oak City residents pay city taxes, and therefore only residents understand how that money could best be used to improve the city. We recommend, then, that the Committee for a Better Oak City vote to restrict its membership to city residents only. We predict that, without the interference of non-residents, the committee will be able to make Oak City a better place in which to live and work."

译 文

Oak City 市民理事会的主要目的是给市政府提建议，帮助把有限的市政经费用在最需要的地方。可是，在最近一些会议上，我们没能做出重要的决定，因为一些理事会成员愚蠢的决定，而这些人压根就不是 Oak City 的居民。那些在 Oak City 工作但在别的地方居住的人无法真正理解本城市的政治和经济。毕竟，只有 Oak City 居民缴税建城，因而也只有他们才知道这些钱如何使用才能促进城市发展。因此，我们建议市民理事会投票将理事会的成员资格限定在本城市居民当中。我们预测，摆脱了非本地居民的干扰，理事会能更好地帮助 Oak City 成为一个适宜居住和工作的地方。

文章结构图

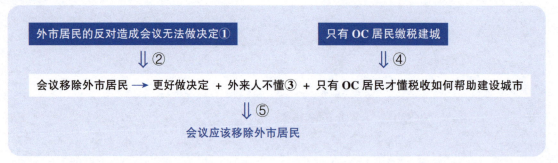

结　　论：The Committee for a Better Oak City should vote to restrict its membership to city residents only.
结论类型：建议型

各步推理分析

①**其他**

Signal：我们没能做出决定，因为外市居民愚蠢的反对

Inference：这是 stated assumption，没有给出任何证据

Assumption：外市居民的反对是愚蠢的

Counterexamples：其实是提案愚蠢，幸好外市居民反对了

Evidence：需要知道到底是什么提案被否定了，以及否定的理由是否合理

②类比类

Signal：谈论的本来是过去的某些会议，但要建议的是未来的会议

Inference：在某些会议上我们没能做出决定是因为外市居民的愚蠢反对 ⟹ 会议移除外市居民将能够更好地做决定

Assumption：所有会议的特点是相似的

Counterexamples：之前的决议是那些参与者不擅长的领域，但还有很多专业领域是他们擅长的，需要他们的意见

Evidence：需要充分考察这些参与者的背景，以判断他们是否会对会议带来积极的影响

③其他

Signal：无

Inference：这是 stated assumption，没有给出任何证据

Assumption：外来务工的人不懂本市政治和经济

Counterexamples：那些外地居民之前是住在该城的，而且很可能在该城工作了很久，非常熟悉这个城市，而且人家有着非常成功的在别的城市制订政策的经验，而且两个城市有非常大的相似性

Evidence：需要知道这些外地参与者在 OC 生活和工作的经历，以判断其对 OC 的了解程度

④ 其他

Signal：therefore

Inference：只有 OC 居民缴税建城 ⟹ 只有 OC 居民懂税收如何帮助城市建设

Assumption：缴税的人最懂税收该怎么用；外地居民不可能了解某地的需求

Counterexamples：缴税和分配税收没有一点关系，因为缴税是被迫的，而研究税收怎么分配是专业的能力；那些外地居民，之前是住在该城的，而且很可能在该城工作了很久，非常熟悉这个城市，而且人家有着非常成功的在别的城市制订政策的经验，而且两个城市有非常大的相似性

Evidence：需要更直接的证据来判断这些外来居民是否具有城市管理的能力

⑤ 建议类

Signal：步骤②③④的结论，以及最终想要在会议中移除外来居民

Inference：在会议上移除外市居民可以更好地做决定 + 外来务工的人不懂得 OC 的政治和经济 + 只有 OC 居民懂得税收如何帮助 OC ⟹ 会议应该移除外市居民

Assumption：不会产生严重的后果

Counterexamples：移除了外市居民，虽然会议的决定方便了，但是这些人是城市重要的投资者，他们就会彻底离开该城，影响城市的发展

Evidence：需要考虑这个决策可能带来的严重副作用

162

The following appeared in a memo from the vice president of a company that builds shopping malls around the country.

"The surface of a section of Route 101, paved just two years ago by Good Intentions Roadways, is now badly cracked with a number of dangerous potholes. In another part of the state, a section of Route 40, paved by Appian Roadways more than four years ago, is still in good condition. In a demonstration of their continuing commitment to quality, Appian Roadways recently purchased state-of-the-art paving machinery and hired a new quality-control manager. Therefore, I recommend hiring Appian Roadways to construct the access roads for all our new shopping malls. I predict that our Appian access roads will not have to be repaired for at least four years."

译 文

Route 101 的一段路面是两年前由 Good Intentions Roadways 所铺，如今破损严重，有着很多危险的坑。在州内的另一个地方，Route 40 的一段路是由 Appian Roadways 四年前铺的，如今仍然状况良好。为了证明自己追求质量，Appian Roadways 最近购买了一台顶级的设备，并且雇用了新的质保经理。因此，我建议雇用 Appian Roadways 来制造我们新购物中心的连接通道。我预测，Appian Roadways 给我们造的道路至少在四年内是不需要再修缮的。

文章结构图

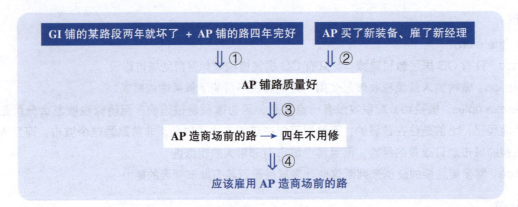

结　论：The company should hire Appian Roadways to construct the access roads for all its new shopping malls.

结论类型：建议型

各步推理分析

①解释型

Signal：通过对比 GI 和 AP 铺的路现在的状态，作者想要将其归结为 AP 注重质量

Inference：GI 铺的某路段两年就坏了，而 AP 铺的路四年完好 ⟹ AP 铺路质量好

Assumption：没有其他解释

Counterexamples：GI 修的路是非常繁华的路段，车流量非常大，而 AP 铺的路使用率非常低，自然不容易造成破损；而且，很有可能 AP 的路有着很好的道路维护，而 GI 的路没有人维护，所以 AP 的路自然保护得好；并且，AP 的路很可能已经经历过修缮；最后，可能 GI 的路是一个非常糟糕的参照物，就算 AP 比 GI 的路好，也不代表 AP 修得真的有多好，只是因为 GI 的路实在是太差了

Evidence：需要排除其他可能的变量对路面质量产生的影响

② 其他

Signal：为了证明 AP 重视质量，作者指出 AP 用了新机器并雇用了新经理

Inference：AP 用了新机器，雇用新经理 ⟹ AP 重视质量

Assumption：用新机器、新经理就意味着公司注重质量

Counterexamples：之前的经理可能非常好，就是工资高，恰恰是因为公司不想在乎质量才换掉了非常合格的员工；可能这种机器虽然非常精良，可是没有人会使用，恰恰不会带来好的质量；可能所有公司都有这样的机器，而 AP 的这种机器比例最低

Evidence：需要知道前后两位经理具体的能力对比；需要知道别的公司是否也有这样优秀的机器

③ 类比类

Signal：谈的本来是之前铺的路，但最终要证明的是未来的路

Inference：AP 重视质量 ⟹ AP 造商场前面的路，则四年不用修

Assumption：AP 修各种路的质量是差不多的；两年来 AP 的水平没有下降

Counterexamples：可能商场前面的路和公路的要求是不一样的，而 AP 并没有修过这种路；可能 AP 这几年员工流动很多，现在已经和过去不一样了

Evidence：需要对比之前的路与未来要铺的路的需求区别；需要知道 AP 这几年的质量变化

④ 建议类

Signal：步骤③的结论，以及最终要建议铺新路雇用 AP

Inference：AP 造商场前面的路，则四年不用修 ⟹ 应该雇用 AP 造商场前面的路

Assumption：没有更好的替代方案；没有副作用

Counterexamples：用 AP 代价高昂，即便质量稍微差一点，两年一修，但可能都不如雇用 AP 来修路代价高；也许还有更好的公司可以雇用

Evidence：需要充分考虑其他可能更有效的解决方案

166

The following appeared as a letter to the editor from the owner of a skate shop in Central Plaza.

"Two years ago the city council voted to prohibit skateboarding in Central Plaza. They claimed that skateboard users were responsible for litter and vandalism that were keeping other visitors from coming to the plaza. In the past two years, however, there has been only a small increase in the number of visitors to Central Plaza, and litter and vandalism are still problematic. Skateboarding is permitted in Monroe Park, however, and there is no problem with litter or vandalism there. In order to restore Central Plaza to its former glory, then, we recommend that the city lift its prohibition on skateboarding in the plaza."

译文

两年前市委投票禁止人们在 Central Plaza 玩滑板。他们认为滑板玩家要为 Plaza 的垃圾和破坏公物现象负责，而这些因素阻碍了人们来 Plaza。但是，在过去两年间，Central Plaza 的游客只有小幅增长，而垃圾和破坏公物问题仍然存在。可是，Monroe Park 就允许玩滑板，并且没有出现垃圾与破坏公物问题。那么，为了将 Central Plaza 恢复到先前的兴旺，我们建议我市取消对 Plaza 滑板的禁令。

文章结构图

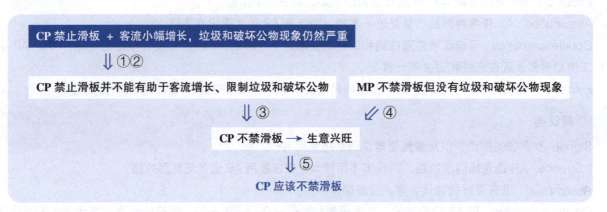

结　　论：The city should lift its prohibition on skateboarding in Central Plaza.
结论类型：建议型

各步推理分析

①解释类

Signal：CP 禁止滑板之后，客流没怎么增加，而作者试图撇清滑板与客流之间的关系
Inference：CP 禁止滑板之后，客流小幅增长 ⟹ CP 禁止滑板并不能有助于客流增长
Assumption：没有其他干扰因素

Counterexamples：首先，客流增加说明滑板对客流有一定副作用；最近经济可能非常不景气，本来就让商店客流难以增加，但若是放开对滑板的禁令，很可能客流会更少；可能是有了禁令，但是禁令执行得不严，人们仍然来玩滑板，恰恰是玩滑板的人造成了这些问题。

② 解释类

Signal：CP 禁止滑板之后，垃圾与破坏公物现象仍然严重，而作者试图撇清滑板与垃圾、破坏公物之间的关系

Inference：CP 禁止滑板之后，垃圾与破坏公物现象仍然严重 $\Rightarrow$ 滑板并不会造成垃圾与破坏公物

Assumption：没有其他解释

Counterexamples：首先，以前的垃圾、破坏公物问题可能更严重，因此，禁止滑板已经带来了效果；其次，很可能滑板禁止之后，这里有了玩其他运动的人，带来了很多垃圾，但这不代表滑板不会造成垃圾问题；而且，可能是有了禁令，但是禁令执行得不严，人们仍然来玩滑板，恰恰是玩滑板的人造成了这些问题。

③ 类比类

Signal：本来谈论 CP 禁止滑板没能帮助生意，但接着直接说允许滑板就能恢复生意

Inference：CP 禁止滑板没能帮助客流增长、限制垃圾和破坏公物现象 $\Rightarrow$ CP 允许玩滑板就能恢复客流

Assumption：滑板能够促进生意

Counterexamples：滑板和生意根本没关系，禁不禁止，生意都不好

④ 类比类

Signal：谈论的本来是 MP，但想证明的是 CP

Inference：MP 不禁滑板没有垃圾 $\Rightarrow$ CP 不禁滑板也没问题

Assumption：公园与广场的情况相似

Counterexamples：公园就是人们游玩的地方，人们不会反感滑板，但是 CP 是人们购物的地方，尤其如果商场比较高档，有人在广场上玩滑板就会让人们不愿意去购物

⑤ 建议类

Signal：步骤③④的结论，以及最终要建议开放对滑板的禁令

Inference：允许玩滑板能恢复客流 $\Rightarrow$ 应该允许玩滑板

Assumption：没有其他解决方案

Counterexamples：开展其他宣传活动，如果是商场，开展促销活动，加大管理以产生更好的用户体验；甚至加强管理，不仅禁止滑板，还遏制一切破坏环境的行为

167

The following appeared as part of an article in a Dillton newspaper.

"In an effort to bring new jobs to Dillton and stimulate the city's flagging economy, Dillton's city council voted last year to lower the city's corporate tax rate by 15 percent; at the same time, the city began offering generous relocation grants to any company that would move to Dillton. Since these changes went into effect, two new factories have opened in Dillton. Although the two factories employ more than 1,000 people, the unemployment rate in Dillton remains unchanged. The only clear explanation for this is that the new factories are staffed with out-of-town workers rather than Dillton residents."

译 文

为了将更多就业岗位带到 Dillton 以及刺激城市萎靡不振的经济，Dillton 市政委员会去年投票降低了该市 15 个百分点的企业税；同时，该市开始为任何愿意迁到 Dillton 的企业支付非常丰厚的搬迁补助。自从这些变化起作用，两家工厂开在了 Dillton。尽管这两家工厂雇用了超过 1 000 名员工，Dillton 的失业率仍然保持不变。对此现象唯一清楚的解释是，这些新工厂雇用了大量外地工人，而不是 Dillton 市民。

文章结构图

两工厂雇用 1 000 人，当地失业率没变

⇩①②③

两工厂雇用的都是外地员工

结　　论：The reason why unemployment rate in Dillton remains unchanged even after two new factories opened there is that the new factories are staffed with out-of-town workers rather than Dillton residents.

结论类型：解释型

推理分析（本文只有一步推理，只能分析该步骤的多个假设）

①**解释类**

Assumption：当地失去工作的人数本不会增加

Counterexamples：当地企业倒闭、裁员更厉害，抵消了两所工厂的贡献

Evidence：需要调查因其他企业倒闭、裁员所造成的工作岗位的减少量

②**解释类**

Assumption：当地总适龄工作人数没有激增

Counterexamples：因为当地适龄人员数量猛增，所以虽然就业的人多了，但是无业的人也多了
Evidence：需要知道当地适龄人员数量的变化

③**解释类**
Assumption：只有雇用外来人员才不会影响当地失业率
Counterexamples：两工厂雇用了大量当地的兼职员工，因此不会显著改变失业率
Evidence：需要知道两工厂雇用的兼职员工的具体比例

> **168** The following appeared in a memo from New Ventures Consulting to the president of HobCo, Inc., a chain of hobby shops.
>
> "Our team has completed its research on suitable building sites for a new HobCo hobby Shop in the city of Grilldon. We discovered that there are currently no hobby shops in southeastern Grilldon. When our researchers conducted a poll of area residents, 88 percent of those who responded indicated that they would welcome the opening of a hobby shop in southeastern Grilldon. Grilldon is in a region of the nation in which the hobby business has increased by 300 percent during the past decade. In addition, Grilldon has a very large population of retirees, a demographic with ample time to devote to hobbies. We therefore recommend that you choose southeastern Grilldon as the site for your next HobCo Hobby Shop. We predict that a shop in this area will draw a steady stream of enthusiastic new HobCo customers."

译　文

我们团队完成了关于 HobCo 模型分店在 Grilldon 城选址的调研。我们发现，目前 Grilldon 东南地区还没有模型店。我们的研究者对该地区的居民做了一项调查，其中 88% 的受访者表示，他们欢迎在 Grilldon 东南地区开一家新模型店。Grilldon 的模型生意在过去十年中增长了 300%。此外，Grilldon 有着巨大的退休人群，这个群体有充足的时间投入模型。因此我们建议你们选择 Grilldon 东南地区作为下一家 HobCo 模型店的地点。我们预测这里开分店会吸引一批稳定的新的 HobCo 客源。

文章结构图

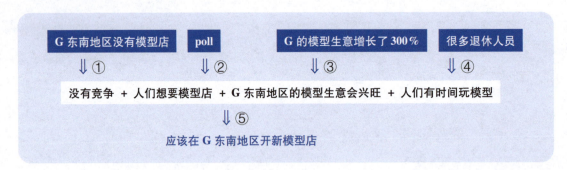

结　　论：HobCo, Inc. should choose southeastern Grilldon as the site for its next HobCo Hobby Shop.
结论类型：建议型

各步推理分析

①其他

Signal：作者指出 G 东南地区目前没有模型店，暗示新开的店将没有竞争者

Inference：G 东南地区没有模型店 ⟹ 新店没有竞争者

Assumption：必须有专门的模型店才能竞争；没有其他模型店计划在这里开店；其他地区的模型店不会形成竞争

Counterexamples：有一些模型俱乐部，还有一些大型商场都有模型销售，会遇到竞争；其次，很可能还有其他公司也觊觎这个市场，正在开设分店；G 可能是个小城，就算模型店不在 G 东南地区，其他地区到这里也不远，其他地方的模型店已经在这里产生了很大影响力

Evidence：需要调查其他非专营店的模型销售情况；需要知道是否有其他地区也将开设模型店

② 证词类

Signal：poll

Inference：调查当中 88% 的人欢迎模型店 ⟹ 人们普遍想要模型店

Assumption：调查有代表性

Counterexamples：喜欢的人才愿意参与调查访谈，其实当地根本就没有多少模型爱好者

Evidence：需要知道该调查是如何选择样本的，从而可以判断其代表性

③ 数据类，类比类

Signal：G 的模型生意增长了 300%，以及谈的本来是 G，但最终要讨论的是 G 东南地区

Inference：G 的模型生意增长了 300% ⟹ G 东南地区的模型生意会兴旺

Assumption：300% 的增长幅度很大；G 东南地区与其他区域经济状况相当

Counterexamples：很可能本来基本就没有模型需求，即便增长了 300% 也不会有多少，根本不足以维持模型店的生意；其次，很可能 G 东南地区是该城市最贫穷的地方，人们根本不会有闲钱来玩模型

Evidence：需要知道实际的模型需求量；需要知道 G 地区人们实际的消费能力

④ 其他

Signal：作者指出这里退休人员多，并指出他们会有很多时间玩模型

Inference：退休人员多 ⟹ 人们会有时间玩模型

Assumption：退休的人就会有充足时间玩模型

Counterexamples：这些人首先经济上保守，其次大部分对于模型并没有任何喜好，他们更会投入一些廉价的娱乐活动中去

Evidence：需要直接调查退休人员对模型玩具的喜好

⑤ 其他

Signal：步骤①②③④的结论，想要证明该在这里开店

Inference：没有竞争 + 人们想要模型店 + G 东南地区的模型生意会兴旺 + 人们有时间玩模型 ⟹ 该在 G 东南地区开模型店

Assumption：没有其他方案

Counterexamples：也许这个城市其他地区更适合开店，或者有别的更适合的城市开分店

Evidence：需要充分考虑其他可能更有效的解决方案

Part 5 Argument 题库逐题精析

169. The following appeared in a newsletter published by the Appleton school district.

"In a recent study more than 5,000 adolescents were asked how often they ate meals with their families. Almost 30 percent of the teens said they ate at least seven meals per week with their families. Furthermore, according to the same survey, teens who reported having the most family meals per week were also the ones least likely to have tried illegal drugs, tobacco, and alcohol. Family meals were also associated with lower rates of problems such as low grades in school, low self-esteem, and depression. We therefore recommend that families have as many meals together as possible. We predict that doing so will greatly benefit adolescents and turn troubled teens away from bad behaviors."

思路相近题目：171

译 文

在最近的一项研究中，有超过5 000名青少年被问到他们与家人一起用餐的频率。差不多30%的少年说他们一周和家人一起用餐至少7次。而且，根据同一份调查，那些最常与家人一起用餐的少年也是最不太可能吸毒、抽烟、酗酒的。与家人一起用餐还与其他一些问题的低发生率相关，比如学业成绩差、自尊心差、抑郁。因此，我们建议家庭成员尽可能多一起用餐。我们预测，这种做法会显著帮助青少年，并帮助问题少年们改正不良行为。

文章结构图

```
调查中说常和家人一起吃饭的孩子通常是不吸毒、不抽烟、不酗酒的孩子
                    ⇓ ①
常和家人一起吃饭的孩子一般不吸毒、不抽烟、不酗酒 + 常和家人一起吃饭的孩子其他问题也少
                    ⇓ ②
         常和家人吃饭 → 孩子出现以上问题少
                    ⇓ ③
         常和家人一起吃饭有利于孩子，且能拯救问题少年
                    ⇓ ④
              家人应该尽可能多在一起吃饭
```

结　　论：We therefore recommend that families have as many meals together as possible.
结论类型：建议型

📝 各步推理分析

① 证词类

Signal：study, said, survey, reported

Inference：调查中说常和家人一起吃饭的孩子通常是不吸毒、不抽烟、不酗酒的孩子 ⟹ 常和家人一起吃饭的孩子一般不吸毒、不抽烟、不酗酒

Assumption：调查可靠，孩子会如实汇报自己和家人一起吃饭的频率

Counterexamples：问问题的人如果表现出对和家人一起吃饭的倾向性，则参加调查的孩子可能为了给别人留下好感而不说实话

Evidence：需要直接调查这些家庭一起聚餐的频率，排除说假话的可能性

② 解释型

Signal：作者试图建立在家吃饭与各种问题少之间的关系

Inference：常和家人一起吃饭的孩子一般不吸毒、不抽烟、不酗酒 + 常和家人一起吃饭的孩子其他问题也少 ⟹ 常和家人一起吃饭可以减少孩子出现以上问题

Assumption：没有其他解释

Counterexamples：很可能在家吃饭与问题少是同一个因素造成的独立结果，比如，可能家庭成员关系好，所以大家愿意在一起吃，也因为家庭成员关系好，所以孩子各方面发展都比较好；类似的，家里的经济条件也可能有作用，家里经济条件差，孩子发展可能受影响，而因为家里缺钱，所以父母可能总需要在外面工作，不能保证与孩子一起吃饭；除此之外，可能不是因为家人一起吃饭，才让孩子优秀，很可能是因为孩子比较优秀，父母才更愿意和他们一起吃饭

Evidence：需要考察其他可能解释该现象的因素

③ 类比型

Signal：讨论的本来是吸毒、抽烟、酗酒的问题，以及成绩差、自尊心差、抑郁等问题的预防，但最后要证明的却是整体上有利于青少年，以及拯救问题少年

Inference：常和家人一起吃饭可以减少孩子出现以上问题 ⟹ 常和家人一起吃饭有利于孩子成长，且能拯救问题少年

Assumption：常和家人一起吃饭有利于孩子成长，且能拯救问题少年

Counterexamples：首先，吸毒、抽烟、酗酒、成绩差、自尊心差、抑郁等问题不代表所有青少年的问题，以上证据不能表明在家吃与其他问题的联系，比如娇惯、缺乏独立性等问题；其次，在家吃也许可以预防这些问题的出现，但对于已经出现这些问题的孩子，在家吃是否可以帮助解决这些问题，以上证据不足以回答

Evidence：需要具体调查家庭聚餐对孩子各方面问题所产生的影响，并且要调查该效果是预防性的还是治疗性的

④ 建议型

Signal：基于和家人一起吃饭有利于孩子成长，且能拯救问题青少年，得出最后建议

Inference：常和家人一起吃饭有利于孩子，且能拯救问题少年 ⟹ 应该尽可能多在一起吃

Assumption：和家人一起吃饭次数越多效果越好；没有其他替代方案

Counterexamples：和家人聚餐有利于孩子们的心理健康可能是因为有了家人足够的陪伴，而这不代表陪伴越多越好，因此没有必要追求每一餐都在一起吃；其次，这也意味着增加陪伴的其他方法也许可以带来同样的效果，比如一起出游、一起参加娱乐活动、一起读书，等等

Evidence：需要充分考察其他可能更有效的解决方案

170 The following appeared in a health newsletter.

"Nosinia is an herb that many users report to be as effective as prescription medications at fighting allergy symptoms. Researchers recently compared Nosinia to a placebo in 95 men and women with seasonal allergies to ragweed pollen. Participants in the study reported that neither Nosinia nor the placebo offered significant relief. However, for the most severe allergy symptoms, the researchers reported that Nosinia was more effective than the placebo in providing relief. Furthermore, at the end of the study, participants given Nosinia were more likely than participants given a placebo to report feeling healthier. We therefore recommend using Nosinia to help with your severe allergy symptoms."

译 文

很多使用者报告说 Nosinia 这种草药和处方药一样能有效地对抗过敏症状。研究者最近对比了 95 名对 ragweed 花粉有季节性过敏的男女，看他们使用 Nosinia 和使用安慰剂后有什么不同。研究参与者们报告说 Nosinia 与安慰剂都不能带来显著的缓解。但是，对于有严重过敏症状的对象，研究者报告说 Nosinia 比安慰剂更能有效地缓解症状。而且，在实验结束时，使用了 Nosinia 的参与者比使用安慰剂的人感觉更健康的概率更高。我们因此推荐大家使用 Nosinia 来帮助应对严重过敏的症状。

文章结构图

根据受试者的报告，使用 N 后比使用 P 后得到更多缓解，感觉更健康
⇓ ①
受试者使用 N 后比使用 P 后症状更轻，更健康
⇓ ②
是 N 的作用让受试者症状更轻、更健康
⇓ ③
N 能缓解所有严重过敏问题
⇓ ④
严重过敏患者应该使用 N

结　　论：We therefore recommend using Nosinia to help with your severe allergy symptoms.
结论类型：**建议型**

各步推理分析

①证词类，数据类

Signal：report，more effective，more likely

Inference：根据受试者的报告，使用 N 后比使用 P 后得到更多缓解，感觉更健康 ⟹ 受试者使用 N 后比使用 P 后更有可能好转

Assumption：两组人群的体验有足够明显的差别；感到缓解和更健康的感觉能够体现过敏症状好转

Counterexamples：作者只说 more relief，more likely，但没有说 how much more，因为一共只有不到 100 名受试者，也许大部分人根本没有严重过敏，而其中得到缓解的人比例可能更低，也许使用 N 后症状得到缓解的人也就比使用安慰剂后好转的人多几个，那么这种区别就完全是误差范围之内的，没有什么实际意义；其次，感到更健康可能根本不是关于过敏上的报告，而可能是精神更好、更兴奋等方面，这完全可能是 N 所产生的神经刺激的结果，但过敏问题仍然严重

②解释类

Signal：作者想要建立服用 N 与症状缓解之间的因果关系

Inference：受试者使用 N 后比使用 P 后症状更轻、更健康 ⟹ 是 N 的作用让受试者症状更轻、更健康

Assumption：没有其他可能解释

Counterexamples：由于作者只说了服用 N 后有更大概率好转，因此很有可能不是每个人都好转，也并不是每个使用了安慰剂的人都没好转，也许作者调查所有好转的人，无论是服用了 N，还是只使用了安慰剂，他们可能会有一些根本上的共性，比如年龄、性别、身体机能等因素，而这些因素才是真正好转的原因

③类比类

Signal：实验中的人都是对 ragweed 过敏的人，但是结论想要证明的是所有严重过敏的人

Inference：是 N 的作用让受试者症状更轻、更健康 ⟹ N 能缓解所有严重过敏问题

Assumption：N 对所有类型的严重过敏有着同样疗效

Counterexamples：很可能不同过敏的机理不完全一样，因此 N 并不能够缓解其他过敏

④ 建议类

Signal：作者试图建议所有严重过敏患者使用 N

Inference：N 能缓解所有严重过敏问题 ⟹ 严重过敏患者应该使用 N

Assumption：能够准确区分严重与非严重过敏；N 不会有更严重的副作用；没有其他更有效的疗法

Counterexamples：首先，文章中只提到了，N 以及安慰剂对过敏的正面作用都不明显，而对严重过敏，N 比安慰剂效果更好，那就存在一种可能性，即 N 对非严重过敏其实可能还会产生加剧的作用，因此意味着，就算 N 对严重过敏有缓解作用，但可能对非严重过敏会雪上加霜，那么人们要服用 N，必须明确判断自己是否属于严重过敏，而文章中没有给出任何明确的判断标准；其次，药物研究必须报告药物的副作用，就算 N 能缓解过敏，但可能会造成其他严重的问题；最后，N 只是比安慰剂略微有作用，但很可能早都有很多过敏药能显著缓解症状，那过敏时正确的做法显然不是去吃 N 了

解密GRE写作
论证思维

Part 6　Argument 精选范文

Part 6 Argument 精选范文

> **1** Woven baskets characterized by a particular distinctive pattern have previously been found only in the immediate vicinity of the prehistoric village of Palea, and therefore were believed to have been made only by the Palean people. Recently, however, archaeologists discovered such a "Palean" basket in Lithos, an ancient village across the Brim River from Palea. The Brim River is very deep and broad, and so the ancient Paleans could have crossed it only by boat, and no Palean boats have been found. Thus it follows that the so-called Palean baskets were not uniquely Palean.
>
> Write a response in which you discuss what specific evidence is needed to evaluate the argument and explain how the evidence would weaken or strengthen the argument.

Sample Essay A: Outstanding

In this argument, the speaker concludes that the so-called Palean baskets were not uniquely Palean. Her conclusion is mainly based on the discovery of such a basket in Lithos, a village separated by a deep and broad river from Palea. According to her reasoning, since no Palean boats have been found, there left but one explanation for this basket—it must not have originated in Palea. Unfortunately, her argument suffers from several unwarranted assumptions that if not supplemented with further evidence, would seriously undermine its cogency.

To begin with, even if the Brim River is now wide and deep, it does not necessarily mean that the ancient people would not have been able to cross it without a boat. Apparently, the author assumes that the river's physical property has not changed drastically over the years and that there were no alternative ways for people to reach the other side. However, perhaps the river used to be quite shallow or did not flow through this area thousands of years ago, and it was only after a violent earthquake or some other geological processes that it became the way it is now. If so, ancient Paleans did not need to cross anything to get to Lithos. It is also possible that the ancient people had other methods to overcome the natural obstacle. For example, they might have crossed the river in winter, when it was completely frozen. Or they might go around the source of the river, if it was not forbiddingly distant. Therefore, more evidence is needed with regard to the river's geography and to local climate information. In fact, an ancient map detailing this region would tremendously help clarify all ambiguities.

Furthermore, even if no Palean boat has been discovered, it does not entail that the Paleans did not have boats to use. Obviously, the underlying rationale behind the author's reasoning is that had there existed Palean boats, evidence would have been unearthed indicating their existence. However, it is possible that archaeological excavation in this region is at its initial stage, so even if no boats have been unearthed so far, they may be discovered later. In addition, made of wood, ancient boats generally decay really fast, so it wouldn't be realistic to find boats in the first place, even if Palea did have boats back then. To really prove that there did not exist any Palean boats, the author should fully evaluate the Paleans' technological ability. If the Paleans had strong craftsmanship and scientific understanding, then it was quite likely that they were able to make boats. Also, indirect evidence from literature, arts and artifacts might also reveal relevant information. For example, documents or novels recording trade between the two neighboring villages would certainly undermine the author's argument.

Last, building on the implication that the Paleans had no boats to cross the deep and broad Brim River, the author suggests that the basket discovered in Lithos could not have come from Palea. However, she has not mentioned whether there are other channels through which the baskets can reach the other side. Perhaps merchants from other regions could use their own boats to deliver these Palean goods elsewhere, whether or not Palea itself had boats. Thus, archaeological or documentary evidence pointing to these possibilities would also serve to challenge the author's argument.

To sum up, through a thorough examination of the author's argument, it is clear that the current evidence is insufficient for a robust conclusion as to where the basket came from. Though the basket might in the end remain non-Palean, her reasoning so far fails to lend adequate support to that statement.

Sample Essay B: Good

The author of the passage concludes that the so-called Palean baskets were not uniquely Palean. Her conclusion is mainly based on the following pieces of evidence. First, a basket similar to the Palean basket was discovered in Lithos. Second, Lithos was separated from Palea by a deep and broad river. Third, no Palean boats have been discovered. But she does not provide enough evidence to fully support the conclusion.

First, she mentions that the Brim River is very deep and broad, so she infers that the ancient Paleans could have crossed it only by boat. She clearly assumes that there is no other method to cross a deep and broad river. However, perhaps the river became frozen in winter, so people could walk across it. Or, people could go around the river's source. Thus, without more evidence to exclude these possibilities, the people could still be able to take the basket from Palea to lithos without having to take a boat.

Second, she also mentions that no Palean boats have been found, implying that the Paleans did not have boats. She clearly assumes that if there were boats, they should have been found by now. However, ancient boats could have been made of wood, so they decayed fast. Consequently, people can't find any direct evidence for their existence, even if they existed. Therefore, the author needs to rely on indirect evidence to exclude the existence of Palean boats.

Finally, even if Paleans had no boats, and the baskets could only reach the other side of the river by boats, it does not necessarily mean that the basket discovered in Lithos did not come from Palea. Perhaps the basket was still made by Paleans. Some Paleans might have travelled to Lithos, and they made the basket in Lithos. Also, people from other places could have had boats. They could have used their boats to carry the baskets from Palea to Lithos. Thus, the author needs to provide more evidence to rule out this possibility; otherwise, she cannot firmly conclude that the baskets were not uniquely Palean.

范文点评

Outstanding 范文与 Good 范文都指出了文章的三个核心推理步骤：

(1) 河宽而深 ⟹ 只能坐船过河；

(2) 没有找到船 ⟹ 没有船；

(3) 只能坐船过河 + 没有船 ⟹ 篮子不属于 L。

两篇文章的首要区别是在反例的全面性上，尤其针对步骤（1）和（2），Outstanding 范文指出了比 Good 范文更丰富的反例。

其次，本题要求讨论作者需要补充的证据，Good 范文只是说明作者要补充证据来处理以上反例，但 Outstanding 范文指出了具体的需要的证据甚至是获取该证据的方式。

两篇范文的语言都做到了表意清楚，基本没有影响读者理解文章意思的语法问题。

7　The following is a recommendation from the Board of Directors of Monarch Books.

"We recommend that Monarch Books open a café in its store. Monarch, having been in business at the same location for more than twenty years, has a large customer base because it is known for its wide selection of books on all subjects. Clearly, opening the café would attract more customers. Space could be made for the café by discontinuing the children's book section, which will probably become less popular given that the most recent national census indicated a significant decline in the percentage of the population under age ten. Opening a café will allow Monarch to attract more customers and better compete with Regal Books, which recently opened its own café."

Write a response in which you discuss what questions would need to be answered in order to decide whether the recommendation is likely to have the predicted result. Be sure to explain how the answers to these questions would help to evaluate the recommendation.

Sample Essay A: Outstanding

　　In this article, the speaker recommends that Monarch Books (MB) replace its children's book section with a café in order to attract customers and to compete with Regal Books (RB), which recently opened its own café. The decision to get rid of the children's book section is mainly based on a recent national census that seems to indicate a gloomy future for children's books. However, the facts presented by the author are neither sufficient to call a death sentence for the children's book department nor to generate optimism with respect to the future of a new café.

　　For starters, the author has not provided any strong evidence as to why opening a new café can help with attracting potential clients. True, MB's competitor RB has recently started its own café. However, we have no idea whether RB's café has contributed to an increase in sales. If RB's café turns out to be a complete failure, then there are probably fewer reasons why MB should start its own café. Also, even if RB's decision proves to be prudent, the author has not provided enough clues for the readers to draw a fair comparison between the two bookstores. Maybe there is no resting area in RB, so when RB's readers want to sit down and take a good look at some books, they can't. In contrast, perhaps not only are there many cafés and restaurants near MB, but MB itself already has sufficient resting spots. Consequently, a new café wouldn't offer its visitors anything that it currently lacks. In short, the author has to answer why specifically she believes a new café can help with increasing customers, or else her motion only sounds overly impetuous.

　　Now, assuming that there is a need to install a new café, where would be the ideal location? The author clearly believes that the space of the current children's book section is the right spot: since according to a recent national census, there is a dramatic decline in the percentage of the population under 10, children's books might become less popular. Unfortunately, behind this tenuous line of reasoning are several crucial questions open to debate. First, it is unclear whether the local child population is decreasing as the national census suggests. It is possible that MB's area is among the few places that are actually seeing a rising number of child population because its superb health care and school system is attracting more young parents to raise their children here. Clearly, the readers would need to see more specific demographic data regarding this particular region.

Second, the author also fails to establish a firm link between child population and the popularity of children's books. How profitable these books are going to be is determined by factors beyond child population. Specifically, it is crucial to know about changes in local household income. If, following an economic boom, many families have more money at their disposal, then even if there are fewer families, each family might spend a lot more on children's books. Also, perhaps because of growing competition in the job market, companies now place higher demand on job seekers' qualification, and consequently, local families care more about their children's education, which in turn can also boost the sales of children's books. Overall, since no data regarding average families' yearly expenses on children's reading materials has been offered, the author's reasoning is so far quite untenable.

Finally, assuming that children's books will not be as profitable as before, it does not directly entail that the children's book section can be removed. It is unknown how big a proportion the sales of children's books takes up out of the stores' overall sales. It is quite possible that even after a sales drop, the children's book section is still going to be the star section of the whole store. Simply put, the author needs to offer data comparing the projected revenue of the children's book department with other departments. Without this information, it remains open which area should give way to the new café.

In sum, perhaps a new café is indeed the way to go for MB, and perhaps the children's book section is the one to cut. Still, the information provided by the author is insufficient to support these recommendations. There is just too much uncertainty to clear up before a robust conclusion can be reached.

Sample Essay B: Good

In this argument, the author recommends Monarch Books to open a café in its book store. However, the evidence is insufficient.

First, given that Monarch has been in business for many years and thus has accumulated a large customer base, the author concludes that the café will attract more customers. In this reasoning, the arguer assumes that the store's reputation or large consumer base in book selling can help its coffee business. Yet, in reality, books and food are totally different things. The book store has accumulated lots of consumers because of a wide selection of books on all subjects. However, it has no experience in restaurant operation at all. How can having various books promote food sales? In fact, people who go to the café may doubt its professionality and choose other more professional cafés. The arguer should provide more information to answer this question.

Second, we can infer from the argument that there is no available space for a café. And the author suggests to discontinue the children's book section because the most recent national census indicated a significant decline in the percentage of the population under age ten. Apparently, the author assumes that the national census can be applied to the store's location. However, the general census is the average trend of the nation, and this particular location may not necessarily conform to the general trend. For example, there may be many primary schools in this area. If so, the population under ten in this area is not decreasing, and discontinuing the children's book section would generate great loss to Monarch Books. Thus, the author should provide the specific characteristics of its location, like how many primary schools, to determine whether the national census can be applied or not.

Finally, the author asserts that a café will allow Monarch to better compete with Regal Books, which recently opened its own café. In this assertion, the author assumes that Regal Books' café gives it competitive advantages. However, Regal Books may not have hired professional baristas. This could lead to bad taste of its coffee and snacks. In turn, the bad taste of could discourage many consumers, possibly disappointing many loyal consumers of the Regal Books. Thus, the presence of the café may not give Regal Books any competitive advantages. Then, there is no reason for Monarch to open a café to compete with Regal. Instead, Monarch should not follow Regal's example and should not open a café in its book store. So, the author should provide the information about the operational situation of the café in Regal.

In short, the author should provide more evidence to address the questions and concerns above to help me to evaluate the recommendation.

范文点评

两篇范文最大的区别就在于讨论步骤的深度上。比如，关于原文对可以关闭儿童图书区域这部分的讨论，Good 范文只意识到全国趋势不见得反映当地趋势；但 Outstanding 范文就非常敏锐地意识到，除了全国与当地趋势的差别，还可能存在儿童人口数量与童书需求之间的差别，甚至是童书需求减弱仍然不能意味着童书部门可以删除。事实上，Outstanding 文章通常就体现在对每步讨论的挖掘深度上，而不体现在它挖掘了更多的步骤。

两篇范文的语言都做到了表意清楚，基本没有影响读者理解文章意思的语法问题。

> Twenty years ago, Dr. Field, a noted anthropologist, visited the island of Tertia. Using an observation-centered approach to studying Tertian culture, he concluded from his observations that children in Tertia were reared by an entire village rather than by their own biological parents. Recently another anthropologist, Dr. Karp, visited the group of islands that includes Tertia and used the interview-centered method to study child-rearing practices. In the interviews that Dr. Karp conducted with children living in this group of islands, the children spent much more time talking about their biological parents than about other adults in the village. Dr. Karp decided that Dr. Field's conclusion about Tertian village culture must be invalid. Some anthropologists recommend that to obtain accurate information on Tertian child-rearing practices, future research on the subject should be conducted via the interview-centered method.
>
> Write a response in which you discuss what questions would need to be answered in order to decide whether the recommendation and the argument on which it is based are reasonable. Be sure to explain how the answers to these questions would help to evaluate the recommendation.

Sample Essay A: Outstanding

According to the article, some anthropologists recommend that all future research on Tertian child-rearing practices be conducted via the interview-centered method. The conclusion mainly rests on Dr. Karp's contention that the interview-centered method is superior to the observation-centered approach, a judgment that in turn relies on a comparison between Dr. Karp's and Dr. Field's respective conclusions about Tertian culture. Unfortunately, the evidence cited in the article is insufficient for the readers to generate a clear preference between the two approaches, and a series of questions should be addressed to really corroborate the anthropologists' recommendation.

For starters, based on her observation, Dr. Field concluded that Tertian children were raised by the entire village, while Dr. Karp's interview implied that, because children on the group of islands including Tertia spent more time talking about their birthparents, Tertian children must be raised by their biological parents. This apparent difference led Dr. Karp to deny Dr. Field's conclusion, but there are three implicit steps where she should have been more critical. First, there is not necessarily a connection between how frequent a child talked about someone and who that child was raised by. It is possible that while she was raised by the whole village, she still recognized her parents, and was emotionally more attached to them, making them more often the theme of her speech. Thus, the interviewer had better propose the direct question of who brought these children up, rather than look for indirect clues.

Second, it is not known whether there are differences between the culture on Tertia and the cultures on adjacent islands. Dr. Karp investigated a group of islands including Tertia, but she did not specifically state if Tertian children responded the way children from other islands did. It is possible that the children from Tertia were among the few interviewees who did not display a sharp discrepancy between the lengths of conversations devoted to their parents and to other adults. To firmly reach a conclusion about Tertia, she should really focus on just Tertia, rather than include other islands that are not necessarily related.

Third, assuming that Dr. Karp was right about Tertian child-rearing culture, it does not instantly contradict Dr. Field's position. After all, Dr. Field's observation was conducted two decades ago, whereas Dr. Karp's interview just took place. It is simply unknown whether there has been a drastic cultural shift during this time. Perhaps within the past twenty years, Tertia had more contact with modern civilization, so it gradually gave up its earlier gregarious customs. As a result, it was only recently that nuclear families became the dominant trend, reconciling the apparent conflict between the two studies. Based on these three aspects, the information in the article is insufficient for the readers to prefer one study result to the other.

Now, building on the implication that Dr. Karp's study was the accurate one, other anthropologists are quick to apply the interview-centered method to future research on Tertian child-rearing culture. Unfortunately, this application does not stand on firm ground either, and there are a couple of important questions to address. First, no evidence is provided as to whether Dr. Karp's study was successful because of the very methodology it adopted. Maybe the interview-centered method is neither superior nor inferior to the observation-centered method. It was perhaps just because Dr. Karp was more careful, patient, and thorough that her interview went smoothly; in contrast, Dr. Field might have been rash in conducting her study, basing her results on just a few observations. Had Dr. Karp chosen to observe, her meticulousness might have rewarded her with the same correct result as well. Thus, a detailed analysis of the two scholars' research processes is needed to further evaluate the validity of the two different methodologies.

Second, because of the apparent success of Dr. Karp's study, the anthropologists assume that the interview-centered approach will always be the better method for every future study on Tertian child-rearing culture. Unfortunately, it remains questionable whether all important information can be obtained by interview. Perhaps it is true that Tertian children were very honest in their interviews, so their answers were extremely helpful to the scholars. However, long isolated from the outside world, adults in Tertia might be very wary of, and thus hostile towards intruders. If so, their responses, if they are willing to respond at all, could be insincere or incomplete, thus making interviews fruitless. Since child-rearing studies need to focus not just on children, but also on parents, this possibility would mean that some other methods have to be adopted to supplement interviews.

Overall, the article has failed to successfully prove that Dr. Field's conclusion is not as trustworthy as Dr. Karp's conclusion, that the interview-centered approach was the key to Dr. Karp's "success", or that Dr. Karp's "success" can be replicated in future research. The anthropologists need to look for further information and resolve all the crucial questions mentioned in order to make their recommendation more convincing.

Sample Essay B: Good

In this article, several anthropologists recommend that future research on Tertian child-rearing practices use the interview-centered method. The recommendation is based on Dr. Karp's recent research, which seems to indicate that the interview-centered method is more reliable than the observation-centered approach used by Dr. Field. However, important questions are left unaddressed, so the argument is not as persuasive as the author intended.

First, it is unclear whether Dr. Karp's conclusion is more believable than Dr. Field's. Dr. Karp's main evidence is that the local children talked about their parents more than about other adults, so she implies that this is because they were reared by their biological parents, not by the entire village. However, there could be other reasons. Do the children speak more about their birthparents just because they are emotionally closer? If they are genetically related, chances are high that they are similar, and more likely to establish a bond. Without addressing this possibility, she cannot simply infer that the children are raised by their birthparents.

Second, because of her research results, Dr. Karp decided that Dr. Field's conclusion must be wrong. However, couldn't they both be correct? After all, the two studies were separated by 20 years. A lot of things can have happened during that time. The local traditions might have changed vastly. It is possible that 20 years ago, children were generally supported by a whole tribe, but today individual families have become the popular trend. Thus, it is important to look into any changes in local convention during this time, before quickly rejecting Dr. Field's study.

Last, because of Dr. Karp's conclusion, other anthropologists now recommend that all future research adopt the interview-centered method. However, are there any other good approaches to adopt besides the two mentioned? Even if not, is the interview-centered method suitable for every study? Readers don't know, and no further evidence is provided. Unless these researchers can demonstrate that the interview-centered approach is always the best choice, their recommendation may actually hurt future investigations.

Overall, the information in the passage is lacking. The aforementioned questions have to be answered before these researchers can successfully show that their advice is worth following.

范文点评

Outstanding 范文非常全面且有条理地讨论了多个论证步骤：

（1）Dr. Karp 访谈中各岛孩子讨论双亲更频繁 ⟹ 各岛孩子由双亲抚养；

（2）各岛孩子由双亲抚养 ⟹ T 岛孩子由双亲抚养；

（3）T 岛孩子由双亲抚养 + Dr. Field 的观察显示 T 岛孩子由全村抚养 ⟹ Dr. Field 基于观察的结论是错的；

（4）Dr. Field 基于观察的结论是错的 ⟹ 研究方法的不同导致 Dr. Field 的失败，Dr. Karp 的成功；

（5）研究方法的不同导致 Dr. Field 的失败，Dr. Karp 的成功 ⟹ 未来所有对 T 岛的育儿文化研究都应该使用访谈法。

与 Outstanding 范文相比，Good 范文只讨论了其中的（1）（3）（5）步骤。显然，Outstanding 范文对原文论证结构的理解要比 Good 范文更深入。

不仅如此，Outstanding 范文对每一步可能是反例的讨论都十分完整，而 Good 范文对步骤（5）的讨论明显欠缺深度，它只是指出 Dr. Karp 的访谈成功不意味着未来所有研究都可以用访谈法，但却没有指出未来研究和 Dr. Karp 研究可能存在的区别。

两篇范文的语言都做到了表意清楚，基本没有影响读者理解文章意思的语法问题。

> **13** In an attempt to improve highway safety, Prunty County last year lowered its speed limit from 55 to 45 miles per hour on all county highways. But this effort has failed: the number of accidents has not decreased, and, based on reports by the highway patrol, many drivers are exceeding the speed limit. Prunty County should instead undertake the same kind of road improvement project that Butler County completed five years ago: increasing lane widths, resurfacing rough highways, and improving visibility at dangerous intersections. Today, major Butler County roads still have a 55 mph speed limit, yet there were 25 percent fewer reported accidents in Butler County this past year than there were five years ago.
>
> Write a response in which you discuss what specific evidence is needed to evaluate the argument and explain how the evidence would weaken or strengthen the argument.

Sample Essay A: Outstanding

The article concludes that Prunty County (PC) has failed in its effort to improve highway safety by lowering its speed limit from 55 to 45 miles per hour on all county highways, and instead suggests that a better alternative is to duplicate the policy of Butler County (BC) from five years ago by undertaking the same kind of road improvement project. Unfortunately, the author's line of reasoning is too tenuous to warrant these statements, or to fully corroborate her recommendation, she should provide additional evidence.

For starters, the author cites the accident rate and reports from highway patrol to prove that PC's earlier efforts turned out to be futile. However, neither lends strong support to that conclusion. First, even though the number of accidents has not decreased, the intensity of the accidents might have. After all, even if one crashes a car, it is less lethal to crash it at a lower speed than at a higher speed. Since the author provides no information regarding how many serious accidents there were before or after the change of policy, it is still quite possible that the reduced speed limit has made driving safer than before.

Second, even though drivers are allegedly speeding, the author has not provided more accurate data as to how many drivers are exceeding the speed limit nor by how much. It is possible that much fewer drivers are transgressing compared with the past, even though there are still many transgressions. More importantly, it is possible that drivers generally drive faster than required, but by a fixed margin. For example, if they normally exceed the speed limit by 10 mph, then before the speed limit change, they would have tended to drive at 65 mph, but now they would run at 55 mph. Under this scenario, they are still driving at a safer speed than before. Thus, instead of just relying on this vague report from the highway patrol, what the author really needs to do is offer more accurate numbers regarding the average speed at which people drive before and after the change of speed limit.

Moreover, granted that setting a cap on driving speed is a useless policy, undertaking a road improvement project is not necessarily a superior alternative. All the evidence the author relies on is experience from BC 5 years ago, and there are serious loopholes. First, to show that BC's experience is worth emulating, the author mentions that there were 25 percent fewer reported accidents in BC this past year than five years ago. However, perhaps because of shortage of funding, the police force is more short-staffed than before. Or perhaps insurance companies have started charging more, making drivers generally less inclined to report minor accidents, in order to avoid further rises in insurance cost. Either way, there could be just as many accidents, but they are just less frequently reported. It is also possible that because of worsening environment or loss of jobs, many BC residents have relocated elsewhere, causing its number of drivers to drop by a large margin. In this situation, the ratio of the number of accidents to the number of residents has perhaps increased, and driving has not been made safer.

Second, assuming that it has become less dangerous to drive on a BC road, it is unclear whether this is due to the road improvement project of five years ago. The author offers no information regarding other possible efforts the BC government might have made which could have contributed to better driving. Perhaps they set up more surveillance cameras and police officers to monitor the roads; they might have increased penalties for speeding and drunk driving; or they might also have raised the bar for passing drivers' tests. Also, the comparison is simply between 5 years ago and last year, and no data has been offered regarding the years in between. Perhaps the seemingly encouraging results of last year were just a result of an abnormally benign winter, with no snow and consequently no ice on roads. Without long term data ruling out these competing factors, it is too hasty to attribute BC's improvement entirely to the road improvement project.

Third, even if BC's efforts paid off, it does not necessarily mean that if PC just imitates the measure, the same results will ensue. The author has not taken into account possible differences the two counties might be facing. Perhaps 5 years ago, BC's main problems were that their roads were rough and narrow, and intersections were often visually blocked, so the road improvement project was a vital decision that helped solve its most urgent problems. In contrast, if most of PC's traffic accidents come from drunk driving, inexperienced drivers, chaotic traffic signals, and so on, then the same road improvement project is quite unlikely to make much difference. Clearly, the author needs to compare the specific problems PC's drivers are facing to those BC encountered years ago. Without sufficient similarities, the proposal to duplicate BC's model is unlikely to yield the same results.

Overall, the information presented in the article is insufficient for the readers to believe that a road improvement project is going to be a better idea than lowering the speed limit. To fully evaluate the two measures, more evidence is desperately needed.

Sample Essay B: Good

The author suggests that Prunty County (PC) undertake the same kind of road improvement project that Butler County (BC) completed five years ago: increasing lane widths, resurfacing rough highways, and improving visibility at dangerous intersections. However, the evidence provided in the passage is insufficient to corroborate this suggestion.

First, the author believes that PC should not lower its speed limits, because last year, the decision to lower speed limits from 55 to 45 miles per hour failed. Her evidence is that the number of accidents has not decreased since, and that highway patrol reported that many drivers are exceeding the speed limit. Clearly, she assumes that the seriousness of these accidents has not changed much, and that the number of drivers exceeding the speed limit has not dropped. However, perhaps there are fewer serious accidents now, so the new regulation has worked. Also, the author does not mention how many drivers used to exceed speed limit. Perhaps there were a lot more in the past. More information is needed to rule out these possibilities.

Second, the author recommends that PC learn from BC, because after BC adopted its road improvement project 5 years ago, there were 25 percent fewer reported accidents this past year than 5 years ago, assuming that this last year was representative, and that all accidents are reported. However, what about the five years in between? Perhaps this last year was an anomaly. Also, maybe there is insufficient police force, so many accidents went unnoticed. The author needs to offer additional information to rule out these possibilities.

Last, the author assumes that PC today and BC five years ago are similar. However, no such information is offered. The two places could be drastically different in size and population. They could have totally different traffic regulations, and their road conditions could also be dissimilar. These could all cause the efforts to fail in PC, even though they worked in BC 5 years ago.

All in all, the author needs to supply the aforementioned information. Otherwise, her conclusion cannot persuade readers.

范文点评

两篇文章最显著的区别在于 Outstanding 范文比 Good 范文更深入地讨论了每个步骤，而 Good 范文很多时候只是一笔带过其反例，甚至没有解释清楚为什么该反例可以削弱原文逻辑。比如，针对 BC 事故减少是不是由 road improvement project 造成的讨论，Outstanding 范文给出了很多种其他可能的解释，比如路面监控、加大惩罚、对驾驶员要求更高，以及最近一年特殊的天气情况；相反，Good 范文只是质疑了报告的可信度，以及最近一年的代表性。更鲜明的是在讨论 BC 的举措是否可以复制到 PC 时，Outstanding 范文清晰地指出了一种可能性，即两个城市事故来源不同，而这种不同如何一步步使得同样的举措在两个地区可以产生不同的效果；相反，Good 范文只是草草说明两城交规可能不同，路况可能不同，但是完全没有解释这种不同为什么会产生重要的影响，难道要让读者自己去想吗？

两篇范文的语言都做到了表意清楚，基本没有影响读者理解文章意思的语法问题。

Part 6 Argument 精选范文

> **15** The following memorandum is from the business manager of Happy Pancake House restaurants.
>
> "Recently, butter has been replaced by margarine in Happy Pancake House restaurants throughout the southwestern United States. This change, however, has had little impact on our customers. In fact, only about 2 percent of customers have complained, indicating that an average of 98 people out of 100 are happy with the change. Furthermore, many servers have reported that a number of customers who ask for butter do not complain when they are given margarine instead. Clearly, either these customers do not distinguish butter from margarine or they use the term 'butter' to refer to either butter or margarine."
>
> Write a response in which you discuss one or more alternative explanations that could rival the proposed explanation and explain how your explanation(s) can plausibly account for the facts presented in the argument.

Sample Essay A: Outstanding

　　In this memorandum, the business manager of the Happy Pancake Restaurant (HPR) mentions that after they changed their butter to margarine, only 2% of customers have complained, and servers also claimed to have received very few complaints. Thus, the manager concludes that the evidence shows that the change has not had significant impact on their clientele. However, without ruling out several alternative explanations, her conclusion could remain, at best, problematic.

　　To begin, despite only 2% of customers having complained, that does not really mean that others are satisfied with the change. The manager assumes that this figure accurately indicates customers' response to the replacement. However, perhaps only a few people ordered food that needed butter. As a result, even though the proportion of complaining customers to all customers is small, the proportion of complaining customers to customers that ordered butter-related dishes could still be high. This scenario, if true, would mean that many of the customers affected by the change did indeed complain.

　　Granted that every dish involves butter, the 2% complaint rate is still not tantamount to a 98% satisfaction rate. The rationale behind the manager's reasoning is that all unsatisfied customers would necessarily file a complaint. However, maybe out of courtesy, most customers did not complain, but simply chose not to patronize the restaurant again. As a result, the manager may still observe very few complaints while the restaurant's business has already suffered a heavy blow. Thus, more information regarding the number of returning customers is needed so as to rule out this alternative possibility.

　　As for the servers' report, it does not lend adequate support to the manager's explanation. This line of reasoning once again is vulnerable to the counterexample that dissatisfied customers may choose to hold back their temper. However, more importantly, servers may not always honestly inform the manager of every negative comment they receive. When a server receives a complaint that she believes is minor, she may address it herself by, say, apologizing to the customer and offering a coupon or a free dessert, instead of reporting it to her superior. Especially if servers' wages or tips are connected with customer feedback, they have all the more reasons not to report every complaint they receive. Obviously, the author's idea that customers either don't distinguish between butter and margarine or that they don't care which one they are given is far from being the only reasonable explanation for her observation.

All in all, the manager's argument is weak, with plenty of loopholes. She needs to take into consideration all aforementioned alternatives before reaching a solid conclusion about the impact of the change.

Sample Essay B: Good

In this memorandum, the author concludes that their customers do not distinguish butter from margarine, or they use the term "butter" to refer to either butter or margarine. However, her inference is based on insufficient evidence, and other explanations could equally account for the information presented.

For starters, the author mentions that after Happy Pancake House restaurants replaced their butter with margarine, only about 2 percent of customers complained, indicating that 98% of people were happy with the change. Clearly, she assumes that 2% is a small amount, and that all unhappy customers would complain. However, maybe most restaurants have a lower proportion of complaints, and the 2% is already high enough to influence the restaurant's reputation. Also, customers don't always complain when they are angry. They sometimes don't bother speaking up; instead, they just leave and never return again. Without evidence ruling out these possibilities, the author's conclusion does not firmly stand.

In addition, the author mentions that many servers have reported that a number of customers who ask for butter do not complain when they are given margarine. Apparently, she assumes that servers are always honest. However, not all servers will tell their bosses about every customer complaint. Perhaps servers who receive the most complaints could be fired or have their wages cut, so they have reason to hide the information. We just don't know if these possibilities are true, unless the author can offer more evidence to clarify the uncertainty.

Last, even if the above possibilities are ruled out, it does not necessarily follow that customers don't distinguish between butter and margarine or use the terms interchangeably. The author assumes that no other explanation exists. However, maybe they are just nice people who are willing to accept everything the restaurant offers. They know the difference, but they just won't say anything. Maybe when they see that they are not given not what they want, they don't use the margarine at all.

In sum, these above possibilities could all equally explain the evidence offered by the out. Without ruling them out, her conclusion cannot stand on firm ground.

范文点评

两篇文章显著的区别在于 Outstanding 范文比 Good 范文更准确地指出了多个其他可能的解释。

(1) 2%的投诉率不来自于人们对人造黄油的满意，而来自于很多顾客没有接触人造黄油；
(2) 人们不投诉不是因为人们满意，而是因为人们懒得投诉；
(3) 侍者反馈的投诉少，不是因为人们不区分黄油与人造黄油，而是因为侍者出于个人原因不反馈收到的投诉。

与其相比，Good 范文指出了 (2) (3) 两种可能性，但 Good 范文在其第四段所给出的可能性只是对其第二段可能性的复制，即人们不投诉不是因为满意，只是不愿意去投诉而已。

两篇范文的语言都做到了表意清楚，基本没有影响读者理解文章意思的语法问题。

Part 6 Argument 精选范文

17

The following is a memorandum from the business manager of a television station.

"Over the past year, our late-night news program has devoted increased time to national news and less time to weather and local news. During this period, most of the complaints received from viewers were concerned with our station's coverage of weather and local news. In addition, local businesses that used to advertise during our late-night news program have canceled their advertising contracts with us. Therefore, in order to attract more viewers to our news programs and to avoid losing any further advertising revenues, we should expand our coverage of weather and local news on all our news programs."

Write a response in which you examine the stated and/or unstated assumptions of the argument. Be sure to explain how the argument depends on these assumptions and what the implications are for the argument if the assumptions prove unwarranted.

Sample Essay A: Outstanding

The business manager proposes that all their news programs devote more time to weather and local news in order to attract more viewers and to avoid losing advertising revenues. The proposal is a response to complaints received about weather and local news coverage, and to the cancelation of several advertising contracts after the station's late-night news program decreased its coverage on weather and local news. However, several crucial assumptions behind the manager's reasoning make it susceptible to potential counterarguments.

First, it is rash to imply that the late-night program's reduced coverage on local and weather news is not a welcome decision among the viewers. Underlying the implication are the essential assumptions that the complaints represent the general opinions of the audience and that these complaints were just about the shortened length of the coverage, not about other aspects of the weather and local news. However, perhaps before last year's coverage adjustment, there used to be a higher rate of viewer discontent; in contrast, the complaints mentioned in the article were few and given by just a couple of insistent audience members whose opinions could hardly reflect a much larger range of satisfied viewers. Also, even if complaints do reflect the popular opinion, it is not known what specifically about the local and weather news coverage they were dissatisfied with. Maybe the length of time was not what they were worried about; instead, they were just displeased with the news anchor's informal outfit, with the biased presentation of stories, or with the frequently incorrect weather predictions. Also, they could be unhappy about the coverage of weather and local news at other viewing hours instead of the late-night slot. Therefore, the manager needs to look into the amount of feedback and its specific contents before she conjures up a recommendation.

In addition, to show that an increased coverage of weather and local news would prevent further loss of advertising revenues, the author must first prove that the station was losing advertising revenues, and that it was due to the reduced coverage of weather and local news. Unfortunately, both statements were assumed rather than proven. True, some contracts were canceled, but more new contracts might have been secured at the same time. Every new policy a TV station implements might end up repelling certain businesses while pleasing others. The manager shouldn't just cite the ones hostile to the shift while ignoring others that were more receptive. Also, assuming that advertising revenues had shrunk, overall is not necessarily attributable to the reduced coverage. A survey among local businesses might show that those which canceled contracts were not displeased with the coverage change, but simply not able to afford a higher charge for commercial slots. Or, the businesses may have disliked the political stance the station recently took towards an election. They might have been displeased with the quality, rather than the quantity of the local and weather news, or with the quality of national and international news. In fact, it is unknown whether the canceled commercials were initially broadcasted during late-night local and weather news, because if not, the author's explanation may simply not be relevant.

Now, granted that the reduction of the late-night local and weather news was a terrible decision that hurt both the audience and advertising revenues, the manager might reasonably decide to increase the time devoted to weather and local news during the late-night slot. However, she cannot hastily assume that the decision would equally apply to other, non-late-night slots. First of all, it is unclear whether day-time viewers share the same interests with late-night viewers. It is possible that the zest for local and weather information is only typical among late-night TV viewers. Second, it is also unclear how much coverage has been devoted to local and weather news in other, non-late-night slots. Perhaps the day-time and prime-time news programs have already sufficiently addressed local events and weather, and the audience is actually looking for information from the entire country and beyond. Thus, a survey of viewer preferences for other time slots would be helpful for a general proposal.

Overall, the manager's argument suffers from too many unwarranted assumptions. She has yet to convince the readers whether the reduced late-night coverage on weather and local news has indeed generated a significant amount of viewer discontent, whether that reduction was the cause of canceled commercial contracts, or whether the situation of late-night coverage can represent other time slots. Without these statements being fully justified, her recommendation remains unpersuasive.

Sample Essay B: Good

The passage recommends that the television station expand its coverage of weather and local news on all their news programs in order to attract more viewers and to avoid losing further advertising revenues. However, underlying in its line of reasoning are several unwarranted assumptions that seriously undermine its persuasiveness.

First, the author mentions that most of the complaints the station received from viewers were concerned with its coverage of weather and local news, assuming that these complaints are representative of the audience. However, perhaps there were few complaints, so even if all of them were about a particular issue, it doesn't really matter much. In fact, perhaps before the reduction in local and weather news, there used to be more complaints. Therefore, without ruling this possibility out, the complaints lend little support to the author's suggestion.

Second, she also mentions that several local businesses have canceled their advertising contracts with the station. Clearly, she assumes that the reduction in weather and local news was the very reason for these cancelations. However, several possible explanations could equally account for these results. Perhaps the station has raised its prices for advertising spots. Maybe these businesses have gone bankrupt. Without considering all explanations, the author has not successfully proven that people would like to see more weather and local news.

Last, granted that viewers and businesses were both unhappy with the reduction in local and weather news, it does not necessarily mean that increasing their coverage is the best way to attract a greater audience and increased advertising revenue. The author assumes that there is no better approach for dealing with the matter. Perhaps the station could hire a more professional news anchor. Maybe it could increase the diversity of its news. Without considering other measures, the author's suggestion appears too simple.

Overall, the aforementioned assumptions all render the author's argument weak. Further evidence is needed to fill these loopholes.

范文点评

两篇文章最大的区别在于其对每个步骤的讨论深度。以观众抱怨这个步骤为例，Good 范文只意识到，存在观众抱怨不能代表普遍意见，也不能代表抱怨增多，但是 Outstanding 范文深刻地认识到了其他可能性的存在，即观众抱怨的可能不是该种新闻的数量，而是该种新闻的质量，而且甚至可能不是该时段的新闻。类似的现象也同样反映在其他部分的讨论当中。

两篇范文的语言都做到了表意清楚，基本没有影响读者理解文章意思的语法问题。

According to a recent report, cheating among college and university students is on the rise. However, Groveton College has successfully reduced student cheating by adopting an honor code, which calls for students to agree not to cheat in their academic endeavors and to notify a faculty member if they suspect that others have cheated. Groveton's honor code replaced a system in which teachers closely monitored students; under that system, teachers reported an average of thirty cases of cheating per year. In the first year the honor code was in place, students reported twenty-one cases of cheating; five years later, this figure had dropped to fourteen. Moreover, in a recent survey, a majority of Groveton students said that they would be less likely to cheat with an honor code in place than without. Thus, all colleges and universities should adopt honor codes similar to Groveton's in order to decrease cheating among students.

Write a response in which you discuss what questions would need to be answered in order to decide whether the recommendation and the argument on which it is based are reasonable. Be sure to explain how the answers to these questions would help to evaluate the recommendation.

Sample Essay A: Outstanding

In this article, the author recommends that all colleges and universities implement the honor code adopted at Groveton College (GC) to combat cheating. Her suggestion is mainly based on the reported decline of cheating after the adoption of the honor code at GC. However, several crucial questions are left unaddressed, and as a result her conclusion is quite unconvincing.

To begin, the author assumes, perhaps unwarrantedly, that students' reports are just as reliable as those from teachers. However, will students honestly report every misconduct they spot, or would they rather choose to cover up for each other? Even if they don't intentionally misreport, do they even have the time and energy to watch out for cheating, since they themselves should be completely engaged in the exams? Without a positive answer to either of these questions, it remains unclear if GC's cheating problem has indeed been alleviated.

Second, granted that the numbers are trustworthy, that cheating incidences have dropped from 30 per year all the way down to 14, it does not necessarily imply a less serious cheating problem. No evidence has been provided as to whether there have been significant changes in total enrollment for recent years. If, the total number of students has remained stable or even increased, the reduced cheating instances might indeed suggest that cheating has become less of an issue for the school. However, if a reputation crisis has caused a devastating blow to enrollment, resulting in a halving of total students, then the ratio of the amount of cheating to the number of students may have even increased, thereby undermining the author's argument.

Besides, even if cheating has in fact been reduced, it remains open whether there are other possible correlates to this shift. Maybe the school has decided on heavier punishments for cheating, maybe it has installed surveillance cameras in every classroom, or the average difficulty of the exams has decreased. Any of these scenarios, if true, would equally explain the diminishing cheating rate. Without sufficient evidence to address these possibilities, the author cannot fairly draw a connection between the code and cheating, and in turn should not confidently apply the measure to other schools.

Furthermore, the author also mentions a campus survey in which students claim that they are unlikely to cheat with an honor code in place. Apparently, she assumes that this survey is trustworthy. In an unlikely scenario in which students are willing to reveal all their dark secrets, this survey does weigh much toward the author's conclusion. Unfortunately, it is quite possible that students want to display their best sides, especially when the survey is not conducted anonymously. If so, then this piece of evidence simply lends no support to the author's conclusion.

Finally, building on the purported success of the honor code in GC, the author immediately alleges that the achievement can be duplicated in other schools. However, it is uncertain how much students of different schools differ. If in this district, all colleges have students that are honest and self-disciplined, then this code could potentially work miracles when imitated. However, perhaps Groveton College is a top institute in the whole region by far. Accordingly, it could have a strict standard for applicant enrollment, especially regarding their moral conduct. In contrast, perhaps most other institutes are relatively loose in this respect. If so, then it explains why the honor code, a system that requires self-discipline to work, could prove successful in Groveton, but it also probably implies a potential failure when implemented in other places. Also, for schools with already few cheating problems, the adoption of a different approach is quite unlikely to yield better results, so the change would be fairly unnecessary.

Overall, the author needs to take into consideration all aforementioned questions and supplement a series of unsupported assumptions before she can legitimately conclude that all schools should follow Groveton College's path.

Sample Essay B: Good

In this passage, the author believes that all colleges and universities should adopt honor codes in order to decrease cheating problems. The honor codes are a set of policies which call for students to agree not to cheat in their academic endeavors, and to notify a faculty member if they suspect that others have cheated. The author's opinion is based on a change in reported cheating problems and a survey from students. However, her argument is filled with unwarranted assumptions that may seriously undermine the cogency of her reasoning.

To begin, the author assumes that the amount of cheating reflected in students' notifications represents the actual amount of cheating. But are the reports truthful? As we can see, students may conceal actual cases of cheating in order to benefit themselves in such an honor code system, so it is reasonable to believe that the amount of cheating is greatly underestimated. What's more, students may be so focused on the exams that they are unable to discern cheating around them. As a result, the author cannot reach an accurate conclusion about the decline of cheating unless she proves that the students' reports truly reflect the actual cheating situation.

Even if the amount of cheating reported by students is accurate, there are other assumptions the author needs to justify. We judge the degree of cheating problems through the ratio of cheating, so the author makes an assumption that the amount of cheating, as she mentioned in her passage, reflects the relative ratio of cheating. However, in many cases, the absolute number does not reflect the relative number exactly. For instance, if the number of students who take the exam decreases dramatically, we cannot determine a change in the proportion of cheating students. As a result, the author needs to provide more details about the number of students who take the exam in order to eliminate the flaws of her assumptions.

Finally, are other colleges' situations similar to Groveton's? In general, if the conditions of the two elements are similar, if something is suitable for the former it can be applied to the latter. However, we all know that each college is unique, because of numerous factors such as policy, location, climate, culture and so on, contribute to the circumstances of the college simultaneously. Given that colleges have such complicated influences, it is extremely arbitrary to apply the situation of Groveton to other colleges. She needs to scrutinize the circumstances of other colleges and, based on those results, apply the honor code only to suitable places.

Overall, all of the assumptions above should be proven or revised in order to make the passage more cogent and reliable.

范文点评

Outstanding 范文非常全面且有条理地讨论了多个论证步骤并分析了其背后的假设：

(1) 学生报告的作弊数 ⟹ 实际的作弊数；
(2) 实际作弊数减少 ⟹ 作弊问题减弱；
(3) 作弊问题减弱 ⟹ honor code 解决了 GC 的作弊问题；
(4) 学生调查 ⟹ honor code 解决了 GC 的作弊问题；
(5) honor code 解决了 GC 的作弊问题 ⟹ honor code 将解决各校的作弊问题。

与其相比，Good 范文只讨论了其中的 (1) (2) (5)。

Outstanding 范文对每一个论证步骤的分析也更加深入，易于读者理解。与其相比，Good 范文的讨论经常只是流于表面。比如，Good 范文对于步骤 (5) 的讨论，只是指出存在各种影响不同学校的因素，却没有真正帮助读者理解为什么不同因素会影响到 honor code 的有效性。

Outstanding 范文语言非常清楚，相比，Good 范文基本没有影响读者理解文章意思的语法问题，但由于其语言抽象，所以有时候读者不能准确捕捉其意图。比如：…the author makes an assumption that the amount of cheating, as she mentioned in her passage, reflects the relative ratio of cheating.

Part 6 Argument 精选范文

22 A recently issued twenty-year study on headaches suffered by the residents of Mentia investigated the possible therapeutic effects of consuming salicylates. Salicylates are members of the same chemical family as aspirin, a medicine used to treat headaches. Although many foods are naturally rich in salicylates, food-processing companies also add salicylates to foods as preservatives. The twenty-year study found a correlation between the rise in the commercial use of salicylates and a steady decline in the average number of headaches reported by study participants. At the time when the study concluded, food-processing companies had just discovered that salicylates can also be used as flavor additives for foods, and, as a result, many companies plan to do so. Based on these study results, some health experts predict that residents of Mentia will suffer even fewer headaches in the future.

Write a response in which you discuss what questions would need to be answered in order to decide whether the prediction and the argument on which it is based are reasonable. Be sure to explain how the answers to these questions would help to evaluate the prediction.

Sample Essay A: Outstanding

According to the passage, some experts predict that residents of Mentia will suffer fewer headaches in the future. The prediction mainly rests on a recent study that seems to show a connection between an increased consumption of salicylates and reduced headache instances, and on several companies' plans to use salicylates as additives in their future food production. Unfortunately, the information presented in the article is insufficient to fully corroborate the prediction, and the author has to address a few more important questions in order to convince readers.

The article starts out by mentioning salicylates' chemical properties, pointing out that they belong to the same family as aspirin, a medicine used to treat headaches. Apparently, it implies that salicylates are likely to possess the same function as aspirin. However, while chemicals of the same family often do share certain properties, it is unknown whether these shared features include the ability to reduce headaches. Perhaps salicylates' similarities to aspirin lie only in taste, solubility, and smell. Without specifying their common properties, the fact that they belong to the same family is not yet a relevant piece of information for evaluating salicylates' potential medical usage.

As for the core evidence the article relies on, the 20-year study, it purports to have found a correlation between rising commercial use of salicylates and a decline in the average frequency of headaches reported by the study participants. However, it is questionable whether headaches have indeed become less frequent; and even if they have been reduced, whether that is attributable to salicylate use. For one thing, perhaps an important reason why there are fewer reports of headaches is that many participants have already passed away; those who are alive may have stopped responding to the research because they grew tired of reporting each instance of discomfort over the course of two decades. For another, even if there are actually fewer headaches, is it attributable to increased salicylates use? Maybe those suffering less from headaches don't have salicylates in their diet at all. Instead, the reduction could be ascribed to improved air quality or a healthier lifestyle. Since the article fails to provide information as to how many participants continued to offer feedback in the study or to whether there were other relevant changes taking place within Mentian population, the link between salicylates and headaches remains tenuous.

Granted that salicylates do help combat headaches, the article immediately goes on to project a future drop in headaches for Mentian citizens, since several companies are deciding to add salicylates to their foods as flavor additives. However, it is unclear whether this decision will directly translate into a higher average intake of salicylates within Mentian population, and if it will, whether the higher intake will necessarily further reduce headache instances. For one thing, how many companies are actually going to do this? How big a market share do these companies take up? How many kinds of foods will end up containing a higher proportion of salicylates? Will consumers welcome the new taste? Readers are not informed. If only a minority of food companies are going to make this trial on only a limited number of foods, and especially if these foods will end up tasting like garbage, then in the long run, Mentian residents will be unlikely to consume more salicylates. Consequently, the article's projection will end up groundless.

For another thing, assuming that Mentian residents will eventually take in a higher volume of salicylates, the article's prediction might still be too optimistic, because the optimum dosage of salicylates is not provided, and because the author fails to address other possible factors that may counteract salicylates' effect. True, a certain amount of salicylates might successfully deal with headaches, but there is a proper dosage for every medicine; even too much water can damage the human body. It is quite possible that at trace levels, the more salicylates people consume, the healthier they will be; however, after reaching a certain threshold, more salicylates will no longer benefit, but hurt their bodies. Thus, it is important for the author to investigate the current average intake of salicylates among Mentian residents, and compare that value with the healthy dosage. Also, there could still be future changes that might compromise salicylates' benefits. If there is going to be a change in the environment, or if people's average pace of life could increase sharply, they may still end up more likely to suffer from headaches.

Overall, the article has not yet offered adequate evidence to fully warrant its projection. Too many assumptions behind its line of reasoning are still open to question, so without addressing them, the author cannot fully convince the readers that there are indeed going to be fewer headaches for Mentian residents.

Sample Essay B: Good

In this article, some health experts predict that residents of Mentia will suffer fewer headaches in the future. However, several questions remain unanswered, so the persuasiveness of this argument is still in doubt.

For starters, the author mentions that salicylates are members of the same chemical family as aspirin, a medicine used to treat headaches, implying that salicylates can help with headaches as well. Clearly, she assumes that every chemical in the same family would have the same function. However, maybe the similarity between salicylates and aspirin is simply their color or taste, while they don't have the same medical function. Therefore, without knowing how similar these two really are, the comparison is quite unconvincing.

Second, the author mentions that a twenty-year study found a correlation between the rise in commercial use of salicylates and a decline in the average number of headaches reported by study participants. Apparently, she assumes that it is the intake of salicylates that explains the decline in headache instances. However, perhaps local residents exercise now more than before; perhaps their environment is cleaner than before. These can also potentially explain the trend. Therefore, she must answer the question of whether there are other phenomena that may explain the trend. Otherwise, the connection between salicylates and headaches is still unclear.

Last, she also states that several food companies are considering using salicylates as flavor additives. Obviously, she assumes that people will like these foods with salicylates. However, they may taste awful; or perhaps the production costs will rise, making these foods pricier than other similar products. If these happen, people will not necessarily consume more salicylates than before. Thus, the author has to provide more evidence to show whether people in Mentia will consume more salicylates than before; otherwise, the companies' plan will not be relevant to the prediction.

Overall, all aforementioned questions are crucial in the evaluation of the author's argument. Without addressing any of them, her conclusion will remain debatable.

范文点评

Outstanding 范文非常全面且有条理地讨论了多个论证步骤：

（1）Aspirin 治头疼 + Aspirin 与 Salicylates 同族 ⟹ Salicylate 能治头疼；

（2）20 年研究发现 Salicylates 商业使用量增多 + 头疼报告减少 ⟹ Salicylates 能够减少头疼；

（3）食品公司计划用 Salicylates 做调味剂 ⟹ Mentia 市民会吃到更多 Salicylates；

（4）Salicylates 能够减少头疼 + Mentia 市民会吃到更多 Salicylates ⟹ Mentia 市民头疼会进一步减少。

与其相比，Good 范文捕捉到了其中的步骤（1）（2）（3）。

其次，Outstanding 范文对多个步骤的分析也比 Good 范文更加深刻，比如步骤（2）和（3）。针对步骤（2），Outstanding 范文指出了头疼报告减少可能是因为人们报告的意愿下降，以及气候、生活习惯的改善。而针对步骤（4），Outstanding 范文的讨论就更加充分了，它指出了使得食品公司的计划不足的多种可能性，以导致人们食用 Salicylates 的量增多。与其相比，Good 范文的讨论显然不够深入。

两篇范文的语言都做到了表意清楚，基本没有影响读者理解文章意思的语法问题。

23

The following was written as a part of an application for a small-business loan by a group of developers in the city of Monroe.

"A jazz music club in Monroe would be a tremendously profitable enterprise. Currently, the nearest jazz club is 65 miles away; thus, the proposed new jazz club in Monroe, the C-Note, would have the local market all to itself. Plus, jazz is extremely popular in Monroe: over 100,000 people attended Monroe's annual jazz festival last summer; several well-known jazz musicians live in Monroe; and the highest-rated radio program in Monroe is 'Jazz Nightly', which airs every weeknight at 7 P.M. Finally, a nationwide study indicates that the typical jazz fan spends close to $1,000 per year on jazz entertainment."

Write a response in which you discuss what specific evidence is needed to evaluate the argument and explain how the evidence would weaken or strengthen the argument.

Sample Essay A: Outstanding

The group of developers claims that a Jazz music club, C-Note, would be a great success in Monroe. Their conclusion is based on several pieces of evidence that seemingly demonstrate the popularity of jazz in Monroe, jazz fans' purchasing power, and the lack of competition against C-Note. However, they need to offer more evidence in order to make their argument cogent.

To begin with, even if there are no nearby jazz clubs, C-Note would not necessarily dominate the local market. If there are other music clubs in Monroe that, though not exclusively playing jazz music, still heavily feature jazz musicians and enjoy a good reputation among local jazz fans, C-Note would still face stiff competition, and its profits might not be as promising as envisioned. Also, if C-Note's services are extremely pricy, its performers are too obscure, or its sound is poor, customers will not have sufficient motive to come. Consequently, even if no local competition exists, fans might still end up driving over 65 miles to a different club rather than visiting C-Note. Therefore, the developers need to do some thorough research on potential competition beyond clubs that specialize in jazz; at the same time, they should provide information regarding the specific plans they have for their proposed club.

As for the three juxtaposed pieces of evidence that seemingly indicate the popularity of jazz, none of them lends strong support. First, the author has failed to show how many out of the 100,000 participants in the jazz festival come from Monroe. It is also questionable how many among the locals who participated were actual jazz fans. If most visitors to the festival came from out of town, or if most came there just to have fun with beer and friends, regardless of the theme, then this figure does really indicate jazz's popularity in Monroe.

Second, the author cites famous jazz musicians living in Monroe without really clarifying why it is relevant to the popularity of jazz. If she can prove that they reside in Monroe because of fans' enthusiasm for jazz or that their music event here has contributed to a booming local jazz industry, then the connection would probably be strengthened. In contrast, if these professionals live here only for its hospitable natural environment, and especially if they are retired from performing or mostly perform elsewhere, then this information would probably be yet another piece of unrelated evidence that hardly justifies the author's claim.

Third, a jazz radio program's high ratings don't reflect the popularity of jazz, either. It is still possible that the program's high quality has earned itself prestige among jazz fans, when the absolute number of jazz fans is still quite low compared with the city's overall population. Additionally, its fervent audience may not even be from Monroe. These scenarios, if proven true, would erase the relevance of the author's evidence. In a nutshell, these three pieces of information are insufficient to justify her claim that jazz is indeed popular in Monroe, so a projection of C-Note's potential success is nowhere near solid.

Finally, granted that C-Note is the only club that features jazz in a city with wide interests in jazz music, the developers' optimism regarding C-Note's potential is still quite unwarranted, because the cited nationwide study does not necessarily reflect Monroe residents' purchasing power. Clearly, the developers take for granted that the nationwide study does represent Monroe, and that a significant portion of money spent on jazz goes to jazz clubs. However, no evidence is provided to justify these assumptions. First, maybe Monroe is the poorest region in the whole country. Thus, despite jazz fans elsewhere being lavish about jazz, those from Monroe might not be. Second, even if jazz fans in Monroe also spend as much as $1,000 a year on jazz music, perhaps most of the expenditure goes to record purchases rather than to club visits. Therefore, the developers need to prove that Monroe's fans would eagerly spend money at jazz clubs, or else C-Note's profitability will still remain a question.

All in all, the developers' argument is filled with unwarranted assumptions. More evidence is needed before the readers can really be sure how lucrative C-Note is going to be.

Sample Essay B: Good

The article claims that a jazz club in Monroe would be a profitable enterprise. However, the author's line of reasoning suffers from several loopholes that need to be supplemented by further evidence.

To begin with, the author believes that the proposed jazz club, C-Note, would have the local market all to itself, since the nearest jazz club is 65 miles away. Apparently, she assumes that C-Note would be able to attract all the nearby jazz fans. However, perhaps the club would book poor performers, its service would be terrible, and its decor outdated. All of this could make the club unattractive to visitors. Therefore, the author has to provide related evidence to address these concerns.

Furthermore, the author guarantees that jazz music is popular in Monroe, because over 100,000 people attended Monroe's annual jazz festival last summer, several well-known jazz musicians live there, and the highest-rated radio program in Monroe is "Jazz Nightly". However, none of these facts are sufficient to prove the popularity of jazz. Maybe most of the visitors to the festival were from out of town, while local residents were quite inactive; the jazz musicians may have retired or have no business in Monroe; the radio program's popularity may be confined within a tiny group of jazz fans, while it has little influence on other people. In short, the author needs more specific evidence to eliminate these possibilities, or else it will remain unclear how well-received jazz is in Monroe.

Finally, the author cites a nationwide study which indicates that the typical jazz fan spends close to $1,000 per year on jazz entertainment. Clearly, she assumes that the study reflects the particular situation in Monroe. However, perhaps Monroe is the poorest region in the country, so even though it has many jazz fans, they are rarely able to afford frequent visits to a jazz club. Thus, the author had better draw a survey on local residents' purchasing power, before she predicts that the jazz club would make money in Monroe.

In conclusion, the article is missing important information on all aforementioned aspects. Thus, the author's claim that C-Note would be profitable does not stand on solid ground.

范文点评

两篇文章都讨论了以下推理步骤：

(1) 附近没有 jazz club ⟹ C-Note 将独享市场；
(2) 100,000 人参加的音乐节 ⟹ jazz 受欢迎；
(3) 知名音乐家 ⟹ jazz 受欢迎；
(4) Jazz Nightly 受到好评 ⟹ jazz 受欢迎；
(5) 全国调查 ⟹ 当地 jazz 粉丝的购买力。

然而，几乎对于每一个步骤，Outstanding 范文都比 Good 范文要分析得更加充分、深入。最鲜明的是对步骤（3）的讨论，Good 范文只是说了这些音乐家可能已经退休了，但我们不知道退休为什么能够削弱原文论证。而 Outstanding 范文就指出了音乐家退休这种可能性，并且指出这意味着这些音乐家并不会带来当地爵士乐的流行。同时，Outstanding 范文还指出音乐家居住此地可能是因为环境好，意味着这些音乐家也不是因为当地爵士乐流行而来此地。于是，这就彻底削弱了原文证据和观点之间的关联。

两篇范文的语言都做到了表意清楚，基本没有影响读者理解文章意思的语法问题。

> **30** The following appeared in a memo from a vice president of Quiot Manufacturing.
>
> "During the past year, Quiot Manufacturing had 30 percent more on-the-job accidents than at the nearby Panoply Industries plant, where the work shifts are one hour shorter than ours. Experts say that significant contributing factors in many on-the-job accidents are fatigue and sleep deprivation among workers. Therefore, to reduce the number of on-the-job accidents at Quiot and thereby increase productivity, we should shorten each of our three work shifts by one hour so that employees will get adequate amounts of sleep."
>
> Write a response in which you examine the stated and/or unstated assumptions of the argument. Be sure to explain how the argument depends on these assumptions and what the implications are for the argument if the assumptions prove unwarranted.

Sample Essay A: Outstanding

The vice president of Quiot Manufacturing (QM) recommends that the factory shorten each of its work shifts by one hour so as to reduce on-the-job accidents. Her claim mainly rests on the following two pieces of evidence. First, QM had 30% more on-the-job accidents last year than the nearby Panoply Industry (PI). Second, PI's work shift is one hour shorter than QM's. However, her argument is filled with assumptions and loopholes that seriously undermine the persuasiveness of her reasoning.

For starters, even if PI reports 30% fewer accidents than QM does, that does not imply that PI has a better safety record. The author unwarrantedly assumes that PI does not have a much smaller staff. True, the 30% difference would be a strong indicator of PI's safer working environment, if PI has as many or more workers than QM does. However, if it later turns out that QM has twice as many workers as PI does, then it is natural to expect that QM's accidents are double to PI's; hence, only having 30% fewer accidents would actually mean that PI is probably not as safe to work in as QM. In short, the author needs to provide specific data that compares the two factories with regard to the size of their work force, or else PI's experience is probably not worth replicating.

Furthermore, by mentioning the different length of work shifts, the author clearly suggests that workers in QM are getting insufficient rest compared with those in PI. However, it is rash to assume that no other factor is in play which may make PI's workers more exhausted. Perhaps their workers have no breaks during shifts, while QM's have many; perhaps their products require intense physical and mental work to assemble, while thanks to QM's automated assembly line, all its workers do is monitor; not to mention, each worker at PI may take more shifts per week. Under these scenarios, PI's workers would actually be the more tired ones, and PI's superior safety record would have to be attributed to factors other than its work length. Thus, to corroborate her reasoning, the author needs to provide additional evidence to rule out other factors that might affect staff fatigue. Perhaps a direct medical test that examines workers' average physical and mental status might provide more relevant data.

Provided that QM's workers are indeed not as well rested as those from PI, and that QM's safety record is inferior to PI's, assuming a causal link between the two events is still contestable. True, if the two factories are not significantly different in their safety regulations, their workers' abilities, or their equipment, then perhaps the assumption is plausible. However, maybe PI's workers are better trained, and thus more skillful, their equipment is more advanced and frequently checked for safety, or their regulations are sounder and carried out more strictly. Any of the above possibilities, if true, would equally contribute to PI's better safety record. Therefore, without ruling them out, she cannot attribute the record to fatigue, and thus her suggestion to reduce one hour per work shift will probably not affect QM's future accident rate.

Now, granted that there is a connection between accident rate and fatigue, applying the shortened work shift to each of QM's three work shifts is still contestable, since it is unclear if the three shifts had contributed equally to the past accidents. The author clearly assumes that the three shifts, need not be distinguished. However, it is quite possible that the evening shift, and especially the late night shift, if there is any, have been the major sources of fatigue, and thus of accidents, whereas the morning shift does not place excessive demand on workers' concentration. Under this scenario, the adjustment does not have to be uniformly enforced throughout all the shifts. Accordingly, what the author needs to do is to investigate specifically the accident rate of each shift, and then to come up a more targeted solution.

In conclusion, many of the reasoning steps in this article are weak, and have unsupported assumptions. The author needs to provide further evidence to supplement all these missing links, or else her recommendation will remain doubtful.

Sample Essay B: Good

In the article, the author recommends that Quiot Manufacturing (QM) reduce each of its three work shifts by one hour to reduce the number of on-the-job accidents. Unfortunately, her argument rests on several unwarranted assumptions that make its reasoning unconvincing.

For starters, based on the fact that QM had 30% more on-the-job accidents than the nearby Panoply Industries (PI), where the work shifts are one hour shorter, the author implies that it is because of the longer work shifts that QM had more accidents. Apparently, the author assumes that no other explanation can account for this data. However, perhaps QM is simply much larger than PI. Perhaps QM's equipment is outdated and thus more dangerous to operate. These differences have to be ruled out in order for the author to draw a connection between the length of work shifts and accident rate.

In addition, to further strengthen the relationship between work hours and accidents, the author cites an expert opinion, that significant contributing factors in many on-the-job accidents are fatigue and sleep deprivation among workers. Apparently, she assumes that the expert's analysis is relevant to QM's particular case. However, maybe QM's work shifts, even though longer than PI's, are not really demanding for the workers, so the workers are not exhausted after their work shifts. Therefore, instead of applying the expert's opinion, the author needs to draw direct evidence based on QM's particular case.

Finally, even if QM's relatively higher accident rate is caused by the longer work shifts, that does not necessarily mean that shortening the work shifts will alleviate the problem. The author assumes that after shortening the work shifts by one hour, workers will get adequate rest. However, it is quite possible that total work load will remain the same, so the shorter work shift means that workers will have to work more efficiently. If so, the intense pressure may still cause the workers to be overly stressed and exhausted. Therefore, without providing more information to address this concern, the author's advice still sounds unconvincing.

Overall, these missing links make the author's reasoning unsound. To further corroborate her suggestion, she has to provide more evidence in order to dispel the aforementioned concerns.

范文点评

Outstanding 范文非常全面且有条理地讨论了多个论证步骤：

（1）PI 报告的事故率低于 QM ⇒ PI 比 QM 更安全；

（2）PI 比 QM 班次时长短 ⇒ QM 比 PI 员工更疲劳；

（3）QM 比 PI 员工更疲劳 ＋ PI 比 QM 更安全 ⇒ 疲劳造成 QM 事故更多；

（4）疲劳造成 QM 事故更多 ⇒ QM 每班次都需要减少时长。

而 Good 范文只是成功地讨论了其中的(3)，略微提到了(1)。其对专家意见的讨论完全是逐句分析的结果，却没有意识到这和 (3) 其实是重复的，并没有本质的区别。Good 范文选择了另一个点讨论，即疲劳造成 QM 事故更多 ⇒ 班次缩短就能减少 QM 事故。这个推理在文中是存在的，但是作者的讨论不能令人信服。就算班次缩短也并不必然减少 QM 事故，但是如果不缩短班次是不可能减少事故的，意味着班次还是需要缩短。于是，这个讨论不足以削弱原文建议的必要性。

两篇范文的语言都做到了表意清楚，基本没有影响读者理解文章意思的语法问题。

Part 6 Argument 精选范文

30 The following report appeared in the newsletter of the West Meria Public Health Council.

"An innovative treatment has come to our attention that promises to significantly reduce absenteeism in our schools and workplaces. A study reports that in nearby East Meria, where fish consumption is very high, people visit the doctor only once or twice per year for the treatment of colds. Clearly, eating a substantial amount of fish can prevent colds. Since colds represent the most frequently given reason for absences from school and work, we recommend the daily use of Ichthaid—a nutritional supplement derived from fish oil—as a good way to prevent colds and lower absenteeism."

Write a response in which you discuss what specific evidence is needed to evaluate the argument and explain how the evidence would weaken or strengthen the argument.

Sample Essay A: Outstanding

　　The article recommends the daily use of Ichthaid, a nutritional supplement derived from fish oil, as an effective way to combat colds and prevent workplace absenteeism. The proposal is largely based on a study which seems to indicate that eating fish can help people avoid colds. Unfortunately, the author's line of reasoning contains several unwarranted assumptions, and without further evidence, the readers cannot effectively evaluate the soundness of her suggestion.

　　The article's main support, and also unfortunately, its main problem, comes from the study it cites. It reports that in nearby East Meria, fish consumption is high, and people visit doctors only once or twice a year to treat colds. These two facts alone cannot firmly establish a connection between fish intake and colds, and there are several reasons why this inference is problematic. First, it is unknown whether most of the fish consumed in East Meria go to the dinner tables of local people. Perhaps because East Meria is a tourist area, most of the fish are consumed by visitors. In addition, a lot of the fish could be processed into products that are sold to other places. Clearly, evidence directly revealing East Merians' dietary preferences would be essential in order to clarify this ambiguity.

　　Second, the frequency that East Merians visit doctors annually to deal with colds is not a strong indication of their health. Colds are minor sicknesses, which people often cope with at home; it is likely that the local people seldom have to consult physicians unless symptoms get worse. Especially if local medical facilities are scarce, or if most physicians there are unqualified, then there are additional reasons why cold patients would prefer to treat themselves. Therefore, the author simply cannot assume that people would all consult doctors for cold treatment, and a random survey directly asking people how often they get colds would be more relevant to the issue.

　　Third, granted that East Merians do eat a lot of fish, and rarely suffer from colds, evidence is inadequate to establish a causal connection between the two phenomena, because alternative possibilities have not been thoroughly examined. Climate in East Meria may be mild and hospitable; local residents may exercise more

447

regularly than people elsewhere; its economy may be strong, so people there could enjoy excellent health care and housing. Overall, without addressing all of the aforementioned uncertainties, the author should not simply assume that no other factors are in play, and if the author cannot effectively build up the correlation between fish and colds, she loses ground in here recommendation of the fish oil product.

Now, even if fish does contribute to a reduction in colds, it does not necessarily cope with absences from schools and workplaces. To substantiate this link, the author has to justify a correlation between colds and absences, but her evidence simply suggests that colds represent the most frequent given reason for absences. However, given reasons may not be the actual causes of absences. Many people try to avoid duty by giving false excuses, and colds are one of the most available excuses. Consequently, even if eating fish does effectively treat colds, it might not make a difference in absenteeism. Thus, to really legitimize her argument, the author needs stronger evidence that establishes a tighter connection between colds and absences.

Finally, assuming that both colds and absences are both effectively dealt with by regular fish intake, are these effects necessarily duplicated by Ichthaid, the fish oil product? Once again, the author provides no scientific data indicating the effects of fish. Perhaps the substances effective for preventing colds simply don't exist in fish oil; or perhaps they are effective only when fish are fresh, and after industrial manufacturing, they become inactive. These possibilities, if true, would add power to skeptics of the medicine, so the author is obligated to offer further information detailing the effective ingredients in Ichthaid.

Overall, within the author's sanguine argument lies too many unwarranted inferences. To truly uphold her recommendation, she has to offer additional evidence, and until then, the readers had better remain doubtful toward Ichthaid.

Sample Essay B: Good

The author recommends the daily use of Ichthaid—a nutritional supplement derived from fish oil—as a good way to prevent colds and reduce absences from work and school. However, to fully evaluate the argument, more evidence is desperately needed.

For starters, the author cites a study which reports that in nearby East Meria, where fish consumption is high, people visit the doctors only once or twice per year to treat colds. Hence, she suggests that eating a substantial amount of fish can prevent colds. Clearly, she assumes that no other factors aside from a diet rich in fish could explain this data. However, perhaps East Merians exercise more often than people elsewhere; perhaps the local climate is mild and uniform, making colds less likely. To fully establish a link between fish and colds, the author has to offer further evidence to rule out these possibilities.

Second, even if fish can help reduce colds, there is no guarantee that Ichthaid can do the same just because it is derived from fish oil. The author apparently assumes that Ichthaid has the same function as fish. However, maybe the key element in fish that helps with colds doesn't lie in its oil. Perhaps during the manufacturing process, all effective elements are decomposed and lose their function. Thus, until relevant information is provided, readers cannot be fully convinced of Ichthaid's potential in dealing with colds.

Last, even if Ichthaid can effectively reduce colds, the recommendation for its daily intake is not necessarily advisable. The author assumes that its side effects are not more significant. However, perhaps some people are allergic to fish oil, so they should stay away from the product. Perhaps using it daily could cause stomachaches or headaches. The author says nothing about Ichthaid's potential harms, but every substance has some side effects. Therefore, to fully dispel consumers' potential worries, the author had better provide more relevant information.

Overall, the argument provides some, but not all important evidence for a thorough evaluation of Ichthaid. Until more evidence is provided, readers should remain skeptical towards the author's recommendation.

范文点评

这两篇文章最大的区别在于对论证步骤的分析深度。同样是讨论研究报告是否能说明吃鱼能防感冒，Good 范文只注意到看感冒少的其他可能解释，而 Outstanding 范文非常透彻地讨论了同一个步骤，分析了鱼消费量与吃鱼量的区别、看感冒与感冒的区别，以及充分考虑了感冒少的其他可能解释。

两篇范文的语言都做到了表意清楚，基本没有影响读者理解文章意思的语法问题。

Part 6 Argument 精选范文

37 A recent sales study indicates that consumption of seafood dishes in Bay City restaurants has increased by 30 percent during the past five years. Yet there are no currently operating city restaurants whose specialty is seafood. Moreover, the majority of families in Bay City are two-income families, and a nationwide study has shown that such families eat significantly fewer home-cooked meals than they did a decade ago but at the same time express more concern about healthful eating. Therefore, the new Captain Seafood restaurant that specializes in seafood should be quite popular and profitable.

Write a response in which you discuss what specific evidence is needed to evaluate the argument and explain how the evidence would weaken or strengthen the argument.

Sample Essay A: Outstanding

In this article, the author concludes that the newly opened Captain Seafood Restaurant (CSR) will become very successful in Bay City. Her prediction rests on several pieces of evidence that seemingly indicate sea food's popularity in the city, as well as on the apparent lack of competition faced by CSR. Unfortunately, because important information is missing, the author's prediction remains problematic.

To begin with, by mentioning the 30% increase in seafood sales in Bay City, the author implies that seafood has become more popular than in the past. Apparently, she assumes that no other factors can adequately explain this increase. If she can show that average food consumption there has not shifted dramatically, then this 30% increase may indeed serve her argument well. However, perhaps population has skyrocketed during that time, perhaps the city has turned into a tourist destination, or perhaps an economic boost has allowed more families to eat out. These factors would naturally stimulate restaurant business. If as a result, most food consumption has surged, with popular foods like vegetables and red meat undergoing a triple in sales, then the 30% increase in seafood consumption does not actually imply its popularity.

To further strengthen the implication that a seafood restaurant is going to be well received in Bay City, the author mentions that a majority of local families are two-income families, and according to a nationwide survey, they generally eat out more, and care more about a healthy diet than in the past. Unfortunately, too much information is lacking, and as a result, the survey cannot really help draw a reliable projection regarding the future of a seafood business. First, it is unclear whether the nationwide survey can represent Bay City's particular situation. Perhaps most parts of the country are quite wealthy, and two-income families generally eat out most of the time. In contrast, because of the staggering local economy, Bay City's average family income is so low that they can rarely afford to dine out. Second, it is uncertain what lifestyle those who express concern about healthful diet would actually choose. Many people still retain an unhealthy way of life because of a weakness of will, even if they say otherwise in a public survey. Last, even if Bay City families eat out more and eat healthily, there is no indication that they specifically favor seafood. Seafood like shrimp and shellfish are a common allergens, and generally high in cholesterol. Because of its relatively bland taste, local chefs may often prepare seafood with excessive butter and cheese. Therefore, seafood dishes are not necessarily healthy; instead, local people's favorite health foods might actually be vegetables, whole grains and fruits. If so, the connection between a healthy diet and seafood is quite flimsy. In a nutshell, without concrete information to help rule out these scenarios, it remains debatable whether a seafood restaurant would be profitable in Bay City.

Last, granted that it is a wise idea to open a seafood restaurant, the author still needs to provide more detailed information comparing the strengths and weaknesses between CSR and potential competitors to make readers optimistic about CSR's future success. By mentioning that no other restaurant specializes in seafood, the author implies that the competition facing CSR is minimal, but the inference is rather tenuous. Restaurants that have a wide range of options can still outshine many other more specialized competitors because the ultimate factor in a restaurant's success lies not in its specialty but in the quality, service, location, and even ambience. In this case, if the author can show that CSR's chefs are reputed masters in cooking seafood and that the restaurant is not vastly overshadowed by competitors in other respects, then readers might have more faith in its promise.

To sum up, if CSR's seafood is superior in every aspect to that of other restaurants, and if seafood is truly a local favorite, then CSR might indeed end up being a successful restaurant. Unfortunately, the evidence from the article is so far quite inadequate to truly persuade the readers of this prediction.

Sample Essay B: Good

The article believes that the new Captain Seafood restaurant (CSR), which specializes in seafood will be popular and profitable. However, the author has yet to provide sufficient evidence for readers to fully evaluate its reasoning.

For starters, she mentions a recent sales study which shows that consumption of seafood dishes in Bay City restaurants has increased by 30 percent during the past five years. However, the data does not necessarily indicate that seafood is now more popular in Bay City than five years ago. The author assumes that no other factors could explain this figure. However, perhaps the local population has increased vastly, or perhaps there are many more tourists today than in the past. These possibilities could be all the cause of the change, so the author needs to provide more information to rule out these circumstances.

Second, according to the author, the majority of families in Bay City are two-income families, and according to a nationwide study, these families tend to eat out more and care more about healthy eating. However, this information does not prove that seafood is a local favorite. The author assumes that eating healthy is related to eating seafood. However, it is possible that most people would choose organic vegetables or whole grains when they think about eating healthily. They may rarely choose seafood because they believe it is high in cholesterol. Therefore, the author needs to do a more specific survey to ask local people how much they prefer seafood. Without more solid information, her argument is prone to counterarguments.

Last, the author mentions that CSR is the only restaurant that specializes in seafood, but it does not necessarily mean that it has no competition. The author assumes that when people want to eat seafood, they prefer a place that specializes in seafood. However, there may be many other restaurants that have good at cooking seafood, even though they may serve many other things as well. In contrast, CSR's seafood may taste awful, even though seafood is all it has. Therefore, the author needs to provide more specific information regarding CSR's quality, or else it will remain unclear how profitable CSR is going to be.

Overall, the author should offer more evidence to address all of the above counterarguments.

范文点评

Outstanding 范文非常全面且有条理地讨论了多个论证步骤:

(1) 海鲜销量增加 ⟹ 海鲜更受欢迎;

(2) 全国调查 ⟹ BC 的情况;

(3) 人们关心健康饮食 ⟹ 人们会健康饮食;

(4) 人们会健康饮食 + 人们会在外吃 ⟹ 人们会吃海鲜;

(5) 没有其他专营海鲜的餐厅 ⟹ CSR 竞争压力小。

与其相比,Good 范文讨论了其中的(1)(4)(5)。

此外,对论证步骤的分析,Outstanding 范文也比 Good 范文更充分一些。比如对(5)的讨论,Outstanding 范文指出影响餐馆受欢迎度的因素可能有很多,比如食物、服务、位置、环境等,只有作者提供的证据显示 CSR 各方面都不差于竞争对手,才可以保证 CSR 的受欢迎度。与其相比,Good 范文的分析就较为单薄。

两篇范文的语言都做到了表意清楚,基本没有影响读者理解文章意思的语法问题。

Part 6 Argument 精选范文

39 The following appeared in a health newsletter.

"A ten-year nationwide study of the effectiveness of wearing a helmet while bicycling indicates that ten years ago, approximately 35 percent of all bicyclists reported wearing helmets, whereas today that number is nearly 80 percent. Another study, however, suggests that during the same ten-year period, the number of bicycle-related accidents has increased 200 percent. These results demonstrate that bicyclists feel safer because they are wearing helmets, and they take more risks as a result. Thus, to reduce the number of serious injuries from bicycle accidents, the government should concentrate more on educating people about bicycle safety and less on encouraging or requiring bicyclists to wear helmets."

Write a response in which you examine the stated and/or unstated assumptions of the argument. Be sure to explain how the argument depends on these assumptions and what the implications are for the argument if the assumptions prove unwarranted.

Sample Essay A: Outstanding

Based on two studies that intend to indicate a correlation between increased helmet usage among cyclists and an increased number of bicycle-related accidents, the article suggests that, since wearing helmets seems to encourage cyclists to take more risks, a better way to reduce serious injuries from bicycle accidents is for the government to educate people about bicycle safety. Unfortunately, the author's reasoning suffers from several assumptions and loopholes which must be justified with further evidence.

The major issue in the article is its overgeneralization of the two studies. The first study indicates that a decade ago, about 35% of bicyclists reported wearing helmets, while today that number has risen to 80%. The other study indicates that bicycle-related accidents have tripled. Clearly, the author would like readers to believe that a helmet-wearing habit actually causes people to be more reckless, and thereby results in more accidents. However, this inference is invalid for several reasons. First, she shouldn't simply assume that all reports from cyclists are trustworthy. It is possible that traffic regulations ten years ago did not require wearing helmets, so those who didn't would honestly concede that they wore no helmet; in contrast, perhaps because of today's stricter requirements, people who don't regularly wear helmets when cycling would still claim otherwise in order to make themselves look more law abiding. Simply put, since the author has not soundly established that helmet use is indeed more common today, she is not in a ready position to evaluate the effect of helmets.

Second, granted that helmet use is indeed more common today, the author clearly assumes that this change is causally connected with a higher rate of bicycle-related accidents. In fact, she explicitly assumes that wearing a helmet provides bicyclists with a false sense of security, which makes them more risk oriented. However, first, it is possible that the increase in accidents is still caused by those who don't wear helmets.

It's true that a smaller proportion of cyclists don't wear helmets, but their absolute number could still have risen, because the local cycling population may have grown tremendously. Consequently, those who don't wear helmets may still be accountable for more frequent bicycle-related accidents. Also, even if many of the helmet wearers are involved in accidents, a more meticulous inquiry might reveal that they rigorously obeyed every traffic regulation; instead, their injuries might alternatively be attributed to the joint effects of crowed roads, reckless car drivers, lack of designated bicycle lanes, and so on. A jam-packed road with more bicycles and more cars would naturally lead to more accidents, especially if the police force is insufficient. In a nutshell, since the author has yet to effectively rule out alternative explanations, people might still be wiser to stick to wearing helmets when cycling.

Building on the implication that helmet use results in more frequent bicycle-related accidents, the author goes on to suggest that to reduce serious injuries, the government should focus less on encouraging helmet use among cyclists. Behind this line of reasoning, she assumes that the number of accidents is directly correlated with the amount of serious injuries. However, granted that helmets do drive people to be more daring, they might still protect them from injuries, especially the more serious ones. Even if cyclists tend to ride faster or cross path with cars when they feel protected, and even if they might end up being hit, helmets can still effectively save them from lethal head injuries; in contrast, while those without helmets might ride safely, they could still be hurt by reckless drivers, and then no helmet probably means no life. Therefore, without data showing how many out of those bicycle-related accidents involve serious injuries, the author cannot simply infer the effect of helmets on serious injuries just from the their effect on accidents.

Last, assuming that wearing helmets is a terrible idea, it is still unclear why education is a better alternative. The author rashly assumes that educating people would be effective, and that no other choice is more appropriate. Perhaps the government has already spent years educating people about riding safely, but it has not worked at all. Instead, local residents may have been suffering from a lack of bicycle lanes, so a better approach would be to install more facilities that suit bicycle-riders. Also, regulations about driving could be implemented to protect riders from cars and buses. It is so far unknown whether these alternative measures have been tested, so without ruling them out, the article's recommendation fails to stand as the optimal solution.

In sum, perhaps education is the ultimate way to go, yet the author's evidence is insufficient to generate that conclusion. The article is vulnerable to attacks on its missing links, and without these assumptions being supplemented, the government had better remain skeptical toward the article's conclusion.

Sample Essay B: Good

In the article, the author recommends that the government concentrate more on educating people about bicycle safety, and less on encouraging or requiring bicyclists to wear helmets. However, her reasoning suffers from several assumptions and loopholes that seriously undermine its cogency.

To begin with, she mentions a ten-year nationwide study, which indicates that, while ten years ago, about 35% of bicyclists reported wearing helmets, today that number has increased to nearly 80%. However, the changed data does not necessarily imply that more cyclists wear helmets today than before. The author assumes that everyone would honestly report his/her behavior, when in reality this is often not the case. Maybe ten years ago traffic regulations did not require wearing helmets, so people would honestly tell surveyors about what they did. In contrast, there might be stricter rules requiring that people wear helmets, so even if some people don't follow the rule, they may still openly lie about it to look better. Therefore, without more direct observation, the author has not provided persuasive evidence to corroborate her reasoning.

Second, the author also mentions that the number of bicycle-related accidents has increased by 200%, and she then attributes this increase to helmet use. Clearly, she assumes that no other factors could equally account for this trend. However, maybe there are many more cars on the road, while road conditions have not improved, so it is perhaps more risky to ride a bike now than before. There might be more bicyclists as well, so increased accidents might simply be a natural result of increased bike riders. In a nutshell, without evidence ruling out these possibilities, the author cannot firmly establish a link between safety and helmet wearing.

Last, even if wearing a helmet does not help reduce accidents, that does not necessarily mean that education is the only way to go. The author assumes that no other solution could better deal with the issue. However, perhaps the local government has already emphasized the importance of safe riding, but that hasn't worked at all. Instead, what it really should do is spend more money on widening the roads, resurfacing them, adding bicycle lanes, and setting stricter car driving regulations. The author cannot offer a strong conclusion without addressing other alternative proposals.

Overall, the author's line of reasoning is weak, and has too many unwarranted assumptions. Only by providing more evidence can she potentially persuade readers to accept her suggestion.

范文点评

Outstanding 范文非常全面且有条理地讨论了多个论证步骤：

（1）报告显示头盔使用增多 ⟹ 头盔使用增多；

（2）头盔使用增多 + 自行车事故增多 ⟹ 头盔使用造成自行车事故增多；

（3）头盔使用造成自行车事故增多 ⟹ 要减少自行车事故中的严重受伤，政府不该靠头盔解决问题；

（4）要减少自行车事故中的严重受伤，政府不该靠头盔解决问题 ⟹ 政府该靠宣传教育。

与其相比，Good 范文只讨论了其中的(1)(2)(4)。

不仅如此，对其中论证步骤的分析，Outstanding 范文的深度也经常胜过 Good 范文。比如对于(2)的讨论，Outstanding 范文指出自行车事故增多可能因为不戴头盔的人群增多，也可能因为汽车司机驾车鲁莽、路面拥堵、缺少自行车道等一系列原因。与其相比，Good 范文的讨论显然简单很多。

两篇范文的语言都做到了表意清楚，基本没有影响读者理解文章意思的语法问题。

Part 6 Argument 精选范文

43

The following is part of a memorandum from the president of Humana University.

"Last year the number of students who enrolled in online degree programs offered by nearby Omni University increased by 50 percent. During the same year, Omni showed a significant decrease from prior years in expenditures for dormitory and classroom space, most likely because instruction in the online programs takes place via the Internet. In contrast, over the past three years, enrollment at Humana University has failed to grow, and the cost of maintaining buildings has increased along with our budget deficit. To address these problems, Humana University will begin immediately to create and actively promote online degree programs like those at Omni. We predict that instituting these online degree programs will help Humana both increase its total enrollment and solve its budget problems."

Write a response in which you discuss what questions would need to be answered in order to decide whether the prediction and the argument on which it is based are reasonable. Be sure to explain how the answers to these questions would help to evaluate the prediction.

Sample Essay A: Outstanding

In this memorandum, the president of Humana University (HU) predicts that the school's newly implemented online degree program will help HU both increase its total enrollment and solve its budget problems. Her optimism is mainly based on nearby Omni University's (OU's) alleged success with its online degree programs. Unfortunately, too many crucial questions are still open to debate, so whether OU's success can be duplicated remains doubtful.

For starters, it is unclear whether the online program is the main explanation for OU's reduced expenses on dormitory and classroom space. The president assumes that certain classes, which would have been conducted in real classrooms in the past have now been moved online, and that certain students who would have sat in actual classrooms are now sitting in front of their computers to take lessons. However, perhaps the online classes are teaching courses that the school didn't have before, and there are just as many traditional classes in real classrooms as before; instead, the reduction in expenses may be due to efforts in energy conservation; the school might have switched to more efficient lighting and heat-control systems. Or the online classes may have completely foundered; enrollment numbers might be so low that a 50% increase would still be negligible, and it would not have affected traditional classrooms; rather, OU's traditional majors may have serious trouble attracting new applicants, in which case the reduced expenditure would simply come from lower enrollment, and not from the online classes. Without ruling out these alternative scenarios, it is uncertain how much the online courses have contributed to the reduced expenses, and thus it also uncertain how promising HU's imitation would be.

Granted that OU's online system did make a huge difference, it is unclear whether it can be duplicated by HU. The president's argument has to rest on a questionable, yet essential assumption, that is, the two schools are similar in their curricula. Unfortunately, perhaps OU's programs focus on social sciences and humanity, such as philosophy, journalism, and literature, which often concentrate on discussion, reading and lectures, and which can all easily be reestablished via the internet. In contrast, if HU's programs are more oriented toward engineering or natural sciences, then online classes would not be able to provide opportunities for lab research and field study, which are both quite essential in these areas of study. As a result, online courses may not generate a boost in enrollment for HU. Therefore, the president has to answer the question of whether there is a big discrepancy between how curricula and majors are set up in the two schools. Otherwise, OU would not necessarily be a perfect model for HU.

Finally, what OU's online program did achieve was a 50% increase in online course enrollment and reduced dormitory and classroom expenses. Assuming that copying the strategy can help HU achieve similar results, the president's optimism regarding increasing enrollment and solving budget problems is still quite unwarranted. Did OU's increased online enrollment come at the expense of a sharper drop in offline course enrollment? If most of the online students attended offline classes in the past, and if those that now take online courses no longer have to enroll offline, then total enrollment may have remained stable, or even decreased. More importantly, is the tuition for online classes significantly lower than that for traditional classes? If so, the shift of students to the Internet could possibly imply a sharply reduced net revenue, leaving the school budget problem just as serious as before. Also, it is not provided whether the school has to spend a lot on installing and maintaining its online systems. If that maintenance fee is too high, it might offset any potential savings from reductions in dormitory and classroom space. These aforementioned factors potentially break the connection between online course enrollment and overall enrollment, and between reduced expenses and reduced budget deficits, more information is needed.

In a nutshell, while online courses may be the new trend for future education, they may not be the solution for every problem a school may face. Without addressing a series of important questions, the president's prediction so far seems overly confident.

Sample Essay B: Good

The article predicts that the newly installed online degree programs will help Humana University (HU) increase its total enrollment and solve its budget problems. Unfortunately, several questions are open to debate, so the author's prediction is still unpersuasive.

For starters, the author mentions that Omni University (OU) showed a significant decrease in expenses for dormitory and classroom space, as the number of students enrolled in online degree programs increased by 50 percent. Thus, she believes that the reduced expenses must be due to online instruction, assuming that the reduction couldn't have been caused by other changes. However, has the school lowered its tuition? Did it hire more prestigious professors? Did it start a new advertising campaign to attract prospective students? The author provides no evidence to rule out these alternative possibilities, so its connection between online courses and expense reduction is weak.

Second, even if OU's online program has contributed to lower expenses, that does not necessarily mean that HU's online program will have the same results. The author assumes that the two programs are similar in several important aspects. However, maybe OU's program focuses on humanities courses, while HU's programs are based on science and technology. If so, then it is unclear whether HU's online classes will be well received. Therefore, to fully substantiate the comparison, the author must address the question of whether HU's online program is going to successfully attract students from real classrooms.

Finally, even if HU's online classes will help reduce its expenses on classroom and dormitory space, that does not necessarily help alleviate its budget problems. The author assumes that the school's revenue would not decline faster, and that increases in other expenses will not compensate for the reduced costs of classroom and dorm maintenance. However, will the online programs charge less than traditional classes? If so, then having students take courses online would probably mean that the school will receive less tuition money. Also, setting up a new online program costs a lot of money, but how much? The author does not indicate. If the cost is excessive, then the school may end up in heavier debt.

Overall, the aforementioned questions are all crucial in corroborating the author's line of reasoning. Only with more evidence can readers be in a position to readily evaluate her prediction.

范文点评

这两篇文章突出的区别是它们对反例的呈现。比如对 OU 的网课能否被 HU 成功模仿这个问题，两篇文章都指出两学校课程可能存在科目区别：OU 可能主要关注文科课程，而 HU 主要关注理工科课程。但是 Good 范文就停留在此，没有详细讲清楚为什么这种科目区别会影响课程未来的吸引力，而 Outstanding 范文就详细阐释为什么文科课程也许更适合网上授课，而理工科课程可能会难以复制到网上。读者没有义务去猜测作者的心理，作者有义务要把其思路说清楚。在这一点上 Outstanding 范文比 Good 范文显然优秀很多。

两篇范文的语言都做到了表意清楚，基本没有影响读者理解文章意思的语法问题。

Part 6　Argument 精选范文

44 The following appeared in a memorandum from the owner of Movies Galore, a chain of movie-rental stores.

"Because of declining profits, we must reduce operating expenses at Movies Galore's ten movie-rental stores. Raising prices is not a good option, since we are famous for our low prices. Instead, we should reduce our operating hours. Last month our store in downtown Marston reduced its hours by closing at 6:00 p.m. rather than 9:00 p.m. and reduced its overall inventory by no longer stocking any DVD released more than five years ago. Since we have received very few customer complaints about these new policies, we should now adopt them at all other Movies Galore stores as our best strategies for improving profits."

Write a response in which you discuss what specific evidence is needed to evaluate the argument and explain how the evidence would weaken or strengthen the argument.

Sample Essay A: Outstanding

The article proposes that Movies Galore's chain stores shorten operating hours, by closing at 6 p.m. instead of 9 p.m., and reduce inventory by no longer stocking any DVDS released more than 5 years ago. The recommendation is a response to declining profits, and is mainly based on the example of one of Movies Galore's chain stores in downtown Marston, which implemented this very policy, and received very few customer complaints afterwards. Unfortunately, the information presented in the article is insufficient for readers to evaluate whether the decision is going to be effective for all Movies Galore's chain stores.

The author starts by ruling out raising prices as an alternative method for increasing profits, based on Movies Galore's reputation for low prices. However, it is curious why a store known for its low prices should never raise prices. If the average commodity price has risen vastly in recent years, it is reasonable for the store to raise prices without jeopardizing its reputation, as long as the price increase is moderate. In particular, if competitors have all increased prices, then Movies Galore can certainly adapt as well. Thus, the author needs to explore these possibilities before hastily eliminating other options.

Now, granted that the store should not increase its prices, would that necessarily imply that reducing operating hours and inventory is the optimal choice to make in order to increase profits? The author seems to think so, especially given that the store in downtown Marston made the first move and received few complaints. However, infrequent complaints do not imply that this store has profited. Dissatisfied customers don't necessarily complain. When they visit Movies Galore after 6 and see that it's closed, they might soon choose a different store. The same might also happen with regard to reduced inventory: fans of old movies might simply go to other movie rental stores without complaining about the small collection offered by Movies Galore. Consequently, reducing operating hours and stock might decrease revenues more than expenses, so profits may dwindle. Therefore, other than the complaint rate, the crucial evidence that would really

459

support the author's point would be an increased profit for that store.

Finally, even if the downtown Marston store did make a profit, it is still questionable whether that success can be duplicated by other stores. It is unclear whether the clientele of different stores are similar. Perhaps the downtown area is a business center with constant visitors and shoppers during the daytime, but if other stores are located in the suburbs, which are normally residential areas, people may visit movie rental stores only after 6 p.m. In this scenario, this very policy would mean that they are not operating at what is supposed to be their busiest hours. Also, maybe the downtown area is filled with people who are young trend followers, so old movies don't matter; in contrast, other places may still have plenty of customers who occasionally want to revisit some old memories, so a decision to eliminate all DVDs released over 5 years ago might end up seriously hurting the store's reputation with its customers. Therefore, without specific information regarding each store's customer preferences, applying the policy throughout all stores is too hasty.

All in all, while the author's proposal may end up being sound, her reasoning so far is not. Too much information is lacking, and without it, readers cannot be sure how the suggestion would turn out.

Sample Essay B: Good

The author recommends that all locations of the chain store Movies Galore reduce their operating hours by closing at 6:00 p.m. rather than 9:00 p.m., and stop stocking any DVDS released more than five years ago. However, more evidence is needed to fully evaluate her line of reasoning.

For starters, the author believes that the stores should not raise prices, because they are famous for low prices. Clearly, she assumes that a store known for its low prices should never raise prices. However, perhaps its fees are so low that their reputation has become a burden. Even if they raise prices moderately, the prices can still be lower than their competitors, and the change wouldn't hurt their reputation. Thus, the author needs to provide specific data comparing Movies Galore and their competitors' prices before she makes this inference.

Second, the author mentions that the branch store in downtown Marston reduced its operating hours and reduced inventory, and that since then, the store has received few customer complaints. However, few customer complaints do not necessarily mean that customers are happy about the change. The statement assumes that all unsatisfied customers would complain. However, in reality, a discontent customer might simply choose other places to rent movies, and Movies Galore's business might have suffered a serious blow. Thus, the author needs to investigate that branch store's profits before suggesting that every branch store imitate the policy.

Finally, even if that particular store in downtown Marston successfully implemented the policy, it does not necessarily mean that other stores should do the same. The author assumes that all the stores are similar in clientele. However, perhaps most clients of that store normally visit before 6:00 p.m., but other stores have a lot of late visitors. Also, maybe that store's most frequently borrowed movies are newly released ones, but other stores have lots of fans of classic movies. Therefore, the author needs evidence regarding customer preferences and habits, or else the suggestion may sound too optimistic.

Overall, evidence is lacking with regard to the author's argument. She needs to do more research before adamantly concluding that every branch store of Movies Galore reduce operating hours and inventory.

范文点评

两篇范文各自都讨论了三个推理步骤：

(1) Movies Galore 以廉价著称 ⟹ 不能提价；
(2) Marston 市中心的分店在减少运营时间和减少库存后收到的抱怨很少 ⟹ 改革带来的顾客满意度没有明显下降；
(3) Marston 市中心分店改革成功 ⟹ 其他分店也应该效仿。

但两篇范文最核心的差别在它们对每一个推理步骤的分析深度上。比如，针对步骤 (1)，Good 范文只是指出，Movies Galore 提了价也可能比竞争对手低，却没有分析为什么会有这种可能性。而 Outstanding 范文就能够帮助读者很清楚地意识到这种可能性存在的情况，即 Movies Galore 本来价格就低，而别的店已经提过价，所以 Movies Galore 适当提价也不会丧失价格优势。类似的，在对步骤 (2) 的讨论中，Good 范文只是分析了运营时间减少的可能影响，但 Outstanding 范文还分析了减少库存所带来的影响。再看步骤 (3)，为了表明 Marston 市中心分店的成功不见得可以推广到其他店，因为各分店面对的客流情况可能不同。Good 范文只是指出，不同分店的客户逛店时间不同，租的电影也不同，但是 Outstanding 范文就分析了为什么会有这种可能性存在，因为处在市中心和处在住宅区可能会对人们产生不同的影响。

两篇范文的语言都做到了表意清楚，基本没有影响读者理解文章意思的语法问题。

Part 6 Argument 精选范文

51 Humans arrived in the Kaliko Islands about 7,000 years ago, and within 3,000 years most of the large mammal species that had lived in the forests of the Kaliko Islands had become extinct. Yet humans cannot have been a factor in the species' extinctions, because there is no evidence that the humans had any significant contact with the mammals. Further, archaeologists have discovered numerous sites where the bones of fish had been discarded, but they found no such areas containing the bones of large mammals, so the humans cannot have hunted the mammals. Therefore, some climate change or other environmental factors must have caused the species' extinctions.

Write a response in which you examine the stated and/or unstated assumptions of the argument. Be sure to explain how the argument depends on these assumptions and what the implications are for the argument if the assumptions prove unwarranted.

Sample Essay A: Outstanding

The article attributes the extinction of several large mammal species on the Kaliko Islands to climate change or other environmental factors. The author reaches this conclusion mainly by excluding the possibility of human impact. Unfortunately, her reasoning rests on several unwarranted assumptions, and more evidence is needed to fully corroborate her claim.

For starters, the author does not believe that human's hunting activity could be responsible for the extinction. For evidence, she points to sites where fish bones had been discarded, assuming that, if humans did hunt large mammals, archaeologists would have discovered similar sites with their remains. However, the author hasn't mentioned what stage archaeological excavation is in, or how much of the islands they have searched. Perhaps researchers are barely starting this project, and have only recently located the site with the fish bones. In fact, most of the islands have not been thoroughly searched, so with a more meticulous examination, they might end up discovering animal bones as well. Also, human traditions might have made archaeological excavation particularly daunting. Since fish are relatively small and easy to transport, humans could have caught the fish and brought them all back to their dwellings; consequently, all the fish bones would have been discarded at a central location, relatively easy to discover. In contrast, large mammals are difficult to carry, so humans would have had to slice their meat and discard their bones wherever they were hunted. Consequently, their bones would be so scattered that they would be nearly impossible to uncover. Another possibility is that humans discarded fish bones because they were useless, whereas they often kept mammal bones, and turned them into ornaments or weaponry. In short, all these possibilities would explain the lack of apparent evidence for human hunting activity.

Granted that humans did not hunt the mammals, it is still rash to exclude human influence as a potential factor. True, as she mentioned, there was no evidence of direct contact between humans and other mammals, but since the ecosystem is a tight net, with each knot directly affected by other joints, humans could still have been responsible for the demise of these large mammals without directly hunting them. Humans could have depleted populations of important small mammals that were the main prey of the larger mammals. Human's slash-and-burn agricultural practices might have eradicated local forests, resulting in loss of habitat for these mammals. Thus, without evidence showing what activities the humans were generally engaged in, it is presumptuous of the author to simply eliminate the possibility of human influence.

Now, granted that there was no way humans could have seriously jeopardized the large mammals' subsistence, directly or indirectly, are climate and environmental factors the only remaining alternatives? The author apparently assumes that there exists no third possibility, when in reality, many other forces could have been in play. The spread of a new virus or bacterial toxin could have eradicated the species. Also, the introduction of non-indigenous plant or animal species could have threatened existing ones by competing with them for local resources. It must be added that these factors could have accompanied the arrival of humans, but they could also have occurred independently. Either way, they would have sufficiently explained the large mammals' disappearance.

In short, while the author's reasoning is superficially reasonable, it still suffers from several unwarranted assumptions. Without providing more evidence to justify these presuppositions, her conclusion could be undermined by a series of alternative possibilities.

Sample Essay B: Good

The article attributes the extinctions of large mammals on the Kaliko Islands to climate change or environmental factors. However, underlying its line of reasoning are several unwarranted assumptions that seriously undermine its soundness.

For starters, the author believes that humans could not have been responsible for the extinctions, because there is no evidence that humans had significant contact with the mammals. Clearly, the author assumes that any significant contact would have left noticeable tracks. However, perhaps after thousands of years of geological change, many traces of human activities have already been buried underneath. Volcanos, earthquakes, fires, and tsunamis could have completely eradicated any detectable evidence. Therefore, without ruling out these possibilities, the author cannot firmly deny the potential impact caused by humans.

In addition, the author mentions that archaeologists discovered sites where fish bones had been discarded, but found no similar sites with mammal bones, so she believes that humans must not have hunted the mammals. Clearly, she assumes that humans would have discarded the animal bones the way they did with the fish bones. However, perhaps fish bones were useless, so they would just throw them away once they consumed the fish. In contrast, animal bones could be used for weapons, tools, or decorations, so humans might have altered them for all kinds of purposes. Consequently, archeologists would not have discovered similar sites. Therefore, the author needs to provide more information to rule out these possibilities, or else the comparison between fish and mammals is not valid.

Finally, even if humans did not play a role, that does not necessarily mean that the extinctions must be attributed to climate or environmental factors. The author assumes that animal extinction can only be caused by these factors. However, viruses and plague can also eradicate species; lack of food, or introduction of new predators may also play a role. Without evidence investigating these possibilities, the author cannot firmly conclude that climate and environmental factors were ultimately responsible.

In sum, the author's argument has made too many unsupported assumptions. She needs to provide more information before legitimately drawing her conclusion.

范文点评

Outstanding 范文非常深入地分析了文章的三个重要假设：

(1) 没有证据就意味着不是因为人类捕猎造成的兽类灭绝；

(2) 没有捕猎就意味着人类不是兽类灭绝的原因；

(3) 不是人类，就一定是环境、气候因素造成的兽类灭绝。

与其相比，Good 范文只讨论了其中的 (1) 和 (3)，只是逐句分析了原文，没有意识到其前两个正文段的讨论其实都只是分析了步骤 (1)。

其次，即便是对于同样的假设，Outstanding 范文的讨论也比 Good 范文更充分，比如针对原文没有发现类似鱼骨遗骸的兽骨遗骸，Good 范文指出这可能是因为鱼骨无法被利用，而兽骨可以；而 Outstanding 范文除了抛出同样的可能性，还指出鱼类容易运输，进而导致人吃掉鱼后可以集中丢弃鱼骨，而狩猎的兽类不容易运输，需要就地处理，导致兽骨无法集中丢弃。

两篇范文的语言使用都做到了表意清楚，基本没有影响读者理解文章意思的语法问题。

72 The following appeared in a memo from the vice president of a food distribution company with food storage warehouses in several cities.

"Recently, we signed a contract with the Fly-Away Pest Control Company to provide pest control services at our fast-food warehouse in Palm City, but last month we discovered that over $20,000 worth of food there had been destroyed by pest damage. Meanwhile, the Buzzoff Pest Control Company, which we have used for many years, continued to service our warehouse in Wintervale, and last month only $10,000 worth of the food stored there had been destroyed by pest damage. Even though the price charged by Fly-Away is considerably lower, our best means of saving money is to return to Buzzoff for all our pest control services."

Write a response in which you discuss what specific evidence is needed to evaluate the argument and explain how the evidence would weaken or strengthen the argument.

Sample Essay A: Outstanding

In this memo, the vice president of a food distribution company recommends that all of their warehouses use Buzzoff Pest Control Company (BO) instead of Fly-Away Pest Control Company (FA) for their pest control services. Her suggestion is based on a comparison of last month's food loss from two warehouses. Specifically, the one in Palm City, protected by FA, witnessed a $20,000 loss of food from pest damages, while the warehouse in Wintervale, protected by BO, only suffered a $10,000 loss. However, these figures, while relevant, cannot provide sufficient grounds for the author's advice.

To begin with, even if the aforementioned data are accurate, it does not necessarily mean that the Palm City warehouse has suffered more heavily from pest damages than the Wintervale warehouse has, because readers are not informed of the total value of food stored in each warehouse. All that we know now is that the Palm City warehouse has lost a higher value of food, but that could be because the warehouse stored more food in the first place, or because the kind of food it stored was more expensive. Either way, the overall value of food in the Palm City warehouse may have started as twice or more than twice that of the Wintervale warehouse, while its overall loss of food was only twice that of the Wintervale warehouse. This possibility would mean that a larger proportion of food in the Wintervale warehouse had been destroyed by pests. Accordingly, rather than FA, BO should probably be the one to blame. Thus, without further information clarifying this uncertainty, the author should probably refrain from assigning blame.

Furthermore, granted that the Palm City warehouse was, in all senses, the one with heavier losses, the connection between its damage and its pest control service is tenuous, because, contrary to what the author assumes, other causes might also adequately explain the greater damage. For example, Palm City might be located in a warm tropical area that is extremely humid, an ideal place for pests to reproduce. In contrast, maybe Wintervale is an inland city at a high altitude, which is inhospitable to insects. As a result, even without a pest control company, it is still natural to expect similar statistical differences. In addition, the two warehouses might have stored different kinds of food. If the food in the Wintervale warehouse naturally stays longer, or is less prone to rot and insect attack, the same result could be expected to occur. Moreover, the food distribution company must have its own staff maintaining the warehouses. If the one in charge of the Palm City warehouse was negligent of his own duties, unable to maintain its hygiene or control the warehouse temperatures or moisture levels, it would also contribute to the loss of goods. More evidence is thus needed to exclude these alternative explanations, or else the switch from FA to BO might end up being futile.

In addition, when suggesting that their warehouses in all cities adopt BO's service, the author rashly assumes that the relative service quality of FA and BO in all cities are the same, and will remain the same in the future. However, it is possible that last month's poor performance was an exception for FA, while generally its service had been much more satisfactory than BO's. It is also possible that Palm City and Wintervale are the only two cities where BO's quality surpasses FA's, because FA just recently set up its branch offices there; yet in all other cities, FA may have long been established as the superior pest control service provider. Therefore, without longer-term observation and data from a wide range of locations, adopting BO's service throughout the company's warehouses is too risky.

Finally, even if BO is better at controlling pests in each city, the food distribution company may still have valid reasons not to adopt its service. As the author has already mentioned, FA's prices are considerably lower, but by how much? If the price difference is already bigger than the projected difference in food loss after using a different pest control service, then of course it is still wise to stick to FA. After all, net profit is a more important figure than cost itself. Thus, the price charged by different pest control services is also relevant to the company's decision, and so related information should be supplemented.

Overall, perhaps the food distribution company will eventually prefer BO's services throughout its warehouse system, and perhaps it will be the rational choice. However, the provided justification is insufficient, and the author's suggestion is, thus far unwarranted.

Sample Essay B: Good

The article proposes that the company return to Buzzoff Pest Control Company for all its pest control services. However, the author needs to present more evidence to fully evaluate the soundness of the argument.

For starters, according to the author, the company's warehouse in Palm City (PC), which is currently serviced by Fly-Away Pest Control Company, has lost $20,000 worth of food to pest damage, in contrast to $10,000 loss in the warehouse in Wintervale (WV), which is serviced by Buzzoff. However, this difference does not prove that the former warehouse suffered heavier loss. The author assumes that the warehouse in PC did not store food with much higher overall value. Yet, perhaps the total quantity of stored food in the PC warehouse was more than twice that in the WV warehouse. If so, it might be the warehouse in WV that actually suffered heavier damage from pests. Therefore, the author needs more specific data regarding the total value of the food stored in each warehouse in order to rule out this possibility.

Second, even if the warehouse in PC had more food damage, that does not necessarily mean that the Fly-Away company was to blame. The author assumes that no other explanation could account for the data. However, perhaps PC and WV have completely different climates and temperatures. If PC is located in a relatively warmer and damper area, then the natural environment, rather than the pest-control company might be the key to the difference in food loss. Thus, the author needs to provide additional information to exclude these alternative explanations.

Finally, even if Buzzoff is better than Fly-Away at controlling pests, that does not necessarily mean that the author's company should return to using Buzzoff's service. She obviously assumes that the higher service fee Buzzoff charges does not offset its superior service. However, perhaps hiring Buzzoff is much more costly than hiring Fly-Away. As result, even though Fly-Away's pest control service is inferior, using its service will be the more financially prudent decision overall. Therefore, the author needs to provide specific data regarding the commission fees of the two pest control companies before drawing a conclusion.

Overall, the article lacks sufficient information for readers to fully evaluate its reasoning.

范文点评

两篇文章最鲜明的区别在它们对论证步骤的挖掘深度上。比如，在讨论是否可以把 Palm City 仓库的损失归结为 Fly-Away 公司的责任时，Good 范文只探索了其他的一种可能性，即气候因素；但 Outstanding 范文在此方面非常敏锐地意识到了其他可能性，比如仓库管理的问题、食品种类的问题。

两篇范文的语言都做到了表意清楚，基本没有影响读者理解文章意思的语法问题。

> **78** In a study of the reading habits of Waymarsh citizens conducted by the University of Waymarsh, most respondents said that they preferred literary classics as reading material. However, a second study conducted by the same researchers found that the type of book most frequently checked out of each of the public libraries in Waymarsh was the mystery novel. Therefore, it can be concluded that the respondents in the first study had misrepresented their reading habits.
>
> Write a response in which you discuss what specific evidence is needed to evaluate the argument and explain how the evidence would weaken or strengthen the argument.

Sample Essay A: Outstanding

In this article, the author cites the results of two studies regarding Waymarsh citizens' reading habits. In the first study, respondents claimed that literary classics were their favorites, while in the second study, it was found out that the most frequently borrowed books from libraries were mystery novels. Based on the apparent contradiction, the author concludes that the first group of respondents lied to the researchers. However, underlying the author's reasoning are several crucial assumptions that call for the provision of further evidence.

To begin with, the author clearly believes that results of the two studies contradict each other, or else she wouldn't have needed to accuse anyone of being dishonest. However, it is quite possible for both results to be valid, and not in conflict with one another. First, it is unclear how researchers categorized literary genres in their investigation. There surely is literature that can be regarded as both literary classic and mystery, so the situation presented in the article does not necessarily mean a contradiction. Perhaps in the first study, there was simply no category entitled "mystery novel", so many works that would have qualified as mystery novels were put by respondents in to the genre of "literary classics". Likewise, in the second study, if genres were more finely defined, many classics could also be described as "mystery novels" "romantic novels" or "detective novels". In addition, the author has not informed the readers of the time when the research was conducted. Perhaps after the first study was completed, a famous mystery novel was adapted into a movie, which quickly became a hit worldwide. In Waymarsh in particular, perhaps a series of promotional campaigns for the movie and the novel were conducted, tremendously igniting local people's interests in mystery novels, and even temporarily changing many people's reading habits. Consequently, the two sets of results were different, but they could have both accurately depicted people's reading habits at a particular time. Therefore, evidence is needed to rule out the above possibilities.

Assuming that the two sets of study results were in fact incompatible, the author was quick to accuse respondents in the first study, clearly taking for granted the reliability of the second study. Unfortunately, no evidence is provided to show whether people tend to purchase or borrow their favorite reading materials. It is highly possible that, on average, people buy and collect their favorite books, while they only borrow books that they want to take a quick look at, so the libraries' checklist doesn't really reflect how much people love these books. Also, many books could be frequently checked out solely for research purposes by a small group of scholars. Thus, the checklist only reflects the reading habits of a particular type of people, rather than Waymarsh citizens in general. In addition, the author has not provided any information regarding the size of the book collections in the libraries. Maybe the only reason that literary classics were not the most frequently borrowed type of books is that local libraries did not offer as many of them as mystery novels. In a nutshell, without ruling out these possibilities, it is impossible to tell which study was indeed the flawed one.

Finally, granted that the second study was the reliable one, if the two sets of results were inconsistent, the first one must indeed be problematic. However, there is no evidence that the only explanation for its unreliability is respondents' dishonesty. In fact, several problems related to its scope can potentially render the research unrepresentative. If they just randomly selected a dozen students to interview, then whatever the respondents said wouldn't suffice to reflect the entire city's reading habits. Or, if they conducted the interview at certain spots, say, a university campus, then the study could represent only a particular type of people. Also, if the interviewees were explicitly told before they were invited to participate in the study that the aim of the research was to investigate the appeal of literary classics in modern society, then the only ones that would take part could be those who were confident that their reading habits fit the research's purpose. In other words, believing that they might be judged, those who rarely read or only read gossip magazines might not feel comfortable sharing their reading habits, so they would be reluctant to even take part in the research; in contrast, those familiar with literary classics might feel what they read was a testament to their elevated taste, so they may be eager to reveal their booklists. In short, without evidence proving that the sample in the first study was representative, the author cannot legitimately blame the respondents for being deceitful.

Overall, the article has offered too little evidence for readers to draw any robust conclusion. Until the author provides all aforementioned information, the best decision to make is to suspend judgment.

Sample Essay B: Good

The author of the passage believes that the respondents in the first study had mispresented their reading habits. However, more evidence is needed to fully evaluate this reasoning.

For starters, according to the first survey, most respondents said that they preferred literary classics as reading material. The author clearly assumes that the respondents selected would have represented the reading habits of all Waymarsh citizens, assuming had they told the truth. However, perhaps they were indeed telling the truth about what they read, but they still would not represent the whole city's reading habits. Their numbers could be small due to surveyors not bothering to collect a large amount of data. The survey could have been conducted outside of libraries, where most respondents have a habit of reading serious books. Thus, without more concrete information regarding how the survey was conducted, readers cannot hastily agree that its respondents were dishonest.

Second, the second study found that the type of book most frequently checked out of each of the public libraries was the mystery novel. However, that does not mean that Waymarsh citizens prefer mystery novels in general, unless the author assumes that the second study is accurate and reliable. People don't necessarily borrow books, especially for the topics that they are most enthusiastic about. Instead, they most likely buy those books to have a copy at home. Consequently, library lists may not reliably reflect people's reading habits. Therefore, the author needs more direct evidence in order to establish a connection between books checked-out from libraries and people's reading habits.

Finally, even if the second study was reliable, that does not necessarily mean that the first was not. The author assumes that the two results were incompatible with each other. However, it is very possible that the two studies were both valid, and that is only because they were conducted at different times that they achieved different results. If a new movie adapted from a mystery novel was released, then it could ignite people's interest in mystery novels. Without evidence ruling out this possibility, the author cannot completely deny the first study.

Overall, the evidence from the passage is insufficient to warrant the author's conclusion. She needs to provide more information in order to fully persuade readers.

范文点评

两篇文章讨论的是同样三个论证假设：
(1) 两次调查结果相矛盾；
(2) 第二次调查是可靠的；
(3) 第一次调查的问题必须是被调查者撒谎，而不是其他原因。

但在每一个论点上，两篇文章的探索深度都有明显区别，Outstanding 范文在每个论点上探索了多种可能削弱原文逻辑的情况。

两篇范文的语言都做到了表意清楚，基本没有影响读者理解文章意思的语法问题。

79 The following appeared in a memo at XYZ company.

"When XYZ lays off employees, it pays Delany Personnel Firm to offer those employees assistance in creating résumés and developing interviewing skills, if they so desire. Laid-off employees have benefited greatly from Delany's services: last year those who used Delany found jobs much more quickly than did those who did not. Recently, it has been proposed that we use the less expensive Walsh Personnel Firm in place of Delany. This would be a mistake because eight years ago, when XYZ was using Walsh, only half of the workers we laid off at that time found jobs within a year. Moreover, Delany is clearly superior, as evidenced by its bigger staff and larger number of branch offices. After all, last year Delany's clients took an average of six months to find jobs, whereas Walsh's clients took nine."

Write a response in which you discuss what specific evidence is needed to evaluate the argument and explain how the evidence would weaken or strengthen the argument.

Sample Essay A: Outstanding

The author of the article sees as a mistake XYZ company's recent decision to switch from Delany Personnel Firm to Walsh Personnel Firm to offer laid-off employees assistance in job seeking. The conclusion is largely based on several facts that seem to indicate that Delany has been superior to Walsh with regard to how fast they help employees find new jobs. However, these facts are insufficient for readers to make an informed judgment as to which company is indeed more up to the task.

For starters, the author clearly implies that Delany has done a great job during the years it was in service, since "last year those who used Delany found jobs quicker those who did not." Unfortunately, it is unclear whether there were other factors in play that could have resulted in the difference between those who relied on Delany and those who did not. Maybe Delany persuaded their clients to accept dead-end, insecure, and low-paying jobs, while others were challenging themselves to look for more lucrative positions in leading corporations. In fact, many of the latter group might not even be looking in the job market, but instead seeking further education to upgrade their skills. If they were willing to settle for undesirable roles, they could have easily secured spots even without Delany's assistance. Consequently, purely based on statistics, the average time taken to find new jobs would be shorter for those that consulted Delany. Thus, to accurately evaluate Delany's success, the author needs to provide more information that addresses the above possibilities.

In contrast, the author suggests that Walsh is a less successful candidate, given that eight years ago when XYZ hired Walsh, only half of the laid-off workers were able to find new jobs under a year. However, first, we have no idea how competitive the job market was back then. If most companies were in the process of laying off their employees to deal with the economic recession, that would mean that Walsh was, in fact, doing an amazing job getting half of its clients re-employed. Second, it is simply unclear whether the other half of the laid-off employees, those who did not manage to find new jobs, actually consulted Walsh at all. If most of these people simply started job hunting on their own, then the fact that they did not find one immediately actually could have indirectly attested to Walsh's capabilities, especially if all those who secured new positions consulted Walsh. Finally, the author cannot assume that Walsh's performance has not improved during the past eight years. Even if it was inadequate years ago, it's possible that, after years of experiences and staff training, now it has advanced into one of the leading companies in job-hunting assistance. Overall, without further information, XYZ's experience with Walsh 8 years ago cannot lend strong support to a judgment about today.

The most relevant piece of information the author offers is a contrast between Delany and Walsh in how fast each helped clients find new positions last year. True, other things being equal, an average of six months compared with an average of nine would suggest that Delany was more preferable than Walsh. However, no evidence has been provided regarding competing explanations for this data. Once again, perhaps Delany tricked its clients into accepting mediocre jobs, while Walsh encouraged its clients to go for desirable positions. Maybe Delany only accepted clients with certain qualifications (language skills, work experience, education background, and so on), meaning that these employees already possessed advantages in job placement; in contrast, perhaps Walsh was willing to offer assistance to all people, whatever their qualifications were. Accordingly, the clients Walsh had would find it easier to be reemployed, and this would have nothing to do with the assistance Walsh provided. Therefore, readers would be more willing to accept the author's conclusion only if she can prove that Delany offers better help than Walsh does to clients with similar backgrounds, applying for similar positions.

In addition to the above facts, the author mentions that Delany possesses a bigger staff and more branch offices than Walsh. However, why staff size and branch offices are even remotely relevant to a company's service quality is not demonstrated at all. Unless the author elaborates on this underlying rationale, this information can neither strengthen nor undermine her argument.

Overall, despite the various facts laid out in the argument, the author has yet to offer sufficient data to really make a sound judgment between Delany and Walsh. Perhaps XYZ's choice is ultimately unwise, but so far, we are not in a position to tell.

▶ Sample Essay B: Good

The article recommends that XYZ Company not switch from Delany Personnel Firm to Walsh Personnel Firm for helping laid-off employees with job placement. However, more evidence is needed for a thorough evaluation of this reasoning.

For starters, the author mentions that last year, those who used Delany found jobs more quickly than did those who did not; in contrast, eight years ago, when XYZ used Walsh, only half of the laid off workers found jobs within a year. Clearly, the author assumes that the job market has not changed much during the past eight years. However, perhaps eight years ago, the economy was receding, so it was quite a difficult task for an employee to find a new job. Therefore, being able to help half of the employees secure a new position could have been quite an amazing achievement for XYZ. In contrast, last year could have been a good year for job seekers. Perhaps the Economy was thriving and new jobs were always available. Therefore, what Delany was able to do was not at all an achievement. Simply put, more evidence comparing the job market eight years ago with that of last year would be useful to evaluate the author's argument.

Second, the author mentions that Delany has a bigger staff and larger number of branch offices, and she believes that these differences indicate Delany's superiority. Clearly, she assumes that only a better company can have a larger staff and more branch offices. However, it is possible that the reason Delany needs so many people is that it runs extremely inefficiently. Also, many of its branches may be functioning poorly, and a large proportion could be facing the possibility of closing. Therefore, without knowing how well these branches are operating, readers will not be fully persuaded by the author's reasoning.

Last, the author mentions that last year Delany's clients took an average of six months to find jobs, whereas Walsh's clients took nine. Apparently, she assumes that the only reason for this statistical difference is Delany's superior ability to help clients. However, many other possibilities could equally account for the data. Perhaps Delaney's clients were better educated, and therefore more qualified for new jobs. Perhaps Delaney tricked its clients into pursuing low-profile jobs. If these were true, then Delaney's clients would easily find new jobs. Therefore, without evidence ruling out these alternatives, the author's conclusion cannot firmly stand.

Overall, the author has to provide additional information to address all aforementioned issues. Until then, readers are very unlikely to be convinced by her reasoning.

范文点评

两篇文章最大的区别是它们对论证步骤的分析深度不同。比如，原文用 Wash 8 年前的案例与 Delaney 去年的案例对比。针对该步骤，Good 范文只讨论了一种可能性，即 8 年来就业市场的变化。但是，Outstanding 范文非常充分地考察了其他多种可能性，比如 Delaney 劝说客户接受很差的工作，8 年前没能再就业的人根本没有使用 Walsh 的服务。

两篇范文的语言都做到了表意清楚，基本没有影响读者理解文章意思的语法问题。

Part 6 Argument 精选范文

125

The following appeared in a letter to the school board of the town of Centerville.

"All students should be required to take the driver's education course at Centerville High School. In the past two years, several accidents in and around Centerville have involved teenage drivers. Since a number of parents in Centerville have complained that they are too busy to teach their teenagers to drive, some other instruction is necessary to ensure that these teenagers are safe drivers. Although there are two driving schools in Centerville, parents on a tight budget cannot afford to pay for driving instruction. Therefore an effective and mandatory program sponsored by the high school is the only solution to this serious problem."

Write a response in which you examine the stated and/or unstated assumptions of the argument. Be sure to explain how the argument depends on these assumptions and what the implications are for the argument if the assumptions prove unwarranted.

Sample Essay A: Outstanding

The author of the article clearly believes that Centerville High School students' driving is making them prone to accidents, since in the past two years, several accidents in and around Centerville have involved teenage drivers. For this reason, after excluding the possibility of students being taught by their parents or by driving schools, the author believes that all CHS students should take mandatory driving courses sponsored by the high school. Unfortunately, the author's rationale is quite problematic, and has several unwarranted assumptions and serious loopholes.

For starters, whether Centerville High School students do drive dangerously is an issue that is worth pondering, and that shouldn't be simply presupposed. For one thing, perhaps the teenage drivers involved in the accidents were not CHS students at all, and most Centerville High School students don't even drive. In addition, even if CHS students were involved, the author cannot just assume that poor driving was the cause of the accidents. Maybe they were not responsible, but the victims of other people's reckless driving: they might have been safe and careful drivers, but they were bumped into by drunk drivers. Without investigating the nature of those accidents, it is possible that the author has made up a non-existent serious problem, and as a result, if the school does open up such a mandatory driving course, it could be a waste of time and money.

Now, granted that these accidents were indeed caused by their students' reckless driving, it is unclear whether a mandatory school course would solve the problem. The author first excludes the possible alternative of the high schoolers being taught by their own parents, because "a number of parents complained that they are too busy to teach." Clearly, the author assumes that these parents' complaints are sincere, and that they represent the voice of most families. Unfortunately, these assumptions are unsupported. Perhaps, these are simply a few lazy parents who just want to shirk their own obligations.

Perhaps some irresponsible parents prefer drinking and partying over parenting their children, bur the school shouldn't give them their way.

The author's reasons for excluding the possibility of a driving school is weak as well. She claims that parents on a tight budget cannot afford driving instruction, but she has not indicated how many parents are facing this problem. Perhaps a majority of families are fully financially prepared to support their children in driving courses. It is simply imprudent to set up a schoolwide course just to meet the needs of a couple of families. In addition, she assumes that those on a tight budget would provide their children with a car to drive, yet another assumption open to debate. If families are so poor as to not be able to pay for their children to go to a driving class, chances are high that their children would also not have a car to drive in the first place. If students from such families generally commute by school bus, then a driving school can still be a solution for the remainder of the students.

Last, granted that parents and driving schools are not the optimal solution to teenagers' driving problems, it remains questionable whether the only option left is a mandatory high school driving course. Highly contestable is the assumption that no other approaches may alleviate this problem. Even if teenagers cannot rely on their parents or on driving schools, they can learn from other adult family members and friends. The author's assumption that everyone has the same needs is also flawed. Many students don't drive, and for them to be required to attend these classes is nothing but a waste of time. Thus, an elective course that caters to those really in need sounds much more effective. In a nutshell, without carefully evaluating a wider range of solutions, the author's decision to open up a schoolwide driving course still remains debatable.

Overall, the information provided by the author is far from sufficient to fully support a decision to launch CHS' own driving course. Without further evidence to justify its several unwarranted assumptions, the author cannot convince readers of the soundness of her reasoning.

Sample Essay B: Good

The author suggests that Centerville High School set up a mandatory driving course for all of its students. However, underlying her line of reasoning are several unwarranted assumptions that seriously undermine the argument's cogency.

For starters, the author mentions that in the past two years, several accidents in and around Centerville have involved teenage drivers. Clearly, she assumes that these accidents are directly attributable to students from Centerville High school. However, perhaps these accidents were just a few sporadic accidents, not caused by the teenage drivers. These teenagers could have been victims rather than villains, and some other adult drivers who drove recklessly had caused the accidents. Therefore, without more specific information regarding the accidents, the author cannot conclude that there is a serious driving problem for Centerville High School students.

Second, the author mentions that many parents complained that they are too busy to teach their children to drive, implying that parents cannot be the solution. Clearly, the author assumes that these parents' complaints are sincere and representative of most parents. However, perhaps these people are just lazy, and wish to assign what should be their own responsibility to someone else. They would rather spend their spare time watching TV or playing poker. Therefore, the author needs to look into the complaints before deciding that the school should carry the obligation.

Lastly, the author claims that parents on a tight budget cannot afford driving schools, so she believes that driving schools are not the solution, either. In contrast, however, she assumes that these relatively poor families would able buy their teenagers cars. However, if parents really cannot afford driving classes for their children, it is quite unlikely that they will be able to buy their children cars. Therefore, without specific information to address the question of how many teenage drivers from the school come from families that cannot afford driving schools, the author cannot simply rule out this alternative solution.

Overall, the article suffers from too many unwarranted assumptions. Without more evidence to supplement these loopholes, the author will fail to persuade readers to accept her proposal.

范文点评

两篇文章最大的区别在于它们对论证步骤的分析深度不同。比如，针对原文排除驾校这个解决方案时，God 范文只是表达了贫困家庭没钱买车这种可能性，而 Outstanding 范文还捕捉到另一种可能性，即该校并没有多少贫困家庭。其次，Outstanding 范文还在整体上捕捉到了一个重要的文章逻辑跳跃，即不能通过排除驾校和家长自己授课之外就认定学校必须要开一个必修的驾驶课。

两篇范文的语言都做到了表意清楚，基本没有影响读者理解文章意思的语法问题。